Lecture Notes in Artificial I

Subseries of Lecture Notes in Computer Science
Edited by J. G. Carbonell and J. Siekmann

Lecture Notes in Computer Science

Edited by G. Goos, J. Hartmanis and J. van Leeuwen

Springer
*Berlin
Heidelberg
New York
Barcelona
Budapest
Hong Kong
London
Milan
Paris
Santa Clara
Singapore
Tokyo*

Ian Smith Boi Faltings (Eds.)

Advances in Case-Based Reasoning

Third European Workshop, EWCBR-96
Lausanne, Switzerland, November 14-16, 1996
Proceedings

Springer

Series Editors

Jaime G. Carbonell, Carnegie Mellon University, Pittsburgh, PA, USA
Jörg Siekmann, University of Saarland, Saarbrücken, Germany

Volume Editors

Ian Smith
Boi Faltings
Federal Institute of Technology (EPFL), AI Lab (LIA-DI)
CH-1015 Lausanne, Switzerland
E-mail: {smith,faltings}@lia.di.epfl.ch

Cataloging-in-Publication Data applied for

Die Deutsche Bibliothek - CIP-Einheitsaufnahme

Advances in case based reasoning : third European workshop ;
proceedings / EWCBR-96, Lausanne, Switzerland, November 14
- 16, 1996. Ian Smith ; Boi Faltings (ed.). - Berlin ; Heidelberg
; New York ; Barcelona ; Budapest ; Hong Kong ; London ;
Milan ; Paris ; Santa Clara ; Singapore ; Tokyo : Springer, 1996
  (Lecture notes in computer science ; Vol. 1168 : Lecture notes in
  artificial intelligence)
  ISBN 3-540-61955-0
NE: Smith, Ian [Hrsg.]; EWCBR <3, 1996, Lausanne>; GT

CR Subject Classification (1991): I.2

ISBN 3-540-61955-0 Springer-Verlag Berlin Heidelberg New York

© Springer-Verlag Berlin Heidelberg 1996
Printed in Germany

Typesetting: Camera ready by author
SPIN 10549187   06/3142 - 5 4 3 2 1 0   Printed on acid-free paper

Preface

Case-based reasoning is an appealing technique for dealing with the knowledge acquisition bottleneck in computer applications. In case-based reasoning, solutions to new problems are found by adapting similar experiences from the past, called cases. This avoids the often tedious formulation of general theories and their representations which are required for conventional computer programs. It also provides an easy way to implement learning by simply adding cases to a library.

However, case-based reasoning creates new issues related to indexing, retrieval, adaptation and maintenance of cases. When is a case relevant for a new situation? How can it be found quickly? How does it need to be changed? How does one maintain a case base? Since case-based reasoning often involves applying computers to tasks which were not previously automated, many of these issues present themselves in different forms.

The papers in this volume were presented at the 3rd European Workshop on Case-based Reasoning held in Lausanne, Switzerland, November 14-16, 1996. We are very pleased with the quality of the results presented in the papers, each of which provides new insights into the challenges posed by the case-based reasoning approach.

Case-based reasoning has been applied successfully in diagnosis (e.g., help desks, estimating, and maintenance) and synthesis (e.g., document creation, design, planning, and natural language interaction). We are very happy that four groups of developers of working industrial applications have agreed to contribute papers describing their systems to this volume, in spite of the fact that their busy schedule does not usually allow for such publications.

We would like to thank the Scientific Committee for their time spent reviewing the articles we received. Without their support, the quality of the workshop would have been diminished. Additional reviewers were Klaus-Dieter Althoff, Josep-Luis Arcos, Eva Armengol, Ralph Bergmann, Isabelle Bichindaritz, Michael Cox, Andrea Bonzano, Friedrich Gebhardt, Christoph Globig, Kathleen Hanney, Thomas Hinrichs, Mark Keane, Ramon López de Mántaras, Hector Muñoz-Avila Sophie Loriette-Rougegrez, Wolfgang Wilke, Geir Willumsen, Ole Martin Winnem and Mark Winter. Also, we are grateful to the Industrial Committee for their assistance in the selection of the Industrial Papers. Finally, we would like to thank Marie Décrauzat and Ruth Stalker for helping us with organizational details.

Lausanne, August 1996 Ian Smith and Boi Faltings

Scientific Committee

Agnar Aamodt	(N)	
Kevin Ashley	(USA)	
Ernesto Costa	(P)	
Padraig Cunningham	(IRL)	
Boi Faltings	(CH)	Co-Chair
Ashok Goel	(USA)	
David Leake	(USA)	
Michel Manago	(F)	
Bernd Neumann	(D)	
Enric Plaza	(E)	
Pearl Pu	(CH)	
Michael Richter	(D)	
Derek Sleeman	(UK)	
Ian Smith	(CH)	Co-Chair
Barry Smyth	(IRL)	
Henry Tirri	(SF)	
Brigitte Trousse	(F)	
Manuela Veloso	(USA)	
Willemien Visser	(F)	
Angi Voss	(D)	
Ian Watson	(UK)	
Stephan Wess	(D)	

Industrial Committee

Ralph Barletta	Inference Corporation	USA
Brigitte Bartsch-Spörl	BSR Consulting	Germany
Betsy Cordingley	British Telecom Laboratories	UK
Rick Magaldi	British Airways	UK
Michel Manago	AcknoSoft International	France
Stefan Wess	Inference Corporation	Germany

Table of Contents

Industrial Applications

How Different Is Different?

Arguing About the Significance of

Similarities and Differences *

Vincent Aleven and Kevin D. Ashley

Intelligent Systems Program,
Learning Research and Development Center, and
School of Law
University of Pittsburgh
Pittsburgh, PA 15260
USA
aleven+@pitt.edu, ashley+@pitt.edu

Abstract

Our instructional program, CATO, uses a model of case-based legal argument to teach law students basic skills of making arguments with cases. CATO represents abstract knowledge about the meaning of the similarities and differences between cases in a Factor Hierarchy, in which the 'factors' used to represent case facts are linked to higher level concerns and legal issues. The Factor Hierarchy enables CATO to identify issues in a problem and to organize multi-case arguments by issues. The Factor Hierarchy also helps to assess and explain the importance of differences in terms of more abstract knowledge, yet in a manner sensitive to the context of the particular problem and case being compared and the argument for which the comparison is made.

We evaluated CATO in a controlled experiment, comparing 7.5 hours of CATO instruction to classroom instruction led by an experienced legal writing instructor. The results indicate that the CATO instruction led to significant improvement in students' basic argument skills, comparable to that achieved by the legal writing instructor. We also found that more is needed in order for CATO to prepare students for a more advanced and complex memo writing task.

1. Introduction

In building 'interpretive CBR' programs (Kolodner, 1993), which generate arguments justifying decisions by comparing problems to past or prototypical cases, a recurrent goal is to design knowledge structures for representing the meaning and significance of relevant similarities and differences among cases. For purposes of explanation and similarity

---

* We would like to thank Kevin Deasy of the University of Pittsburgh School of Law for graciously giving every possible cooperation to the evaluation study of the CATO program and Steffi Brüninghaus of the Graduate Program in Intelligent Systems for her very valuable contributions to the same experiment. The research described here has been supported by grants from the National Science Foundation, West Publishing Company, Digital Equipment Corporation, Tektronix, the National Center for Automated Information Research, and the University of Pittsburgh ECAC Advanced Instructional Technology Program. We gratefully acknowledge their contribution.

assessment, it is important for a program to know not only that a similarity or difference is significant but also why it is significant in terms of more abstract knowledge.

Although knowledge that a similarity or difference is significant can be represented by numerical weighting schemes, knowledge of why it is significant, must be represented symbolically in terms of abstract knowledge. The symbolic representation should capture the general purposes and strategies for drawing analogies and distinctions among cases as a guide to decision-making. A reasoner may, for instance, analogize a problem to positive case examples and contrast it with negative examples as a way of arguing that a problem is governed by a general principle, policy, or normative concern. Without this kind of abstract knowledge, a program cannot explain why a similarity or difference matters and thus cannot adequately justify or explain its conclusions (Ashley, 1992).

The challenge of representing such abstract knowledge, however, is to insure that the abstractions can be applied in a context-sensitive manner. In general, context sensitivity in case comparison means knowing which similarities and differences are the most salient in different circumstances: which should a reasoner focus upon and which should it ignore. Although a principle, policy or normative concern may lead one to conclude generally that a particular factual circumstance is very important, in the context of a particular problem and case, that assessment may be tempered by the co-occurrence of other factual circumstances and other applicable principles, policies or concerns, the arguer's rhetorical viewpoint and the dialectical role in which the arguer is engaged (Ashley, 1989; Ashley & Rissland, 1988; Ashley & McLaren, 1995).

2. The Factor Hierarchy

In this paper, we present a hierarchical knowledge structure, the Factor Hierarchy, as a method for representing in part the meaning and significance of relevant surface-level similarities and differences among cases in terms of more abstract concepts. The Factor Hierarchy helps to assess and explain the importance of differences in terms of more abstract knowledge, yet in a manner sensitive to the context of the particular problem and case being compared and the argument for which the comparison is made. The Factor Hierarchy relates its lowest level information, 'factors', to its highest level, 'issues', representing the normative concerns of a particular body of law. Factors are domain-specific expert knowledge of stereotypical collections of facts which tend normally to strengthen or weaken a conclusion that a side should win a particular kind of legal claim (Ashley, 1990). In this work, we are interested in factors which tend to strengthen or weaken a side's legal claim for trade secret misappropriation. Trade secret law is intended to protect commercial competitive information to the extent that an employer has taken steps to maintain the confidentiality of such information.

Each abstract factor represents two opposing conclusions about a legal or factual issue: a pro-plaintiff and a pro-defendant conclusion. For example, factor F102 Efforts-To-Maintain-Secrecy in Figure 1 represents a conclusion that 'Plaintiff took efforts to maintain the secrecy of its information' but also a conclusion that 'Plaintiff showed a lack of interest in maintaining the secrecy of its information.' The Factor Hierarchy contains 26 base-level factors for trade secrets law, 16 abstract factors, 5 of which are top-level legal issues, and 51 links. The factors, issues, and abstract factors have been gleaned from the Restatement (First) of Torts, s 757, which many jurisdictions have adopted as an authoritative statement of the law of trade secrets, as well as from cases and secondary sources.

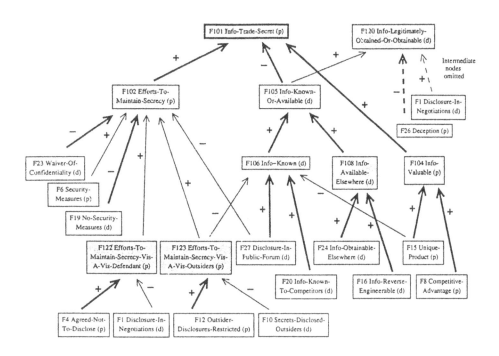

Figure 1. Part of CATO's Factor Hierarchy.

A positive link in the hierarchy indicates that a factor lends support to a more abstract factor, in other words, that it tends to favor a conclusion for a particular side on an issue. A negative link indicates that a factor tends to favor an opposite conclusion. Links can be strong (thick links) or weak (thin links), indicating the level of support that they represent. In Figure 1, for example, all of the factors and abstract factors linked to F102 provide evidence for or against the conclusions associated with F102, which itself provides evidence concerning the more abstract issue of whether the information is a trade secret, F101. The links are assumed to be self-evident, grounded in the common sense of the legal claim. CATO cannot justify the links in its arguments.

A case or legal problem often presents evidence for and against a particular high-level conclusion. The Factor Hierarchy is not used primarily to resolve such conflicts, but instead to guide the use of cases to make arguments about these conflicts. However, to avoid generating awkward arguments, CATO must be (and is) able to resolve some conflicts related to abstract factors. For example, if in a given case plaintiff disclosed its information to defendant (pro-defendant factor F1 Disclosure-In-Negotiations), this indicates that defendant obtained the information through legitimate means (pro-defendant conclusion associated with factor F120 Info-Legitimately-Obtained-Or-Obtainable). However, if it is also known that in the same case, defendant deceived plaintiff in order to gain access to plaintiff's information (i.e., if pro-plaintiff factor F26 Deception is also present) then obviously defendant did not use legitimate means and it would even be somewhat disingenuous to argue that it did. Thus, CATO must interpret F1 as support for the pro-defendant conclusion of F120, but not if F26 is also present. CATO achieves this by using information about link strength to evaluate the support for an abstract factor in a case[1]. Note that this notion of support is nonmonotonic.

The CATO program, an intelligent tutoring system designed to teach law students to make arguments with cases (Aleven & Ashley, 1994; 1995; Ashley & Aleven, 1992), employs the Factor Hierarchy in a number of ways. In teaching students to analyze problems, CATO teaches them to determine which factors apply to the problem and to find and compare cases which share factors with the problem. A relevant similarity is a factor shared by a case and the problem. A relevant difference is an unshared factor which can help an opponent to show that the case is stronger than the problem and, thus, not a good guide for how to decide the problem. CATO uses the Factor Hierarchy to lead students to reason about the significance of these relevant similarities and differences and to organize their arguments comparing a problem to cases in terms of the high-level issues.

As an intelligent case-based tutorial program, CATO differs from CREANIMATE (Edelson, 1993) and SPIEL (Burke & Kass, 1994) which focus on retrieving relevant stories to illustrate or explore issues with which a student is grappling. By contrast, CATO teaches students a process of reasoning with cases in which they will draw and justify inferences about a problem by comparing it to past cases, focusing on the relevant similarities and differences.

AI/CBR programs have employed a variety of hierarchical structures to represent the significance of surface-level similarities and differences in terms of more abstract concepts and techniques for taking contextual circumstances into account in making determinations of salience. Unlike GREBE (Branting, 1991), CATO's Factor Hierarchy represents the significance of a similarity or difference not in terms of the fact that an authority deemed it to be criterial but explicitly in terms of a model of why a decision-maker reasonably could deem it to be important. Unlike PROTOS (Bareiss, 1989), whose category structures collapse significance into a numerical sum, CATO's Factor Hierarchy enables the program to generate symbolic arguments about the significance of similarities and differences. CATO's Factor Hierarchy is most like CASEY's causal inference network (Koton, 1988) except that the two are used in dramatically different ways. CASEY's network enables the HEART FAILURE program actually to solve problems in the domain; CATO's Factor Hierarchy is a partial model designed to facilitate interpreting cases. Furthermore, the Factor Hierarchy helps CATO assemble multiple cases into an argument about a problem. CASEY employs its network to build and assess an explanation based on only one case at a time. ACCEPTER's abstraction nets (Leake, 1991) are designed to represent general patterns of explanation and support a wider range of alternative interpretations of an event (such as the death of a race horse); CATO focuses on comparatively few, more specifically case-based explanation patterns and provides domain-specific expertise for instantiating those patterns realistically. TRUTH-TELLER's Reasons Hierarchy (Ashley & McLaren, 1995) represents principled and un-principled reasons for telling the truth at various levels of abstraction. While normative

---

[1] A factor *F supports* an abstract factor *A* in a given case *C*, if there is a path from *F* to *A* such that for every node *X* on the path, either the path from *A* to *X* is strong (i.e., is made up of strong links only), or there is no strong path to *X* from any opposing factor in *C* (i.e., from a factor that favors the opposing side as compared to·*F*).

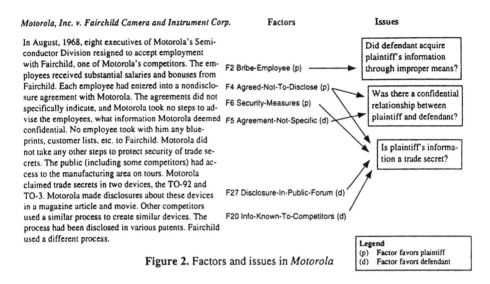

Motorola, Inc. v. Fairchild Camera and Instrument Corp.

In August, 1968, eight executives of Motorola's Semi-conductor Division resigned to accept employment with Fairchild, one of Motorola's competitors. The employees received substantial salaries and bonuses from Fairchild. Each employee had entered into a nondisclosure agreement with Motorola. The agreements did not specifically indicate, and Motorola took no steps to advise the employees, what information Motorola deemed confidential. No employee took with him any blueprints, customer lists, etc. to Fairchild. Motorola did not take any other steps to protect security of trade secrets. The public (including some competitors) had access to the manufacturing area on tours. Motorola claimed trade secrets in two devices, the TO-92 and TO-3. Motorola made disclosures about these devices in a magazine article and movie. Other competitors used a similar process to create similar devices. The process had been disclosed in various patents. Fairchild used a different process.

Factors

F2 Bribe-Employee (p)

F4 Agreed-Not-To-Disclose (p)

F6 Security-Measures (p)

F5 Agreement-Not-Specific (d)

F27 Disclosure-In-Public-Forum (d)

F20 Info-Known-To-Competitors (d)

Issues

Did defendant acquire plaintiff's information through improper means?

Was there a confidential relationship between plaintiff and defendant?

Is plaintiff's information a trade secret?

Legend
(p)   Factor favors plaintiff
(d)   Factor favors defendant

Figure 2. Factors and issues in *Motorola*

reasons are relevant to legal reasoning and factors are relevant to practical ethical reasoning, it remains for future work to integrate these somewhat differently focused hierarchies. CATO's Factor Hierarchy could supplement the approach in CABARET (Rissland & Skalak, 1991) which related individual factors to various sub-issues in deciding a taxpayer's claim, each sub-issue corresponding to a different open-textured term of the relevant statutory rule. A Factor Hierarchy for each term, or possibly one for the statutory rule as a whole, could represent more abstract reasons why the particular factors mattered in the determination of the statutory term. It could also help track factors which bore on more than one sub-issue. BankXX (Rissland, et al., 1996) relates factors to legal theories employed by courts in deciding claims. These links are used mainly to guide search, not to explain the significance of similarities and distinctions.

3. Using the Factor Hierarchy to Identify Issues and Organize Arguments

CATO's Factor Hierarchy is instrumental in teaching students to make arguments with cases about legal problems. For example, Figure 2 shows a legal problem in which plaintiff Motorola, Inc. complained that the Fairchild Corporation, the defendant, had misappropriated trade secrets incorporated in its TO-92 and TO-3 devices. A student presented with this problem faces the task of constructing an argument to support plaintiff's trade secrets claim or to deny the claim on defendant's behalf. The argument must be supported by relevant past cases, selected from the CATO Database, which contains, for each of 147 trade secrets cases, a textual summary and a list of applicable factors. In the more interesting problems, students need multiple cases to discuss all issues presented by the problem and to address the strengths and weaknesses related to each issue. They must compare the problem to various candidate cases retrieved from the CATO database, evaluate how best to use these cases in an argument, and marshal the most relevant cases to produce a coherent (written) argument. Using its Factor Hierarchy, CATO can demonstrate various steps of the process. In this section, we present an example illustrating how CATO uses its Factor Hierarchy to identify some issues in the *Motorola* problem and discusses these issues one by one in an argument based on multiple cases.

Argument for Plaintiff in the *Motorola, Inc. v. Fairchild Camera and Instrument Corp.* problem

Plaintiff should win a claim of trade secrets misappropriation. Plaintiff's information is a trade secret [F101], a confidential relationship existed between plaintiff and defendant [F114], and defendant acquired plaintiff's information through improper means [F110].

Plaintiff's information is a trade secret

Plaintiff's information is a trade secret [F101]. Restatement 1st of Torts s 757, and Comment b, factors 1-6 (1939). In the current problem, defendant entered into a nondisclosure agreement [F4] and plaintiff took measures to keep its information secret [F6]. This shows that plaintiff took efforts to maintain the secrecy of its information [F102]. In *B.F. Goodrich Co. v. Wohlgemuth*, 117 Ohio App. 493, 192 N.E.2d 99 (1963), there was similar evidence that plaintiff's information is a trade secret [F101], and plaintiff won. In *Goodrich*, which held for plaintiff, defendant entered into a nondisclosure agreement [F4] and plaintiff took measures to keep its information secret [F6], as in the current case.

The fact that plaintiff disclosed its information in a public forum [F27] does not preclude a conclusion that plaintiff's information is a trade secret. *Brown v. Fowler*, 316 S.W.2d 111 (Tex.Civ.App.1958). This is especially so where, as in the current problem, plaintiff adopted security measures [F6] and defendant entered into a nondisclosure agreement with plaintiff [F4].

The fact that plaintiff's information was known to competitors [F20] does not necessarily rule out a conclusion that plaintiff's information is a trade secret. *Kamin v. Kuhnau*, 232 Or. 139, 374 P.2d 912 (1962).

To justify a favorable decision on an issue:
Point to strengths related to issue, say why they matter.
Show cases in which these strengths led to favorable outcome.
Discuss weaknesses related to issue; point to strengths that may compensate.
Show cases that had favorable outcome in spite of weaknesses.

A confidential relationship existed between plaintiff and defendant

... [argument justifying decision for plaintiff on this issue]

Defendant acquired plaintiff's information through improper means

... [argument justifying decision for plaintiff on this issue]

Figure 3. Argument organized by issues, generated by CATO

A student analyzing *Motorola* may represent the strengths and weaknesses related to *Motorola*'s trade secrets claim using the factors shown in Figure 2. CATO finds three issues related to these factors, following links in the Factor Hierarchy from the *Motorola* factors upwards to the issues at the top of the hierarchy[2]. Note that one of the *Motorola* factors (F4 Agreed-Not-To-Disclose) is linked to multiple issues. Note also that for two of the three issues, there are conflicting factors. This is typical. CATO uses the issues to guide the organization of an overall argument based on multiple cases. Figure 3 shows an argument generated by CATO for plaintiff in *Motorola*, supported by three cases won by plaintiff *(Goodrich, Brown,* and *Kamin)*. CATO argues that a conclusion favoring plaintiff is warranted on all three issues and hence on the top-level question of whether trade secret misappropriation occurred. CATO's discussion of each issue follows a basic rhetorical format: State strengths and emphasize them; then deal with any weaknesses, beginning with the ones that appear to be least damaging.

To argue that plaintiff's information is a trade secret, for example, plaintiff points to pro-plaintiff factors related to this issue (F4 and F6) and emphasizes why these factors matter, pointing to abstract factors in the Factor Hierarchy found at intermediate levels. (References to factors and abstract factors in the argument have been marked.) Plaintiff

---

[2] Actually, CATO looks up the applicable issues in a table. But with one exception, this leads to the same result as would be found by traversing the Factor Hierarchy.

Generate Multi-Case Argument Organized By Issues
To generate an argument organized by issues, for a side in a problem, using a given (small) set of cases:

Identify issues

Find all issues related to the problem factors. For each issue, collect related strengths and weaknesses. For the strengths, find reasons why they matter (intermediate abstract factors in the Factor Hierarchy).

Organize cases by issues

For each issue *I*

Determine which of the given are relevant to *I* (i.e., have factors related to *I*). For each relevant favorable case, determine which of its strengths and/or weaknesses are related to *I*.

For each weakness related to *I*, check if there are compensating strengths in the problem. Also, check which of the given cases are counterexamples for the weakness (cases with favorable outcome even though they have the weakness).

Check which relevant cases have counterexamples among the given cases (i.e., cases that are more on point or as on point with respect to *I*).

Do the same for the opposing side. (If generating an issue-based argument in response to another one, it is necessary to reconstruct how cases were used in the argument being responded to.)

Generate English text for argument organized by issues

For each issue *I*

Draw attention to strengths related to *I*, citing reasons why they matter and relevant cases. Deal with weaknesses related to *I*, citing compensating strengths and counterexamples.

When arguing on behalf of defendant, distinguish cases cited by plaintiff when discussing *I* and cite counterexamples.

Figure 4. CATO's method for generating multi-case arguments

also analogizes *Motorola* to a case *(Goodrich)* in which the same strengths were present and (allegedly) led to a pro-plaintiff conclusion on this issue. (In fact, we cannot infer from CATO's factor representation of *Goodrich* whether the court in *Goodrich* actually addressed this issue and decided it in plaintiff's favor. But in common law legal argumentation, one is free to re-interpret the court's decision rationale.) To deal with the weaknesses (i.e., pro-defendant factors) related to the issue, CATO cites cases in which plaintiff won in spite of the presence of these weaknesses. It also points to strengths in *Motorola* that may compensate for these weaknesses, strengths which share with the weakness one or more intermediate abstract factors in the Hierarchy.

Figure 4 outlines CATO's method for generating multi-case arguments. Given a problem, a side to argue for (plaintiff or defendant), and a (small) set of past cases selected from the database, CATO identifies issues in the problem, organizes the cases on the basis of the strengths and weaknesses that they have related to each issue, and uses a set of text templates to generate an English argument. For example, in generating the argument for plaintiff in *Motorola*, CATO determines with respect to the issue of whether plaintiff's information is a trade secret that *Goodrich* shares plaintiff's strengths with *Motorola* (F4 and F6), whereas *Brown* and *Kamin* share weaknesses (F27 and F20, respectively). It uses *Goodrich* to emphasize strengths and *Brown* and *Kamin* to downplay weaknesses. In sum, key to organizing an argument by issues is knowing which issues to raise and what strengths and weaknesses (factors) of the problem and past cases are related to these issues. The Factor Hierarchy provides just the right kind of information.

4. Using the Hierarchy to Reason About the Significance of Distinctions

Much legal argument involves debating whether a case is really the same as the problem or not. One side analogizes the problem to a case, the opponent distinguishes the problem. The first side downplays the significance of the similarities, the opponent emphasizes them. The dialectical process is one of characterizing and recharacterizing the relevant features of the problem and case in terms of their legal significance in support of an argument either that the cases should be decided alike or differently.

With the information contained in the Factor Hierarchy, CATO can teach students to make arguments emphasizing and downplaying distinctions, using its own arguments as examples. *To emphasize a distinction,* CATO states why the distinction matters and argues that this reason is not present in the other case (i.e., the case in which the distinguishing factor does not apply), or even, that there are contrasting factors in the other case that oppose that reason. Thus, it argues that the distinction is indicative of a 'deeper' difference between the cases. *To downplay a distinction,* CATO also states why the distinction matters, but now points out that this reason is also supported in the other case, by factors similar to the distinction. In effect, it argues that even though there is an apparent distinction, at a deeper level a parallel can be drawn between the two cases.

In Figure 5, we illustrate these heuristic techniques with examples of arguments CATO made comparing a single case, the *Sandlin* case, to three different problems. In each argument, CATO is either emphasizing or downplaying the significance of the same distinction, a factor (F27) which the *Sandlin* case did not share with any of the three problems, namely, the 'secrets' in *Sandlin* were disclosed in a public forum. By comparing the examples, one can see how widely CATO can interpret the significance of a factor using information contained in the Factor Hierarchy and information about the context of the comparison. In Figure 5, CATO has compared three problem situations to the *Sandlin* case, *Arco*, *Space Aero*, and *Den-Tal-Ez*. At the top of each comparison, one sees a comparison of the factors in each problem or case and an indication of whether the factors are relevant similarities (=) or distinctions (*). Note that the pro-defendant factor F27 Disclosure-In-Public-Forum is a distinction in all three comparisons.

The significance of the distinction varies across the three problems, however. In the context of the *Arco* problem, it is not very important as indicated by the fact that defendant has arguments downplaying its significance, but plaintiff has no arguments for emphasizing it. In the *Den-Tal-Ez* problem, by contrast, the distinction is very important; plaintiff has arguments emphasizing the distinction but defendant has no arguments downplaying it. In the *Space Aero* problem, there are arguments in both directions, illustrating that CATO can even use its abstractions to emphasize a distinction for one side and downplay it for the other in the same problem. The differences across the three problems reflect the problems' different circumstances: *Arco* has uniformly pro-defendant factors, *Space Aero* has a mix of pro-defendant and pro-plaintiff factors, and all but one of *Den-Tal-Ez*'s factors favors the plaintiff. In other words, CATO arguing on behalf of the defendant, has a variety of opportunities to argue that in *Arco* there are similar pro-defendant factors to make up for the lack of F27. In *Den-Tal-Ez* it has few. Conversely, CATO arguing on behalf of the plaintiff, has a variety of opportunities to argue that in *Den-Tal-Ez* there are pro-plaintiff factors starkly contrasting with the presence in *Sandlin* of F27. In *Arco*, it has none.

Arco
- F10 Secrets-Disclosed-Outsiders (d)
- F19 No-Security-Measures (d)
- F20 Info-Known-To-Competitors (d)

Sandlin (d)
- F1 Disclosure-In-Negotiations (d)
- F10 Secrets-Disclosed-Outsiders (d)
- F16 Info-Reverse-Engineerable (d)
- F19 No-Security-Measures (d)
- **F27 Disclosure-In-Public-Forum (d)**

Defendant's argument downplaying the significance of distinction F27:
In *Sandlin*, plaintiff disclosed its information in a public forum [F27]. This was not so in *Arco*. This however is not a major distinction.

First, in *Arco*, plaintiff made disclosures to others outside its business [F10] and plaintiff did not adopt any security measures [F19]. Therefore, in both cases, plaintiff showed a lack of interest in maintaining the secrecy of its information [F102].

Second, in *Arco*, plaintiff made disclosures to others outside its business [F10] and plaintiff's information was generally known in the industry [F20]. It follows that in both cases, plaintiff's information was known outside plaintiff's business [F106].

Plaintiff's argument emphasizing the significance of distinction F27:
None.

Space Aero
- F1 Disclosure-In-Negotiations (d)
- F8 Competitive-Advantage (p)
- F15 Unique-Product (p)
- F18 Identical-Products (p)
- F19 No-Security-Measures (d)

Sandlin (d)
- F1 Disclosure-In-Negotiations (d)
- F10 Secrets-Disclosed-Outsiders (d)
- F16 Info-Reverse-Engineerable (d)
- F19 No-Security-Measures (d)
- **F27 Disclosure-In-Public-Forum (d)**

Defendant's argument downplaying the significance of distinction F27:
In *Sandlin*, plaintiff disclosed its information in a public forum [F27]. This was not so in *Space Aero*. However, this difference is not significant.

First, in *Space Aero*, plaintiff disclosed its product information in negotiations with defendant [F1] and plaintiff did not take any measures to protect the information [F19]. Therefore, in both cases, plaintiff showed a lack of interest in maintaining the secrecy of its information [F102].

Second, in *Space Aero*, plaintiff disclosed its product information in negotiations with defendant [F1]. Therefore, in both cases, defendant obtained or could have obtained its information by legitimate means [F120].

Plaintiff's argument emphasizing the significance of distinction F27:
In *Sandlin*, plaintiff disclosed its information in a public forum [F27]. This was not so in *Space Aero*. This is an important difference. It shows that in *Sandlin*, plaintiff's information was known in the industry or available from sources outside plaintiff's business [F105]. Other factors in *Sandlin* also show this: Plaintiff made disclosures to others outside its business [F10] and plaintiff's information could be ascertained by examining or reverse engineering plaintiff's product [F16]. By contrast, in *Space Aero*, the information apparently was not known or available outside plaintiff's business [F105]: Plaintiff's product was unique on the market [F15].

Den-Tal-Ez
- F1 Disclosure-In-Negotiations (d)
- F4 Agreed-Not-To-Disclose (p)
- F6 Security-Measures (p)
- F21 Knew-Info-Confidential (p)
- F26 Deception (p)

Sandlin (d)
- F1 Disclosure-In-Negotiations (d)
- F10 Secrets-Disclosed-Outsiders (d)
- F16 Info-Reverse-Engineerable (d)
- F19 No-Security-Measures (d)
- **F27 Disclosure-In-Public-Forum (d)**

Defendant's argument downplaying the significance of distinction F27:
None.

Plaintiff's argument emphasizing the significance of distinction F27:
In *Sandlin*, plaintiff disclosed its information in a public forum [F27]. This was not so in *Den-Tal-Ez*. This is a clear and striking distinction.

First, it shows that in *Sandlin*, plaintiff showed a lack of interest in maintaining the secrecy of its information F102]. Other facts in *Sandlin* further support this: Plaintiff disclosed its product information to outsiders [F10] and plaintiff did not take any measures to protect the information [F19]. On the other hand, in *Den-Tal-Ez*, plaintiff took efforts to maintain the secrecy of its information [F102]: Defendant entered into a nondisclosure agreement with plaintiff [F4] and plaintiff adopted security measures [F6].

Second, it shows that in *Sandlin*, defendant obtained or could have obtained its information by legitimate means [F120]. Other factors in *Sandlin* also show this: Plaintiff disclosed its information to parties outside its business [F10] and plaintiff's product information could be learned by reverse-engineering [F16]. In *Den-Tal-Ez*, by contrast, defendant may have acquired plaintiff's information through improper means [F120]: Defendant deceived plaintiff to gain access to the information [F26].

Figure 5. CATO's arguments about the significance of the F27 distinction in the context of comparisons of the *Sandlin* case to three different problems

We also see that CATO interprets the distinction based on the F27 Disclosure-In-Public-Forum factor differently (i.e., relates it to different abstract factors) depending on the context. In all three comparisons, CATO 'interprets' plaintiff's public disclosures (F27) in *Sandlin* as lack of interest in secrecy on plaintiff's part (F102). In the *Arco* comparison, the public disclosures (F27) are interpreted also as evidence that the information is known outside plaintiff's business (F106), to downplay the distinction. In the *Space Aero* and in *Den-Tal-Ez* problems, F27 is interpreted as as evidence that defendant could have obtained the information legitimately (abstract factor F120 Info-Legitimately-Obtained-Or-Obtainable), for purposes both of downplaying and emphasizing the factor.

In downplaying or emphasizing distinctions, CATO does not simply recite similar or contrasting factors. Rather, it searches the Factor Hierarchy for paths from the distinction upward through the abstract factors which best enable it to realize the goal of either downplaying or emphasizing the distinction. It recharacterizes the cases in terms of these abstract factors, and it marshals the evidence in favor of the recharacterization. In the *Arco* comparison, for instance, CATO elaborates two abstract, gestalt-like senses in which *Arco*'s factors are quite similar to those in *Sandlin* despite the absence in *Arco* of F27. In both cases, CATO maintains, there is evidence that the plaintiff showed a lack of interest in maintaining security and that plaintiff's information was known outside its business. In the *Den-Tal-Ez* comparison, CATO elaborates two abstract senses in which that problem contrasts sharply with *Sandlin*. First, it points out a variety of evidence (factors) that *Sandlin*'s plaintiff lacked an interest in maintaining security and, by contrast, a variety of evidence that the plaintiff in the problem did maintain security. Second, it marshals the evidence that *Sandlin*'s defendant could have obtained the information legitimately and contrasts it with the evidence that the defendant in the problem may have used improper means.

In order to generate the most persuasive arguments, CATO tries to draw as broad a parallel or contrast between cases as possible. It covers as many different characterizations of the distinction as possible and all evidence it can find in the form of similar or contrasting factors related to each characterization. For example, in the *Arco/Sandlin* comparison, CATO focuses on two different interpretations of the F27 distinction, corresponding to abstract factors F102 and F106, and mentions all similar factors in *Arco* that are related to these focal abstractions. Also, as CATO's arguments emphasizing the F27 distinction in the *Space Aero* and *Den-Tal-Ez* illustrate, in emphasizing a particular interpretation of a distinction, CATO lists as many corroborating factors for that interpretation as it can find. For example, in the *Space Aero* comparison, in plaintiff's argument emphasizing the distinction, CATO mentions all factors in *Sandlin* that show that plaintiff's information was known outside plaintiff's business (F105), not just the distinction. Similarly, in downplaying the significance a distinction, CATO shows undercutting factors, factors in the same case as the distinction that would lead one to believe that a particular interpretation of the distinction may not be warranted and hence should not be seen as a significant difference between the cases. This is not illustrated in the examples.

These examples illustrate that CATO's arguments are sensitive to context, specifically, the problem to which a case is being compared, as well as the viewpoint from which the argument is made (whether one wants to downplay or emphasize the distinction). In different contexts, CATO relates the same distinction to different abstractions. It may consider the same distinction to be very significant in one context, but insignificant in another.

Downplay Distinction

A *focal point* for downplaying a distinction is a tuple *(P, X, Y)*, where *P* is the *focal abstraction* (an abstract factor in the Factor Hierarchy), *X* a set of *similar factors in the other case*, and *Y* a set of *undercutting factors in the same case*.

To downplay distinction *D* of case C_1 as compared to case C_2 where *D* favors side *S:*

Select focal points for downplaying *D*

    Find similar factors in C_2 (the other case)

        Return all tuples *(P, [X_1, ... , X_n], Ø)* where the X_i are all pro-*S* factors in C_2 that have *P* as a most specific ancestor shared with *D*. *P* must be supported in C_2 for *S* (necessarily by one of the X_i).

    Find undercutting factors in C_1 (the case with *D*)

        Return all tuples *(P, Ø, [Y_1, ... , Y_m])* where the Y_i are all con-*S* factors in C_1 that have *P* as a most specific ancestor shared with *D*. *P* must be supported in C_1 for the side opposing *S* (necessarily by one of the Y_i).

Organize focal points

    Join together focal points with the same focal abstraction

        Among the focal points selected in the previous steps, replace any pair *(P, X, Ø)* and *(P, Ø, Y)* by a new focal point *(P, X, Y)*.

    Filter out unsuitable factors and focal points

        For each focal point *(P, X, [Y_1, ... , Y_m])*, remove undercutting factors Y_i that apply in C_2 (and hence, are shared between C_1 and C_2). If the focal point has no similar or undercutting factors left, remove it.

    Consolidate focal points whose focal abstractions are ancestor and descendant

        For each pair of focal points (P_1, X_1, Y_1) and (P_2, X_2, Y_2) such that P_2 is an ancestor of P_1, replace X_2 by $X_2 \cup X_1$ and Y_2 by $Y_2 \cup Y_1$. Afterwards, remove the focal points whose focal abstractions are descendants of focal abstractions of other units.

    Order the focal points

        Order the focal points according to an estimate of strength, so that strongest points come first in the argument: (1) FPs *(P, X, Y)* where *P* is not supported by *D* in case C_1. (2) FPs *(P, X, Y)* where both *X* and *Y* are non-empty. (3) FPs *(P, Ø, Y)*. (4) FPs *(P, X, Ø)*.

Generate English text for focal points

    For each focal point, select and fill out argument templates.

Figure 6. Algorithm for downplaying a distinction

CATO's algorithm for downplaying a distinction is shown in Figure 6. CATO first selects and organizes the 'focal points,' then generates an argument by filling out a set of templates, translating each focal point into a paragraph of text. The key step is selecting the focal abstractions, similar factors, and undercutting factors that make up the focal points. To find similar factors, CATO selects from the Factor Hierarchy all abstract factors that are a most specific common ancestor[3] of (1) the distinction to be downplayed

---

[3] The notion of a most specific common abstraction has been used to compute the similarity of corresponding case features (Kolodner, 1993, p. 346). CATO uses its Hierarchy not to compute whether one pair of feature values matches better than another, but to find the factors and abstractions that allow it most effectively to justify that a difference is significant or is not. These justifications involve multiple features and abstractions selected (and sometimes consolidated) from a hierarchy with a nonmonotonic notion of support. Kolodner notes (p. 347) in this connection that "[a] problem arises in abstraction hierarchies when items are abstracted several different ways." CATO provides a symbolic approach to that problem in the context of interpretive CBR tasks.

and (2) one or more factors in the other case that favor the same side as the distinction. Undercutting factors are selected analogously. For example, to generate the argument downplaying the F27 distinction in the *Arco/Sandlin* comparison (see Figure 5), CATO has selected F106 as a focal abstraction and F10 and F20 as similar factors in the other case *(Arco)*; F106 is a most specific common ancestor of F27 and both F10 and F20. CATO consolidates focal points if the focal abstraction of one is more specific than that of the other. This heuristic policy enables CATO to combine similar points into a shorter argument and to avoid certain repetitive or not so clever arguments. The downside is that sometimes, interesting information from lower down in the hierarchy is lost.

The algorithm for emphasizing a distinction is similar. The focal points for emphasizing a distinction consist of a focal abstraction, a set of contrasting factors in the other case, and a set of corroborating factors in the case that has the distinction. The corroborating and contrasting factors share with the distinction the focal abstraction as a most specific ancestor. The focal points are organized in the same four steps as when downplaying a distinction, although the filtering step is more elaborate. Text is generated using templates designed to draw a contrast between two cases.

5. Evaluation of CATO Instruction

In February, 1996, we conducted an empirical evaluation of how effective instruction with CATO is compared to small group instruction by an experienced legal writing instructor. Our experiment took place in the context of a real first-year, second semester legal writing class and involved 30 law students, all drawn from a particular legal writing instructor's three sections. The subjects were assigned at random into an experimental group (16 students) and control group (14 students). Each group used the same 'Casebook', a traditional-looking law school casebook chapter dealing with trade secret law, presenting five important case opinions each followed by a set of argumentation problems. Students in both groups were responsible for reading the Casebook as homework.

Over a three week period, using the Casebook as his text, the legal writing instructor taught the control group in 3 subgroups of 4 to 10 students each. The control group students participated in six classroom sessions, including two in which the students made oral arguments in class. Prior to the oral argument classroom sessions, the students broke down into teams to prepare for the arguments. Altogether the control group spent about 7.5 hours on task (not including the time spent reading the Casebook).

During the same three weeks, instead of attending their regular legal writing class, the experimental group received a comparable period of instruction with CATO in nine fifty-minute sessions conducted in a specially prepared CATO lab at the Law School. The experimental group students worked with CATO in groups of two. In addition to the Casebook, students used a workbook which instructed them how to use the CATO program to help them analyze the argumentation problems at the end of each section in the Casebook.

The CATO instruction employed the Factor Hierarchy in a variety of ways. The Factor Browser tool used the Factor Hierarchy to provide students with information about factors. Its lists of factors were organized under issues according to the Factor Hierarchy links and the textual descriptions of each factor's meaning were generated directly from information contained in the Factor Hierarchy. The Argument Maker Tool employed the Factor Hierarchy in exercises specially designed to encourage students to downplay or

	Basic Argument Skills		Memo Writing		
	Pre-Test	Post-Test	Prev.	Post-Test	
Experimental Gr. Avg.	60	C-	70	C+	63	70	B-
Control Gr. Avg.	55	D	68	C	63	79	B+
CATO answers	81	B+	87	A-		62	C

Table 1. Results of the Basic Argument Skills Tests and Legal Memo Writing Assignment

emphasize distinctions like those illustrated above in Figure 5. The Argument Maker also showed students examples of multi-case legal arguments it generated using the Factor Hierarchy to organize the argument according to issues.

The experiment contained two assessment vehicles intended to measure what students may have learned in the course of instruction: (1) Basic Argument Skills Tests and (2) a Legal Memo Writing Assignment. The first assessment vehicle measured any differences among the students' abilities to perform the basic argument skills which CATO was designed to teach. It comprised in-class, pre- and post-test written exams in which students were presented with a problem situation and two short cases and asked to make brief (one-page) written arguments about the problem using the cases. The pre- and post-tests were graded by the legal writing instructor in a blind evaluation according to a set of criteria to which the instructor agreed in advance and regarded as important substantive criteria. We also included answers generated by the CATO program which were transcribed into handwriting and presented in the same format as a student's answer.

The Legal Memo Writing Assignment measured any differences in the students' ability to write a long (six page) legal memorandum about a trade secret problem using six pre-selected cases. It comprised a take-home writing assignment which the students had about a week to prepare. The memo task was much more complex than the in-class pre- and post-tests, requiring more written composition and rhetorical skills and presenting a more complex configuration of cases to integrate into the memo. The instructor graded the memos in a blind evaluation according to an agreed-upon set of criteria. This time, however, he was grading a take-home writing assignment for which students had ample time, rather than an in-class, fifty-minute exam. As a control, we used the students' previous grades in the major writing assignment of the previous semester. Again, we included a memo generated by CATO and presented as a student's answer. This memo was similar to the arguments organized by issues shown in Figure 3.

The results of the Basic Argument Skills Tests are shown in Table 1. The improvement from pre-test to post-test within each group is significant ($p < .05$), indicating that each group learned something from their respective instruction. On the pre-test and post-test, there was no significant difference between the experimental and control group. In addition, the improvement scores (post-test grade minus pre-test grade) do not differ significantly between the experimental group and control group. CATO's answers were ranked among the best student answers.

The results of the Memo Writing Assignment are shown in Table 1. Here, the control group did significantly better than the experimental group ($p < .05$). On the memo writing assignment of the previous semester, there had been no significant difference between the groups. CATO's answer was well below average.

6. Discussion and Conclusion

The Basic Argument Skills test results indicate that the CATO instruction leads to a significant improvement, comparable to that achieved by an experienced legal methods instructor with small groups. The results should be assessed in the light of two considerations: First, the student subjects were all members of a special legal writing session and comprised those students judged most in need of specialized attention and support in legal writing and analysis by virtue of their underprivileged backgrounds or long absences from a school environment. Second, the legal writing instructor is the director of that special program as well as of all the Law School's legal writing instructors, and a very experienced, dedicated teacher who enjoys an excellent rapport with his students. Since the Factor Hierarchy was an important component of CATO's instruction and was reflected in CATO's answers to the pre- and post-tests, the evaluation supports the conclusion that the Factor Hierarchy is an effective device for representing some aspects of the meaning of factors and the significance of similarities and differences.

The Memo Writing Assignment results indicate that CATO's instruction needs more to deal adequately with long legal memo writing assignments. The CATO instruction focused on the basic argument skills. There was little time left to spend on its multi-case arguments, and, as it turned out, CATO's examples of such arguments were not ideal for this pedagogical purpose. As indicated by CATO's low grade and the grader's comments, CATO's answer did not reflect the format and organization the grader expected. He said the memo was 'on track —but serious problems with organization and presentation,' and the 'paper lacks overall structure —too fragmented'. It is important to note that the students had considerable knowledge of this instructor's expectations which they learned during their first semester with this same legal writing instructor. CATO did not have this knowledge. The fact that many experimental group students had better grades than CATO —some had considerably better— indicates that students did draw on their old knowledge.

The Factor Hierarchy probably played some role in CATO's low grade on the memo and, since CATO's instruction employed examples like its memo, in the lower grades of the experimental group students. Not all uses of the Factor Hierarchy were bad. CATO used it to link facts (or factors) to high-level concerns and issues. Since the instructor did not criticize CATO's argument for linking the wrong facts to the wrong issues, the Factor Hierarchy passed an important test. CATO also used the Factor Hierarchy, however, to break down the problem into issues. The instructor thought that there were too many issues, and he did not see how the discussion of each issue added up to an overall conclusion that plaintiff should or should not win. In one respect, this is due to a wrong choice by CATO's designers in the top-level organization of CATO's multi-case arguments. We chose to organize them in terms of plaintiff's argument, defendant's argument, and plaintiff's response rather than the instructor's preferred 'issue1, issue2, etc.'. That could be changed without affecting the Factor Hierarchy.

In another respect, however, the limitations of CATO's text organization and generation routines become more apparent in the longer memo text and especially as it was called upon to deal with more cases. (Hence the instructor's criticism of a 'fragmented discussion.') Apparently, CATO is not so adept at integrating the discussion of this large a number of cases (or conversely, in limiting the discussion to a single most relevant case for each point). Here, more of synthesis of the various cases may be required. The arguer may need to provide more of a rationale for deciding the issue despite the conflicting factors and in light of the cases. For this, the Factor Hierarchy's evidential links are certainly important but may not be sufficient.

In sum, the Factor Hierarchy seems to be a useful device for representing the meaning of factors and for reasoning about the significance of similarities and differences among cases. As a component of the CATO program's instruction, it helped achieve good results in teaching basic argumentation skills. In a more complex memo-writing exercise, however, its organizational links between factors and issues appeared to be inadequate. The test was not conclusive, however, because, we believe, we can improve CATO's arguments considerably, and probably its instructional performance, without changing the Factor Hierarchy.

References

Aleven, V. and Ashley, K. D. (1995) Using a Well-Structured Model to Teach in an Ill-Structured Domain. In *Proc. 17th Annual Conf. Cognitive Science Society*. pp. 419-424. Lawrence Erlbaum Assoc.: Mahwah, NJ.

Aleven, V. and Ashley, K.D. (1994) An Instructional Environment for Practicing Argumentation Skills. In *Proc.12th Nat. Conf. on Artificial Intelligence (AAAI-94)*. pp. 485-492. Seattle, WA. July.

Ashley, K.D. (1992) Case-Based Reasoning and its Implications for Legal Expert Systems. In *Artificial Intelligence and Law* . Vol. 1, No. 2, pp. 113-208. Kluwer. Dordrecht, Netherlands.

Ashley, K.D. (1990) *Modeling Legal Argument: Reasoning with Cases and Hypotheticals*. The MIT Press / Bradford Books, Cambridge, MA.

Ashley, K.D. (1989) Defining Salience in Case-Based Argument. In N.S. Sridharan, editor, *Proc., 11th Internat. Joint Conf. on Artificial Intelligence (IJCAI-89)*. pp. 537--542. Morgan Kaufmann: San Mateo, CA.

Ashley, K.D. and Aleven, V. (1992) Generating Dialectical Examples Automatically. In *Proc., Tenth Nat. Conf. on Artificial Intelligence (AAAI-92)* pp. 654--660. AAAI Press/The MIT Press: Menlo Park, CA, Cambridge, MA.

Ashley, K.D. and McLaren, B. M. (1995) Reasoning with Reasons in Case-Based Comparisons. In *Proc. First Internat. Conf. on Case-Based Reasoning (ICCBR-95)* Lecture Notes in Artificial Intelligence 1010 Veloso, M. and Aamodt, A. (ed.) pp. 133-144. Springer: Berlin. Sesimbra, Portugal. October.

Ashley, K.D. and Rissland, E.L. (1988) Waiting on Weighting: A Symbolic Least Commitment Approach. In Proc., American Association for Artificial Intelligence, *7th Nat. Conf. on Artificial Intelligence (AAAI-88)*. pp. 234--239. Morgan Kaufmann: San Mateo, CA.

Bareiss, E. R. (1989) *Exemplar-Based Knowledge Acquisition A Unified Approach to Concept Representation, Classification, and Learning*. Academic Press, San Diego, CA, 1989. Based on PhD dissertation, 1988.

Branting, K. L. (1991) Building Explanations From Rules and Structured Cases. In the *Journal of Man-Machine Studies*. 34, 797-837.

Burke, R. and Kass, A. (1994) Tailoring Retrieval to Support Case-Based Teaching. In *Proc. Twelfth Nat. Conf. on Artificial Intelligence (AAAI-94)*. pp. 493-498. Seattle, WA. July.

Edelson, D.C. (1992) When Should A Cheetah Remind You of a Bat? Reminding in Case-Based Teaching. In *Proc., Tenth Nat. Conf. on Artificial Intelligence (AAAI-92)* pp. 667-672. AAAI Press/The MIT Press: Menlo Park, CA, Cambridge, MA.

Kolodner, J. (1993) *Case-Based Reasoning*. Morgan Kaufmann Publishers, Inc., San Mateo, CA.

Koton, P. (1988) Using Experience in Learning and Problem Solving. PhD thesis, MIT.

Leake, D. (1991) An Indexing Vocabulary for Case-Based Explanation. In *Proc., Ninth Conference on Artificial Intelligence (AAAI-91)* pp. 10-15. AAAI Press/The MIT Press: Menlo Park, CA, Cambridge, MA.

Rissland, E. L. and Skalak, D. B. (1991). CABARET: Rule Interpretation in a Hybrid Architecture. In the *Journal of Man-Machine Studies*. 34, pp. 839-887.

Rissland, E. L., Skalak, D. B., and Friedman, M.T. (1996) Evaluating a Legal Argument Program: The BankXX Experiments. *Artificial Intelligence and Law*. To appear. Kluwer: Dordrecht, Netherlands.

Towards CBR for Bioprocess Planning

Robert J. Aarts and Juho Rousu

VTT Biotechnology and Food Research
P.O. Box 1500, FIN–02044 VTT, Finland
{Robert.Aarts, Juho.Rousu}@vtt.fi

Abstract. We present the current status of a recipe planner for bioprocesses. This case-based reasoner adapts previously successful recipes for each batch of the process. In this domain, recipe planning is difficult as actual numerical values of recipe parameters are crucial but quantitative information is scarce. However, adaptation, although far from trivial, is less complicated than planning from scratch. Like other case-based reasoners the system learns from experience, whenever the casebase grows. Therefore we expect that planners will automatically tune themselves to different plants. Case adaptation is fully automatic; process operators were never trained for this task. For adaptation, the case-based reasoner calls upon a semi-qualitative model of the process. The model, casebase and index are integrated and allow for indexing on inferences made by the model. All the software is implemented in an object-oriented framework that can be rapidly instantiated for different processes.

1. Introduction

Biotechnical process industries have a need for tools that support the implementation of modern manufacturing practice. Flexible production strategies and total quality management require efficient planning of process recipes. In this context *planning* is the process of selecting appropriate values for those process parameters that need to be decided *before* every batch of the process. Examples of such parameters are the choice and amounts of ingredients, setpoint profiles, process start and finish times, etc. The set of planned parameters has often been called the process *recipe*. Current practice is to modify recipes only when several, consecutive, batches yield unsatisfactory results. Planning of bioprocess recipes is very difficult, and recipe modification is perceived as risky. A minor change in one parameter of the recipe might prevent a particular problem, but may simultaneously cause several others. In other words, bioprocess planning problems are hard to decompose and therefore difficult. However, it is expected that batchwise adaptation of recipes will reduce product quality variations, allow more flexible policies for the purchase of raw materials and will increase overall plant productivity. Moreover it is expected that process efficiency increases, to be reflected in a reduction of waste (raw material, energy).

Some of these expectations originate from the development of a prototype planner for mashing temperature programmes developed at VTT (Aarts, 1992). Mashing is the first process step in the production of beer and the temperature programme the most important part of the recipe. That prototype was based on a constraint satisfaction approach and was successfully tested in laboratory and pilot scale (Aarts *et al.*, 1993). However, it had two notable shortcomings. First, that system needed tuning of the rules and fuzzy sets that were used to infer the constraints. Second, this prototype planned only the temperature program used for mashing. Although this is the most important element of the recipe, it was thought that planning of additional recipe parameters could be beneficial. Fortunately, the prototype clearly demonstrated the possible benefits of recipe planning and construction of a new prototype was started, around the case-based reasoning (CBR) paradigm. As it was expected that recipe planning could be beneficial for a number of different processes, the new system was constructed as a generic bioprocess recipe planner that could be specialised.

This paper will describe the different parts of the system, using the new planner for mashing as an example. First we will motivate the use of CBR and give an outline of the system. Next, we will describe and motivate the use of a qualitative model in indexing and adaptation of cases. Related work and some of the problems encountered during development will be discussed and the nature of the various types of knowledge in this domain will be analysed. Finally, we will present some ideas for additional futures, some of which may provide some challenges for the CBR community.

2. System

2.1 Problem Description and Motivation for Using CBR

In our system a complete case typically consists of a product specification, a product analysis, a list of ingredients, a vessel, and a recipe. The planner should construct a recipe given the product specification, and possibly (some of) the ingredients and the vessel. As stated above, such planning problems are hard to decompose. As Kolodner (1993) pointed out, with CBR one preserves most of a successful solution, so CBR was thought to enable planning of *complete* recipes, including setpoint profiles, ingredients and perhaps scheduling aspects. This as opposed to constructing only a temperature programme. Another reason to venture into CBR was the desire to have a learning system, i.e. a planner that would benefit and learn from feedback and adapt itself to a particular plant for a process.

Upon closer examination, the domain lends itself quite naturally to a CBR approach. A single batch is a quite clearly defined case. Each batch has a goal, the product specification. As a case, a batch has a context formed by the (quality of the) ingredients available, the vessel or other resources to be used, or the current production schedule. In most processes the product specification is rather constant; the most common reason for recipe modification is variation in the quality of the raw materials. Batches for the same product, made from very similar quality ingredients, are made using the same standard recipe; cases with a similar context have a similar solution. Finally, batches with an exceptional context, and causing severe problems, are usually remembered as cases by plant personnel.

To our disadvantage, knowledge about recipe adaptation is usually scarce, as the industry only rarely modifies recipes. On the other hand, ample experience is available; most processes run many batches per year or even per week. In addition, a large body of, mainly qualitative, biotechnological knowledge is valid for many processes. The idea then, was to combine somehow that qualitative process knowledge with the quantitative information that is implicit in the experience from many batches.

Although the system can be easily specialised for different bioprocesses, we will focus on one such specialisation, the planner for mashing. Most of the software is rather generic, mashing specific parts will be indicated.

2.2 Case Representation

A case is represented as a quite large, hierarchical, object. The product specification is represented as a set of constraints that the product analysis should satisfy. Product analyses, ingredients and vessels are represented as objects, i.e. as instances of predefined classes. All these objects are created by the system from standard database tables that usually reside in the production management system of the plant. The recipe is represented as a, possibly non-linear, action based plan. Some of the actions that may be included are: addition of an ingredient, adjunct, or additive; and heating or cooking steps. A mashing temperature programme consists of *rests* (keeping the mash at a constant temperature), interleaved with *rises* (Fig 1). Each rest has a temperature and a length. Rises have a start temperature, slope and end temperature. Most often, the rises are completely determined by the rests; the temperature of the mash is increased as fast as possible. The temperature of the mash is always increased, never decreased.

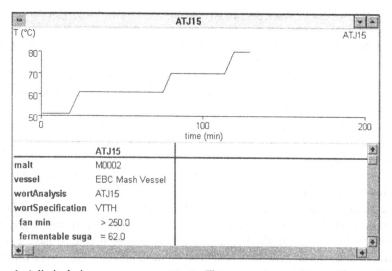

Figure 1. A limited view on one case, a Mash. The temperature program with rest and rises is shown as well as some of the features of the case.

A large number of classes for case representation were implemented, many of which are abstract superclasses that can be subclassed for particular (kinds of) processes. Some examples are:

a Mash ⇒ (is a kind of) Bioprocess ⇒ Case;

MashTun ⇒ Vessel ⇒ Resource;

Enzyme ⇒ Protein ⇒ MacroMolecule ⇒ Chemical ⇒ Component.

As in any object oriented system instances of subclasses inherit the variables and behaviour defined for superclasses.

Cases are stored in a *casebase*. Currently cases are not generalised in any way. This may be necessary, and desirable in the mashing planner, as one brewhouse typically produces 7-8 mashes per day. A meaningful casebase would include several years of experience, that is thousands of cases. Our current solution is to rely on the external relational database for the complete case description and construct the case objects as needed on the fly. So when the casebase is saved each Case is replaced by a degenerate StoredCase that only contains the ID of the mash. Pointers from the index to Cases are made to point to the StoredCases (see also section 2.4).

2.3 Qualitative Model

A substantial part of the process knowledge is represented in a (semi-) *qualitative model*. This model is process specific and has to be created for each application. The model should be able to guide adaptation of recipes. The representation used for this model is based upon Qualitative Process Theory (Forbus, 1984). Within a bioprocess there are active (QPT) processes that may *influence* process *variables*. Processes are only active when certain conditions are met. In our representation, variables again may influence the activity of processes. Hence, the model can be viewed as an influence graph, not unlike the representation used (for cases!) in CADET (Sycara *et al.*, 1992). Processes have a degree of activity and influences may have weights. The absolute value of these weights is of little importance, their sole purpose is to indicate that one influence may be more important than another (Fig. 2).

This kind of model is a very effective way to represent a large amount of knowledge. A network of processes, influences, conditions and other nodes, represents the paths between causes and effects. It can be traversed forward to predict, and backwards to find means to an end.

Naturally, model construction is a significant effort. To facilitate this task a library of building blocks for the model is provided, again as a class library. In this library the more abstract classes provide the functionality to integrate model based reasoning with case based reasoning. The subclasses specialise the kinds of links that can be made from one model node to another. This "construction-set" approach may facilitate future implementation of a module for learning of the model from the cases.

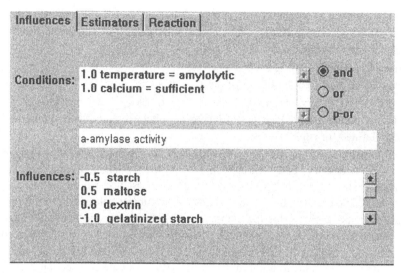

Figure 2. The model editor showing one node of the model. This node represents an EnzymaticReaction, a kind of FunctionalProcess. This reaction only takes place when the conditions are satisfied. If there is α-amylase activity the amount of starch will decrease and the concentrations of the sugars maltose and dextrin will increase. The influences of α-amylase activity on gelatinised starch and dextrin are more pronounced.

2.4 Case Indexing and Retrieval

The system maintains an index in the form of a tree. Root nodes in the tree represent a statement that can be made about the case. Evaluation of the statement for a particular case results in a truth value. If this value exceeds a threshold, children of the node are evaluated recursively. The recursion bottoms out at *leaf nodes*. Leaf nodes point to all cases for which the leaf node evaluated to 'true' when the case was added to the case base. The link from a leaf node to a case records the truth of the leaf node for that particular case. If the current case activates a leaf node then, that leaf node activates all the cases that once activated that same leaf node. The index can perhaps been viewed as a "spreading activation" network. When the index is given a target case, the cases in the case base are ordered on their degree of activation.

The entries or items in the index are not given *a priori*, but originate from the cases. Subclasses of Case implement methods that will return index entries in a hierarchical fashion just like the index itself. Most often the case will return an index that reflects its object structure. The planner itself may compute additional entries. The mashing planner for instance, uses the model to infer activities of processes during various plan steps, provided the case was completed (has a plan). Similar use of a process model for indexing was employed in CASEY (Koton, 1989).

Any time a case is added to the case base the whole set of entries is compared to the current index. Novel entries are added to the index, whereas (active leave nodes of) entries that are already in the index are made to point to the new case.

Further flexibility is provided by *selectors*. Selectors are used to represent different points of view for retrieval. For instance, cases with a similar 'goal' can quickly be found by activating only the 'goal' selector. Each selector activates some of the links from index leaves to cases. These links only activate a case if both the leaf node and at least one of its selectors are activated. Special selectors may be defined for different processes or configurations. Our current mashing system uses selectors for 'goal', 'situation', 'plan' and 'observations'. The selectors for 'goal' and 'situation' are activated when a new target case is given. This ensures that case with a similar product specification and context will be highly activated.

When the product analysis becomes available and problems such as specification violations were encountered, it may be beneficial to activate the selectors for 'situation' and 'plan' in order to find cases with similar contexts and recipes. If this kind of problems are important and frequent one could define a selector for 'specification violations'. An interesting alternative would be to activate the selector for 'observations'.

When feedback is available, the model is used to generate explanations for observed results and problems. These explanations are added to the index, under control of the selector for observations. Activation of this selector will then retrieve cases where problems occurred for similar reasons. The explanations for problems can be used to guide future adaptation.

2.5 Adaptation

When the mash planner is given a new target case without a plan, it first indexes the case using the selectors 'goal' and 'situation'. The previous batches in the case base have then been ranked in order of similarity as described above. Initially the recipe of the most similar case is then used as a template, i.e. is copied into the target case. Next the target case and the template case are analysed for their differences. This is done by comparison of the activation of index leaf nodes by the target and template. If there is a different activation, the cases must be different in the aspect represented by the leaf node. Such a leaf node returns an instance of `CaseDifference`. This is another abstract superclass with subclasses such as: `AimIncrement` and `PropertyDecrement`.

After construction of the differences, potential pitfalls of the copied plan are fetched. The problems, if any, that were observed for the template are analysed. If observed `ConstraintViolations` hold for the target they are added to the pitfalls, as are all other observed problems.

Once the differences and pitfalls are constructed the actual adaptation starts. The model is asked to construct an `AdaptationGoal` for each difference and pitfall. Relevant nodes for the kind of `CaseDifference` are selected, then the net is traversed along the influences up to process nodes that can be influenced by such a difference, or influence an outcome. Each `AdaptationGoal` is given an *importance*, based upon the size of the difference or the severity of the pitfall. Identical goals are then combined; each `AdaptationGoal` has one or more *justifications*, one for each difference or pitfall that may be taken care of when the goal can be met.

Next, the model is asked to construct `Adaptations` for each `Adaptation-Goal`. This is done by another search trough the model network; in backward fashion towards nodes that are linked to an `Action` (e.g. to a rest by a `Measurement` of the temperature). Next, the obtained list of possible adaptations is processed. If some adaptation makes another adaptation redundant, the later is not made. On the other hand, if some adaptation introduces a constraint violation it is undone.

2.6 Interfaces

The user interface of the system is, once again, provided as a class library. This library implements a number of editors and viewers. Some of these can be specialised for a particular application, but most can be used as is, as long as process specific classes implement some user-interface related methods. A significant part of the user interface is provided as hypertext that is generated on-the-fly by the various objects mentioned above and by *explanations*.

The qualitative model and object oriented representation of cases enable rather decent explanation facilities. The model can construct `Explanations` for e.g. a particular `Adaptation`. `Explanations`, `Observations`, and most other objects can provide short hypertext fragments that so far have been perceived as quite informative.

Apart from a user interface, the system has an interface to the production management system used. Nowadays production management and material flow systems are often realised as a relational database. The system should be linked to such databases but of course, that link has to be configured for each specific database.

2.7 Implementation and Current Status

The system was implemented in Visual Smalltalk (Parcplace-Digitalk) for Windows NT. It consists of a large number of related class libraries. The major goal of this high degree of object orientation is to facilitate rapid development of process or plant specific applications. The set of all the classes for case and model based reasoning, explanations, the user interface, etc., forms a *framework* (Johnsson & Russo, 1991) for bioprocess planning. It is our intention to expand the libraries for case representation and model construction into a serious *ontology* (Gruber, 1991) for bioprocesses, not unlike other recent ontologies for manufacturing (Fox *et al.*, 1993) and design (Alberts, 1993).

Our current class libraries cover mashing. In order to get a feel for the effort needed for specialisation of the framework to another process, a prototype planner for production of rye-bread was developed. At a slight level of abstraction, this process is quite similar; the structure of rye-bread production batches is virtually identical to those of mashes. But the material and product analyses are all different. After a morning session with two domain experts, it was possible to construct a reasonable process model, using the existing model construction blocks, in the afternoon of the same day. Another half day was needed to write the subclasses necessary for construction of cases from a database. Once these were available an, admittedly primitive but working, prototype was ready for testing. This exercise clearly demonstrated the power a framework approach. It also brought out some minor flaws in the design of the libraries; code that actually is generic had been defined in process specific (mashing) classes.

The mashing planner is currently being tested in a large pilot plant. The earlier (constraint-based) mash planner was tested in our laboratory and smaller pilot plant (Aarts *et al.*, 1993). Computer generated recipes were used to make three different worts from five different malts. Analysis of the worts revealed that the prototype planner worked surprisingly well. These earlier tests have been used as (28) cases for the new planner. Some of the test cases were included in the casebase and the planner was asked to construct a recipe for one or more of the other tested situations. In all trials the case-based planner constructs very similar, but not always identical, recipes as the earlier prototype for all situations; even when a casebase with only a few cases is used. For some situations the new planner constructed slightly different recipes than the earlier prototype. Some of these modified recipes are an attempt to improve the wort quality, whereas in some other cases the new recipe seems a viable alternative to an earlier successful recipe (in such a case that successful recipe was of course not included in the casebase, otherwise it would have been used as is). In addition the planner was used to construct recipes for malts not used in previous tests and for blends of malts. These recipes seem valid and were not rejected by human experts. However, only actual production of the wort, and subsequent fermentation of the wort to beer, will validate the planner. The confidence in the current planner is illustrated by the fact that it is tested directly in a pilot plant with a working volume of several thousand litre, whereas the constraint-based prototype was tested only at 50 litre scale.

Although the planner works quite satisfactorily, there are various parts of the reasoning system that could most likely be improved. In addition, the library of bioprocess components could be extended enormously, this would enable the construction of more sophisticated models.

3. Discussion

This system offers several advantages. First, such a planner enables a radically different, but attractive, way of operating a bioprocess. As recipe planning is such a "revolution" there are no human experts; so perhaps the quality of plans does not have to be extremely high. On the other hand, the recipe has to yield a satisfying product, of course. It is very likely that a recipe is not unique; i.e. more than one recipe would yield an acceptable product. We learned that funding and fielding an AI application that *enables* a novel mode of operation is definitely easier and more interesting than working on an application that tries to replace humans.

A second advantage, is that the planner indeed is able to adapt previous solutions all by itself. The inclusion of a qualitative process model into the system was crucial for this purpose. Perhaps adaptation knowledge for a particular process can be represented in rules, but in this domain it would be very hard to acquire such rules. A qualitative model can relatively easily be obtained from literature and experts, and the library of model components facilitates the implementation of such a model.

Aamodt (1994) pointed at the likelihood of power from integration of case- and model-based reasoning. Although the presented model representation is somewhat inconsistent, and perhaps even clumsy, its integration with the case-based reasoning system certainly works. Overall adaptation is somewhat complex, but still relatively fast. More importantly, no specific *adaptation* knowledge has to be defined for a specific planner. The qualitative model, that describes the process, has the adaptation knowledge in an implicit form. The division of adaptation into the construction of adaptation goals, followed by the construction of adaptations that meet these goals, was very effective. Direct construction of adaptations would require a much more global form of model-based reasoning with an accompanying requirement for process specific adaptation knowledge apart from the model *per se*. The mechanism for adaptation was recently improved by using adaptation *cost* as a criterion for solution evaluation (Rousu & Aarts, 1996).

The currently used representation of the model knowledge fits the domain of bioprocess planning very well. Although we have not used the system in other domains, it can be expected that the same, or a very similar representation can be used in other domains, where *processes* can be identified, such as medicine or chemical industry. In other domains, e.g. electronics, a device oriented representation such as used in CADET (Sycara *et al.*, 1992) and IDEAL (Bhatta *et al.*, 1994) may be more suitable. CADET uses a simpler form of influences but an otherwise very similar kind of graph for model representation. Within IDEAL a rich *structure-behaviour-function* representation is used. A crucial difference is that both CADET and IDEAL have devices as cases with specific qualitative models for each case, whereas our system has a single, but quite large model (approx. 50 nodes), that should explain all the cases (batches). Note that IDEAL also employs small global models for principles, such as laws of thermodynamics. Naturally, when the task of the system centres around devices, it is useful to represent those devices explicitly. In our system the task is focused on process recipes; a brewhouse produces several batches per day whereas the devices (vessels) within a particular plant last for decades.

The examination of *pitfalls* was found to be very effective. With a model or other causal knowledge available it certainly is worthwhile to record problems. As in CHEF (Hammond, 1990) and IDEAL (Bhatta *et al.*, 1994), the causal knowledge of the model in our system can be used to generate explanations for observed problems. These explanations directly hint at possible adaptations of the recipe. Unlike CHEF, our system does not revise a recipe when negative feedback becomes available, only when that recipe is being used as a ball-park solution.

There seems to be an interesting relation between the knowledge contained in cases and model knowledge. Good case representations should perhaps explicitly represent those aspects that can not (yet) be captured in a model. Cases could be viewed as exceptions to the general "theory" represented by the model. Think of our planner with an empty case base but with a qualitative model. It reminds us of a fresh graduate, it has an up-to-date theory of the domain but no experience. Experience in the form of actual cases provides quantitative information and brings about the limits of the theory. For bioprocesses at least this seems to be the case, but similar issues may be important in recent work on pest management (Hastings *et al.*, 1995) and fruit treatment (Verdenius, 1997).

Another reason for the interest in this kind of planners is that no other tools for bioprocess recipe *planning* are available to the biotechnical industry. However, many bioprocesses are very sensitive to their history; erroneous process states can normally not be corrected. This makes it essential to design a correct process recipe *a priori* (a planning approach) instead of adjusting process setpoints after recognition of deviations and problems (on–line control). However, in some processes it may be possible, and indeed effective, to adjust the recipe (plan) during the course of the process. This has been referred to as an agent approach (Hammond *et al.*, 1993) to planning; the planner is an agent taking care of the process. The application for rye-bread production, briefly mentioned before, should be such an agent. In practice industrial production of rye-bread is a continuous, not a batch process. Here, a solution (and extension of the framework), would be to regard observed deviations and problems together with their solution, current situation and process history as a case. The system should then come up with a remedy for the problem; the output is no longer a recipe but a recipe modification. An interesting challenge is to develop a system for a process consisting of a combination of batch and continuous unit operations.

4. Possibilities and Challenges

Having a model also enables computation of interesting aspects to index on, although the current system does not yet makes much use of this. One obvious possibility lies in using the planner for additional tasks, such as diagnosis. The system could retrieve cases that could be expected to have a similar behaviour as a target case, and then compare such cases with the target case that resulted in an actual problem. A similar situation exists when product analysis becomes available.

Because of the model, explanations for a variety of aspects are easy to construct. A very interesting extension would be to use cases to *learn* the model. Pioneering work by DeJong (1994) hints at how this could be achieved. The model would be asked to construct explanations for the observed result (product analysis) of the case, given the plan and the situation, that is. If the model can indeed explain all the observations, the model is valid. If however, the model cannot explain an observation, it obviously need to be revised. Another reason to revise the model could be rejection of a proposed recipe by the user. DeJong (1994) worked with very simple models where it was possible to search the space of possible model extensions and select the simplest model that could explain all observations. In a real application, that does not seem feasible, perhaps model revision can be done by a case-based reasoner, or actually by the machinery already in the planner.

A planner, such as the mashing planner described here, may have other functions than just planning a recipe for every batch. The planner could also be used in production development, especially if model learning is available. The specification and perhaps ingredients for a novel product would be unlike any other case. However if the product is not too different, the planner could construct a, probably poor, recipe. Execution of the recipe however results in an additional case and possibly in an improved model. Again a recipe for the same new product could be planned but now the system has one case and a better model to rely on.

Another role of such a planner could be in training. A planner that has been in use for a while builds a kind of "corporate" memory, a useful asset as such. This idea could be extended even further; a large company could have a central planner that is used by its many plants. The planner would effectively transfer experience from one plant to another.

References

Aamodt, A. (1994). Explanation-driven case-based reasoning, In S. Wess, K. Althoff, M. Richter (eds.): *Topics in Case-based reasoning*. Springer Verlag, pp 274-288.

Aarts, R. J. (1992). *Knowledge-based systems for bioprocesses*. Technical Research Centre of Finland, Publications 120, 116 p.

Aarts, R. J., Sjöholm, K., Home, S. & Pietilä, K. (1993). Computer-planned mashing. *Proc. of the European Brewery Convention Congress, Oslo, 1993*, pp. 655–662.

Alberts, L. K. (1993). *YMIR: an ontology for engineering design*, PhD-thesis, ISBN 90-9006128-2.

Bhatta, S., Goel, A. & Prabhakar, S. (1994). Innovation in Analogical Design: A Model-Based Approach. *Proc. of the Third International Conference on AI in Design, Aug. 1994, Lausanne, Switzerland*.

DeJong, G. F. (1994). Learning to plan in continuous domains. *Artificial Intelligence* **65**: 71–141.

Forbus. K.D. (1984). Qualitative Process Theory. *Artificial Intelligence* **24**: 85–168.

Fox, M., Chionglo, J.F., & Fadel, F.G. (1993). A Common Sense Model of the Enterprise. *Proceedings of the 2nd Industrial Engineering Research Conference, Norcross GA*: Institute for Industrial Engineers, pp. 425–429.

Gruber, T. R. (1991). The Role of Common Ontology in Achieving Sharable, Reusable Knowledge Bases. *Principles of Knowledge Representation and Reasoning: Proceedings of the Second International Conference, Cambridge, MA*, Morgan Kaufmann Publishers Inc., pp. 601–602.

Hammond, K. (1990). Explaining and Repairing Plans That Fail. *Artificial Intelligence*, **45**:173–228.

Hammond, K., Converse, T. & Marks, M. (1993). Toward a Theory of Agency. In: *Machine Learning Methods for Planning*, Minton, S. (ed), Morgan Kaufmann Publishers Inc., San Diego, pp. 351–396.

Hastings, J.D., Branting, L.K. & Lockwood, J.A. (1995), Case Adaptation Using an Incomplete Causal Model. In: Veloso, M. & Aamodt, A. (Eds.): *Case-based reasoning research and development: 1st Intl. Conf. ICCBR-95, Sesimbra, Portugal, Oct. 1995*, Springer, pp. 181–192.

Johnson, R. E. & Russo, V. F. (1991) *Reusing Object Oriented Designs*. University of Illinois tech. report UIUCDCS 91–1696.

Kolodner, J. (1993). *Case-Based Reasoning*. Morgan-Kaufmann Publishers, Inc., San Mateo CA, 668 p.

Koton, P. (1989). *Using experience in learning and problem solving*. Massachusetts Institute of Technology, Laboratory of Computer Science (Ph.D. diss., October 1988), MIT/LCS/TR-441.

Rousu, J. & Aarts, R.J. (1996). Adaptation Cost as a Criterion for Solution Evaluation. In this volume.

Sycara, K., Guttal, R., Koning, J., Narasimhan, S. & Navinchandra, D. (1992) CADET: a Case-based Synthesis Tool for Engineering Design, *Intl. J. Expert Systems*, **4**:2.

Verdenius, F. (1997). Managing Product Inherent Variance During Treatment. Accepted for publication in: *Computers & Electronics in Agriculture*.

On the Role of Abstraction in Case-Based Reasoning

Ralph Bergmann and Wolfgang Wilke

University of Kaiserslautern,
Centre for Learning Systems and Applications (LSA)
Dept. of Computer Science,
P.O.-Box 3049, D-67653 Kaiserslautern, Germany
E-Mail: {bergmann,wilke}@informatik.uni-kl.de

Abstract. This paper addresses the role of abstraction in case-based reasoning. We develop a general framework for reusing cases at several levels of abstraction, which is particularly suited for describing and analyzing existing and designing new approaches of this kind. We argue that in synthetic tasks (e.g. configuration, design, and planning), abstraction can be successfully used to improve the efficiency of similarity assessment, retrieval, and adaptation. Furthermore, a case-based planning system, called PARIS, is described and analyzed in detail using this framework. An empirical study done with PARIS demonstrates significant advantages concerning retrieval and adaptation efficiency as well as flexibility of adaptation. Finally, we show how other approaches from the literature can be classified according to the developed framework.

1 Introduction

Traditionally, case-based reasoning (CBR) approaches retrieve, reuse, and retain cases in a representation at a single level of abstraction. In this predefined representation, cases, new problems, as well as general knowledge must be represented. Recently, some researchers have started to investigate the use of abstraction in CBR (e.g., [19, 12, 3, 4, 5, 20, 2], cf. also [13], p. 576). However, a clear picture of how CBR can benefit from abstraction has not be drawn till now.

In AI, the use of abstraction was originally inspired by human problem solving (cf. [14]) and has already been successfully used in different fields such as theorem proving, model-based diagnosis or planning [9]. The basic idea that emerges from different approaches to using abstraction in CBR is to supply a CBR system with cases at different (higher) levels of abstraction. Thereby, the CBR process can be supported in the following ways:

- Abstraction can reduce the complexity of a case, i.e., it can simplify its representation, e.g. by reducing the number of features, relations, constraints, operators, etc. This simplification usually reduces the effort required for similarity assessment and/or solution adaptation.
- Cases at higher levels of abstraction can be used as a kind of prototypes, which can be used as indexes to a larger set of related, more detailed cases. Such indexes can help to improve the efficiency of the retrieval.

- Cases at higher levels of abstraction can even be used as a substitute for a set of concrete cases. Thereby, the size of the case base may be reduced significantly, which improves the efficiency of retrieval.
- Abstraction can also be used as a means of defining the semantics of similarity. Similarity can be defined as equality on a certain level of abstraction. The lower the level of abstraction on which two cases are identical, the higher the similarity.
- Abstraction can increase the flexibility of reuse. Adapting abstract solutions contained in cases at higher levels of abstraction can lead to abstract solutions suitable for a large spectrum of concrete problems.
- Abstraction and refinement, on their own, can be used as a method for solution adaptation. Like in hierarchical problem solving, an abstract solution (or parts of a solution) contained in a case can be refined towards a solution to the new problems that may be radically different from the original concrete solution contained in the cases.

These advantages seem to be particularly valuable in situations in which a large number of cases is available, the similarity assessment is very expensive, or flexible adaptation is required. However, abstraction is inevitably connected with a loss of information. When reasoning primarily with abstract cases, this loss of information must be compensated by other kinds of (general) knowledge which can lead to an increased effort in knowledge engineering.

2 Reusing Cases at Several Levels of Abstraction

We now present a general framework for reusing cases at higher levels of abstraction covering the CBR phases [1] retrieve, reuse, and retain. This framework is particularly suited for synthetic problem solving tasks such as case-based configuration, design, or planning. Typically, these tasks are characterized through a vast space of potentially relevant solutions and a relatively low coverage of this solution space by the available cases.

2.1 What are Abstract Cases?

While cases are usually represented and reused on a single level, abstraction techniques enable a CBR system to reason with cases at several levels of abstractions. Firstly, this requires the introduction of several distinct levels of abstraction.

Levels of abstraction Each level of abstraction allows the representation of problems, solutions, and cases as well as the representation of general knowledge that might be required in addition to the cases. Usually, levels of abstraction are ordered (totally or partially) through an abstraction-relation, i.e., one level is called *more abstract* than another level.

A more abstract level is characterized through a reduced level of detail in the representation, i.e., it usually consists of less features, relations, constraints, operators, etc. Moreover, abstract levels model the world in a less precise way, but still capture certain, important properties.

In traditional hierarchical problem solving (e.g., ABSTRIPS [17]), abstraction levels are constructed by simply dropping certain features of the more concrete representation levels. However, it has been shown that this view of abstraction is too restrictive and representation dependent [4, 11] to make full use of the abstraction idea. In general, different levels of abstraction require different representation languages, one for each level. Abstract properties can then be expressed in completely different terms than concrete properties [2].

Different Kinds of Cases Based on the level of abstraction, we can distinguish between two kinds of cases: *concrete cases* and *abstract cases*. A *concrete case* is a case located at the lowest available level of abstraction. An *abstract case* is a case represented at a higher level of abstraction.

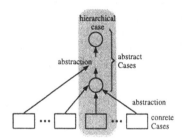

Fig. 1. Different kinds of cases

If several abstraction levels are given (e.g., a hierarchy of abstraction spaces), one concrete case can be abstracted to several abstract cases, one at each higher level of abstraction. Such an abstract case contains less detailed information than a concrete case. On the other hand several concrete cases usually correspond to a single abstract case (see Fig. 1). These concrete cases share the same abstract description; they only differ in the details.

Instead of having cases located at a single level of abstraction, one case (called *hierarchical case*) can also contain information at several or all levels of abstractions that are available.

2.2 Acquisition of abstract cases

We can distinguish different ways in which abstract or hierarchical cases are built in order to be stored in the case base.

Abstract cases available The first, and simplest scenario is one, in which case data is naturally available at several appropriate levels of abstraction. This can be the situation if, for example, data is modeled in an object-oriented language and stored in an object-oriented database. The abstraction present in the class hierarchy (inheritance) can then lead to different levels of abstraction and data base instances provide data for abstract or hierarchical cases.

Automatic generation of abstract cases In most situations, cases are only available in a single representation which can be considered the concrete level. Consequently abstract or hierarchical cases must be abstracted out of these concrete cases. In certain situations, such a *case abstraction* can be done automatically. This usually requires general knowledge about ways of mapping cases onto higher levels of abstraction.

Manual generation of abstract cases If abstract cases are neither available nor generated automatically, they must be abstracted manually from concrete cases. This option requires a very high effort, that – we think – cannot be justified in most applications.

2.3   Abstract Cases in Retrieval

Abstract cases located at different levels of abstraction can be used as hierarchical indexes to those concrete (or abstract) cases that contain the same kind of information but at a lower level of abstraction. An *abstraction hierarchy* can be constructed in which abstract cases at higher levels of abstraction are located above abstract cases at lower levels. The leaf nodes of this hierarchy contain concrete cases (see Fig. 2). During retrieval, this hierarchy can be traversed top-down, following only those branches in which abstract cases are sufficiently similar to the current problem. This kind of memory organization is similar to the *memory organization packets* (MOPs) [18].

This approach to indexing, however, makes an assumption concerning the similarity assessment. It requires that a problem cannot be similar to a concrete case unless it is at least similar to this case at a higher level of abstraction. This assumption holds particularly, if similarity is defined *based* on the level of abstraction, which can be done as follows:
A problem p is more similar to the concrete case C_1 than to the concrete case C_2 if the lowest level of abstraction on which p matches C_2 is higher (more abstract) than the lowest level of abstraction on which p matches C_1.

2.4   Reuse of Abstract Cases

There are different ways of using the information provided in abstract cases for solving the current problem.

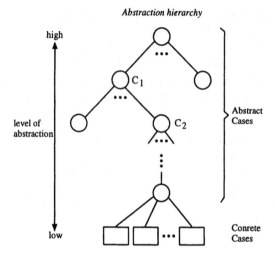

Abstraction hierarchy

high

level of
abstraction

Abstract
Cases

Conrete
Cases

low

Fig. 2. Abstraction hierarchy for indexing cases

No reuse of abstract solutions Abstract cases are only used as indexes to concrete cases. For problem solving, concrete cases are used exclusively.

Abstract solutions as result The CBR system retrieves and reuses abstract cases. The abstract solutions contained in the abstract cases are not refined to more concrete levels but are directly returned as output. The interpretation of abstract solutions is up to the user.

Refinement of abstract cases The CBR system retrieves and reuses abstract cases and refines abstract solutions to the concrete level. The refined solution is then presented to the user. For her/him it is transparent, whether the solution presented by the system stems directly from a matching concrete cases or whether the solution is obtained through the refinement of an abstract case.

Please note that abstraction and refinement is already a technique for solution adaptation. If available concrete cases are abstracted (e.g., automatically) to abstract cases and then getting retrieved and refined, a new solution to a new problem will be constructed. The higher the level of abstraction of the reused abstract case, the more may the newly refined solution differ from the solution contained in the original case.

We can distinguish different methods for realizing such a refinement:

Generative refinement of abstract cases This refinement is done by generative problem solving methods, e.g. hierarchical problem solving. For automatically performing this refinement task, additional general domain knowledge is usually required.

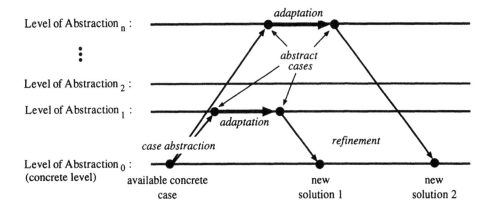

Fig. 3. Adaptation of abstract cases

Case-based refinement of abstract cases This refinement itself is done in a case-based way, avoiding partially the need for additional general knowledge. However, case-based refinement requires cases that describe how the individual elements, the abstract solutions are built of, can be refined at a more concrete level.

2.5 Adaptation of Abstract Cases

Besides the possibility to realize adaptation by refining abstract cases, adaptation can also be done on a single level of abstraction (see Fig. 3). The spectrum of known methods for solution adaptation in CBR (for an overview see e.g., [6, 10, 24]) can also be applied to abstract cases prior to the refinement. Thereby, the flexibility of reuse can be increased, i.e., an abstract case covers a larger area in the solution space.

2.6 Forgetting cases

The reuse of cases at several levels of abstraction also provides a frame for realizing case deletion policies [21]. Cases deletion is particularly important to avoid the utility or swamping problem [22, 8] that occurs when case bases grow very large. When reusing abstract cases for indexing and reuse, case deletion can efficiently be realized through a pruning of the abstraction hierarchy. If certain concrete cases are removed from the case base, the abstract cases that remain accessible can still cover the set of target problems previously covered by the deleted concrete case. However, this requires effective ways of refinement such as generative or case-based refinement. For selecting cases to forget, the savings due to the reduced retrieval effort must outweigh the additional effort for refining more abstract cases.

kind of stored cases:	abstract	abstract & concrete	hierarchical	
acquisition of abstract cases:	cases available	manual generation	automatic generation	
abstract cases for indexing:	no		yes	
reuse of abstract solutions:	no	abstract result	generative refine.	case based refine.
adaptation of abstract solutions:	no		yes	
case deletion policy:	no		yes	

Table 1. Framework for reusing abstract cases. The left column shows the facets and the right part displays the possible values.

2.7 Summary of the Framework

Table 1 summarizes the various facets of the framework for reusing abstract cases. Existing approaches can be described and analyzed and new approaches can be designed using this framework.

3 PARIS: Using abstraction in case-based planning

Now, we briefly describe a concrete case-based reasoning system, called PARIS[1] [3, 4, 2] that uses abstraction for case-based planning. PARIS was designed as a generic (i.e., domain independent) case-based planning system but with a particular area of application domains in mind: manufacturing planning in mechanical engineering. Here, a plan is a sequence of manufacturing steps that must be performed in order to produce a particular mechanical workpiece. Planning in this domain can be viewed as classical STRIPS [7] planning: a (manufacturing) *operator* transforms a certain *state* (current workpiece) into a successor state (workpiece after the manufacturing step). The planning task is to find a sequence of operators which transform a mold (initial state) into the desired workpiece (goal state). Since finding such a plan is known to be a NP-complete problem, several case-based approaches have been developed already that allow to make use of additional knowledge (in the form of previous cases) during planning [23].

The task of a case-based planning system in this domain is to produce a manufacturing plan (solution) for a new workpiece (problem) by reusing previous manufacturing cases. We have identified, a set of CBR specific requirements that are important in this domain [2]:

- ability to cope with vast space of solution plans
- construction of correct solutions

---

[1] PARIS stands for *plan abstraction and refinement in an integrated system*.

- flexible reuse due to large spectrum of target problems
- processing of highly complex cases
- only concrete planning cases available (e.g. in archives of a company)

Abstract Planning Cases In PARIS, *abstract planning cases* are *generated automatically, stored* together with the concrete cases in the case-base, *used for indexing* during retrieval, and they are *adapted* and *refined automatically* during the reuse-phase. Different levels of abstraction are realized by different *planning domains*, each of which consists of its own set of operators and its own representation of states (i.e., workpiece descriptions in our domain). Abstract operators and states are described using more abstract terms than concrete operators. This typically requires also a reduced number of predicates. While a concrete planning case consists of a sequence of operators from the concrete level, an abstract planning case consists of a sequence of operators form the abstract level. Each abstract operator that occurs in an abstract case stands for a sub-sequence of concrete operators of the corresponding concrete case. In [4] a comprehensive formal model of case abstraction is explained in detail.

Example Figure 4 presents an example of the relationship between a concrete case and an abstract case in the manufacturing domain. Here, the concrete planning domain contains operators and predicates to describe the detailed contour of workpieces and individual manufacturing operations (e.g., cutting a certain area) that must be performed. The abstract domain abstracts from the detailed contour and represents larger units, called complex processing areas, together with the status of their processing (e.g. not processed, roughly processed, or completed). The left side of Figure 4 shows a section of a concrete case, depicting how a step-like contour with two grooves is manufactured by a sub-plan consisting of 6 steps. The abstract case, shown in the middle of this figure, abstracts from the detailed contour and just represents a complex processing area named A that includes raw (step-like contour) and fine (grooves) elements. The corresponding abstract plan contains 2 abstract steps: processing in a raw manner and processing in a fine manner.

Acquisition of Abstract Cases Engineering departments which develop manufacturing plans manually, usually record them (e.g., in a database) for documentation purposes. These plans contain all details necessary for manufacturing the workpiece; they represent concrete cases only. Because manual abstraction of such cases seems to be a tremendous effort, abstract cases are generated automatically from a given concrete case. For this purpose, a domain-independent case abstraction algorithm has been developed [4, 2]. Given a concrete and an abstract planning domain, this algorithm computes abstract cases from a given concrete case.

Refinement of abstract cases In PARIS an abstract solution contained in an abstract case is refined automatically to a concrete level solution, as explained in

36

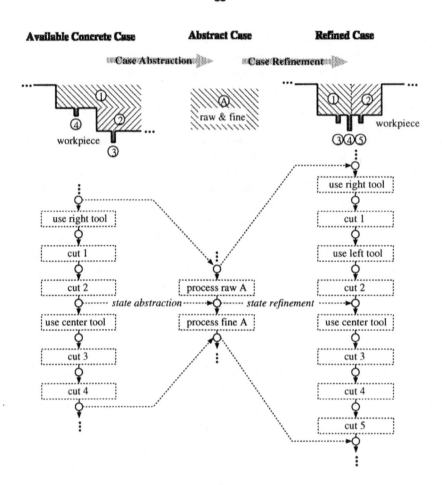

Fig. 4. Example of generating and refining abstract cases.

detail in [4, 2]. The right side of Figure 4 shows an example of such a refinement. Please note that the contour of the two workpieces differs drastically at the concrete level. However, the abstract case matches exactly because the 5 atomic contour elements in the new problem can be abstracted to a complex processing area with raw and fine elements. During refinement, the abstract opertors of the abstract case are used to guide the generative planner to find a refined solution to the problem. Therefore, each abstract state is used as a kind of sub-goal. The planner starts with the concrete initial state from the new problem description and searches for a sequences of concrete operators leading to a concrete state that can be abstracted to the first abstract state in the abstract case. The resulting operator sequence is a refinement of the first abstract operator. All remaining abstract operators are then sequentially refined in the same way. In the portion of the case shown in Figure 4, the abstract operator *process raw A* is refined to a sequence of four concrete steps which manufacture area 1 and 2. The next abstract operator is refined to a four-step sequence which manufactures the grooves 3, 4, and 5.

We can seen that the abstract case decomposes the original problem into a set of much smaller subproblems. Due to this decomposition, the effort for problem solving is drastically reduced compared to a pure from scratch problem solver.

Adaptation of Abstract Cases PARIS performs solution adaptation also at a single level of abstraction. For that purpose, an abstract or concrete case is *generalized* into a generalized case (similar to a schema or script). Such a generalized case does not only describe a single problem and a single solution but a *problem class* together with a *solution class*. Such classes are realized by introducing *variables* into the initial and goal state as well as into the plan. Additionally, a generalized case contains a *set of constraints* that restricts the instantiation of these variables. PARIS includes an algorithm for automatically generalizing concrete or abstract cases into schemas [2] by applying explanation-based generalization [15]. Adaptation with generalized cases is done by finding an instantiation of the variables such that instantiated generalized case matches the target problem to be solved. In PARIS, matching (similarity assessment) and adaptation is done by a constraint satisfaction problem solver (see [2] for details). The effort for solving this constraint satisfaction task can be very high: in the worst case it is exponential in the number of constraints and the size of the problem class. Typically, the representations at a higher level of abstraction are less complex than representations at lower levels. Consequently, generalized cases at higher levels of abstraction contain less constraints and the problem class is composed of a small number of prepositions. Therefore, adaptation of abstract cases requires less effort than adaptation of concrete cases.

Retrieval with Abstract Cases In PARIS, abstract and concrete cases are stored in the case base which is organized by an abstraction hierarchy. The idea for constructing this hierarchy is based on the following condition: *a case C_1 is located above C_2 (cf. Fig. 2) if for every problem p holds that if C_2 is adaptable for p (at some level of abstraction) then C_1 is adaptable for p as well.* If this condition can be fulfilled, retrieval will be improved, because if C_1 is *not adaptable* for solving p, then none of the cases in the sub-tree below C_1 can be adaptable and must consequently not be accessed. In PARIS such an abstraction hierarchy is built and updated incrementally [2]. During retrieval, this hierarchy is traversed top down. If an abstract case is adaptable for the new problem, the successor nodes are investigated, otherwise the successors not considered and the retrieval proceeds with the next node of the same level.

Case Deletion Policy In PARIS a utility problem can occur, if the representation (e.g., the concrete domain) is very complex such that matching and

Table 2. Comparison of matching and adapting concrete and abstract cases

kind of cases	number of constraints	run-time in sec.	percentage of failures
concrete cases	76.3	95.97	42 %
abstract cases	21.5	1.11	0 %

adaptation of generalized cases through the constraint propagation becomes very costly. In this case, refining an abstract case at a higher level of abstraction can involve less effort than adapting a case at a lower level. To cope with this problem, a case deletion policy is realized which works by pruning sub-trees of the abstraction hierarchy [2]. A sub-tree is pruned if matching and adapting abstract or concrete cases contained in this sub-tree requires more effort than refining a more abstract available case. These efforts are estimated through measuring the run-time for matching and adaptation and the run-time for solution refinement based on the problems already contained in the case base.

4 Experimental Evaluation

We now present the results of an experimental study on the benefits of using abstraction in CBR. This study was done using the fully implemented PARIS system in the domain of manufacturing planning for rotary symmetric workpieces on a lathe (see [4] for details of the domain). For the experiments, 100 concrete cases were generated randomly. From these concrete cases 28 abstract cases at four levels of abstraction could be generated.

Improving Efficiency of Similarity Assessment and Adaptation The purpose of the first experiment was to evaluate how the effort for similarity assessment and adaptation decreases with higher levels of abstraction. For this purpose, we measured the run-time for matching and adapting concrete and abstract generalized cases. A time limit of 200 seconds was imposed. Table 2 shows for abstract and concrete cases, the average number of constraints to be considered during constraint propagation, the average run-time for matching and adapting, and the percentage of failures due to exceeding of the time limit. As expected, these results show a strong decrease in the run-time for abstract cases which is due to the reduced complexity of abstract cases compared to concrete cases.

Improving Retrieval by Abstract Cases The purpose of the second experiment is to evaluate the speedup in retrieval time when using abstract cases (organized in an abstraction hierarchy) for indexing. We built up a case-base with 100 concrete and 28 abstract cases. The abstract cases were used as indexes only. We measured the time for retrieving (including matching and adapting)

Table 3. Retrieval with abstract cases

retrieval method	average retrieval time	percentage of failures
sequential retrieval	185	76 %
retrieval with abstract cases	127	58 %

Table 4. Reuse of abstract cases vs. reuse of concrete cases

Reuse method	size of training set	average problem solving time	percentage of unsolved problems
reuse abstract cases	5	56	16%
	10	49	13 %
reuse concrete cases	5	157	71 %
	10	154	68 %

a concrete case with the abstraction hierarchy and compared it to the time for a sequential retrieval of concrete cases. Table 3 shows the average results for retrieving 100 different cases. We can see a good improvement in the retrieval time as well as a reduction in the number of failures due to exceeding of the time limit.

Problem Solving Performance The purpose of this experiment is to evaluate the overall problem solving performance and competence for reusing abstract cases vs. reusing concrete cases. From the 100 available cases, we have randomly chosen 10 training sets of 5 cases and 10 training sets of 10 cases. Table 4 shows the average problem solving time and the average percentage of solved problems (within a time limit of 200 seconds) for the training sets of the two different sizes and the different kinds of reuse. These average numbers are computed from the 10 training and testing sets for each size. We can recognize a (statistically) significant improvement through reusing abstract case.

Flexibility of Reuse The purpose of this experiment was to evaluate the flexibility of the reuse. For each of the 100 cases, we evaluated how many of the problems in the remaining 99 cases could be solved through reuse of this case within the time limit of 200 seconds. We compared the flexibility of reusing concrete and abstract cases separately. Figure 5 shows the results plotted for each case. On the abscissa, the 100 cases are ordered according the complexity. Case No. 1 is the simplest case with a plan composed of 4 operators and Case No. 100 is the most complex case containing 18 operators. The ordinate shows the number of problems (of the remaining 99 cases) for which this case can be reused. Again, we can see a strong advantage when reusing abstract cases.

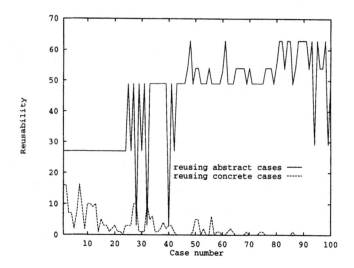

Fig. 5. Flexibility of reuse

Table 5. Case deletion policy

Case deletion policy	average problem solving time	percentage of unsolved problems
disabled	69	28 %
enabled	36	6 %

Case Deletion Policy Finally we evaluated the impact of the case deletion policy. For that purpose, we trained the system with all available cases and used the same cases for testing it again. In one run, the case deletion policy was active, in the other run it was disabled. Table 5 shows the average problem solving time as well as the number of problems solved within the 200 second time limit. We can identify a (statistically) significant improvement caused by the case deletion policy.

Conclusion from experiments These experiments clearly demonstrate the benefits we hoped to gain from introducing abstraction into case-based reasoning (cf. section 1). However, these experiments are performed in a very specific scenario (planning task, domain: process planning for rotary symmetric workpieces, particular representation). Whether these results can be generalized for different tasks and domains still has to be proven. However, the results obtained by Branting and Aha [5] – also for a planning task – strongly support our results.

kind of stored cases:	*abstract*	*abstract & concrete*		*hierarchical*
		PARIS DEJA-VU	COVER CLOSEST	PRIAR MOCAS

acquisition of abstract cases	*cases available*		*manual generation*	*automatic generation*
	PRIAR COVER DEJA-VU CLOSEST			PARIS MOCAS

abstract cases for indexing:	*no*	*yes*
	MOCAS PRIAR	PARIS COVER CLOSEST DEJA-VU

reuse of abstract solutions:	*no*	*abstract result*	*generative refine.*	*case based refine.*
		MOCAS	PARIS PRIAR COVER	DEJA-VU CLOSEST

adaptation of abstract solutions:	*no*	*yes*
	COVER	PARIS CLOSEST PRIAR MOCAS DEJA-VU

case deletion policy:	*no*	*yes*
	COVER CLOSEST PRIAR MOCAS DEJA-VU	PARIS

Table 6. Comparison of other approaches using the framework

5 Related Work

We now discuss related work with respect to the general framework introduced in section 2. Table 6 shows the result of classifying the following approaches according to the framework:

- Déjà Vu [19, 20]: design of control software,
- PRIAR [12]: domain-independent action planning,
- MoCAS [16, 3]: model-based case adaptation for diagnosis of technical systems,
- COVER and CLOSEST [5]: algorithms for hierarchical A* search.

We can see that there is no approach that is limited to the reuse of abstract cases. All approaches that reuse cases at several levels of abstraction always include the concrete level. However, the experiments with PARIS have shown that it is often not useful to reason with concrete cases, if abstract cases are available.

Almost all current approaches assume that cases are available at several levels of abstraction. PRIAR, COVER, and CLOSEST are based on a hierarchical problem solver. Consequently, cases at all levels of abstraction are available when problems become solved. PARIS and MoCAS are the only system which supports the automatic generation of abstract cases out of concrete ones.

Not all approaches make use of abstract cases as a means for indexing. Some approaches does not address the retrieval problem in deep (e.g. MoCAs and PRIAR).

MoCAs seems to be the only system that directly returns abstract solutions to the user. The reason for this is that in the diagnostic domain, abstract solutions correspond to a complex component that may be replaced completely. All approaches that refine cases by a generic method are built on the integration of a from-scratch problem solver.

Almost all systems make use of the advantage that adapting an abstract case is simpler than adapting a concrete case. COVER explicitly renounces adaptation for experimental purposes.

Till now, PARIS is the only system that makes use of a case deletion policy. This policy has shown to significantly improve the performance of the system (cf. section 4).

The presented framework for reusing cases at several levels of abstraction shows in its facets different possibilities of how abstraction can be incorporated into CBR. Unfortunately, there are only a few systems available that make full use of the abstraction idea. Most of them are in the area of planning. Future research should try to use this framework for developing similar approaches for different tasks and domains (e.g. configuration) to validate the positive results gained so far.

Acknowledgements

The authors want to thank Klaus-Dieter Althoff and Hector Munioz for helpful remarks on earlier versions of this paper. This research was partially funded by the Commission of the European Communities (ESPRIT contract No. 22196, the INRECA II project, *Information and Knowledge Reengineering for Reasoning from Cases*). The partners of INRECA II are AcknoSoft (prime contractor, France), Daimler-Benz (Germanz), tecInno (Germany), Irish Medical Systems (Ireland) and the University of Kaiserslautern (Germany). This work is also partially funded by the "Stiftung Rheinland-Pfalz fuer Innovation".

References

1. A. Aamodt and E. Plaza. Case-based reasoning: Foundational issues, methodological variations, and system approaches. *AI Communications*, 7(1):39–59, 1994.
2. R. Bergmann. *Effizientes Problemlösen durch flexible Wiederverwendung von Fällen auf verschiedenen Abstraktionsebenen*. PhD thesis, University of Kaiserslautern, 1996.
3. R. Bergmann, G. Pews, and W. Wilke. Explanation-based similarity: A unifying approach for integrating domain knowledge into case-based reasoning. In S. Wess, K.-D. Althoff, and M.M. Richter, editors, *Topics in Case-Based Reasoning*, volume 837 of *Lecture Notes on Artificial Intelligence*, pages 182–196. Springer, 1994.
4. R. Bergmann and W. Wilke. Building and refining abstract planning cases by change of representation language. *Journal of Artificial Intelligence Research*, 3:53–118, 1995.

5. K. Branting and D. Aha. Stratified case-based reasoning: Reusing hierarchical problem solving episodes. In *Proceedings of the International Joint Conference on Artificial Intelligence*, pages 384–390, 1995.

6. P. Cunningham, D. Finn, and S. Slattery. Knowledge engineering requirements in derivational analogy. volume 1 of *LNAI*, pages 234–245. Springer Verlag, 1994.

7. R. E. Fikes and N. J. Nilsson. Strips: A new approach to the application of theorem proving to problem solving. *Artificial Intelligence*, 2:189–208, 1971.

8. A. G. Francis and A. Ram. The utility problem in case-based reasoning. In *Proceedings AAAI-93 Case-Based Reasoning Workshop*, 1993.

9. F. Giunchiglia and T. Walsh. A theory of abstraction. *Artificial Intelligence*, 57:323–389, 1992.

10. K. Hanney, M. Keane, B. Smyth, and P. Cunningham. Systems, tasks and adaptation knowledge: Revealing some revealing dependencies. In M. Veloso and A. Aamodt, editors, *Case-based Reasoning Research and Development*, volume 1010 of *Lecture Notes in AI*, pages 461–470, 1995.

11. R. C. Holte, T. Mkadmi, R. M. Zimmer, and A. J. MacDonald. Speeding up problem solving by abstraction: A graph-oriented approach. Technical report, University of Ottawa, Ontario, Canada, 1995.

12. S. Kambhampati and J. Hendler. A validation-structure-based theory of plan modifications. *Artificial Intelligence*, 1992.

13. J. L. Kolodner. *Case-Based Reasoning*. Morgan Kaufmann, 1993.

14. M. Minsky. Steps toward artificial intelligence. In E. Feigenbaum, editor, *Computers and Thought*. McGraw-Hill, New York, NY, 1963.

15. T. M. Mitchell, R. M. Keller, and S. T. Kedar-Cabelli. Explanation-based generalization: A unifying view. *Machine Learning*, 1(1):47–80, 1986.

16. Gerd Pews and Stefan Wess. Combining case-based and model-based approaches for diagnostic applications in technical domains. In *Proceedings EWCBR93*, volume 2, pages 325 – 328, 1993.

17. E.D. Sacerdoti. Planning in a hierarchy of abstraction spaces. *Artificial Intelligence*, 5:115–135, 1974.

18. R. C. Schank. *Dynamic Memory: A Theory of Learning in Computers and People*. Cambridge University Press, New York, 1982.

19. B. Smyth and P. Cunningham. Deja vu: A hierarchical case-based reasoning system for software design. In *ECAI-92*, pages 587–589, 1992.

20. B. Smyth and M. Keane. Retrieving adaptable cases. In S. Wess, K.-D. Althoff, and M. M. Richter, editors, *Topics in Case-Based Reasoning*, pages 209–220. Springer, 1994.

21. B. Smyth and M. Keane. Remembering to forget: A competence-preserving case deletion policy for case-based reasoning systems. In Chris S. Mellish, editor, *Proceedings of the International Conference on Artificial Intelligence*, pages 377–383. Morgan Kaufmann Publishers, 1995.

22. M. Tambe and A. Newell. Some chunks are expensive. In *Proceedings of the 5th International Conference on Machine Learning*, pages 451–458, 1988.

23. M. Veloso, H. Munioz, and R. Bergmann. Case-based planning: Selected methods and systems. *AI Communications*, 1996. (in press).

24. A. Voss. Exploiting previous solutions - made easy. ftp://ftp.gmd.de//GMD/ai-research/Publications/Fabel/Prev-sol-voss.ps.gz, 1995.

ISAC: A CBR System for Decision Support in Air Traffic Control[1]

Andrea Bonzano* **, Pádraig Cunningham*, Colin Meckiff**

*Reasoning Research Project
Department of Computer Science
Trinity College Dublin
College Green
Dublin 2
Ireland
{Andrea.Bonzano,Padraig.Cunningham}@cs.tcd.ie

**Eurocontrol Experimental Centre
91222 Brétigny Sur Orge
France
Colin.Meckiff@eurocontrol.fr

Abstract. The conflict resolution task performed by air-traffic controllers appears a suitable task for automation using CBR. This is because human competence seems to involve recognising situations and reusing solutions. In this paper we present our experiences in developing a CBR system to support this conflict resolution task. We discuss the problems of case representation: the macro problem of what should constitute a case and the micro problem of how to characterise a case. We evaluate some alternative case representations and identify a representation with one aircraft per case that is extendible to describe conflicts with multiple aircraft.

1. Introduction

In this paper we describe the application of CBR to a real world problem in air traffic control. This application is interesting in itself because of the safety critical issues involved. It is also of particular interest from a CBR viewpoint because of the question of what should constitute a case in this problem domain. At this stage in the progress of CBR research this question is chestnut that has exercised many researchers. CBR is intuitively appealing because it manifestly reflects one of the important ways in which humans solve problems. However the represent-retrieve-reuse model of CBR is often difficult to apply in situations where human competence is obviously reuse-based. This difficulty is almost always associated with the granularity of retrieval and the question of what should constitute a case.

ISAC is a case-based decision support system for conflict resolution in air traffic control (ATC). A conflict occurs in ATC when two or more aircraft pass too close together. It is the air traffic controller's job to resolve potential conflicts by adjusting the trajectories of the aircraft. This decision involves: selecting the aircraft to manoeuvre, deciding on the type of manoeuvre and determining the details of the manoeuvre. The choice of aircraft to manoeuvre and the type of manoeuvre depend on several factors including:

---

1. This research was carried out with the support of Eurocontrol Experimental Centre at Brétigny, a European centre for research and simulation in Air Traffic Control.

the geometry of the conflict, the capabilities of the aircraft, their position relative to their destination, etc. At the moment ISAC assists in the first two stages of this decision making process. The motivation in designing ISAC has been to reduce the decision making burden on controllers. This is of particular importance for the future as air traffic volumes increase. The current version of ISAC can resolve conflict between pairs of aircraft. However, an important design consideration has been that it should be extendible to problems involving three or more aircraft. In a CBR context this involves more complex types of case reuse. It implies that, for reasons of domain coverage, monolithic cases describing individual conflicts are not practicable.

Later in this paper we evaluate some alternatives to this monolithic case structure. In Section 2 we will describe the air traffic control problem in detail. We will also describe HIPS, a next generation visualisation aid for controllers and explain how ISAC interacts with that system. In Section 3 we will present the overall architecture of ISAC and in Section 4 we will describe the alternative case representation options that have been considered. We conclude in Section 5 with an evaluation of the effectiveness of these alternatives.

2. The problem of air traffic control

Despite the fact that modern aircraft are packed with sophisticated electronic equipment, air traffic control has always been more of an art than a science. Ground-based control essentially consists of people following the progress of aircraft represented by points (derived from radar data) on a flat display screen. The simple nature of the data available means that the controllers themselves are required to build and maintain a "mental picture" of extrapolated 4D traffic based on experience and other rather ill-defined heuristics. Having done this, the controller must mentally compare every pair of predicted trajectories to determine whether any pair of aircraft will pass within the minimum permitted separation - in which case he is required to intervene in some way to resolve the potential conflict.

Such an unscientific approach to ATC is, however, becoming less and less acceptable. Pressure for change is coming from two sources: firstly, the ATC world, as elsewhere, is undergoing an information explosion - controllers potentially have access to gigabytes of data of every sort, and the possibility to communicate with aircraft and other ground systems in ways, and at speeds, which were unimaginable when their practices were conceived. Secondly, airlines are demanding greater efficiency and quality of service from the air traffic control providers: efficiency, because ATC currently accounts for about 15% of the price of a ticket, and quality of service to allow airlines to increasingly fly their preferred (and presumably near-optimal) flight paths - this is difficult using today's practices and structures.

The problem cannot, however, be approached from a uniquely technical viewpoint. Removal of the "artisanal" aspects of ATC, particularly with regard to the task of preventing metallic contact between aircraft, touches the very heart of the profession. This means that any enhancement of the controller's skills by some type of automation must be done in a way which is sympathetic to current practices and therefore acceptable to controllers.

A number of attempts have been made to model conflict resolution activity by capturing and reproducing the rules by which controllers operate. This has inevitably failed because of the difficulty of defining clear and consistent sequences of actions. In this context it therefore seems natural to consider the use of case-based reasoning, since one of the strengths of the technique is not having to model the problem/solution domain in detail, as long as it is possible to identify the key elements involved in the process, together with an idea of their relative importance.

2.1   Principles of ATC

Commercial aircraft are controlled by ground-based air traffic controllers from the moment the engines are started at the origin of the flight to the moment the engines are stopped at the destination. To facilitate the control task once the aircraft is en-route, the airspace is divided into horizontally and vertically bounded sectors, each sector normally being the responsibility of two controllers. The size of a sector depends on the amount of traffic to be processed, the number of aircraft per hour normally being limited to around 30. This means that in areas of high traffic density the sectors will tend to be smaller, giving an average transit time of around 6 or 7 minutes, whereas in low density areas with larger sectors transit time can be around 20 minutes. Apart from national boundaries, the shape of the sector is normally a function of route structure - a sort of road system in the sky normally followed by commercial aircraft - designed so that, for example, major route crossing points do not occur near the edges of the sectors.

When an aircraft is about to enter a sector, the controller(s) responsible for that sector will be somehow notified of its arrival, and this should correspond more or less with its appearance on the synthetic radar display. A short time later they assume responsibility for the aircraft, a complementary release of responsibility having taken place in the upstream sector - the bilateral agreement of the conditions for transfer from one sector to another is known as coordination, and actually represents a substantial part of the controller's workload.

It is then up to the controllers to see the flight through the sector, and clearly the principle concern is that the aircraft transits the sector conflict-free. There is, however, a secondary requirement which is to provide the aircraft with a cost and time-efficient passage.

2.2   Conflicts and conflict resolution

Internationally agreed rules exist defining separation standards below which aircraft are said to be "in conflict". The values of these separations vary according to a number of factors such as the type of controlled airspace e.g. near an airport, oceanic etc. (Note that "conflict" is not synonymous with "collision": for our purposes a conflict is rather the infringement of the applicable separation minima.) Minimum horizontal separations are typically 5 nautical miles (1 Nm=1852 m) in radar controlled regions and either 1000ft or 2000ft vertically, depending on altitude.

In practice controllers will often apply significantly larger separations, mainly due to the difficulties they have in accurately visualising future trajectories and conflict situations. This has a number of implications: for example a manoeuvre applied to resolve a conflict may end up significantly larger than is actually necessary (i.e. non-optimal), and, indeed, there will often be unnecessary intervention where, had the aircraft continued on their existing trajectories, there would not actually have been a loss of separation.

One of the most important advances in computer support for air traffic controllers in the next few years will be the provision of relatively accurate predictions of future aircraft trajectories. Such a development should, in principle, allow clearer visualisation of where aircraft will go, and in particular whether they will be in conflict. Even with such information, however, it is not immediately obvious how controllers can use it.

2.3   The HIPS System

One system which presents this information in a usable way is HIPS (Highly Interactive Problem Solver), a system developed at the Eurocontrol Experimental Centre. HIPS is a novel support tool which comprises two main parts: firstly, it displays conflict situations relative to one selected aircraft in a time-independent way, and secondly, it provides a means for the controller to modify trajectories to find solutions to conflicts. Space does not permit to describe HIPS techniques in detail, so a simple example will be used to show the principles.

Consider Figure 1. The aircraft which interests us, EEC123, is traversing our airspace from left to right. Unfortunately, its trajectory is in conflict with that of another aircraft, EEC456, which is travelling in a northerly direction. The part of our trajectory for which there is a loss of separation between ourselves and EEC456 is marked with a thicker line. If we now imagine that we want to solve this conflict by changing EEC123's heading, we could attempt various new headings assuming a certain point as our start of turn, and for each one we could check for conflicts and again mark any loss of separation in bold.

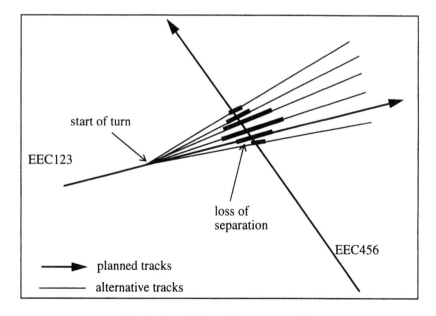

Fig. 1. A possible conflict representation.

Having tried a number of possibilities the next step is to group together all the bold lines to produce a single "no-go" zone as shown in Figure 2. This provides an immediate and powerful visual device by which the controller can rapidly see that in this case the conflict can be solved by a relatively small southward or larger northward deviation to EEC123.

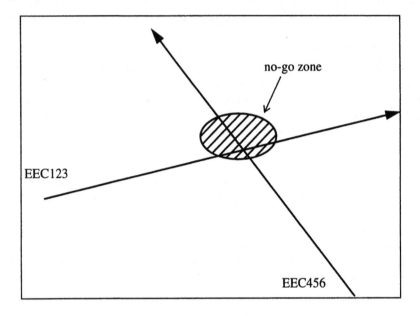

Fig. 2. How HIPS represents the conflict.

The above illustration assumes linear constant-speed trajectories, with the start-point of the manoeuvre already known. Unfortunately these assumptions are unrealistic in real life, which means that the techniques used for generating the diagrams are actually quite complex.

As well as generating a horizontal view, we can use a similar approach to produce diagrams for vertical and speed dimensions, giving a total of three pictures. This HIPS interface is shown in Figure 3. The Plan View Display represents the synthetic radar screen - this is the information that is available to the controller in the current generation of ATC systems. In HIPS this is augmented with the three other perspectives on the conflict. In each of these windows the conflict region is shown in dark grey (normally in red or yellow). In each case the subject trajectory can be manipulated by simple mouse interaction to determine the exact magnitude of the heading, speed or altitude change(s) required.

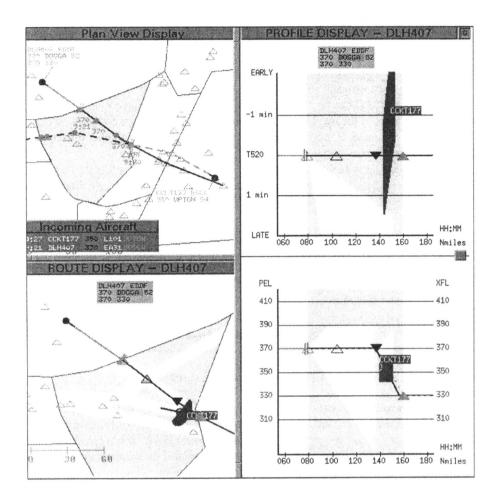

Fig. 3. The HIPS interface.

2.4 Conflict Resolution support for HIPS

One of the main advantages of the HIPS approach is that it does not, of itself, attempt to present complete solutions. It presents information to the controller in a way that he can (hopefully) understand, and it is then up to him to find solutions. This is a key advantage of the approach, and has been important in gaining a degree of acceptance. It has meant, however, that there are still a number of steps to be taken between the time when a potential conflict is recognised, and the implementation of the solution. In particular, the controller must:

- evaluate the conflict situation and decide which aircraft he is going to manoeuvre
- decide which type of manoeuvre is appropriate
- determine the details of the manoeuvre (e.g. turn right 10 degrees, go 10 knots faster etc.).

These decisions imply the examination of the horizontal, altitude and speed display for each aircraft involved in the conflict. The aim of ISAC (Intelligent System for Aircraft Conflict resolution) is to automatically highlight the display corresponding to the best manoeuvre of the best aircraft. This means that ISAC has to decide which is the aircraft that has to be manoeuvred and the type of manoeuvre to avoid the conflict. The solution given by ISAC can be accepted by the controller who will complete it with a deeper specification of the manoeuvre. Alternatively, it may be discarded because it is considered not adequate. If this happens, the controller will choose another display of the six available.

The main advantage in having an intelligent system behind HIPS is that the controller's workload is reduced. Moreover, the system could suggest a manoeuvre that didn't come to the controller's mind, but is more efficient.

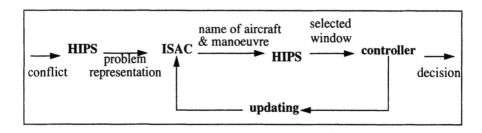

Fig. 4. How ISAC is embedded in HIPS.

The conflict resolution process is shown in Figure 4. When HIPS detects the conflict, it sends the description to ISAC: i.e. the flight plan and performance of the aircraft involved, the shapes of the no-go zones etc. Using this data, ISAC selects the aircraft to manoeuvre and the type of manoeuvre. Then HIPS highlights the display to be used by the controller in determining the final detail of the manoeuvre.

The controller has full visibility of all the data and has full responsibility for the manoeuvre that will be communicated to the pilot. ISAC presents only a "suggestion" of what is the best manoeuvre based on the conflict solutions stored in its knowledge base.

3.   System Architecture

The current version of ISAC operates as a decision support system. It can be argued that this is the natural role for a CBR system (Kolodner, 1991). It is certainly important for its acceptance in the ATC culture that it should be a support system rather than an expert system. This means that the emphasis in ISAC is on case retrieval. However it will be seen in Section 4, there is some complexity in the reuse process in the aggregation of solutions when more than one solution is retrieved.

The retrieval process is shown in Figure 5. A key criterion in the design of the retrieval mechanism in ISAC is that it should be very fast. When a controller selects a conflict in HIPS for resolution, ISAC needs to suggest a solution very quickly. The retrieval mechanism that we have settled upon is a two stage process. These two stages reflect the fact that the case features are divided into constraints and ordinary features. The characteristics of the domain dictate that there are some features that must be matched if cases are to be considered similar. These features are considered constraints and the base filtering stage in retrieval selects cases that match on these constraints. The objective in the next stage is to select cases that match best on the remaining features. The outcome is equivalent to k-Nearest Neighbour (k-NN) retrieval but is implemented as a spreading activation process for reasons of speed.

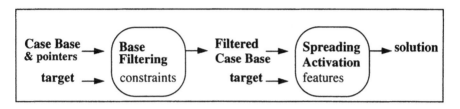

Fig. 5. The case retrieval architecture in ISAC.

During the HIPS start-up, ISAC loads the case base into memory and builds a web of pointers among the cases that will speed up the retrieval process. The Base Filtering mechanism discards from the case base all the cases whose constraints do not match exactly the target. This step is necessary because of the characteristics of the domain but it also has the advantage that it reduces the size of the case base before the comparatively expensive spreading activation stage. The pointers link all the cases that have the same value for a given parameter. During retrieval, activation passes along these links. The importance of the different features are weighed and activation is proportional to is importance. This implements a type of eager k-NN retrieval. This is appropriate because there will be a large number of retrievals in a session.

In ISAC the solution can come from one or more cases and is compound manipulable (following the convention introduced in Hanney et al., 1995). At the moment there is no adaptation because the solution required does not specify the detail of the manoeuvre and the case coverage should be sufficiently extensive that any structural transformation is not required.

4. Case Base and Case Description

Most of the development effort in ISAC has focused on the case representation. There were two problems here: the macro problem of what should constitute a case, and the micro problem of how to characterise a case.

4.1 Case Representation

It can be seen in Figure 4 that when a conflict is to be addressed a case representation is passed from HIPS to ISAC. All the data concerning the conflict are available in HIPS and are converted into parameters that describe a conflict. The conversion process eliminates useless data and transforms some others into more abstract and elaborated parameters. For example, the number of passengers on an aircraft is discarded and the coordinates of the no-go zones are meaningless per-se, but become useful if related to the aircraft trajectory. If ISAC is to propose a good solution to the conflict all relevant information must be available at this point and it must be transformed into a perspicuous representation. Determining this representation has involved extensive dialogues with ATC controllers and then the manipulation of the data from HIPS to produce the correct representation. Some examples of important parameters are:

- Horizontal Conflict Configuration: This is a general description of the conflict as one of: facing, catching, crossing, etc. It is handled as a constraint.
- Horizontal Intention: Where is the destination of the aircraft compared with its current heading?
- Near To Boundary: How close is the aircraft to exiting the sector?
- Left Exit No Go Zone: By how much does the aircraft need to turn left to avoid the no-go zone?

The process of determining these parameters is iterative with the selection of new parameters being driven by the analysis of errors at each iteration. Still it is difficult to determine a comprehensive set of important parameters from dialogues with the controllers. This difficulty is exacerbated by considerable differences in how individual controllers view conflicts. In the end there is a compromise between what is considered an important criterion and what can be extracted from the geometric information from HIPS.

4.2 Case Structure

The motivation behind the development of ISAC is to reduce the decision making burden on controllers in order to support operation in situations of increased traffic. This future scenario also implies more complex conflicts involving more than two aircraft. A key design criterion has been to develop a case representation that will be extendible from two aircraft conflicts to conflicts involving three or more aircraft. This militates against having a single conflict as the basic unit of retrieval. For reasons of economy in case coverage we want solutions in two-aircraft conflicts to be reusable in three-aircraft conflicts, and so on. This means that conflicts should be decomposable so that the basic unit of retrieval is an individual aircraft in a conflict.

This problem of representing cases describing two conflicting entities has already been faced in the CBR literature in two classical systems, Mediator (Simpson, 1985) and Persuader (Sycara, 1987), and more recently in Truth-Teller (Ashley, 1995). In all these systems, perhaps because they describe interaction between humans, there is a vocabulary to characterise the "type" of conflict and this is critical in determining the solution. This is less true in ATC where the solutions depend on the arrangement of the aircraft and the context of the individual aircraft as described by their flight plans. The conflict between two aircraft can be described roughly with one or two global parameters but the final solution depends on a lot of dependent variables related to a single aircraft. For this reason the approach adopted in ISAC is somewhat different to the above systems, with an emphasis placed on some parameters that describe an aircraft on its own.

While our ultimate objective in developing ISAC is to have a single aircraft as the unit of case retrieval we have considered three case organisations in detail. We have evaluated two alternatives with two aircraft per case and one alternative with one aircraft per case. The option of storing the two conflicting aircraft in the same case (TwoInOne) is the most obvious because it reflects the controller's way of examining a conflict, but it presents the problem of deciding which is the first aircraft in the conflict description. Let us suppose that a conflict between two aircraft A1 and A2 is stored in the case-base in the form A1A2. If the same conflict is to be solved again, HIPS will give ISAC the description of A1 and A2, but ISAC could build either target A1A2 or target A2A1, inverting the order. If this happens the probability of finding the correct case A1A2 in the case base is very low. This problem is called the "symmetric problem". An obvious, but time and space consuming, solution to the symmetric problem is to build the two cases A1A2 and A2A1 for each conflict in the case base, that means a case base that is twice the size it needs to be. This means that, in our implementation, retrieval will take twice as long. Alternatively, we may build two targets P1P2 and P2P1 for each conflict between P1 and P2 and repeat the retrieval process twice, that means a doubled retrieval time. The advantage of both these solutions is that there is no knowledge loss. We actually evaluated the first option with the bloated case-base.

An alternative solution is to produce a set of rules that will decide which is the first and the second aircraft in the case description. These rules will have to be applied during the case-base construction and every time a new target problem is presented. After the rules are applied, the case is said expressed in the "canonical form". The advantage of this process is that neither the retrieval time nor the case base dimension is doubled. This involves the risk of loss of information as we can see from the experiments results.

The final means of representing a conflict is by storing the information on each aircraft, plus a general description of the conflict, in a separate case (OneInOne). The information of the other aircraft involved in the conflict is implicit in the environment description in the form of the no-go zones (see Table 1). This moves us towards a Hierarchical CBR situation (Smyth & Cunningham, 1992) where problems are represented by multiple cases. This has the big advantage that the number of aircraft that can be involved in a conflict is not limited to two. Moreover, the "symmetric problem" is avoided. However we found it more difficult to come up with a set of parameters that capture all the details.

Evidently this last approach requires that a conflict be represented as two (or more) target cases and that there should be a retrieval for each one. This requires a policy for the extraction of the final solution from the two sets of matching cases, because the two solutions could lead to an incongruence. In fact, this is a delicate issue. Let us suppose that in the case base there are two conflicts A-B and C-D which are represented in four cases A, B, C, D. If a new conflict is X-Y, ISAC will build two cases X and Y and will start the retrieval process. If the conflict X-Y is, in general, more similar to the conflict A-B, it does not imply that the retrieved cases will be A and B, because the retrieval results depend on the individual aircraft matching. Our current policy is to select the highest scoring case but more experimentation is required on this issue.

Table 1. Example of an aircraft description in the OneInOne case representation.

```
CaseName            CCKT177_2764
HorConflConf        crossing
SameDestination     no
AltitudeNow         lower
AltIntention        StableDescend
HorizIntention      LeftLeft
Speed               faster
DimAltZone          big
Performance         worse
CloseToBoundaries   yes
MilesDone           1741
MilesToDo           147
RightExitNoGo       53.03
RightAvailable      36.97
LeftExitNoGo        26.15
LeftAvailable       63.85
ReqLevFree          Above&Below
Faster              0.53
Slower              1.58
InFrontDirect       yes
InFrontMoreSpace    yes
@s hor3*alt2
```

It can be seen that all the values are symbolic (enumerated). This is the result of the iterative research done with the controller. Initially the case representation contained a lot of numeric values but it became evident that the controller considered values in ranges so it was decided that symbolic values were more suitable.

5. Evaluation

ISAC is currently in the second phase of its evaluation. In the first phase it was evaluated on what might be called iconic conflicts. These were artificially constructed conflicts and the case-base captured all the basic ways in which two aircraft can approach too close together. There are two components to a solution in ISAC. It must nominate the aircraft to manoeuvre (A, B or A&B) and it must select the type of manoeuvre (horizontal, altitude or speed). After some refinement of the case representation ISAC performed very well in this initial evaluation. With a case-base of 50 conflicts and a set of 10 parameters, using a leave-one-out evaluation strategy, all three case organisations described in section 4.1 were able to produce good solutions in greater than 95% of the cases.

It is clear that these artificially constructed cases do not capture the full complexity of real ATC conflicts. When this case organisation was evaluated on conflicts taken from real traffic samples the number of completely acceptable solutions dropped to little over 51% and either the correct aircraft or the correct manoeuvre was selected in little over 70% of cases (i.e. 70% were half right). In resolving conflicts in real situations with complex trajectories there are details that were not represented in this initial case representation. With a refining of the acquisition of the parameters and with the acquisition of a new case base, coming from more realistic conflicts, these two numbers reached 75% and 85% with the OneInOne case organisation.

In the Figures 6 and 7, we report the results obtained from a case base of 51 conflicts described with 18 basic parameters (some of these parameters are duplicated in the TwoInOne case representation). It should be noted that the evaluation and refinement process is still ongoing. We are confident that we will be able to produce solutions that will be accepted by the controller in greater than 95% of situations.

A lot of work still has to be done on extending the case base, because 50 conflicts are not enough to characterise all the possible ATC conflicts, and on the parameters acquisition, because it is not always obvious how to convert into numbers what the controller sees on the radar screen.

In addition to improving our case representation in our evaluation process we are also interested in discovering which parameters are particularly predictive and which should be handled as constraints. In Figure 6 we show that handling one of the parameters as a constraint improves the competence of the system slightly. This is in addition to improving the retrieval time.

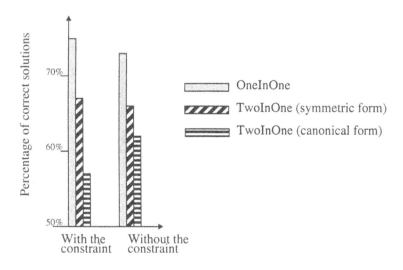

Fig. 6. Advantages in using the constraints.

We are also interested in simplifying the case representation so that the case description would involve less parameters. To this end we have evaluated the discrimination power of all the parameters using the mechanism used in ID3 (Quinlan, 1986) and have evaluated retrieval while ignoring less discriminating parameters. In Figure 7 we can see that removing one parameter actually improves performance but after that, performance begins to deteriorate.

From both Figures 6 and 7 it can be seen that the performance of the canonical form is worse than the performance of the symmetric form because of the loss of information. Nevertheless, we still think that the option of using the canonical form is not to be discarded because, with a more effective policy for ordering the aircraft, the results may improve.

Conclusions and Future Work

The performances of CBR systems in general and of ISAC in particular depend on how well the case is described and on how densely and homogeneously the case space, i.e. the set of all the possible conflicts, is populated.

To populate our case space it was first necessary to list what were the most common and realistic conflicts - these we called "gold standard cases". These cases should cover all the case space. Using the terminology of (Smyth, 1995) these cases should be pivotal, i.e. if a pivotal case is deleted the competence of the system is reduced, but the regions of these pivots should cover all the case space.

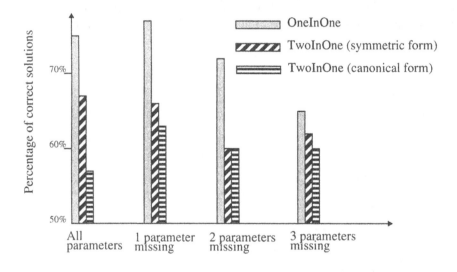

Fig. 7. Performance compared to the number of parameters.

The idea to create from scratch a traffic sample containing all the gold standard conflicts was rejected after some tests: the controllers judged the environment too unrealistic and thus the solutions given. It was necessary to introduce a more realistic display environment and the use of more elaborated traffic samples (coming from real-time simulation) to finally bring to the controller an environment that could enable him to give "reliable" solutions. We are now close to settling on a definitive case representation. Once this final case representation has been determined, our long term objective is to extend the system to tackle conflicts with more than two aircraft.

Acknowledgments

We would like to thank Nigel Makins and Andrew Barff for sharing their expertise in Air Traffic Control with us.

References

Ashley K.D., McLaren B.M., (1995), Reasoning with Reasons in Case-Based Comparisons, Case-Based Reasoning Research and Development, Lecture Notes in Artificial Intelligence, M. Veloso & A. Aamodt (eds), pp133-144, Springer Verlag.

Hanney K., Keane M., Smyth B., Cunningham P., (1995), Systems, tasks and adaptation knowledge: Revealing some revealing dependencies, Case-Based Reasoning Research and Development, Lecture Notes in Artificial Intelligence, M. Veloso & A. Aamodt (eds), pp461-470, Springer Verlag.

Kolodner J.L., (1991), Improving Human Decision Making Through Case-Based Decision Aiding, AI Magazine, Vol. 12, No. 2, Summer 1991, pp52-68.

Meckiff C. and Gibbs P., (1994), PHARE Highly Interactive Problem Solver, EEC Report 273/94 [on request to Colin.Meckiff@eurocontrol.fr].

Quinlan J.R., (1986), Induction of Decision Trees, Machine Learning, 1, 81-106.

Simpson R.L., (1985), A Computer Model of Case-Based Reasoning in Problem Solving: An Investigation in the Domain of Dispute mediation, PhD thesis, Georgia Institute of Technology, TR. GIT-ICS-85/18.

Smyth B., Cunningham P., (1992), Déjà Vu: A Hierarchical Case-Based Reasoning System for Software Design, in Proceedings of 10th. European Conference on Artificial Intelligence, Vienna, Austria, ed. Bernd Neumann, Wiley & Son, pp587-589.

Smyth B. and Keane M.T., (1995), Remembering to forget: A competence-preserving deletion policy for CBR systems, C Mellish (Ed.), Fourteenth International Joint Conference on Artificial Intelligence. Los Altos: Morgan Kaufmann.

Sycara E.P., (1987), Resolving Adversarial Conflicts: An Approach to Integrating Case-Based and Analytic Methods, PhD thesis, Georgia Institute of Technology, TR. GIT-ICS-87/26.

Structural Similarity and Adaptation

Katy Börner[1], Eberhard Pippig[1], Elisabeth-Ch. Tammer[1], Carl-H. Coulon[2]

[1] HTWK Leipzig, FB IMN, PF 30066, 04251 Leipzig, GERMANY
katy | eberhard | tammer@informatik.th-leipzig.de
[2] FIT, AI Research Division, 53754 Sankt Augustin, GERMANY
coulon@gmd.de

Abstract. Most commonly, case-based reasoning is applied in domains where attribute value representations of cases are sufficient to represent the features relevant to support classification, diagnosis or design tasks. Distance functions like the *Hamming-distance* or their transformation into similarity functions are applied to retrieve past cases to be used to generate the solution of an actual problem. Often, domain knowledge is available to adapt past solutions to new problems or to evaluate solutions. However, there are domains like architectural design or law in which *structural case representations* and corresponding *structural similarity functions* are needed. Often, the acquisition of adaptation knowledge seems to be impossible or rather requires an effort that is not manageable for fielded applications. Despite of this, humans use cases as the main source to generate adapted solutions. How to achieve this computationally? This paper presents a general approach to structural similarity assessment and adaptation. The approach allows to explore structural case representations and limited domain knowledge to support design tasks. It is exemplarily instantiated in three modules of the design assistant FABEL-Idea that generates adapted design solutions on the basis of prior CAD layouts.

1 Introduction

To provide support in a complex real world domain like design, case-based reasoning (CBR) has been suggested as an appropriate problem solving method [14, 17, 13, 15]. In CBR, a new problem is solved analogously to past experiences (cases). That is, cases similar to the problem are retrieved, the set of best cases is selected, a solution is derived and evaluated and the new problem along with its solution is stored in memory [17, 25]. In most CBR applications past experiences have no inherent structure and are described by fixed sets of attribute value pairs. Traditionally, case adaptation is guided by static libraries of hand-coded adaptation rules. If model-based knowledge about the domain is available it may be used to constrain the reasoning process (retrieval as well as adaptation) or to evaluate solutions.

In design, cases correspond to arrangements of physical objects represented by CAD layouts and refer to parts in real buildings. The topological structure (which does not reflect the function or behaviour of objects) inherent in such layouts needs to be considered during reasoning. Complex case representations, however, increase the computational expense in retrieving, matching, and adapting cases. Efficient memory organization directly tailored to analogical reasoning becomes essential. Additionally, design is a weak theory domain. Hardly any information about the relevance of features guiding the selection of similar cases is available. The adaptation of prior layouts mainly corresponds to adding, eliminating, or substituting physical objects. Because of the variety and the possible number of combinations of these modifications, adaptation knowledge is difficult to acquire by hand. In the project FABEL approaches have been developed that define the *structural similarity* [6, 16] between structured case representations (graphs) by their maximal common subgraphs (*mcs*). Given a new problem the structurally most similar case(s) are retrieved. One out of several *mcs* is transferred and the remaining case parts are taken over as needed. Additionally, the *mcs* may be used to represent and access classes of cases in an efficient manner. The remaining case parts can be seen as proper instantiations of *mcs*, i.e., as a special kind of adaptation knowledge that allows to adapt past cases to solve new problems. In such a way adaptation knowledge can be automatically extracted out of past cases reducing the effort needed for knowledge acquisition enormously.

This paper outlines the application domain and task and introduces the basic functionality required to support various design tasks. Based on this three concrete approaches are presented that apply structural similarity assessment and adaptation to provide this functionality in an efficient way. The approaches differ by focusing on specific parts of the CBR-scenario. Finally, related work will be discussed and conclusions will be drawn.

2 Application Domain and Task

The application domain used to motivate, illustrate, and evaluate the approaches to structural similarity and adaptation is architectural design. In particular we are concerned to support the design of rectangular building layout. Here, past experiences (cases) correspond to arrangements of physical objects represented by CAD layouts and refer to parts in real buildings. Each object is represented by a set of attributes describing its geometry and its type (e.g. fresh air connection pipe). Concentrating on the design of complex installation infrastructures for industrial buildings, cases correspond to pipe systems that connect a given set of outlets to the main access. Pipe systems for fresh and return air, electrical circuits, computer networks, phone cables, etc. are numerous and show varied topological structures. As for the retrieval, transfer, and adaptation of past cases to new problems not the geometry and type of single objects but their topological relations are important.

Due to this, objects and their (topological) relations need to be represented and considered during reasoning. Therefore, the approaches described in this article use a *compile* and *recompile* function to translate attribute value representation of objects and their relations into graphs. In general, objects are represented by vertices and relations between objects are represented by edges.

Reasoning, i.e. structural retrieval and adaptation proceeds via graph-based representations. A *recompile* function translates the graph-based solution into its attribute-based representation that may be depicted graphically to the architect. Concentrating on different aspects of structural similarity assessment and adaptation different compile functions are appropriate, resulting in different graph representations of cases and corresponding expressibility power and reasoning complexity. They are explained in detail in section 4.1 to 4.3. As an example see Fig. 1 which shows a problem and its solution. Some of the spatial relations (*touches, overlaps, is_close_to*) used by TOPO to represent cases structurally are visualized by arrows.

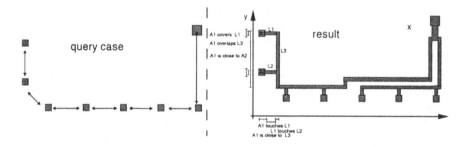

Fig. 1. Domain example: A problem and its solution

Given a base of cases represented by graphs, reasoning proceeds as follows: First, one or a set of cases that show a high structural similarity to the problem needs to be *retrieved* out of the case base. Here structural similarity is defined via the maximal common subgraph (*mcs*) of a case and a problem. Assuming that cases and problem may share more in common than their maximal common subgraph, structural *adaptation* proceeds by transferring and combining case parts that connect unconnected problem objects to the *mcs*.

3 Required Functionality

The required functionality (informally defined in the last section) will be defined via the mappings needed to transfer a set of cases and a problem into one or a set of problem solutions.

We give some basic notions and notations first. A graph $g = (V^g, E^g)$ is an ordered pair of vertices V^g and edges E^g with $E^g \subseteq V^g \times V^g$. Let $mcs(G)$ denote the set of all maximal common subgraphs of a set of graphs G, with respect to some criteria. If there is no danger of misunderstanding, the argument of *mcs* will be left out. Let Γ be the set of all graphs, and O be a finite set of objects represented by attribute values for geometry and type. $\mathcal{P}(\Gamma)$ denotes the powerset of Γ, that means the set of all subsets of Γ.

The mappings needed to accomplish the required functionality are depicted in Fig. 2 and are explained subsequently. In order to access and interact via CAD layouts (that are represent by attribute value pairs) but to reason via topological structure there must be a way of translating attribute value representations of cases into graph representations and reverse. Therefore, a *compile* function has to be defined that maps the attribute value representation of a set of objects representing a case or a problem into its structural representation:

$$compile : \mathcal{P}(O) \rightarrow \Gamma.$$

Inversely, the function *recompile* maps the graph representation of a set of objects denoting a solution into their attribute value representation:

$$recompile : \Gamma \rightarrow \mathcal{P}(O).$$

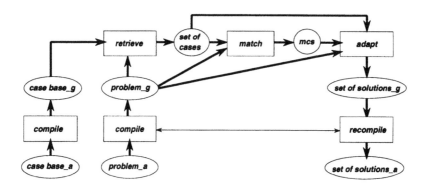

Fig. 2. Mappings required to accomplish the required functionality

The concept of structural similarity allows the selection of one or more cases, that are suitable for solving a problem. It is used by the function *retrieve*, that maps a set of cases (i.e. the case base) and a problem into a set of candidate cases that are applicable to solve the problem:

$$retrieve : \mathcal{P}(\Gamma) \times \Gamma \rightarrow \mathcal{P}(\Gamma).$$

Retrieve itself uses (sometimes repeatedly) a function named *match* that maps two graphs into their maximal common subgraphs *mcs*:

$$match : \Gamma \times \Gamma \rightarrow \mathcal{P}(\Gamma).$$

As for adaptation, vertices and edges of the selected set of candidate cases are transferred and combined to complement the problem into a set of solutions:

$$adapt : \mathcal{P}(\Gamma) \times \Gamma \times \Gamma \rightarrow \mathcal{P}(\Gamma).$$

The function *adapt* also itself will be influenced by the function *match* such that a single element of *mcs* is used for adaptation.

Because of the finity of the object set and the existence of the *compile* function, we can restrict the last four mappings to finite domains, i.e., Γ may be replaced by $compile(\mathcal{P}(O))$.

4 Three Approaches to Structural Similarity and Adaptation

This section introduces three approaches that provide the defined functionality using structural similarity assessment and adaptation. The approaches differ in the compile and recompile functions applied. Different graph representations (trees to arbitrary graphs) are used to represent cases illustrating the tradeoff between expressibility and match complexity. Different ways of memory organization are used and several retrieval and adaptation strategies are proposed. The approaches are compared at the end of this section.

4.1 TOPO

The main feature of TOPO is the case-based extension and correction of rectangular layouts.

Compile and Recompile: The *compile* function used by TOPO detects binary topological relations of various types. The type of a relation is determined by the application dependent attributes of involved objects and their 3-dimensional topological relation. TOPO's *compile* function projects each layout to the three axes and the 3-dimensional relation is a combination of the relations detected for each dimension. For each projection 8 different directed relations can be detected. They are similar to the temporal relations of [1], but additionally distinguish several classes of distances between disjoint intervals. Therefore, a given object may be in one of 16 relationships for each dimension leading to $16^3 = 4096$ different 3-dimensional relationships [12].

Building a graph out of objects and relations, one must decide which ones should be the vertices and which ones the edges. Depending on this decision different subgraphs of graph representations of two layouts become isomorph. As described and discussed in [12] TOPO uses the relations as vertices and the objects as edges because it allows to detect weaker, but larger, correspondencies between two layouts.

Retrieval: The *matching* function searches for the maximal common subgraphs of two graphs. In order to solve a similar task, the problem of finding a maximal clique of a graph, various NP-complete algorithms has been developed [2]. A clique is a complete subgraph of a graph (every vertex is connected with every other one). Instead of searching for a common subgraph of two graphs TOPO searches for a maximal clique in one graph representing all possible matchings between the two graphs, called their *combination graph.*

Building the combination graph: Using the transformation in [3], the vertices in the combination graph represent all matchings of compatible vertices in the source graphs. Figure 3 shows an example. The source graphs f and g contain objects of type a and b connected by directed relations. The type of a relation is defined by the types of its source and target objects. Two vertices are connected in the combination graph if and only if the matchings represented by the vertices do not contradict one another. The matchings $(R_2(a,b) \Leftrightarrow R_8(a,b))$ and $(R_5(b,b) \Leftrightarrow R_{10}(b,b))$ are connected because both relations occur in both source graphs in the same context. Both are connected by a shared object of type b. $(R_2(a,b) \Leftrightarrow R_8(a,b))$ and $(R_1(b,a) \Leftrightarrow R_6(b,a))$ are not connected because the matched relations share an object of type a in graph f but do not share any object in graph g.

The maximal clique in this combination graph and the corresponding maximal subgraphs are marked in black.

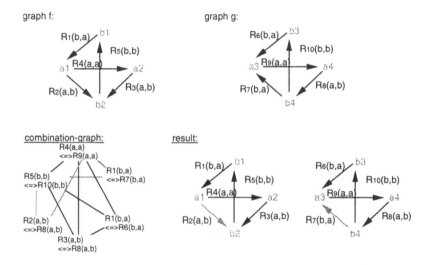

Fig. 3. Transformation of the problem of finding the maximal common subgraph to the problem of finding a maximal clique in a graph. The maximal clique and the corresponding matching are marked in black.

A general maximal clique algorithm: The algorithm of [11] (for further use called *max-clique_{BK}*) finds all cliques in a graph by enumerating and extending all complete subgraphs. It extends complete subgraphs of size k to complete subgraphs of size $k + 1$ by adding iteratively vertices which are connected to all vertices of the complete subgraph.

As an improvement [12] describes, how to reduce the search space by searching for matchings of connected subgraphs only and combining them in a second step.

The function retrieval: TOPO includes no own retrieval function but supplies the retrieval module ASPECT [20] with two different similarity functions. Given a similarity function and a query case, ASPECT guarantees to find the most similar source case without the need to compare all cases.

Given two cases, the first similarity function returns the size of the maximal common subgraphs relative to the minimum size of both graphs. Because a maximal common subgraph cannot be larger than the smaller one of both graphs the result is always a rational number between 0 and 1. In order to avoid the np-complete search for the maximum common subgraphs a second similarity function is defined. It compares the sets of relations occuring in both cases. The result is the number of compatible relations relative to the minimum number of detected relations of both cases leading to a result, which is also between 0 and 1. The second similarity function obviously returns an upper bound of the first similarity function, but has no np-complexity.

Adaptation: TOPO extends, refines and corrects layouts by case adaptation. Because there exists no theory dividing a layout statically into problem part and solution part, TOPO uses the heuristic that every object of the source case which is not found in the query case might be part of the solution. After determining the common subgraph of the graph representation of a query and a case it offers to transfer all objects from the source case to the query case which are connected to the common part by a path of topological relations. In order to use this path of topological relations to determine the position of the transferred object in the query, TOPO uses the recompile functions. The user may specify the parts to be transferred by selecting types of desired objects.

During transfer TOPO may change the size of transferred objects to preserve topological relations. For example a window is resized in order to touch both sides of a room. To avoid geometries which are impossible for an object, TOPO limits the resizing to geometries which occurred in the case base.

The adaptation described so far is additive only and this is the main aim of TOPO. A second way of using TOPO is transformative. TOPO searches in the query case for objects constituting an unusual topological relationship. For this reason TOPO creates a statistic about the frequency of topological relations occurring in the case base for each type of objects. For example, 100 percent of the outlets in the case base touch pipes and 2 percent of the chairs touch a shelf. In case of detecting unusual relationships between objects of a query, TOPO asks the user whether the position of one or both of the objects should be changed or not. If the position of an object is confirmed to be changed, TOPO searches for an object of the source case compatible to the object of the query which is related to compatible objects, but by more frequent topological relations. Using the recompile functions of those more frequent relations the new position of the object of the query case is determined. As an example let us suppose, that TOPO detected the unusual relation *used air outlet inside used air connection pipe* in a query case like in Fig. 5 and the user confirmed the position of the outlet to be changed. TOPO searches for a part of the source case, where there is an object which is compatible to the outlet and related to another object which is compatible to the connection pipe. Probably it would find an outlet which touches a connection line. Therefore, it would transfer the relation *touching* and accordingly reconstruct the position of the outlet of the query case.

4.2 MACS

In order to apply our structural concept the module MACS uses an appropriate representation of domain objects which focuses on their structure. Therefore, domain objects translated into unconstrained graphs. The preference of MACS involves to structure the case base dynamically based on the structural similarity of graph-based cases and to realize a fast retrieval over such a structured case base.

Compile and Recompile: Analogous to the other approaches the function *compile* guarantees the transformation of an attribute value represented case into its graph representation (see [4] for examples). We represent cases very close to the graphical representations which are in accordance with former reflections about the graph structure of the domain elements. There are mainly two ways to interpret a layout fragment:

- All architectural objects which appear in the layout are represented as vertices. It is possible but not necessary to label the vertices with a type name of the object and with additional qualitative and quantitative attributes. The edges are used for expressing the topological relationships between neighboring vertices and, possibly, are labeled with a type name of the topological relationship together with additional attributes.
- If the layout contains a certain amount of spanning objects like pipes or beams then it is more suitable to represent the spanning objects as edges and the remaining objects as vertices and, if it is necessary, to label with their type name and necessary additional attributes.

The function *recompile* transforms vertices and edges of an adapted graph into objects and relations of a concrete layout. In case of labeled graphs this mapping is unique. Otherwise the problem of nonunique mappings has to be solved.

Organization of the Case Base: In this approach, we consider arbitrary graphs which may be either directed or undirected and, possibly, labeled or unlabeled. Computing structural similarity is essentially based on graph matching which actually means computing the maximal common isomorphic subgraphs. The module MACS uses a backtracking algorithm [23] that realizes the function *match* to compute maximal common subgraphs of two arbitrary graphs [24]. A maximal common subgraph of two graphs denotes their *structural similarity*. Because of our key concept of structural similarity, for any collection of graphs $C \in \mathcal{P}(\Gamma)$, we use $mcs(C)$ to denote the set of maximal common subgraphs of all graphs in C with respect to counting vertices and edges (cf. [24]).

In general, the structural similarity of a set of graphs is not unique. Therefore, it may be represented by a set of graphs. Let us introduce some *selection operator* $E : \mathcal{P}(\Gamma) \rightarrow \Gamma$ to determine a unique representative $\Theta \in mcs(C)$ for each class C.

Usually, the peculiarities of the application domain lead to a couple of preferable selection operators. There are some illustrative possibilities, e.g.

- *other similarity concepts* based on labels of vertices or edges of graphs within $mcs(C)$,
- *graph–theoretic properties* which characterize structures preferred in the domain.

When $mcs(C)$ and E are given, the structural similarity of any class C of graphs may be written as $\sigma(C) = E(mcs(C))$ in the sense of [10].

Because of NP-completeness of the subgraph isomorphism problem, that is the computing of a common isomorphic subgraph, classical case retrieval is extremely expensive, if every member of a usually huge case base is potentially queried. The performance of this search can be increased by prestructuring the case base in case classes, i.e. clustering.

Preferably, a given case base CB is clustered with respect to structural similarity, i.e. graphs of a close structural relationship are grouped together and represented by a graph describing their structural similarity. Let us assume that a case base CB is separated in n partitions or classes where the finite number n may be approx. $\sqrt{N}$ with $N = | CB |$. Each class CB_i $(i = 1, ..., n)$ consists of a set of graph-represented cases and is determined by a graph Θ_i which is called its *representative*.

Fast Retrieval over a Structured Case Base: We may assume that the case base is partioned in n finite classes and that a representative of every class is computed by $\Theta_i = \sigma(CB_i)$, $(i = 1, ..., n)$ with an optimal value of $n \approx \sqrt{N}$.

There is a basic scenario for retrieving similar cases to a given problem (the query case g). The *fast retrieval* proceeds in two steps:

1. The retrieval yields a maximal similar representative Θ_i to the given query case. The resulting class is indexed by some i^*. (Note that there may be several maximal results being mutually incomparable.)
2. Over the set CB_{i^*} of preferred cases, retrieval is performed again to return the ultimate result.

The fast retrieval allows to reduce the number of necessary comparisons to $2n$ in the average case. Usually, the result is a set of cases of CB_{i^*} having a structural similarity of maximal size. Those are returned for further reasoning procedures like case adaptation. The advantage over conventional approaches is quite obvious.

In case of MACS, the result of retrieval is a set of *source* cases denoted by $S_{i^*} \subseteq CB_{i^*}$. Each case $g_{i^*}^j \in S_{i^*}$ has the property that each element of $mcs(\{g_{i^*}^j, g\}) = match(g_{i^*}^j, g)$ has the equal number of vertices and edges, i.e. the size of structural similarity of each graph of S_{i^*} and the query case is identically.

Adaptation: The selected cases are proposed one after the other to a checking algorithm or to the user, who selects the most suitable one.

In general we have smaller query cases than source cases, hence it is possible that a chosen source case solves a problem itself. Otherwise, the selected source case have to be adapted to the problem. Normally, in CBR *adaptation* means the transformation of a chosen source case using informations which are included in a knowledge-base and several kinds of substitutions of a query case.

The module MACS realizes a structure modification of query cases doing simple substitutions exclusively which result is the supplemented query case. We may distinguish two basic scenarios to realize the function *adapt* for a query case g:

1. We select a source case $g'_{i\bullet} \in S_{i\bullet}$. Further, let h be a structural similarity of g and the chosen source case $g'_{i\bullet}$. Using the result of $match(g, g'_{i\bullet})$, we get a mapping list of corresponded vertices of g and $g'_{i\bullet}$ which define the graph h. The *adapted graph* (solution) is generated from graph g by adding all walks in $g'_{i\bullet}$, which have not an isomorphic mapping in g but which begin and end with vertices of h. These walks may be sequences of edges which are incident with vertices not corresponding to a vertex of g excluding the begin and end vertices.

2. We use the whole set $S_{i\bullet}$ for adaptation. Let h be a structural similarity of g and $S_{i\bullet}$. An *adapted graph* (solution) is generated from graph g by adding all walks of graphs of $S_{i\bullet}$ that have the same property as described above. The user will have to choose between using all graphs of $S_{i\bullet}$ or special graphs only.

The module MACS provides the first variant of adaptation exclusively. It would require a different scenario to realize the second variant of adaptation. Especially, the creation of some choosing heuristics based of a different graph representation or the specification of extensive user interaction would be necessary.

4.3 CA/SYN

Conceptual analogy (CA) is a general approach that relies on conceptual clustering to facilitate the efficient use of past cases in analogous situations [7]. CA divides the overall design task into *memory organization* and *analogical reasoning* both processing structural case representations. In order to ground both processes on attribute value representations of cases a *compile function* and a *recompile function* need to be defined.

Compile and Recompile: The function *compile* guarantees the unique transformation of an attribute value represented case into its structural normal form, i.e., a tree. Especially suited for the design of pipelines, *compile* maps outlets into vertices and pipes into edges. Inversely, *recompile* maps vertices and edges into outlets and pipes. Geometrical transformations like rotation are considered.

Representing the main access by a square, outlets by circles, interconnecting points by circles of smaller size and pipes by line segments, Fig. 4 (left bottom) illustrates six cases representing pipe systems. Each of them shows a tree like structure. The main access corresponds to the root (R), outlets correspond to leaves (L). Crosspoints of pipes or connections of pipe segments are represented by internal vertices (I). Pipes correspond to edges. Each object is placed on the intersecting points of a fixed grid (not shown here) and can be uniquely identified by its x and y coordinates and its $type \in \{R, I, L\}$. Pipes connect objects horizontally or vertically. Thus a case can be represented by a set of vertices and a set of edges representing *connected_to* relations among these objects. Formally, a *case* $c = (V^c, E^c)$ is a tree. A *case base* CB is a finite set of cases. A typical design *problem* provides the main access, the outlets, and perhaps some pipes, i.e., it is a forest. A *solution* of a problem contains the problem objects and relations and eventually adds intermediate vertices from past cases and provides the relations that are required to connect all outlets to the main access.

Memory Organization starts with a case base (CB) providing a significant amount of cases as well as a structural similarity function σ.

To explain memory organization some basic definitions will be given first. A *case class* CC is a nonempty subset of CB. Let $mcs(CC)$ be the (unique) maximum common, connected subgraph of the cases in CC containing the root vertice. The structural similarity[3] is defined as $|E^{mcs}|$ divided by the total number of edges in the cases of CC:

$$\sigma(CC) = \frac{|E^{mcs}|}{|\cup_{c \in CC} E^c|} \in [0, 1].$$

Given a case base and a similarity function σ a *case class partition* CCP is a set of mutually disjoint, exhaustive case classes CC: $CCP = \{CC_i \mid \bigcup_i CC_i = CB \wedge \forall i \neq j(CC_i \cap CC_j = \emptyset) \wedge \forall i \neq j((c_1, c_2 \in CC_i \wedge c_3 \in CC_j) \rightarrow \sigma(c_1, c_2) \geq \sigma(c_1, c_3) \wedge \sigma(c_1, c_2) \geq \sigma(c_2, c_3))\}$. A *case class hierarchy* CCH is the set of all partitions CCP^v of $CB = \{c_1, .., c_N\}$: $CCH = (CCP^0, CCP^1, ..., CCP^{N-1})$.

Given a set of cases $CB = \{c_1, .., c_N\}$, represented by trees, memory organization starts. Nearest-neighbor-based, agglomerative, unsupervised conceptual clustering is applied to create a hierarchy of case classes sharing cases of similar structure. It begins with a set of singleton vertices representing case classes, each containing a single case. The two most similar case classes CC_1 and CC_2 over the entire set are merged to form a new case class $CC = CC_1 \cup CC_2$ that covers both. This process is repeated for each of the remaining $N-1$ case classes, where N is the number of cases in CB. Case class merging continues until a single all-inclusive cluster remains. Thus at termination a uniform, binary hierarchy of case classes is left.

Subsequently, a concept description $K(CC)$ is assigned to each case class CC. The concept represents the $mcs(CC)$ (named prototype) of the cases in

---

[3] Note that the structural similarity function is commutative and associative. Thus it may be applied to a pair of cases as well as to a set of cases.

CC and a set of instantiations thereof, along with the probability of these instantiations. The probability of an instantiation corresponds to the number of its occurrences in the cases of CC divided by the total number of cases in CC. The *mcs* denoting the structure relevant for similarity comparisons will serve as an index in the case base. The instantiations (subtrees) denote possibilities for adaptation. Probabilities will direct the search through the space of alternative instantiations.

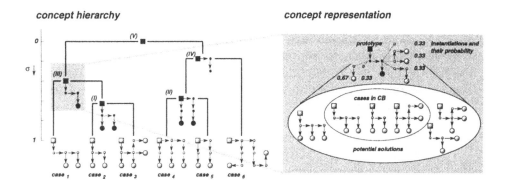

Fig. 4. Concept hierarchy and concept representation

In such a way, large amounts of cases with many details can be reduced to a number of hierarchically organized concepts. The concrete cases, however, are stored to enable the dynamic reorganization and update of concepts.

Analogical Reasoning is based on concepts exclusively. Given a new problem, it is classified in the most applicable concept, i.e., the concept that shares as many relations as possible (high structural similarity) and provides instantiations that contain the problem objects that are not covered by the prototype (adaptability)[4]. Thus instead of *retrieving* one or a set of cases, the function *classify* maps a concept hierarchy $K(CCH)$ and a problem p into the most applicable concept $K(CC)$.

Next, the *mcs* of the most applicable concept is transferred and instantiated. Instantiations of high probability are preferred. Each solution connects all problem objects by using those objects and edges that show the highest probability in the concept applied. In general, there exist more than one solution. The set of solutions for a problem and a case base may be denoted by $S_{CB,p}$. Instead of *adapting* one or more cases to solve the problem, the function *instantiate* maps the concept representation $K(CC)$ and the problem into a set of adapted solutions $S_{CB,p}$.

---

[4] Note that the most similar concept may be too concrete to allow the generation of a solution. See also [22] for a discussion and experiments on adaptation-guided retrieval.

Finally, the set of solutions may be ordered corresponding to a set of preference criteria: (1) max. structural similarity of the solution and the concept applied, (2) max. probability of edges transferred, and (3) min. solution size.

If the solution was accepted by the user, its incorporation into an existing concept changes at least the probabilities of the instantiations. Given that the problem already contained relations, it might add new instantiations or even change the prototype itself. If the solution was not accepted, the case memory needs to be reorganized to incorporate the user provided solution.

Fig. 4 (left) depicts the organization of cases into a concept hierarchy. N cases are represented by $2N - 1$ case classes resp. concepts $K(CC)$. Leave vertices correspond to concrete cases and are represented by the cases themselves. Generalized concepts in the concept hierarchy are labeled (I) to (V) and are characterized by their *mcs* (prototype) denoted by black circles and line segments. The representation of concept no. (III) representing $case_1$ to $case_3$ is depicted on the right hand side of Fig. 4. The instantiation of its prototype results in $case_1$ to $case_3$ as well as combinations thereof. Given a new problem, the most applicable, i.e., most similar concept containing all problem objects is determined. The set of problems that may be solved by concept no. (III) corresponds to the set of all subtrees of either concrete or combined cases, containing the root vertice.

The general approach of *Conceptual Analogy* has been fully implemented in SYN, a module of a highly interactive, adaptive system architecture [8]. Its compile and recompile function is especially suited to support the geometrical layout of pipe systems. See [6, 9] for a detailed description of the implementation.

4.4 Example

Figure 5 provides an example of structural similarity assessment and adaptation. Depicted on the top is the query case or problem, the middle presents a source case used by TOPO to generate the adapted solution on the right hand side. The bottom line illustrates the application of a concept to generate a design solution. The problem contains a set of supply accesses, a main access as well as some pipes. In the source case, all accesses are connected by pipes.

As for the application of TOPO (middle), dark arrows denote spatial relations of the maximal common subgraph of the graphs of both cases. If there is no maximum common subgraph, one is chosen by chance. The paths of relations connected to the chosen common subgraph are transferred incrementally to generate the adapted case.

It is not always desirable to transfer all paths, as the ones leading to outlets A and H. Therefore, the designer is asked before transfer, or he can repair the layout, or domain-specific heuristics must be applied. During transfer TOPO may change the size of transferred objects to preserve spatial relations. For example a window is resized in order to touch both sides of a room. To avoid geometries which are impossible for an object, TOPO limits the resizing to geometries which occurred in the case base.

The application of MACS may retrieve to the same source case as the one used by TOPO requiring a higher match complexity and the handling of non-uniform mappings. The application of MACS *adapt* function transferes all pipes that are necessary to connect all problem outlets. Again the problem of non-unique mappings needs to be solved.

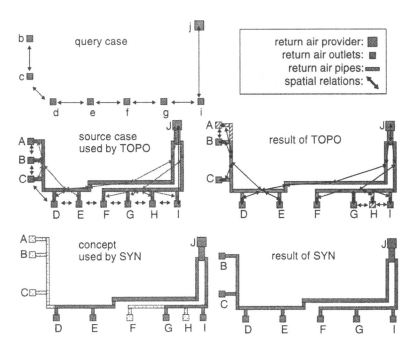

Fig. 5. Examples of structural similarity assessment and adaptation

Instead of transferring parts of a single case, SYN selects the most applicable concept of the respective concept hierarchy. This concept shows the highest structural similarity of its cases and contains all problem objects. It is characterized by its prototype (dark grey) and its instantiations (light grey) on the left hand side. The prototype is transferred to the query case connecting outlets D, E, G, and I to the main access J. The remaining problem outlets B, C, and F are connected via appropriate instantiations resulting in a correctly adapted solution.

4.5 Comparison

All three approaches use structural similarity assessment and adaptation to retrieve and transfer case parts to solve new problems. However, the approaches differ in their focus on different parts of the CBR-scenario. Subsequently the strength and limitations of each approach and its domain specific and domain independent parts are discussed.

First of all it must be noticed that the definition of the compile and recompile function strongly depends on the domain and task to support. The higher the required expressability of structural case representations the more complex are graph matching, i.e., the less efficient are retrieval and adaptation. The application of labeled graphs (TOPO) or trees (SYN) allows to invert the function *compile* to *recompile*. This can not be guaranteed for arbitrary graphs (MACS). Whereas the representation of cases by trees (SYN) guarantees unique *mcs*, this does not hold for graph representations, as in TOPO or MACS. Domain specific selection rules need to be defined or extensive user interaction is necessary to select the most suitable *mcs*. This may be advantageous during retrieval allowing the selection of different points of view on two graphs (being the *mcs* and a problem) but may not be acceptable for memory organization.

While TOPO does no retrieval at all, MACS and SYN retrieve a set of cases from a dynamically organized case base. MACS uses a two-level case organization. The lower level contains the concrete cases grouped into classes of similar cases. The upper level contains graphs describing the *mcs* of classes of similar cases. It does a two stage retrieval selecting the most similar *mcs* first and searching in its cases for the most similar concrete case(s). SYN uses a hierarchical memory organization, i.e., a case class hierarchy. Each case class is represented intentionally by a concept representing the unique *mcs* and *instantiations* which denote possibilities for adaptation as well as their *probabilities*. Given a new problem, the most applicable concept of the concept hierarchy is searched for.

In order to compare graph representations, MACS and TOPO need to apply graph matching algorithms (cliquen search and backtracking) that are known to be NP-complete. For this reason TOPO uses ASPECT for retrieval, reducing retrieval to one computationally expensive match between a selected case and the problem. MACS case organization allows to reduce the number of matches required to search through N cases to $N \times \sqrt{N}$. The restriction to trees (SYN) reduces expressibility but offers the advantage to match efficiently.

An important peculiarity of the module TOPO is to investigate the compatibility of object types and relation types of layouts. The case adaptation of TOPO searches for an object of the source case compatible to the object of the query which is related to compatible objects, but by more frequent topological relations. Using the recompile functions of those more frequent relations the new position of the object of the query case is determined.

The preference of MACS involves to structure the case base dynamically and to realize fast retrieval. MACS is suitable to investigate the possibilities of learning the partition of a case base with respect to the structural similarity and their representatives. MACS realizes a simple variant of case adaptation by adding all walks of the source case, which have not an isomorphic mapping in the query case but begin and end with vertices of their *mcs*.

CA/SYN definitely concentrates on efficient structural case combination. Therefore, the approach integrates the formation of hierarchically organized concepts (i.e., concept hierarchies) and the application of these concepts during analogical reasoning to solve new problems. It is unique in its representation of concepts by the *mcs* and its *instantiations* plus *probabilities*. Its definition of applicability allows the efficient selection of the most similar concept that is neither too general not to concrete and guarantees the generation of a problem solution. The instantiation of its *mcs* is guided by the probabilities of these instantiations, resulting in the optimal solution.

5 Related Work and Discussion

Interactive design systems as ARCHIE [19] or CADRE [15] do either support retrieval or adaptation of past designs. Systems like CASEY, KRITIK or IDEAL [5] integrate case-based and model-based reasoning to support retrieval as well as adaptation. They require model-based knowledge which is not available in our domain. Cases are most commonly represented by fixed sets of attribute value pairs. Static libraries of hand-coded adaptation rules are used to transform past cases into new solutions.

There is a number of CBR approaches that apply conceptual clustering techniques in organizing their case base. The *Prototype-Based Indexing System* (PBIS) proposed by [18] uses an incremental prototype-based neural network to organize cases into groups of similar cases and to represent each group of cases by a prototype. The JANUS CBR Shell [21] applies a Cohonen network to automatically organize cases into disjoint case classes corresponding to similar attribute values. It represents these classes by reference cases. Both systems do a two stage retrieval. Firstly, the prototype/reference case pointing to a case class is selected. Secondly, this case class is searched for the most similar concrete case. Its solution is presented as the actual classification. However, both systems are restricted to attribute value representations of cases and support classification tasks.

To our knowledge, the approaches introduced in this paper are unique in their handling of structural, i.e., graph-based case representations, their definition and application of structural similarity functions and the structural adaptation of cases without further domain knowledge. They enable to reuse highly structured cases of varying sizes to support design tasks. As for memory organization, conceptual clustering techniques can be advantageously applied to reduce reasoning complexity. The representation of case classes by their *mcs* or by concepts, effectively short cuts much of the memory retrieval effort that would be necessary to check each past case separately for structural similarity. The complexity of structural mappings can be handled in an economical manner and realistic response times become possible.

6 Acknowledgements

Thanks to D. W. Aha, K. P. Jantke, M. M. Richter, A. Voß and the anonymous referees for their many critical comments that helped shape this research. The research was supported by the German Ministry for Research and Technology (BMBF) within the joint project FABEL under contract no. 413-4001-01IW104.

Project partners in FABEL are German National Research Center of Computer Science (GMD), Sankt Augustin, BSR Consulting GmbH, München, Technical University of Dresden, HTWK Leipzig, University of Freiburg, and University of Karlsruhe.

References

1. J. Allen. Towards a general theory of action and time. *Artificial Intelligence*, 23:123–154, 1984.
2. Luitpold Babel and Gottfried Tinhofer. A branch and bound algorithm for the maximum clique problem. *ZOR – Methods and Models of Operations-Research*, 34:207–217, 1990.
3. H. G. Barrow and R. M. Burstall. Subgraph isomorphism relational structures and maximal cliques. *Information Processing Letters*, 4:83–84, 1976.
4. Brigitte Bartsch-Spörl and Elisabeth-Ch. Tammer. Graph-based approach to structural similarity. In Angi Voß, editor, *Similarity concepts and retrieval methods*, pages 45–58. GMD, Sankt Augustin, 1994.
5. S. Bhatta and A. Goel. From design cases to generic mechanisms. *AI EDAM*, 10, 1996.
6. Katy Börner. Structural similarity as guidance in case-based design. In Wess et al. [25], pages 197–208.
7. Katy Börner. Conceptual analogy. In D. W. Aha and A. Ram, editors, *AAAI 1995 Fall Symposium Series: Adaptation of Knowledge for Reuse*, pages 5–11, November 10-12, Boston, MA, 1995.
8. Katy Börner. Interactive, adaptive, computer aided design. In Milton Tan and Robert Teh, editors, *The Global Design Studio – proceedings of the 6th international conference on computer-aided architectural design futures B95*, pages 627–634, Singapore, 1995. Centre for Advanced Studies in Architecture, National University of Singapore.
9. Katy Börner and Roland Faßauer. Analogical Layout Design (Syn*). In Katy Börner, editor, *Modules for Design Support*, pages 59–68. GMD, Sankt Augustin, June 1995.
10. Katy Börner, Klaus P. Jantke, Siegfried Schönherr, and Elisabeth-Ch. Tammer. Lernszenarien im fallbasierten Schließen. Fabel-Report 14, GMD, Sankt Augustin, December 1993.
11. C. Bron and J. Kerbosch. Finding all cliques in an undirected graph. *Communications of the ACM*, 16:575–577, 1973.
12. Carl-Helmut Coulon. Automatic Indexing, Retrieval and Reuse of Topologies in Architectural Layouts. In Milton Tan and Robert Teh, editors, *The Global Design Studio – proceedings of the 6th international conference on computer-aided architectural design futures*, pages 577–586, Singapore, 1995. Centre for Advanced Studies in Architecture, National University of Singapore.
13. Eric A. Domeshek and Janet L. Kolodner. A case-based design aid for architecture. In *Proc. Second International Conference on Artificial Intelligence in Design*, pages 497–516. Kluwer Academic Publishers, 1992.
14. Ashok K. Goel. *Integration of case-based reasoning and model-based reasoning for adaptive design problem solving*. PhD thesis, Ohio State University, Columbus, Ohio, 1989.

15. Kefeng Hua and Boi Faltings. Exploring case-based building design – CADRE. *AI EDAM*, 7(2):135–144, 1993.

16. Klaus P. Jantke. Nonstandard concepts of similarity in case-based reasoning. In H. H. Bock, W. Lenski, and M. M. Richter, editors, *Information Systems and Data Analysis: Prospects–Foundations–Applications*, pages 29–44. Springer Verlag, 1994.

17. Janet L. Kolodner. *Case-Based Reasoning*. Morgan Kaufmann, San Mateo, 1993.

18. M. Malek and B. Amy. A pre-processing model for integrating CBR and prototype-based neural networks. Technical report, Working Paper TIMC-LIFIA-IMAG Grenoble, 1994.

19. M. Pearce, A. K. Goel, J. L. Kolodner, C. Zimring, L. Sentosa, and R. Billington. Case-based design support: A case study in architectural design. *IEEE Expert*, pages 14–20, October 1992.

20. Jörg Walter Schaaf. "Fish and Sink"; An Anytime-Algorithm to Retrieve Adequate Cases. In Manuela Veloso and Agnar Aamodt, editors, *Case-based reasoning research and development: first International Conference, ICCBR-95, proceedings*, pages 538–547. Springer, Berlin, October 1995.

21. Ingo Schiemann and Ansgar Woltering. Organisation großer Fallbasen in der TUB-JANUS Shell zum effizienten Retrieval geeigneter Fälle. In Richter M. M., editor, *Workshop Fallbasiertes Schließen: Grundlagen und Anwendungen, Deutsche Expertensystemtagung XPS-95*, LSA-95-02, pages 30–36, 1995.

22. Barry Smyth and Mark T. Keane. Retrieving adaptable cases: The role of adaptation knowledge in case retrieval. In Wess et al. [25], pages 209–220.

23. Kathleen Steinhöfel. Backtrack Algorithmus zur Suche des größten gemeinsamen Teilgraphen. HTWK Leipzig, 1995. Dokumentation.

24. Elisabeth-Ch. Tammer, Kathleen Steinhöfel, Siegfried Schönherr, and Daniel Matuschek. Anwendung des Konzeptes der Strukturellen Ähnlichkeit zum Fallvergleich mittels Term- und Graph-Repräsentationen. Fabel-Report 38, GMD, Sankt Augustin, September 1995.

25. Stefan Wess, Klaus-Dieter Althoff, and Michael M. Richter, editors. *Topics in Case-Based Reasoning – Selected Papers from the First European Workshop on Case-Based Reasoning (EWCBR-93)*, volume 837 of *LNAI*. Springer Verlag, 1994.

Justification Structures for Document Reuse[*]

L. Karl Branting[1], and James C. Lester[2]

[1] Department of Computer Science
University of Wyoming
Box 3682
Laramie, WY 82071
karl@index.uwyo.edu
[2] Department of Computer Science
North Carolina State University
Box 8206
Raleigh, NC 27606
lester@adm.csc.ncsu.edu

Abstract. Document drafting—an important problem-solving task of professionals in a wide variety of fields—typifies a design task requiring complex adaptation for case reuse. This paper proposes a framework for document reuse based on an explicit representation of the illocutionary and rhetorical structure underlying documents. Explicit representation of this structure facilitates (1) interpretation of previous documents by enabling them to "explain themselves," (2) construction of documents by enabling document drafters to issue goal-based specifications and rapidly retrieve documents with similar intentional structure, and (3) maintenance of multi-generation documents.

1 Introduction

Documents play an increasingly important role in all sectors of society. Legal documents precisely stipulate complex relationships between parties; government documents set forth regulatory requirements and procedures; and software documentation provides both specifications and usage recommendations. Because of the ubiquity of complex, formal documents, document interpretation and maintenance has become an issue of significant economic and legal import.

Complex documents are typically created by modifying previous documents. For example, adaptation and reuse of previous documents is an almost universal practice in U.S. law firms. Document reuse is beneficial because it promotes stylistic and substantive consistency and reduces drafting time.

However, document reuse requires access to the original intentions underlying the document, which may not be readily apparent from the document's

---

[*] This research is supported in part by grants from the National Center for Automated Information Research and by NSF Faculty Early Career Development Grant IRI-9502152.

surface text. For example, when both parties to a contract agree that modifications should be made, the assumptions behind the original contract must be reconstructed to determine the precise textual changes required. Thus, complex documents suffer from many of the same problems as legacy software: as the context for which a document was created changes, the document becomes outdated and requires revision. Problems of document maintenance are exacerbated by the frequent personnel changes that characterize large institutions, where many documents are created. Without access to a document's authors, the intent behind particular clauses may be lost, impeding interpretation and modification.

To address these problems, we propose a *self-explaining documents* framework. We say that a document containing a given discourse is "self-explaining" if it contains an explicit representation of the illocutionary and rhetorical structure underlying the discourse. Because self-explaining documents record intentional knowledge, they offer significant potential for the interpretation and maintenance of complex, multi-generation documents. In particular, they can explain why a particular clause was included, suggest how an existing document should be modified to apply to slightly different circumstances, and present arguments for the pros and cons of alternative clauses.

This paper presents a framework for the use of justification structures for document reuse. Section 2 describes three document management tasks that require self-explaining documents. Section 3 proposes a dual justification structure that combines illocutionary and rhetorical structures to represent document intent. Section 4 presents a computational architecture for interactive self-explaining document systems that assist users in constructing and querying documents, and Section 5 illustrates the envisioned behavior of the system when applied to the domain of will drafting. We are currently exploring the self-explaining document framework in the context of routine judicial orders. Section 6 describes the implementation plans for this work, and Section 7 outlines related work.

2 Applications of Self-Explaining Documents

Three tasks can be distinguished requiring knowledge of the illocutionary and rhetorical structure of texts: document drafting, document analysis, and document maintenance. Given a set of specifications—the formality of document specifications can range from formal, quasi-legal descriptions to sketchy, informal notes—the task of *document drafting* is to prepare a document that satisfies both the illocutionary goals of the specifications and the genre-specific rhetorical conventions. Document drafters typically operate in an iterative fashion, gradually refining the document until it satisfies the constraints noted above and, perhaps, meets with the approval of a client.

As stated above, drafting of complex documents is typically performed by modifying existing documents. The task of drafting by means of document reuse can be summarized as follows:

Given:

– A set of goals to be accomplished by the document to be drafted.
– A library of existing documents.

Do:

– Retrieval. Find the existing document(s) (or combination of document components) that best satisfy the current goals.
– Comparison. Display the differences, if any, between, the goals achieved by the retrieved document(s) and the current goals.
– Adaptation. Remove the portions of text whose only purpose is to satisfy goals that aren't present in the current situation (excision), and add text to satisfy any of the current goals not satisfied by the retrieved text (augmentation).

While document drafting is primarily a synthetic task, *document analysis* centers around interpretation. Here, the goal is to ascertain the intent of particular clauses, to identify documents that are similar, and to perform comparative analyses. In the course of conducting an analysis, users must be able to quickly locate relevant documents and precisely establish illocutionary analogies between statements in a given document and those in archival documents.

Document maintenance is concerned with revision. Because the overriding goal of maintenance operations is to revise an existing document to reflect new specifications, this task typically combines elements of both drafting and analysis. Existing versions of documents must be interpreted in light of new circumstances, and new sections or clauses are created to address the new context.

Because drafting, analysis, and maintenance are tightly interleaved in practice, an effective self-explaining document systems should offer a uniform communication mechanism that (1) employs a single representational vocabulary for specifying and querying documents, and (2) enables users to interleave specification and querying operations with ease.

A complete document management system[3] should enable users to pose four classes of queries:

– *Intentional Identification:* Why was a given segment of a document included?
– *Intentional Achievement:* What types of document segments in a given genre will achieve a given goal?
– *Intentional Exemplification:* What are some examples of archival document segments that achieve a given goal?
– *Intentional Comparison:* To what segments of archival documents is a given document segment most similar? What are the intentional similarities and differences between two documents (at the most specific abstraction level at which they differ)?

---

[3] We use "document management" as the super-ordinate concept for document drafting, document analysis, and document maintenance.

As users engage in document-building and document-querying dialogues, they should be able to shift effortlessly between discussions of abstract document features (*e.g.*, the predicates employed in illocutionary and rhetorical structures) and specific segments of particular documents (both documents under construction and archival documents).

The next section describes the representation requirements for the document drafting, analysis, and maintenance tasks.

3 Representational Requirements

The primary emphasis of most work in discourse analysis and generation has been on texts having communicative goals. However, documents are often intended to accomplish various other illocutionary goals, including eliciting information, persuading, memorializing events such as reciprocal communications, or accomplishing performative goals, such as creating or revoking legal, social, or institutional relationships. Self-explaining documents therefore require a rich vocabulary of illocutionary goals.

However, the illocutionary goal structure of a document is not *per se* sufficient to completely determine the selection and configuration of text. In general, the illocutionary goal structure leaves unspecified rhetorical features such as (1) the order of the textual elements that satisfy various illocutionary subgoals, and (2) textual elements and stylistic constraints imposed by the particular genre of the text. Accordingly, self-explaining documents must include the rhetorical structure of documents as well in order to answer intentional identification and comparison queries.

The minimum representational requirements for self-explaining documents therefore include the following:

- A taxonomy of illocutionary goals sufficiently expressive to permit retrieval of documents, comparison of documents, and explanation of document components. The necessary granularity of the leaf nodes of this taxonomy depends on the requirements of the particular document genre and the pragmatics of the user's application.
- A taxonomy of rhetorical goals.
- A representation of templates at a level of granularity corresponding to the leaf nodes of the illocutionary goals. The substitutable elements of text templates should be tagged with a data-type so that entire documents, or document components, can be viewed either as uninstantiated templates or as fully instantiated texts.
- A set of link annotations, *e.g.*, annotations providing the legal authority under which a given legal goal is satisfied by a given set of performative subgoals, and annotations explaining why a given rhetorical goal is satisfied by a particular set of subgoals in a given document genre.

To illustrate, a simplified representation of the illocutionary structure of a will is shown in Figure 1. The root illocutionary goal is to make a bequest.

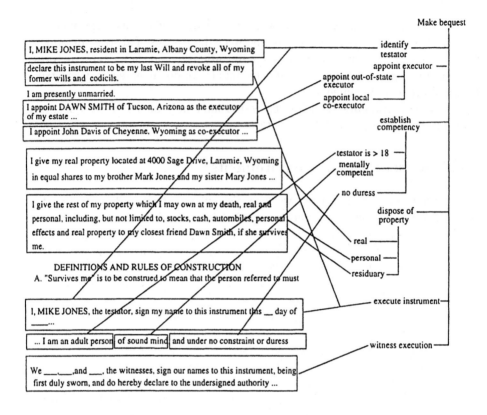

Fig. 1. A simplified representation of the illocutionary structure of a will.

Achieving this goal requires the operators displayed as children of the root: identify the testator, appoint an executor, etc. Each leaf illocutionary goal is connected to a text segment intended to achieve that goal. Not shown are the annotations explaining why (*i.e.*, citing the legal authority under which) making a bequest has the requirements shown.

A simplified representation of the rhetorical structure of the will is shown in Figure 2. Unlike the illocutionary structure, the rhetorical structure is closely connected to the surface text of the document. Together, the annotated illocutionary and rhetorical goal structures constitute the *justification structure* of a document.

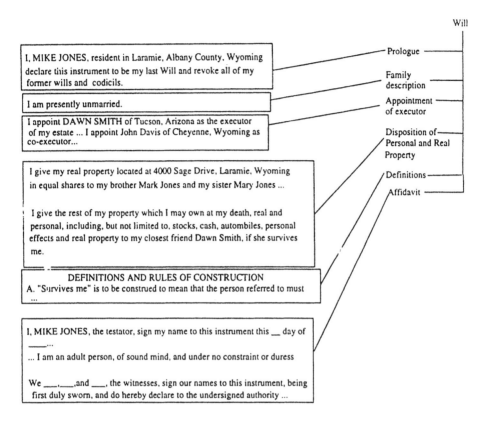

Fig. 2. The rhetorical structure of the will.

4 An Architecture for Self-Explaining Document Management

The previous sections described the tasks of document analysis, reuse, and maintenance, and argued that self-explaining documents, that is, documents containing explicit justification structures, are important for these tasks. This section proposes a *justification-based* framework for self-explaining document management. It uses the justification structures described in Section 3 as the basis for all transactions—both between the user and the system, and between all components within the system.

All communication between users and the document system transpires within the *document studio*, a workspace *cum* dialogue system in which specifications are constructed, new documents are edited, and retrieved archival documents are displayed. For each document currently under construction, the document studio maintains a *document object*, which consists of the evolving justification structure, the surface text, and the mapping between them. Before the document is complete, the surface text may be only partially reified.

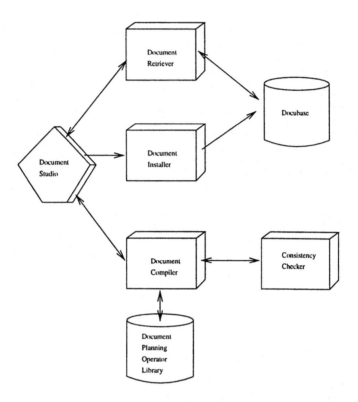

Fig. 3. An architecture for self-explaining document management.

When the user issues a request to create a new document, he or she is prompted for the document genre (*e.g.*, contracts) and sub-genre(s) (*e.g.*, employment contracts). Users may then pursue one of two construction modes: *ab initio* or adaptive. If they opt for *ab initio*, the system will engage them in a *specifications-gathering* dialogue. First, it will use the genre and sub-genre types to identify the operators in the *document planning operator library* that are relevant to the construction task at hand. Next, it will employ a hierarchical planning technique to decompose the root illocutionary goals and root rhetorical goals by querying the user. As users respond to questions about the illocutionary goals to be achieved, subsumptive operators are identified and their predicates are instantiated with user-specified values. This process bottoms out for leaf goals, which are entity and relationship variables that are instantiated with the specifics of the current document specification.

When users select the adaptive construction mode, the system engages them in a *similarity-identification* dialogue. In an iterative refinement process, it will request users to characterize the illocutionary and/or rhetorical goals to be achieved. The document studio will pass these to the *document retriever*, which will use them to locate similar documents in the *docubase*, the library of archival documents. The docubase employs justification indices that map illocutionary and rhetorical goals to document objects that achieve these goals. As a consequence, the document retriever can quickly identify archival documents whose intent is similar to that desired by a user. These documents are then presented in the document studio, and the user either deems them acceptable or annotates individual segments as being desirable or undesirable. This feedback, along with refined specifications at the goal level, is used to obtain archival documents that more closely meet the user's needs.

Once the most relevant archival documents have been located, the user adapts them to his or her current needs. Adaptation is performed by comparing the justification structure of the retrieved text to the current illocutionary and rhetorical goals. Text segments whose only purpose is to satisfy goals absent from the current situation are *excised, i.e.,* identified and removed. If the user has goals that are not satisfied by the retrieved text, retrieval is performed on other documents to find text segments that can satisfy that goal. Retrieved text segments are abstracted and reinstantiated with values appropriate for the user's goals.

Adaptive construction offers two benefits over *ab initio* construction. First, it can provide significant efficiency gains, particularly if intentionally similar documents can be located. Second, adaptation conserves justification structures across documents. This property is critical for document drafting tasks in which (1) complex large-scale (perhaps multi-volume) documents must achieve a global consistency, (2) multi-generation documents must retain a semantic (as opposed to merely a syntactic) similarity across generations, or (3) "hyper-formal" documents must make declarations that achieve complicated illocutionary goals while simultaneously adhering to strict legal or regulatory rules and attending to baroque stylistic conventions.

To permit maximum expressiveness, at any time users may compose and insert their own text segments. Though critical, this capability is problematic for inference unless the system constructs a justification (sub-)structure for the user's text. It must therefore either infer the justification structure of the newly entered text or engage in a dialogue with the user in which the illocutionary and rhetorical structure are interactively ascertained. Given the limitations of NLP, the latter alternative is adopted. Accordingly, the system integrates the new text into the justification structure by engaging in a *text characterization* dialogue in which the user is asked to categorize the text with the appropriate illocutionary and rhetorical representational vocabulary.

When users wish to see the effects of their specifications, they request a document compilation. Upon request, the document studio passes the justification structure developed up to this point—note that depending on the stage of completion, it may or may not be completely instantiated—to the *document compiler*, which employs a top-down planning mechanism to construct as much of the justification structure as the current information will permit. This structure is then passed to the *consistency checker*, which inspects the structure for constraint violations with respect to the selected genre and sub-genres. The resulting surface text, together with formatting specifications and the constraint violations, are then passed to the document studio, which displays the properly formatted document and reports any constraint violations.

At any time, users can highlight specific regions of a document and request that rationale behind the segment be explained. The document studio will inspect the justification structure associated with the document object to identify the sub-trees of the illocutionary and rhetorical structures that are associated with the specified segment. It will then display the justifications, both in tree form and in textualized form. Users may also highlight a region of the document and request to view similar text segments of archival documents. The document studio will extract the selected sub-trees of the justification structure and pass these to the document retriever, which will identify analogous segments in the docubase. Finally, users may view a document's entire justification structure. They can specify for it to be displayed in either an *abstracted* mode, where the variables remain uninstantiated, in an *instantiated* mode, where all bindings are displayed, or in a *juxtaposed* mode, where the justification structure and its mapping to the surface text are displayed side by side.

5   Example: Use of Self-Explaining Documents

Suppose that an attorney, Clarice Darrow, a general practitioner, wishes to draft a will for a client, Mary Baker, who desires to devise her home to husband, John Baker, and to provide for the guardianship for her minor children, Sally and Bill, if her husband should predecease them. Suppose that Clarice wishes to find an existing will to adapt to meet her current goals. The attorney's interaction with the system might consist of the following steps:

1. Retrieval: finding an existing document that can be adapted for the current situation.
   (a) Illocutionary goal identification. Darrow first identifies the illocutionary goals that she wishes the document to achieve. The system's interface may include a check-sheet, interviewing procedure, or domain-specific expert system to elicit goals from the user in a process of iterative refinement. The system should be able to infer any necessary subgoals of the specified goals. A simplified illocutionary goal tree is shown in Figure 4. This goal tree shows, *e.g.*, that in order to make a bequest, it is necessary for the testator to establish competency, and this in turn requires establishing three subgoals: age; mental competency; and absence of duress.
   (b) Indexing. The most closely matching existing documents under a user-modifiable similarity metric are then located and retrieved. Suppose that the will shown in Figure 1 is one of the documents retrieved.
2. Comparison. The user, Clarice, must now determine how the retrieved document should be modified to apply to the current situation. This requires comparing the illocutionary goal tree for the current situation, shown in Figure 4, with the goal tree for the retrieved document. This comparison is shown in Figure 5. This comparison indicates that the retrieved document

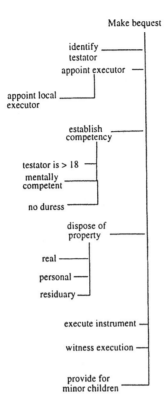

Fig. 4. An illocutionary goal hierarchy.

differs in that (1) it achieves the appointment of an executor by appointing an out-of-state executor together with a local co-executor, whereas the current goal tree satisfies this goal by appointing a local executor, and (2) the retrieved document doesn't provide for minor children.

3. Adaptation: modifying the retrieved document to satisfy the current illocutionary goals.

   (a) Excision. Text whose only purpose is to satisfy goals that aren't present in the current situation should be identified and removed. For example, text whose purpose is to appoint a local co-executor is not necessary in the current situation and is removed.

   (b) Augmentation. For each goal that does not appear in the retrieved text (such as provide for minor children), present the user with examples of text from other documents that can satisfy that goal. This requires retrieval not at the level of granularity of the entire document, but at a much finer granularity. In this case, just those portions of several previous wills that provide for guardianship are retrieved. For example one retrieved segment might be the following portion from the will of Eleanor Silver: "In the event that my wife, Eleanor Silver, should predecease me

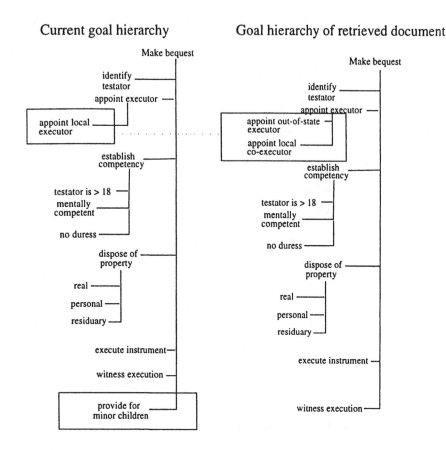

Fig. 5. A comparison of the given goals with the illocutionary structure of the retrieved document.

before my children, Sarah and Martha achieve their majority, I appoint my brother, Elmer Goldsmith, to be guardian ..." The user can view these test segments and select the most appropriate segment in view of (1) the illocutionary structure of the text segment itself, (2) any annotations attached to the text segment at the time of their creation, or (3) stylistic preferences of the user.

(c) Substitution. Since substitutable elements of all items in the docubase are tagged with type labels using standard template techniques, retrieved segments can be abstracted and reinstantiated. In the current example situation <testator: Mary Baker> to be substituted for corresponding values in the retrieved text, e.g., <testator: Eleanor Silver>. The result of the substitution is a self-explaining document that satisfied the current set of illocutionary goals.

4. Storage. The final document, which may embody components from multiple previous documents, is added to the document library indexed by illocutionary and rhetorical goal structure.

6 Implementation Plans

We are currently exploring the application of justification structures to document reuse in the context of Colorado Court of Appeals show-cause orders. Jurisdictional show-cause orders are issued during jurisdictional screening, a process of determining whether the requirements for an appeal have been satisfied. If there appears to be a jurisdictional defect, a staff attorney drafts a show-cause order that sets forth the apparent defect and orders the appellant to rebut the defect within a fixed time period or face dismissal of the appeal. Show-cause orders are produced in relatively high volume (several hundred per year), are complex enough to require drafting by an attorney, but have sufficient stylistic and substantive consistency to facilitate reuse.

Our research agenda is as follows. We are currently engaged in developing the domain theory for show-cause orders (the objects and predicates that define the illocutionary and rhetorical structures). When this process is complete, we will undertake the construction of each component of the architecture. To supply a uniform representation for all of the knowledge structures, all illocutionary structures, rhetorical structures, and planning operators will be implemented in a unification-based constraint system [Elh91]. As a result of the single representation, all adaptation procedures (document compilation and consistency checking) will be performed with a single mechanism: constraint propagation. Although this brings with it an initial development overhead, we expect to witness significant software engineering benefits in the form of rapid extensions to the domain theory. Finally, once the system for show-cause orders is complete, we will run extensive empirical evaluations to measure the gains in efficiency and correctness.

7 Related Work

Indexing and adaptation are central to any case-based approach to problem solving. Early case-based reasoning systems, *e.g.,* [Kol84, SW86, PBH90], typically addressed tasks, such as classification, that require little or no adaptation. By contrast, more recent CBR research has often addressed tasks such as design, planning, or configuration, that require complex adaptation, *e.g.,* [Vel92, BS95, SK95, BA95]. Document drafting typifies a design task requiring complex adaptation for case reuse. The research described in this paper is intended to formalize the knowledge required for document reuse, just as the projects cited above identified knowledge required for reuse of other types of design, planning, and configuration cases.

Our model of document justification structures draws on four different lines of research: discourse structure analysis; the theory of argumentation; explanation generation; and automated document drafting. The primary focus of research in discourse structure has been accounting for the coherence of expository or other communicative text through hierarchical structures of rhetorical and other discourse relations, *e.g.,* [GS86, Hob79]. The formalization of inter-sentential discourse relations is a key requirement for the development of self-explaining documents.

The most directly relevant portion of research in discourse structure is speech act theory. Initiated by J.L. Austin, who was primarily concerned with explicit performatives [Aus62], speech act theory addresses the illocutionary content of discourse, that is, the goals that a speaker intends to accomplish through that discourse [Gri75, Sea69]. Illocutionary analysis is essential for self-explaining documents because few documents have an exclusively communicative purpose. Instead, as emphasized above, documents are often intended to elicit information, persuade, memorialize events, or to accomplish performative goals.

The theory of argumentation addresses texts intended to persuade, establish, or prove. For example, Toulmin [Tou58] analyzed argumentative texts in terms of the concepts of warrant, ground, conclusion, backing, and qualification. This model has been widely applied to the analysis [Mar89, ZS95] and creation [BCS95] of legal documents. Argument structure, like other forms of illocutionary goal structure but unlike rhetorical structure, does not directly address the "surface" form of texts. This line of research is particularly relevant to the analysis of the illocutionary structure of persuasive or dispositive documents such legal briefs and judicial decisions [Bra93].

The explanation community has extensively studied the process of planning and realizing text given a set of discourse specifications. Over the past decade, their work research on discourse planning [McK85, Par88, Hov90, Hov93, Caw92, Sut93, Moo95, LP96] has produced a variety of techniques for determining the content and organization of many genres of text. Perhaps because of the necessity of coping with the myriad underlying rhetorical, illocutionary, and argument structures in discourse generation, this work has yielded a variety of mechanisms for determining the content and organization of multi-sentential text, a key capability of self-explaining documents.

Automated document drafting research is the fourth relevant research area. Two important areas of automated document drafting research are automated legal drafting and automated report generation. A large number of automated legal drafting systems have been developed in recent years, but most involve creation of text templates that are then instantiated to create particular documents [Lau92]. Some progress has been made in exploiting explicit representations of the relationship between generic documents and document instances and of constraints among document components [DS95]. However, there is a growing recognition in the Law and AI community that a declarative representation of the knowledge underlying the selection and configuration of textual elements is essential for the development of tools that embody the expertise of legal drafting experts [Gor89, Lau93].

The automated report generation community has addressed another form of text production from an underlying domain structure: the derivation of technical documentation from program traces generated during software development or use [MRK95, KMR93]

8 Summary

Document drafting typifies a design task requiring complex adaptation for case reuse. This paper has proposed a self-explaining document framework that uses explicit knowledge of the document's illocutionary and rhetorical structure for indexing and adapation. We are currently instantiating the framework in the context of judicial show-cause orders. It is our hypothesis that, by equipping documents with a justification structure that includes both illocutionary and rhetorical components, self-explaining document systems can assist document designers with constructing, maintaining, and interpreting complex documents.

References

[Aus62] J. Austin. *How to do things with words*. Oxford U. Press, New York, 1962.

[BA95]   K. Branting and D. Aha. Stratified case-based reasoning: Reusing hierarchical problem solving episodes. In *Proceedings of the Fourteenth International Joint Conference on Artificial Intelligence(IJCAI-95)*, Montreal, Canada, August 20–25 1995.

[BCS95] T. Bench-Capon and G. Staniford. PLAID - proactive legal assistance. In *Proceedings of the Fifth International Conference on Artificial Intelligence and Law*, pages 81–88, 1995.

[Bra93] L. K. Branting. An issue-oriented approach to judicial document assembly. In *Proceedings of the Fourth International Conference on Artificial Intelligence and Law*, pages 228–235, Amsterdam, The Netherlands, June 15–18, 1993. ACM Press.

[BS95]   B. Bartsch-Sporl. Towards the integration of case-based, schema-based and model-based reasoning for supporting complex design tasks. In *Lecture Notes in Artificial Intelligence*, pages 145–156, Sesimbra, Portugal, October 1995. Springer.

[Caw92] A. Cawsey. *Explanation and Interaction: The Computer Generation of Explanatory Dialogues*. MIT Press, 1992.

[DS95]   A. Daskalopulu and M. Sergot. A constraint-driven system for contract assembly. In *Proceedings of the Fifth International Conference on Artificial Intelligence and Law*, pages 62–70, 1995.

[Elh91] M. Elhadad. FUF: The universal unifier user manual version 5.0. Technical Report CUCS-038-91, Department of Computer Science, Columbia University, 1991.

[Gor89] T. Gordon. A theory construction approach to legal document assembly. In *Pre-Proceedings of the Third International Conference on Logic, Informatics, and Law*, pages 485–498, Florence, 1989.

[Gri75] H. Grice. Logic and conversation. In P. Cole and J. Morgan, editors, *Syntax and Semantics 2: Speech Acts*, pages 41–58. Academic Press, New York, NY, 1975.

[GS86]   B. Grosz and C. Sidner. Attention, intention, and the structure of discourse. *Computational Linguistics*, 12(3), 1986.

[Hob79] J. Hobbs. Coherence and co-reference. *Cognitive Science*, 3(1):67–82, 1979.

[Hov90] E. H. Hovy. Pragmatics and natural language generation. *Artificial Intelligence*, 43:153–197, 1990.

[Hov93]   E. H. Hovy. Automated discourse generation using discourse structure relations. *Artificial Intelligence*, 63:341–385, 1993.

[KMR93]   T. Korelsky, D. McCullough, and O. Rambow. Knowledge requirements for the automatic generation of porject management reports. In *Proceedings of the Eigth Knowledge-Engineering Conference*. IEEE Computer Society Press, September 20–23 1993.

[Kol84]   J. Kolodner. *Retrieval and Organizational Strategies in Conceptual Memory: a Computer Model*. Lawrence Erlbaum Associates, Hillsdale, NJ, 1984.

[Lau92]   M. Lauritsen. Technology report: Building legal practice systems with today's commericial authoring tools. *Law and Artificial Intelligence*, 1(1), 1992.

[Lau93]   M. Lauritsen. Knowing documents. In *Fourth International Conference on Artificial Intelligence and Law*, pages 185–191, Amsterdam, 1993. ACM Press.

[LP96]   J. C. Lester and B. W. Porter. Scaling up explanation generation: Large-scale knowledge bases and empirical studies. In *Proceedings of the Thirteenth National Conference on Artificial Intelligence*, Portland, Oregon, to appear 1996.

[Mar89]   C. Marshall. Representing the structure of a legal argument. In *Proceedings of the Second International Conference on Artificial Intelligence and Law*, pages 121–127, Vancouver, B.C., June 13-16 1989.

[McK85]   K. R. McKeown. *Text Generation: Using Discourse Strategies and Focus Constraints to Generate Natural Language Text*. Cambridge University Press, 1985.

[Moo95]   J. D. Moore. *Participating in Explanatory Dialogues*. MIT Press, 1995.

[MRK95]   K. McKeown, J. Robin, and K. Kukick. Generating concise natural language summaries. *Information Processing and Management*, 1995. Special Issue on Summarization.

[Par88]   Cécile L. Paris. Tailoring object descriptions to a user's level of expertise. *Computational Linguistics*, 14(3):64–78, September 1988.

[PBH90]   B. W. Porter, E. R. Bareiss, and R. C. Holte. Concept learning and heuristic classification in weak-theory domains. *Artificial Intelligence*, 45(1–2), 1990.

[Sea69]   J. Searle. *Speech Acts: An Essay in the Philosophy of Language*. Cambridge University Press, Cambridge, 1969.

[SK95]   B. Smyth and M. Keane. Experiments on adaptation -guided retrieval in case-based design. In *Lecture Notes in Artificial Intelligence*, pages 313–324, Sesimbra, Portugal, October 1995. Springer.

[Sut93]   D. D. Suthers. *An Analysis of Explanation and Its Implications for the Design of Explanation Planners*. PhD thesis, University of Massachusetts, February 1993.

[SW86]   C. Stanfill and D. Waltz. Toward memory-based reasoning. *Communications of the ACM*, 29(12), 1986.

[Tou58]   S. E. Toulmin. *The Uses of Argument*. Cambridge University Press, 1958.

[Vel92]   M. Veloso. *Learning by Analogical Reasoning in General Problem Solving*. PhD thesis, Carnegie Mellon University, 1992.

[ZS95]   J. Zeleznikow and A. Stranieri. The split-up system: Integrating neural networks and rule-based reasoning in the legal domain. In *Proceedings of the Fifth International Conference on Artificial Intelligence and Law*, pages 185–194, 1995.

Adaptation-Guided Retrieval in EBMT:
A Case-Based Approach to Machine Translation

Bróna Collins, Pádraig Cunningham.
Dept. of Computer Science, Trinity College, Dublin 2, Ireland.
email: bcollins@cs.tcd.ie

Abstract. In this paper we describe a methodological analysis of EBMT (Example-Based Machine Translation) based on a CBR (Case-Based Reasoning) perspective. This analysis focuses on adaptation. We argue that, just as in CBR, the overall power of an EBMT system is its ability to adapt examples retrieved to suit the new problem translation. Here we describe a technique whereby reusability is a function of the abstract "adaptability" information stored in the cases. This information is exploited during both the adaptation and retrieval stages.

1. Introduction

Adaptation-guided retrieval is an important emerging notion in CBR research (Smyth & Keane, 1993; Leake, 1995; Smyth, 1996). In this paper we explore the relevance of this idea in the related area of example-based machine translation (EBMT). The motivating principle in adaptation guided retrieval is that cases are retrieved in CBR in order to be reused. This retrieval is normally based on the similarity of selected features. In the end this similarity is acting as a proxy for the adaptability of the retrieved case. This is not necessarily a good thing because semantic similarity may not always signal ease of adaptation. Adaptation guided retrieval (AGR) recognises this and emphasises retrieval based on adaptability. This means that the adaptability of a case should be a key consideration in case retrieval and selection.

We argue that this policy is particularly appropriate in example-based MT. Because of the *sparse data* problem in EBMT (Gale & Church, 1993; Moonjoo, 1995) an EBMT system must have a sophisticated adaptation mechanism. In addition, adaptation is complicated by translation divergences that are brittle in reuse. This means that a translation example involving a target language segment that is structurally different to the source language segment can only be adapted with great care. An AGR policy in EBMT is useful because it helps retrieve cases that can be adapted safely. In this paper we present an approach to EBMT that quantifies this concept of 'safety' and makes it a key criterion in case selection. We describe *ReVerb*, an EBMT system that implements this idea. We illustrate that ReVerb retrieves adaptable cases in the translation of software manuals from English to German.

In section 2 we provide an overview of EBMT and present our model of EBMT that emphasises the transformations in EBMT that dictate the adaptability of a translation case in a particular context. In section 3 we describe the overall architecture of ReVerb and in section 4 we describe how adaptation-guided retrieval works in ReVerb. In section 5 we illustrate how ReVerb adapts cases, followed by an evaluation in section 6.

2. EBMT

Example Based Machine Translation (EBMT) is the marriage of MT and Case Based Reasoning (CBR) techniques (see Nagao, 1984; Sumita, 1995). It involves translating the source language (SL) into the target language (TL) via *remindings* from previous translation cases. Natural language translation can be seen as a heavily memory-dependent problem, especially when the text at hand is a *sublanguage*, (a subset of language which is specific to one domain, e.g. the language of software documentation). Professional translators often get the feeling that much of their skill is wasted on translating very repetitive passages of text. The motivation for EBMT is thus clear: when faced with a novel sentence, chances are that the expert translator will have translated something very similar before, will recognise this (matching and retrieval), and will make the changes necessary (adaptation) to produce a good translation. Approaches differ with respect to the amount of linguistic processing performed on the example texts. At one end of the spectrum are string-based approaches (Nirenburg 1995, MacLean, 1993) in which examples are retrieved on the basis of string similarity only and the input is covered by combining substrings retrieved from different cases, giving preference to longer substrings. Combining substrings in this linguistically unprincipled manner inevitably leads to the problem of 'boundary friction' -a well recognised problem in EBMT literature, but the technique has the advantage that a huge data base of examples can be built easily. Other approaches incorporate shallow syntactic indexing (Juola 1994, Cranias 1995) and then use clustering techniques or simulated annealing during retrieval. At the linguistic end of the scale, language is usually represented in tree forms which typically represent the 'dependency relations' between syntactic constituents and then tree operations (e.g. deleting and replacing subtrees) are performed in order to cover the input string (Sato 1990). The surrounding context of the subtree is taken into account, along with the number of tree operations which the template must undergo, when choosing candidate translation examples.

In ReVerb, translation examples consist of aligned sentences/ clauses which are extracted from a bilingual corpus, abstracted to a dependency level of syntactic representation, and then cross-linked during the indexing stage. Linking the respective SL and TL sentence sub-parts, or, "chunks" (where a 'chunk' is a syntactic constituent consisting of one or more words, e.g. "on the screen" is an adverbial chunk) in this way results in a translation process which accounts for structural and lexical divergences that may have occurred during initial human translation of the corpus. Thus, the *ReVerb* system uses shallower linguistic processing to that of Sato and Nagao, and, instead of calculating the exact tree operations necessary to adapt the chosen case for both the source and target language at run-time, ReVerb compares flat lists of features and values and chooses the case which will unify best with the input. ReVerb's templates contain variables which indicate the chunks can be replaced, which increases the likelihood of the input and examples unifying because in these positions, only the features (syntactic functions) and not the values (actual words) have to match. In Sato's approach, the context of the original case is taken into account when inserting it into a new tree. This means that subtrees are replaced by subtrees coming from a similar syntactic and semantic environment, which is desirable. However, it does not guarantee that the resulting tree is syntactically correct in the case of the target language. Hacking a tree on the basis of subtree similarity in the source language can never be guaranteed to result in a correspondingly hacked up target language tree with its syntactic structure still intact. This is the problem which our approach seeks to address in particular.

One way of addressing this problem is by quantifying just how "dependent" chunks within a sentence are on other chunks, not only with respect to other chunks in the sentence (within-language dependency) but also with respect to its mapping to the target text (between-languages dependency). A high dependency of either kind is penalised and receives a low-*adaptability* score.

This linking information – represented as features attached to each word – is also used for building the system's lexicon as examples are added to the case base. As words are associated with the cases in which they appear, thus giving them an explicit context, the system can exploit this by using only those words in the dictionary that were previously translated in a similar (syntactic) context to the present translation problem. Once this detailed linguistic information has been stored during the generalisation phase, the system can then proceed with the typical CBR cycle of indexing the input sentence, matching it against the case-base, retrieving a best-match, and then adapting this example to suit the new problem. At run-time, the system treats case-data as it would any other data set composed of frame-structured features and values, i.e., it does not assume any linguistic knowledge.

2.1 Mappings in EBMT

In general, an EBMT system architecture will contain the following data in the example base:

SL   Source Language in original string form.
TL   Target Language in original string form.
SLA   Source Language Abstraction.
TLA   Target language Abstraction.

The SL is abstracted into the SLA by means of some standard linguistic processing, likewise the TL (see Figure. 1). The SLA and TLA representations are then linked at the sub-sentential level. The level of linguistic abstraction will determine how substrings can be linked. After a syntactic analysis of the example SL and TL, the resulting SLA and TLA parse-trees can be linked, i.e. the syntactic constituents are linked (see Iida, 1991). A higher level of abstraction is that of syntactic functionality or dependency; each syntactic constituent has a certain role to play in a sentence, whether this be the subject or object or verb. Dependence relations are often expressed in hierarchical trees and this level of abstraction tells us which constituents affect which others in a sentence, for example, the subject of a sentence/clause always has to agree with the main finite verb. A node's position in a dependency tree can determine the respective contexts of the SLA and TLA nodes (see Sato 1990).

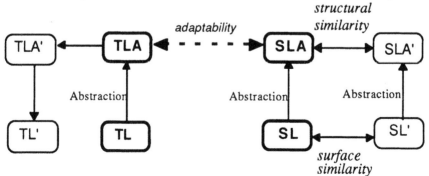

Fig.1. Multi-level correspondences between an input sentence(SL') and a given example(SL)

In order to define a subsentential mapping between two natural languages it is not sufficient to link two nodes which have the same syntactic feature. Translators often find it necessary to express SL words as different syntactic functions in the TL in order to create a grammatically or even stylistically correct TL. For example, the verb, say, in the SLA, may be realised as the subject in the TLA. Such divergences are the main obstacles to MT and there have been several attempts to formalise the problem (see Dorr, 1993; Streiter, 1995) but they inevitably suffer from the knowledge-acquisition bottleneck problem. In CBR, the idea is to compare enough previous translations so that useful generalisations fall out of the data. Therefore, one needs firstly to link two constituents on the basis of their *lexical* meaning and then to determine how the corresponding TLA constituent was realised syntactically compared to the SLA. Each case therefore is a description of a TLA derivation. A scoring mechanism can be used to penalise SLA → TLA mappings where the syntactic function was changed. A case base of such derivations constitutes a subset of contrastive linguistic data, which, if suitably generalised, can be regarded as an abstract model of translation for the SLA and TLA in that particular domain. More importantly for our purposes, it represents how *adaptable* each translation case is, for only cases with good SLA → TLA mappings can be adapted to compensate for any differences between the SL and the SL'.

EBMT Systems which base their retrieval mechanisms on *both* similarity and adaptability would then differentiate between the following scenarios given a case base of examples and an input sentence representation, SL'. Here, we ignore the surface similarity (of two sentences, SL' → SL) but see Section 4 for a discussion of the Base Filtering Stage.

- Good SLA' → SLA   Good SLA → TLA   :Retrievable and adaptable
- Poor SLA' → SLA   Good SLA → TLA   :Difficult to retrieve, easy to adapt.
- Good SLA' → SLA   Poor SLA → TLA.   :Easy to retrieve but adaptation is *unsafe*. This means that even if only one TLA word needs changing, it will probably affect other constituents. What is more, this effect may not be determinable.
- Poor SLA' → SLA   Poor SLA → TLA.   :The case will not be retrieved.

Imitation of the retrieved example may involve nothing more than simple word substitution or it could involve integration of standard MT techniques (Kaji, 1992) (Sumita, 1991). A good way to proceed is to determine where simple chunk substitution is "safe" with respect to the above named dependencies and to perform it as much as boundary friction will allow.

3. ReVerb

3.1   Overall Architecture

The overall CBR model adopted for this work is best understood by consideration of Figure 2 following (adapted from Bergmann, 1995). While providing a coherent organisation for all the necessary components of a full EBMT system, we presently concentrate on only three components of this model, namely: *Case Organisation, Case Retrieval,* and *Case Adaptation* (described in sections 3, 4 and 5 respectively). The central philosophy of CBR employed in the design of these components is that of *Adaptation Guidance* (see Smyth & Keane 1993, Leake 1995, Smyth 1996) –that is, these components are geared toward generating data structures (e.g., cases and chunks of cases) that are most likely to be adaptable at later stages of processing.

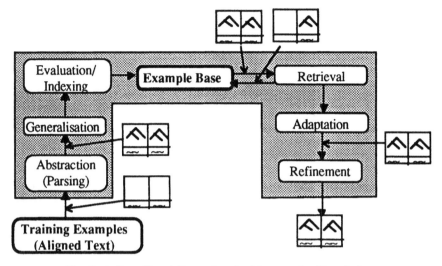

Fig. 2. A Case-Based-Reasoning Architecture for Translation

3.2. An Associative Model of Case-Memory

The case-base is derived from a corpus of bilingual English/German *CorelDRAW-6* manuals. Each case is represented in a uniquely-labelled frame which in turn contains a number of "chunk"-frame pointers. A frame-based language KRELL is used to represent the cases. KRELL is a generic frame-management system in which specific knowledge bases may be implemented. Since a case must be retrieved from memory on the basis of its string/word content, each such word is defined in ReVerb's frame-structured memory, providing pointers to the chunks and cases in which it is employed; as illustrated in Figure 3 below. The links between case frames, chunk frames, and word frames are bidirectional, with associated *demon* procedures to ensure their consistency after any updates or deletions (see Cunningham & Veale 1991).

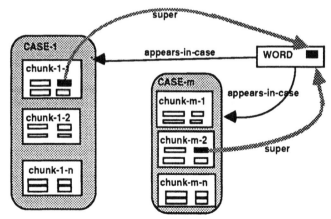

Fig. 3. Concepts linked in the ReVerb translation memory

3.3. Aligning the Examples

While we are against case-decomposition in general, due to the boundary friction problem it causes, in some situations it is perfectly safe (and advisable) to split a given SL sentence into its component clauses if there is a direct mapping into its TL counterpart, as in the following example taken from the CorelDRAW corpus:

1)   <1: When blending on a path > <2: you can specify the spacing between the intermediate shapes>
<1: Beim †berblenden entlang einer Strecke> <2: können Sie den Abstand zwischen den Zwischenformen festlegen>
(gloss: <During the blending along a path > <can you the spacing between the intermediate-shapes specify >)

Such separate clauses can then be combined with the clauses arising from other sentences in the corpus without experiencing the ill effects of boundary friction, because it has already been established that the clauses in question are independent of the sentence in which they originally occurred. In our test corpus of 200 examples, about 50% of the sentences consist of two or more clauses and of those, about 10% could be split up in this manner.

3.4. Abstraction

The model of EBMT described in section 3.1 supports different levels of abstraction. At present, a surface syntactic structure is obtained for the English component of each case by passing it through the constraint based grammar *engcg* of Voutilanien (1995). This grammar tags its input with morphological and categorial information, while also annotating words with the correct syntactic function. It does not completely parse the input, as syntactic functions are not used for building a hierarchical representation of the sentence. Attachment ambiguities may thus be ignored completely. However this under-specification leaves us with a problem, namely that some fertile words have two syntactic functions. Post processing of the grammar output is currently necessary to eliminate this ambiguity of syntactic function.

3.5. Linking

ReVerb uses a *mappability scale* of 0 .. 3 to classify the different levels of correspondence that may exist between chunks (see Fig. 4.). A mappability of 3 is granted only if the correspondence is perfect: i.e., all the words in an SLA chunk are mapped in 1:1 fashion to the TLA. A mappability of 2 indicates there is a morphological difference in the words surrounding the *head* (H) of the chunk, but that the syntactic functions are the same. Morphological variation would include many-to-one mappings in either direction, inflection, case-marking, additional particles, etc.). A mappability of 1 indicates that the SLA : TLA chunks differ in syntactic function, but have a lexical correspondence which would be awarded a 3 or 2 mapping had the syntactic function been the same, while zero is reserved for chunks which exhibit no SLA:TLA commonality. Because it cannot be discerned what these 'zero' chunks are linked to in the TL, it is dangerous to make any changes to them. In general, their function in the TL is incorporated into one of the chunks of mappability 1 or 2 in such a way as to make a dictionary-based connection impossible.

If the *head-word(SL_chunk)* ≡ *head-word(TL_chunk)* for some chunk pair then

If the *syntactic-function(SL chunk)= syntactic-function(TL_chunk)* then

If the other words in SL chunk have a 1:1 mapping to the TL chunk

then score = 3 .

else score = 2.

else score = 1.

else score = 0.

Fig. 4(a). The linking algorithm

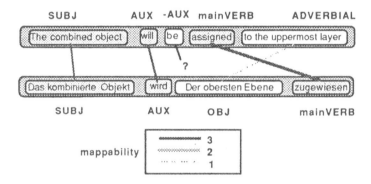

Fig. 4(b). Linking the abstracted SL and TL

3.6 Generalisation of Cases for Indexed Retrieval

Generalisation of cases (see figure 2) in ReVerb is achieved by a process of *case templatisation*, whereby a case template is generated by combining either the source text of each chunk, or a representative variable encoding the syntactic function of that chunk. Variablisation is performed by substituting SL elements of a given level of mappability/adaptability (or higher) with their *part-of-speech* (POS) tags; the intuition at work here is that the higher a chunk's mappability, the safer it will be to adapt at a later stage. As an example, consider that the SL string *"Move allows you to move the active window with the direction keys on the keyboard"* which is generalisable at four levels of variablisation, each level corresponding to a different mappability score (0 ... 3), as follows:

Level 0: SUBJ -0 FMAINV-1 OBJ -2 NFMAINV-3 OBJ-4 ADVL-5 ADVL-6
Level 1: SUBJ -0 FMAINV-1 OBJ -2 NFMAINV-3 OBJ-4 ADVL-5 ADVL-6
Level 2: SUBJ -0 *allows*   OBJ -2 NFMAINV-3 OBJ-4 ADVL-5 *on the keyboard*
Level 3: *Move   allows   you   to move   the active window with the*
                                               direction keys on the keyboard

The success of this indexing scheme in syntax-based retrieval was tested on a case base of 210 cases at different levels of chunk variablisation. The results, shown in Figure 5 following, give an indication as to the trade-off between precision and recall.

One can observe that as the mappability threshold for generalisation increases, the recall potential, or average number of retrievable cases, decreases. At the very safe mappability level of 3, therefore, a case-base of 20,000 cases would by our calculations contain 20 very adaptable templates.

Fig. 5. This graph illustrates the probability of any two cases (from our 214 case memory) matching at different levels of variablisation. As we increase the mappability threshold for variablisation, the percentage of matches drops considerably.

4. Retrieval in ReVerb

ReVerb currently utilises two different levels of case retrieval, using both surface and structural criteria; our aim is to compare the nature of the cases retrieved at each level independently, given the same input, to determine if string-based retrieval can act as a useful filter for subsequent structural retrieval. This arrangement is illustrated in Figure 6. We shall now consider each of these levels in turn:

4.1. String Matching Retrieval : Phase 1

At run time, the user inputs a sentence, or clause, for which examples must be selected from the corpus. No linguistic judgements are made by the system regarding this input: only exact words are matched, and near morphological neighbours (e.g. "object" and "objects") are not considered. Frame *demons* will activate all cases containing exact word matches, allocating the highest scores to those cases which have been activated the greatest number of times. This brute-force technique omits all consideration of part of speech criteria, syntactic dependency, or word count of the input, but any information stored in each case (e.g., POS, head, syntactic function, linear order and mappability of the SL: TL) can be exploited if the user so wishes. The first pass is not reliable in and of itself, but is subsequently used as a loose-grain filter to select candidates for the structural matching stage, Phase 2.

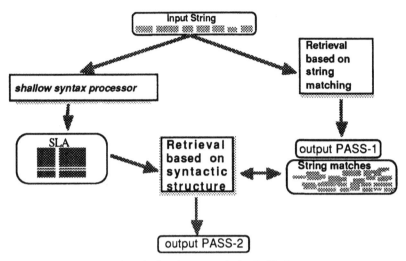

Fig. 6. Retrieval levels in ReVerb

4.2. Activation Passing for Retrieval

In the loose-grain stage, retrieval can be regarded as a process that satisfies the constraints imposed by a memory probe (i.e., the input). Marker passing is a suitable technique for retrieval at this level, which is well documented in AI literature (see Charniak 1983; Hendler 1989), and is used here to give any retrieved case a similarity score relative to the input. Activation passing is appropriate because it propagates simple numeric values throughout memory. The scoring mechanism can be viewed then as involving three phases:

Initiating Activation: The input case places activation on all nodes which contain the same words.

Summing Activation: Activation is propagated from each individual word to the chunks which contain that word.

Selection Criterion: Activation is propagated upwards from the chunk to the case which contains it such that the collection of chunk activations will produce a score of similarity for that case.

4.3. Activation Passing for Syntactic Retrieval: Phase 2

For structural retrieval, the input sentence is first pre-chunked, such that each chunk has an explicit head-word. The algorithm described below initiates activation from each word in the chunk, giving the head word an increased weighting to reflect its pivotal role in the chunk. The summation of activation proceeds as for the purely string based retrieval method, save that adaptability/mappability scores are integrated into the calculation of activation levels.

Initiating Activation: From the head word $H(CS_i)$ of each chunk CS_i, issue forth a wave of activation of a fixed level (1.0) say. For every non-head word of each chunk, also initiate a wave of a lower level (e.g. 0.2)

Summing Activation: When an activation wave of strength I reaches a memory chunk CS_j of an example $E_K<S:T>$, add I to the internal activation of E_K. Then add the mappability score for CS_j to produce the adaptability-based activation.

Selection Criterion: When all waves have terminated, collate in a list and sort (in descending order) the internal activation levels of each visited example E_K. return the first R examples on this ordered list.

5. Adaptation

By adaptation, we mean here on-line, or run-time adaptation of the TLA frame of a retrieved example to accommodate any differences between the input SL and the example SL'. We restrict our present discussion to the dependency-syntactic level of case representation. No changes are made to the syntactic structure (the linear ordering of syntactic functions) during adaptation. ReVerb employs the following assumption:

> If the SL' and SL are very similar at a string and grammatical level, and the SLA to TLA mappability is good, then the corresponding adaptation of the TLA will result in the TL' whose meaning is that of the SL', or else the SL' is divergent.

If an SL' and an SL sentence are extremely similar on a syntactic level and yet semantically totally different, then they will almost always have different patterns of syntactic links to the target language. Awareness of this fact will prevent a translator from blindly replacing the offending word with the new word because (s)he knows that in the TL, it will not just be a matter of replacing the corresponding word there. ReVerb will always choose an example which can be adapted easily at a syntactic level. So, if the input sentence (unlike the straightforward example) actually requires a divergence, caused by a certain verb, say, then the resultant translation will not be correct and the user will have to correct it and it will be stored as a new case. This stored example will have a poor mappability but it will be specialised for that particular verb. Now, if a new input sentence also has this divergency-causing verb in it and the surrounding context is sufficiently similar to render the example retrievable, then the poor mappability of the example is less likely to result in a poor translation this time around.

5.1. Using the Corpus as A Bilingual Dictionary

If a chunk has been seen before by the system it will be stored in the system's bilingual lexicon, which is simply a table of word-frames which are linked, in turn, to their host cases and thus to their TL-equivalents within those cases. In other words, no effort goes into building the lexicon as it is a by-product of ReVerb's case-memory organisation. Chunks which have a high mappability score (3 being best) are preferred by the system, as are those which have the same syntactic function as the problem word (2+), and we are currently experimenting with incorporating a chunk's context as an added contributor to the score.

The new target word (i.e., in German) is then inserted into the new TLA structure (a copy of the old TLA example), and assumes the same syntactic function, linear order and syntactic category as the original. If the system lexicon is used, the mapping score of the substitution is used as a basis for quality determination. Depending on whether the mappability of the substitution is 3,2 or 1, the system awards a local *translation quality* of 100%, 67% and 33% respectively. The translation quality of a chunk which does not need to be substituted by lexical lookup is similarly determined on the basis of its SL': TL' mappability. In this way a *global translation quality* can be compositionally determined for the whole sentence.

If the system has not previously "seen" a particular SLA chunk to be adapted, then a bilingual dictionary outside the system has to be consulted. In this case, the word will be in its root form and so the system must consult the morphological markings on the original example's TL words to modify the dictionary entry correspondingly. The result of this process is a new case representation from which the TL string can be trivially generated without linguistic processing, by simply concatenating the chunk contents of the TLA representation in their correct linear order. In effect, this is the *strong assumption* of section 5 at work: stringing the adapted TLA chunks together according to their original linear order in this way allows the target language syntax and meaning to be preserved.

6. Evaluation

Our experiments to adapt input structures have produced encouraging results in that the output translations are quite accurate and helpful to the user. The input sentences we have used are taken from the case base itself –that is the SLA components of the cases are used to index the case base. At this stage, we are primarily interested in the correct adaptation of each struture with respect to its nearest structural matches in the case base, provided there are any. For some 74% of cases at present, however, there are no exact structural matches even when all of the chunks are variablised (level 0). This indicates how varied English language structures can be, even in the subdomain of software documentation where sentences and clauses tend to be short. Of the 24% SLAs which do retrieve structurally similar examples, the results of the matching and adaptation modules are outlined in sections 6.2 and 6.3 respectively. The base-filtering (phase 1) is discussed in section 6.1 but it is clear that it will only prove its usefulness when the case base has been scaled up. We evaluate the system by examining the respective TLA' templates retrieved at successive levels of adaptability in terms of their grammaticality and stylistics. This indicates how useful the system will be as an interactive tool for machine translation.

6.1   Phase 1 Retrieval

The first retrieval phase acts as a base-filter which extracts a group of candidate translations which are then input into phase two. At present, the case base is too small for the retrieved examples to be significantly similar but when the data is scaled up to, say, 20,000 examples then this stage will become more useful.

6.2   Phase 2: Structural Comparison and Adaptability

From an AGR viewpoint, this is the more interesting phase. Only adaptable templates will be retrieved. The threshold adaptability level with respect to the SLA' can be set to 3, 2, 1 or 0 depending on whether the user wishes to include templates with only high-level chunk mappings(3) or to include all templates(0), the latter being equivalent to mere similarity-guided retrieval. The system's performance at each level of adaptability is evaluated on the basis of the quality of output sentences, that is, the number of mistakes found in the output translations, as judged by a human evaluator (see figure 7). The 'translation score' is ReVerb's prediction regarding translation quality, based on its knowledge about chunk similarity and mappability.

Mappability level of templates' variables	Number of matching pairs in 214 cases	Human evaluation (Average #mistakes per translated case)	ReVerb's own evaluation (translation score)
0	104	2.57	47.2%
1	50	1.28	55.3%
2	8	0.25	90.2%
3	6	0.00	100%

Fig. 7. Results of matching ReVerb's 214 cases against each other

6.2.1 Retrieval at adaptability threshold: 3

At this highly restrictive level, only those templates are retrieved whose SLA differences are all reconcilable by adapting a chunk of mappability 3. This usually involves a simple noun-phrase substitution (see Figure 8).

Result: 6 matches in 214 cases

Quality: perfect translations

```
[CASE-92] Found Match of strength 2 with [CASE-93]
SL': ENTER A PREFIX TO BE ATTACHED TO THE DIMENSION TEXT HERE
SL: ENTER A SUFFIX TO BE ATTACHED TO THE DIMENSION TEXT HERE
TL: GEBEN SIE HIER EIN SUFFIX EIN DAS DEM DIMENSIONSTEXT
ANGEHAENGT WERDEN SOLL
 Direct: SOLL
 Direct: DAS
 Direct: EIN
 Direct: SIE
 Direct: GEBEN
 Adapt: A PREFIX :was (A SUFFIX) :lookup (OBJ) = (EIN PRAEFIX) :quality
1.0
 Direct: WERDEN
 Direct: ANGEHAENGT
 Direct: DEM DIMENSIONSTEXT
 Direct: HIER
Translating case [CASE-93] ...
TL': GEBEN SIE HIER EIN PRAEFIX EIN DAS DEM DIMENSIONSTEXT
ANGEHAENGT WERDEN SOLL
```

Fig. 8. Adaptation at Level 3 of a highly similar Example

6.2.2 Retrieval at adaptability threshold: 2

At this level, one or more of the SLA chunks which need adaptation is different in *word-form* to the TLA, but syntactic functionality is isomorphic.

Result: 8 matches in 214 cases

Quality: Same as for threshold 3, but is dependent on the chunk's translation being correct in the lexicon for the context of the new case.

6.2.3 Retrieval at adaptability threshold: 1

Here, the SLA chunks that need adaptation have different corresponding syntactic functions in the TLA.

Result: 50 matches in 214 cases

Quality: Varies from perfect (no mistakes) in some 36% of the cases to mediocre (3 errors or less) in most others. What is very interesting here is that almost two-thirds of the cases (62%) had only one error or less, which would be easy for even an inexperienced translator to correct. Only 2% of the cases had more than 3 errors. The most common problem is the verb positioning and the incorrect form of the verb appearing in the adapted case. Another common problem is that of prepositions vanishing because an ADVL chunk containing a preposition is suddenly replaced by a SUBJ or OBJ chunk then the preposition will be overwritten by a single noun.

6.2.4 Retrieval at adaptability threshold: 0

One or more chunks in the SLA have no lexically determinable links to the TLA.

Result: 104 matches in 214 cases

Quality: Words which needed adaptation were often not recorded in the system dictionary. The translation quality suffered from extra TLA' words being present which were irrelevant to the SLA'. Also, linear order and word-forms of many chunks were incorrect, especially verbs.

7. Conclusions & Future Work

In testing our experimental system, *ReVerb*, we found that it can accurately adapt exemplar TLA templates when the corresponding SLA exemplar has sufficient structural similarity to the input sentence. Indeed, the CorelDRAW corpus contains several examples of such near-mappings, which are typical of computer software manuals. We have implemented the system in such a way as to be extensible in the following important respects. Firstly, we wish to bring such near-misses within the reach of the system. For instance, the input sentence may differ from a memory exemplar only in the addition (or omission) of a trailing temporal adjunct such as "yesterday". Redundancy rules governing the organisation of the case base can easily generate new well-formed cases from old by deleting or adding such constituents (if they have a 3 mapping between SLA and TLA), thus increasing the coverage of the case-base while avoiding an over-complication of the system's matching algorithms.

Secondly, we wish to refine the on-line adaptation process so that mappings of 2 and 1 will cause specialised adaptation operators to come into effect which will refer to the POS knowledge stored in the cases, or will use a derivational analysis approach to reconciling SLA → TLA differences and transmitting them to the TL. Finally, the mechanisms are already in place for semi-automatic case creation from bilingual text, so our long-term aim is to increase the number of cases until such time that the process can proceed completely automatically. This will require that all possible structures will be present in the case base, perhaps in generalised form, and also most (contextualised) words which one may expect to find in the given application domain. Our results have lead us to believe that there is an upper limit to the number of generalised templates necessary for producing perfect translations with the help of specialised adaptation specialists. On reaching this limit, a system could perform fully automatic MT. In the meantime, however, we are confident AGR can produce translation tools which assist users –who are not necessarily bilingual –in producing high quality translations of software documentation texts.

8. References

Bergmann R., Wilke W., (1995)   Building and Refining Abstract Planning Cases by change of Representation Language, *Journal of AI Research*, **3**, 53-118.

Charniak, E. (1983). Passing Markers: A Theory of Contextual Influence in Language Comprehension. *Cognitive Science* **7**. 171 -190.

Collins, B., Cunningham, P. (1995) A Methodology for EBMT. *4th Int. Conference on the Cognitive Science of Natural Language Processing,* Dublin 1995.

Cranias, L., Papageorgiou, H., Piperdis, S. (1995) A Matching Technique in EBMT. *The Computational Linguistics Archive,* cmp-lg/9508005.

Cunningham, P. , Veale, T. (1991). Organizational issues arising from the integration of the Concept Network & Lexicon in a Text Understanding System, *Proceedings of IJCAI'91,* Morgan Kaufmann, 986-991.

Dorr, B.J. (ed.) (1993) *Machine Translation: A View from the Lexicon.* MIT Press.

Hendler, J. A. (1989). Marker Passing over Micro-Features: Toward a Hybrid Symbolic/Connectionist Model, *Cognitive Science* 13(1).

Juola, P. (1994). Corpus-based Acquisition of Transfer functions using Psycholinguistic Principles, *in the proceeding of NeMLaP-1, New Methods in Language Processing,* UMIST 1994.

Kaji, H.,Kida, Y., Morimoto, Y. (1990) Learning Translation Templates from Bilingual Text. *COLING* 1992, Nantes. 672-678.

Leake, D. (1995). Adaptive similarity assessment for case-based explanation. International Journal of Expert Systems, 8(2): 165-194.

Moonjoo, K., Young, S.H., Choi, K. (1995) Collocation Map for overcoming Data Sparseness. *EACL 1995,* Dublin. 53-59

Nagao, M. (1984). A framework for mechanical translation between Japanese and English by analogy principle. In *A. Elithorn & R. Banerji (Eds.), Artificial and Human Intelligence.* NATO Publications.

Nirenburg, S. C. (Ed.). (1995). The Pangloss Mark III machine translation system *(Tech. Rep. No. CMU-CMT-95-145).* Pittsburgh: Carnegie Mellon University, Center for Machine Translation

Sato, S., Nagao, M. (1990) Toward Memory-based Translation. *COLING '90.*

Sumita E. , Tsutsumi, H. (1988) A translation aid system Using Flexible Text retrieval Based on Syntax Matching. TRL Research Report, IBM.

Smyth, B. (1996) *Case-Based Design.* PhD Thesis, Trinity College Dublin.

Smyth, B., Keane, M.T. (1993) *Retrieving Adaptable Cases.* Topics in Case-Based Reasoning, Springer Verlag. 209-220.

Streiter, O. (1995) Patterns of Derivation, *TMI-95,* Leuven, 1995.

Voutilainen, A. (1995) A syntax-based part-of-speech analyser. *Proceedings of the EACL, Dublin* 1995

Dynamically Creating Indices for Two Million Cases: A Real World Problem

J. Daengdej[1], D. Lukose[2], E. Tsui[3], P. Beinat[4], and L. Prophet[5]

Distributed Artificial Intelligence Center[1,2]
Department of Mathematics, Statistics and
Computing Science,
University of New England,
Armidale, NSW 2351, Australia

Expert Systems Group[3,4,5]
Continuum (Australia) Ltd.,
201 Miller Street,
North Sydney, NSW 2060,
Australia

E-Mail: {jirapun I lukose}@neumann.une.edu.au, esg@continuum.com.au[3,4,5]
Tel: +6 (067) 73 3574[1]   Fax: +6 (067) 73 3312[1,2]

Abstract

Efficiently indexing and retrieving cases from a very large case library are
major concerns when building a Case-Based Reasoning (CBR) system.
Most CBR research has focused on representation of cases, how to identify
features that should be used for retrieval; and similarity measurement between values of attributes. In this paper, we propose a method for *dynamically* creating indices, and, also different similarity-measurement methods
for different types of attributes. We also discuss the use of a relational database for representing cases, taxonomy knowledge, and spatial information. Our real world problem domain consists of *2* million incomplete insurance cases, with *30* different attributes. Even though all of these are
valid cases, only *10* percent of these policies have lodged claims. These
situations create a very complex case base for reasoning and problem solving. In response to this complexity, the approach adopted in building our
CBR system involves a considerable amount of statistical pre-analysis of
the contents of the case base to generate *domain knowledge* that could be
used by the "Dynamic Index Creation Mechanism". The main contribution
of this paper is in describing the techniques used in our CBR system to dynamically create indices for the purpose of effective case retrieval .

Keywords: Case-Based Reasoning, Indexing, Retrieval, and Relational
Database.

1. Introduction

Identifying a set of attributes which are suitable to be used as indices, and can be
used for retrieving similar cases, is a difficult process when building an efficient
Case-Based Reasoning (CBR) system [5][9][15]. Various techniques have been
applied for identifying appropriate indices. For example, using inductive algo-

rithms and decision tree concepts [4][5][10][12]. Alternatively, Fox and Leake [9] used introspective reasoning to monitor the system's reasoning process and to identify new attributes for better indexing in the future, if required. Nevertheless, identifying a *complete* set of indices in advance is difficult [6] and in doing so, it will certainly limit the flexibility of the system. There are two million cases in our data set. Each case consists of *30* attributes. Some attributes contain up to 2000 different values. The problem of identifying a set of indices in advance has become much more difficult in our case study because there is a very large number of possible combinations that can be used as indices.

Two major concerns in our work are: how to retrieve a set of similar cases only for a particular situation from a very large number of historical cases; and how the system can produce a reliable solution out of these historical cases. In this paper, we will discuss only the first issue. Our approach is to dynamically create indices (i.e., identifying the most appropriate attributes to be used in case retrieval) for *each situation* at runtime. This approach is applied in our CBR system called *RICAD* (Risk Cost Adviser). RICAD identifies an appropriate insurance premium for new customers based on its calculated *risk cost*. For example, what is the premium for insuring a man who is 27 years old, drives BMW 325I, and lives in North Sydney. The most interesting issue in this research is the development of the *indexing mechanism*, using the existing relational database environment. This process involves extending the existing record retrieval technique (i.e., which is based on exact matching), to enable it to handle partial matching, which is an essential requirement of the CBR approach. Since matching processes in CBR systems are mostly based on partial match [15], identifying an appropriate range of values for each attribute is essential so that only similar cases are retrieved for a particular situation. This is a novel approach compared to the conventional methods (i.e., check list method (e.g., nearest neighbor), or explanation based method (eg., redundant discrimination network)).

The outline of this paper is as follows. Section 2 will attempt to describe our case study to provide the reader with sufficient background to appreciate the complexity of the problem domain. Following this, Section 3 attempts to provide the reader with some explanations of reasons for adopting CBR, and the relational database systems, for building RICAD. Section 4 will then discuss the two main areas of research in this paper: *organising qualitative and quantitative data*, and *dynamically creating indices*. Finally, some sample run are outlined in Section 5, and finally, the conclusion and a direction for future research can be found in Section 6.

2. Problem description

Our problem domain consists of approximately two million cases, which have been supplied by an insurance company. Each case is a policy record from the personal automobile insurance line, and consists of a number of descriptive attributes, and the total cost of claims for that policy for a set period. Claims in this context are generally the result of accidents and theft. Not all policies have claims, in fact only a small minority have a claim within the policy period (generally one year). Thus, for any given set of descriptive attributes there will exist a number of cases with zero claims cost, and a much smaller number (approximately ten percent) with claims costs. The risk cost is defined as the average cost of claims incurred for each set of descriptive attributes, *including* the cases for which no claims were incurred. If the cases all span one year, then the average risk cost is merely the total cost of claims divided by the number of policies, for each set of descriptive attributes. Thus, the risk cost will vary as the descriptive attributes vary. Each case consists of *30* attributes. Two attributes: *Post code* and *Vehicle code* contain approximately *600* and *2000* discrete values, respectively. Recall that of these two million records, only approximately ten percent of them have a non-zero claims cost. This means that if one enters a new case into the system, the system may find hundreds of cases that are applicable, but only approximately ten percent of them have a non-zero answer[*]. The problem becomes worse when those cases contain largely different values of claims cost due to the unpredictiveness of accidents and theft. For example, as outlined in Table 1, case numbers *1, 2, 3, 5, 6, 8, 10, 11, 13, 14*, and *15* are identical, but they are associated with completely different claims cost. This leads on to another very important research issue in this project which is not discussed in this paper. That is, finding a reliable solution from the claims cost of all similar cases. The current approach adopted to resolve this problem involves the use of Central Limit Theorem [17]. After applying various statistical analyses to our data set and taking into account the domain specific heuristic from the insurance experts, we found that the weighting of each attribute will change according to the values of the attribute of the situated case. For example (with reference to cases listed in Table 1), assume that after conducting statistical analysis, and based on the domain specific heuristic, the most important attribute (that which has the highest weight value) is *driver age*, where age between *18-22* years old has very *high* risk, while age between *31-55* years old has *low* risk. In addition, assume that *Ford XR-6* and *Nissan 300-ZX* are categorized into the same group, which is *high* risk; while on the other hand, assume that *Toyota Corolla* and *Nissan Pulsar* are categorized into the same group, which is *low* risk.

With reference to the example cases listed in Table 1, if a new case with a *20* year old person driving a *Toyota Corolla* is encountered by RICAD, then case numbers *1, 2, 3, 5, 6, 8, 10, 11, 13, 14*, and *15* should be retrieved. (In the table above only a small number of cases have been included. In the real data set there will be approximately ten times as many cases with zero claims cost, which will naturally be retrieved as well).

---

[*] Note that there is in fact no significant deviation from a representative sample.

Case No.	Vehicle Model	Driver Age	...	Suburb	Sum Insured	Claims Cost
1	Toyota Collora	19	...	Newtown	18000	0
2	Toyota Collora	19	...	Newtown	18000	3,120
3	Toyota Collora	19	...	Newtown	18000	0
4	Nissan Pulsar	20	...	Newtown	18000	700
5	Toyota Collora	19	...	Newtown	18000	0
6	Toyota Collora	19	...	Newtown	18000	0
7	Ford XR-6	32	...	St. James	60000	820
8	Toyota Collora	19	...	Newtown	18000	0
9	Nissan Pulsar	34	...	St. James	18000	700
10	Toyota Collora	19	...	Newtown	18000	0
11	Toyota Collora	19	...	Newtown	18000	0
12	Nissan 300-ZX	44	...	Redfern	60000	2,150
13	Toyota Collora	19	...	Newtown	18000	0
14	Toyota Collora	19	...	Newtown	18000	0
15	Toyota Collora	19	...	Newtown	18000	12,000

Table 1: Example of Cases

On the other hand, if a new customer is *33* years old, and drives *Nissan 300-ZX*, then case number *7* and *12* should be considered. Note that case number *9* should *not* be retrieved even though it contains an age applicable to the new problem. This is because age between *31-55* years old has very little effect on the risk cost, while a high-performance car has a much more significant effect. For these reasons, we want RICAD to be able to dynamically create its indices for each situation. This is because different attributes may be considered as *highly* significant depending on the situation (eg., *age = 19*). On the other hand, the same attribute may turn out to be the *least* significant in another situation (eg., *age = 58*). Identifying all possible indices in advance is not possible since there are thousands of possible combinations that can be used as indices. The following section describes the architecture of the system, and the reason why the CBR approach with the use of a relational database is appropriate for this project.

3. Description of the RICAD System

3.1. Architecture

One of the main reasons for implementing a mechanism for dynamically creating indices is to provide RICAD with high flexibility in order to produce the most accurate answer possible. In addition, as mentioned in Section 2, some qualitative attributes consist of up to 2,000 different discrete values. It is very difficult to identify all possible sets of indices in advance. Figure 1 shows the architecture of RICAD. It consists of 7 major components described below:

1. *Pre-Analysis Mechanism*

   This mechanism is used by the knowledge engineer to periodically carry out statistical analyses on the cases in the case base, (taking into account the domain expertise) and to revise the domain knowledge base.

2. *Dynamic Index Creation Mechanism*

   This mechanism first analyses the incoming case by utilizing the previously identified domain knowledge to determine a set of significant attributes for this case. Secondly, for each of these significant attributes, it determines the range of values. This range of values allow RICAD to create fuzzy or partially match SQL queries. Finally, it generates the appropriate SQL query for case retrieval purposes. The mechanism is made up of the following three components:

   (a) *Significant Attribute(s) Identifier* : When a new case is received by RICAD, this component uses heuristic rules to identify all significant attributes which should be used as indices by the system. The outcome of this process is a set of significant attributes that will be passed forward to the next component called the Range Identifier.

   (b) *Range Identifier* : Since the system must be able to retrieve partially matched cases, this process uses *similarity measurement* knowledge to identify an appropriate range of values that must be used in the case retrieval process. The result of this process contains all selected attributes, together with their suitable ranges.

   (c) *SQL Query Generator* : This process generates executable SQL statement which will be used for retrieving all similar cases from the database.

3. *Case Retrieval Mechanism*

   This mechanism simply consists of the SQL Processor applied to the cases stored in the relational database.

4. *Confidence Identification Mechanism*

   This mechanism will calculate the mean and standard deviation of the claim cost, together with the number of cases that need to be retrieved to obtain a reliable value for the risk cost.

5. *Risk Cost Calculation Mechanism*

   This mechanism simply calculates the average risk cost of the retrieved cases. This is the risk cost that RICAD will recommend for the case at hand.

6. *Case Ranking Mechanism*
This mechanism is only activated when RICAD has retrieved more cases than required. In this situation, it will attempt to rank each of these cases based on the similarity measure (most to least similar case). It then selects a sufficient number of cases from the top of the list, and eliminates the remaining. It then passes these cases to the Risk Cost Calculation Mechanism to obtain the average risk cost for the case at hand.

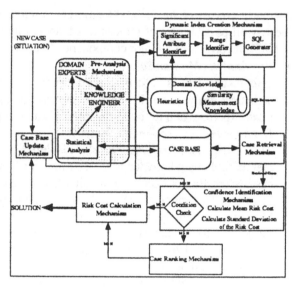

Figure 1: Architecture of RICAD

7. *Case Base Update Mechanism*
This mechanism takes the new case and the solution produced by RICAD and adds these into the case base for future use.

In reference to Figure 1, you will also observe that the *Confidence Identification Mechanism* passes control to different mechanisms according to the following rules:

Control Passed to $\begin{cases} \text{Dynamic Index Creation Mechanism} & \text{if } M < N \\ \text{Risk Cost Calculation Mechanim} & \text{if } M = N \\ \text{Case Ranking Mechanism} & \text{if } M > N \end{cases}$ where M is the number of similar cases retrieved, while N is the number of cases that need to be retrieved to obtain sufficiently reliable values for the risk cost. If $M > N$, RICAD will then iteratively activate the Significant Attribute Identifier in order to create new SQL query that allow more similar cases to be retrieved.

3.2. Reasons for using CBR Approach

There are a number of reasons for using the CBR approach in developing RICAD. Firstly, CBR does not require an extensive amount of expert knowledge, but relies on previous cases which are readily available [14][15][16][23]. In other words, CBR approach appropriate for situations where well-understood knowledge is not available, or the domain is not completely understood [18]. Secondly, similar to other analogical reasoning techniques, CBR systems reuse previously solved cases [15]. Since we are dealing with a very large data set, calculating solutions from scratch for solving every problem can be computationally very expensive. The system must be able to improve its problem solving capabilities (by re-using previously solved cases) from each consultation. This involves inserting the processed case into its case library [13]. Finally, CBR systems can provide explanations for proposing a particular solution by keeping track of its reasoning trace.

One of the advantage of using a CBR approach in this project is its ability to improve its problem solving capabilities by utilizing previously solved cases. As mentioned previously (c.f., Section 2), for any given case, there will be a *large* number of similar (or even identical) cases found in the case base, but each of them may be associated with completely different solutions (i.e., risk cost). Since the number of cases that RICAD have to reason with is very *large*, the reasoning process is computationally very expensive. The RICAD reasoning process involves searching for similar cases, performing statistical analyses on the retrieved cases, and finally calculating the risk cost. Reducing the systems reasoning time is achieved by storing all solved cases back into the case base, and referring to these cases in the first instance before re-computing a solution for a similar case. This approach reduces the need to re-compute a solution for every new case. As long as there are no additional cases added into the case base as part of its historical cases, RICAD's approach for re-using previously solved cases will enhance it's speed. There is no need to go through the complete reasoning process if it will lead to the same solution. It is faster to propose the solution of a previously solved case.

3.3. Reducing Search Space

An appropriate organisation of cases can lead to efficient search and retrieval of cases [15]. Since we were dealing with a very large case base, we intended to enhance the efficiency of this system by decreasing the search space. Contemporary literature outline two approaches in reducing the search space. Firstly, generating an index tree which has a set of applicable cases at the leaf node (eg., [5]). Secondly, nearest neighbor techniques can be applied to the data set, and information derived from this experiment can be utilized to enhance the searching. These two approaches have not been experimented with this particular data set. These tasks are part of the future work to be carried out on this project. The approach adopted for reducing search space is by partitioning cases into several groups based on values of some attributes. Some examples are *Driver sex* (M or F), *Use of Vehicle* (Private or Commercial), or *Type of Finance* (Bank, Finance, or None). Database technologies have been applied successfully in building real-world CBR applications (eg., [2, 20]). Representing cases in a hierarchical fashion (eg., [11, 22]) or using complex indices may result in efficient retrieval, but it can only be applied to problems with a small number of indices. For example, CYRUS only permits a small vocabulary of indices [1]. From our experiment, it is not practical to load all 2 million cases into the hierarchical structure even with a *very simple* index structure. Furthermore, from a Management Information System (MIS) point of view, confidential data, such as customer records, should be kept securely in the database. By using a Database Management System (DBMS), the security of data can be tightly controlled. Also, duplication of data into the secondary storage for any purpose is not appropriate [20]. Allowing the CBR system to directly interact with cases in the database can help developers to avoid the problem of duplicating the cases at run-time. Thus, the approach we have adopted in this project is to use ORACLE DBMS [8] for storage and retrieval of cases and the associated domain knowledge.

4. Organizing qualitative and quantitative attributes

The domain knowledge used by RICAD consists of both qualitative and quantitative attributes. There are a number of issues which must be considered in order to identify the appropriate representation structure for each type of attribute. Firstly, for a *qualitative* attribute, we must identify the type of relationship between the values of a particular attribute and the values of the solution-attribute, called the *claim cost* (e.g., taxonomic or spatial relationship). Secondly, we must organize the values for all attributes by using an appropriate structure. For example, if the relationship between the values of a particular attribute is taxonomic then we or-

ganize all values in an *hierarchical* structure. On the other hand, if it is a spatial relationship (which we found in the *post code* attribute) then we organize its values in a spatial structure. Finally, an appropriate similarity measurement method has to be identified for each type of representation structure. Figure 2 depicts examples of hierarchical and spatial organization of *Car Model* and *Post Code*, respectively. In Figure 2, cars are or-

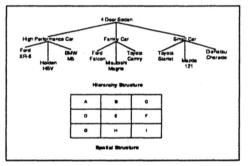

Figure 2: Example of the Taxonomic and Spatially Structured Knowledge in RICAD

ganized based on a hierarchy of car types, and in doing so, we find for example that a *Ford XR-6* is categorized as similar to a *Holden-HSV* rather than a *Ford Falcon*. Also from the spatial structure, area *I* is closer (thus considered to contain a similar population category) to area *E*, *F*, and *H* rather than area *A*, *B*, *C*, *D*, and *G*.

For a quantitative attribute, Reategui and Campbell [19] used a fuzzy overlapping intervals technique to find similarity. Fuzzy set concepts have also been applied by Jeng and Liang [13] for a similar purpose. In most cases, all quantitative values are grouped by using a qualitative scale (e.g., [13, 19]). For example, *age* between *17* to *40* years old can be grouped into 4 consistent groups: *17-22*, *23-*

28, 29-34, and *35-40* years old. In the RICAD system, we apply a simple *constantly-decreasing technique* to measure the similarity between two quantitative attributes.

For example, as depicted in Figure 3, if the case at hand has value of age equal to *37* years old, then historical cases which have value of age equal to *37* years old will match perfectly with the case at hand (the score of matching is equal to *1*), otherwise the matching score of historical cases will decrease depending on its distance from the considered value (in this case, the value is *37*).

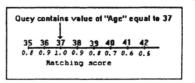

Figure 3: Example of the *Constantly-Decreasing technique*

5. Dynamically creating indices

RICAD's reasoning process starts when a new case arrives. For every new case, the "Significant Attribute Identifier" will attempt to identify a set of significant attributes. To identify these attributes, RICAD uses two types of information: *weight value*, and *risk level*. Weight value for each of the attributes can be obtained from the domain experts, or can be determined by applying inductive programs. It is used to rank the attributes (i.e., from the most influential to the least influential attribute). For example, in our case study, the domain experts considered the attribute *age* to be the most influential attribute. The second most influential attribute is *car model*. Since there are *30* attributes that have to be considered in the system's reasoning process, attribute *age* will have highest weight value (weight value equal to *30*), and *car model* will have weight value equal to *29*. The least important attribute will have weight equal to *1*.

On the other hand, risk level information is obtained by sorting all values of a particular attribute based on average risk cost. For example, Table 2 shows the result of sorting the attribute age. In our case study, the actual values of age are between *17* to *94* years. There is a total of *53* different values of age (*94 - 17*). Thus, the risk level is divided into *78* different levels. The highest risk level (i.e., that which has the highest average risk cost) in this case is equal to *78*. On the other hand, the lowest risk level is equal to *1*. From the example in Table 2, age *62* years will have the lowest risk level (a risk level of *1*) since it has the smallest average risk cost. However, age *18* years has the highest risk level (risk level is *78*) since it has the highest average risk cost. This form of ranking is carried out for all the attributes.

By using these two types of information described above, RICAD can identify significant attributes that will be used as indices for retrieving similar cases. As mentioned previously, there is a very high possibility that similar cases which are retrieved will contain largely different solutions (see Table 1). Finding similar cases is **not**

Rerk (Risk level)	Age	Average Risk cost
1	62	189.75
2	66	189.81
:	:	:
32	51	228.41
33	52	229.05
:	:	:
78	18	591.44

Table 2: Example of ranking for attribute *age* based on their associated average *risk cost*

a major problem in this data set. The difficulty is how to find only similar cases that have the least amount of different in their solutions (claim cost) to reason with. RICAD finds similar cases by relaxing value of a certain attribute of the new case. For example, if case contains age equal to 30, the first adjustment may result in retrieving cases with age 29 and 31. As shown in Table 2, attribute-value pair that has high risk level always lead to high value of the risk cost. This implies that attribute-value pair that has high risk level have also greatly affected to the final risk cost. Adjusting value of these attributes should be done carefully. RICAD find only cases that have small different in their claim cost by cautiously adjust value of these attributes. This is why identifying which attribute(s) contributes to high risk is an important part of RICAD reasoning process. At this stage, attribute-value pair of the new case that have their risk level higher than approximately 66 percent of the highest risk level is considered to be high risk attribute-value pair. The identification of significant attributes is done in two phases. In the *first* phase, all attribute-value pairs that have their risk level *more than or equal* to 2/3 of the highest risk level for that particular attribute are identified. All attributes that have their risk level *less* than 2/3 of the highest risk level will be kept in the *ignored-attributes* list. The *second* phase is only invoked if the number of significant attributes identified in the first phase is *less* than two. An example of how RICAD uses all this knowledge to identify significant attributes is found at the end of this section. The model, and the corresponding algorithm (i.e., in Figure 4) used for finding all significant attributes-value pairs in similar case retrieval, is shown on left hand side:

Phase1:

$$\sum_{n=1}^{30} \begin{cases} \text{add}(A_n, Accepted\ List) & \text{if } R_n \times 2/3M_n \\ \text{add}(A_n, Ignored\ List) & \text{otherwise} \end{cases}$$

Phase 2: *Rank Attributed-Value pairs in the Ignored_List; and Select two top ranked Attribute-Value pairs*

In the model, A_n is the nth Attribute-Value pair, R_n is a risk level for A_n, and M_n is the highest risk level for

A_n. For example, assume a new case with age = 51. Further, assume that the attribute age is the 7th attribute to be considered by the *Significant Attribute Identifier* (i.e., A_7), then, based on Table 2, the risk level of age for this case is *32* (i.e., $R_7 = 32$). The highest risk level for attribute age is *78*. Thus, $M_7 = 78$. In this example, R_7 is not more or equal to $2/3M_7$. Therefore, age will not be considered as a significant attribute for this new case for the purpose of retrieving similar cases from the case base. Thus, attribute *age* will be added into the *Ignored_List*. Every attribute that is added into the *Ignored_List* is normalized according to the following formula:

$$X_n = W_n * (R_n / M_n)$$

where W_n is a pre-defined weight of the nth attribute, M_n is the highest risk level for the nth attribute, and X_n is the significance value of the nth attribute. Thus, for our example, the significant value for age is *7.35* (i.e., $X_7 = 12.30$).

```
FOR  each ($A_n$) DO
      IF $R_n$ 2/3$M_n$ THEN add($A_n$, Accepted_List);
      ELSE $X_n$ = $W_n$ * ($R_n$ / $M_n$); add($A_n$, Ignored_List);
END_FOR
IF number (Accepted_List) < 2 THEN select_two_highest (rank(Ignored_List));
```

Figure 4: Algorithm for identifying the indices

For a more complete explanation on how the *Significant Attribute Identifier* works, we will consider *3* attribute-value pair cases rather than *30* attribute-value pair cases, as in our actual case study. Table 2 represents the risk level for *Age*, while Table 3 and Table 4 list the risk level for *Car Model* and *Suburb*, respectively. Let us assume that the new case is as follows: a *51* years old man, drives *Ford XR-6*, and lives in a suburb called *Newtown*. In addition, assume that the weight of attribute *Age* is *30*, *Car Model* is *29*, and *Suburb* is *28*. The first attribute-value pair (i.e., A_1) that will be considered for the significance test is *age*. By using the information listed in Table 2, and applying the algorithm outlined in Figure 4, we get R_1 to equal *33* (i.e., the risk level of age *51* years old). Since R_1 is less than 2/3 of M_1 (2/3 of 78 is equal to *52*), the attribute *age* and its value will not be added in the *Accepted_List*. Instead, the X_1 value will be calculated (i.e., $X_1 = 12.30$), and *age* will be added into the *Ignored_List*.

On the other hand, the remaining two attribute-value pairs (i.e., *Car Model* and *Suburb*) are found to be significant (i.e., $R_2 = 815, R_3 = 70, M_2 = 1130$, and $M_3 = 76$), and will be added into the *Accepted_List*. Table 5 shows the result of the calculation for each of these 3 attributes and their values.

Car Model	Risk Level
:	:
Ford XR-6	815
:	:
Holden HSV-215	899
:	:

Suburb	Risk Level
:	:
Newtown	70
North Sydney	23
:	:
Redfern	72

Table 3: System's Knowledge
(*Car Model* and their *Risk Level*)

Table 4: System's Knowledge
(*Suburb* and their *Risk level*)

Attribute	Value	Weight	Risk (R)	Max risk (M)	(2/3) M	Risk (X)
Age	51	30	33	78	52	12.3000
Car Mod	Ford XR-6	29	815	1130	745.80	20.9159
Suburb	Newtown	28	70	76	50.16	25.7895

Table 5: Results of calculation based on above algorithm

The attribute *Age* and its value are called *ignored-attribute*. If there is only *1* attribute with its *R* value greater than (2/3) of *M*, then the system may reconsider all ignored-attributes again by sorting all of them and use two attributes that have the highest *X* values. Once the significant attribute-value pairs have been selected, the *Range Identifier* will decide on an appropriate range of values that should be used in the retrieved process. This is where similarity measurement knowledge is taken into account. For each of the significant attributes, the *Range Identifier* uses two forms of information to find the appropriate range for each of these attributes. They are: the knowledge representation scheme and its associated similarity measurement method. For example, the attribute *Car Model* is represented in a hierarchical manner[#] (c.f., Figure 2). The similarity measurement method used for *Car Model* is *semantic distance* [21].

Figure 5 and 6 depicts the user interface of RICAD. In Figure 5, the case at hand is a female driver aged 36, living in St. James, drives Nissan Pulsar, borrowed money from the bank, and uses her car for private use. Since our domain knowledge does not categorize St. James as a dangerous suburb, and categorizes Nissan Pulsar as Low risk car, the generated SQL statement does not include these values. Alternatively, the man in the case at hand outlined in Figure 6 lives in a high risk area, and he drives a high risk car, these attribute-values are included in the generated SQL statement.

[#] Hierarichal representation is used despite some of its shortcomings (e.g., unbalanced hierarchy, possibilities of building a lattice instead of a hierarchy, completeness of the hierarchy, and consistency of judgment on the contents of the hierarchy).

As seen in the descriptions and examples outlined above, by providing RI-CAD with necessary knowledge, it could dynamically create a set of appropriate indices. The major advantage of this approach is that the users do not have to identify all possible combination of indices for RICAD.

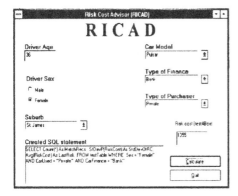

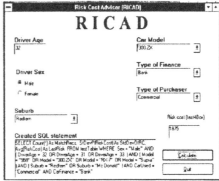

Figure 5: Case with person living in a save suburb, and driving a low risk car

Figure 6: Case with a the person living in high risk area, and driving a high risk car

6. Conclusion and Future Work

In this paper, the authors described a complex real-world domain for identifying risk cost when insuring clients. The complexity of this domain results from two-million valid cases that are categorized as claimed and unclaimed cases. In addition, each cases consist of *30* attributes (i.e., combination of both qualitative and quantitative attributes), some of which may have up to *2000* distinct values. Furthermore, after carrying out pre-analysis of the data set, and in consultation with the domain experts, it has been identified that different attributes play significant roles in different situations. Thus, the CBR system outlined in this paper (i.e., RI-CAD) take into account all of these variability when proposing a solution. In this paper, we have only addressed the issues related to identifying the domain knowledge, representation of both the quantitative and qualitative information, similarity measurements, and dynamically creating indices for different situations (i.e., based on the case at hand).

There are still a large number of issues that need to be considered in this very challenging project. The fundamental requirement of RICAD is to achieve the high-performance (i.e., based on accuracy and speed in proposing solutions) required by an online system. Evaluation processes are in progress at the moment. We hope to obtain some evaluation data in the next 6 months. With the availability of these data, we could begin to identify probable areas for improvement (i.e., techniques, components, and mechanisms). At this stage, based on human experts,

RICAD can correctly identify the set of indices for all tested cases. It can also accurately adjust its indices when more cases are required. However, the current implementation of RICAD does not taken into account the time spend in the case retrieval process. This is one of two major issues in RICAD. The system, at this stage, only concentrates on creating the right set of indices. It does not have a mechanism that aids the database management system in order to reduce its searching time. In addition, the second important issue is how to calculate a reliable solution from these retrieved cases. The approach taken at this stage is simply to calculate the average value of all claim costs found. A future direction of this research is to find a statistical model that will allow RICAD to propose its solution with known degree of confidence.

Acknowledgments

We would like to take this opportunity to thank all the members of the Distributed Artificial Intelligence Center (DAIC) at The University of New England, and members of the SIG-CBR at Continuum Australia Ltd., who have helped us in revising this paper. Our special thanks to Ms Meg Vivers for checking English expression. Finally, our sincere thanks to the directors of Continuum Ltd., for approving the publication of this paper.

References

1. Aamodt, A., and Plaza, E. *Case-Based Reasoning: Foundational Issues, Methodological Variations, and System Approaches,*. AI-Communications, Vol. 7, No. 1, 1994.
2. Allen, J.R.C., Patterson, D.W.R., Mulvenna, M.D., and Hughes, J.G. Integration of Case Based Retrieval with a Relational Database System in Aircraft Technical Support, *Proceedings of the First International Conference, (ICCBR-95)*, Springer, October, 1995.
3. Allenmang, D. Combining Case-Based Reasoning and Task-Specific Architectures, *IEEE Expert*, pp. 24-34. October, 1994.
4. Auriol, E., Manago, M., Althoff, K.D., Wess, S., and Dittrich, S. Integrating Induction and Case-Based Reasoning Methodological Approach and First Evaluation, *Proceedings of the Second European Workshop on Case-Based Reasoning (EWCBR 94)*, Springer, 1994.
5. Barletta, R. A Hybrid Indexing and Retrieval Strategy for Advisory CBR systems Built with ReMind, *Proceedings of the Second European Workshop on Case-Based Reasoning (EWCBR 94)*, Springer, 1994.
6. Bhatta, S. and Ram, A. Learning Indices for Schema Selection. *Proceedings of the Fourth Florida Artificial Intelligence Research Symposium*, pp. 226-231, Coca Beach, Florida, April, 1991.

7. Cheeseman, P., and Stutz, J. Bayesian Classification (AutoClass): Theory and Results, *Advances in Knowledge Discovery and Data Mining*, Usama M. Fayyad, Gregory Piatetsky-Shapiro, Padhraic Smyth, and Ramasamy Uthurusamy, Eds. The AAAI Press, Menlo Park, 1995.

8. Colston, L. SQL Plus: User's Guide and Reference (Version 3.0), Oracle Corporation, USA, 1989.

9. Fox, S., and Leake, D.B. Learning to Refine Indexing by Introspective Reasoning, *Proceedings of the First International Conference on Case-Based Reasoning*, Springer, 1995.

10. Goss, K. Preselection Strategies for Case-Based Classification, *Proceedings of the 18th German Annual Conference on Artificial Intelligence*, Springer, 1994.

11. Hammond, K.J. *Case-Based Planning*, Academic Press, 1989.

12. Hansen, J.V., Meservy, R.D., and Wood, L.E. Indexing Tree and Pruning Concepts to Support Case-Based Reasoning, *International Journal on Management Science*, Pergamon, Vol. 22, No. 4, pp. 361-369, 1994.

13. Jeng, B.C., and Liang, T-P. Fuzzy Indexing and Retrieval in Case-Based Systems, *Expert Systems with Applications*, Vol. 8, No. 1, pp. 135-142, 1995.

14. Kang, B.H., and Compton, P. A Maintenance Approach to Case, *Proceedings of the Second European Workshop on Case-Based Reasoning (EWCBR 94)*, Springer, 1994.

15. Kolodner, J. *Case-Based Reasoning*, Morgan Kaufmann. 1993.

16. Mizoguchi, R., and Hiroshi, M. Expert Systems Research in Japan, *IEEE Expert*, pp. 15-23, August, 1995.

17. Mood, A., Graybill, F., and Boes, D. *Introduction to the Theory of Statistics*, McGraw-Hill, 1974.

18. PW. *Technology Forecast: 1996*, Price Waterhouse World Firm Service BV, p. 460, 1995.

19. Reategui, E.B. and Campbell, J. A Classification System for Credit Card Transactions, *Proceedings of the Second European Workshop on Case-Based Reasoning (EWCBR 94)*, Springer, 1994.

20. Shimazu, H., Kitano, H., and Shibata, A. Retrieving Cases from Relational Data-Bases: Another Stride Towards Corporate-Wide Case-Base Systems, *Proceedings of the 13th International Joint Conference on Artificial Intelligence (IJCAI-93)*, Vol. 2, Chambery, France, pp. 909-914, 1993.

21. Sowa, J. F. *Conceptual Structure: Information Processing in Mind and Machine*, Addison Wesley, Reading, Mass., 1984.

22. Sycara, K. Using Case-Based Reasoning for Plan Adaptation and Repair, *Proceedings of the Case-Based Reasoning Workshop, DARPA*. Clearwater Beach, Florida. Morgan Kaufmann, pp. 425-434, 1988.

23. Takahashi, M., Oono, J-I., and Saitoh, K. Reusing Makes It Easier: Manufacturing Process Design by CBR with Knowledge Ware, *IEEE Expert*, pp. 74-80, December, 1995.

Case Memory and the Behaviouristic Model of Concepts and Cognition

Werner Dubitzky, John G. Hughes, David A. Bell

School of Information and Software Engineering
University of Ulster, Jordanstown, Ireland
{ w.dubitzky, jg.hughes, da.bell } @ulst.ac.uk

Abstract. Since the advent of case-based reasoning (CBR) in the early eighties, two schools seem to have emerged: One that is more concerned with the cognitive aspects of CBR, and another, arguably more applied school, which views CBR as an AI 'workhorse', as it were, that can provide solutions to real-world problems. The former school is sometimes associated with the US, and the latter with Europe. This work, to some extent, attempts to reconcile the two camps. It proposes the behaviouristic or cognitive (as opposed to metaphysical) concept notion as conceptual framework for CBR. It does so by reviewing the three most intensely researched concept models, and relating them to the CBR paradigm. Two of the more recently evolved concept views—the probabilistic exemplar and prototype view—are then put forward as epistemologically sound foundation to model a memory of cases. Extending this core model by means of a complementary possibilistic dimension, a rich and flexible case-knowledge representation framework is developed that addresses issues like expressiveness, extendibility, context effects, and uncertainty. This scheme is called PERCEPT.

1 Introduction

Without concepts, mental life would be chaotic. If people perceived each entity as unique, they would be overwhelmed by the enormous diversity of what they experience, unable to remember but a fraction of what they encounter. A *concept* or *class* captures the notion that many objects or events are alike in some important respects, and can therefore be thought about in the same or similar ways. Once an entity has been assigned to a class on the basis of its perceptible properties, a concept also allows to infer some of its non–perceptible attributes. Having, for example, chosen perceptible attributes like size, shape and material to decide an object is a book, it can be inferred that, among other things, the object contains pages and textual information. This idea of inferibility is based on the assumption that all instances of a given concept are subject to the same, or similar, underlying mechanisms (eg, cause–effect relationships) which may or may not be completely known.

In a memory–based model of cognition, like CBR, this process of relating a thus far not encountered object or event to a known concept or class is crucial [1,2].

Intra-mental concepts (henceforth referred to as concepts), like cases and case indices, are evolving structures that are *memory–based* [3,4,5,6,1,7,8]! A memory is *not* a static repository of concept intensions and instances, rather, a memory is dynamic, a constantly growing body of concepts derived from an agent's interaction with and experience in the world. Striking and intriguing as the similarity between the notion of concepts and a memory–based theory of cognition may be, most CBR researchers have failed to explicitly deal with concepts. One exception is the work of Porter and Bareiss [9,10]. This lack of appreciation for the nature of concepts is reflected in, for example, the explosion of indices in MOP–based (memory organisation package) and context–plus–index memory models, where new 'generalised episodes' (ie, concepts) are created excessively. Psychological studies, on the other hand, suggest that concepts enjoy a relatively high degree of within–individual, and to a lesser extent, across–individual stability [4].

A case memory organisation strategy has to be expressive, efficient, effective, flexible and epistemologically adequate [4,5,6,11,10,12,13].

Because of its importance for human thinking and its affinity to the fundamentals of CBR as a theory cognition, the notion of a concept is proposed as an epistemologically adequate platform for the representation of case–knowledge. The proposed case memory model is based on the *prototype* and *exemplar* 'view' of concepts [3,4]. These views assume that instances of a concept vary in the degree to which they share certain properties, and therefore vary in the degree to which they are members of the concept. To capture uncertainty that may prevail in case properties (hence cases), the prototype/exemplar concept scheme is extended via a possibilistic dimension. Finally, to deal with contextual idiosyncrasies of case/concept properties, an explicit scheme is introduced into the model that can handle such context effects [14].

The remainder of the paper reviews the three commonly differentiated views of concepts (Section 2), and the equally important issue of concept properties (Section 3). A concept-centred model is then proposed as a framework to model a case memory (Section 4 and 5). In Section 6 this model is extended to capture possibilistic uncertainty. Section 7 concludes with a brief summary and future issues.

2 Concepts and Concept Properties

How people acquire and process concepts has been, and still is, researched quite intensively [4,15]. These studies revolve around the *structure* and *function* of concepts, and how concepts could be modelled. The three major concept 'views' proposed in the literature are: classical view, prototype view, and exemplar view. The prototype and exemplar views are to address the problems found in the more and more frequently criticised classical view which dates back to Aristotle. In the classical view it is held that all instances of a concept share common properties, and these common properties are necessary and sufficient to define the concept. The prototype view, on the other hand, assumes that instances of a concept vary in the degree to which they share certain properties, and as a result vary in the degree to which they represent the concept (this view is sometimes called *probabilistic* view). Finally, the exemplar view, which constitutes a more extreme departure from the classical view, holds that there is no single representation of an entire concept or class, but only specific representations of the concept's exemplars or instances.

Intensional concept *summaries* and extensional concept *exemplars* are characterised by *properties*. Properties can be divided into *holistic* and *component* types [16,4]. The former kind of property is somewhat restricted to certain types of applications it is not further considered in this work. A component property is one that helps to describe a concept but does not usually constitute a complete description of the concept. Component properties describe *partial* and (abstracted) *global* aspects of a concept. Usually, two types of component properties are distinguished: qualitative, featural properties (*features*) and quantitative, dimensional properties (*dimensions*). By addressing issues associated with both property representations, this work proposes a flexible case property concept that, amongst other things, allows for context effects and uncertainty management.

2.1 What, then, is a Concept?

Although it is debated which of the concept views one should endorse, there exists some agreement on the *function* of concepts. Concepts provide a *taxonomy* of entities and events in the world, and concepts are used to express *relations* between classes in that taxonomy. Two sub–functions of the taxonomic function have received much attention in the literature: *categorisation* and *conceptual combination*. Both functions are of predominant importance for the case memory architecture of the PERCEPT system.

A concept's categorisation function is concerned with the concept's role as a pattern–recognition device. This means that concepts are used to classify or categorise novel entities and draw inferences about such entities. To possess a concept C is to know something about the properties of the instances of C, this knowledge can be used to categorise novel entities. The relation to CBR is best illustrated by a quote from Kolodner [1]: 'The key question such a model [CBR] is always asking itself is not "What knowledge applies to this situation?" but "Where should I store this experience?" or, in other terms, "How should I categorise this situation?"'

Once an object x has been recognised as a member of the concept C, the knowledge about x's properties (constraints on and relationship between them) serves as basis to infer certain, not directly perceptible 'aspects' of x. It is obvious that such intra–concept inference capabilities are related to CBR tasks like adaptation and similarity assessment. These processes rely on a concept exemplar (stored base case) to draw inferences about a new concept member (query case). The categorisation function, then, is an evident candidate for the realisation of an explicit reasoning regime.

The combination function is responsible for expanding the taxonomy by combining existing concepts or properties into novel ones. For example, the DoublePawn concept in chess is formed from the concepts Pawn and File and a set of constraints. This aspect of concepts corresponds directly to the extendibility requirement stated earlier.

While the taxonomic functions involve intra and inter–concept structural relationships (physical and logical) between concepts and concept exemplars, the relation function is concerned with more 'functional' relations, such as causality, function, implication, time, constraint, and predicate, that may hold between concepts and their instances [12].

Both functional and taxonomic (structural) relationships between concepts form the basis for drawing certain inferences from representations, they are therefore essential for the proposed concept–centred reasoning model.

2.2 The Classical Concept View

In the classical view of concepts it is held that the representation of a concept is a *summary* description of the entire class, rather than descriptions of various exemplars or subordinates of that class. Representing the concept Bird, for example, would not state separate definitions for different species (like Robin and Chicken) nor for specific instances. This approach of condensing a concept into a single summary representation has the advantage that little information needs to be stored.

Another fundamental assumption underlying the classical view holds that (1) the properties that represent a concept are singly *necessary* and (2) jointly *sufficient* to define that concept.

Necessary and sufficient properties are sometimes referred to as *defining* properties. A singly necessary property requires that each exemplar of that concept must have this property. To illustrate, every legal chess position must involve exactly two kings (a white and a black king). A set of jointly sufficient properties demands that every object having that set must be an instance of the concept in question. For example, a chess position containing only pawns (and two kings) must be an exemplar of the concept PawnEnding.

The classical view has been heavily criticised throughout its existence; two of its most frequently recognised 'defects' are its inability to handle abstract properties, and the fact that for many concepts a commonly agreed set of defining properties cannot be found (decades of analysis have failed to turn up the necessary and sufficient properties for even simple concepts like Bird)

Take, for example, the concept Game. What is a necessary property for this concept? It cannot be competition between teams or even competition between two individuals, for there are games that can be played by a single person, eg, solitaire. Similarly, the property must have a winner is not essential for all games, eg, the child's game ring–a–ring'o–roses.

Insisting on defining properties, the classical view denies the fact that in most but a few cases the *relationships* between a concept and its properties are characterised by some degree of uncertainty [17]. Instead, for example, to define the Game concept by the property must have a winner, it seems more realistic to replace that property by something like is likely to have a winner or usually has a winner.

2.3 The Prototype Concept View

Paralleling the classical view, the first assumption of the prototype (or probabilistic) concept view holds that a concept is represented by an intensional summary description of the entire class. In its second assumption it is held that the representation of a concept *cannot* be restricted to a set of necessary and sufficient properties. Rather, the properties that represent a concept are *salient* ones that have a significant *probability* of occurring in exemplars of the concept.

The binary or *featural* property flies, for example, could be used to represent the concept Bird Although some birds do not fly (eg, chicken), flies is a very relevant or salient, and a relatively frequently occurring property of Bird instances.

Both the property's relevance and its probability of occurring in concept exemplars is explicitly reflected in the concept representation by a *relevance weight* or simply *weight*. In addition to flies, a continuous or *dimensional* property like wingspan may be employed to represent Bird In contrast to featural properties—describing a *modal* property of a class (ie, presence/absence of a property)—dimensional properties like wingspan characterise an *average* or *mean value* of a concept's property. A weight used in conjunction with a dimensional property not only expresses its relevance and probability of occurring, but also the importance of variations in the associated dimension. To illustrate this, and the resulting categorisation procedure, consider the simplified prototype representation of the Bird concept in Table 1.

Table 1: Prototype representation of the Bird concept.

Property Weight	Property Name	Property Value	Property Type
1.00	winged	(*present*)	featural
0.80	flies	(*present*)	featural
0.50	wingspan	*40* [cm]	dimensional

Table 1 depicts the concept Bird which is represented by the properties winged, flies and wingspan. The property winged carries a weight of 1.00, this indicates that winged is a *necessary* property of Bird (save pathological cases, an entity that has no wings cannot possibly be a bird). Bird's other featural property, flies, is a non-essential one (eg, penguins are birds but do not fly), it has, however, some significance and likelihood to occur with exemplars of the Bird concept. This is expressed by the weight 0.80. Both properties, winged and flies, do not assume actual values, rather, an entity either *has* such a property (wings attached to it, the capability to fly) or it does not. In case the property is present in an entity, it contributes, according to its weight, to the entity's recognition as a member of the concept. The dimensional property wingspan may or may not be a necessary one; its associated weight (0.50) reflects its saliency, probability of occurring, *and* importance of variations around its mean value (40 cm).

The categorisation procedure of the *classical* view requires that an entity x, to be recognised as an exemplar of concept C, contains *all* defining properties represented in C. Due to the fact that the *prototype* view allows for non–necessary properties (explicitly reflected by property weights), its processing requirements for the classification function differ from that of the classical view: An entity x is categorised as an instance of the concept C if, and only if, x possesses some critical sum m of the weighted properties of C. This means that the prototype scheme, as opposed to the classical model, admits of exemplars to have partial membership degrees!

Revolving around the notion of *central tendency* (modal or mean), the prototype view sacrifices some economy of the classical view, however, it does suggest an increased richness in abstracting information. And, most importantly, it offers an answer to the single most important failure of the classical view, namely the lack of progress in specifying defining properties for many (natural, artificial, ontological and scientific) concepts. Because the prototype view does not require necessary and sufficient properties, this issue is immaterial.

Compared with the classical view, the prototype view of concepts does not seem to suffer from any major conceptual defect. However, Smith and Medin themselves and others have pointed out fuzzy set theory (possibility theory) as a natural complement to the probabilistic (prototype and exemplar) concept models [4,18,19]. This theme is taken up again in Section 6.

2.4 The Exemplar Concept View

In the exemplar view of concepts the stand is taken that concepts are represented, at least in part, by some of their exemplars rather than by an abstract summary. Supported by experimental evidence, the critical claim in this view is that exemplars usually play the dominant role in categorisation because they are more accessible than the summary information. However, it is to be noted that in many exemplar–based schemes a subordinate concept is also considered as an 'exemplar'. For example, Robin is an exemplar of the concept Bird. So there *is*, after all, some room for abstractions in this view; it would not appear to be very viable otherwise.

Since general exemplar–based concept models leave little room for abstractions and allow a high degree of disjunctiveness they have the tendency to make every single instance an explicit part of the concept representation. This seems highly implausible and counter–intuitive for such a model would impose an inefficient processing and storage regime on the concept memory. So–called *best examples* or *focal instances* exemplar models have been developed and empirically studied to account for the major drawback of the general model [4]. The essential assumption in these models holds that the exemplars used to explicitly represent a concept are *those* that share some critical number of properties with other exemplars of the concept. This relates to the CBR issue of which cases should be retained by the system—once it encounters and solves new cases—so as to improve its quality of performance.

Taking in account the best–examples assumption, two fundamental procedures for the exemplar view's categorisation function have been put forward and studied.

(1) All exemplars E in the representation of a concept C are retrieved and compared with the query item x. If, and only if, x sufficiently matches at least one exemplar in E, then x is judged to be a member (instance or subordinate) of C.

(2) An entity x is categorised as an instance or subconcept of concept C, if and only if, x retrieves (based on some measure of similarity) a critical number of the exemplars E in C.

Besides the obvious correspondence to the intra–class case selection phase in CBR, it is interesting to note that both classification procedures allow an entity to be members of more than one class!

In the exemplar view, in contrast to the classical model, each concept representation is explicitly disjunctive, at least in part, as each exemplar (instance or subordinate) of a concept is described by properties that do not necessarily have to be shared by other exemplars. Also, the exemplar view does not require that a property of one exemplar should be a property of other exemplars of the concept; that is, the properties need not be necessary ones. And since a concept is disjunctive, there is no need for sufficient properties. It follows that the exemplar view explicitly includes the notion of non–necessary properties.

Unlike the intuitively appealing prototype view, some aspects of the exemplar view seem to provoke objection. With respect to the proposed CBR framework, some of these points are briefly discussed.

If the prototype view is so efficient and conceptually sound, why then retain exemplars in the first place? Besides the argument that exemplars are easier accessed, another reason is provided by CBR research (and the general inferential function of concepts): an exemplar (or case) forms the basis to draw useful inferences about *similar* exemplars. To achieve the same capability a concept representation solely based on an abstracted summary would have to represent inferential knowledge powerful enough to capture *all* possible instances of the concept. This seems unrealistic; and rule-based schemes have proven the drawbacks of such models.

3 Concept Properties

Concept properties are used to model concepts, *and* to make apparent relationships *between* concepts. On the basis of common or shared properties, an inter–concept relationship structure, also called concept taxonomy, can be established. Such a structure constitutes one of the most vital and powerful conceptual machineries of an intelligent agent.

Properties are employed to describe partial and global aspects of concepts. Examples for global properties, describing the concept Car, are age and means of transport; both are used to characterise entire Car instances irrespective of other properties. Partial properties, on the other hand, refer to constituent parts of the entity in question, examples include number of doors, has engine.

Highly critical for the organisation (and indexing) of a concept (or case) memory is the issue of *constraining* properties [4,5,1,7]. One such constraint follows directly from the main purpose of properties, namely that to make apparent relationships between concepts. According to this, a property is a useful one if it reveals many *inter*–concept relationships. Take, for example, the property animate. This property makes it possible to 'see' a stronger relationship or similarity between, for instance, the concepts Chicken and Collie than between, say, Chicken and Daisy.

Besides their conceptual value, shared properties allow economic representation of concept taxonomies (inheritance). Of course, a property should not be too general, that is, apply to all concepts in a conceptual domain, for then it would be of no discriminative value. Similarly, a too specific a property barely contributes to conceptual richness or profound efficiency.

Finally, a general constraint on properties is concerned with the *absolute judgement* phenomenon [20,19]: 'Seven plus or minus two' represents the greatest amount of information an observer can give about an object on the basis of an absolute judgement. An expert chess player, for instance, would hardly state 15 or more salient characteristics to be present in even a complex middle game position.

3.1 Concept Properties and Context

A complex conceptual space is often divided into *contexts* and *sub–contexts* [4,14]. Across such contexts the interpretation or meaning of properties may differ according to the prevailing circumstances.

To illustrate, consider the concept People and four of its instances "Carlos", "Franz", "Tomohiro" and "Chin-Lai". Let all People exemplars share the dimensional property height with an identical instance value of 180 cm. By means of the property nationality—also shared by the four instances—two geographical contexts, Europe and Asia, can be derived. Within the European context the meaning of the property-value pair ⟨ height, *180* ⟩ may be interpreted as *tall*, and within the Asian as very tall. To model this situation, two subordinate concepts could be introduced (eg, European,

Asian) with 'specialised' properties (eg, european_height, asian_height). This solution, however, compromises the desired generality of properties!

From this example it can be seen that a main function of contexts is to resolve the *ambiguity*—or indeed *uncertainty*—induced by the generality of properties or concepts, ie, contexts effectively *restrict* concepts and properties.

3.2 Features

One way to characterise a concept's component properties is by qualitative or featural properties, called *features*. The Bird concept, for example, may be described by the features is big, has wings, can fly, has feathers, etc. Features, then, capture qualitative variations of concepts; two concepts differ with respect to a feature if one concept has it and the other does not have it. The advantage of a feature–based representation regime is its simplicity.

An obvious shortcoming of the featural approach is that it cannot properly explain and handle quantitative variations of properties. Humans, on the other hand, often have a fairly accurate idea about these variations [4]. A big turkey, for example, may weigh something between 15 and 25 pounds. Related to this issue is the variation of 'truth' (degree of possibilistic certainty) that is often inherent in vague quantitative features (eg, big), and in seemingly non–quantitative features like can fly [17,18]. Although some proposals have been made, purely feature–based representation systems have little to offer in this respect [4].

3.3 Dimensions

Another way to represent concept properties is by quantitative or dimensional properties, also called *dimensions*. The essential assumption of the dimensional approach is that concepts that have the same relevant dimensions (eg, wingspan for Chicken and Eagle) can be represented as points in a multidimensional *metric space* (which has the desirable properties *minimality*, *symmetry*, and *triangular inequality*). Dimensions capture quantitative variations of concepts; for two concepts to differ with respect to a particular dimension, one concept must score a higher value on that dimension than the other.

The weight associated with each dimension (eg, $w_{wingspan} = 0.40$) reflects the relevance of variations along the corresponding dimension. Two basic categorisation methods exist:

(1) To recognise an entity x as a member of a concept C, x must achieve a critical weighted sum of dimensions. This method focuses on the C's mean values $m_i(C)$.

(2) To recognise an entity x as a member of a concept C, the distance $d(C, x)$ between the concept C and an entity x must be equal or less than some threshold t_C.

Here the emphasis is on the processing of concepts as units and distances between them, rather than on the values of the individual dimensions.

Obviously, the advantage of the dimensional approach is its ability to capture quantitative variations of properties. By means of the metric space assumption, dimensions allow a categorisation model which is based on distances, rather than on the presence/absence of features.

A drawback of dimensional properties is that they do not support explicit relationships between properties such as the aggregation relation between blood_pressure and its constituents systolic and diastolic.

Although dimensions can be used to 'simulate' qualitative properties like animate or flies, they, similar to their featural counterparts, cannot capture the (possibilistic) uncertainty inherent in symbolic expressions of this kind. Related to this is the issue of *imprecise quantities* such as roughly 200, tall, big, etc—as opposed to qualities like flies. Imprecise quantities are the rule rather than the exception, they may origin from different sources: imprecise, incomplete or non-obtainable information, or partial ignorance [18,19].

Finally, similar to the featural approach, dimensions do not address any context effect issues, eg, constraining the values a dimension may assume in a particular context.

4 PERCEPT: A Concept-Centred CBR Model

Concepts seem to play a central role in the way humans organise and use knowledge about the world. In the previous sections it has been shown that there is a great deal of overlap between fundamental CBR issues and the findings in concept research. Concepts (and concept exemplars) as well as cases (and case organisation structures) arise from the interaction of an experiencer with the world. They have to be learned, organised and stored in a concept or case *memory* so that they can be accessed and used when needed. Such a memory organisation strategy has to be efficient, effective, flexible and epistemologically adequate [4,5,6,11,10,13]. Efficiency is concerned with 'acceptable' storage and retrieval times of cases. Effectiveness has to do with the relevance or usefulness of the retrieved cases. Flexibility refers to the extendibility and modifiability of an existing concept space. And epistemological adequacy means that the *semantic* gap between the system's and expert's memory organisation should be minimal.

Because of its importance for human thinking and its affinity to the fundamentals of CBR as a model of human cognition, the notion of a concept is proposed as the representation framework for modelling case–knowledge [10]. This scheme, called PERCEPT, is described below.

5 Case Concepts and Memory Organisation

The two primary functions of a case memory are to serve as a repository to store cases, and to efficiently access relevant case clusters and cases. With the increase in number and complexity of cases and case properties, more sophisticated memory organisation strategies are needed to achieve efficient and effective retrieval. This work proposes a case memory architecture that revolves around *case concepts*. Via inter–concept relationships a natural means is provided to economically conceptualise a potentially large variety of case types (in a specific domain) into a taxonomy of cases. Intra–concept relationships and components serve to describe, constrain and represent structural and operational aspects of a case concept, and provide a 'link' to the exemplars or cases stored under that concept.

Because of their superiority over the classical view, the prototype *and* exemplar concept views are chosen as a basis to model case–knowledge concepts in the

PERCEPT architecture. The combination of the two models is in line with suggestions by Smith and Medin themselves and others [4]—people seem to represent a single concept via both a probabilistic summary representation and exemplars. The complementary nature of such a combined summary/exemplar representation corresponds well to the orthogonal breakdown of a case memory (memory organisation and content).

So a prototype–view–based intensional concept *summary* is used to conceptualise—structurally and operationally—the entire case memory space into regions or clusters of similar cases. Besides its obvious structural and taxonomic utility, the main purpose of such a summary is its operational, *inter*–concept categorisation function. Essentially, a taxonomy of case concept summaries can be thought of as an inter–class classification system, it assigns an unclassified item to none, to one or to more of the concepts it contains.

In CBR, once a case concept has been deemed relevant to the problem at hand (query case), the exemplars or cases (stored under the concept) that are most similar to the query case need to be selected. Basically, such a selection process carries out an *intra*–concept classification task by establishing the query case's conceptual location l amongst the stored cases of the class [9].

By resorting to a combined (prototype) summary/exemplar concept representation, the PERCEPT scheme overcomes one of the most critical aspects that troubles the exemplar view, namely its lack of handling cross–exemplar relationships. If described in the summary representation of the concept C, then a property is probabilistically distributed over the exemplars of the C in accordance with the property weight. For example, nine out of ten Bird exemplars share the property flies.

6 Case Concepts and Their Properties

In the PERCEPT scheme, case–knowledge components (properties and cases) around self–contained, operational entities (objects and object classes). This approach facilitates the representation of 'intelligent' properties that subsume both the features as well as dimensions. The same underlying abstraction mechanisms allow the representation of properties' context dependencies and afford a flexible regime for the specification of property values. Furthermore, through fuzzy–set–based *property concept frames*, PERCEPT provides a powerful means to explicitly manage uncertainty associated with case properties (see below).

6.1 What makes an Expressive, Versatile Case Property?

Both probabilistic concept models, the prototype as well as the exemplar view, fail to capture *possibilistic* uncertainty that may be inherent in some of their properties. Possibilistic uncertainty—unlike probabilistic uncertainty which relates to the randomness of a property's occurrence and to ambiguity—deals with the vagueness or *fuzziness* present in a system (concept, property, situation, event, etc). Here the *existence* of a property such as *high* is assumed (eg, the die faces 3, 4, 5 and 6 are interpreted as *high*), but the *extent* to which the property is present has to be gauged (eg, $die(3) \rightarrow high/0.4$ or $die(5) \rightarrow high/0.8$). Possibilistic uncertainty, then, deals with sets whose boundaries are not sharply defined (eg, $high = \{3/0.4, 4/0.6, 5/0.8, 6/1.0\}$), ie, *fuzzy sets*. Fuzzy set theory has been proposed to represent the meaning and capture the uncertainty associated with qualitative (or inexact quantitative) concepts frequently expressed via *linguistic terms* like *flies, high, many*, etc [19]. A fuzzy set *A* is usually defined by a *membership function* $\mu_A(x)$ which maps elements *x* of some *universe of discourse U* into the unit interval [0, 1]. Formally: $\mu_A(x): U \rightarrow [0, 1]$, where $x \in U$. As an example consider the Bird concept and its fuzzy property *flies* represented by the fuzzy set labelled *flies* in Figure 2.

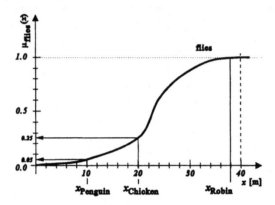

Figure 1: Fuzzy property flies.

The fuzzy set *flies* in the diagram is defined by the membership function $\mu_{flies}(x)$; where *x* corresponds to the distance an object is able to fly. According to $\mu_{flies}(x)$, only entities that are able to travel in the air for at least 40 meters fully possess the property *flies*, eg, for $x_{Robin} > 40$, ie, $\mu_{flies}(x_{Robin}) = 1.00$. The *flies* property can be attributed to Chickens and Penguins as well, but to a lesser degree, eg, $\mu_{flies}(x_{Chicken}) = 0.25$.

To be epistemologically adequate and representationally expressive, a concept scheme must capture the possibilistic uncertainty of its properties. The PERCEPT approach embodies this idea through the explicit incorporation of a property's characterising membership function in the summary representation of case concepts. Table 2 below demonstrates this by means of the simplified description of the Bird concept (the *characterising* membership function of a property is called *c-function*).

Table 2: Bird concept and fuzzy properties.

Weight	Name	C-Function	Modal/Mean Value
1.00	winged	$\mu_{winged}(x)$	*present*
0.80	flies	$\mu_{flies}(y)$	*present*
0.50	wingspan	$\mu_{around\_40}(z)$	40

The table above shows how modal and mean property *values* (rightmost column), used to *describe* concepts in the probabilistic view, are replaced by c-functions, eg, $\mu_{winged}(x)$. What is critical for the categorisation function of the Bird concept is the fact that all three c-functions evaluate to *membership degrees* in the interval [0, 1]. Actual membership degrees, derived from the property *values* x_i of an unclassified entity (query case) X, together with the corresponding weights w_i serve as basis to compute the X's overall concept membership m_C via, for example, $m_C(X) = \Sigma_{i=1..n} w_i \times \mu_C(x_i)$.

Allowing properties to assume the symbolic values *present* and *not-present*, and interpreting the membership degree 1 as featural *match* (eg, $\mu_{winged}(present) = 1$) and 0 as *mismatch* (eg, $\mu_{winged}(not\text{-}present) = 0$), a membership function can represent featural properties—ie, more quantitative properties like winged—as special case. The meaning of imprecise quantities such as medium is also captured and explicitly modelled by c-functions, eg, the c-function $\mu_{around\_40}(x)$ may be defined as follows: $\mu_{around\_40}(x) = 1/40\ x$, for $0 < x \leq 40$, and $-1/40\ x + 2$, for $x > 40$.

The function $\mu_{around\_40}(x)$ illustrates that c-functions subsume the dimensional *mean* value concept as special case, for example, $(\mu_{around\_40}(40) = 1) \Rightarrow precise\ match$, and, $(\mu_{around\_40}(20) = 0.5) \Rightarrow partial\ match$. It is obvious that linguistic expressions like *around 40* (along with the definition of their membership function) are more suitable and flexible than exact numbers for the description of properties like wingspan, intelligence, anxiety, stress, height, etc, which, when determined and used in practice, are subject to several sources of uncertainty [19].

The example above illustrates how the PERCEPT concept scheme represents possibilistic uncertainty that is inherent in concept properties and therefore in the concepts themselves. However, extending the mean–value–based concept representation via the notion of c-functions raises some questions.

(1) The c-function of a (more quantitative) property like flies 'expects' a precise numerical value as argument, for instance, 20 [meters] representing the distance an entity is able to fly. Applicable in some circumstances, this way of specifying property instances may be too restricted in others. Often it is preferred or even necessary to use:

(a) vague quantitative values to specify properties, for example (with f_i being an instance of the flies property), $f_1 := short$ [a short distance], $f_2 := roughly\ 50$ [a distance of roughly 50 m], and $f_3 := long$ [a long distance].

(b) more qualitative values where the numeric connotation is not readily recognised. The flies property, for instance, may be replaced by a more general, hence more desirable, property like locomotion with possible linguistic *values*, for example (with l_i being an instance of the locomotion property), $f_1 := nose\text{-}dives$, $f_2 := leaps$, and $f_3 := flies$.

Case (b) also captures the featural values *present* and *not-present*. To allow such a flexible way of specifying and processing properties, the PERCEPT scheme deploys *polymorphic properties*, and, for the property representation on the concept summary side, the notion of a *property concept frame*. Amongst other things, a property concept frame consists of a set of membership functions, including the c-function, and the property's weight.

(2) Given the membership-function–based concept representation approach, the comparison of properties becomes a non–trivial affair [19,]. Take, for example, the *flies* property and the c-function $\mu_{flies}(x)$ depicted in Figure 1. Comparing a query case property value $x_q = 15$ (ie, $\mu_{flies}(x_q) \approx 0.12$) with the corresponding base case values $x_{b_1} = 10$ and $x_{b_2} = 20$ (ie, $\mu_{flies}(x_{b_1}) = 0.05$, and $\mu_{flies}(x_{b_2}) = 0.25$) reveals that x_q is *conceptually* closer to x_{b_1} than x_{b_2}!

The issues outlined in (1) and (2) are handled and represented via *polymorphic properties* and property *concept frames* (defined on concept summary level). Some conceptual aspects of these components are introduced below. More detailed definitions may be found in [21,22,23].

To capture the context effects of properties, concept descriptions should contain information that allows the interpretation of one and the same property type according to its idiosyncrasies under varying contexts [14,17]. In the PERCEPT scheme a property describing a concept is associated with a property concept frame which represents components such as the property's relevance weight and c-function. Table 3 illustrates the idea of a concept description that uses properties and property concept frames.

Table 3: Property-based concept description (Bird) and property concept frames.

Property Name	Property Concept Frame		
	weight	c-function	v-function$_i$
flies	0.80	$\mu(x)_{\text{flies}}$	...
wingspan	0.50	$\mu(x)_{\text{around\_40}}$	...

By assigning different property concept frames, for different contexts, to the same property (identified by the property type or name) it is possible to reflect the context–specific characteristics of the property without compromising its generality.

For example, let the concept People and two of its subordinates (European and Asian) establish the respective contexts. Further, suppose that the property height is shared by European and Asian, and the European height is be associated with the property concept frame $frame^{height}_{European}$, and in Asian with $frame^{height}_{Asian}$ (see Figure 2).

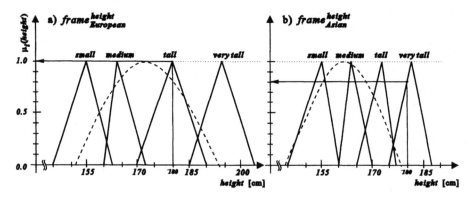

Figure 2: Context–dependent property concept frames.

Through *value membership functions*, called v-functions (solid-lined), the *frame of discernment* of the height concept frame is conceptualised into linguistic categories such as 'tall'. Thus, in the European context, a People case x, for which the height value $x_h = 180$ [cm] is determined, may be assessed as $\langle tall, 1.00 \rangle$ (part (a) of diagram), and as $\langle very\ tall, 0.80 \rangle$ in the Asian context (part (b) of diagram). The point is that no new property, eg, european_height and asian_height, needs to be used, thus the desirable generality constraint of the height property can be preserved. The dashed membership functions in Figure 2 represent *c-functions* (see below).

6.2 Case Properties and the Freedom of Expression

Two aspects of PERCEPT's case properties can be distinguished: the *description* of the property on the concept summary level, and the *values* a property may assume. In the previous section the focus has been on the description side, this section concentrates on the instance values of properties.

Through v-functions (value membership functions) PERCEPT provides a means for *specificational polymorphism*. This means that instance values of *polymorphic primitive properties* can be specified in various formats. The supported specification formats are: *real number, linguistic term, graded linguistic term,* and *fuzzy predicate.*

In circumstances where exact information about the property in question is available, the real number format is used, eg, $height := 183$. However, such a property value is still *interpreted* within the conceptual and contextual confines of the corresponding concept frame!

Both linguistic term formats are deployed if precise information about the property under consideration cannot be readily obtained, eg, $height := tall$ and $height := \langle tall, 0.80 \rangle$. For each property there exists a limit as to what linguistic terms can be used (absolute judgement phenomenon). This format, somewhat forcing the specifier to use linguistic notions that correspond to well–established concepts in a domain, is suitable for less experienced users as well as for expert system users.

Finally, the fuzzy predicate encoding provides the specifier of cases with an unconstrained mechanism to explicitly express his or her subjective belief in the certainty or exactness of property values like *about 60, old, hazardous,* etc, eg, $height := \langle 175, 190, \mu_{approximately\_180}(x) \rangle$. The fuzzy predicate format, as opposed to the linguistic term formats, is intended for users that have a deeper understanding of the domain in question (ie, domain experts).

It is obvious that the provision of polymorphic properties imposes some special processing requirements, notably on those algorithms involving property comparison. A detailed discussion and definition of PERCEPT's case property mechanisms is found in [21,22,23].

7 Conclusions

This paper presented, in some detail, the topology and components of an expressive case-knowledge architecture, called PERCEPT, which realises a framework for a memory of cases based on the combined prototype/exemplar view of behaviouristic concepts [4], and possibility theory [17]. Because its sound empirical basis, the advantage of this scheme lies in its epistemological adequacy. Via a fuzzy-set-based extension to the core model, the architecture provides an explicit uncertainty management regime, and specificational polymorphism. Furthermore, through context frames (weight, v-functions, c-function), a means is provided to explicitly represent and process the contextual idiosyncrasies of case properties.

References

1. J.L. Kolodner, K.C. Riesbeck. *Experience, Memory, and Reasoning*. Hillsdale, NJ, 1986.
2. J.L. Kolodner. *Case–Based Reasoning*, Morgan Kaufmann Publishers, Inc., CA, 1993.
3. E.E. Smith, E.J. Shoben, L.J. Rips. Structure and Process in Semantic Memory: A Featural Model for Semantic Decisions. *Psychological Review*, 81, pp214-241, 1974.
4. E.E. Smith, D.L. Medin. *Categories and Concepts*. Harvard University Press, 1981.
5. R.C. Schank. *Dynamic Memory: A Theory of Learning in Computers and People*. Cambridge University Press, 1982
6. J.L. Kolodner. *Retrieval and Organizational Strategies in Conceptual Memory*. Hillsdale, N.J., 1984.
7. K.J. Hammond. *Case-Based Planning: Viewing Planning as a Memory Task*. Academic Press, 1989.
8. A. Ram A. Indexing, Elaboration and Refinement: Incremental Learning of Explanatory Cases., *Machine Learning*, 10(3):201-248, 1993.
9. R. Bareiss, B. Porter, C. Wier. PROTOS—An Exemplar-Eased Learning Apprentice. *2nd Knowledge Acquisition for Knowledge-Based Systems Workshop*, 1987.
10. B. Porter, R. Barreiss, R. Holte. Concept Learning and Heuristic Classification in Weak Theory Domains. *Artificial Intelligence*, vol. 45 (1-2), pp229-263, 1990.
11. J.S. Aikins. Prototypical Knowledge for Expert Systems, *Artificial Intelligence* vol. 20, pp163-210, 1983.
12. A. Aamodt. *A Knowledge-Intensive Approach to Problem Solving and Sustained Learning*. PhD dissertation, University of Trondheim, Norwegian Institute of Technology, 1991.
13. A. Aamodt. Case-Based Reasoning: Foundational Issues, Methodological Variations, and System Approaches. *AICOM*, vol. 7, 1, 1994.
14. Y. Cheng. Context-Dependent Similarity. *Uncertainty in Artificial Intelligence 6*, vol. 12, pp41-47, North-Holland, NY, 1991.
15. R.E. Stepp, R.S. Michalski. Conceptual Clustering of Structured objects: A Goal-Oriented Approach. *Artificial Intelligence*, 28, pp43-69, 1986.
16. A. Tversky. Features of Similarity. *Psychological Review*, vol. 84, pp327-252, 1977.
17. Ruspini, E.H., "Possibility as Similarity: The Semantics of Fuzzy Logic", in *Uncertainty in Artificial Intelligence 6*, pp271, North-Holland, 1991.
18. Klir, G.J., T.A. Folger, *Fuzzy Sets, Uncertainty and Information*, Prentice Hall, Englewood Cliffs, NJ, 1988.
19. S-J. Chen, C-L. Hwang. *Fuzzy Multiple Attribute Decision Making, Methods and Applications*, Springer Verlag, 1992.
20. G.A. Miller. The Magic Number Seven, Plus or Minus Seven. *Psychological Review*, vol. 6, 3, pp81, 1965.
21. W. Dubitzky, A. Schuster, J.G. Hughes, D.A. Bell. Conceptual Distance of Numerically Specified Case Features. *2nd New Zealand International Two–Stream Conference on Artificial Neural Networks and Expert Systems*, pp210-213, 1995.
22. A. Schuster, W. Dubitzky, K. Adamson, J.G. Hughes, D.A. Bell. Processing Similarity between a Mix of Crisply and Fuzzily Defined Case Features. submitted to *Second International ICSC Symposium on Fuzzy Logic and Applications*, 1997.
23. W. Dubitzky. *Uncertainty Management in Case-Based Reasoning: A Concept-Centred Approach*, PhD thesis, to be submitted by autumn 1996.

Supporting Object Reuse Through Case-Based Reasoning *

Carmen Fernández-Chamizo, Pedro Antonio González-Calero,
Mercedes Gómez-Albarrán and Luis Hernández-Yáñez

Dep. Informática y Automática. Universidad Complutense de Madrid
28040 Madrid, Spain
email: cfernan@dia.ucm.es

Abstract. In this paper we address the problem of locating the appropriate component in an object-oriented software repository along with the issue of extending the component to adapt it to particular requirements. In order to give support to both types of tasks, we use a CBR approach which allows to profit from past experiences with the use of the repository, and to integrate different knowledge sources under the same representation scheme. This approach has been evaluated through a prototype implementation, which addresses the reuse of a general purpose Smalltalk repository.

1   Introduction

Software reuse is considered as the best potential approach to bring about the gains of productivity and quality that the software industry needs [3]. However, there are several methodological and technical problems that hinder reuse [5]. Object-Oriented Programming has been proposed as the best hope for facing these problems and promoting widespread software reuse [19]. However, the concepts that provide the great strengths of this paradigm introduce new difficulties in program analysis and understanding [26]. Inheritance, polymorphism and dynamic binding complicate the tracing of dependencies, and the dispersion of functionality into different components makes global understanding difficult.

Case-Based Reasoning (CBR) [6] is a problem solving paradigm that uses knowledge of relevant past cases to interpret or to solve a new problem case. Case-based techniques constitute a natural approach to represent the experience acquired in the design of past software applications. Therefore, CBR can be used to support software reuse, specially when dealing with object-oriented design where software development usually relies on previously developed object classes.

In this paper we address the problem of locating the appropriate component in an object-oriented software repository along with the issue of extending the component to adapt it to particular requirements. In order to support both types of tasks, we use a CBR approach which allows the integration, under the

---

* This work is supported by the Spanish Committee of Science & Technology (CICYT TIC94-0187)

same representation scheme, of different knowledge sources about components. This approach has been evaluated through a prototype implementation, which addresses the reuse of a general purpose Smalltalk repository.

Section 2 describes the CBR approach used to support object-oriented reuse. Section 3 describes the case representation. Measures used to assess similarity between components are presented in Section 4. Retrieving and adapting processes are described in Section 5. Related work and conclusions are presented in Section 6.

2 A CBR Approach to Support Object Reuse

Effective software reuse [23] requires mechanisms that help to (a) specify reuse needs, (b) retrieve reuse candidates from a component repository which meet, at least to some extent, the reuse needs, (c) assess the ability of each retrieved candidate to satisfy the reuse needs, and select the best-suited candidate, if any, (d) modify the selected candidate, if necessary, and (e) integrate the modified candidate into the current project.

In this paper, we are concerned with the retrieval and adaptation tasks. Usually, knowing the behavior, structure and interrelationships of the components is necessary to evaluate the adequacy of a selected component, or to adapt it to the given reuse specification. So, component understanding problem underlies both tasks.

The inherent difficulty of component understanding is increased due to component extensibility, defined as the ability of a component to be easily modified to better meet a particular need [16]. General purpose class repositories extensibility is due to subclassing and inheritance mechanisms, which allow multiple variants to coexist, cooperate, and be easily constructed.

The problem with extensible systems is that they can not be arbitrarily extended, since some restrictions and dependencies must be met in order to preserve the consistency of the system. Object-oriented languages allow the user to subclass any class and to specialize any method, but in many cases arbitrary replacement will destroy the integrity of any actual system.

Traditional approaches to support software retrieval can basically fall into two categories, automatic indexing and knowledge-based. The automatic indexing approach takes the natural language documentation of the component and automatically extracts a set of indices to characterize it. [12], [14] and [20] describe systems based on this approach. With these techniques, retrieval is in general efficient, but help with selection and correct usage must be found outside the retrieval system.

On the other hand, in the knowledge-based approach, the characterization of the component is done manually by human experts, following a pre-established model of the domain. Knowledge-based systems pay attention to the component understanding problem but, as a trade-off, they require domain analysis and a great deal of pre-encoded, manually provided semantic information. Some knowledge-based systems for software reuse are described in [4], [7] and [13].

In terms of retrieval efficiency, it is hard to decide which approach is better, automatic indexing or knowledge-based, because there are no comparable empirical results about the performance of systems based on them. But, if we are interested in supporting adequately the component understanding problem, domain-oriented knowledge-based techniques are needed.

When designing a general purpose class, the designers have in mind the potential extensions of this class that will be consistent with their design. Accordingly to these potential extensions, many design decisions are taken and many design commitments are established. Our proposal consists of (1) identifying this design knowledge, and (2) representing it explicitly, along with all the knowledge about behavior and structure of the class that may be required to reuse it. The high grade of parallelism between the selection of a component from the repository and the extension of this component to meet the particular requirements of the problem, and the tasks of selection and adaptation of cases in a CBR system has made us follow a CBR approach to support software reuse.

What exactly is meant by a case and how it is represented are two key issues in CBR. In our approach, a case is a reusable component or a programming recipe. An object repository basically consists of two types of components: classes and methods. Both kinds of entities are not independent but they reflect two different reusability issues: reuse of abstract data types and procedural reuse. We have defined cases corresponding to classes and cases corresponding to methods, and we have stated explicitly the different relationships between them.

In addition to these cases we have included another kind of cases corresponding to programming recipes. Some object-oriented environments include a "cookbook", a collection of recipes, or prototypical examples, about the way of implementing some usual operations. These operations correspond to code fragments which can make use of different methods and classes. These cookbooks are usually very useful because they organize the operations in a conceptual way, close to the user's cognitive model, so that the programmer does not need to know the actual repository organization.

Considering software components and programming recipes as cases is a specially suitable approach when dealing with commercial repositories. We can describe the components by using the attributes which are relevant to reuse, and we can state the granularity level of the description according to the required level of reuse. Some other approaches, for example those which use a formal specification of the components, require a repository specifically designed for its use and they can not be applied to existing commercial environments.

We have applied this approach to support software reuse in VisualWorks [22], a Smalltalk programming environment. We have selected Smalltalk because it is the fastest growing object-oriented programming language [25] and because becoming truly proficient with the Smalltalk environment is no simple achievement [2] and requires a good support. This work is a part of a wider project to promote software reuse in general purpose object-oriented libraries, the Object Reuse Assistant (ORA) project. Several systems using and combining different approaches have been developed in the last years [8], [9], [10].

3 Case Representation

A software component may be described by either its function (input-output relation, the "what") or its structure (the "how"). Usually, a programmer that wants to reuse a component repository asks for a component that fulfills a given purpose ("what"). So, to retrieve a component, it is necessary to specify its functional properties rather than to specify its structure. Therefore, for matching purposes, software components are described by their functional properties. However, in order to estimate the structural changes needed to adapt a component to new requirements, we need to have a model of the relation between functional requirement and component structure.

Representing the function or the structure of a component involves an encoding process in which a set of relevant properties are selected to characterize the components. This encoding process inevitably results in a loss of information, because not all the component properties can be represented. The choice of the encoding methods and of the matching algorithms involves a number of trade-offs between cost, complexity, and retrieval quality.

In our approach, each case is represented by giving three features: its description, its associated solution and the justification of its solution.

Case description corresponds to the functional description of the component. We have used two different encoding methods to overcome some of the drawbacks related to the loss of information. So we obtain two case descriptions: lexical descriptions which are obtained from the component documentation by using automatic free-text indexing techniques, and conceptual descriptions, introduced by a human expert who describes the component functionality in an existing conceptual framework.

Case solution corresponds to the code of the component which will be presented to the user when required. It is represented directly, without further processing, as an ASCII string.

Case justification is an explicit representation of the component structure. It corresponds to a description of the code properties relevant to reuse. In particular, it includes the dependencies on other components and its use restrictions. All this information is fundamental to support the component reuse and adaptation.

Conceptual descriptions and case justification are represented in LOOM, a language and environment for knowledge representation and reasoning [17], descendant of the KL-ONE system. LOOM has the ability of automatically classifying a structured concept with respect to a taxonomy of other concepts. We decided to use LOOM instead of a specific CBR tool because of its flexibility and its facility to be integrated in a Common Lisp program. Moreover, commercial tools have limited capacities and give little support to generalization and adaptation activities [1]. The whole case representation is integrated under the Common Lisp environment and it is accessible from a single interface.

3.1 Lexical Description

The lexical description of a case is obtained from the natural language documentation of the corresponding software component by using automatic indexing techniques [24]. We perform a statistical analysis of the word distribution in the repository documentation. This analysis allows to identify the different terms appearing in the documents. A term is a word in a *word-stem* form, that is, a word where inflectional endings have been removed. The stemming process has been performed using the morphological parser of the Wordnet lexical data base [21].

Each case is represented by means of a profile or term vector in a n dimensional vector space, being n the number of different terms that appear in the whole repository documentation. The i-th component of the term vector representing the case c_j stores the weight, wc_{ij}, of the term t_i in the documentation associated with that case. The weight, wc_{ij}, of a term, t_i, in a case, c_j, is defined as follows

$$wc_{ij} = tf_{ij} \cdot w_i$$

being tf_{ij} the frequency of t_i in c_j, and w_i the weight of t_i.

The definition of term weight is based on the quantity of information concept. The best indexing terms are those with a high quantity of information [24]. These terms are those that occur frequently in the individual case but rarely in the rest of the cases. The weight of a term t_i is given by

$$w_i = \log\left(\frac{N}{df_i}\right)$$

being N the number of cases and df_i the number of cases where t_i appears.

3.2 Conceptual Description

For each case, a conceptual description is created by using a conceptual framework obtained from the domain analysis. This conceptual framework is a global ontology of programming knowledge, implemented in LOOM as a frame network where every node represents a *concept*. Concepts are restricted by a number of *slots* that relate them to other nodes in the network.

The description of a given class will be an instance of the c-class concept defined in Loom as

```
(defconcept c-class
    "A class in Smalltalk"
  :is-primitive (:and c-object
                    (:the r-has-data-specification
                          c-data-specification)
                    (:the r-has-restriction c-restriction)
                    (:all r-has-method c-method)))
```

This definition shows that an instance of the c-class concept is connected, through r-has-data-specification, with an instance of c-data-specification concept. The c-data-specification concept defines the objects represented by the class. The r-has-restriction relation connects the class with an instance of c-restriction which represents the constraints to be considered when implementing the class. Finally, r-has-method relates the instance of c-class to the instances of c-method representing the methods defined in the class.

Therefore, describing a class involves defining an instance of c-class, an instance of c-data-specification and as many instances of c-method as operations are defined in the class. The instance of c-class acts as an element that connects all the different parts of the description. It does not provide any information. For example, the instance representing the case related to the Bag class in Smalltalk would be

```
(tell (about i-Bag c-class
              (r-has-data-specification i-Bag-data)
              (r-has-restriction i-Bag-restriction)
              (r-has-method i-Bag-remove-)
              (r-has-method i-Bag-remove-ifAbsent-)
              ...
       ))
```

The specification of the class objects should describe the kind of objects represented by the class making use of the available terminology. For instance, OrderedCollection class represents a collection of objects sorted by the sequence in which these objects are added and removed from it. The elements of an OrderedCollection can be accessed using an external key, its position in the collection. This class can be used to implement queue and stack data types. The instance representing the specification of objects in this class is defined as

```
(tell (about i-OrderedCollection-data
              c-keyed-collection
              (r-key-type i-integer-data)
              c-ordered-collection
              (r-order-type i-external-order)
              c-variable-size-collection
              c-allow-duplicates-collection
              c-any-element-type-collection))
```

being i-integer-data the instance that represents the specification of the object integer number and i-external-order the only instance of the c-external-order concept. The system deduces that it must be an instance of c-integer-key-collection because it is a key accessed collection (instance of c-keyed-collection) and it has integer keys (it is connected with the instance of c-external-order through the r-order-type relation). At the same time, it must be an instance of c-externally-ordered-collection since it is an ordered collection (instance of c-ordered-collection) with an external order (r-order-type i-external-order).

The next step in creating a class description is the definition of its method descriptions. Methods will be described by means of the c-method concept. In the same way as the c-class concept was used to gather the different aspects of the class description, the c-method concept will gather the aspects of the method description. We define the method concept as

```
(defconcept c-method
    "A method in Smalltalk. A function in Smalltalk terminology"
    :is-primitive (:and c-software-entity
                        (:exactly 1 r-method-of)
                        (:the r-has-operation-specification
                               c-operation-specification)))
```

The characteristics that describe a method are the class where it is defined and its operation specification. Note that previous definition does not explicitly refer to the class which defines the method because the representation language does not allow circular definitions. To overcome this drawback, the reference can be introduced in the definition of the relations that connect the instances of the two concepts. We define the r-has-method relation that connect a class with its methods and we use this relation when defining the c-class concept. On the other hand, we define the inverse of the r-has-method relation, r-method-of, and we establish that a method can only be implemented by one class (:exactly 1 r-method-of). If an instance of c-class is connected with a c-method instance through the r-has-method relation, the system can automatically infer that the c-method instance is connected with the c-class instance through the r-method-of relation.

The second constraint that appears in the method description refers to the specification of the operation carried out by the method. This constraint shows that a c-method instance is connected with a c-operation-specification instance via the r-has-operation-specification relation. The c-operation-specification instance linked to a method instance is created using the operation description terminology obtained from the domain analysis. Thus, for example, the specification of the operation carried out by the remove:ifAbsent: method in the Bag class would be

```
(and c-remove-ifAbsent- (r-source i-Bag-data-spec))
```

This specification uses a more abstract operation specification (c-remove-ifAbsent) defined as

```
(defconcept c-remove-ifAbsent-
    :is-primitive (:and c-remove-element
                        (:filled-by r-has-object-specification
                                    i-literal-object-spec)
```

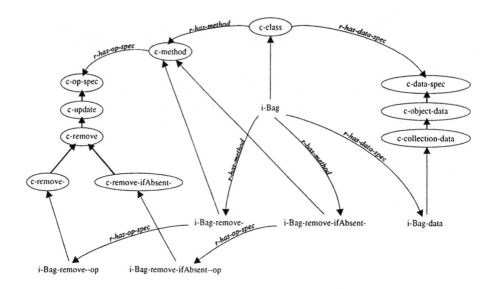

Fig. 1. Class representation

```
(:filled-by r-has-action-on-fail
            i-execute-block)))
```

All methods remove:ifAbsent: defined in different classes are instances of this more abstract operation. This generic specification shows that the remove: ifAbsent: operation removes an object, specified in a literal way, from a collection (c-remove-element), and, if the operation fails, a block of code is executed.

Figure 1 shows a partial view of the concepts in the conceptual framework used to describe classes and methods, along with a specific example consisting of the instances defined to represent a given class, the Bag class.

Next we address the issue of describing cases corresponding to operations that are not related to any particular method. For example, in the cookbook of VisualWorks [22] there are "recipes" to "Find elements in a collection", to "Store text in a file", or to "Associate an icon with a window". Its description is merely an operation description, like the ones used in describing methods. These cases will be represented as instances of the c-operation concept defined as

```
(defconcept c-operation
  :is-primitive (:and c-software-entity
                 (:the r-has-operation-specification
                  c-operation-specification)))
```

The only difference between the c-operation concept and the c-method concept is that the former is not related to any class. The operation description is represented as an instance of the c-operation-specification concept with a specific operation modified by several attributes.

3.3 Case Justification

In order to reason about the code we need not only the real code, but also a structured representation of it. The case justification is a representation of the code properties that are relevant to the component reuse.

To include the justification inside the case representation, we add to the previous definition of the c-class concept a slot that relates each class to its code properties (:the r-has-code c-code-class). We also add the slot (:the r-has-code c-code-method) to the previous c-method definition. In the same way, we modify the instances that represent operation cases adding the slot (:the r-has-code c-code-operation).

Each c-code-class instance basically stores its superclass name, the class category it belongs to, the methods it implements and the variables it defines. c-code-method instances store its method category, the class which implements the method and the messages it sends. This structured representation is automatically obtained from the code using an information extractor we have developed. This automatically extracted information is combined with the hand-coded knowledge about other reuse constraints:

- Design decisions and commitments. For example, class libraries are designed in such a way that certain groups of methods must remain consistent, i.e. these methods have to be overridden together or not at all.
- Feasible customizations. Abstract classes are used in reusable libraries to gather together the common functionality of a number of classes. Typically, in abstract classes some methods are implemented in terms of other non implemented methods, which are the responsibility of the subclass. When designing abstract classes a number of possible specialization parameters are in the mind of the designer, but this information does not appear explicitly in the implementation. We elicit that knowledge and represent it in the cases.
- Dependencies among implementations. One of the design guidelines in object-oriented programming is "do not duplicate functionality". This commitment leads to a cleaner architecture where every class has a well defined functionality, and where many components rely, through a client relationship, on the functionality provided by classes located in different places of the class hierarchy. In our case base these dependencies are explicitly represented for two purposes: to help in understanding the implementation; and to assist in the adaptation of methods by accessing to functionally related components which are close according to the conceptual similarity measure.

In order to build a complete representation of the code, method and class representations come along with the representation of other entities like variables, and method and class categories.

4 Similarity Measures

We have used two measures to assess similarity between components, one for each case description: lexical and conceptual. Each one of these measures will guide a different retrieval process as we will describe in the next section.

Similarity between lexical descriptions is obtained using the *vector space model calculus* where the similarity between two *documents* is given by the cosine of the vectors that represent those documents.

Similarity between conceptual descriptions is defined as the similarity among the entities of the case base that represent the cases. The similarity between two entities is obtained as the sum of two factors: the similarity among the concepts of which those entities are instances and the similarity among the slots defined in the entities.

To define a similarity measure on concepts we use an idea taken from the vector space model. We consider that every concept of the conceptual framework is an attribute, and the attributes of a concept are: itself and its superconcepts. We state that the more attributes two concepts have in common the closer they are. To implement this high level idea we associate with each concept a vector of $0|1$ values in the following way:

Given the set $C = \{1, \ldots, N\}$ of concepts defined in the knowledge base, for each concept $c_i \in C$ we define a vector v_i such that:

$$\forall c_i : i \in \{1, \ldots, N\} : \exists v_i : \underline{\text{vector}} \ [1 \ldots N] \ \underline{\text{of}} \ 1|0$$

$$v_i(j) = \begin{cases} 1 \text{ if } c_i \prec c_j \\ 0 \text{ otherwise} \end{cases}$$

The symbol $\prec$ is used to denote the subsumption relationship.

Once the vectors have been built, we can compute the similarity between two concepts as the cosine of the angle formed by the vectors which represent them:

$$\text{sim}(c_i, c_j) = \frac{v_i \cdot v_j}{\|v_i\| \cdot \|v_j\|}$$

It can be proved that this expression is equivalent to the following one, the one that we really use to compute the similarity among concepts:

$$\text{sim}(c_1, c_2) = \frac{|\bigcap \text{super}(c_1, C)\text{super}(c_2, C)|}{\sqrt{|\text{super}(c_1, C)|} \cdot \sqrt{|\text{super}(c_2, C)|}}$$

where the function $\text{super}(c, C)$ computes the set of concepts in C which are superconcepts of the concept c.

The second factor in the similarity between entities is the similarity among the slots defined on them. A slot is defined by a relation (*role*) and a set of entities (*filler*). If we say that entity o has the slot (r, F) we mean that it has been asserted or inferred in the conceptual framework that relation r holds between entity o and every entity in the set F. When computing the slot-based similarity of two entities, o_1 and o_2, we consider comparable only those slots with the same relation, so that, the similarity between the slot (r_1, F_1) of o_1 and the slot (r_2, F_2) of o_2 is computed as the similarity between the sets F_1 and F_2 if $r_1 = r_2$ and 0 otherwise.

When comparing groups of entities we recursively apply the function of similarity among entities by comparing every entity of one set with every entity of the other and accumulating the maximum of the results. The rationale of this decision can be explained with an example. Given two instances, o_1 and o_2, of the concept c-class we want to compare the set of entities that fill the relation r-has-method on those instances. For every method, m_{1i}, implemented by the class represented by o_1 (i.e., for every instance of c-method related with o_1 through the relation r-has-method) we are interested in comparing it with the most similar among the methods implemented in the class represented by o_2 (i.e., the instance of c-method related with o_2 through the relation r-has-method).

Finally, the similarity between two entities is computed as follows:

$$\text{sim}(o_1, o_2) = \begin{cases} \text{sim}(t(o_1), t(o_2)) & \text{if } \forall r \in R : v(o_1, r) = \emptyset \wedge v(o_2, r) = \emptyset \\ \frac{1}{2}\left(\text{sim}(t, (o_1), t(o_2)) + \frac{\sum_{r_i \in R} \text{sim}(v(o_1, r_i), v(o_2, r_i))}{|\{r \in R | v(o_1, r) \neq \emptyset \vee v(o_2, r) \neq \emptyset\}|}\right) & \text{otherwise} \end{cases}$$

where the set R denotes the set of relations defined in the conceptual framework and the functions $t(o)$ and $v(o, r)$ obtain the concepts of which the entity o is an instance, and the set of entities connected with the entity o through the relation r, respectively. And the similarity between two sets of entities $O_1, O_2 \subseteq O$, is given by the expression:

$$\text{sim}(O_1, O_2) = \begin{cases} 0 & \text{if } O_1 = \emptyset \vee O_2 = \emptyset \\ \dfrac{\sum_{o_i \in \min(O_1, O_2)} \max_{o_j \in \max(O_1, O_2)} (\text{sim}(o_i, o_j))}{|\min(O_1, O_2)|} & \text{otherwise} \end{cases}$$

where the min of a couple of sets is the set with the minimum cardinality, and the max, the set with the maximum cardinality.

5 Case Retrieval and Adaptation

We implement two retrieval algorithms associated with the two kinds of case descriptions, lexical and conceptual, and their corresponding similarity functions.

For the lexical description the user poses a query in natural language. This query is enriched with the synonyms of the terms it contains. These synonyms are obtained from the Wordnet lexical data base. The resulting enriched query is indexed using the same mechanism applied to the documents of the repository documentation, building a term vector. This vector is then compared with the vectors of all the documents in the corpus and those which result in a bigger similarity are retrieved. This process is not as expensive as it could seem since we build an inverted file, with access by term, and we only compute the similarity with those documents that have at least one term in common with the query.

For the conceptual description, the user must build an instance of the concept c-class along with an instance to represent the data specification of the desired class, and as many instances of c-method as operations he/she wishes that class to implement. In the construction of the instances the user is guided through a number of menus dynamically built from the contents of the case base.

Once the user has specified his/her needs using a conceptual description, the system retrieve those instances of c-class closer to the description of the query, in terms of the similarity function described above. The cost of comparing the query with every description defined in the case base would be intolerable. The solution is let the content of the case base guide the search.

First, we build a query including all the constraints defined in the user query and retrieve all the instances that verify them, if any. This first query would retrieve those cases matching all the user needs, or, at least, those specified in the instance representing the query. But, in general, no such case will be present in the case base. Therefore, we have to relax the restrictions of the original query, using more and more abstract concepts in it, until the number of candidate cases retrieved goes beyond a given threshold. It can be proved that this process of relaxation will retrieve first those instances closest to the original query.

We have tested these retrieval algorithms with Smalltalk beginners. Our preliminary results show that, in many cases, the retrieval performance is similar in both algorithms (even though they retrieve different components). However, in other cases there is a big difference in the quality of the retrieved cases. In general, lexical retrieval introduces more noise due to its blind text exploration. For example, when the user asked for "add an element to a set" the conceptual algorithm retrieved Set>>add:, the more relevant method to that query. However, the lexical algorithm retrieved that method in the fifth position of the candidate list, obtaining in the first places Collection>>grow: and Collection>>withAll:, two methods of the Collection class which bear no relation to the question posed by the user.

After the retrieval process, the user can inspect and interact with the information associated with any of the retrieved cases. Figure 2 shows the graphical interface implemented for this purpose. This interface comprises a number of different *views* designed to provide a smooth interaction with the different types of information included in case justifications. The figure shows the *code dependencies view*, including a graphical pane with mouse-sensitive nodes representing classes and methods, a text pane displaying code and comments of the component, and two list panes displaying functionally related methods and those methods the one being inspected depends on. As stated above, the availability of all these types of information assists to the user in component understanding and adaptation.

6   Related Work and Conclusions

The idiosyncrasy of object-oriented components has required a careful study of the knowledge to be represented, along with the adequate indexing mechanisms. We have shown that the special characteristics found in class repositories, due to their extensibility properties, need some specific representation features not addressed by other systems found in the component-based software reuse lit-

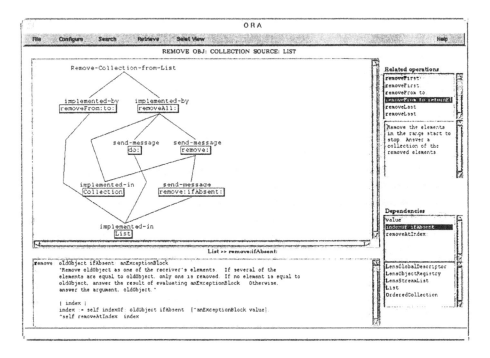

Fig. 2. The graphical interface

erature. So, the GTE [13] environment, while facing a wider problem (system evolution, library-based reuse, library population, and library improvement) uses a pattern-matching process which would be inappropriate for general purpose class libraries, due to the dispersion of functionality. IPSEN [4] is constructed around a notion of software architecture not present in the general purpose class libraries we have used. Comet [18], using LOOM as the representation language, also needs a highly specified application domain to support the software adaptation process it is intended to guide. Finally, the system described in [14] is (in spite of its title) not a knowledge-based system but an automatic indexing system. In that system, the domain knowledge (the class hierarchy) is only used to locate the free-text documentation associated with the methods and classes, when it is not directly available.

With regard to other systems that use CBR approaches to reuse software components we can mention the CAESAR system [11]. CAESAR works with repositories of mathematical functions. This domain is very well defined and the problems of retrieval and adapting components are simplified. Case description is based on facets and the emphasis is put on the testing capabilities of the system instead of on a deep understanding of the components.

Finally, the CBR approach described in [15] deals with the same problem considered here (reuse in an object-oriented repository) but in a very simplified way. Component retrieval is based on the name of the component, without taking into account any other kind of semantic similarity. Although some of its features are interesting, it uses an oversimplified conception of software components as construction blocks that limits its applicability in a real repository.

In this paper we have presented a CBR approach to support software reuse in an object-oriented environment. The main advantages of our approach are:

- The integration, under the same representation scheme, of different knowledge sources about components: code, natural language documentation, and domain knowledge provided by human experts.
- The use of two differents retrieval algorithms in order to combine the more useful features of each one.
- The connection of the description of component implementations (case justification, the "how") to the related programming concepts (conceptual description of the cases, the "what"), facilitating the location and understanding of the required component.

Future work will focus on the component adaptation process in order to give a more active support to the user, not only displaying the detected constraints but also guiding the whole process.

References

1. Althoff, K., Auriol, E., Barletta, R. & Manago, M., 1995. *A Review of Industrial Case-Based Reasoning Tools*, AI Intelligence.
2. Auer, K., 1995. "Smalltalk Training: As Innovative as the Environment". *Communications of the ACM*, vol. 38, 10.
3. Biggerstaff, T. J. & Richter, C., 1987. "Reusability Framework, Assessment, and Directions". *IEEE Software*, vol. 4, 2.
4. Börstler, J., 1994. "IPSEN: An integrated environment to support development for and with reuse", in *Software Reusability* (Schäfer, W., Prieto-Díaz, R. and Matsumoto, M., eds.), Ellis Horwood.
5. Caldiera, G. and Basili, V.R. 1994. "The qualification of reusable software components", in *Software Reusability* (Schäfer, W., Prieto-Díaz, R. and Matsumoto, M., eds.), Ellis Horwood.
6. DARPA: Machine Learning Program Plan, 1989. "Case-Based Reasoning". *Procs. of the Case-Based Reasoning Workshop*.
7. Devanbu, P., Ballard, B.W., Brachman, R.J. and Selfridge, P.G., 1991. "LaSSIE: A Knowledge-Based Software Information System", in *Automating Software Design* (Lowry, M.R. and McCartney, R.D., eds.), AAAI Press/ The MIT Press.
8. Fernández-Chamizo, C., González-Calero, P. A. & Gómez-Albarrán, M., 1995a. "Promoting Software Reuse through Explicit Knowledge Representation", in *Progress in Artificial Intelligence*, Lecture Notes in Artificial Intelligence, 990 (Pinto Ferreira, C. & Mamede, N., eds.), Springer Verlag.
9. Fernández-Chamizo, C., González-Calero, P. A., Hernández-Yáñez, L & Urech-Baqué, A., 1995b. "Case-Based Retrieval of Software Components". *Expert Systems with Applications*, vol. 9, 3.

10. Fernández-Chamizo, C., Hernández-Yáñez, L., González-Calero, P. A. & Urech-Baqué, A., 1993. "A Case-Based approach to Software Component Retrieval". *Symposium on Case-Based Reasoning and Information Retrieval*, Standford University, AAAI Spring Symposium Series, March 1993.

11. Fouqué, G. & Matwin, S., 1992. "CAESAR: a system for CAse basEd SoftwAre Reuse", *Procs. of the Seventh Knowledge-Based Software Engineering Conference*. IEEE Computer Society Press.

12. Frakes, W. B. & Nejmeh, B. A., 1987. "Software Reuse through Information Retrieval". *Procs. of the 20th Annual HICSS*, Kona, HI.

13. Gish, J.W., Huff, K.E. and Thomson, R., 1994. "The GTE environment-Supporting Understanding and Adaptation in Software Reuse", in *Software Reusability* (Schäfer, W., Prieto-Díaz, R. and Matsumoto, M., eds.), Ellis Horwood.

14. Helm, R. and Maarek, Y. S., 1991. "Integrating Information Retrieval and Domain Specific Approaches for Browsing and Retrieval in Object-Oriented Class Libraries". *OOPSLA-91*.

15. Katalagarianos, P. & Vassiliou, Y., 1995. "On the Reuse of Software: A Case-Based Approach Employing a Repository", *Automated Software Engineering*, vol. 2, 55-86.

16. Kiczales, G. and Lamping, J., 1992. "Issues in the Design and Specification of Class Libraries". *OOPSLA '92*.

17. MacGregor, R., 1991. "The evolving technology of classification-based knowledge representation systems", in *Principles of Semantic Networks: Explorations in the Representation of Knowledge* (Sowa, J. ed.), Morgan Kaufmann.

18. Mark, W., Tyler, S., McGuire, J., & Schlossberg, J., 1992. "Commitment-Based Software Development". *IEEE Trans. on Software Eng.*, vol.18, 10.

19. Meyer, B., 1987. "Reusability: The Case for Object-Oriented Design". *IEEE Software*, vol.4, 2.

20. Mili, H., Rada, R., Wang, W., Strickland, K, Boldyreff, C., Olsen, L., Wott, J., Heger, J., Scherr, W. and Elzer, P., 1994. "Practitioner and SoftClass: A Comparative Study of Two Software Reuse Research Projects", J. *Systems and software*, vol. 27, May 1994.

21. Miller, G. A., Beckwith, R. Fellbaum. C., Gross, D. & Miller, K., 1993. *Five Papers on Wordnet*, Cognitive Science Laboratory, Princeton University, CSL Report 43.

22. ParcPlace, 1994. *VisualWorks User's Guide and Cookbook*. ParcPlace Systems, Inc.

23. Rombach, H.D. and Schäfer, W., 1994. "Tools and environments", in *Software Reusability* (Schäfer, W., Prieto-Díaz, R. and Matsumoto, M., eds.), Ellis Horwood.

24. Salton, G. & McGill, M. J., 1983. *Introduction to Modern Information Retrieval*, McGraw- Hill, New York.

25. Shan, Y., 1995. "Smalltalk on the Rise". *Communications of the ACM*, vol. 38, 10.

26. Wilde, N. and Huitt, R., 1992. "Maintenance Support for Object-Oriented Programs". *IEEE Trans. on Software Eng.*, vol. 18, 12.

Meta-Cases: Explaining Case-Based Reasoning

Ashok K. Goel and J. William Murdock

Artificial Intelligence Group
College of Computing
Georgia Institute of Technology

Abstract. AI research on case-based reasoning has led to the development of many laboratory case-based systems. As we move towards introducing these systems into work environments, explaining the processes of case-based reasoning is becoming an increasingly important issue. In this paper we describe the notion of a meta-case for illustrating, explaining and justifying case-based reasoning. A meta-case contains a trace of the processing in a problem-solving episode, and provides an explanation of the problem-solving decisions and a (partial) justification for the solution. The language for representing the problem-solving trace depends on the model of problem solving. We describe a task-method-knowledge (TMK) model of problem-solving and describe the representation of meta-cases in the TMK language. We illustrate this explanatory scheme with examples from INTERACTIVE KRITIK, a computer-based design and learning environment presently under development.

1 Background, Motivations and Goals

One goal of AI research on case-based reasoning is to develop theories for designing useful and usable interactive case-based environments. In an interactive case-based environment, a human may acquire knowledge by navigating and browsing a case library, address a problem in cooperation with a case-based system, or learn about problem solving by observing the problem solving in the case-based system. The goal of designing case-based interactive systems that are both useful and usable raises the issue of *explaining* the reasoning of the case-based system. This issue is especially important in moving laboratory case-based systems into real work environments.

Explanation of reasoning is a recurrent theme in AI research. Consider, for example, the history of AI research on knowledge systems. Starting with MYCIN (Shortliffe 1976), which probably was the first useful and usable knowledge system, explanation became an increasingly important issue. In the context of MYCIN, for example, AI researchers first built an explanatory interface called GUIDON for tutoring medical students (Clancey 1987). Explanations in GUIDON initially were expressed in the language of goals, production rules, and rule activation and selection. But the need for generating useful and usable explanations soon led to the theory of heuristic classification (Clancey 1985) that provided a task-level account of MYCIN's reasoning. This task-level model in turn led to the development of a new system called NEOMYCIN, and to an new explanatory interface called GUIDON-WATCH. In parallel, other AI researchers developed general task-oriented theories of knowledge-based problem-solving, for example, Chandrasekaran's theories of Generic Tasks (Chandrasekaran 1988) and Task Structures (Chandrasekaran 1989). Chandrasekaran, Tanner and Josephson (1989) in particular argued that explanations in interactive knowledge-based systems need to capture the functional and strategic content of problem solving at the task level.

Before we go further with this discussion, it may be useful to make some key distinctions. First, by "explanation," we mean a system's capability of generating *self-explanations*, not its ability to generate abductive explanations of external data. The generation of self-explanation is a meta-task that involves introspective meta-reasoning. Second, self-explanation includes both justification of generated solutions and justification of knowledge used in generating the solutions in addition to explanation of problem solving. In this paper, we focus on explanation of problem solving. Third, explanation in an interactive system involves the issues of content of explanations and modality of interaction. This paper focuses on explanatory content.

We are exploring the issue of explaining case-based reasoning in the context of an interactive design and learning environment called INTERACTIVE KRITIK. INTERACTIVE KRITIK directly evolves from a family of autonomous systems called KRITIK (Goel 1991, 1992; Goel and Chandrasekaran 1989, 1992). KRITIK and its successor systems combined case-based and model-based reasoning for functional design of physical devices: the high-level computational process is case-based, and structure-behavior-function device models provide (i) a model-based vocabulary for indexing, retrieving and storing design cases, and (ii) a set of model-based strategies for adapting a design case and evaluating the modified design. KRITIK3 provides both the case base and the case-based reasoner for INTERACTIVE KRITIK.

Our earlier work on case-based reasoning has naturally led us to the notion of *meta-cases* for the meta-task of explanation. A meta-case contains a trace of the processing in a problem-solving episode. We use the term 'meta-case' to distinguish it from an 'object-case' that may specify, say, a specific design. Our idea of a meta-case is related to Chandrasekaran's (1989) notion of Task Structures. A task structure of a problem solver specifies a recursive task-method-subtask decomposition that sets up a virtual architecture for the problem solver. The architecture is virtual because more than one method may be applicable to any (sub)task in the task structure. When a specific problem is presented to this virtual architecture, specific methods get selected, specific subtasks get spawned, and specific branches in the virtual architecture get instantiated. A meta-case corresponds to a specific instantiation of this virtual architecture for a particular problem. It follows that a meta-case is represented in the language of tasks and methods.

The goal of this paper is describe the notion of meta-cases, and to illustrate the use of meta-cases for explanation in interactive systems through examples from INTERACTIVE KRITIK. The rest of this paper is organized as follows: in the next section, we describe a task-method-knowledge theory of problem solving, and, in section 3, we present an illustrative example from INTERACTIVE KRITIK. In section 4, we describe INTERACTIVE KRITIK and present an illustrative example from INTERACTIVE KRITIK. In section 5, we compare our work to related research and conclude the paper.

2 Task-Method-Knowledge Specification of Meta-Cases

AI research on knowledge systems has led to several task-oriented theories of problem solving, knowledge acquisition and explanation, for example, (Chandrasekaran 1988, 1989; McDermott 1988, Steels 1990; Wielenga, Schreiber and Breuker 1992). Although the different theories vary in many details, they all specify the content and organization of problem solving in terms of domain-independent classes of goals (called tasks) and task-specific patterns of inference (called methods). Chandrasekaran's (1989) theory of Task Structures provides the starting point for our work on modeling and explaining case-based reasoning. The main difference between our work and his theory is that our theory makes the content, form, organization of knowledge and its functional role in problem solving more explicit. For this reason, we call it the Task-Method-Knowledge (TMK) theory.

A task-method-knowledge (TMK) model of a specific problem solver has three main elements. The first element, the task, can be characterized by the types of information it takes as input and gives as output. For example, a common design task takes as input a specification of the functions desired of an artifact, and has the goal of giving as output a specification of the structure for the artifact that can deliver the desired functions. The second element in the TMK model is the method. A method can be characterized by (i) the type of knowledge it uses, (ii) the subtasks (if any) it sets up, and (iii) the control it exercises over the processing of subtasks. For example, the method of case-based reasoning uses knowledge of past cases, sets up the subtasks of retrieval, adaptation, evaluation and storage, orders these subtasks as listed here, and controls their processing so that the last three subtasks are processed only if the retrieval task fails to access an exactly-matching case that directly provides a solution to the given problem. In general, a number of methods may be applicable to a given task. The third element in the TMK model is knowledge. A specific type of knowledge can be characterized by its content, by its form of representation, and by its organization. To illustrate, consider the example of diagnostic knowledge. In some domains, models that specify how a device works may be available. In an interactive system, this knowledge system this knowledge may be represented in the form of directed acyclic graphs (DAGs) and the DAGs may be organized in a hierarchy, for example, an abstraction hierarchy.

Note that the task-method decomposition in a TMK model is recursive: since a method used for addressing a task spawns subtasks, the same task-method decomposition gets repeated for each of the subtasks. This recursive decomposition bottoms out when, for a given subtask, knowledge is available that directly solves the subtask, i.e., the knowledge directly corresponds to input-output specification of the task. We will use the term *procedure* to refer to this kind of method: a procedure does not spawn any subtasks. Also, we will use the term *strategy* to refer to subtrees in the task-method decomposition: a strategy is a specific task-method decomposition. Informally, a task in the TMK specification correspond to "goals" and the leaf-level subtasks correspond to the "operators" in means-ends analysis. Stroulia and Goel (1994a, 1994b) provide a semi-formal notation for representing tasks, methods, procedures, strategies, and knowledge.

A meta-case contains the trace of processing in a problem-solving episode. The TMK theory of problem solving provides a language for meta-cases in terms of tasks, methods and knowledge.

3   An Illustrative Example

To illustrate TMK models, we will briefly describe here the TMK model for KRITIK3, which provides the foundation for INTERACTIVE KRITIK. The primary task addressed by KRITIK3 is the extremely common functions-to-structure design task in the domain of physical devices. The functions-to-structure design task takes as input the functional specification of the desired design. For example, the functions-to-structure design of a flashlight may take as an input the specification of its function of creating light when a force is applied on a switch. This task has the goal of giving as output the specification of a structure that satisfies the given functional specification, i.e., a structure that results in the given functions.

KRITIK3's primary method for accomplishing this task is case-based reasoning. Its case-based method sets up four subtasks of the design task: *problem elaboration*, *case retrieval*, *design adaptation*, and *case storage* as illustrated in Figure 1. Note this figure shows only some of the high-level tasks and methods in KRITIK3's TMK model; it does not show the detailed decomposition of each task-method branch, nor does it show the kinds of knowledge that are used by the different methods. The rectangles in the figure represent tasks while the ovals represent methods; points beneath some of the rectangles/ovals in the figure indicate further decomposition of the tasks/methods.

The task of problem elaboration takes as input the specification of the desired function of the new design. It has the goal of generating a probe to be used by design-retrieval for deciding on a new case to use. KRITIK3 uses domain-specific heuristics to generate probes based on the surface features of the problem specification. The task of case retrieval takes as input the probes generated by the problem elaboration component. It has the goal of accessing a design case and the associated SBF model whose functional specification is similar to the specification of desired design. KRITIK3's case memory is organized in a discrimination tree, with features in the functional specifications of the design cases acting as the discriminants. Its retrieval method searches through this discrimination tree to find the case that most closely matches the probe.

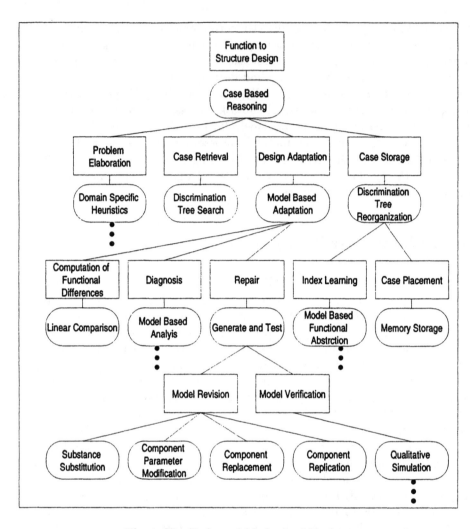

Fig. 1. The Tasks and Methods of KRITIK3

The task of design adaptation takes as input (i) the specification of the constraints on the desired design, and (ii) the specifications of the constraints on and the structure of the candidate design. It has the goal of giving as output a modified design structure that satisfies the specified constraints. KRITIK3 uses a model-based method of design adaptation which divides the design task into three subtasks: *computation of functional differences*, *diagnosis*, and *repair*. The idea here is that the candidate design can be viewed as a failed attempt to accomplish the desired specifications. The old design is first checked to see how its functionality differs from the desired functionality. The model of the design is then analyzed in detail to determine one or more possible causes for the observed difference. Lastly, KRITIK3 makes modifications to the device with the intent of inducing the desired functionality.

The method of repair used by KRITIK3 is *generate and test*. This method sets up two subtasks of the repair task: *model revision* and *model verification*. The task of model revision takes as input (i) the specification of the constraints on the desired design, and (ii) the model of the candidate design. It has the goal of giving as output a modified model that is expected to satisfy the constraints on the desired design. KRITIK3 knows of several model revision methods such as the substitution of one component for another or the replication of a component. KRITIK3 dynamically chooses a method for model revision at run time based on the results of the diagnosis task. Depending on the modification goals set up by the diagnosis task, the system may also use more than one model-revision method.

The task of model verification takes as input (i) the specification of the constraints on the desired design, and (ii) the specification of the structure of the modified design. It has the goal of giving as output an evaluation of whether the modified structure satisfies the specified constraints. KRITIK3 qualitatively simulates the revised SBF model to verify whether it delivers the functions desired of it.

The task of case storage takes as input (i) a specification of the case memory, and (ii) a specification of a new case. It has the goal of giving as output a specification of the new case memory with the new case appropriately indexed and organized in it. Recall that KRITIK3's case memory is organized in a discrimination tree. The system uses a model-based method for the task of storing a new case in the tree. This method sets up the subtasks of *indexing learning* and *case placement*. The SBF model of the new design case enables the learning of the appropriate index to the new case. This directly enables the task of case placement.

4 INTERACTIVE KRITIK

INTERACTIVE KRITIK is an interactive design environment that illustrates both KRITIK3's case-based reasoning and the device designs generated by the system (Goel et al 1995; Gruei1994). When completed, INTERACTIVE KRITIK is intended to serve as a constructive design and learning environment. At present, when asked by a human user INTERACTIVE KRITIK can invoke KRITIK3 to address specific kinds of design problems. In addition, INTERACTIVE KRITIK can provide explanations and justifications of KRITIK3's reasoning and results, enable the human user to explore the system's design knowledge, and also enable the user to access a library of meta-cases for examining specific reasoning traces. In this section, we describe only how INTERACTIVE KRITIK explains the case-based reasoning in KRITIK3, not the device designs the system generates.[1]

4.1 Explanation of Case-Based Reasoning in INTERACTIVE KRITIK

INTERACTIVE KRITIK's architecture consists of two agents: a case-based design

---

[1] INTERACTIVE KRITIK's explanation of devices is described in (Goel et al 1996).

agent in the form of KRITIK3 and an user interface agent[2]. The architecture of INTERACTIVE KRITIK is illustrated in Figure 2; in this figure solid lines represent data flow while dotted lines represent control flow.

Kritk3   Interface Agent

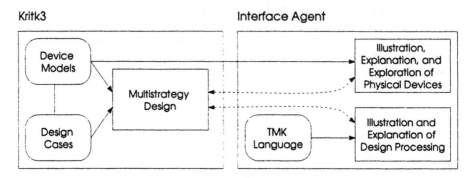

Fig. 2. INTERACTIVE KRITIK's Architecture

The interface agent in INTERACTIVE KRITIK has access to all the knowledge of KRITIK3 including its design cases and device models. It uses KRITIK3's structure-behavior-function (SBF) models of physical devices to graphically illustrate and explain the functioning of the devices to the users. It uses the TMK model of KRITIK3's case-based reasoning to graphically illustrate and explain how the system generates a new design. The trace of this reasoning is available for inspection in the form of a meta-case.

The application of multi-strategy case-based reasoning in INTERACTIVE KRITIK is illustrated to the user on several interrelated screens. Figure 3 shows the first task screen in INTERACTIVE KRITIK. It informs the user that the current task is the Design task. It also shows that KRITIK3 is planning to use the Case-Based Reasoning method, and displays the subtasks that are set up by this method: Problem Elaboration, Case Retrieval, Design Adaptation, and Case Storage.

INTERACTIVE KRITIK provides a set of screens for presenting the user with information about the input and output of the subtasks and uses highlighting features to inform the user of the reasoning state: which tasks have already been performed, what is the current task and what subtasks are left. For example, Figure 4 shows the representation of the subtasks set up by the *Model-Based Adaptation* method used for the *design adaptation* task. It illustrates a deeper level of KRITIK3's task-method decomposition.

4.2 Reflection on Case-Based Reasoning in INTERACTIVE KRITIK

INTERACTIVE KRITIK makes available its reasoning traces in the form of meta-cases. The TMK representation of the trace of reasoning enables the user to

---

[2] The interface is built using the Garnet tool (Myers and Zanden 1992).

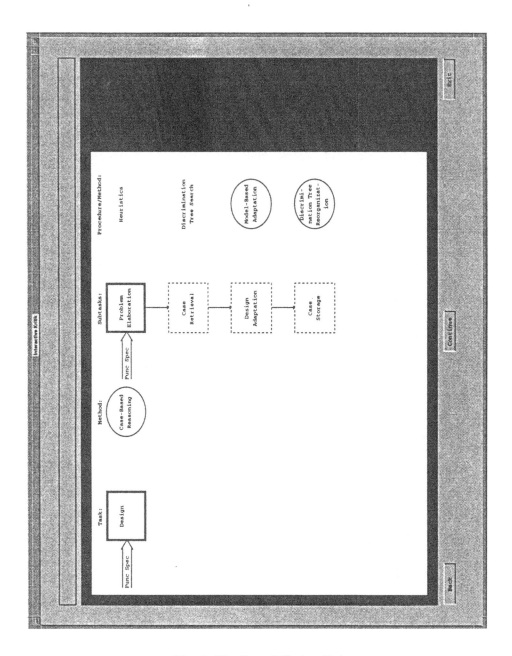

Fig. 3. The Overall Design Task

158

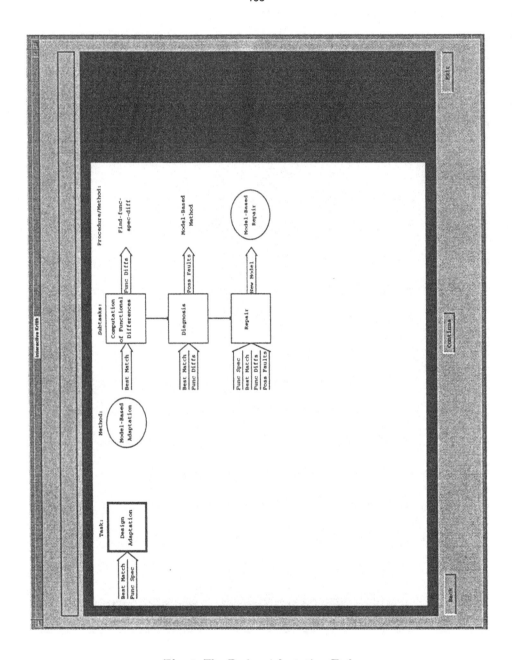

Fig. 4. The Design Adaptation Task

inspect each task, method, knowledge source, and reasoning state. This enables the user to reflect on the design reasoning. For example, the user can examine the TMK reasoning trace and detect potential flaws in it.

The user can also ask INTERACTIVE KRITIK for a justification for some kinds of reasoning choices. As an example, consider the situation in which INTERACTIVE KRITIK is given a problem, INTERACTIVE KRITIK invokes KRITIK3 to solve the problem, and, during the course of reasoning, KRITIK3 retrieves a design case from its case memory. The meta-case for this design episode shows the user the probe KRITIK3 had prepared to retrieve a case and the case the system actually retrieved from its case memory. The user can now ask why did KRITIK3 retrieve this particular design case. Since the reasoning trace explicitly specifies the probe prepared by KRITIK3, and how the system's retrieval method probed the case memory - the branches it followed, the matches it made, and their results. In this way, the trace provides a justification for why the particular case best matches the given problem.

5 Discussion

In this section, we compare our work with related research on explanation in interactive case-based environments. In addition, we critique INTERACTIVE KRITIK and point to further work needed on it.

5.1 Related Research

We already have pointed out the relationship between our work on explanation of case-based reasoning and task-oriented theories of problem solving and explanation. In particular, our use of the TMK model for explaining case-based reasoning is an extension of Chandrasekaran, Tanner and Josephson's (1989) use of Task Structures for explanation of control strategies. The literature on the use of task models of problem solving for explanation and reflection is vast (e.g. (Arcos and Plaza 1994)), and we will not cover it here in its full generality. Instead, we focus on the relationship of our work with other interactive case-based problem-solving and design environments.

AI research has led to the development of several paradigms of case-based reasoning and numerous laboratory case-based systems. Kolodner (1993) provides a recent summary of the main paradigms and a compilation of the major systems. Maher, Balachandran and Zhang (1995) provide a recent summary of major case-based design systems, such as their own CADSYN and CASECAD systems, CADET (Sycara et al 1991), CADRE (Hua and Faltings), and FABEL (Voss et al 1994). None of these interactive design environments provide any kind of explanatory interface. This is also true of our own earlier work on interactive case-based design aiding systems such as Archie (Pearce et al 1992), AskJef (Barber et al 1992) and ArchieTutor (Goel et al 1993). These systems provided human designers with access to design case libraries in different domains. AskJef, for example, used multi-media (text, graphics, animation and sound) for enabling the navigation and browsing of a library of annotated design cases in the domain of software interface design. While the case annotations provided an explanation of the designs, they did not provide an adequate explanation of case-based reasoning itself.

The JANUS system of Fischer et al (1992) and BOGART system of Mostow (1989) are two notable exceptions to this. Like INTERACTIVE KRITIK, both JANUS and BOGART provide explanation in the form of reasoning traces. Unlike INTERACTIVE KRITIK, the reasoning traces in both are part of the object cases themselves. Fischer et al have advocated that interactive design environments should provide access not just to a catalog of past designs but also to the reasoning that led to the specific designs in the catalog. Their JANUS system adopts the issue-based view of group problem solving (Rittel 1972), and provides a user with a trace of the issues that arose in a past design problem-solving episode, the arguments made for and against various design choices, and the justifications for the design decisions. Fischer et al argue that the issue-based trace of past design problem-solving episodes enables the user to make arguments for and against a specific design choice in the context of new problems, and, thus, empowers the user to create more effective designs.

Mostow adopts a similar stance towards the knowledge content of design cases in interactive design environments. Based on Carbonell's (1983, 1986) framework of derivational analogy, Mostow's BOGART system provides a user with traces of past design problem-solving episodes in the language of goals, operators, and heuristics for goal decomposition and operator selection. He argues that this derivational record of the problem solving in a past design case enables the user to more effectively transfer knowledge from the past case to the new problem.

While INTERACTIVE KRITIK shares this explanatory stance with JANUS and BOGART, we believe that the usefulness and usability of the reasoning traces used in these earlier systems are limited. The difficulty with the JANUS scheme is that it uses an informal language for representing the trace: what is (and what is not) a valid design issue, a valid argument for a design choice, a valid justification for a design decision? This informal specification may be the best that can be accomplished in recording the design rationale, i.e., the trace of decision making in a group. But in the case of explaining problem solving in an interactive system, it is possible to automate the process of explanation generation. And the difficulty with the BOGART scheme is that it represents the trace at too low a level of abstraction, e.g., operators, operator selection, and operator selection heuristics. This makes for a poor explanatory interface. Our argument mirrors Clancey's argument against the explanatory interface of his own Guidon system, which too explained problem solving in the language of goals, rules, rule activation, and rule activation heuristics. Thus JANUS's language for representing traces of design problem solving is too informal to be automated, and BOGART's language is too low level to be useful or usable in an interactive setting. The TMK language for specifying meta-cases in INTERACTIVE KRITIK, we believe, addresses both shortcomings.

5.2 Critique

There is still a great deal of work to be done on INTERACTIVE KRITIK's user interface. As we mentioned in the introduction, so far we have focused on the content and generation of explanations, not on the display and presentation of explanations. Some issues which would need to be addressed before INTERACTIVE KRITIK can be used as a practical tool include the improved display of explanations, the building of better graphical representations, and provision of additional interaction capabilities. We recognize that INTERACTIVE KRITIK needs to be formally evaluated in a real world setting. But this kind of evaluation too requires additional work on the user interface.

5.3 Conclusions

Explanation is an important issue in the design of interactive case-based environments. In fact, if past experience in use of knowledge systems in real work environments is any guide, then explanation of problem solving is a critical issue in moving case-based systems out of the laboratory. Past experience with knowledge systems also indicates that explanations need to capture the functional, strategic and knowledge content of reasoning at the *task level*.

Meta-cases that contain reasoning traces of problem solving provide one way for explaining case-based problem solving. But to be useful and usable, meta-cases need to specify the trace at the task level. The Task-Method-Knowledge is a general task-level model of problem solving that sets up a virtual architecture for the problem solver. Meta-cases correspond to a specific instantiation of this virtual architecture for a particular problem. This insures that the meta-cases specify the task-level content and organization of reasoning. INTERACTIVE KRITIK demonstrates the computational feasibility of using meta-cases for explaining case-based reasoning.

Acknowledgments

Sambasiva Bhatta, Andrés Gómez, Murali Shankar, and Eleni Stroulia contributed to the programming of KRITIK3, while Michael Donahoo, Andrés Gómez, Gregory Grace, and Nathalie Grué contributed to the programming of INTERACTIVE KRITIK. This work has benefited from many discussions with T. Govindaraj and Margaret Recker. It has been funded in part by a grant from the Advanced Research Projects Agency (research contract #F33615-93-1-1338) and partly by internal seed grants from Georgia Tech's Educational Technology Institute, College of Computing, Cognitive Science Program, and Graphics, Visualization and Usability Center.

References

Arcos, L. and Plaza, E. A Reflective Architecture for Integrated Memory-Based Learning and Reasoning. In *Lecture Notes in Artificial Intelligence - 837*, pp. 289-300, Berlin: Springer-Verlag, 1994.

Barber, J., Jacobson, M., Penberthy, L., Simpson, R., Bhatta, S., Goel, A., Pearce, M., Shankar, M., and Stroulia, E. Integrating Artificial Intelligence and Multimedia Technologies for Interface Design Advising. *NCR Journal of Research and Development*,6(1):75-85, October 1992.

Carbonell, J. Learning by Analogy: Formulating and Generalizing Plans from Past Experience. *Machine Learning: An Artificial Intelligence Approach*, R. Michalski, J. Carbonell, and T. Mitchell (editors). Palo Alto, CA: Tioga, 1983.

Carbonell, J. Derivational Analogy: A Theory of Reconstructive Problem Solving and Expertise Acquisition. *Machine Learning: An Artificial Intelligence Approach, Volume II*, R. Michalski, J. Carbonell, and T. Mitchell (editors). San Mateo, CA: Morgan Kauffman, 1986.

Chandrasekaran, B. Generic Tasks as Building Blocks for Knowledge-Based Systems: The Diagnosis and Routine Design Examples. *Knowledge Engineering Review*, 3(3):183-219, 1988.

Chandrasekaran, B. Task Structures, Knowledge Acquisition and Machine Learning. *Machine Learning*, 4:341-347.

Chandrasekaran, B. Design Problem Solving: A Task Analysis. *AI Magazine*, 59-71. Winter 1990.

Chandrasekaran, B., Tanner, M., and Josephson, J. Explaining Control Strategies in Problem Solving. *IEEE Expert*, 4(1):9-24, 1989.

Clancey, W. Heuristic Classification. *Artificial Intelligence*, 27(3): 289-350, 1985.

Clancey, W. *Knowledge-Based Tutoring: The Guidon Program*. Cambridge. MA: MIT Press, 1987.

Fischer, G., Grudin, J., Lemke, A., McCall, R., Ostwald, J., Reeves, B. and Shipman, F. Supporting Indirect Collaborative Design with Integrated Knowledge-Based Design Environment. *Human-Computer Interactions*, 7(3):281-314, 1992.

Goel, A. A Model-based Approach to Case Adaptation. *Proc. Thirteenth Annual Conference of the Cognitive Science Society*, Lawrence Erlbaum Associates, pp. 143-148, August 1991.

Goel, A. Representation of Design Functions in Experience-Based Design. *Intelligent Computer Aided Design*, D. Brown, M. Waldron, and H. Yoshikawa (editors), North-Holland, pp. 283-308, 1992.

Goel, A. and Chandrasekaran, B. Functional Representation of Designs and Redesign Problem Solving. *Proc. Eleventh International Joint Conference on Artificial Intelligence*, Morgan Kaufmann Publishers, pp. 1388-1394, 1989.

Goel, A. and Chandrasekaran, B. Case-Based Design: A Task Analysis. In *Artificial Intelligence Approaches to Engineering Design, Volume II: Innovative Design*, Tong and D. Sriram (editors), Academic Press, pp. 165-184, 1992.

Goel, A., Pearce, M., Malkawi, A. and Liu, K. A Cross-Domain Experiment in Case-Based Design Support: ARCHIETUTOR. *Proc. AAAI Workshop on Case-Based Reasoning*, pp. 111-117, 1993.

Goel, A., Gomez, A., Grue, N., Murdock, J. W., Recker, M., and Govindaraj, T. Design Explanations in Interactive Design Environments. In *Proc. Fourth International Conference on AI in Design*, Palo Alto, June 1996.

Gru, N.é. Illustration, Explanation and Navigation of Physical Devices and Design Processes. M.Thesis, S., College of Computing, Georgia Institute of Technology, June 1994.

Hua, K. and Faltings, B. Exploring Case-Based Building Design - CADRE. *AI(EDAM)*, 7(2):135-143, 1993.

Kolodner, J. *Case-Based Reasoning*, Sam Mateo, CA: Morgan Kauffman, 1993.

McDermott, J. Preliminary Steps Towards a Taxonomy of Problem Solving Methods. *Automating Knowledge Acquisition for Expert Systems*, S. Marcus (editor), Kluwer, Boston, MA, 1988.

Maher, M. L., Balachandran, M. B., and Zhang, D. *Case-Based Reasoning in Design*, Erlbaum, Hillsdale, NJ, 1995.

Mostow, J. Design by Derivational Analogy: Issues in the Automated Replay of Design Plans. *Artificial Intelligence*. 1989.

Myers, B. and Zanden, B. Environment for rapidly creating interactive design tools. *Visual Computer*, 8:94-116, 1992.

Pearce, M., Goel, A., Kolodner, J., Zimring, C., Sentosa, L. and Billington, R. Case-Based Design Support: A Case Study in Architectural Design. *IEEE Expert*. 7(5):14-20, 1992.

Rittel, H. On the Planning Crisis: System Analysis of the First and Second Generations. *Bedriftsokonomen*, 8:390-396, 1972.

Shortliffe, E. Computer-Based Medical Consultation: MYCIN, New York: American Elsevier, 1976.

Steels, L. Components of Expertise. *AI Magazine*, 11(2):29-49, 1988.

Stroulia, E. and Goel, A. A Model-Based Approach to Reflective Learning. In *Proc. 1994 European Conference on Machine Learning*, Catania, Italy, April 1994, pp. 287-306; available as *Lecture Notes in Artificial Intelligence 784 - Machine Learning*, F. Bergadano and L. De Raedt (editors), Berlin: Springer-Verlag, 1994.

Stroulia, E. and Goel, A. Reflective Self-Adaptive Problem Solvers. In *Proc. 1994 European Conference on Knowledge Acquisition*, Germany, September 1994; available as *Lecture Notes in Artificial Intelligence - A Future for Knowledge Acquisition*, L. Steels, G. Schreiber, and W. Van de Velde (editors), Berlin: Springer-Verlag, 1994.

Voss, A., Coulon, C-H, Grather, W., Linowski, B., Schaaf, J., Barstsch, Sporl, B., Borner, K., Tammer, E., Durscke, H., and Knauff, M. Retrieval of Similar Layouts - About a Very Hybrid Approach in FABEL. *Proc. Third International Conference on AI in Design*, Lausanne, pp 625-640, August 1994.

Wielinga, B., Schreiber, G. and Breuker, J. KADS: A Modelling Approach to Knowledge Acquisition. *Knowledge Engineering*, 4:5-53, 1992.

A Two Layer Case-Based Reasoning Architecture for Medical Image Understanding

Morten Grimnes and Agnar Aamodt

Department of Informatics
Norwegian University of Science and Technology
N-7034 Trondheim, Norway

Abstract. The paper describes a novel architecture for image understanding. It is based on acquisition of radiologist knowledge, and combines low-level structure analysis with high-level interpretation of image content, within a task-oriented model. A case based reasoner working on a segment case-base contains the individual image segments. These cases with labels are considered indexes for another case based reasoner working on an organ interpretation case base. Both are Creek type case based reasoners, here operating within a propose-critique-modify task structure. Methods for criticizing suggested interpretations by way of explanation, and how interpretations may be modified, are presented. An example run illustrates the system architecture and its key concepts.

1 Introduction

Image understanding has turned out to be a very difficult application task for AI methods. Methods exist that are able to do edge detection, and to some extent object identification, but methods for interpreting and understanding the content and meaning of whole pictures are less developed [Chellappa 92]. In the research reported here we address the interpretation of medical images, and in particular CT images. Computer Tomography (CT) is a widespread medical imaging technique which scans and displays a cross-section of the body using a type of X-rays. The images are mainly used for diagnostic purposes, as part of the overall patient examination procedure. The interpretation is therefore highly influenced by other patient data and the expectations they set up. We are exploring ways to combine lower-level segment identification with a higher level interpretation and understanding of the image as a whole. A segment, in this context, refers to an area of the image corresponding to an anatomical object or a significant part of one, for example an area picturing a liver.

At the core of our approach are two case-based reasoners, one for segment identification and one for the more wholistic interpretation of the image, corresponding to two layers of the system architecture. CBR covers a wide range of specific methods, ranging from syntactic pattern recognition type of methods [Wess 94][Aha 95], to knowledge-intensive methods oriented towards semantic and pragmatic contents [Leake 93][Aamodt 94a]. This makes CBR potentially suitable for both low and higher level image analysis, and for exploring the interfacing and the cooperative interpretation effort between the two layers. CBR methods at each of the two layers will accomplish different subtasks of the overall diagnostic task. This calls for a task oriented architecture, in which the medical diagnosis task is broken down into subtasks, and each subtask assigned to a particular part of the system. Methods are in turn assigned to each subtask, and each method specify the type and form of knowledge (cases as well as more general knowledge) that it requires. This results in an explicit problem solving and learning architecture targeted at the medical, diagnostic, image interpretation task.

Although simple diagnostic tasks best can be viewed as classification problem solving, the type of diagnosis we talk about here cannot. Detailed medical diagnosis involves planning of the diagnostic process as well as hypotheses construction, testing, reformulation, etc., making it more like a synthesis task than a pure classification one. In our case, the lack of a predefined, fixed set of image interpretations, and the complex process of arriving at an interpretation, has lead us to look into methods for construction and design problem solving to describe the overall image interpretation process. This type of method decomposes the top-level diagnostic image interpretation task into subtasks for which more detailed case-based methods in turn can be specified.

The focus of the paper is how explanation-driven case based reasoning methods (the Creek approach [Aamodt 91][Aamodt 94a]) fruitfully can be employed in the task of understanding abdominal CT images, within an architecture of two distinct but cooperating case bases. The next section gives a brief review of methods relevant for medical image understanding in general. Section 3 introduces the two-layered architecture within the framework of a generic design task model, and relate the subtasks to the reasoning methods within a Creek CBR system. In section 4 the task model of our system, named *ImageCreek*, is detailed, and the corresponding reasoning methods are described through an example. Discussion and status of research close the paper.

2 Methods for Tomographic Image Understanding

2.1 Medical image interpretation systems

There are a large number of medical image interpretation systems in the literature. Conventional image interpreting architectures [Swett 93][Gonzales 92] have also been employed in interpreting abdominal CT images [Englmeier 93]. Unfortunately, these architectures are characterized by performance brittleness and a lack of learning capability. A sufficient degree of system robustness as well as an ability to continuously learn from problem solving experiences are important for open-textured, weak-theory domains such as ours.

Beyond the conventional approaches, some systems focus on architectural aspects, others on knowledge modeling methods. Recent examples of architectural variations are a blackboard system with a hypothesize-and-test reasoning cycle for the radiological domain [Davis 91], an architecture based on genetic programming in which learning plays an important role [Teller 95], and a flexible architecture where image interpretation is viewed as a planning task [Gong 95]. Examples of systems where knowledge modeling plays an important role are the ERNEST system that has been applied to the interpretation of scintigraphic images and MRIs [Kummert 93], two systems on cranial MRI interpretation that feature knowledge modeling [Vernazza 87][Menhardt], a blackboard architecture featuring four diagnostic strategies in the radiological domain [Rogers 95], and a belief network based diagnostic decision aid on MRI liver lesions [Tombropoulos 94]. Characteristic of all the latter systems is that they lack a learning component.

In case-based reasoning there are a few examples of systems that are concerned with medical images. In the ROENTGEN system [Berger] therapy planning based on tomographic images is the object of reasoning. Radiologic image retrieval based on image captions and content related queries is the focus in the MacRad system [Macura 95]. None of these systems attempt to interpret images. The authors know of only one case based system that interprets medical images. This is the SCINA system [Haddad 95], which is based on the commercially available ESTEEM CBR tool. The system features a rule base for case adaptation and a case is represented as a matrix of integers. It seems the system features a limited possibility of knowledge modeling and is likely to experience the above mentioned brittleness problems.

Several support tools for general image analysis exist. In the implemented version of ImageCreek we are use the publicly available Khoros (version 2.0, from Khoral Research Inc.) image processing environment, for segmenting the image from the CT scanner.

2.2 Acquisition and modeling for abdominal CT understanding

Together with a radiology expert, a knowledge level analysis of the domain was made, as described in [Grimnes-96a]. In interpreting abdominal CT images radiologists tend to consider each projected anatomical entity separately, while at the same time combining the diagnostic hypotheses and findings for each entity into a complete image interpretation (see also [Wegener 92]). Wholistic aspects of the image and considerations pertaining to how well findings and hypotheses for each entity fit in with each other are crucial as well [Grimnes 96b].

Medical diagnosis in general is a complex type of diagnosis, which is tightly linked to examination procedures, diagnostic hypothesis formulation, testing and modification of hypotheses, etc. Often a preliminary diagnostic interpretation is arrived at which then has to be confirmed or rejected through a non-risky treatment regime. A task analysis of the abdominal CT interpretation problem reveals a type of problem and a set of tasks that in their scope and complexity to a larger degree conforms with solution synthesis than simple solution classification into a limited set of predefined categories. Our knowledge analysis and modeling approach is to a large extent based on the Components of Expertise framework [Steels-90], and some experiments performed within the Creest workbench [Winnem 96] (an extension of the KREST knowledge modeling tool [Steels 93] that incorporates the CreekL knowledge representation language). Our work has also been strongly influenced by the Generic Tasks [Chandrasekaran 93] and CommonKADS [Wielinga 93] methodologies. However, unlike the latter methodologies we put a strong emphasis on reducing the dependency on top-level modeling in favor of bottom-up, iterative model development - both in the system development phase and through sustained learning during system operation [Aamodt-95]. Our "world model" is decomposed into:

- A **Task** model where we principally look at the question of "what" is to be achieved and how specific tasks may be broken down into subtasks.

- A **Method** model where we look at how the tasks may be realized and how control flow is handled. In modeling methods we address the question of "how".

- A **Domain Knowledge** model where we specify what kind of knowledge is necessary for achieving the tasks in terms of the available methods.

2.3 Integrated problem solving and sustained learning

The ImageCreek architecture is designed and implemented within the Creek system for knowledge-intensive case-based problem solving and learning. Cases, as well as general domain knowledge and information are captured in the frame-based representation language CreekL. A knowledge model represented in CreekL is viewed as a dense semantic network, where each node (concept) and each link (relation) in the network is explicitly defined in its own frame. A concept may be a general concept, a case, or a heuristic rule, and may describe domain objects as well as problem solving methods and strategies. The case-based method of Creek relies heavily on an extensive body of general domain knowledge in its problem understanding, similarity assessment, case adaptation, and learning.

The underlying case-based interpreter in Creek contains a three-step process of 1) activating relevant parts of the semantic network, 2) explaining derived consequences and new information within the activated knowledge structure, and 3) focusing towards a conclusion that conforms with the task goal. This "activate-explain-focus" cycle, is a general mechanism that has been specialized for each of the four major reasoning tasks of the CBR cycle [Aamodt 94b]. This is illustrated in Figure 1.

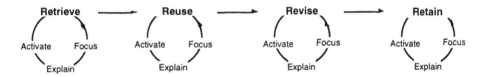

FIGURE 1. The CBR process and the explanation engine

The extensive, explanation-driven way of utilizing general domain knowledge in the CBR subtasks is a feature that distinguishes Creek from most other CBR systems.

A Creek system has the potential to learn from every problem solving experience. If a successful solution was directly copied from, or just slightly modified on the basis of a previous case, the reminding to that case from each relevant feature is strengthened, and no new case is stored. If a solution was derived by significantly modifying a previous solution, a new case is stored and difference links between the two cases are established. A new case is also created after a problem has been solved from rules or from the deeper knowledge model alone. The user is assumed to actively take part in both the problem solving and learning processes, e.g. by assessing hypotheses that the system cannot confirm or reject itself, supplying missing information, etc.

3 A system architecture for medical image understanding

3.1 A generic task model for medical image understanding

Inspired by work on Generic Design Tasks [Chandrasekaran 90], and in view of our knowledge acquisition findings, we have adapted a *"propose-critique-modify"* generic problem solving method. The method breaks down the top-level task of suggesting a diagnosis based on the CT image, into the four main subtasks:

- **Propose.** *Task* is to propose possible solutions. *Input* is a problem description and context. *Output* is a ranked list of possible solutions with normalized justifications. The solutions mark the spectre of likely and less likely solutions.

- **Verify.** *Task* is to verify that the solution(s) proposed fits the problem description. *Input* is a set of top ranked solutions and problem description. *Output* is a verified solution or failure with normalized justifications.

- **Critique.** *Task* is to look at what failed and propose a strategy for how the solution may be modified so as to better fit the problem description. *Input* is a normalized justifications on why verification failed, the failed solution in question and problem description. *Output* is a solution amendment strategy.

- **Modify.** *Task* is to realize the amendment strategy. *Input* is an amendment strategy, the failed solution, normalized justifications and problem description. *Output* is an amended solution.

3.2 A two layer approach to medical image understanding

In light of how radiologists seem to work and how current image processing algorithms are designed, we propose a two-layered architecture, corresponding to two case bases storing two different kinds of experience and supporting two different kinds of solutions. One layer lays on top of the other and both employ the *propose-verify-critique-modify* framework distinctly:

- The **Segment ImageCreek** Task layer (**SICT**). At this level we work with image segments (i.e. subsets of the image sharing some similarity) in isolation.

  i. In the *case base*, a case is a description of a segment possibly together with a tentative pathologic/anatomical hypothesis as well as any previously rejected hypotheses with justifications. In this paper we use the term *segment hypothesis* denoting such a label (i.e. a case description of part of an image). Some of the hypotheses may be pathological labels, others may be normal anatomical labels and some may neither be pathological nor anatomical due to imaging or therapeutic artifacts.

  ii. The type of *method* associated with this layer is to only look at one segment description at a time and suggest a segment hypothesis of each single segment.

- The **Wholistic ImageCreek** Task layer (**WICT**). At this level we work with the entire image in question. We try to reach an overall image interpretation where all the different segments with suitable segment hypotheses fit in with each other and with the general problem description context.

  i. In the *case base*, a case is a set of segments with diagnostic segment hypotheses together with the problem description not pertaining to single segments only, as well as any previously rejected segment hypotheses with justifications. In this paper we use the term *image interpretation* denoting such a case description.

  ii. The type of *method* associated with this layer is to look at the broader aspects and the totality of the all the segment hypotheses in light of the problem description context and the findings not pertaining to a particular segment only.

4 The abdominal CT image understanding task

4.1 The generic model instantiated

We have instantiated the generic *"propose-verify-modify"* method with its *propose-verify-critique-modify* subtasks in light of the two case based reasoning layers described in section 3.2. The resulting task structure is illustrated in Figure 2. At the WICT level the object that is proposed, verified, possibly criticized and modified is an image interpretation. At the SICT level the object is a segment hypothesis. The input-output requirements are described in Table 1 based on the generic design in section 3.1.

There are two subtasks of the top ImageCreekTask (Figure 2) that will not be further described here. They are:

- **AcquireProblemDescription** - This task achieves three principal functions. It acquires all kinds of non-image findings like patient details and examination specifics. It furthermore plans an appropriate image segmentation procedure based on the non-image findings and finally executes the plan (segments the image). This task is outside the scope of this article.

- **ImageCreekLearn** - Top level task for the learning process in ImageCreek, corresponding to the Retrieve task in Figure 1. This task is not covered in this article, but briefly it is a combination of failure driven learning and case integration initiated at the end of a case based reasoning cycle. The expert may be requested to volunteer new knowledge in case of reasoning problems.

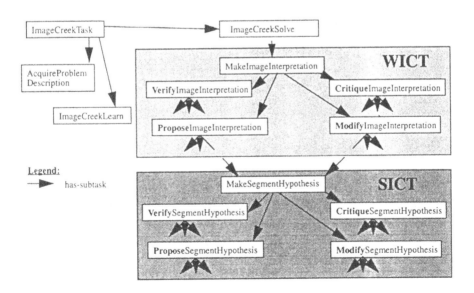

FIGURE 2. The two layer propose-verify-critique-modify task hierarchy in ImageCreek

Task	Input	Output
ProposeImageIn-terpretation	Input image interpretation case findings, Domain Knowledge	Ranked list of previous image interpretations (cases), context activated knowledge, normalized justifications
ProposeSegment-Hypothesis	Input segment case findings, Domain Knowledge	Ranked list of previous segments with hypotheses (cases), context activated knowledge, normalized justifications
VerifyImagenter-pretation	Proposed image interpretation cases, input image interpretation case, context activated knowledge	Normalized justifications and verification decision
VerifySegmentHy-pothesis	Proposed segmentation cases, input segmentation case, context activated knowledge	Normalized justifications an verification decision
CritiqueImageIn-terpretation	Normalized criticism, proposed image interpretation case, input image interpretation case	Modification strategy or failure
CritiqueSegment-Hypothesis	Normalized criticism, proposed segmentation case, input segmentation case	Modification strategy or failure
ModifyImageInter-pretation	Modification strategy, ranked list of proposed image interpretations, input image interpretation case, normalized justifications	New interpretation case or failure with resegmentation flag set or unset
ModifySegmentHy-pothesis	Modification strategy, ranked list of proposed segments with segment hypotheses, input segment case, context activated knowledge	New segment hypothesis or failure

TABLE 1. Input and output for the Propose, Verify, Critique and Modify tasks

4.2 The SICT-WICT interface

The interaction between the segment and wholistic level is a core issue in the architecture (see Figure 3). The interaction takes place basically through two interfaces:

1. In **proposing an image interpretation**: We achieve ProposeImageInterpretation by first generating possible image interpretations (GenerateInterpretations). Generation is achieved by direct reminding to earlier cases (ProposeInterpretationFrom-InterpretationCases) and by hypothesizing new diagnostic labels for all the segments output from the image processing subsystem (ProposeInterpretationBy-SegmentIntegration). The process of finding diagnostic segment hypotheses for the various segments is the main task of SICT (section 3.2). The MakeSegmentHy-

pothesis task is the main SIC Task whereas MakeSegmentHypotheses is a task that combines a set of segments that are assigned the same diagnostic segment hypothesis into one complex entity.

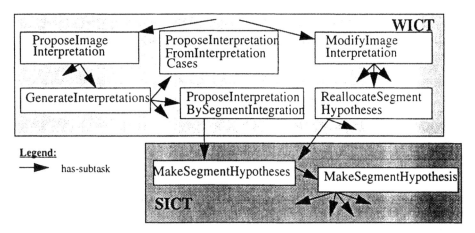

FIGURE 3. The SICT-WICT interface

2. In **modifying an image interpretation**: One way of modifying a solution is to alter parts of it. This is the task of ReallocateSegmentHypothesis. ReallocateSegment-Hypotheses looks at the justifications of the image interpretation and bases it´s judgement on how well a segment hypothesis seems to fit in on this. The ones having the weakest justifications are picked, and MakeSegmentHypotheses is requested to suggest new segment hypotheses for these.

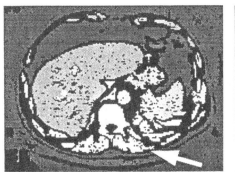 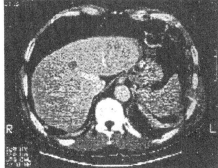

FIGURE 4. The segmented version (left) of an example input image (right). Arrow indicates example segment (section 4.3)

4.3 Proposing an image interpretation.

Below we illustrate key aspects of this reasoning process by presenting excerpts from an example run of ImageCreekSolve. Let´s assume we have acquired a problem description (AcquireProblemDescription in figure 2) of the right image in Figure 4.

The description is the input problem case to the ImageCreek system and includes general non-image findings pertaining to the patient and examination:. The image segmentation produced by Khoros comes as additional input.

icase-b1-1-t001

...   ...

has-sex	male	has-exam-modality	ct
has-age	seventies-years	has-exam-machine-id	rit-old-ct
has-earlier-diagnosis	lung-cancer	has-contrast-injection-type	prolonged
has-earlier-diagnosis-time-ago	ayear-threeyears-ago	has-contrast-time	portovenuous
has-social-condition	retirement-home	has-ct-slicethickness	ten-mm
has-habit	smoker	has-ct-angle	zero-degrees

...   ...

Image interpretations are suggested by the subtask GenerateInterpretations (Figure 3). The task is achieved in two principal ways, through case remindings from findings - so that ProposeInterpretationFromInterpretationCases is able to retrieve a set of earlier cases, or by hypothesizing a diagnostic label for each image segment. Let us take a closer look at the latter:

Based on the problem description, a number of segments cases are retrieved. One of the cases looks like:

scase-b1-1-42-bp

instance-of	no-heart-or-kidney-level-scase	has-ventral-bb	dorsal
has-size	spine-size	has-intensity	sixties-hu
is-left-right	narrow-lr-centre	has-stdev	stdev-large-hu
is-ventral-dorsal	dorsal	has-contrast-injection-type	prolongued
has-orientation	left-right	has-contrast-time	portovenuous
has-eccentricity	slightly-eccentric	has-exam-purpose	routine-search-for-abnormality
has-left-bb	left-centre	has-ct-bodysection	nokidney-noheart-level-region
has-right-bb	narrow-lr-centre		

ImageCreek does two things to each of these segment cases early in the ProposeImageInterpretation process:

1. Each segment receives a diagnostic hypothesis. This is the overall goal of SICT and in our example the segment scase-b1-1-42-bp is assigned this hypothesis (MakeSegmentHypothesis achieves this):

   has-segment-hypothesis   c-nok-noh-left-erector-spinae

2. In each segment there are certain findings that are relevant to the interpretation of the entire image. These are extracted and integrated into the input image interpretation case. This is achieved by ProposeInterpretationBySegmentIntegration. The *transformed* **scase-b1-1-42-bp** then looks like:

...		...	
has-left-erector-spinae-scase	(scase-b1-1-42-bp)	has-left-erector-spinae-left-bb	left-centre
has-left-erector-spinae-hypothesis	c-nok-noh-left-erector-spinae[a]	has-left-erector-spinae-right-bb	narrow-lr-centre
is-left-erector-spinae-left-right	narrow-lr-centre	has-left-erector-spinae-ventral-bb	dorsal
is-left-erector-spinae-ventral-dorsal	dorsal	has-left-erector-spinae-dorsal-bb	extreme-dorsal
...		...	

a. The erector spinae is a muscle adjacent to the spine. The abbreviation c-nok-noh is simply an abbreviation of contrast-no-kidney-no-heart-level which is indicates the entity´s position in an anatomical classification hierarchy.

Findings pertaining to the image segments undergo several transformations, some in AcquireProblemDescription, others in MakeSegmentHypotheses. They therefore rely on image segmentation functions. Further, they get associated with a medically relevant segment hypothesis. This has consequences:

• We cannot simply accept the findings as true by default. Findings pertaining to image segments must be **questioned** and possibly **rejected**

• In rejecting findings we need a mechanism for **evaluating the quality of the findings** as well as **handling the rejection**. This is partly what we try to do in Critique-ImageInterpretation and ModifyImageInterpretation respectively.

4.4 Testing and Verifying an image interpretation

In ProposeImageInterpretation the generated interpretations are tested for relevance in terms of explaining how serious syntactic differences between solution (retrieved cases) and problem description (input case) are. In VerifyImageInterpretation we generate expected findings of the retrieved case and explain how these are met in the input case. This task, as well as the other high-level tasks, have their own detailed subtask structure not elaborated here.

The explanation process is handled by a particular task (the GenericExplanation-Task) which uses the domain knowledge base and a context-based spreading mechanism (a type of bounded beam search) and search from a set of support concepts to a set of concepts to be explained. The search results in an explanation path with a certain combined explanation strength. This is a computed value, where the most important role is played by the explanatory strength of each relation that is part of the path.

• An example: In the transformed scase (above) a represented segment was hypothesized to be a left-erector-spinae which is not present in the retrieved scase. In light of the retrieved findings, can we justify that left-erector-spinae should be present as a segment hypothesis? A justification task (JustifyInputFindings), using the GenericExplanationTask, gives us:

(((START C-NOK-NOH-LEFT-ERECTOR-SPINAE) (IS-COMPLETELY-DORSAL-OF C-NOK-NOH-COLON) (IS-COMPLETELY-LEFT-OF C-NOK-NOH-RIGHT-ERECTOR-SPINAE)) 0.8640000000000001)

The explanation structure as shown is a dump from an execution run. It shows an explanation chain, built up of concept-relation-concept triplets, and assigned the resulting explanation strength as a numerical value.

All explanations are stored as part of the image interpretation case. A decision is made whether to accept the image interpretation or reject it. In our example it is accepted and will be subject to verification.

A part of the verification task is to look at the solutions proposed (essentially the set of segment hypotheses generated by ProposeInterpretationBySegmentIntegration), generate expectations from these and justifying whether these are met.

- In our example one of the retrieved segment hypotheses were right-erector-spinae. The GenericExplanationTask states that given a right-erector-spinae, we should expect a spine as well:

  (((START C-NOK-NOH-RIGHT-ERECTOR-SPINAE) (IS-COMPLETELY-RIGHT-OF C-NOK-NOH-COLON) (IS-COMPLETELY-VENTRAL-OF C-NOK-NOH-SPINE)) 0.7635266498559999)

  This and other expectations are summed up in the list of expected findings:

  ((C-NOK-NOH-RIGHT-ERECTOR-SPINAE 0.8640000000000001) (C-NOK-NOH-FIRST-LEFT-RIB 0.8) (C-NOK-NOH-COLON 0.8) (C-NOK-NOH-SPINE 0.7635266498559999) (C-NOK-NOH-SPLEEN 0.8552960000000001) (C-NOK-NOH-AORTA 0.7672) (C-NOK-NOH-LEFT-ERECTOR-SPINAE 0.8) (C-NOK-NOH-GALL-BLADDER 0.88) (C-NOK-NOH-LIVER 0.7031799999999999))

  The task JustifyExpectedFindings receive the list of expected findings not occuring in the input case, and try to explain how they are similar to the input findings, in a similar manner to what JustifyInputFindings earlier did.

4.5 Criticizing an image interpretation

In the present version of ImageCreek this function exists only as an early design. The task is split into two subtasks:

- **DiagnoseInterpretationFailure**: The method we chose looks at the source, the severity and kind of criticism in classifying the failure:

  i. If criticism is relatively even on all segments tag the criticism as **Even**. Otherwise, tag it **Uneven**.

  ii. If the total of criticism is very strong, tag the criticism **Strong**. Otherwise tag it **Moderate**.

  iii. If the criticism is strong from the ProposeImageInterpretation step tag the criticism **StructuralCriticism** otherwise tag it **SolutionCriticism**.

- **Proposing an amendment strategy**: Some tentative rules we propose are:

  i. In case criticism is **Uneven** or **Moderate** propose segment reallocation.

ii. In case criticism is **Even** or **Strong** propose finding a new image interpretation.

iii. In case criticism is **StructuralCriticism** count this as an argument for a finding a new image interpretation.

iv. In case criticism is **SolutionCriticism** count this as an argument for a proposing segment reallocation.

v. If this is second (or more) time verification fails from segment reallocation, propose finding a new image interpretation.

vi. If this is second (or more) time verification fails from finding new image interpretations, propose image resegmentation.

4.6 Modifying an image interpretation

ModifyImageInterpretation have four ways of attempting to modify the failed and verified image interpretation.

1. From ModifyImageInterpretation we receive the collected criticism of the verified image interpretation. Each finding pertaining to a segment is related to a particular segment hypothesis (e.g. has-left-erector-spinae-dorsal-bb is related to the c-nok-noh-left-erector-spinae hypothesis. All findings pertaining to such a segment hypothesis are grouped together and a total criticism factor for that particular segment hypothesis is calculated.

2. If an identified segment hypothesis has a corresponding set of input segment cases these are identified and the segments together with the segment hypothesis is added to the CandidateSegments set. The segment hypothesis is included and named the ForbiddenHypothesis so that MakeSegmentHypotheses shall know that it must not associate the particular segments with this segment hypothesis again.

3. All identified segment hypotheses are named CandidateHypotheses. Control is left to MakeSegmentHypotheses.

As control is resumed the new segment hypotheses are integrated into the input image interpretation case and control is left to ModifyImageInterpretation which will leave control to ImageCreekSolve, which in turn will make the input case subject for renewed verification.

5 Discussion

The ImageCreek architecture crucially depends on a number of assumptions to ensure robustness and problems solving quality. Among the more important are:

1. **Case representation.** The findings in segment cases must show to be well chosen in that they (i) ensure a reasonable feature cluster separability (linear separability is not necessary) and (ii) serve as relevant indices such that the Propose subtasks at WICT and SICT level are able to generate a high quality set of solutions.

2. **Image segmentation robustness.** The correspondence between an image segment and an anatomical entity must be reasonably true. That means that it must not happen too frequently that there is no such one-to-one correspondence. If this happens the system will gracefully degrade in performance. To ensure that this one-to-one correspondence is generally true, a method of intelligent planning of image segmentation processing must be devised and the underlying image processing functions must be reasonably stable.

3. **Learning capability.** Not only must revised cases be retained for future retrieval but there must be a method correcting problem solving anomalies and integrating new knowledge. The ImageCreek prototype knowledge base is already less than trivial to maintain and to be able to make the architecture scalable, methods for knowledge base maintenance are crucial.

The principal strong sides of the ImageCreek approach are:

- **Domain knowledge language.** ImageCreek relies heavily on explanations in problem solving. The explanations are based on the domain knowledge. Care has been taken to make a knowledge base ontology that is as close to the radiologist´s language as possible. This ensures a quality control in that the radiologist more easily can verify the explanations from ImageCreek and that learning indices and from failures can be evaluated by a radiologist with minimum ImageCreek experience.

- **Context sensitive problem solving.** Our knowledge acquisition shows that the diagnostic image interpretations of a radiologist are highly sensitive to findings pertaining to the patient´s general characteristics, referring physician, clinical history and current diagnoses and medications. The ImageCreek system ensures that such concerns appropriately influences the image interpretation process.

- **Integrated problem solving and learning.** Every solved problem is an experience to learn from in ImageCreek. Since we base our architecture on Creek methods we profit from the methology´s ability to learn and solve in tandem. Problem solving and learning is involving the user interactively.

Looking at the literature we feel that the systems that are closest in having appropriate solutions for our domain are the ERNEST system [Kummert 93] and the VIA-RAD system [Rogers 95]. Both are realized and well evaluated. ERNEST seem to scale up reasonably well, is fairly close to the expert in terminology. The system has a way of explaining it´s actions but these justifications are mere user presentations and do not influence the problem solving itself. Control is handled in an elegant and generic fashion. In VIA-RAD much the same is the case. It is unclear as to how well it would scale up and it features a domain knowledge language that is fairly close to the expert´s. The systems´ principal weakness are their lack of learning from experience. It is unclear to what an extent either system would be sensitive to problem solving context.

6 Status

Currently the problem solving part of the architecture is past the early design stage and the key aspects are implemented in a prototype. The image processing subsystem is in a similar stage. ImageCreekLearn is in an earlier design stage where initial implementation is due to begin soon. The image processing subsystem runs on a Unix Solaris system and is an integration of c based Khoros library routines and custom made shell scripts. The other part of the prototype system is written in a combination of the CreekL representation language and standard Common Lisp for Macintosh.

Image understanding is a difficult task, where methods for integration of low-level and higher-level image analysis and interpretation is called for. This represents a challenge for both the AI and the image understanding communities. Given the problem of developing sufficiently strong general domain knowledge models in these domains, a case-based approach is a plausible suggestion. The results of our research so far clearly indicates that this also is a promising approach.

7 Acknowledgment

We would like to thank Pinar Øzturk for valuable input on aspects of the architectural model. Particularly the ideas on the Generic Explanation Task are inspired by her work. Furthermore we are indebted to Arnt Lockert, Ståle Heitmann and Ole Martin Winnem for implementing a number of Creek methods and the Creest modeling tool. Finally we acknowledge the invaluable input of our collaborators at the Regional Hospital of Trondheim, in particular Medical Drs. Asbjørn Ødegård and Klaus Schipper.

8 References

[Aamodt 91] Aamodt A., *A Knowledge-Intensive, Integrated Approach to Problem Solving and Sustained Learning*, Ph.D. thesis, May 1991, Dept. of Computer Systems and Telematics, University of Trondheim, Norway

[Aamodt 94a] Aamodt A., Explanation-Driven Case-Based Reasoning, pp. 274-288 in *Topics in case-based reasoning* by Wess S. et al. (eds.), Springer 1994, pp. 274-288.

[Aamodt 94b] Aamodt A. and Plaza E, Case-Based Reasoning: Foundational issues, methodological variations, and system approaches, *AI Communications*, Vol 7, no.1, pp. 39-59.

[Aamodt 95] Aamodt A., Knowledge acquisition and learning by experience - the role of case specific knowledge, in *Machine Learning and Knowledge Acquisition*, Academic Press 1995, ISBN 0-12-685120-4, pp. 197-245.

[Aha 95] Aha, D., Weighting features, In Veloso, M. and Aamodt, A. (eds.) *Case-based reasoning research and development*, First International Conference, ICCBR-95, Sesimbra, Portugal, October 1995, Springer Verlag, 1995, pp 347-358.

[Berger] Berger J., Roentgen: Radiation Therapy and Case-based Reasoning, Artificial Intelligence Laboratory, University of Chicago, Chicago, Illinois 60637.

[Chandrasekaran 90] Chandrasekaran B., Design Problem Solving: A Task Analysis, *AI Magazine*, Winter 1990.

[Chandrasekaran 93] Chandrasekaran B. and Johnson T., Generic Tasks and Task Structures: History, Critique and New Directions in David, J.-M. et al. (eds.),*Second Generation Expert Systems*, Springer 1993, ISBN 3-540-56192-7.

[Chellappa 92] Chellappa R and Kashyap, R.L., Image understanding, In Shapiro, S.C (ed.), *Encyclopedia of artificial intelligence,* Vol 1, John Wiley & Sons, 1992pp 641-663.

[Davis 91] Davis D. and Taylor C., A Blackboard Architecture For Medical Image Interpretation, *SPIE* Vol. 1445 Image Processing (1991).

[Englmeier 93] Englmeier K. et al., Model Based Image Interpretation of Spiral CT Scans of the Abdomen, pp. 44-51, in *Artificial Intelligence in Medicine* by Andreassen S., Engelbrecht R and Wyatt J. (eds.), IOS Press 1993.

[Gonzales 92] Gonzales R. and Woods R., *Digital Image Processing*, Addison Wesley 1992, ISBN 0-201-50803-6.

[Grimnes 96a] Grimnes M. and Ødegård A., Knowledge acquisition for robust image understanding: Knowledge use in CT image understanding, Report at dept. of Informatics, NTNU, ftp://sophus.ifi.unit.no/YarcWorld/public/papers-reports/kacq.kn-use.19-01-96.ps

[Grimnes 96b] Grimnes, M., Knowledge breadth in CT image diagnosis, Submitted for publication, 1996.

[Gong 95] Gong L. and Kulikowski C., Composition of Image Analysis Processes Through Object-Centered Hierarchical Planning, *IEEE Transactions on Pattern Analysis and Machine Intelligence*, Vol. 17, No. 10, October 1995.

[Haddad 95] Haddad M. et al., SCINA: A Case-Based Reasoning System for the interpretation of Myocardial Perfusion Scintigrams, Dept. of Cardiology, University of Vienna, AKH Wien, Vienna, Austria, email: haddad@vm.akh-wien.ac.at

[Kummert 93] Kummert F. et al., Control and explanation in a signal understanding environment, *Signal Processing* 32 (1993) 111-145

[Leake 93] Focusing construction and selection of abductive hypotheses. In *IJCAI, 1993*, pp. 24-31. Morgan Kaufmann.

[Macura 95] Macura R. and Macura K., MacRad: Radiology Image Resource with a Case-Based Retrieval System, pp. 43-54, in Veloso M. and Aamodt A. (eds.), *Case-Based Reasoning Research and Development*, Springer 1995, ISBN3-540-60598-3

[Menhardt] Menhardt W. et al., Knowledge Based Interpretation of Cranial MR Images, Philips GmbH, Forschungslaboratorium Hamburg POBox 540840 D-2000 Hamburg 54, FRG

[Rogers 95] Rogers E., VIA-RAD: a blackboard-based system for diagnostic radiology, *Artificial Intelligence in Medicine* 7 (1995), pp. 343-360

[Schalkoff 92] Schalkoff R., *Pattern Recognition. Statistical, Structural and Neural Approaches*, Wiley 1992, ISBN 0-471-55238-0

[Steels 90] Steels L., Components of Expertise, *AI Magazine* summer 1990.

[Steels 93] Steels, L., The component framework and its role in reusability, In David, J-M. et al. (eds.), Springer 1993, ISBN 3-540-56192-7, pp. 273-298.

[Swett 93] Swett H. et al., Computer Vision and Decision Support, pp. 273-313 in *The Perception of Visual Information* by Hendee W. and Wells P. (eds.), Springer 1993

[Teller 95] Teller A. and Veloso M., PADO: A new learning architecture for object recognition, *Symbolic visual learning*. Oxford University Press, 1995.

[Tombropoulos 94] Tombropoulos R. et al., A Decision Aid for Diagnosis of Liver Lesions on MRI, Section on Medical Informatics, Stanford University School of Medicine, 1994 AMIA

[Vernazza 87] Vernazza G.L. et al., A Knowledge-Based System for Biomedical Image Processing and Recognition, *IEEE Transaon Circuits and Systems*, Vol. cas-34, no. 11, November 1987

[Wess 94] Wess, S., Althoff, K-D., Derwand, G., Using k-d trees to improve the retrieval step in case-based reasoning, In Wess. S., Althoff, K-D., and Richter, M.M. (eds.) *Topic in case-based reasoning*, Springer Verlag, 1994, pp. 167-181.

[Wegener 92] Wegener O., *Whole Body Computed Tomography*, 2nd ed., Blackwell scientific pub. 1992, ISBN 0-86542-223-0

[Wielinga 93] Wielinga B. et al., Towards a Unification of Knowledge modeling Approaches, in David, J-M. e al. (ed), *Second Generation Expert Systems*, Springer 1993, ISBN 3-540-56192-7.

[Winnem 96] Winnem O., Integrating knowledge level and symbol level modeling - The Creest Workbench, MSc thesis, Dept. of Informatics, Norwegian University of Science and Technology - NTNU, Trondheim, 1996.

Learning Adaptation Rules From a Case-Base

Kathleen Hanney and Mark T. Keane

Dept. of Computer Science, Trinity College Dublin, Dublin, Ireland
E-mail: kathleen.hanney, mark.keane@cs.tcd.ie

Abstract. A major challenge for case-based reasoning (CBR) is to overcome the knowledge-engineering problems incurred by developing adaptation knowledge. This paper describes an approach to automating the acquisition of adaptation knowledge overcoming many of the associated knowledge-engineering costs. This approach makes use of inductive techniques, which learn adaptation knowledge from case comparison. We also show how this adaptation knowledge can be usefully applied. The method has been tested in a property-evaluation CBR system and the technique is illustrated by examples taken from this domain. In addition, we examine how any available domain knowledge might be exploited in such an adaptation-rule learning-system.

1 Introduction

Part of the success of case-based reasoning (CBR) has been attributed to its reduced knowledge engineering requirements. Case-based reasoning researchers point out that cases are often available for free in existing database records. Furthermore, these cases contain a lot of implicit knowledge about causal dependencies and the relative importance of different features in a domain. However, this optimistic picture of CBR can really only be sustained for retrieval-only systems. Unlike cases, adaptation knowledge is not usually readily available and the development of such knowledge involves knowledge acquisition difficulties akin to those found in traditional expert system design. The simplest and most widely-used form of adaptation knowledge acts to resolve feature differences between a target problem and a retrieved case [3]. For example, in the Déja vu system, which deals with the design of plant control programs for steel mills [7, 8], many feature differences can arise between problem specifications and retrieved cases. A problem specification could require a two-speed buggy to pick up a load from one location and deliver it to another location, whereas the best retrieved case might only describe how a one-speed buggy carries out these actions. Déja vu has a specific adaptation rule to deal with this buggy-speed feature-difference; this rule notes that two-speed buggies have to be slowed before they stop, whereas one-speed buggies do not and modifies the solution of the one-speed buggy case to reflect this difference. This speed-difference rule is typical of CBR adaptation rules. These rules tend to be domain-specific and have to be hand-coded by the system developer. Hence, the knowledge-engineering effort expended in one domain tends not to be re-usable in other domains (although see [8, 10] for some exceptions). Furthermore, the knowledge engineering task in coding adaptation knowledge is non-trivial. The knowledge engineer has to predict the feature-differences that are likely to arise between known cases and all possible future problems and then determine the solution changes produced by these differences. Indeed, the latter will often require a deep understanding of the problem domain. If CBR is to deliver on the promise it clearly shows, then solutions to this knowledge engineering problem will have to be found. This view is supported by the current interest in adaptation and the worries being raised about its tractability (see e.g. [11]). In this paper, we look at one possible solution to this problem, we pursue the possibility that adaptation knowledge might be acquired automatically from case knowledge. We are aware that there are many types of adaptation rule that carry out different roles in CBR systems; however, as a first pass, we tackle the learning of feature-difference-based adaptation rules. In the next section, we review this and other approaches to adaptation-knowledge acquisition, before describing a technique for learning adaptation knowledge (section 3) and presenting some preliminary experimental evidence on this technique (section 4). Later, we show how domain knowledge aside from the case-base aids adaptation rule learning (section 5).

2 Learning Adaptation Knowledge

Ideally, CBR systems should be able to learn adaptation knowledge automatically from knowledge sources that have minimal knowledge-engineering requirements. There appear to be three main methods for learning adaptation knowledge; methods that exploit (i) other domain knowledge, (ii) an expert user or (iii) the case-base. The first two solutions have been examined in the literature but we know of no attempt to use the last method to learn adaptation rules.

2.1 Using Domain Knowledge to Learn Adaptation Rules

Leake et al. (see [4, 5]) report on one method that uses other domain knowledge to learn adaptation knowledge. The system is given general adaptation knowledge strategies which when applied result in specific adaptation cases and these adaptation cases are stored for future use. Adaptation is viewed as a combination of transformation and search. When differences arise between the current problem and the retrieved case, case-based adaptation is attempted and if no suitable prior cases are found rule-based adaptation is used. For example, when using rule-based adaptation to adapt a reaction-plan for the environmental problems in a factory building to an air-quality problem in a school, DIAL uses a general role/filler mismatch transformation to adapt the 'notify-union' step and finds 'parents' to be a suitable substitute for 'union' based on role similarities. DIAL can then create an adaptation case from this information for future use (see [2] for another example of adaptation rule learning from domain knowledge). The problem with this method is that it does not appear to reduce the knowledge engineering load. In particular, the handcoding of general transformation strategies may be too expensive. One possible advantage of this approach is that domain knowledge could already be available in another knowledge based system developed for other purposes.

2.2 Interactive Adaptation Rule Learning

DIAL supplements its learning of adaptation rules with the second method of exploiting the user's knowledge. An expert user can judge whether certain feature differences matter and may even identify the need for further plan adaptation (see e.g., repair in Persuader [10]). It make a lot of sense to keep users in the learning loop as a "free" source of knowledge, as long as they are asked the right sort of questions. At the very least, an interactive approach to adaptation can reduce the knowledge engineering load. However, if the intended user of the system is non-expert then we may want to constrain what the system will learn. The user is a very useful source of adaptation knowledge but it may often be possible to supplement this type of learning with learning from other sources.

2.3 Learning Adaptation Rules from the Case-base

A third possible solution, which, to our knowledge, has not been examined before in the CBR literature, is to use the knowledge that is already available in the system, namely the case-base itself. (Related work in the growing area of knowledge discovery in databases includes the generation of association rules from databases [1]). It is possible to compute all the feature-differences that exist between cases in the case-base and examine how these differences relate to differences in case solutions. From this analysis, it should be possible to automatically learn a set of adaptation rules. The implicit assumption here is that the differences that occur between cases in the case-base are representative of the differences that will occur between future problems and the case-base (see [9], for more on this assumption). As we shall see, further processing might have to be carried out to determine which of these rules are actually used by the system. However, even if this solution is only approximate, it may be sufficient because it reduces significantly the knowledge engineering load. So far, the approach has been implemented for flat cases with ordinal, boolean or symbolic features and numeric, boolean or symbolic solutions. In the next section, we describe the method used in more detail.

3 Learning Adaptation Rules from a Case-base and Applying them

We have developed an algorithm, for learning and applying adaptation rules. It takes a case-base and performs pair-wise comparisons of its cases. The feature differences between each pair of cases are noted and become the antecedent part of a new adaptation rule, with the consequent part of this rule being the difference between the solutions of both cases. Methods for constraining case-comparison and subsequent refinement and generalisation of the generated rule set as well as rule application are described below.

3.1 Representing Adaptation Rules

Information about the adaptation rules created by case comparison is contained in two sets of rules: C-rules and F-rules. C-rules are the basic adaptation rules that associate a change in case feature values with solution changes. Each rule has seven slots: rule identifier, features, values, context, solution-change, gen, and confidence-rating. The 'features' slot contains those features with different values in the case pair. The 'values' slot contains the value pairs of the features in the features slot. The 'context' slot contains those feature values that the case pair share that have an impact on solution change. The 'solution-change' is the rule consequent and is an expression of the change is the solution. In the case of numeric solutions it could be simply additive. For symbolic solution it is a transition from one class to another class. The 'gen' slot notes whether the rule was generalised. The main advantage of generalisation is that it broadens the applicability of the specific adaptation rules. The system induces a more general adaptation rule given several similar but non-identical, specific rules. The 'confidence-rating' entry has further significance later on; at present, it is sufficient to say that it is important to weight the confidence in adaptation rules based on several factors. Its role can be accounted for by the the fact that the more frequently an association is observed, the more likely it is to be true.

F-rules just record the frequency of groups of feature value differences. There may be more than one consequent change associated with the same feature changes. In this domain, two rules are considered to be duplicates if they have exactly matching antecedents (i.e., feature differences) and broadly similar consequents. If the solution is symbolic duplicates must have both matching antecedents and consequents. Whether or not context must match depends on the domain. There is no requirement for the solutions of duplicates to match exactly because it is important for the system to handle noisy data. Each C-rule has a corresponding F-rule which has information about the number of times its set of value differences was found, the case-pairs on which it is based and the consequents of each occurence of the rule. The motivation for the use of F-rules is to curtail the size of the C-rule list while keeping account of rule frequency and consequent variation.

3.2 Reducing the Number of Adaptation Rules Generated

A key consideration in adaptation rule generation by case comparison is to limit the number of adaptation rules generated. First, one can limit the number of cases considered by the algorithm; in the experiments carried out we limit the number of cases compared, to reduce the number of rules generated. If a similarity metric is available it may be used to find cases for comparison. Case pairs within a given measure of similarity are compared. If a similarity metric is not available and requires too much effort to obtain another test for case comparison is proposed in which we make use of the fact that the retriever returns a case within a certain degree of similarity to the target for adaptation. The solution is to let the retriever determine candidates for case comparison. A threshold number of differences between cases is determined below which case pairs will be compared. This threshold is found by using each case in the case-base as target and finding the number of differences between the target and highest ranked retrieved case. The threshold for identification of candidates for comparison can be gauged by examining the number of differences found between the target and retrieved cases in n retrievals where n is the case-base size.

The rule-set can also be reduced by deleting duplicate rules. The knowledge expressed by a set of duplicated rules can be expressed by a single rule which characterises the deleted duplicates; this rule inherits the 'features', 'values' and 'gen' entries from the duplicate rules and the value of the soln-change entry is some average of the solutions in the individual rules (clearly, what constitutes an average solution will change from one domain to another). The rule also receives a confidence rating that reflects the number of duplicates it captures (the higher the rating the more duplicates it captures).

3.3 Generalisation of Adaptation Rules

Generalisation has an important role to play in filling gaps in the rule-set; it allows a general pattern to be induced from a set of specific rules, producing a wider coverage of possible differences. One of the generalisation heuristics used for generalising rule antecedents is Michalski's [6] closing interval rule. However, it should be remembered that even the applicability of this rule depends on feature-values being ordinal or continuous. The above rule states that if two descriptors of the same class differ in the values of only one linear descriptor, then the descriptions can be replaced by a single description whose reference is the interval between the two values. Rules may also be generalised by removing constraints on context. Application of this generalisation rule results in rule antecedents like:

if the no-of-bedrooms changes by 2 in the range of 2-bed-rooms to 6-bed-rooms

Rule consequents can be generalised by taking the average (for numeric solutions) and the most common class change for symbolic solutions. Rules may be generalised by removing unnecessary contextual constraints. For example, a given feature difference might always result in the same solution change regardless of the context in which it occurs.

Note, that since the space of generalisations is huge, the system does not perform generalisations over all of the rules it creates. Rather it only finds generalisations of rules when applying the adaptation rules to a given problem. That is, it only generalises on demand when applying its adaptation rules (see next section).

3.4 Adaptation Rule Application

Apart from learning adaptation rules, we have devised mechanisms for applying these rules when given a target problem. When a case has been retrieved for a target problem and the differences between the two noted, an attempt is made to find rules in the rule-base that match the general form of these differences. Initially, the system searches for the full list of differences occurring together in a single rule. If no single rule can resolve all the differences it looks for a set of rules. The set of differences is reduced by looking at all possible ways of dropping a difference from the list of original differences. Then a search is made for all possible shorter antecedents. Reduction of the differences continues by dropping one difference from the list of differences and finishes with a search for rules handling one difference only. This search method gives all the rules that could potentially resolve one or more differences between the base and target case. Generalisation is then applied to this set of rules. The generalised rules are then filtered to exclude rules that are no longer applicable due to scope constraints on their feature values. The resulting set contains the building blocks for solving the adaptation; that is, the list of rules that resolve the differences between the retrieved and target cases. This set contains those rules that match differences in the difference list exactly and those generalised rules applicable to the differences. Whether or not the adaptation rules need to be ordered depends on the solution type and the domain.

The rule set may contain rules with matching antecedents and conflicting consequents. When applying such rules, the rule whose base cases are closest to the target are chosen. When more than one rule is applicable, we need some way to select a rule from the set of applicable rules. Where the differences between the target and best case are only partially resolved, the set of rules which handle the most differences is chosen. Where all the differences between target and best match case have been resolved this decision is based on three factors (listed in order of precedence):

- *specificity*: Given a list of differences to resolve, preference is given to rules that include as many of these differences as possible. For example, if four differences are to be resolved we prefer a rule that can tackle all four differences as opposed to four rules that handle one difference each. (This heuristic is important in systems where the feature values interact.)
- *confidence rating*: the rule with the highest confidence rating is used.
- *concreteness*: Specific rules have primacy over general rules, because generalisation is not guaranteed to be correct.

Using these criteria an adaptation path is constructed from selected rules. If unhandled-differences still remain then other methods must be used, like relying on an expert user to institute the changes. Alternatively, a new adaptation path may be constructed from the set of rules applicable to the differences. If the best match case cannot be fully adapted the user can choose to try the next best match until a satisfactory solution is found. There is a trade-off here between a full adaptation of a similar previous case and a partial adaptation of a case more similar to the target problem. This iterative method is especially useful when adaptation rule application is ordered since it was found that the requirement for finding a full adaptation path with a certain ordering is harder to meet.

4 Learning Adaptation Knowledge from Cases: Experiments using a Pure Inductive Approach

To determine whether the method was at all feasible a relatively simple system was used in the empirical tests. In Hanney et al's [1] taxonomy of CBR systems, the simplest CBR system performing adaptation has an atomic solution (i.e., a single value, numeric or symbolic) and solves problems using a single adapted case. Therefore, the chosen system had these characteristics with the added constraint that feature changes in a case had local, non-interacting effects on the solution value. This type of system is representative of many simple systems currently used in CBR industrial applications. The CBR system was created from an expert system for property evaluation; the expert system was used to create the case-base and to determine correct answers to problems. The CBR version of this system had 1000 cases in its case-base and used a standard, spreading-activation retrieval algorithm. The 1000 cases were generated randomly; that is, features values were selected for each possible slot of a case and then the expert system was used to provide the solution answer for this set of features. Figure 1 shows a sample case:

feature	value
location	loc3
nr-bed-rooms	3-bed-rooms
nr-rec-rooms	2-rec-rooms
kitchen	medium-kitchen
structure	detached
nr-floors	1-floor
condition	excellent-condition
age	mature-age
facilities	facilities-far
price	75000

Fig. 1. Sample Case from the Property Evaluation Domain

It is probably true to say that a "real" case-base for this system might have a greater clustering of cases than our randomly generated case-base. However, a more clustered case-base would probably make adaptation-rule learning easier because there would be better structure in it. For present purposes, it is sufficient to note that this case-base might be a little harder to learn rules from than a real one. For illustration purposes, an adaptation rule generated by the system is shown below. The basis for this rule is case 1000 compared with case 792 (see figure 2).

If kitchen changes from bad-kitchen to good-kitchen and number of reception rooms changes from 3 reception rooms to 6 and condition changes from medium condition to bad condition then the house value decreases by 4000

Case_1000		Case_792	
location	loc4	location	loc4
nr-bed-rooms	6-bed-rooms	nr-bed-rooms	6-bed-rooms
nr-rec-rooms	3-rec-rooms	nr-rec-rooms	6-rec-rooms
kitchen	bad-kitchen	kitchen	good-kitchen
structure	semi	structure	semi
nr-floors	2-floors	nr-floors	2-floors
condition	medium-condition	condition	bad-condition
age	mature-age	age	mature-age
facilities	facilities-far	facilities	facilities-far
price	73500	price	69500

Fig. 2. A Compared Case Pair

4.1 Experimental set-up

In all the experiments, the CBR property-evaluation system was used. It has 1000 cases and was presented with 3 sets of 100 randomly-generated test problems. These problems were solved by retrieving and adapting cases from the case-base, using the learned adaptation-rules. In order to rate the performance of the CBR system, the dependent variable was how close the CBR system's answer was to the expert system's answer. The formula used to measure this deviation is

$$E = \frac{\sum_{i=1}^{N} \frac{|estimate(i)-rbs(i)|}{rbs(i)}}{N} \qquad (1)$$

N is the number of test cases, rbs(x) is the the expert system's solution and estimate(x) is the CBR system's solution. If the CBR system is being successful then most of the test problems should deviate minimally from the expert-system's solution.

4.2 Experiment 1

In the first experiment, the system does simple case comparison with no generalisation and uses no other domain knowledge. A threshold value of 4 differences was used to identify candidate case pairs. Alternatively, a similarity metric could be used. We can justify the usage of this threshold by the assumption that case coverage is good and the retriever retrieves a case sufficiently close to the target. The threshold is estimated by using each case in the case-base as target and finding the number of differences that exist between the case retrieved from the case-base with this target removed. It was found that there was almost always no more than 4 differences between the target and retrieved cases so only rules with a cardinality of 4 or less were generated.

Three test sets of 100 cases were used to evaluate the relative performance of the retrieval only system and the system with adaptation. The percentage error (calculated using formula 1 above) for the retrieval only system ranged from 0.077 to 0.133 whereas the percentage error of the system performing adaptation was considerably less ranging from 0.001 to 0.003. It is also interesting to examine the number of exactly correct results given by the system performing adaptation. Whereas the retrieval only system found on average only 3 exactly correct solutions the system performing adaptation found the exactly correct solution on 95 per cent of test problems. The above experiment shows that adaptation knowledge can be acquired automatically and that it results in significant performance improvements over a system lacking such rules. In the next section, we describe how the addition of domain knowledge effects adaptation rule learning.

5 Using Domain Knowledge to Support Adaptation Rule Learning from Cases

Often, there are known regularities in the domain which are not evident from an examination of the case base. We demonstrate how this knowledge can be utilised to guide adaptation rule learning. First, each of the general categories of domain knowledge types is described. Second, we show how this domain knowledge can be effectively exploited. Third, the effects of domain knowledge on adaptation rule application are examined.

5.1 Types of Domain Knowledge

Four types of domain knowledge are considered: known adaptation rules, knowledge of feature relevance, knowledge of contextual constraints and knowledge of interactions between adaptation rules. Each of these knowledge types is described below and one example of each type is provided.

- *Known Adaptation Rules* are adaptation rules already known by the system designer. For example, a change in structure from terraced to semi-detached results in a price increase of 7000
- *Irrelevant Features* are features that have no effect on the solution. In our domain, some features are always irrelevant while other features are irrelevant if certain contextual constraints hold. An example of a rule containing knowledge about feature irrelevancy is the rule, *if location is location 1 or location 2 then distance from facilities has no effect on the solution*

- *Contextual Dependencies* Sometimes, the solution changes arising from a feature value change depend on the context. For example, in our experimental domain, the addition of a bedroom in location 1 (a good location) results in a larger price increase than in location 6 (a medium location).
- *Feature Interaction* It is known that the effects of some features are non-interacting. Features are non-interacting if differences in those feature values occurring together have the same effect as the sum of the effects of those differences occurring separately.

5.2 Domain Knowledge Constrains Adaptation Rule Learning

Previously known adaptation rules prevent the acquisition of rules produced by case comparison if a predefined adaptation rule matches exactly the antecedent of a rule suggested by case comparison. Here, case comparison is not productive since the rule is already known and no learning occurs. Adaptation knowledge has an effect on what is learned from case comparison when the antecedent list of the predefined adaptation rule is contained in the antecedent list of the suggested rule. Here learning is possible by subtracting the known adaptation rule from the rule suggested by case comparison. For example, if the result of case comparison is the rule [1], and [2] is a known adaptation rule, then the new rule [3] may be inferred.

if d1 and d2 then soln change is X [1]
if d1 then soln change is Y [2]
if d2 then soln change is X-Y [3]

In this way, the differences handled by the known adaptation rule along with its effects on the solution are removed from the rule obtained from case comparison. The result is a new rule which might not be obtained using cases alone. The existence of irrelevant case features complicates the rule acquisition process because feature relevance has a direct effect on the contents of a rule's antecedent. The value of knowledge about feature relevance is illustrated with an example. Consider case[1] and case[2] in figure 3 below.

In case[1], features *d*, *a f* are irrelevant (given in feature relevance rules). In case[2], features *d*, *a*, *f* and *r* are irrelevant. The change in condition from *gc* to *bc* is responsible for *r's* being irrelevant in case[2]. Now a simple comparison of case[1] and case[2] might suggest the rule [c [gc → bc]] → decrease 4000.

This rule is erroneous because it includes the side effects of feature relevance by failing to note that feature *r's* irrelevance in case[2] has a positive effect on the solution. (In fact the difference in solution for the single change [gc → bc] is a decrease of 7000). The problem then is to find whatever context features are responsible for the attenuated effect of the change in context in this case pair. Clearly, it is not desirable, during case comparison, to put all the differences and context features in the rule antecedent. In order to maximise rule applicability, we require only the feature differences and context changes that justify the solution change. Knowledge of any other feature differences or context is

[1]			[2]		
	c	gc		c	bc
	l	11		l	11
	a	ya		a	ya
	b	4b		b	4b
	k	mk		k	mk
	f	1f		f	1f
	r	3r		r	3r
	s	ss		s	ss
	d	ff		d	ff
	p	107000		p	103000

Fig. 3. Case Pair Illustrating the Effect of Irrelevant Features

unnecessary and imposes undesired constraints on applicability. We use a simple technique that relies on knowledge about causal dependencies between features to find minimal rules. Like feature relevance knowledge, contextual knowledge plays a role in the selection of rule context components. Knowledge about contextual constraints guides the generation of rule context components. Failure to take these constraints into account may result in rules with over generalised applicability. The problem of finding the right context during case comparison is illustrated by the case pair in figure 4.

[3]			[4]		
	c	mc		c	mc
	l	18		l	16
	a	ya		a	ya
	b	1b		b	1b
	k	bk		k	bk
	f	1f		f	1f
	r	2r		r	2r
	s	ss		s	ss
	d	fv		d	fv
	p	29500		p	40500

Fig. 4. Case Pair Illustrating the Effect of Contextual Dependencies

In case [3], the impact of the values of the features b and d are governed by contextual constraints. In case [4] they have the usual effect on the solution. Case[4] is identical to case[3] apart from the location. However, this change from *18* in case[3] to *16* in case[4] means that the values of features *b* and *d* have different effects in these two cases. The rule associating the change (18 → 16) with the solution differences is erroneous since it does not take into account the different contributions of features *b* and *d* to the final solutions in both cases. Straight comparison is therefore insufficient for this case pair. The problem is to identify the context features responsible for the reduced increase in solution caused by this solution change. (It is sufficient to note that normally, this change in feature *l* results in a bigger solution increase). The procedure used to identify necessary context features relies on knowledge of causal dependencies between features. In the case of non-interacting features, the sum of the effects of differences occurring separately is equal to the effect of those differences had they occurred together. Knowledge about non-interacting features helps constrain the number of adaptation rules learned. For example, if the rules [9] and [10] below have already been learned and if a case comparison suggests the rule [11] there is no need to retain this proposed rule since it may be deduced that the consequent of rule [11] is the sum of the consequents in rules [9] and [10]. Note that it is more desirable to have a group of rules with small antecedents than an equivalent longer rule since smaller rules have more extensive applicability.

Rule 9: diff1 and diff2 → effect on soln X
Rule 10: diff3 → effect on soln Y
Rule 11: diff1 and diff2 and diff3 → effect on soln Z

So, in general, if the differences between two compared cases are all non-interacting, a search is made of the adaptation rule-base to find a group of rules whose collective applicability is equivalent to the consequent of the proposed rule.

5.3 Effects of Domain Knowledge on the Adaptation Rule Application Process

The rule application process is effected by domain knowledge in the following ways:

- *irrelevant features* may be removed from the list of differences between the target and best matching case and only the remaining differences need be resolved.
- *contextual dependency* means that when assessing the applicability of a rule, context too must be checked. A rule may be applied if either the feature value constraints in the rule antecedent are satisfied or the context of the rule is unspecified.
- *adaptation rules* allow the reduction of differences because the system applies domain adaptation rules before learned rules.

There are six possible outcomes for adaptation rule application in this system. First, if the target case is already in the case-base the solution of the duplicate case in the case-base is given and no further action is necessary. Second, the differences between the target and best match cases may be resolved entirely by domain knowledge. For example, the differences between the best-match and target cases may be found to be irrelevant or solvable by domain adaptation rules. Third, a sufficiently similar best match case may not be found for a target case making adaptation impossible. Fourth, there may be no applicable adaptation rules. This happens if none of the differences between the best match and target cases are resolved by the learned adaptation rules. Five, the differences between the target and best match cases may be only partially resolved by adaptation rules. In this case, the remaining unresolved differences are presented to the user for further processing. Six, all the differences between the best match and target cases may be resolved by adaptation rules (either learned rules or a combination of learned and domain adaptation rules).

5.4 Experiment 2

A new case-base containing 1000 cases was randomly generated for this experiment and the same 3 sets of 100 test cases were used for the three conditions of this experiment. The major difference between this case base and the earlier one was that it contained implicit contextual constraints. In addition, the cases also contained features that were sometimes or always irrelevant. In this way, two types of domain knowledge, contextual constraints and feature irrelevance directly influence case generation. The experiment examines the effect of domain knowledge on rule learning and application in three conditions involving separate tests on a retrieval-only system, a system which learns adaptation rules with no domain knowledge, and a system that uses all four types of domain knowledge during adaptation rule learning.

Using formula 1 the percentage error was measured for each of the three conditions. The percentage error of the retrieval only system ranged from 0.071 to 0.098. The application of adaptation rules generated without using domain knowledge brought the percentage error to within the range 0.019 to 0.032. Interestingly, the third set of tests which used adaptation rules generated using domain knowledge gave a higher percentage error; between 0.030 and 0.042. From these results it would seem that the addition of domain knowledge has a negative effect on results. However if we examine the number of exactly correct solutions the benefits of domain knowledge are more evident. Using adaptation rules generated without domain knowledge the average number of exactly correct solutions was 38 per test set. The addition of domain knowledge brought this figure to 71 per test set. The results show that a good approximation of the solution may be obtained without domain knowledge but that domain knowledge can significantly improve adaptation accuracy.

6 Conclusions

A method for adaptation rule learning has been described. The technique manipulates cases alone or a combination of cases and domain knowledge. Our results show that case-comparison can improve on the performance of a retrieval system without costly knowledge engineering. In the domain illustrated here, rule consequents are additive. The approach can be extended to handle other types of solution change, e.g. multiplicative changes. We then showed how domain knowledge can be exploited in adaptation rule learning. The results show that best adaptation accuracy is obtained when all domain knowledge is used during adaptation rule learning. The use of domain knowledge can help prevent incorrect adaptation by allowing the system to enforce constraints on adaptation rule applicability. The success of our approach relies on the existence of a well populated case-base. Further tests are necessary to see if this conclusion holds for other more complex domains and an extension of the approach to other types of adaptation knowledge would be useful.

References

1. Agrawal R., Mannila H., Srikant R., Toivonen H., Verkamo A.: Fast Discovery of Association Rules. In Fayyad U., Piatetsky-Shapiro G., Smyth P., Uthurusamy R. (Ed.) Advances in Knowledge Discovery and Data Mining. *AAAI Press / The MIT Press* (1996)
2. Hammond K.:Case-Based Planning: Viewing Planning as a Memory Task. *Boston: Academic Press* (1989)
3. Hanney K., Keane M.T., Smyth B., Cunningham P.: Systems, Tasks and Adaptation Knowledge: Revealing some Revealing dependencies. In Proceedings of the First International Conference on Case-based Reasoning (1995) 461–470.
4. Leake D.: Combining Rules and Cases to Learn Case Adaptation. In Proceedings of the Seventeenth Annual Conference of the Cognitive Science Society, (1995)
5. Leake D., Kinley A., Wilson D.: Learning to Improve Case Adaptation by Introspective Reasoning and CBR. In Veloso M., Aamodt A.: (Eds.) Case-based Reasoning Reasoning Research and Development: Lecture Notes in Artificial Intelligence 1010. *Springer Verlag* (1995) 229-240.
6. Michalski R.: A Theory and Methodology of Inductive Learning. In R. Michalski, J. Carbonell, T. Mitchell (Ed.) Machine Learning: An Artificial Intelligence Approach Vol. 1. *Morgan Kaufmann* (1983)
7. Smyth B., Cunningham P.: Déja vu: A Hierarchical Case-Based Reasoning System for Software Design. In Proceedings of the 10th European Conference on Artificial Intelligence. Vienna, Austria (1992)
8. Smyth B., Keane M.T.: Retrieving Adaptable Cases: The Role of Adaptation Knowledge in Case Retrieval. In Topics in Case-Based Reasoning: Lecture Notes in Artifical Intelligence 837. *Springer Verlag* (1994) 209-220
9. Smyth B., Keane M.T.: Remembering to Forget: A Competence-Preserving Deletion Policy in Case-Based Systems. In Proceedings International Joint Conference on Artificial Intelligence, Montreal. (1995)
10. Sycara E.P.: Using Case-Based Reasoning for Plan Adaptation and Repair. In Proceedings: Case-Based Reasoning Workshop (1988) 425-434.
11. Veloso M., Aamodt A.: (Eds.) Case-based Reasoning Reasoning Research and Development: Lecture Notes in Artificial Intelligence 1010. *Springer Verlag* (1995)

An Evolutionary Agent Model of Case-Based Classification

Ye Huang[†]

Faculty of Computer Studies and Mathematics
University of West England
Bristol BS16 1QY
United Kingdom
Email: huang@btc.uwe.ac.uk

Abstract: This paper proposes an agent model of case based classification. The idea is to allow cases, and more generally memorized problem solving experiences, to take a more active role in future problem solving. This is achieved through the so called memory agents which are selected cases with their own reasoning mechanisms. The proposed model of memory agents enables context sensitive classification, leading to a better overall classification accuracy. Memory agents enable localized incremental learning. The resulting system is therefore able to cope with the dynamic environment where class distribution may change over time. Evolutionary agent learning outperforms linear search and simple re-enforcement learning methods. Further, the agent model of memory indicates an important direction of study for memory based reasoning. It focuses attention on cases as agents with knowledge and intention rather than something passively waiting to be retrieved. The agent model provides a more suitable vehicle for integrating different AI techniques to form hybrid systems where different parts of the problem are better suited by different kinds of reasoning method.

1 Introduction

For any automatic reasoning systems, three basic features are desired: correctness, efficiency and flexibility. The correctness refers to the ability to find the right solution or to make the correct prediction. The efficiency concerns with the memory consumption and the response time required to find a solution. The flexibility implies that the system is able to adapt itself to the changing environment.

Case based reasoning (CBR) scheme, which is based upon the principle of reusability, has the potential of achieving the correctness with efficiency by avoiding unnecessary, time consuming deductive reasoning process. Ultimately, knowledge about the domain can be embodied by a set of specific cases. As a consequence, the knowledge elicitation bottle neck in rule based systems may be relieved in CBR systems. However, although

---

† The author thanks Dr. P. Sharpe, Dr. L. Bull, Mr. N. Ireson and Dr. R. Miles for their useful input during numerous discussions.

collecting specific cases is easier than eliciting rules, finding and maintaining representative cases have always been challenging problems in developing CBR systems.

To achieve the correctness and the efficiency, cases stored in the case base must be carefully selected in the first place before a CBR system can be used. This is partly due to the memory limitation and the constraints on retrieval time. But more importantly, using carefully chosen representative cases reduces the complexity of reasoning tasks occurs at a later stage of case based reasoning, which can be costly and time consuming [Huang & Miles 95]. The philosophy behind is to emphasis the cases storing and recalling rather than case adaptation. Complicated case adaptation process, which may incur the knowledge elicitation process, should and can be avoided in many CBR systems.

To achieve the flexibility feature, extra complexity of case base construction and maintenance is added on. CBR systems should be able to replace obsolete cases by new cases in order to reflect the dynamics of the changing environment. The difficulty is how this can be achieved smoothly, efficiently and automatically without having to repeat the case base construction process all over again.

This paper proposes a multiple evolutionary agent model to tackle these problems. A basic class of decision making problem, the classification problem, is used to demonstrate the proposed ideas. Briefly speaking, we are to classify new cases based upon a given set of pre-classified cases. The objectives of the model are first to maintain only a small representative case base while achieving a reasonable accurate classification. Second, the model should be able to adjust itself in the light of new classification results.

By introducing the concept of memory agent, which has its own decision preference and learning mechanism, these objectives are achieved by optimizing agents' distance thresholds, weight systems and also by allowing agents to move their location in the case space and to reside in locations corresponding to hypothetical cases. In the classification problem, homogeneous case representation is presumed. Many real problems, e.g. credit control problem in financial industry [Thomas, et al. 92], fit this homogeneous representation assumption. For other problems, e.g. engineering design task, the agent model can be used together with the hierachical case representation [Smyth & Keane 95] where components of cases will be represented as agents.

The rest of the paper is organised as follows: Section 2 reviews some of the related work in generating representative cases. In section 3, the evolutionary agent model and its components are described. Section 4 outlines how the agent model works with the classification problem. In section 5, the anticipated behaviours of the agent model is described. Section 6 concludes the paper.

2 Related Work

Work on the edited nearest neighbour rules (ENNR) has addressed the problem of generating an initial set of representative exemplars. The ENNR algorithms aimed at finding an optimal subset of cases within the case space while maintaining the prediction accuracy. The iterative condensation algorithm (ICA) proposed in [Swonger 72] derives a subset of the training set eliminating unnecessary cases while maintaining the prediction accuracy. Using the ICA, the resulting subset tends to be those cases which are near to the appropriate decision boundaries between the various class distributions. A different approach from the ICA is the modified NNR [Wilson 72] which, during its editing stage, abandons the cases which do not agree with their majority neighbour, thus reducing the original training set. It is suggested that only a few pre-classified samples are required to approach the Bayesian asymptotic performance. The prototype based NNR [Chang 74] allows merging of multiple input training case to create prototype. By doing so, the number of cases required are greatly reduced. The prototypes are the central points of clusters of cases belonging to the same class.

Using generalized exemplars is another way of achieving a reduced number of stored cases. A nested generalized exemplar (NGE) is represented by a hyper-rectangle which is an axis-parallel multidimensional rectangle and is formed to cover a cluster of cases belonging to the same class [Salzberg 91]. Storing hyper-rectangles instead of the original set of case greatly reduces the size of the case base while maintaining the classification accuracy. The AASM model [Racci & Avesani 95] further improves the NGE by associating each case or hyper-rectangle with a local metric weight, allowing the distance measure to be context sensitive. This is in line with the findings presented in [Aha & Goldstone 92]. The local metric forms an integrated part of the exemplars and is learnt in a reinforcement fashion.

These searching algorithms are conducted in a linear fashion, either in the elimination of unnecessary cases, in the formation of hyper-rectangles or in the reinforcement learning of local distance metric. It is a well recognized fact that linear optimization algorithms may be trapped in a local optima. In general, "linearization can lead to results which are far away from the true optimum" [Back et al. 91]. To overcome this difficulty, some work has been carried out in combining adaptive search techniques, i.e. genetic algorithms (GAs), and the nearest neighbour rule. The PLEASE system [Knight & Sen 95] uses a GA to construct appropriate prototypes from the training cases. The GA evolves the number of prototypes per class and their positions in the input case space. The resulting classifier is reported to be better than several nearest neighbour classifiers. In the GA-WKNN model [Kelly & Davis 91], the GA is used to learn real-valued global weights associated with individual attributes. This work exploits the advantage of the non-linear, parallel optimization approach.

The main disadvantage of these GA models is that the component granularity is not fine enough to allow individual cases to be optimized or to adjust itself to reflect the region it represents. This can result in difficulties in achieving the global optima through the collaboration of cases.

To overcome the drawbacks of the ENNR algorithms, i.e. the linear iterative optimization difficulties, the proposed agent model exploits the implicit parallelism of the GA which optimizes a target by simultaneously searching many regions of the search space [Grefenstette 89]. In addition, the proposed multiple memory agent model will allow each individual agent to be able to adjust itself to reflect the region it represents. Different agents may have different behaviour patterns and learning strategies. This extra layer of granularity is aimed to allow the system to be more flexible in dealing with complicated decision problems.

3 An Agent Model of Memory

Previous work on CBR views cases as passive objects waiting to be retrieved to assist further decision making or problem solving. A case does not adapt to newly acquired information. The decision as to which cases are to be retrieved is carried out by a global mechanism and individual cases have very little affect on future case selection[†]. In many situation, this global mechanism can not accurately reflect local contexts. Regions having different characteristics will have to make compromises. This is due to the fact that the global mechanism cannot use local information independently, and it can only model the problem space homogeneously. This can sometimes lead to poor performance.

We would like the memorized case to play a more active role to increase the flexibility of the case retrieval process, each case should reflect the context within which it resides and cases cooperate with each other to achieve some global goals. Studies on intelligent agents provide a model that fit these requirements. Agents are autonomous beings that have some control over their actions. They are able to react to the changes in the environment and are able to interact with other agents. In addition, agents are not just responding to their environment, they bear their own goals and are able to take initiative [Wooldridge & Jennings 95].

3.1 Memory Agents

In the agent model of memory, the conventional concept of case is extended to that of the memory agent. Memory agents are able to carry out a list of tasks such as bidding for a problem case, self adjustment in the light of the results of bidding and evolution towards its most suitable location and bidding region in the case space. The conventional case base in the agent memory model becomes a set of cooperative agents.

---

† An exception of this is the frequency parameter, W_h, in Salzberg's EACH system which reflects the success rate of a case [Salzberg 91]. But W_h is adjusted only at the training stage.

A memory agent has four parts. The first part is referred to as the data elements of the agent. The contents of the data elements record the current status of the agent. The second part relates to the "pro-activityness" property [Wooldridge & Jennings 95]. It expresses the intention or the self interests of each agent. The activity part of the agent describes what the agents do. The fourth part is a mechanism which allows the agent to adapt to its environment. This adaptation mechanism implements the autonomy of the agent allowing changes to its status and the way it acts.

A. Data elements:
  - a vector of values indicating where the agent is located in the case space;
  - a weight system determining the neighbourhood relationships;
  - a distance threshold which determines the agent bidding region;
B. Local goals (pro-activity):
  - high classification accuracy;
  - large coverage;
C. Activities:
  - Bidding for a new problem;
  - Classify new cases if bidding is successful;
  - Self-adjustment according to the classification result;
  - Communicate with other agents;
D. Autonomy:
  - Evolution mechanism; Each memory agent has its own genetic features affecting how it may evolve.

3.2 Evolving Memory Agents

Our goal is to find a set of agents which are able to classify cases in the case space accurately. Genetic algorithms (GAs) as an adaptive searching technique is used. The GA is a model of machine learning which simulates the mechanisms of evolution in nature and provides robust and powerful search mechanisms [Goldberg 89]. In GAs, points in the solution space are represented by a string of bits, the chromosomes. Simulated sexual reproduction is carried out by applying recombination operators, such as crossover, to the selected parent solutions. The selection is based on a fitness function and the next generation of solutions are generated from those with higher fitness. In this way, solutions represented by the chromosomes will converge to an optima.

In the memory agent model, each agent runs its own GA to search for the best location in the case space and for the best weight system associated with the agent. This method is different from other systems which use GAs to generate prototypes or exemplars for nearest neighbour classification rule [Punch et al. 93]. These systems use a universal GA to achieve a global optima. In the agent model proposed here, the GA is used to achieve local optima for each agent. The global optima is achieved through agent cooperation. The advantage of the approach is that each agent can be refined in accordance with the region with which it is associated. This make the optimization process context sensitive, thereby achieving a better classifier. This reflects of the more general idea of context dependent learning in case based system [Aha & Goldstone 90].

The agent chromosome contains three types of information which are described in section 3.1 as the *data elements*. These are: information about the location of the agent in the problem space; the weight associated with the agent; and the distance threshold which determines the region this agent controls.

The genetic operators, crossover and mutation, work in the following way. For the location genes, mutations are carried out by randomly changing a small fraction of the original gene. This operation allows the next generation to be able to move away from the original location where the parent agent sits; Crossovers are carried out in a conventional way, i.e. a random set of location genes are swapped between parent chromosomes to generate a next generation chromosome.

For the weight genes, the method used in the GA-WKNN model [Kelly & Devis 91] is adopted. The difference is that the weight system in the agent model is localized to a region associated with an agent, while in the GA-WKNN it is global. This allows the agent model to generate context dependent weights for each dimension of the problem space.

The distance threshold gene is mutated in the same way as the location genes. There is no crossover operation applied to it.

The fitness of the chromosome was assigned in the following way. The distance threshold and the weights form a region around the location expressed by the agent location gene. The homogeneity of the classes of all the training cases falling into that region is used as the fitness value. The homogeneity is measured by the standard entropy function $p_i \log p_i$, where p_i is the proportion of the ith class.

3.3 Communication between Memory Agents

Agent communication is designed to enable agent cooperations to achieve some global objectives. For the classification task, the global objectives are to achieve higher global coverage and higher classification accuracy, and to minimize the number of agents.

Communication allows agent to adjust themselves according to how other agents perform. Currently, only a very simple communication method, broadcasting, is used. Volume and direction controls are fixed for simplicity reason. The general principle is that each agent tries to gain its local interest in order to survive and agents are forced to cooperate and compete with each other to achieve maximum global interests.

When an agent has successfully bid for a new case and made a prediction on the class of the new case, the result of whether the classification is correct or not, together with the case itself, are broadcast to enable other agents to adjust themselves.

A memory agent, upon receiving a message, adjust itself in the following way. If the new case does not fall into the agent's bidding region, there will be no adjustment. Otherwise, there are two possibilities: If the message indicates that the message sending agent has correctly classified the case, then the recipient agent modifies its weight system so that the distance between the agent location and the new case are increased. This is motivated by the idea of avoiding overlapping agents. It is a simple way of resolving agents' interest conflict. If the message sending agent made a wrong classification, the weight system of the receiving agent is modified to decrease the distance if the receiving agent can classify the new case correctly.

The weight system modification follows the simple reinforcement rules:
   For each dimension i of the problem space,

$$w_i = w_i + d * | x_i - y_i |$$ to increase the distance between X and Y.
$$w_i = w_i - d * | x_i - y_i |$$ to decrease the distance between X and Y.

   here the w_i is the weight of ith dimension of the problem space and the d is a parameter determining how radical the adjustment is going to be. $X(x_1,...x_n)$, $Y(y_1,...,y_n)$ are two cases.

The bid winning agent will also adjust itself according to the classification result. If it makes a wrong classification, its weight system will be adjusted to increase the distance between the agent's location and the wrongly classified case. Otherwise, adjustment is made to decrease the distance.

4 Classification with the Memory Agent Model

There are three key issues involved in building a memory agent based classification system: the first is the initial training or generation of the agents; the second is the issue of incremental learning or continuous evolution of agents; and the third one is the actual classification of new problem cases.

An agent based classification system contains a set of memory agents. Initially, this set of agents are generated using a genetic prototype generating method described in [Knight & Sen 95]. The continuous evolution process is carried out in a batch fashion to avoid computational expensiveness. In practice, the evolution stops once the agent genes reach a relative stable state measured by a statistical variance parameter. The resulting set of agent is then used to carry out the classification task. A system parameter records the up to date unsuccessful classification rate indicating how well the current set of agents has been doing. If this parameter reaches a certain threshold, agents involved in these unsuccessful classification will begin their evolution processes to self-adapt themselves in order to fit those failed cases. In between the evolution stages, agents may adjust themselves using method described in section 3.3, based on the results of the classifications that have just been carried out.

For the classification task, each agent acts like a independent local classifier. When a new case to be classified is presented to the system, agents will either make a bid to classify it or take no action at all, depending on the agents' statuses. A global auction mechanism decides which agent wins the bid. The memory agent which is successful in the bidding has the right to classify the problem case. After classification, it sends out a message to other memory agents. Other agents may adjust themselves accordingly.

Globally, there are three ways the agent structure may change:

- It is possible that no agent has made a bid for a new case. In this instance, the training case becomes a new memory agent.
- Agents close to each other and which give the same classification may merge to form new agents.
- An agent which has successfully bid a large enough number of cases and gave a near evenly split classification will die, give up its bidding region for new or other agent to take over.

5 Expected Behaviour

Experimental system incorporating the memory agent model is still under development. Some planned experiments are reported in this section to illustrates the key ideas. Although the agent model has been aiming at solving real world problems, such as the insurance claim assessment problem in the context of the present project, however for simplicity reasoning, artificially generated data sets are used in this paper. This allows controls be easily placed on the distribution of the classes and the agent model be tested and evaluated more strictly.

The data used in the following experiments contains points in a two dimensional Euclidian space. the data is automatically generated following a designed class distribution There are only two classes concerned in the problem.

The objectives of the experiments are to examine how the agent model performs in regard to the following issues:

- Ability to generate a proper agent structure which produce good classification accuracy, given a set of training data.
- Adaptation ability to the changing environments, in particular, to the changes on class distribution.

The first test is to examine whether a set of agents can be formed to achieve a reasonable classification accuracy. The distribution of the class is depicted in figure 1. It is anticipated that a small number of agents will be generated as indicated in the figure. This agent structure will give a satisfactory overall classification accuracy.

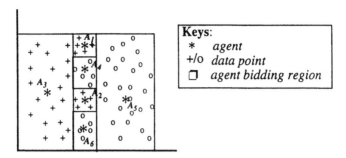

Figure 1. Agent Structure

The second experiment is to examine the reaction of agents towards the changes in the class distribution. It is anticipated that when the class distribution is changed from that in figure 1 to the one in figure 2, agents will make corresponding changes to their weight systems, to the locations which they reside as well as to the bidding region. As illustrated in figure 2. agent A_1 in figure 1 has changed to agent $A_{1'}$. It is also intended to test in this experiment the effect of allowing agents to move to locations which correspond to hypothetical cases as against the strategy which only allow agents to move to locations corresponding to training cases. It is anticipated that the former strategy will result in a better classification system.

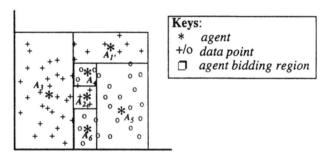

Figure 2. Adaptation to a changing environment

The third experiment concerns the issue of merging two agents to form a new agent, resulting in a reduced number of agents and a better classification coverage and accuracy. In figure 3, the class distribution presented in Figure 1. is changed in the way that merging agent A_1 and agent A_2 would be desirable. The anticipated agent structure is shown in figure 3.

There are many other issues need to be addressed and tested. It is hoped that experiments will be completed in the near future and comparisons carried out with the performances of other related models described in section 2.

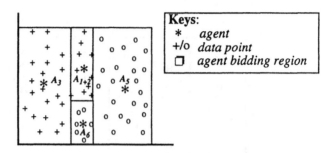

Figure 3. Merging agents to form a new agent structure

6 Conclusion

This paper proposes an agent model of memory for case based classification. The idea is to allow cases, and more generally memorized problem solving experiences, to take a more active role in future problem solving. The advantages[†] are that, first, memory agents will be able to handle problems particular to their bidding regions, leading to better overall classification accuracy. Second, memory agents will be able to make localized incremental learning in terms of changing agent locations and bidding regions. Global learning is achieved by changing agent structure. These enable the system to cope with dynamic environments where class distributions are changing. As a consequence, the difficult case base maintenance task in case based system may be solved automatically. Third, the evolutionary approach to learning enables the agent based system to outperform those based on linear search and simple reinforcement learning methods.

In addition, it is believed that the agent model of memory indicates a promising research direction for memory based reasoning. Instead of treating the cases in the case base as passive mass of past experiences, the agent model extends cases to active agents with knowledges and intentions. This may even be more important for problem domains such as design and planning, where case adaptation is more in need than in the classification domain. In these domains, past problem solving experience may be decomposed and partitioned to form agents to tackle particular parts of the problem in the future. This extend the idea of the hierarchical case based reasoning [Smyth & Keane 95].

Case based systems have hardly ever been just "case based reasoning" *per se*. There is always some sort of hybrid nature in a CBR system, especially when adaptation is involved [Hunt & Miles 94]. The agent model can provide a suitable vehicle for integrating different AI techniques to form hybrid systems, especially when different parts of the problem are better suited to different kinds of reasoning methods.

---

†. These claims are indirectly based on the work on nearest neighbour rules and genetic algorithms, more direct evidences supporting these claims are expected after experiments are fully carried out.

References

Aha, D. and Goldstone, R. L. 1992. Concept Learning and Flexible Weighting. *Proceedings of the 14th Annual Conference of the Cognitive Science Society. pp 534 - 539.*

Aha, D. and Goldstone, R. L. 1990. Learning Attribute Relevance in Context in Instance-Based Learning Algorithms. *Proceedings of the 12th Annual Conference of the Cognitive Science Society. pp 141 - 148.*

Back, T., Hoffmeister, F. and Schwefel, H. 1991. A Survey of Evolution Strategies. *Proceedings of the 4th International Conference on Genetic Algorithms. pp 2 - 9.*

Chang, C. 1974 Finding Prototypes for Nearest Neighbor Classifiers. *IEEE transactions on Computer, Volume C-23, Number 11, pp 1179 - 1184.*

Goldberg, D. E. 1989. *Genetic Algorithms in Search, Optimisation and Machine Learning.* Addison-Wesley.

Grefenstette, J. J. and Baker, J. E. 1989. How Genetic Algorithms Work: A critical look at implicit parallelism. *Proceedings of the 3rd International Conference on Genetic Algorithm. pp 20 -27.*

Kelly Jr., J. D. and Davis, L. 1991. A Hybrid Genetic Algorithm for Classification. *Proceedings of the 12th IJCAI. pp 645 - 650.*

Huang, Y. and Miles, R. 1995. A Case Based Method in Solving Relatively Stable Dynamic Constraint Satisfaction Problems. *Proceedings of the first International Conference on Case Based Reasoning, pp 481 - 490.*

Hunt, J. and Miles, R. 1994. Hybrid Case-Based Reasoning. *Knowledge Engineering Review, 9.*

Knight, L. and Sen, S. 1995. PLEASE: A prototype learning system using genetic algorithms. *Proceedings of the 6th International Conference on Genetic Algorithms. pp 429 - 435.*

Punch, W. F., Goodman, E. D., Pei, M., Shun, L., Hovland, P. and Enbody, R. 1993. Further Research on Feature Selection and Classification Using Genetic Algorithm. *Proceedings of the 5th International Conference on Genetic Algorithms. pp 557 - 564.*

Ricci, F. and Avesani, P. 1995. Learning a Local Similarity Metric for Case-Based Reasoning. *Proceedings of the first international conference on CBR. pp 301 - 312.*

Salzberg, S. 1991. A Nearest Hyperrectangle Learning Method. *Machine Learning 6. pp 277- 309.*

Smyth, B. and Keane, M. 1995. Experiments On Adaptation-Guided Retrieval In Case Based Design. *Proceedings of the first International Conference on CBR. pp 313 - 324.*

Swonger, C. W. 1972. Sample Set Condensation for a Condensed Nearest Neighbor Decision Rule for Pattern Recognition. S. Watanabe (Ed.). *Frontiers of Pattern Recognition. pp 511 - 519.*

Thomas, L. C., Crook, J. N. and Edelman, D. B. 1992. *Credit Scoring and Credit Control.* Oxford University Press.

Wilson, D. L. 1972. Asymptotic Properties of Nearest Neighbor Rules Using Edited Data. *IEEE transactions on Systems, Man and Cybernetics, Volume SMC-2, Number 3, pp 408 - 421.*

Wooldridge, M. and Jennings, N. R. 1995. Intelligent Agents: Theory and Practice. *The Knowledge Engineering Review, Vol. 10:2. pp 115 - 152.*

Using Description Logics for Knowledge Intensive Case-Based Reasoning

Gerd Kamp

Fachbereich Informatik, University of Hamburg,
Vogt-Koelln-Str.30, 22527 Hamburg, Germany

Abstract In this paper we argue that description logics with their object-oriented representation based on a declarative semantics and their powerful inferences are a good base for building similarity-based systems. But in existing description logic systems it is not possible to formulate and use knowledge about concrete domains (e.g. data types like numbers, strings, sets of symbols). Based on Baader and Hanschke's theoretical work on "admissible concrete domains" we realized CTL, an extensible description logic system that is able to integrate such concrete domains via a generic interface to existing implementations of such data types. Initially, we coupled a CLP($\mathcal{R}$)-system in order to realize sound and complete inferences over systems of linear inequalities. This concrete domain is especially useful within the area of second-level corporate support, a domain whose requirements initiated our investigations on description logics and which we will use for our illustrating examples.

1 Motivation

1.1 Second Level Support – Diagnosis as similarity based retrieval

Diagnosis is most often considered as a classification problem [Pup91, Ric95] using a description of a *diagnostic case* of the form *"case = problem + solution"* where the problem is given by a set (vector) of symptom values, and the solution is the diagnosis. The underlying hypothesis for the use of CBR is then expressed as: *"similar symptoms $\Rightarrow$ similar (same) diagnosis"*. Case-based diagnosis is therefore often realized as the task of finding the n most similar cases, and computing the diagnosis by some voting procedure on these n-nearest neighbors. This view is also the base for the most successful application area of CBR: Help-desks (see e.g. [Weß96]). Available help-desk systems normally use an attribute-value vector description and some numerical similarity function. This results in a system guiding the user in its search for the problem solution and is therefore especially suited for users that are unexperienced in the problem domain, e.g. first-level support persons such as help-desk operators.

The situation is different if one is to support technicians or other experts of "second-level support" [Kam94b, Kam94a]: Technicians need a system that they can use in a number of different ways. For instance they are responsible for a whole range of different devices, and they are also responsible e.g. for the regular maintenance of the devices etc. In a scenario that is geared towards use in multiple situations it is not possible to define a *singular* case representation and a *singular* similarity measure. Every intended type of usage needs a either a different representation, e.g new "secondary" attributes as in Richter [Ric95] or a different similarity measure. In addition, the technicians are able to identify the attributes[1] that are deemed relevant in a specific situation. Hence, they want to be in control over the sets of attributes and the retrieval function used in the retrieval. In the extreme case this can be an exact match on a single attribute (e.g. if they want to retrieve all the devices made by a certain manufacturer). Therefore, second-level support systems impose the following requirements:

1. *Object-oriented domain description.* In order to structure and represent the knowledge that is needed for the different intended types of use (e.g. the different device types), we need an object-oriented representation scheme. Since everything could be deemed relevant in a specific situation, no class of object could be considered as "the case": All objects have to be treated equally by the retrieval mechanism.

2. *Flexible query language.* Instead of a fixed similarity measure a flexible query language must be provided to enable the user to describe the current situation and his interests.

3. *Extensibility of the domain description.* Since new kinds and types of devices may be introduced or new types of usage may arise, in addition to the possibility to add new knowledge by adding new cases, the domain description itself must be extensible.

4. *Declarative Semantics.* Similarity measures, usually more or less complicated numerical functions of the attribute values, have no transparent semantics and therefore only a limited explanatory value. Since experts are able to understand the result of the retrieval to a greater degree than novices, a comprehensible and coherent semantic of the similarity measure is needed. Whereas laymen are grateful for every little tip, experts are scrutinizing the result. A result that is without foundation, or reduced to a numerical value is not satisfying.

5. *User driven system.* Because the user is an expert, he wants to be in control. A second-level service support system has to leave the initiative to the technician, it serves as a system that provides the information the technician wants to have in a particular situation.

All this leads to a model of case-based diagnosis that is considerably different from the "classical" model presented above: A case-based second-level support system has to be a *flexible information system*, that is able to deduce new information from a given set of informations. The actual problem is solved if we have provided enough information to enable the user to solve his problem[2]. Hence, the case retrieval must act in some sense like a data base system. A query formulated within some query language (e.g with some specified values of attributes) is

---

[1] At least they think they can.

[2] This is similar to the basic approach of information retrieval, where the user has some kind of information need and uses a system in order to retrieve new information.

answered by a set of objects which match with the given values. But in contrast to existing data base systems, we have to look for all objects which match by similarity and not exactly. Clearly, such a flexible information system is not only suitable for second-level support, but rather a general approach to similarity-based retrieval.

1.2 Integration of Knowledge

In technical domains a vast amount of knowledge has been gathered. CBR should not try to substitute this knowledge when it is available. If we know some rules or functional dependencies for sure, we should use them rather than a set of cases which behave according to that rule[3]. Therefore we must be able to firstly represent that knowledge, and secondly use it for indexing and retrieval. In particular, in a second-level support system it should be possible to represent the following kinds of knowledge may be relevant:

1. The different *types of components*, e.g. wheels, gear-wheels, chains, along with their *attributes* like force F, radius r and torque M.
2. The *structure* of assemblies, e.g the kinematic structure of the mechanisms using kinematic pairs.
3. *Physical laws* like $M = r \times F$ and *constraints* imposed on the attributes like $F \geq 0$ and $r > 0$.
4. The *normal and faulty behaviors* (often called models in consistency-based diagnosis) of components and assemblies, e.g. the propagation of torques from one wheel to another ($M_1 = M_2$) in a rotational pair.

To clarify, we are not claiming that the integration of case-based reasoning and model-based reasoning is novel, there are already quite a number of systems that combine case-based and model-based reasoning in the area of design (e.g. [SCN91, Goe88]) and diagnosis (e.g. [PW93]). We argue that it is necessary to use complex descriptions and integrate model-based reasoning in order to build second-level support systems, and that the methods based on attribute-value vectors and similarity measured used for case-based diagnosis today are insufficient. However, the above systems all use methods of qualitative physics and make use of some external system for model-based reasoning. We have chosen to model the attributes using scalar numeric values resulting in quantitative models of behavior. Most similar to our requirements is the approach presented in [Mad95], that uses a (in principle quantitative) bond graph method for the description of the design cases.

Our goal is to show that description logics with expressive concrete domains provide a general framework for the flexible information system depicted in the previous section. That framework was inspired by the need to express and integrate the above knowledge. It allows us to do so within the same mechanism, there is no external procedure doing the model based reasoning. Moreover, it is not restricted to only these kinds of knowledge.

---

[3] For a discussion of the use of case-bases vs. general knowledge see [Ric95].

2 Description Logics for similarity-based retrieval

Based on considerations similar to the ones presented in the previous section we developed AMS, a second-level support system [Kam94a, Kam94b], that employs an object-oriented representation formalism and a flexible query language based on a hierarchy of comparing relations. Other projects (e.g. [Weß95]) extended the attribute-value vector based techniques and similarity measures to hierarchic object structures. In our search for feasible extensions of these systems we were guided by their[4] following shortcomings:

1. *Seamless integration of knowledge.* Whereas it is possible to integrate device knowledge into object-oriented systems, it is not clear how the integration of physical laws and models of behavior could be done in a uniform way.
2. *Declarative Semantics.* While the definition of a set of comparing relations in [Kam94b] provided a flexible query language, it was only a step towards a declarative semantics. Whereas the semantics could be given declaratively at the attribute level, the semantics at the object level could only be given in a operational way.
3. *Automatic Indexing.* Whereas the syntactical indexing of cases (e.g. assigning a bucket in a k-d tree) could be done automatically, a semantic index like the membership of an object to a certain class must be assigned by the user.

In the following we will show that description logics with expressive concrete domains overcome these shortcomings.

2.1 Description Logics

Description logics (DL) have a long tradition (originating from the KL-ONE [BS85] system) in organizing information with a powerful representation scheme and clearly defined model-theoretic semantics. Description logics consist of two parts: a so called TBox[5] containing terminological knowledge and an ABox[6] containing assertional knowledge. Since we can not elaborate on the basics of description logics, we only give a brief introduction in the following and refer the reader to the respective literature (e.g. [BBH+92]) for a more detailed introduction.:

Definition 1 (TBox). *Concept terms* allow for a structured (object-oriented) representation of a relatively large fragment of first order-logic. Starting with primitive concept and role terms, new concepts terms can be constructed from others by a set of concept forming operators. There are mainly three categories of such operators [Han93]:

- *Boolean operators* (e.g. (and C_1 ...), (or C_1 ...), (not C_1))[7]

---

[4] especially AMS's.

[5] Terminological Box.

[6] Assertional Box.

[7] Throughout this paper we make use of the KRSS syntax, a proposed standard in the field of DL.

- *Role Forming operators* (e.g. composition of roles (compose r_1 r_2)).
- *Operators on Role Fillers* (e.g. quantification (some r C), (exists r C)).

Terminological axioms in the form (define-concept CN C) associate a concept name CN with a concept term C and are used to define the relevant concepts[8] of an application. Terminological axioms are therefore an extension to the class definitions of an object-oriented CBR approach[9]. A *TBox* ($\mathcal{T}$) is a finite set of terminological axioms.

Remark. Different terminological systems implement languages with different sets of operators and hence with different expressiveness.

Definition 2 (ABox). Concrete objects are realized as *instances* (individuals, objects) of concepts. New instances o can be introduced into the ABox via (define-distinct-individual o), and assertions α concerning the membership of an instance o to a concept C , or about existing relations (functions) between two objects o_1 and o_2 can be made through (state (instance o C)) resp. (state (related o_1 o_2 r)). The set of assertions constitutes the *ABox* $\mathcal{A}$.

What distinguishes a description logic approach to CBR from pure object-oriented ones, is that one is able to formally define a declarative model-theoretic semantics for the T- and ABox constructs by means of an interpretation function $^{\mathcal{I}}$, e.g. (and C_1 C_2)$^{\mathcal{I}} = C_1^{\mathcal{I}} \cap C_2^{\mathcal{I}}$. This semantics allows to give a formal definition of a number of powerful inferences, providing "intelligent" (semantic) access to information, that is independent from the syntax.

Definition 3 (DL Inference Services (I)). In our context the following inference services are of particular interest:

- *Consistency Test* An ABox (w.r.t. a TBox) is consistent iff. it has a model, i.e. $\mathcal{A}^{\mathcal{I}} \neq \emptyset$.
- *Concept Classification* is a TBox inference service that calculates the *subsumption hierarchy*, i.e. the subconcept-superconcept relationships between concepts. A concept C_1 *subsumes* another concept C_2 iff. for C_2 is also a model for C_1 (i.e. $C_1^{\mathcal{I}} \supseteq C_2^{\mathcal{I}}$).
- *Object Classification* is an ABox inference service that determines, given an object o of the ABox, the set of most specific concepts $\overline{C}(o) = \{C_1, \ldots, C_n\}$ that this object belongs to, i.e. $\overline{C}(o) = \{C_i \in \mathcal{T} \mid \{\mathcal{A} \cup \neg(o : C_i)\}^{\mathcal{I}} = \emptyset \wedge C_i$ minimal in $\mathcal{T}$ w.r.t. subsumption$\}$.
- *Retrieval* is dual to the object classification problem. Given an concept term C, the set of TBox objects (instances) $\overline{O}(C) = \{o_1, \ldots, o_m\}$ that are members of C, is returned.

---

[8] In the following the term concepts refers to concept terms as well concept names.

[9] The class hierarchy of object oriented systems could be translated into purely conjunctive concept terms with the slot definitions resulting in appropriate role definitions.

In addition to these well known inference services weak variants of the object classification and the retrieval are useful for similarity based retrieval.

Definition 4 (DL Inference Services (II)). Weak object classification in contrast delivers the set $\underline{C}(o)$ of the most general concepts the object may be specialized to if new information is added, i.e. $\underline{C}(o) = \{C_i \in \mathcal{T} \mid \{\mathcal{A} \cup (o : C_i)\}^{\mathcal{I}} \neq \emptyset \wedge C_i$ maximal in $\mathcal{T}$ w.r.t. subsumption$\}$. Weak retrieval returns the set of objects $\underline{O}(C) = \{o_1, \ldots, o_m\}$ for which it is possible that they are members of the concept.

Remark. Recent work in the area of DL focused on determining the computational properties of different description languages (i.e. sets of concept terms). Since all inference services are defined based on the consistency test of an ABox it is sufficient to find an algorithm for this problem. It has been shown that there exist sound and complete algorithms to determine the consistency of an ABox for a number of description languages. These algorithms are inspired by the tableaux calculus. But only a few available systems like KRIS and TAXON currently employ them. Most systems (e.g. LOOM and CLASSIC) instead use incomplete structural subsumption algorithms, and since they they don't reduce subsumption to the consistency test of an ABox a number of the other inferences is unavailable.

2.2 Ctl

It has become clear that description logics with their object-oriented description language and their powerful inferences are a good base for building knowledge-intensive CBR systems. Similar considerations led to the investigation of DL for CBR in [AA94] and [Koe94]. [AA94] uses LOOM with its expressive language but its very incomplete inferences[10] in a legal domain, whereas [Koe94] uses a very restricted language that allows for polynomial algorithms in helping a user working with the mail system of a Unix box. Neither their approaches, nor DL in the form presented above are suitable for building second-level support systems. Moreover, they can't be used to overcome the above mentioned shortcomings of object-oriented systems. The reason is the following: Initially, and the way presented above, description logics are operating only on the *abstract domain*. In order to refer to concrete values of attributes such as a force F or a name n one needs in addition *concrete domains*, comparable to the basic data types of the object-oriented schemes.

Definition 5. A *concrete domain* $\mathcal{D}$ is a relational structure, consisting of a set $dom(\mathcal{D})$, the domain of $\mathcal{D}$, and a set $pred(\mathcal{D})$, the predicate names of $\mathcal{D}$. Each $p \in pred(\mathcal{D})$ is associated with an arity n_p and an n_p-ary predicate $P^{\mathcal{D}} \subseteq dom(\mathcal{D})^{n_p}$.

Available DL systems such provide either no concrete domains at all or realize a single concrete domain over numerical values. Only comparisons with constant

---

[10] We would consider LOOM a frame-system rather than a DL.

values are possible, allowing simply for the definition of intervals [KW96]. It is impossible to define the simplest equations between univariate linear polynomials like $x = y + 1$ or $d = 2 \cdot r$. Not to mention linear multivariate polynomials like $p = 2 \cdot (l + w)$ or nonlinear polynomials like $M = r \cdot F$. Therefore they are far to inexpressive in order to represent the physical laws and models of behavior from Section 1.2 or other background knowledge.

In a first attempt to realize more expressive concrete domains we tried to use an escape mechanism that is provided by Loom (and Classic). They allow to define more complex relations between objects via arbitrary lisp functions. Obviously, these relations must be neglected during the TBox inferences, resulting in incomplete systems. Moreover, the undirectedness of the relations and therefore the physical laws and constraints must be simulated within their respective lisp functions, making this approach unusable. This experiences led us to the conclusion that the integration of additional and more expressive concrete domains is only usable, if the advantages of description logics, namely the declarative semantics and sound and complete inferences could be preserved. The theoretical foundations for such a scheme of so called *admissible concrete domains* were developed by Baader and Hanschke [BH91, Han93] and used in TAXON [11]. We present only the major results:

Definition 6. A concrete domain is *admissible* iff. (i) it is *closed under negation*, i.e. $\forall P \exists Q \ (Q = dom(\mathcal{D})^{n_P} \setminus P, P, Q \in pred(\mathcal{D}))$, (ii) it contains a name $\top_\mathcal{D}$ for $dom(\mathcal{D})$ (i.e. $\forall d \in dom(\mathcal{D})(\top_\mathcal{D}(d) = true)$), and (iii) the *satisfiability problem of finite conjunctions is decidable*. The finite conjunction $K = \bigwedge_{i=1}^{k} p_i(\mathbf{x}_i)$ is *satisfiable*, iff. there exists an assignment of the variables such that K becomes true.

Theorem 7. *Let $\mathcal{D}$ be an admissible concrete domain. Then there exists a sound and complete algorithm which is able to decide the consistency problem of an ABox for the description language $\mathcal{ALCF}(\mathcal{D})$.*

The task of the integration of data types such as numbers and strings is now reduced to finding admissible concrete domains over their respective domains, e.g. $\mathbb{Q}, \mathbb{R}$ etc. Without proof (see [BH91, KW96]) we present the following results:

Theorem 8. *The theory of the elementary algebra over the reals is an admissible concrete domain.*

Theorem 9. *Systems of (in)equalities between multivariate polynomials of degree at most n are an admissible concrete domain, especially systems of (in)equalities between linear multivariate polynomials are an admissible concrete domain.*

As we have seen above, the implementation of TAXON only provides a numerical domain that is restricted to comparisons with constants. The main criterion for an admissible concrete domain is the existence of a decision procedure for

---

[11] To our knowledge TAXON is the only available system that does so.

finite conjunction of concrete predicates. Based on TAXON we therefore developed CTL, a DL system that provides a well-defined interface that allows us to use existing implementations of such decision procedures [KW96]. In addition, we extended the consistency test within CTL. Normally, the consistency test returns a boolean value, but in our scenario[12] the actual model is of interest, as it provides among other things the value restrictions of the component parameters. Since a terminological system based on a tableaux method explicitly generates a model, the consistency can be modified to return the computed model along with the calculated parameter restrictions.

The language of the description logic has to be extended in the following way (for details see [KW96]):

Definition 10 (Concrete Domains). *Predicate terms P describe concrete predicates.* They are either a predicate name PN or a list $(\langle \text{name}_{\mathcal{D}} \rangle \ (x_1 \ldots x_n) \ \langle \text{expr}_{\mathcal{D}} \rangle)$ consisting of a domain identifier $\langle \text{name}_{\mathcal{D}} \rangle$ and a list of variables $x_1 \ldots x_n$. The expression $\langle \text{expr}_{\mathcal{D}} \rangle$ is written in a syntax understood by the decision procedure of the concrete domain $\mathcal{D}$, and actually defines the concrete predicate. define-constraint assigns a name PN to a predicate term P. Further (constrain $R_1 \ldots R_n P$) is an additional concept term operator with the following semantics:

$$(\text{constrain } R_1 \ \ldots \ R_n P)^{\mathcal{I}} =$$
$$\{a \mid \exists b_1, \ldots, b_n ((a, b_1) \in R_1^{\mathcal{I}} \wedge \cdots \wedge (a, b_n) \in R_n^{\mathcal{I}} \wedge (b_1, \ldots, b_n) \in P^{\mathcal{I}})\}.$$

In order to integrate the knowledge of Section 1.2 we coupled a CLP($\mathcal{R}$)-system with CTL. This gives us an admissible concrete domain that allows us to completely handle systems of linear inequalities, and to handle systems of nonlinear inequalities if they become linear due to the restriction of an appropriate number of parameters during the inference process.

3 Similarity-based Retrieval

The above inferences services can be used for similarity-based retrieval and for the realization of the flexible information system we sketched in Section 1.1. In the following we present a number of methods for similarity-based retrieval. The methods differ on the basic inference that they employ, and therefore in the size of the ABox the consistency test is working on. Since concept classification does not consider any concrete ABox objects, the ABox consists only of that entries that are obtained by translating the TBox into an equivalent ABox. Object classification adds the objects mentioned in the query. Retrieval finally works on the all objects. Since the complexity of the consistency test is directly determined by the size of the ABox, the chosen basic inference determines the time needed for the similarity-based retrieval. On the other hand fewer inferences are drawn since the ABox is smaller. Therefore the different retrieval methods provide a

---

[12] as well as at least in other applications in technical domains such as configuration.

means to choose between using little background knowledge and (hopefully) compensating that with large amounts of cases and using lots of background knowledge and reducing the size of the case base.

Methods based on retrieval The inference service that is most obvious to use is the retrieval service. Methods based on it work as follows:

1. *Query formulation* The query is formulated as a concept term C_q.
2. *Calling the retrieval inference* Determination of the sets $I'(C_q) = \overline{O}(C_q)$, $I''(C_q) = \underline{O}(C_q)$ bzw. $I'''(C_q) = (\overline{O}(C_q), \underline{O}(C_q))$.
3. Display $I'(C_q)$ (resp. $I''(C_q)$ or $I'''(C_q)$.

Remark. In a naive implementation the membership of all objects $o_j \in \mathcal{A}$ would be tested wrt. C_q in step 2. The number of objects to be tested can be reduced by calling object classification on C_q first, and then testing only those objects contained in the subtree below C_q. This too can be a time consuming process. Therefore one can implement methods that approximate retrieval based on concept classification.

Methods based on concept classification Prerequisite for methods based on concept classification is the previous indexing of all $o_j \in \mathcal{A}$ based on retrieval[13]. Because of this, concept classification is used at best, if only queries at an existing set of objects are formulated and no new objects are introduced to the ABox simultaneously.

1. *Preprocessing* For each $C_j \in \mathcal{T}$, call the retrieval $O(C_j)$ and the index the returned instances. Use either strong $I'(C_j) = \overline{O}(C_j)$, weak retrieval $I''(C_j) = \underline{O}(C_j)$ or a combination of both $I'''(C_j) = (\overline{O}(C_j), \underline{O}(C_j))$ as an index .
2. *Query formulation* Since the query language and the concept description language are identical, an arbitrary concept term C_q can be used as query formulation. Use the concept classification C_q to determine its position in the concept hierarchy, i.e. calculate the sets of its direct upper neighbors $\overline{C_q} = \{\overline{C_{q_1}}, \ldots, \overline{C_{q_n}}\}$ and and direct lower neighbors $\underline{C_q} = \{\underline{C_{q_1}}, \ldots, \underline{C_{q_m}}\}$.
3. *Calculate the retrieval result* The result of the query C_q is calculated as a combination of the stored retrieval results $I^*(\overline{C_q})$ resp. $I^*(\underline{C_q})$. Good approximations for $\overline{O}(C_q)$ and $\underline{O}(C_q)$ are:

$$\overline{O'}(C_q) = \bigcap \overline{C_q} \qquad \underline{O'}(C_q) = \bigcup \underline{C_q}.$$

4. *Display the result.*

---

[13] Other methods could be used too, but then the consistency of the result could not be guaranteed.

Methods based on object classification As we have seen in Section 2.1 object classification is an procedure for the automatic semantic indexing of ABox objects $o_j \in \mathcal{A}$ wrt. the concept descriptions $C_k \in \mathcal{T}$. Therefore object classification is the method of choice if one is actually adding objects to the ABox and is interested in already existing objects within $\mathcal{A}$ that are similar. The method works as follows:

1. *Add assertions about objects o_j* New assertions (e.g. values of parameters) about an object o_j trigger automatically a reclassification and therefore a reindexing of o_j.
2. *Reindex the o_j* Use either the strong $I'(o_j) = \overline{C}(o_j)$, or the weak variant $I''(o_j) = \underline{C}(o_j)$ of object classification, or a combination of both $I'''(o_j) = (\overline{C}(o_j), \underline{C}(o_j))$.
3. *Determine similar objects* Based on weak and strong object-classification a number of similarity measures can be defined:
   (a) *Identical indices.* The most simple, pure relational similarity measure returns all the objects as similar that have the same set of indices as the query object. Let $I^* \in \{I', I'', I'''\}$ and $\aleph_M$ be the characteristical function of M. Then
   $$sim_{I^*}(o_k) = \aleph_{I^*(o_l)=I^*(o_k)}(o_k);$$

   Since the user is an expert and is able to formulate the query very precisely. This, together with the inferences drawn by the classification process ensure that even this simple similarity measure is sufficient for most purposes.
   (b) *Relative fraction of indices*
   $$sim_{I^*}(o_l, o_k) = \frac{|\,I(o_l) \cap I(o_k)\,|}{|\,I(o_l) \cup I(o_k)\,|}, \qquad I^* \in \{I', I'', I'''\}$$
   (c) *Tree Distance between the index sets*

Remark. Because o_j is related to a set $o_{k_1}, \ldots, o_{k_n}$ these objects must be reclassified and reindexed. In the "worst-case" the classification of a singular object o_j triggers the reclassification of the whole ABox $\mathcal{A}$, a time consuming process. But normally only a fraction of the objects is affected: "Conventional" CBR systems make the independence assumption that different cases are not related to each other and their implementation (e.g. their similarity measure) is based on that assumption. Since we don't have an explicit "case" object, we don't have such a strict independence assumption, the independency of objects is implicitly described by the relations within the ABox, and the affected objects is determined by the transitive hull of the objects related to the query objects.

4 Example

Lets suppose one wants to support a second-level support person responsible for mechanisms consisting of wheels or gear-wheels such as bike drive-trains. As an example of such a mechanism we use the simple bike drive-train depicted

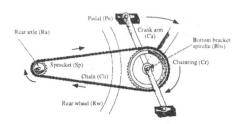

Figure1. A simple bike drivetrain

in Figure 1. As we have seen in Section 1.2, we must be able to describe the different component types of a mechanism as well the kinematic structure. In kinematics this is normally done with links and kinematic pairs [Reu76, ISO94].

Representation In order to describe the drivetrain of Fig.1, it is sufficient to define rotational links and tension links as specializations of general links. The terminology in Fig.2a) a defines a link as something that carries a force: link.force. Rotational links (rotational-link) are links that in addition have attributes for a radius (rot.radius) and a torque (rot.torque). link.force and rot.torque are not negative, rot.radius is strictly positive. In order to describe the structure of a mechanism, kinematic pairs are used. A kinematic-pair describes the connection between two links: pair.link1 and pair.link2. Depending on the degrees of freedom of the relative motion of the links and the type of connection different types of pairs can be identified. In the terminology shown in Fig.2b) we restrict us to the description of pairs between two rotational-links (rot-pair) and pairs between one rotational-link and one tension-link (rot-tension-pair). Until now, the description of links and pairs would also have been more or less possible in object-oriented representation schemes. One notable exception is the following. We are able to describe rot-tension-pair via an or construct, something that is not possible in object-oriented systems. We now turn our focus on the representation of the other kinds of background knowledge mentioned in Section 1.2. First, we are not aware of any approach that seamlessly integrates background knowledge like laws of physics into the CBR system. One approach to the direct integration of background knowledge into object-oriented CBR systems is that of Bergmann et.al. [BWVW96]. But they are only able to make use of directed rules, instead of omni-directional relations. Within CTL the integration of the law of torque is simply a matter of slightly modifying the definition of rotational-link in the way shown in Fig.2c). Adding this constraint enables us to determine the value of the third parameter, no matter which two parameters are given, nor which value they have.

In addition to the component types and the structure of the device, descriptions of the correct as well as the different faulty behaviors are needed. The terminology in Fig.2d) describes the correct behavior of rotational-pairs and rot-tension-pairs. Whereas the torque is propagated in ok-rot-pair, ok-rot-tension-pair

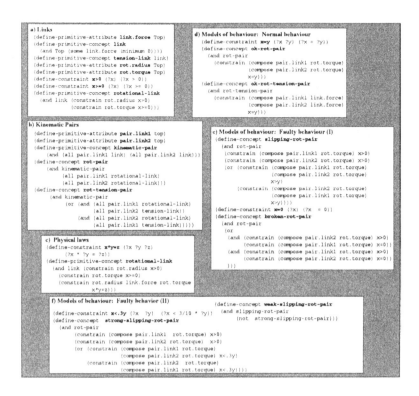

Figure2. Representation of simple mechanisms

propagates the force. The terminology in Fig.2e) shows some exemplary faulty behaviors of a rotational pair. A pair is slipping (slipping-rot-pair) if both torques are strictly positive and different. A pair is broken (broken-rot-pair) if one torque is strictly positive, the other zero. A second developer might distinguish between strong and weak slipping pairs (strong-slipping-rot-pair resp. weak-slipping-rot-pair) as it is depicted in Fig.2f). Note that we are able to describe the weak slipping pair as the negation of a strong one, another thing that is not possible within object-oriented representations. This allows for a simple description of a weak slipping pair, and reduces the sources of possible faults. It further eases the modification of the knowledge base, e.g. a change of the limit between strong and weak slipping.

Automatic semantic indexing Object-oriented CBR systems like the one presented in [Weß95] most often make use of an automatic indexing scheme based on a syntactic criterion, in order to build up the index structure. Also they most often use a index structure designed for multidimensional structures based on a totally ordered dense data type like $\mathbb{R}$. Nearly all index structures devised so far for this kind of data (e.g. k-d-trees, R*-trees, ...) use axis-parallel rectangles to approximate the semantic concepts (see Fig.3a). This works reasonably well for a great deal of situations. But they are inappropriate for a number of more complex situations. Consider for example the models of behavior introduced above. Due to $M_1 = M_2$, ok-rot-pair is nearly impossible to approximate via axis-parallel rectangles[14] (see Fig.3b). The same applies to slipping-rot-pair. Moreover, since the different concepts are directly touching each other and they make up a partition of the whole data space, it is difficult to overcome the shortcomings of the basic indexing structure with an appropriate numerical similarity measure. Note that broken-rot-pair is equivalent to $M_1 \cdot M_2 = 0 \land M_1 > 0 \land M_2 > 0$. Therefore it is not possible to even classify broken-rot-pair using a similarity measure based on a weighted sum.

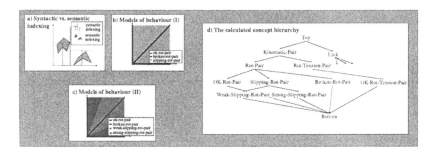

Figure3. Indexing

Fig.3b) and Fig.3c) also give a visual clue to the concepts of an interpretation function and concept subsumption. The shaded areas are the possible interpretations of a concept, and a concept C_1 is subsumed by a concept C_2 if its shaded area is totally enclosed by the shaded area of C_2. Fig.3d) shows a part of the concept hierarchy that is automatically computed via the concept classification inference service. There a few facts that could be read off from this graph:

1. All concept definitions are different from **bottom**. Therefore all definitions are satisfiable. This guarantees that no model of behavior is mistakenly defined in a way that there exists no parameter combination that leads to this behavior (e.g. through a parameter restriction like $x > 0 \land x < 0$).
2. All concept definitions are distinct from each other. This means that there are no two models of behavior that are equivalent, something that could easily happen when two model libraries are merged.
3. Strong and weak slipping pairs are modeled as specializations of **rot-pair** and not of **slipping-rot-pair**. Situations like this are very likely if different people are simultaneously developing models of behavior, or when the model libraries are complex. The classification service detected the missing subsumption relation between **slipping-rot-pair** and **strong-slipping-rot-pair**. In other situations it may be the case that a computed subsumption relation is not missing but accidental in a sense that it is caused by some error or laxness in the description of the models of behavior.

---

[14] At least over the attributes $M1, M2$.

Remark. Such Errors are very likely in large and complex model libraries. Therefore the detection of these errors is crucial for the development of such libraries. Since all inferences are sound and complete[15] in CTL, we can guarantee that all missing and accidental subsumption relations in the model library are detected.

We will now give a brief example how our representation together with the object classification delivers automatic semantic indexing.

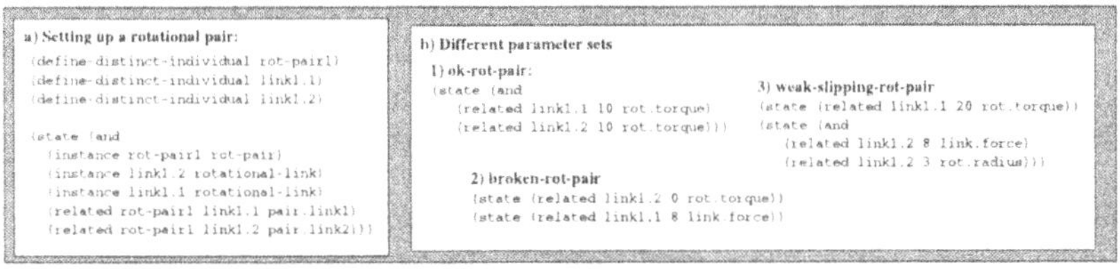

Figure4. Object classification

Giving two identical torques as parameter values as in Fig. 4b1) leads to the classification as an **ok-rot-pair**, as it should be expected. The classification process becomes more clear if one uses the parameter values of Fig. 4b2). The first assertion, together with the law of torque and the constraint that a radius is strictly positive enforces that the torque of link1.1 is strictly positive. Therefore the second assertion, giving a zero value for the torque of link1.2 suffices to classify **rot-pair1** as a broken-rot-pair. Note that only 2 of the 6 parameters are needed for correct classification. The example in Fig 4b3) finally illustrates how the **rot-pair1** can be classified as a **weak-slipping-rot-pair**. This is possible due to the calculation of the torque of link1.2 via the law of torque and the calculation of the ratio of the two torques. This example also illustrates the role of weak object classification. After the second assertion **broken-rot-pair** can be excluded from the list of possible behaviour models since – using the same argumentation as above – the torque of link1.2 is strictly positive. Hence both torques of **rot-pair1** are strictly positive and it is impossible that it is a **broken-rot-pair**.

5 Summary and outlook

In this paper we have argued that description logics (DL) are well suited for similarity based retrieval and can be successfully used for implementing second-level support systems. Actual work has its focus on integrating additional concrete domains such as symbols and texts, and to enhance the expressiveness of the concrete domain over the numbers by incorporating decision procedures based on quantifier elimination [Wei96].

References

[AA94]   K. D. Ashley and V. Aleven. A logical Representation for Relevance Criteria. In K.-D. Althoff S. Weß and M. M. Richter, editors, *Topics in Case-Based Reasoning*, pages 338–352, 1994, Springer Verlag.

---

[15] at least for linear systems of inequalities in our current implementation

[BBH⁺92]   F. Baader, H. Bürckert, B. Hollunder, A. Laux, and W. Nutt. Terminologische Logiken. *KI*, (3):23–33, 1992.

[BH91]   F. Baader and P. Hanschke. A Scheme for Integrating Concrete Domains into Concept Languages. Research Report RR-91-10, DFKI, Kaiserslautern, Germany, April 1991.

[BS85]   R. J. Brachman and J. G. Schmolze. An overview of the KL-ONE knowledge representation system. *Cognitive Science*, 9(2), 1985.

[BWVW96] Ralph Bergmann, Wolfgang Wilke, Ivo Vollrath, and Stefan Weß. Integrating General Knowledge with Object-Oriented Case Representation and Reasoning. In *Proc. 4th GWCBR*, pages 120–127, Berlin, Germany, 1996. Humboldt Universität Berlin.

[Goe88]   Ashok Goel. Integrating Model-Based-Reasoning and Case-Based Reasoning for Design Problem Solving. In *Proc. AAAI-88*, 1988.

[Han93]   P. Hanschke. *A Declarative Integration of Terminological, Constraint-Based, Data-driven, and Goal-directed Reasoning*. Dissertation, Universität Kaiserslautern, 1993.

[ISO94]   ISO. *ISO 10303 Part 105: Kinematics*. ISO, 1994.

[Kam94a]   Gerd Kamp. AMS - A Case-Based Service Support System. In R. V. Rodriguez F. D. Anger and M. Ali, editors, *Proc. of the IEA/AIE94*, pages 677–683, Austin, TX, 1994. Gordon and Breach Science Publishers.

[Kam94b]   Gerd Kamp. Integrating Semantic Structure and Technical Documentation in Case-Based Service Support Systems. In K.-D. Althoff S. Weß and M. M. Richter, editors, *Topics in Case-Based Reasoning*, pages 392–403, 1994. Springer Verlag.

[Koe94]   Jana Koehler. An Application of Terminological Logics to Case-based Reasoning. In Proc. KR94, Bonn, Germany, 1994.

[KW96]   Gerd Kamp and Holger Wache. CTL – a description logic with expressive concrete domains. Technical report, LKI, 1996.

[Mad95]   T.N. Madhusudan. A Bond graph based approach to Case-based synthesis. CMU-RI-TR-95-29, Carnegie Mellon University, July 1995.

[Pup91]   Frank Puppe. *Einführung in Expertensysteme*. Springer, 1991.

[PW93]   Gerd Pews and Stefan Wess. Combining Case-Based and Model-Based Approaches for Diagnostic Applications in Technical Domains. In *Proc. EWCBR'93*, pages 325–328, 1993.

[Reu76]   F. Reuleaux. *The Kinematics of machinery - outlines of a theory of machines*. Macmillan & Co, New York, NY, 1876.

[Ric95]   Michael M. Richter. The Knowledge Contained in Similarity Measures. Invited Talk ICCBR95, 1995.

[SCN91]   Katia Sycara, D. Navin Chandra, and S. Narasimhan. A transformational approach to case-based synthesis. *AI EDAM*, 5(1), 1991.

[Weß95]   Stefan Weß. *Fallbasiertes Problemlösen in wissensbasierten Systemen zur Entscheidungsunterstützung und Diagnostik*. PhD thesis, Universität Kaiserslautern, Kaiserslautern, Germany, January 1995.

[Weß96]   Stefan Weß. Intelligente Systeme für den Customer-Support. *Wirtschaftsinformatik*, 38(1):23–31, 1996.

[Wei96]   Volker Weispfenning. Applying Quantifier Elimination to Problems in Simulation and Qptimization. Technical Report MIP-9607, Universität Passau, Passau, Germany, April 1996.

Applying Case Retrieval Nets to Diagnostic Tasks in Technical Domains

Mario Lenz[1], Hans-Dieter Burkhard[1] and Sven Brückner[1,2]

[1] Dept. of Computer Science, Humboldt University Berlin, Axel-Springer-Str. 54a,
D-10117 Berlin, Email: {lenz,hdb}@informatik.hu-berlin.de
[2] P.S.I. AG, Heilbronner Str. 10, D-10711 Berlin

Abstract. This paper presents *Objectdirected Case Retrieval Nets*, a memory model developed for an application of Case-Based Reasoning to the task of technical diagnosis. The key idea is to store cases, i.e. observed symptoms and diagnoses, in a network and to enhance this network with an object model encoding knowledge about the devices in the application domain.

Keywords: Technical diagnosis, case retrieval, memory structures

1 Introduction

In the area of Case-Based Reasoning (CBR), a major focus of research in recent years has been on the development of techniques allowing for an efficient retrieval of relevant cases in a given problem situation. This has led to a number of sophisticated techniques for this subtask, as for example indexing techniques ([11]); *kd*–trees ([14, 15]); the *"Fish–and–Sink"* approach ([12]); the CRASH memory model ([3]); and *Knowledge-directed Spreading Activation* (KDSA, [16]).

As an alternative memory model we have developed the model of *Case Retrieval Nets* (CRNs [9]), which are particularly suitable for analytic CBR tasks, such as classification, diagnosis, and decision support ([6, 8]). The goal of this article is to present *Objectdirected Case Retrieval Nets* (OCRNs), an extension of CRNs especially for the purpose of technical diagnosis: The task was to develop a case-based diagnosis-assistance-system for a heterogeneous computer network. A major characteristic in this environment is that broad knowledge about the physical devices exists and has to be taken into account when performing inferences. However, this knowledge does not suffice for a model-based approach and hence we decided to apply CBR enhanced by an object model.

This paper is organized as follows: Section 2 reviews the basic ideas of *Case Retrieval Nets* while not really going into details about this model (cf. [5, 9] for broader investigations). In Section 3 the focus is set on applications in the area of technical diagnosis and an extended model of CRNs especially suitable for this task is introduced. Sections 4 to 6 discuss related work and give an outlook on future work.

2 A Brief Review of *Case Retrieval Nets*

This section will give an informal review of the ideas of *Case Retrieval Nets* as far as it facilitates the understanding of the extended model given in Section 3. A brief formal description is given in Appendix A, detailed descriptions can be found, for example, in [9].

2.1 Structure of a CRN

The most fundamental item in the context of CRNs are so-called *Information Entities* (IEs). These may represent any basic knowledge item, such as a particular attribute-value-pair or an observable symptom.

A *case* then consists of a set of such IEs, and the *case base* is a net with nodes for the IEs observed in the domain and additional nodes denoting the particular cases. IE nodes may be connected by *similarity arcs*, and a case node is reachable from its constituting IE nodes via *relevance arcs*. The idea is illustrated for the TRAVEL AGENCY domain ([7]) in Figure 1.

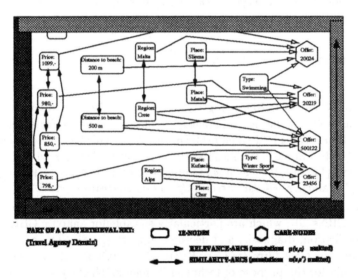

Fig. 1. Example of a CRN in the TRAVEL AGENCY domain: A case is a special travel offer, denoted by a case descriptor, e.g. <Offer 20219>. It consists of a set of corresponding IEs giving the specification of that offer, in case of <Offer 20219> the IE nodes <Type:Swimming>, <Price:980>, <Place:Matala>, <Region:Crete>, <Distance to beach:500 m> are connected with that case node.

Given this structure, case retrieval is performed by

1. *activating* the IEs given in the query case,
2. *propagating* this activation according to similarity through the net of IEs and
3. collecting the achieved activation in the associated case nodes.

Different degrees of similarity and relevancy may be expressed by varying arcs weights. In Figure 1, for example, a query asking for a bathing holiday and not too far from the beach will cause the IE nodes <Type:Swimming>, <Distance to beach:200 m> and <Region:Crete> to be initially activated. Using similarity arcs, other IE nodes, such as <Region:Malta> and <Distance to beach:500 m>, will be activated afterwards and hence the three case nodes <Offer 20024>, <Offer 20219>, <Offer 500122> will each get some activation the amount of which depends on arc weights. Special preferences may be expressed by initial weights, similarity weights and relevance weights, respectively. A first suggestion by the system might include alternative solutions which are pruned after a decision by the customer for either of them.

This simple example already points out some essential features of the CRN memory model:

- CRNs can handle only *partially specified queries* without loss of efficiency (most case retrieval techniques have problems with partial descriptions and *unknown* resp. *missing values*).
- CRNs require the application of a composite similarity measure, i.e. that similarity of two cases is determined according to the similarity of the features describing the cases. CRNs are particularly useful if varying similarity between different values of certain attributes has to be taken into account.
- Case retrieval is seen as a kind of *case completion*, i.e. whatever part of a case will be given as a description, the retrieval algorithm will deliver the remaining part and thus *complete* the case.
- In contrast to, for example, classification tasks there is no *a priori* distinction between a *description* of a problem and a *solution*[3]. This implies that a diagnosis is a part of a case just as the description of a symptom is. Hence, one may determine the diagnosis for a given set of symptoms — but one may also search for the symptoms (typically) associated to particular diagnoses.
- CRNs can be tuned to express different similarities/relevances at run time (by simply changing related arc weights), while other techniques need a new compilation step.
- Insertion of new cases (even with new attributes) can be performed incrementally by injecting related nodes and arcs.

2.2 More Sophisticated Retrieval Procedure

While the formal description of CRNs allows for a detailed investigation of the approach in terms of theoretical properties (such as *completeness* and *complexity*), it suffers from the drawback that during similarity propagation (Step 2 on page 15 in Appendix A) activation is propagated from the initially activated IEs to *all* IE nodes having non-zero similarity. In situations where a set of highly

---

[3] This is in some sense similar to queries to a database where arbitrary parts of the database record may be specified to obtain other parts — however, CRNs do not contain something like a *primary key* to support efficiency.

similar cases exists, it will be more reasonable to subsequently extend the scope of IEs and to include less similar IEs only if a sufficiently similar case has not yet been found.

> *As an example imagine being in a foreign city, having a map of the city, and looking for the nearest underground station: After having found the current location on the map (which is straightforward, e.g. by using the index of streets), one would probably search the region near the current location (e.g. the same quadrant on the map). If some stations are found one can compare them to select the nearest. Otherwise, i.e. if there was no station, one will extend the scope (e.g. consider neighboring quadrants, too) until at least one station is contained in it.*

The method of *Lazy Propagation of Similarity* as introduced in [10] formalizes this idea and allows to further reduce the retrieval effort without loosing completeness[4]. OCRNs, as introduced in the main body of this paper, provide another means for directing the spread of activation.

2.3 Improved Structuring

According to flat case representations, the simple model of BCRN has considered IEs as atomic entities. However, one often has the opportunity to organize the different attribute values (or IEs) in such a way that certain *concepts* can be utilized. This is the idea of *Microfeature CRNs* which employ a number of domain specific *microfeatures* to support similarity assessment between different IEs. When taking this approach, an IE is no longer necessarily an atomic, *non-decomposable Information Entity*, as described in Section 2, but rather represents the granularity chosen for describing cases. Each IE may, however, be a collection of further properties, concepts, or microfeatures. The major difference between microfeatures and concepts in the traditional sense is that microfeatures may be related to each other in terms of similarity, too. This is usually not applied to concepts.

As an example consider the TRAVEL AGENCY domain again: Here each particular destination is represented by an IE which, in turn, has a set of microfeatures, such as `location`, `climate`, `landscape` etc. (cf. Figure 2). The `locations` of two different IEs, for example, may then be compared; and the similarity concerning the various microfeatures, or *aspects*, is utilized to determine the similarity between two IEs.

This approach to similarity assessment not only eases maintenance of the CRN, but also allows for a convenient way to incorporate a notion of *context* in similarity assessment: As in different situations different aspects are important,

---

[4] The term *completeness* will only be used informally here. Basically, this means that no case will be discarded during the retrieval process which would have been retrieved, for example, by using a flat search through the case base. For a more formal definition cf. [14, p.160]

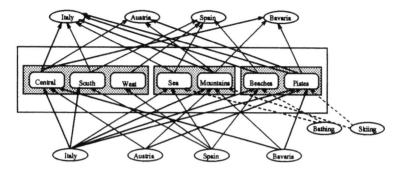

Fig. 2. Utilizing microfeatures (middle level) to determine similarity of IEs (upper level) in the TRAVEL AGENCY domain (case nodes not displayed).

the influence of the various microfeatures to the similarity of IEs will vary — giving rise to a context-sensitive similarity measure (see dotted lines in Figure 2).

As with the improved retrieval method, OCRNs provide another approach for structuring the entire set of IEs according to existing knowledge about the domain.

3 Utilization of CRNs for Technical Diagnosis

After the basic ideas of CRNs and some possible extensions have been reviewed above, this section is concerned with the application of CRNs for diagnostic purposes, in particular for technical diagnosis. For this, we will describe *Objectdirected Case Retrieval Nets* (OCRNs), an extension of CRNs with domain-dependent knowledge.

3.1 Extended CRNs: OCRNs

The goal of OCRNs is to further extend the basic memory model by integrating available domain knowledge into the CRN. While this domain knowledge will be weak and incomplete for sufficiently complex applications, it may nevertheless provide some useful guidance to the retrieval procedure. For example, details about the considered physical devices in an environment, their relationships, and their associated faults may be used

- in an early stage of retrieval: to focus on a specific set of devices with which the fault may be connected;
- in a later stage of retrieval: to guide the search for additional symptoms allowing for an efficient differential diagnosis.

In this approach, the domain knowledge will be encoded in terms of an *object model* containing details about the devices under investigation and their relationships. This *object model* will be placed on top of a BCRN, which contains case nodes (describing previously observed failures) and IE nodes (encoding particular symptoms). Figure 3 shows an example of a simple OCRN for technical diagnosis.

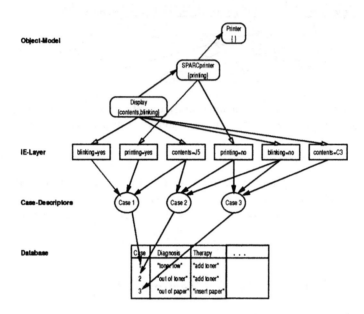

Fig. 3. Example OCRN: IEs represent symptoms and cases describe diagnostic episodes. Knowledge about physical devices is placed on top of the BCRN.

3.2   Formal Definition of OCRNs

Definition 1 An *Objectdirected Case Retrieval Net* (OCRN) is defined as a structure $[O, E, C, \rho, \psi, \eta, \Pi]$ with

O is the finite set of *object nodes*, each object has 2 different kinds of activation (positive inform α^p, negative inform α^n);

E is the finite set of IE nodes, each IE has 2 activation-values (retrieval α^p, differential α^n);

C is the finite set of case nodes, each case has an activation α;

ρ is the *relevance function*

$$\rho : E \times C \to \mathcal{R}$$

describing the (static) relevance $\rho(e, c)$ of the IE e to the case denoted by c;

ψ is the *generalization function*

$$\psi : O \to \mathcal{P}(O)$$

describing with $p \in \psi(o)$ that o inherits features from p or that o is part of p;

η is the *realization function*

$$\eta : E \to O$$

meaning with $\eta(e) = o$ that the IE e provides a value to one of the attributes describing the object o;

Π is the set of *propagation functions* π_n for each node $n \in O \cup E \cup C$ with

$$\pi_n : \begin{cases} R^E \to R & : & n \in E \cup C \quad \text{(similarity and relevance propagation)} \\ R^{E \cup O} \to R & : & n \in O \quad \text{(inform propagation)} \end{cases}$$

□

Definition 2 Consider an OCRN with $C = \{c_1, \cdots, c_{s_c}\}$, $E = \{e_1, \cdots, e_{s_e}\}$, $O = \{o_1, \cdots, o_{s_o}\}$.

- The *activation of an IE-node* $e \in E$ at time $t+1$ is given by

$$\alpha_{t+1}^p(e) = \alpha_0^p(e)$$

that is, positive activation does not change over time, and

$$\alpha_{t+1}^n(e) = \begin{cases} \pi_e(\rho(e, c_1) * \alpha_t(c_1), \cdots, \rho(e, c_{s_c}) * \alpha_t(c_{s_c})) & : & \alpha_t^p(e) = 0 \\ 0 & : & \alpha_t^p(e) \neq 0 \end{cases}$$

- The *activation of a case-node* $c \in C$ at time $t+1$ is given by

$$\alpha_{t+1}(c) = \pi_c(\rho(e_1, c) * \alpha_t^p(e_1), \cdots, \rho(e_{s_e}, c) * \alpha_t^p(e_{s_e}))$$

- Finally, the *activations of an object node* $o \in O$ at time $t+1$ are given by

$$\alpha_{t+1}^p(o) = \pi_o(\overline{\alpha_t^p}(e_1), \ldots, \overline{\alpha_t^p}(e_{s_e}), \overline{\alpha_t^p}(o_1), \ldots, \overline{\alpha_t^p}(o_{s_o}))$$

and

$$\alpha_{t+1}^n(o) = \pi_o(\overline{\alpha_t^n}(e_1), \ldots, \overline{\alpha_t^n}(e_{s_e}), \overline{\alpha_t^n}(o_1), \ldots, \overline{\alpha_t^n}(o_{s_o}))$$

where $\overline{\alpha_t^p}(n), n \in E \cup O$ is a shorthand for

$$\overline{\alpha_t^p}(n) = \begin{cases} \alpha_t^p(n) & : & n \in E \wedge \eta(n) = o \\ 0 & : & n \in E \wedge \eta(n) \neq o \\ \alpha_t^p(n) & : & n \in O \wedge o \in \psi(n) \\ 0 & : & n \in O \wedge o \notin \psi(n) \end{cases}$$

and accordingly for $\overline{\alpha_t^n}(n)$.

□

Similarly to the basic model (see Appendix A), the initial activation α_0 is set according to the description of the query case, that is IE nodes are activated (with value 1) if and only if they occur in the query case description. All other nodes are initially inactive.

Remarks and Requirements on the Definition

- The object model has to be an acyclic, directed graph.
- Each element of E contains an attribute-value pair to describe one aspect of a case.
- The elements of O (the objects in the object model) contain a set of attributes. Attributes of an object can be found, together with a specifying value, in elements of E. These IEs are then realizations of the object.
- $[E, C, \sigma, \rho, \Pi|_{E \cup C}]$ with

$$\sigma(e_i, e_j) = 1 \begin{cases} 1 & : & e_i = e_j \\ 0 & : & else \end{cases}$$

forms a *Basic Case Retrieval Net*. $\Pi|_{E \cup C}$ denotes the propagation-functions of the elements of E and C, $\alpha^p(e), e \in E$ is the activation used in the BCRN.

3.3 Retrieval in OCRNs

As already pointed out, the knowledge encoded in the object model may be used to provide some useful guidance during case retrieval. Very briefly, retrieval of appropriate diagnostic cases is performed by:

1. Activating the IEs corresponding to the initially observed symptoms
2. Performing spreading activation as in BCRNs to access a set of possible faults
3. Selecting a set of hypothetic cases with associated diagnoses as indicated by the highest activated case nodes (if this allows for an unambiguous diagnosis, retrieval can be aborted)
4. Choosing additional IE nodes representing symptoms not yet determined and associated to at least one of the hypothetical cases (these will be referred to as the *relevant* symptoms)
5. Performing a spreading activation process into the object model to access those object nodes, which contributed to the activation of the hypothetical cases and can provide further information about relevant symptom(s)
6. Selecting the most specific object from the latter set
7. Determining the set of most *useful* symptoms (i.e. those symptoms which provide a maximum information to differentiate between the diagnoses of the hypothetical cases) and presentation to the user
8. Using the obtained answers for activating further IEs and restart in Step 2

Steps 1 through 3 correspond to the retrieval process as defined in the formal model of BCRNs (cf. Appendix A). While in BCRNs retrieval is stopped at this stage, a further spreading activation process is used in OCRNs to allow for a differential diagnosis (Steps 4 through 8).

Selecting the most specific object in step 6 means finding the object node in the object model the positive and negative inform-activation (α^p and α^n) of which are both non-zero and that there is no less general object (according to ψ) with that property.

The method to specify the most *useful* symptoms in step 7 is to determine how many of the set of the hypothetic cases would receive additional activation through the determination of one of these symptoms. The less this number is for one symptom, the more *useful* it is. In a second test the number of other symptoms which would be excluded in determining a symptom is computed. Here a higher value indicates a higher *usefulness* of a symptom.

The determined usefulness of the symptoms can be used to exclude all but the most useful one from the presentation, or, in a more informative way, it can be used to order the set of symptoms.

3.4 Two Example Sessions

For the following two example runs consider the simple OCRN from Figure 3 again. It consists of a three-node object model extending the BCRN containing 6 IEs and 3 case-descriptors.

First Example: Immediate Solution

The query ("The SPARCprinter-display shows C3") is posed by activating the corresponding IE: ($\alpha^p(\text{Display.contents} = \text{C3}) := 1$). There is no similarity between the activated IE and other IEs, hence no other IE gets an activation. Through the relevance-relation, activation is spread to the case-descriptor of case 3 only. This allows for the unambiguous diagnosis that the SPARCprinter has run out of paper and it is suggested to insert some more (cf. Figure 4).

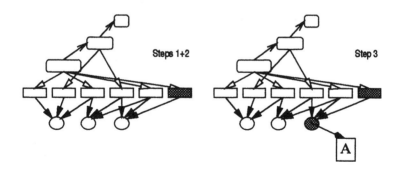

Fig. 4. The OCRN from Figure 3 suggesting an immediate solution

Second Example: Differential Diagnosis

When the printer is not printing at all, **SPARCprinter.printing=no** will be the initially activated IE (step 1 in Figure 5). The set of hypothetic cases activated through the relevance of that IE contains the case-descriptors for the cases 2 and 3 (step 2). Hence, an unambiguous diagnosis is not possible and other symptoms have to be found. In step 3, all those IEs being relevant to the hypothetic cases but not having received a retrieval-activation receive a differential-activation. Step 4 shows the object in the object model which is the most specific one with both activations greater than zero. In the first approximation, the set of symptoms is determined (step 5) which contains all IEs which are realizations of that object or its specifications. In step 6, some symptoms are excluded from the question-set. For example, symptoms are excluded, if there exists an activated IE providing information about an attribute excluding the symptom, such as the IE `SPARCprinter.printing=yes` in the example. What follows, is the ordering of the symptoms according to their *usefulness* as explained in Section 3.3. So in step 7, the user is asked for the display contents and whether the display is blinking.

4   Related Work

Case Retrieval Nets in general and OCRNs in particular inherit a number of techniques from other approaches to case retrieval and from completely different areas. A few of these will be mentioned here briefly:

The *similarity* and *propagation functions* of Definitions 1 and 3 indicate that CRNs/OCRNs share some ideas with recurrent Neural Networks. In particular, the computations performed locally in each node support this comparison. However, in CRNs each node represents a particular symbol (IE or case), and it is the activation of single nodes that matters — not entire patterns of activation. In OCRNs the difference is even more crucial as the propagation of activation is highly directed and concerns only those nodes which have a strong relationship to the symptoms and failures inferred so far (cf. Section 3.3).

kd–trees ([14, 15, 1]) employ a pre-structuring of case memory into a decision tree like structure. The structuring of the domain represented in a kd–tree can be found in OCRNs, too: The devices of the application domain are grouped according to their specific properties and relationships. However, these structures are limited to the object nodes of the domain while failures (case nodes) and symptoms (IE nodes) are still encoded in a net structure allowing for higher flexibility.

The "Fish–and–Sink" strategy ([12]) developed within the FABEL project also employs a net–like structuring of the case base. However, the nodes here directly correspond to cases which are connected via links representing their similarity concerning particular *aspects* of the domain. The IEs of CRNs do not have a counterpart. FISH–AND–SINK works by determining the utility of an arbitrary case and applying the obtained result to other cases *near* the original selected one. The major advantage is that a cheap to compute *aspect distance* can be used to estimate the usefulness of cases and to avoid the (expensive) computation of the *view distance*.

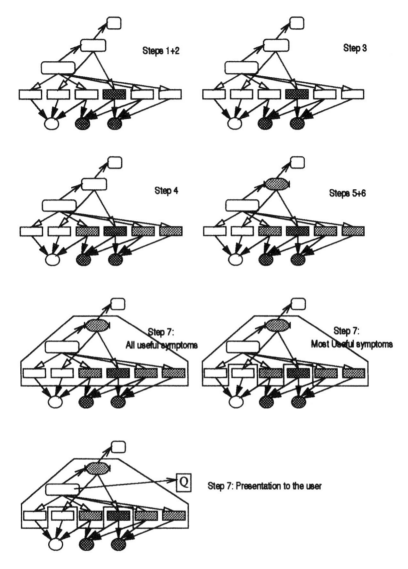

Fig. 5. Process of differential diagnosis in the example OCRN of Figure 3

The CRASH system ([3, 4]) uses an activation passing scheme for case re-trieval, too. The major difference to (B)CRNs is that during similarity propa-gation activation is propagated through a network of *world knowledge*. On the one hand, this allows for the integration of a deep background knowledge into the case retrieval system. On the other hand, it makes retrieval highly complex if this *world knowledge* is sufficiently broad. Also the acquisition of this knowl-edge may cause severe problems. Obviously, OCRNs fall in between BCRNs and

CRASH: Here, a limited *world knowledge* is used to guide the spread of activation and focus on a number of highly relevant symptoms and failures. The acquisition of that knowledge is straightforward as it consists of simple descriptions of the devices under consideration.

Knowledge-directed Spreading Activation (KDSA) ([17, 16]) is an improved variant of basic spreading activation algorithms. In KDSA the spreading activation process is performed in several steps, too: Each time an analogue has been retrieved from memory, the quality of it is evaluated by a heuristic mapping component. Based on the degree of usefulness determined by this mapping component, some *"... search control module modifies the direction of subsequent spreads of activation into more promising areas of the knowledge base"* ([16]). KDSA has been designed mainly for cross-domain analogies where the goal is to retrieve *"... semantically distant analogies"*. This differs from our standpoint in so far as we assume that the goal of retrieval is to access previously encountered cases describing problem situations in the same domain. Given this assumption, the task of the heuristic mapping component of KDSA (namely to determine how close a retrieved case is to the query) can be fulfilled by simply assessing the similarity between the query and the retrieved case — that's exactly what *Case Retrieval Nets* do. What's more, retrieval in OCRNs is *knowledge-directed* in so far as knowledge about the physical devices and their associated malfunctions is used to guide the spread of activation.

5 Summary

The main goal of this article was to present an application of the model of *Case Retrieval Nets* to the task of technical diagnosis. Summarizing we can state that:

- The basic concept of CRNs can be enhanced with application specific knowledge encoded in an object model. This object model can be used to provide useful guidance to the case retrieval process.
- Retrieval using CRNs is based on a sound formalism, in particular completeness can be guaranteed.
- CRNs support flexible case retrieval as cases are considered as sets of IEs — hence each part of a case may be used to retrieve other parts and no *a priori* distinction between a *problem description* and a *solution* is necessary.
- Construction and maintenance (insertion, deletion of cases) is straightforward and computationally cheap.

A prerequisite for the applicability of CRNs is that a composite similarity measure is applied, i.e. that similarity of two cases is determined according to the similarity of the features describing the cases. In more detail, CRNs are useful if similarity between different values of certain attributes is taken into account — although Tversky's *Contrast Rule* ([13]) may be implemented, too. However, in the latter approach the similarity function is reduced to the identity checking function.

On the other hand, CRNs (and thus OCRNs, too) are probably not applicable in more synthetic tasks, like case-based planning or design. Here, the goal is often to *construct* a suitable solution to a problem case, rather than to *find* a case having a similar description.

6 Outlook

After a first implementation of the OCRN model using the $\mathcal{K}$appa development system, one of the next steps will be to collect enough case-material for testing the Computer-Fault-Diagnosis system.

Furthermore the extension of the OCRN with rules will be examined. Different types of rules and their integration with the case-based reasoning approach of OCRNs will be considered, e.g. completion-rules (cf. [2]), constraints and user-interaction-rules.

The third branch which will be followed will be the improvement of the user-interaction. In particular, the use of user-profiles and resource-adaptive systems will be investigated.

Acknowledgments

We would like to thank Prof. Dr. Bernd Böhme and Dr. Uwe Starke from P.S.I. AG, Berlin, for their cooperation in the development of the OCRN model. Furthermore, we obtained a lot of useful hints and suggestions from Mike Brown, currently with Siemens AG (Erlangen).

References

1. E. Auriol, S. Weß, M. Manago, K.-D. Althoff, and R. Traphöner. INRECA: A seamlessly integrated system based on inductive inference and case-based reasoning. In M. M. Veloso and A. Aamodt, editors, *Case-Based Reasoning Research and Development (Proceedings of the First International Conference on CBR, ICCBR-95)*, Lecture Notes in Artificial Intelligence 1010, pages 371–380. Springer Verlag, 1995.
2. R. Bergmann, W. Wilke, I. Vollrath, and S. Weß. Integrating general knowledge with object-oriented case representation and reasoning. In H.-D. Burkhard and M. Lenz, editors, *4th German Workshop on CBR — System Development and Evaluation —*, pages 120–127, Berlin, 1996. Humboldt University.
3. M. G. Brown. *A Memory Model for Case Retrieval by Activation Passing*. PhD thesis, University of Manchester, 1994.
4. M. G. Brown. An underlying memory model to support case retrieval. In S. Weß, K.-D. Althoff, and M. M. Richter, editors, *Topics in Case-Based Reasoning, Proceedings EWCBR-93*, pages 132–143. Springer Verlag, 1994.
5. H.-D. Burkhard and M. Lenz. Case Retrieval Nets: Basic ideas and extensions. In H.-D. Burkhard and M. Lenz, editors, *4th German Workshop on CBR — System Development and Evaluation —*, pages 103–110, Berlin, 1996. Humboldt University.

6. H.-D. Burkhard and P. Pirk. Technical diagnosis: Fallexperte-D. In H.-D. Burkhard and M. Lenz, editors, *4th German Workshop on CBR — System Development and Evaluation —*, Berlin, 1996. Humboldt University.

7. M. Lenz. Case-based reasoning for holiday planning. In W. Schertler, B. Schmid, A. M. Tjoa, and H. Werthner, editors, *Information and Communications Technologies in Tourism*, pages 126–132. Springer Verlag, 1994.

8. M. Lenz, E. Auriol, H.-D. Burkhard, M. Manago, and P. Pirk. CBR für Diagnose und Entscheidungsunterstützung. *Künstliche Intelligenz, Themenheft Fallbasiertes Schließen*, 10(1):16–21, 1996.

9. M. Lenz and H.-D. Burkhard. Case Retrieval Nets: Basic ideas and extensions. In *accepted for: KI-96*, 1996.

10. M. Lenz and H.-D. Burkhard. Lazy propagation in Case Retrieval Nets. In W. Wahlster, editor, *Proceedings 12th European Conference On Artificial Intelligence*, pages 127–131, Los Angeles, 1996. John Wiley and Sons.

11. E. L. Rissland, D. B. Skalak, and M. T. Friedman. Case retrieval through multiple indexing and heuristic search. In *Proceedings 13th International Joint Conference On Artificial Intelligence*, pages 902–908, 1993.

12. J. W. Schaaf. "Fish and Sink": An anytime-algorithm to retrieve adequate cases. In M. M. Veloso and A. Aamodt, editors, *Case-Based Reasoning Research and Development (Proceedings of the First International Conference on CBR, ICCBR-95)*, Lecture Notes in Artificial Intelligence 1010, pages 538–547. Springer Verlag, 1995.

13. A. Tversky. Features of similarity. *Psychological Review*, 84:327–352, 1977.

14. S. Weß. *Fallbasiertes Problemlösen in wissensbasierten Systemen zur Entscheidungsunterstützung und Diagnostik*. PhD thesis, Universität Kaiserslautern, 1995.

15. S. Weß, K.-D. Althoff, and G. Derwand. Using *kd*-trees to improve the retrieval step in case-based reasoning. In S. Weß, K.-D. Althoff, and M. M. Richter, editors, *Topics in Case-Based Reasoning, Proceedings EWCBR-93*, pages 167–181. Springer Verlag, 1994.

16. M. Wolverton. An investigation of marker-passing algorithms for analogue retrieval. In M. M. Veloso and A. Aamodt, editors, *Case-Based Reasoning Research and Development (Proceedings of the First International Conference on CBR, ICCBR-95)*, Lecture Notes in Artificial Intelligence 1010, pages 359–370. Springer Verlag, 1995.

17. M. Wolverton and B. Hayes-Roth. Retrieving semantically distant analogies with knowledge-directed spreading activation. In *Proceedings AAAI-94*, 1994.

A   A Formal Model of CRNs

In this appendix we will give a (brief) formal description of *Case Retrieval Nets* allowing for a detailed investigation of the approach.

Definition 3 A *Basic Case Retrieval Net* (BCRN) is defined as a structure $N = [E, C, \sigma, \rho, \Pi]$ with

E is the finite set of IE nodes,

C is the finite set of case nodes,

σ is the *similarity function*

$$\sigma : E \times E \to \mathcal{R}$$

which describes the similarity $\sigma(e', e'')$ between IEs e', e'',

ρ is the *relevance function*

$$\rho : E \times C \to \mathcal{R}$$

describing the relevance $\rho(e, c)$ of the IE e to the case node c,

Π is the set of *propagation functions*

$$\pi_n : \mathcal{R}^E \to \mathcal{R}.$$

for each node $n \in E \cup C$. □

Definition 4 An *activation* of a BCRN $N = [E, C, \sigma, \rho, \Pi]$ is a function
$\alpha : E \cup C \to \mathcal{R}$. □

Definition 5 Consider a BCRN $N = [E, C, \sigma, \rho, \Pi]$ with $E = \{e_1, ..., e_s\}$.
Let be $\alpha_t : E \cup C \to \mathcal{R}$ the activation at time t.
The *activation* of IE nodes $e \in E$ at time $t + 1$ is given by
$$\alpha_{t+1}(e) = \pi_e(\sigma(e_1, e) \cdot \alpha_t(e_1), ..., \sigma(e_s, e) \cdot \alpha_t(e_s)),$$
and the activation of case nodes $c \in C$ at time $t + 1$ is given by
$$\alpha_{t+1}(c) = \pi_c(\rho(e_1, c) \cdot \alpha_t(e_1), ..., \rho(e_s, c) \cdot \alpha_t(e_s)).$$ □

To pose a query, the activation of all IE nodes may start with

$$\alpha_0(e) = \begin{cases} 1 & : \quad \text{for the IE nodes } e \text{ describing the query case} \\ 0 & : \quad \text{else} \end{cases}$$

Given α_0 and Definition 5 it is well-defined how the activation α of each node $n \in C \cup E$ has to be computed at any time. In particular, case retrieval by propagation of activations can be performed as a three-step process:

1. Given the query case, α_0 is determined for all IE nodes.
2. The activation α_0 is propagated to all IE nodes $e \in E$:
   $$\alpha_1(e) = \pi_e(\sigma(e_1, e) \cdot \alpha_0(e_1), ..., \sigma(e_s, e) \cdot \alpha_0(e_s)).$$
3. The result of step 2 is propagated to the case nodes $c \in C$:
   $$\alpha_2(c) = \pi_c(\rho(e_1, c) \cdot \alpha_1(e_1), ..., \rho(e_s, c) \cdot \alpha_1(e_s)).$$

The result of the retrieval for a given query activation α_0 is the *preference ordering* of cases according to decreasing activations $\alpha_2(c)$ of case nodes $c \in C$.

Note that the retrieval methods in OCRNs, as discussed in this paper, utilize the same scheme but further enhance it by allowing for a *feedback* of (diagnostic) case nodes to the symptoms encoded as IE nodes associated to them.

Plans as Structured Networks of Hierarchically and Temporally Related Case Pieces

Luís Macedo (*), Francisco C. Pereira (**), Carlos Grilo (**), Amílcar Cardoso (**)

(*) Instituto Superior de Engenharia de Coimbra, 3030 Coimbra, Portugal
(macedo@alma.uc.pt)
(**) Dep. Eng. Informática, Univ. Coimbra, Polo II, 3030 Coimbra, Portugal
(francisco@alma.uc.pt, grilo@alma.uc.pt, amilcar@dei.uc.pt)

Abstract. This paper describes a representation of plan cases as a structured set of goals and actions. These goals and actions are the unit pieces that form a case. These case pieces are related each other by hierarchical and temporal links (explanations) forming a tree-like network. We give importance not just to explicit links, i.e., links between case pieces which are concretely known, but also to implicit ones, i.e., possibly unknown links between case pieces. Each case piece is explained by antecedent links and explains other case pieces by consequent links. The retrieval of a case piece is mainly guided by its links and by its surrounding case pieces. Our concept of case piece usefulness is briefly explained. We discuss the benefit of reusing and directly accessing small case pieces from multiple cases for improving the Case-Based Reasoning (CBR) systems' capability and efficiency to solve problems. We explain the importance of stepwise refinement in plan cases and also the role that temporal representation can take in the meaningful and coherent construction of planning problem solutions.
An application in musical composition domain is presented. We also show how a musical composition task can be treated as a planning task.

1 Introduction

Considering cases as set of pieces (Barletta & Mark, 1988), also called snippets (Kolodner, 1988; Redmond, 1990; Sycara & Navinchandra, 1991) or footprints (Veloso, 1992; Bento, Macedo & Costa, 1994) instead of monolithic entities, can improve the results of a CBR system in that solutions of problems may result from the contribution of multiple cases.

Moreover, structured representations of cases (Plaza, 1995) allow treating pieces of cases as full-fledged cases, minimising the problems that appear when using parts of multiple monolithic cases, particularly, the lot of effort taken to find the useful parts in them.

Although many CBR systems select out cases that are most similar to the new problem, other selection criteria may prove more effective. E.g., Kolodner (Kolodner, 1989) has considered that the most useful cases are those that can address the reasoner's current goal, which means that they may not be the most similar ones.

Knowledge-based retrieval systems (Koton, 1989) are a consequence of combining nearest neighbour and knowledge-guided techniques. These systems are characterised by the use of domain knowledge to the construction of explanations for why a problem had a particular solution in the past. Explanations are necessary to similarity judgement (Barletta & Mark, 1989; Cain, Pazzani & Silverstein, 1991; Veloso, 1992; Bento & Costa, 1994). CBR is appropriate for domains where a strong theory does not exist but past experience is accessible. This leads to the consideration of cases imperfectly explained (Bento, Macedo & Costa, 1994).

A plan is a specific sequence of steps (or actions) with the aim of a goal achievement. Case-Based Planning (CBP) systems reuse past sequences of actions from past plans to construct new ones. Some systems like CELIA (Redmond, 1990), MEDIATOR (Simpson, 1985), JULIA (Kolodner, 1989; Hinrichs, 1988), PRODIGY/ANALOGY (Veloso, 1992), and CAPlan/CbC (Munõz-Avila & Huellen, 1995) break up the goal into smaller sub-goals, enabling plan construction by composition of sub-plans. This leads to an hierarchical representation of plan cases (Khemani & Prasad, 1995). The case representation is similar to a tree where each node is a goal and its sons the sub-goals, or at the latest level, the actions of the plan. Each goal (or action) depends on other goals. This is particularly evident in structured domains (Munõz-Avila & Huellen, 1995).

In this paper we will focus on a structured representation for plan cases as a set of implicitly and explicitly, hierarchically and temporally related case pieces. Each one of these case pieces is considered, for indexing, matching, retrieving and validation purposes, as an individual case, which facilitates the reuse of parts of multiple cases to construct a new solution.

To represent time, we adopt a kind of "pseudo-date" scheme (Allen, 1991; Grilo, Pereira, Macedo & Cardoso, 1996), which provides an efficient and expressive mean to represent and reason about time relations, even when dealing with incomplete information, as when incrementally constructing a solution from the adaptation of ill-related pieces. As we'll exemplify in Section 5, this kind of representation also facilitates the retrieving process.

Our approach to case representation is presented in the next section. In section 3, we introduce the retrieval and plan generation processes. Section 4 presents an application in the music composition domain. We also explain how a music composition process may be seen as a planning task. A short example of new case generation is presented in section 5, and the handling of "pseudo-dates" is also exemplified. In section 6 we discuss some of the advantages of our approach. At last, a conclusion about our work is made in section 7.

2 Case Representation

2.1 Case Structure

Within our approach a case plan is a set of goals and actions organised in a hierarchical way (Figure 1): a main goal (the main problem) is refined into subgoals (the sub-problems), and so on, until reaching the actions (the leaf nodes of the tree[1]) that satisfy the goals.

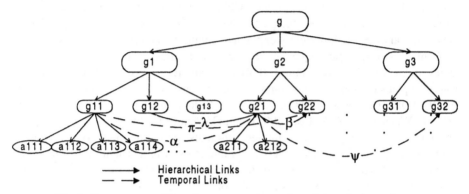

Fig. 1. Case structure. The g_i's represent the goals and the a_i's the actions.

In our model, each node of the hierarchical structure corresponds to a case piece. To complete the case structure, there are links between case pieces, representing causal justifications, or explanations. Some of these links maintain the hierarchical case structure, others reflect causal temporal relations between case pieces. Thus the existence of a case piece in a plan case is causally explained by several case pieces of the same plan case.

A measure of importance (strong, weak or medium) is given to each explicit link, according to its weight in the explanation of the consequent case piece.

Considering the hierarchical links only (represented in Figure 1 by continuous arrows), the inherent meaning of the represented structure is: g, the main goal of the plan (or the main problem), is achieved by sequentially achieving sub-goals (sub-problems) $g1$, $g2$ and $g3$. Each one of these sub-goals is also broken up into other sub-goals. For example, $g1$ is broken up into $g11$, $g12$ and $g13$, and $g2$ into $g21$ and $g22$. To achieve the goal $g11$ the actions $a111$, $a112$, $a113$ and $a114$ must be sequentially executed by this temporal order.

Besides being explained by the goal-refinement process, through hierarchical links, a case piece may also be explained through a temporal link (represented in Figure 1 by discontinuous arrows). For example, $g21$ (sub-goal of $g2$) is a consequence of case pieces $g11$ and $g12$, which is represented by the temporal links labelled α and λ, respectively.

As the case pieces form a tree-like structure we adopt the tree characteristic terminology to facilitate the description of our approach. Thus, we say that a case piece is a node and belongs to a level (e.g., in Figure 1, case pieces $g1$, $g2$ and $g3$ belong to level 1; case piece g belongs to the level 0). We also consider that father, son, brother, etc., relations exist between case pieces (e.g., in Figure 1, case piece g is father of case piece $g1$, $g1$ is son of g and brother of $g2$ and $g3$).

---

[1]Although the actions are represented by the leaf nodes, some of their properties (attributes) are inherited from (the attributes of) their hierarchical ascendants.

We adopt Allen's period-based approach to represent time[2] (Allen, 1989), and associate a period to each case piece of the tree. A case piece's position in the tree is represented by an address ("pseudo-date") (see next section). Therefore, we may establish a correspondence between addresses and periods in a manner that simplifies the task of obtaining temporal relations (*starts*, *meets*, etc.) between case pieces, which is helpful for the temporal reasoning needed for plan generation, and also facilitates the use of causal temporal relations in the retrieval process.

2.2 Case Pieces

A case piece has seven types of information describing its relevant aspects: a name that uniquely identifies the case piece, the name of the case to which the case piece belongs, the case piece address, the constraints, a set of attribute/value pairs, the antecedents and the consequents.

The address of a case piece in level n is represented by $N_n:N_{n-1}:...:N_0$[3], where each $N_i \in \aleph_0$ (from now on we will call offsets to the N_i's). An offset $L=N_i$, $0 \le i$ $<n$, means that the case piece with that address has a predecessor in level i of the tree which is the L-th son of its father (with the exception of the case piece in level 0, which has no ascendants and so its offset is always 0). The offset $J=N_n$ means that this case piece is the J-th son of its closer ascendant. Every case piece propagates its address to its descendants, that is, if the case piece's address is $N_n:...:N_0$, its M-th son's address will be $M:N_n:...:N_0$.

This representation embeds in its syntax, explicitly, the position that a case piece and its ascendants occupy in the tree relatively to the others, and, implicitly, the hierarchical level that the case piece occupies in the tree.

It is worth noting that the case pieces do not have all the same duration, and in consequence, each address is not committed with a fixed portion of time. We can say that a case piece has the length of its descendants, and that if it has not descendants, it has an intrinsic value (in the last level, the length of the actions that compose it).

Another information in a case piece is a *set of attribute/value pairs* describing several properties which characterise the case piece.

The constraints are also attribute/value pairs, but play the role of determining whether or not the case piece is a candidate to occupy a free position in a solution, depending on whether or not they are coherent with the attributes of the free position's hierarchical ascendants.

Antecedents and *consequents* are causal links that follow, respectively, from and to other case pieces. Antecedent links show how a case piece is explained by the existence of other case pieces (e.g. in Figure 1, *g21* is explained by *g11* and *g12* through the links labelled α and λ, respectively, and by *g2* through a father link). Consequent links show how a case piece explains the existence of other case pieces

---

[2] We do not make any commitment about the discreteness or the continuity of time.

[3] Allen, uses ':' to represent the "meets" relation. In our representation, ':' is a composition operator.

(e.g., in Figure 1, *g21* partially explains *g22* and *g32* through links β and ψ, respectively, and *a211* and *a212* through father links).

Each antecedent or consequent link is classified into another two main kinds of links: hierarchical and temporal ones.

Hierarchical links reflect the case pieces refinement (e.g., in Figure 1, there is a hierarchical link between goal *g* and goal *g1* because *g1* is a subdivision of *g*).

A temporal link expresses a causal explanation between two temporally disjoined case pieces (e.g., in Figure 1, case piece *g21* is explained by case piece *g11*). The explanation embeds the causal temporal relation between the case pieces.

Sometimes the type of relation between antecedent fact(s) and the consequent one may be unknown. This lack of a complete theory is common in CBR (Bento, Macedo & Costa, 1994). This idea leads to another classification of the links between case pieces: we say that a link between the case pieces *a* and *b* is explicit if we known the relation between *a* and *b*, and implicit if we do not. In Figure 1, *g13* implicitly (and temporally) explains *g21*. There is not a concrete link between them, but it is coherent to assume that the existence of *g21* is, probably, partially due to the previous occurrence of *g13*. We may also say that *a* implicitly (and hierarchically) explains *g21*, although there is not a direct relation between them.

We call the case piece *context* to the set of case pieces that surrounds it. We distinguish eight types of contexts according to the kind of link existing between the case piece considered and the surrounding ones. Thus, each one of these surrounding case pieces is included in one of the following contexts (the name of the context reflects the classification of the link to the case piece): antecedent-hierarchical-implicit context, antecedent-hierarchical-explicit context, antecedent-temporal-implicit context, antecedent-temporal-explicit context, consequent-hierarchical-implicit context, consequent-hierarchical-explicit context, consequent-temporal-implicit context or consequent-temporal-explicit context.

For example, in Figure 1, the contexts of *g21* are: antecedent-hierarchical-implicit context = {*g*}; antecedent-hierarchical-explicit context = {*g2*}; antecedent-temporal-implicit context = {*g13*}; antecedent-temporal-explicit context = {*g11*, *g12*}; consequent-hierarchical-implicit context = {}; consequent-hierarchical-explicit context = {*a211*, *a212*}; consequent-temporal-implicit context = {*g31*}; consequent-temporal-explicit context = {*g22*, *g32*}.

Since there is not any direct link between implicitly related case pieces, it is necessary to define a frontier to limit the number of case pieces of the implicit contexts. We assume that this frontier involves the nearest case pieces. To each implicit type of context, we defined a user-configurable parameter with the maximum distance a case piece may be to belong to a context of that type.

3 Retrieval and Plan Generation Processes

A new problem to be solved by the CBR system may comprise a set of linked case pieces. At least the main goal (the root case piece) must be included, with its name, address, constraints and attributes instanciated.

The meaning associated to a problem description composed by the main goal is the following: the system must find a structured plan solution to achieve the goal. If the problem also includes sub-goals or actions with the same instanciated information types, then the meaning of the problem description is augmented by the following: the system must find a structured plan solution to achieve the goal; the solution must achieve the specified sub-goals and perform the specified actions. Thus a problem may be a partial structured solution given by the user. The system just have to coherently complete it.

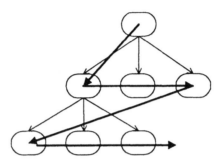

Fig. 2. Case generation order.

After giving the system a new problem, this is subdivided into several ones. Each one of these sub-problems is considered and solved individually, taking into account the previously solved ones.

Let's give a sketch of the process. First, the main goal is considered. Since the complete information about this goal is not already known (for example, the number of sub-goals that are necessary to achieve it or the links that follow from it may be unknown), the main goal that best matches the considered one is retrieved from a case in memory. The next step is retrieving the main goal's sons from memory, starting by the oldest, assuming its context (currently, the retrieved main goal), its attributes and its address as indexes. Following this, each one of these main goal's sons is considered and its sons are retrieved from memory through a similar process. This procedure is repeated until the actions (the lowest level case pieces of the tree-like structure) are obtained. Figure 2 shows the sequence of the new case generation process.

The retrieving of a case piece from memory involves the following steps (given the context, the attributes and the address of the next free position on the new case[4]):

1) selection of the candidate case pieces from memory, eliminating those whose constraints are incompatible with the attributes of the free position's ascendants, and those which do not belong to the same level of the free position;

---

[4] The attributes of the free position may have already been instanciated by the user (notice that the problem may be a partial solution).

2) application of a similarity metric[5] to each candidate case piece selected in step 1, taking into account the similarities between the given context, attributes and address and the context, attributes and address of the candidate case piece;
3) ranking of the case pieces by its similarity metric value;
4) selection of the most useful case piece;
5) validation of the addition to the solution of the selected case piece.

From the above algorithm it can be seen that the weighted similarity metric used for selection of a case piece takes into account the next three similarities
- *attributes similarities*, which are computed by the following way. Considering that α is the set of attributes of the considered free position on the new case, and β the set of attributes of the candidate case piece, then, the similarity between α and β is $Y=[2*L(\alpha \cap \beta)]/ [L(\alpha) + L(\beta)]$, where $L(x)$ is a function that computes the length of the set x;
- *address similarities*, which are the result of two address similarity contributions: the absolute address similarity and the relative address similarity. The former one is 1 or 0, depending on whether or not the similarity between the two compared addresses is exact. The second one, takes into account the similarity of the temporal positions of the case pieces relatively to the beginning and to the end of the case. This temporal position is mapped into a interval between 0 and 1. Therefore, if a case piece is at the beginning of the case it has the relative temporal position 0, if it is in the middle 0.5, etc. These positions are then compared;
- *context similarities*. As was said above, we consider eight types of contexts. Each type of the free position's context is compared with the correspondent candidate case piece's context. Each type of context is an ordered set of case pieces, as we exemplified in section 2. The order is hierarchical or temporal, depending on the type of context. Therefore, the comparison between two correspondent contexts is performed taking into account not just their intersection, but also the similarity of the case piece's order. This means, for example, that the contexts $c1 = \{a,b,c\}$ and $c2 = \{b,c,a\}$ (where a, b and c are case pieces), although their intersection is total, are not totally similar, because they have just one similar sequence of case pieces: c follows b.

In order to obtain meaningful case pieces associations, the similarity metric gives different weights to different context similarities. For example, it gives a bigger weight to explicit link's similarities than to implicit ones.

The selection of the most useful case piece involves the computation of a similarity metric value for it and the consideration of the degree of matching the needs of the goal being achieved (Kolodner, 1989). Thus, the most useful case piece may not be the one with the most similarities. We think that this issue depends on the domain. Since our domain is music composition, an important parameter to consider is the originality of the new case, i.e, it is important that the new case has novel associations of case pieces, which are not present in the previous cases in memory. These novel associations may be required just in some hierarchical levels.

---

[5] e.g., Bento's quantitative metric (Bento & Costa, 1994).

Therefore each one of the hierarchical levels has a selection criterion, which is defined by the user. This criterion determines which case piece is selected from the ranking. E.g., in level 1 the case piece selected is the totally similar, while in level 4 the case piece selected is the most but not totally similar.

After its selection, a case piece is submitted to a validation process consisting in the verification of incompatibilities between the selected case piece and the partially constructed solution for the given problem. At this point, there may be provisional links that follow from earlier case pieces, pointing to the free position. We call them *suggestions*, as they correspond to proposed but not definitive links. If an incompatibility exists between a suggestion and an antecedent link of the selected case piece there are two choices: (i) try to adapt it, relaxing the validation by ignoring the less important of the incompatible links (e.g., if the suggestion is strong and the antecedent link of the selected case piece is weak, the validation step substitutes the second link by the former one in the selected case piece, and then this case piece is added to the new case); (ii) if it was not possible to adapt it, select another one and apply the validation step to it.

4 An Application in Musical Composition Domain

As studied by Lerdahl and Jackendoff (1983), Balaban (1992) and Honning (1993), music is a domain in which "structure", "hierarchy" and "time" are more than occasional keywords. Music is indeed a highly structured and organised world. As stated by Balaban, any music can be represented by a hierarchy of temporal objects (an object associated with a temporal duration), in such a way that each one has, as descendants, a sequence of sub-objects that starts and ends at the same start and ending point as the object's. Figure 3 shows an example.

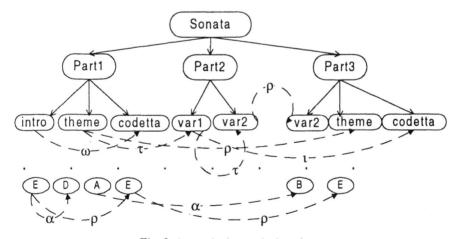

Fig. 3. A case in the music domain.

In such a structure, we may say that each object has a temporal duration associated with it. We also may infer from that structure temporal relations between the objects. For instance, in Figure 3, we may infer (using Allen's approach (1983)) that Part2 is *during* Sonata, *met-by* Part1, *meets* Part3, and is *started* by var1.

Apart from these temporal relations, there are also causal ones in music (represented in Figure 3 by discontinuous arrows), since many musical objects may be causally explained by, for instance, concretely known transformations of some other object (e.g., repetition, variation, inversion, transposition, etc). For example, in Figure 3, the temporal link between theme of Part1 and var1 of Part2 may represent a variation transformation which, when applied to theme originates var1. These temporal relations are represented in the antecedents and consequents informations fields of a case piece.

Each musical object has several properties which are represented in our approach by attribute/value pairs (e.g., {ton='I', meas=2/4} meaning that tonality is 'I' and that measure is binary).

Additionally, each musical object has also a set of constraints, which are conditions that must not be contrary to the attributes of its ascendants, when it is added to the new case (e.g., if a case piece has the set of constraints a = {meas=2/4, ton='II', etc} then it must not be a descendant of a case piece which tonality is, for example, 'I'). Thus the role of constraints is to maintain the coherence of the new musical piece hierarchy, since they disallow the hierarchical association of case pieces with incompatible properties.

The goal of our application is to use analysis of music pieces as foundation for a generative process of composition, providing a structured and constrained way of composing novel pieces, although keeping the essential traits of the composer's style. We use analysis of music pieces from a seventeenth century composer.

We have concluded that considering music as a plan, with the organisational characteristics described earlier, and the act of composing as CBP, might be an interesting way of generating new music from old ones. In fact, music structure has the basic conditions to be considered as a normal plan structure.

5 An Example

In this section we illustrate the new case generation in music domain.

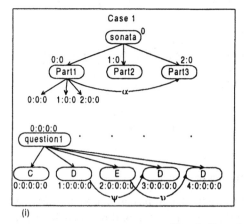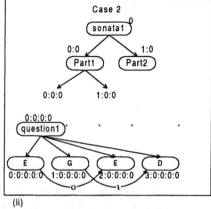

Fig. 4. Cases in memory.

243

At the beginning, the system's memory has two musical cases (represented in Figure 4)[6].

The problem given to the system (represented by the PROLOG fact case_node(new_case, sonata2, 0, [], [ton='I',meas=2/4, style=sonata], [],[])) is to come up with a music sonata (style=sonata) characterised by having binary measure (meas=2/4) and tonality 'I'' (ton='I').

First, a case piece with more similarities with the one represented in the problem is retrieved from a case in memory.

The system retrieved the main goal of case 1 since it is the one with more similarities with the main goal of the problem. At this point the solution is the one presented in Figure 4 - (i).

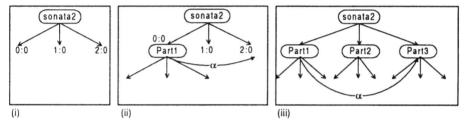

Fig. 5. New case generation.

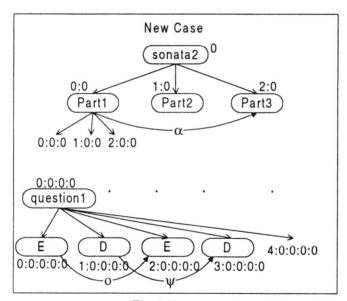

Fig. 6. New case.

Next step is retrieving a case piece from memory to be placed on the new case free position with address 0:0.

---

[6] Because of the extent of musical cases we have to represent incomplete ones.

This free position belongs to the first level of the tree. Therefore, the candidates are those ones belonging also to the first level of the two cases. There are five candidates: Part1, Part2 and Part3 from case 1, and Part1 and Part2 from case 2. Part2 from case 2 is eliminated since it has the constraint ton='II', which is incoherent with the attribute ton='I' of case piece Sonata2.

To apply the similarity metric, the system has to compute the context of the free position 0:0 and of all candidates. It takes use of the address to more easily perform this task. Thus, for example, the surrounding case pieces of Part2 (address 1:0 of case 1) are obtained as follows: the father is obtained deleting the first offset (1); the immediately younger brother is obtained subtracting 1 to the same first offset and maintaining the rest of the address, etc.

The system ranked the candidate case pieces by the following decreasing similarity order: Part1 (address 0:0 of case 1), Part1 (address 0:0 of case 2), Part2 (address 1:0 of case 1) and Part3 (address 2:0 of case 1). The selection of one of these pieces depends on the used criterion for this hierarchical level, which is to select the most similar case piece. Therefore Part1 (0:0 of case 1) is chosen. Since it has not incompatibilities with the other case pieces of the current solution, it is added to it (Figure 5 - (ii)). It can be seen that exist a suggestion between addresses 0:0 and 2:0.

Next step is the retrieval of a case piece for the new case free position with address 1:0, and then to 2:0. The system chose Part2 and Part3 from case 1, respectively (Figure 5 - (iii)). At this level, as a consequence of the selection criterion be to select the most similar case piece, there are no originality in the new case, since it is equal to case 1.

From Figure 6, which presents the final new case, it can be seen that the system selected the note E (address 0:0:0:0:0 of case 2) for position addressed with 0:0:0:0:0, since the selection criterion was to select the second most similar case piece in the ranking (the first is C from address 0:0:0:0:0 of case 1). To the address 1:0:0:0:0 it selected D (address 1:0:0:0:0 of case 1), since G (address 1:0:0:0:0 of case 2) is the most similar. And so on.

Consequently, at this level and using this criterion, the system obtained novel associations of case pieces. If the criterion was to select the less similar case piece, then more novel associations were made, and therefore, the new case was more original, but probably, it was also more bizarre.

6 Discussion

Our approach to case representation has some similarities with CELIA's (Redmond, 1990) which are mainly: cases are stored in pieces; there are links between case pieces to maintain the structure of the case; case pieces are accessed taking into account the case piece context; a case is constructed with case pieces of multiple cases.

However there also some key differences. The major ones are: rather than considering just hierarchical links we also assume the existence of temporal ones; rather than considering just explicit links we also assume the existence of implicit ones; we use a representing time technique based on "pseudo-dates" (the case pieces' addresses).

Our representational approach exhibits several advantages for CBP (some of them are common to CELIA's advantages).

Storing cases as individual pieces facilitates the access to all useful case pieces from several cases, improving the efficiency of retrieval. CBR systems dealing with monolithic cases have two steps to access the useful parts of previous cases: they need to retrieve the whole case and then they take a lot of effort to find its relevant part(s).

Moreover, the retrieval efficiency is increased by a simplified search of the case piece context, provided by using the addresses. In fact, the properties of the address and the links of the case piece together allow a fast collecting of the surrounding case pieces (case pieces of the context).

An issue worth of addressing is the case pieces size, because CBR systems' efficiency and capability to solve new problems depend on that. It could be expected that a system dealing with smaller case pieces would be less efficient than one dealing with bigger ones (or with no case pieces at all), because of the greater number of retrieval operations that have to be performed. However, this drawback is overwhelmed by providing direct access to the case pieces in memory, avoiding unnecessary processing.

We also think that the capability of a CBR system to solve problems grows when the case piece size decreases: using smaller case pieces, we may dispose of a higher number of combinations to construct the solution. The usefulness of a case is also improved because it is considered in terms of case pieces and not in terms of the all case. This means that, for example, a case as a all may have little usefulness to construct the new case, but may have a highly useful case piece for a free position of that new case, and then, may contribute with a case piece to it. If considered as monolithic cases, because of it little usefulness, that case probably would not be considered to contribute for the generation of the new case.

Some CBR systems do not consider temporal links between events. Figure 7 and 8 show the importance of these links to construct meaningful and coherent cases using case pieces assembling. Supposing we have two candidate pieces (8 and 9) to be put in the new case place represented by a discontinuous circle in Figure 8, retrieved, respectively, from case x and case y. Case piece 8 (case x in Figure 7) is temporally explained by case pieces 6 and 7, and hierarchically explained by case piece 2. Case piece 9 (case y in Figure 7) is temporally explained by case piece 5, and hierarchically by 3. The free position of the new case (Figure 8) is temporally suggested by 6 and 7, and hierarchically by 3. Thus, if we take into account just hierarchical links we select piece 9, but considering also temporal links then piece 8 is chosen (it is assumed that equal weights is given to all contexts in the similarity metric and that the address, and attributes contributions are not considered). So, piece 8 has a higher similarity value than 9. Thus, the system selected 8, and consequently, the case constructed is more coherent than if piece 9 was chosen. If we selected 9 instead of 8 the new case was more original, since we were making more novel case pieces associations (9 was original linked with two case pieces (6 and *7*), while *8* is just original linked with one (*3*)), but is also with more probabilities a more bizarre one. This idea means that the selection order of case pieces determines the solution's originality.

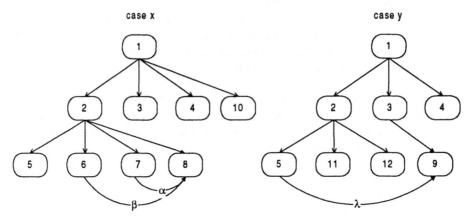

Fig. 7. Cases in memory.

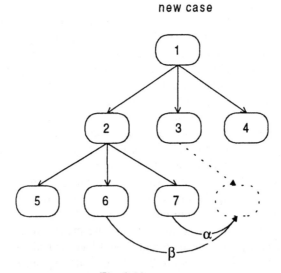

Fig. 8. New case.

Our system can be used for solving problems in structured planning domains. In these domains, we distinguish two main kinds of problems: problems that do not require original solutions, i.e., if the same problem is proposed in different times it must have the same solution; and problems constrained to have original and useful solutions, i.e., the same problem has different solutions if proposed to the system in different times. The problem of finding an algorithm to a programming problem just need one solution (although it may have more). The problem of finding the less extent route between two sites in a city can have just one solution. Thus, these are examples of the former kind of problems. In contrary, the problem of composing a sonata or writing a scientific fiction book, must not have previous solutions. These are examples of the second kind of problems.

To be applied for the first kind of problems, our system must have in every levels the criterion of selecting the most similar case piece, while to be applied for the second kind, the criterion must be, at least in one level, to not select the totally similar case piece. Thus, we may conclude that in these kind of problems the most useful case piece (Kolodner, 1989) is the one: (i) which gives more original case pieces associations to the new case; (ii) and that does not confront the coherence and meaningfulness of the new case.

7 Conclusions

We have presented an approach to representing structured plans as a combination of a tree-like network with a pseudo-dating scheme. Under this approach cases comprises a set of linked pieces.

Three main classifications of links were reported: implicit/explicit links; temporal/hierarchical links; and antecedent/consequent links.

These link classifications determine eight types of case piece contexts in which the retrieval process to new case generation is based.

As shown, musical composition can be considered as a planning task and is an appropriate domain to our approach. However, in this domain and other similar ones like story making or cook recipes generation, we think it is important to assume that a useful case piece (or case) may not be the one with the best similarity metric value but instead the one which gives coherently meaningful originality to the new case.

This approach is already implemented and is in test phase.

Acknowledgements

We would like to thank to Anabela Simões and António Andrade, teachers at the Coimbra School of Music for their valuable contribution, and the anonymous reviewers of this paper for their helpful comments.

References

Allen, J., (1983) - Maintaining Knowledge about Temporal Intervals. ACM 26(11), pp. 932-843.

Allen J., and Hayes, P., (1989) - Moments and Points in an interval-based temporal logic. Computational Intelligence, An International Journal, Vol. 5.

Allen J., and Hayes, P. J. (1991) - Time and Time Again: The Many Ways to Represent Time. International Journal of Intelligent Systems, Vol. 6, pp. 341- 355.

Balaban, M., (1992) - Musical Structures: Interleaving the Temporal and Hierarchical Aspects in Music. In Understanding Music with IA: Perspectives in Music Cognition, MIT Press, pp. 110 - 138.

Barletta, R., Mark, W., (1988). Breaking cases into pieces, in Proceedings of a Case-Based Reasoning Workshop, St. Paul, MN.

Barletta, R., Mark, W., (1989). Explanation-Based Indexing of Cases, in Proceedings of a Case-Based Reasoning Workshop.

Bento, C. and Costa, E., (1994). A Similarity Metric for Retrieval of Cases Imperfectly Explained. In Wess S.; Althoff, K.-D.; and Richter, M. M. (eds.), Topics in Case-Based Reasoning - Selected Papers from the First European Workshop on Case-Based Reasoning, Kaiserslautern, Springer Verlag.

Bento, C., Macedo, L. and Costa, E., (1994). RECIDE - Reasoning with Cases Imperfectly Described and Explained, in Second European Workshop on Case-Based Reasoning..

Cain, T., Pazzani, M. and Silverstein, G., (1991). Using Domain Knowledge to Influence Similarity Judgements, in Proceedings of a Case-Based Reasoning Workshop, Morgan-Kaufmann.

Grilo, C., Pereira, F. C., Macedo, L. and Cardoso, A. (1996). A Structured Framework for Representing Time in Generative Composing System, International Conference on Knowledge Based Computer Systems'96. (submitted)

Hinrichs, T., (1988). Towards an Architecture for Open World Problem Solving, In Proceedings of a Workshop on Case-Based Reasoning, San Mateo, CA, Morgan Kaufmann.

Honning (1993). Issues in the representations of time and structure in music. Contemporary Music Review, 9, pp. 221-239.

Khemani, D., Prasad, P., (1995). A Memory-Based Hierarchical Planner, in Proceedings of the First International Conference on Case-Based Reasoning, Sesimbra, Portugal.

Kolodner, J., (1988). Retrieving events from a Case Memory: a parallel implementation, in Proceedings of a Case-Based Reasoning Workshop, San Mateo, CA, Morgan-Kaufmann.

Kolodner, J., (1989). Judging Which is the "Best" Case for a Case-Based Reasoner, in Case-Based Reasoning: Proceedings of a Workshop, Florida, Morgan-Kaufmann.

Koton, P., (1989). Using Experience in Learning and Problem Solving, Massachusets Institute of Technology, Laboratory of Computer Science (Ph D diss., October 1988), MIT/LCS/TR-441.

Lerdahl, F. and Jackendoff, R. (1983). A Generative Theory of Tonal Music. Cambridge, Mass.: MIT Press.

Munõz-Avila, H., Huellen, J., (1995). Retrieving Cases in Structured Domains by Using Goal Dependencies, in Proceedings of the First International Conference on Case-Based Reasoning, Sesimbra, Portugal.

Plaza, E., (1995). Cases as terms: A feature term approach to the structured representation of cases, in Proceedings of the First International Conference on Case-Based Reasoning, Sesimbra, Portugal .

Redmond, M., (1990). Distributed Cases for Case-Based Reasoning; Facilitating Use of Multiple Cases, In Proceedings of AAAI.

Simpson, R., (1985). A Computer Model of Case-Based Reasoning in Problem Solving. PhD thesis, Georgia Institute of Technology, Atlanta, GA.

Sycara, K., Navinchandra, D., (1991). Influences: A Thematic Abstraction for Creative Use of Multiple Cases, in Proceedings of a Case-Based Reasoning Workshop.

Veloso, M., (1992). Learning by Analogical Reasoning in General Problem Solving, Ph D thesis, School of Computer Science, Carnegie Mellon University, Pittsburgh, PA.

The Transfer Problem in Analogical Reuse

N.A.M. Maiden

Centre for Human-Computer Interface Design,
City University, London, UK.
Tel: +44-171-477-8412
E-Mail: N.A.M.Maiden@city.ac.uk

Abstract

Analogical reuse, as one form of case-based reasoning, has been shown to aid specification of requirements for computer systems. This paper reports an investigation in which 5 inexperienced software engineers transferred a reusable specification to produce a solution for an analogical software engineering problem. The software engineers exhibited mental laziness as well as analogical reasoning during reuse, and made errors consistent with poor analogical understanding. Results indicate the need for intelligent assistance during reuse of requirement specifications. First, malrules derived from errors during reasoning provide the basis for problem diagnosis. Second, strategies to guide analogical comprehension and transfer strategies are needed. These malrules and strategies have been designed as part of the AIR toolkit. More general implications for case-based design are then discussed.

Keywords: requirements engineering, analogical reasoning, case-based reasoning, software reuse.

1 Introduction

Requirements engineering is a complex technical, social and cognitive activity in need of tool-based assistance (Jarke et al. 1993). One solution is analogical reuse of requirement specifications across domains to define requirements of new systems. Analogical specification reuse, as one form of case-based reasoning, can provide the domain and method knowledge necessary for tasks like structuring, scoping and completing requirements specifications which less experienced software engineers find difficult (e.g. Guindon 1990, Sutcliffe & Maiden 1992). Effective reuse of matched specifications has been demonstrated (Sutcliffe & Maiden 1990), however adaptation of complex analogical specifications defies automation, and little is known about how software engineers understand and reuse specifications. Unfortunately studies of program reuse (e.g. Detienne 1992), comprehension (e.g. Pennington 1987) and debugging (e.g. Holt et al. 1987) indicate that understanding unfamiliar software is difficult, even for experts, while analogical problem solving in even simple domains has proven problematic (e.g. Gick & Holyoak 1983, Ross 1987, 1989, Novick & Holyoak 1991).

Studies of cognitive processes during software reuse (e.g. Neal 1989, Detienne 1992) indicate that inexperienced software engineers, who have the most to gain from reuse, copy using lexical properties rather than understand the specification and analogical match (Sutcliffe & Maiden 1990). Similar findings were reported in object-oriented reuse (Lange & Moher 1989) and physics problem solving by students who copied example solutions from textbooks (Chi et al. 1989).

However, further studies of the cognitive processes during analogical reuse are needed to determine reuse malrules as an empirical basis for the design of intelligent requirements engineering tools. To this end the paper reports an empirical investigation of reuse of analogical specifications by inexperienced software engineers.

Potential problems during analogical reasoning are three-fold. First, analogical recognition has proven difficult between problems without salient surface similarities (Keane 1987, Ross 1989). Second, induction of mental schemata requires assistance in the form of explanation of the analogical match (Gick 1989). Third, good analogical understanding does not always lead to effective analogical transfer (Novick & Holyoak 1991). Therefore, the cognitive processes underlying analogical specification reuse need to be investigated to provide a sound empirical basis for the design of tools intended to support such reuse. This paper reports the analogical understanding (Gick & Holyoak 1983) and reasoning strategies of inexperienced software engineers to determine how they do, or do not, understand and transfer specifications.

2 Method

Protocol analysis was used to investigate the analytic and reuse behaviour of 5 inexperienced software engineers (3M & 2F Masters students in Business Systems Analysis) with a maximum of 3 years programming experience obtained from commercial and academic backgrounds. Subjects used SSA (Structured Systems Analysis, De Marco 1978) to specify an air traffic control (ATC) system. The problem statement described an existing air traffic control system, problems with this system and functional requirements for a new system. This problem statement was defined using text supported by informal diagrams showing air spaces, radar screens and flight plans. Subjects were assisted during the task by provision of a flexible manufacturing system (FMS) specification which was analogous to the ATC system. They were informed that the FMS specification could assist specification of the ATC system but were not given details of the analogical match. This was regarded as typical of support provided by current requirements engineering tools. The problem statement and reusable specification ensured that subjects were given the domain knowledge necessary to develop a specification.

2.1 Experimental Material

All subjects read the 820-word problem statement. The FMS specification was represented using DFD notation supplemented by short narratives describing the system objectives and main processes (see Appendix A). Subjects had access to both documents throughout the exercise. For those readers unfamiliar with structured analytic techniques, De Marco defines a DFD as "a network of related functions showing all interfaces between components" (p342). DFDs are made up of only four basic elements: data flows represented by named arcs, processes represented by circles, data stores represented by parallel lines, and data sources and sinks represented by curved rectangles. DFDs show a road map of the input-process-output interconnections from sinks. The method follows a process of top-down functional decomposition. Each process fulfils a goal and is decomposed into lower-level diagrams with sub processes, see Appendix A.

2.2 Experimental Design

Subjects were requested to think aloud and their verbal protocols were captured by video cameras which also recorded drawing and reading behaviour. Subjects were advised to take their time and not be afraid of verbalising too much, following Ericsson & Simon's (1984) practice. Subjects' instructions were read by the experimenter, and each subject was recommended to reuse the analogical specification to develop two (context and level-0) data flow diagrams to complete the ATC specification in the time allowed.

Subjects were given 75 minutes to develop context and level-0 data flow diagrams as a pilot study indicated that this was sufficient time to complete the task. All subjects were informed of this time limit. Each subject recorded a concurrent protocol during the task then the experimenter retrospectively elicited analytic strategies and mental and non-mental behaviour. First, a written questionnaire was used to elicit subjects' analogical understanding. Second, 15 minutes verbal questioning elicited analytic and reasoning strategies and investigated specific hypotheses and errors. It was controlled by a checklist of behaviours expected during the task, following Ericsson and Simon's practice.

2.3 The Analogy

The analogy between the ATC and FMS domains allows considerable specification reuse. The main concept in both is the functional requirement to keep objects apart and ensure that they follow a predetermined plan to their destination. This was manifest as aircraft protected by an air space which no other aircraft is permitted to enter and guidance by a flight plan to their destination. Similarly products were protected by track sections which are only permitted to contain one product at a time and controlled by a production plan which directs each product. Furthermore, object movement in both domains was guided by a remote human controller. However, the two domains were also different, for example a two-dimensional space in the FMS domain and a three-dimensional space in the ATC domain. These differences mean that there is no complete set of mappings between the two domains. Indeed, most complex analogies between problem domains in software engineering are like this, therefore the inclusion of unmappable components represented a realistic challenge.

2.4 Analysis

Protocol transcripts were analysed twice: (i) categorising mental behaviours represented in speech segments, usually sentences and incomplete utterances (see Ericsson & Simon 1984 for further details); (ii) identification of analytic strategies using a taxonomy based on criteria of mental and non-mental (physical) activity. During the first pass, protocol utterances were categorised to identify mental reasoning behaviours and associated non-mental behaviours. Reasoning was defined as verbalising the generation, development, testing, confirmation, modification and discarding of hypotheses about the problem, its proposed specification or the source domain (e.g. "the aircraft risk colliding, hence the warning process must be automatic, and it must inform the air traffic controller with warning messages displayed on the radar screen"). Each reasoning utterance was further categorised to identify subjects' topic focus: reasoning about the target (ATC) domain, reasoning about the source (FMS) domain, reasoning about analogical mappings between the source and target domains, and; reasoning about general concepts which do not describe the target or source domains, or the analogical links between them.

Reasoning utterances were distinguished from other mental behaviours, such as assertions, by the degree of inference applied, concurrent non-mental behaviour (e.g. reading behaviour suggested assertions) and the tone and vocal inclination of the verbalised utterance. Other mental behaviours include assertions, planning and diagram-based testing. Non-mental behaviours were:

Information acquisition -	searching for and retrieval of data in the requirements document or the reusable specification;
Structured diagramming -	physical construction of the system specification, recorded as a data flow diagram;
Note taking -	physical note taking and highlighting not related to construction of the data flow diagram.

Non-mental behaviour was categorised as occurring concurrently with mental behaviour. During a second-pass categorisation analytic strategies were based on mental and non-mental behaviour and the purpose of subject's activity. They were classified using eight strategies:

Gather information -	read the target document or the reusable specification;
Summarise data -	summarise the contents of the target document or the reusable specification;
Construct with reuse -	reuse the FMS specification to develop a structured diagram representing the specification to the ATC system;
Construct without reuse--	develop a structured diagram representing the ATC specification without reusing the FMS specification;
Revise -	redraw the ATC specification;
Evaluate against the target -	test the subject's specification against the target requirements in the problem document;
Evaluate against the analogy -	test the subject's specification against the reusable specification;
Summarise specification -	test the subject's specification without accessing the requirements document or the reusable specification.

Ericsson & Simon (1984) have suggested protocol analysis is a useful technique for eliciting sequential models of human problem solving. The consistent verbalisation of our subjects suggests that reports were generally representative of underlying mental behaviour, although this cannot be guaranteed.

2.5 Protocol Categorisation

Protocol categorisation was validated through cross-marking by two independent observers with experience of protocol analysis. Each observer allocated a behavioural category to each utterance in 3 randomly-selected protocols. Inter-observer agreement was 83% of all categorised protocol utterances, and differences between observer categorisations were reconciled. Analytic strategies in three different protocols were also categorised independently, then observers reconciled differences between categorisation of strategies to develop a common definition and application of analytic strategies used to categorise all protocols.

2.6 Specification Completeness

Completeness scores were allocated to each subject's specification to measure their success or otherwise in solving the problem. A solution specification and marking scheme was developed by two expert software engineers who had considerable knowledge of the analogy. Specification completeness was measured using a list of necessary components and focused on semantic specification features rather than the syntax of the data flow diagramming notation. Specification components included processes, system inputs and outputs, external entities and data store accesses in the expert's specification. Subjects received a score if a component was included in the data flow diagram.

3 Results

All 5 subjects developed a solution to the ATC problem. Completeness scores are shown in Table 1. All subjects produced much of their solutions during periods of reuse. Subjects N3 and N5 developed more complete solutions than other subjects but did not spent more time reusing the specification. Analysis of verbalised planning of the problem solving process revealed that subjects did not use method knowledge such as SSA (De Marco 1978) to structure the analytic process (average 25.2 instances of general planning behaviour, 2.8 instances of method planning behaviour). Indeed N3 and N5 ignored such method plans (total of 1 planning utterance) and relied on the reusable specification to guide their behaviour, a conclusion in line with retrospective comments by these subjects.

Analytic strategies were counted for whether or not each strategy was exhibited by each subject within each 5 minute time period, see Figure 1. Strategies indicated, in general, an initial period of information gathering before the solution was developed by reuse, then tested by summarising the solution or evaluating it against the target. The average length of time spent by subjects on strategies revealed the importance of information gathering and reuse, while subjects spent least time constructing and revising their solutions and evaluating it against the analogy.

subject	completeness scores (out of maximum of 44)					
	total score	cons. with reuse	cons no reuse	summ soltn	eval. target	eval. analgy
N1	27	11	14	2		
N2	22	20		1	1	
N3	32	32				
N4	24	23				1
N5	32	30	1		1	

Table 1. Completeness score totals, and completeness scores by strategy for all subjects

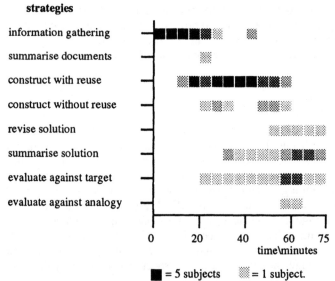

Figure 1. Number of subjects using a strategy within 5 minute periods

The effect of using different strategies on solution completeness was measured by the number of components added during bouts of each strategy. Reuse led to the most effective production of subject's solutions, indicating that all 5 subjects recognised the analogical match to some degree, although N1 constructed some of the solution from the problem text, without reuse. On the other hand, testing strategies led to few additions or changes to solutions, see Table 1. Subjects' reuse, information gathering and construction behaviour were examined in more detail.

3.1 Reusing the Reusable Specification

Construction with reuse was examined during transfer of the larger level-0 DFD. Each subject's approach was categorised as top-down (reuse processes first) or incremental (reuse each process and its inputs\outputs in turn), then each bout of reuse was analysed to determine the number of solution components (processes, data stores, external entities, inputs and outputs) transferred to the solution, see Table 2. Incremental reuse was exhibited more by subjects N3 & N5 who produced the more complete solutions. Analysis of their verbalisations also revealed that these subjects reasoned about more candidate reusable components than did other subjects.

subject	number of components reasoned about	number of components reused incrementally
N1	36	3
N2	37	0
N3	41	14
N4	32	0
N5	44	14

Table 2. Number of components transferred incrementally during reuse of the level-0 DFD, and number of components reasoned about during the task

Solution specifications and transcripts of subjects' reasoning and behaviour were examined to determine which solution components were transferred from the reusable specification. Each reusable component was categorised as either reused or not. All subjects reused at least 4/6 FMS processes but transfer of other reusable components varied. N3 and N5 transferred on average 65.5% of all reusable data store accesses, external entities, inputs and outputs. In contrast, other subjects transferred on average 13.8% of such components then abandoned reuse in favour of other strategies. Reasons for this given during retrospective questioning revealed that N1 needed more target domain knowledge to build the solution, N2 adopted an iterative testing cycle and N4 redrew his solution in order to better understand it.

Previous studies had indicated the likelihood of mental laziness during specification reuse (Sutcliffe & Maiden 1990). Four of the 5 subjects claimed an important role for copying and word substitution. During the task N2 considered but rejected word substitution, however retrospective questioning claimed a copying strategy "to see how far I could get". Indeed, this subject used word substitution to transfer 4 of the processes in the level-0 DFD. N4 claimed during the task that it was sufficient just to alter to reusable specification. Subjects N3 and N5 also admitted to mental laziness: N3 retrospectively claimed to have copied and substituted words throughout reuse while N5 admitted to copying components and changing their names towards the end of task. Furthermore, no subject exhibited evidence of strategies for deliberate learning, verbalised as planning behaviour, to avoid mental laziness during reuse.

3.2 Reading the Reusable Specification

Subject behaviour and responses to retrospective questions revealed three different approaches to reading the requirement specification: (i) subjects N1 and N4 gathered information from both the DFD and text; (ii) subject N2 found the DFDs too confusing and read the text only; (iii) subjects N3 and N5 failed to notice the third page containing additional text intended to aid domain understanding. N3 claimed afterwards that the DFD was the solution to all her problems, so it was unnecessary to read on. All subjects read one page at a time rather than gather information from all three pages of DFDs and text at the same time.

3.3 Constructing the Solution Specification Without Reuse

One subject (N1) constructed the entire context-level and much of the level-0 DFD solution. This led to solution completeness equivalent to that of the less successful reusers (N2 & N4). Construction took place once specification reuse had been tried and abandoned. Retrospective questioning revealed that, despite N1's earlier claims, the reusable specification provided only a partial solution so this subject "needed to analyse the ATC problem some more". N1 also claimed to have reached the level of the analogical match where it was no longer of any help.

3.4 Reasoning During Information Gathering and Reuse

Subjects' verbalised reasoning provided further clues about their reuse and information gathering behaviour. The topic focus of reasoning behaviour was analysed by categorising each reasoning utterance as an inference about the target or source domain or the analogical mappings between them. All subjects reasoned most about the target domain and least about the source domain, see Table 3. Totals of reasoning about the source domain were low, averaging 9.8 reasoning utterances per subject.

subject	number of reasoning utterances		
	target	analogy	source
N1	119	15	0
N2	192	46	28
N3	107	50	3
N4	162	78	5
N5	147	71	13

Table 3. Totals of reasoning utterances by subject

Life histories for each hypothesis were traced by their thematic content until eventual rejection or resolution. Reasoning utterances were categorised as generate, develop, test, confirm, modify and discard. Sequential dependencies between reasoning behaviours for all subjects were analysed to construct a network model of the temporal relationships between categories. Frequencies greater than 1% of the total are shown in Figure 2. More transitions occurred within target utterances and within analogical utterances than between target and analogical utterances, and there was little difference between transition frequencies from analogical to domain reasoning, and vice versa. There was also little inter-individual difference in subjects' patterns of reasoning behaviour.

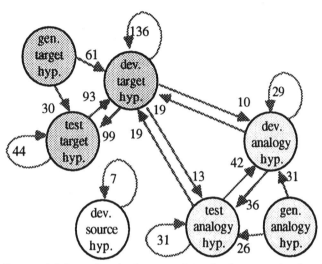

Figure 2. Sequential dependencies between hypothesis categories for all subjects

3.5 Analogical Understanding

Subject's recall of analogical mappings at the end of the task was also examined to determine their understanding of the analogical match. A questionnaire requested mappings in the target domain for each component in the source domain. Subjects recognised on average only 51.5% of the possible correct analogical mappings. Subjects N2 and N4 mapped fewer incorrect analogical mappings while N3 made as many incorrect as correct mappings. However, there were no order-of-magnitude differences between the totals of correct and incorrect mappings, so a qualitative analysis of recalled mappings was undertaken.

The total of correct and incorrect mappings for major components in the reusable specification is shown in Table 4. All subjects recognised correct mappings with the production controller, infra-red sensors, production plan and occurrence of two products in the same track section but not with any other source components. One subject failed to map product to aircraft despite its importance to the analogical match. This indicated poor analogical understanding, in keeping with earlier evidence for copying and word substitution during reuse.

analogical mappings		correctly mapped	incorrectly mapped
source domain	target domain		
production Controller	air traffic controller	5	0
infra-red Sensors	radar	5	0
production Plan	flight plan	5	0
2 products in same track section	2 a/c in same air space	5	0
product	aircraft	4	1
misdirected product	aircraft off course	3	0
production floor layout	airways	3	1
production operator	pilot	3	2
delayed product manufacture	delayed flight	2	1
manufacture of a product	flight	2	1
lost product manufacture	missing flight	0	1
production track	air corridor	2	3
production track section	air space	1	2
machine	air space	0	2
job	flight step	0	4

Table 4. Retrospective analogical mappings - not all subjects gave a mapping for each source domain component. No mapping was not counted as an incorrect mapping

Subjects also made incorrect mappings with other source domain components, see Table 4. In particular subjects were unable to map the correct components to physical components of the production planning domain (production track, track section and machine). Subjects made 3 correct but 7 incorrect mappings with these 3 components. Subjects also failed to map individual production jobs to flight steps (0 correct, 4 incorrect). Therefore, subjects' analogical understanding at the end of the task appears to have been mixed, with good understanding of 5 or 6 mappings but not mappings between elements of the physical structure of the two domains.

3.6 Errors During Analogical Reasoning

One aim of this investigation was to determine malrules which explain errors which arise during analogical comprehension and transfer. Subjects' qualitative analogical mappings verbalised during the task were examined. An error was defined as either: (i) an analogical mapping which was inconsistent with mappings inferred by the authors of this paper who had 'generated' the analogical match, or; (ii) inferences about the source domain which were inconsistent with assumptions made the authors. Verbalised analogical errors were categorised into three types. No-mapping errors occurred when a correct analogical mapping was rejected. Surface-similarities errors were incorrect analogical mappings with syntactic similarities between the mapped objects. False-mapping errors represented all other types of incorrect mapping. Total numbers of error types were similar for all subjects:

- surface-similarities errors were the least common potential source of incorrect analogical mappings. Examples include mapping the reusable data store *machine type* to the solution data store *aircraft type* (shared label *type*) and mapping the reusable data store *job* to the solution data store *flight* (input data flow *job completed* mapped to input data flow *flight completed*);
- subjects exhibited 14 instances of false mappings, for example *production operators* were mapped to *air traffic controllers* rather than *pilots* because these external entities enter information about *new* products and new aircraft to the system;
- subjects exhibited 15 instances of incorrect rejection of analogical mappings within the bout of reasoning topic focus. Most errors could be attributed to lack of reasoning about the source domain.

These error patterns provide the basis for error diagnosis using a set of malrules during analogical reuse.

4 Summary

Results reported in this paper demonstrate that less experienced software engineers can reuse analogical specifications during requirements engineering, however a number of problems arose:

- the software engineers transferred the major components of the specification (processes) but transfer of other components (data stores, data flows, external entities, inputs and outputs) was problematic;
- systematic reuse, guided by the syntactic structure of the notation, led to more reasoning about and transfer of these components;
- no software engineer reasoned about all components available for transfer, or transferred all components which were reasoned about;
- software engineers transferred components which were not understood, through copying and word substitution;
- some software engineers did not read the entire reusable specification prior to reuse;
- the reusable specification was not used to test solutions;
- there was little reasoning about the source domain;
- there was a poor recall of most analogical mappings, despite their importance in the analogical match;
- software engineers made diverse errors during mapping and comprehension which are consistent with poor analogical understanding.

Despite these problems, specification reuse was still more effective than construction of solutions from scratch, as N1's solution suggested and previous studies (Sutcliffe & Maiden 1990) indicate. However, these problems, if typical of those encountered by the wider population of software engineers, must be addressed before successful and large-scale analogical reuse is feasible.

5 Discussion

Our basic finding that analogical reasoning is difficult and that novice problem solvers turn to syntactic mappings is not new. There is strong evidence that analogical recognition between semantically-remote domains is difficult (e.g. Keane 1987, Ross 1987, 1989). Indeed, when two domains share surface but not structural features, incorrect transfer is stronger for novices than for experts in a domain (e.g. Novick 1988). However analogical specification reuse, unlike problems used in previous studies of analogical reasoning (e.g. Heit & Rubinstein 1994), is an ill-structured task and our results were more complex, indicating both analogical reasoning and mental laziness by all 5 software engineers. Our software engineers appeared to transfer parts of the analogical specification using both correct and incorrect mappings which exploited the close analogical fit between the two domains. However much of the analogical specification was not transferred at all.

Another difference with previous studies was the use of structured notations to represent the analogical solutions. The more complete solutions of N3 and N5 can be attributed to detailed incremental transfer using this syntactic structure. Such transfer can be linked to reasoning about more candidate components for reuse, recognition of more analogical mappings and greater component reuse. If this was the case, the use of graphic notations for solution representation also has implications for case-based reasoning in other complex design activities such as architecture (Voss & Schmidt-Belz 1993) or industrial design engineering (Kruger 1993). These domains use graphical notations as the principle representation. Incremental transfer using the notation structure (e.g. rooms in architectural plans or circuits in electronic circuit board design) might also ensure greater reuse, more analogical mapping and more reasoning about features for reuse, although these predictions remain to be investigated through further empirical research.

As predicted, our software engineers did not appear to exhibit good understanding of the problem prior to solution transfer. Indeed, the software engineers appear to have used minimal knowledge to undertake the task. Three out of 5 did not read the entire specification and all exhibited little verbalised reasoning about the source domain. Neither was there evidence for separating learning about the source domain from solving the target problem. Rather, evidence indicates that learning might have taken place in parallel. Reasoning about the source domain appears to be driven by the need to transfer a component to solve the target problem. Furthermore, software engineers exhibited poor recall of mappings between physical elements of the two domains. One possible reason is that formation of analogical mappings between the two-dimensional FMS domain and three-dimensional ATC domain was difficult, thus possibly indicating the limitations of the analogical match.

Comprehension problems notwithstanding, ineffective transfer appears to have been due more to a lack of systematic reasoning than to errors during reasoning.

Analyses revealed fewer errors than anticipated from previous findings (Sutcliffe & Maiden 1990). Indeed, failure to map components accounted for more observed errors than did surface similarities. This indicates that analogical transfer between ill-structured problems varies, unlike the all-or-nothing transfer in simpler analogical problem solving (e.g. Ross 1989). Difficulties arise in controlling the transfer process, which is not surprising given the scale and complexities of this process. The next stage is to explore this assertion with a wider population of engineers for different engineering discplines and case-based design scenarios.

6 The AIR Toolkit

Effective analogical reuse must overcome problems such as mental laziness, poor analogical mapping and ineffective analogical transfer. The AIR toolkit aids understanding and transfer of analogical specifications. Details for this toolkit are available in Maiden & Sutcliffe (1994). Design features linked to empircal findings reported in this paper are:

* guidance for systematic analogical transfer to direct reasoning topic focus is combined with hiding parts of the specification not being transferred to avoid opportunistic transfer and word substitution, as exhibited by experienced software engineers (Maiden & Sutcliffe 1992);
* a set of tool-initiated incremental transfer strategies which exploit the syntactic structure of graphical notations. Similar strategies were identified for successful transfer of JSD process structure diagrams (Sutcliffe & Maiden 1990);
* use of the analogical specification as a template for transfer, through direct modification of the analogical specification, changing or deleting names of reusable components using understood analogical mappings (Maiden & Sutcliffe 1992);
* promote analogical reasoning prior to transfer of components: (i) understand the relevant features of the source domain through reference to other documentation; (ii) systematic formation of the analogical mapping, using graphical notations for expressing mappings; (iii) validation of the analogical transfer through reference to existing mappings;
* guidance for systematic testing of requirement specifications using the transferred analogical specification, for example through side-by-side, zoom-out representations of the analogical and target specifications to encourage browsing.

Step-by-step guidance and partial exposure to the specification is expected to encourage analogical reasoning and avoid mental laziness. It is assisted with malrules derived from observed analogical errors to produce a simple, enumerated bug model for analogical reuse. One interesting research direction will be to undertake usability studies of existing case-based tool design such as CLAVIER and ARCHIE to see whether designers exhibit the same mapping malrules, and whether these malrules have a significant effect on the design task.

7 Implications for Case-Based Reasoning

This paper reports effective if problematic analogical reuse of requirement specifications and proposes co-operative assistance for requirements engineers to avoid observed problems. Similar studies of analogical reuse by experienced software engineers (Maiden & Sutcliffe 1992) revealed that analogical understanding is difficult regardless of experience, therefore this co-operative assistance is expected to assist requirements engineers of all levels of experience.

Although our research is, in essence, case-based reasoning for requirements engineering, it also can have implications for CBR for other design disciplines such as architecture (e.g. Kolodner 1993). Both are ill-structured problems with complex cases which are amenable to graphic representation but not to machine-based adaptation due to the problem domain complexity. Although some researchers have identified the importance of case adaptation (e.g. Smyth & Keane 1993) there has been little recognition for the need for human involvement (Kolodner 1993) or issues which that implies. Guidance for such adaptation becomes imperative because evidence such as that reported in this paper reveals that case adaptation is difficult. As such this paper can act as a guide which demonstrates one direction for future research in case-based reasoning. The author is in the process of repeating the reported studies for case understanding and adaptation in other domains such as kitchen and building design.

Acknowledgements

The authors would like to thank the MSc students in Business Systems Analysis at the City University for their co-operation. This work was funded by UK Science and Engineering Research Council Grant 88803006.

References

Chi M.T.H., Bassok M., Lewis M.W., Reimann P. & Glaser R., 1989, 'Self-Explanations: How Students Study and Use Examples in Learning to Solve Problems', *Cognitive Science* 13, 145-182.

De Marco T., 1978, *Structured Systems Analysis and Specification*, Prentice-Hall International.

Detienne F., 1992, 'Acquiring Experience in Object-Oriented Programming: Effect on Design Strategies', in *Cognitive Models and Intelligent Environments for Learning Programming*, ed. E. Lemut, B. du Boulay and G. Dettori, Springer-Verlag.

Ericsson K.A. & Simon H.A., 1984, *Protocol Analysis*, MIT Press.

Gick M.L. & Holyoak K.J., 1983, 'Schema Induction and Analogical Transfer', *Cognitive Psychology* 15, 1-38.

Guindon R., 1990, 'Designing the Design Process: Exploiting Opportunistic Thoughts', *Human-Computer Interaction* 5, 305-344.

Heit E. & Rubinstein J., 1994, 'Similarity and Property Effects in Inductive Reasoning', *Journal of Experimental Psychology: Learning, Memory and Cognition* 20(2), 411-422.

Holt R.W., Boehm-Davis D.A. & Schultz A.C., 1987, 'Mental Representations of Programs for Student and Professional Programmers', in *2nd Workshop of Empirical Studies of Programmers*, ed. G. Olson, S. Sheppard and E. Soloway, Ablex, 33-46.

Jarke M., Bubenko Y., Rolland C., Sutcliffe A.G. & Vassiliou Y., 1993, 'Theories Underlying Requirements Engineering: An Overview of NATURE at Genesis', Proceedings of IEEE Symposium on Requirements Engineering, IEEE Computer Society Press, 19-31.

Keane M., 1987, 'On Retrieving Analogues When Solving Problems', *The Quarterly Journal of Experimental Psychology* 39A, 29-41.

Kolodner J.L., 1993, 'Case-Based Reasoning', Morgan-Kauffman.

Kruger C., 1993, 'Cognitive Aspects of Reuse in Industrial Design Reengineering', Proceedings of Workshop of 13th IJCAI Conference 'Reuse of Designs: An Interdisciplinary Cognitive Approach', INRIA Technical Report, Domaine de Voluceau, Rocquencourt, BP105, 78153 Le Chesnay, France.

Lange B.M. & Moher T.G., 1989, 'Some Strategies of Reuse in an Object-Oriented Programming Environment', Proceedings of CHI'89, ed. K. Bice & C. Lewis, ACM Press, 69-73.

Maiden N.A.M. & Sutcliffe A.G., 1992, 'Exploiting Reusable Specifications Through Analogy', *Communications of the ACM*, **34(5)**, 55-64.

Maiden N.A.M. & Sutcliffe A.G., 1994, 'Requirements Critiquing Using Domain Abstractions', Proceedings of IEEE Conference on Requirements Engineering, IEEE Computer Society Press, 184-193.

Neal, L.R., 1989, 'A System for Example-Based Programming', Proceedings of CHI'89 Conference, ACM Press, 63-68.

Novick L.R., 1988, 'Analogical Transfer, Problem Similarity, and Expertise', *Journal of Experimental Psychology: Learning, Memory and Cognition* **14(3)**, 510-520.

Novick L.R. & Holyoak K.J., 1991, 'Mathematical Problem Solving by Analogy', *Journal of Experimental Psychology: Learning, Memory, and Cognition* **17(3)**, 398-415.

Pennington N., 1987, 'Comprehension Strategies in Programming', in 2nd *Workshop of Empirical Studies of Programmers*, ed. G. Olson, S. Sheppard and E. Soloway, Ablex, 100 - 113.

Ross B.H., 1989, 'Distinguishing Types of Superficial Similarities: Different Effects on the Access and Use of Earlier Problems', *Journal of Experimental Psychology: Learning, Memory and Cognition* **15(3)**, 456-468.

Ross B.H., 1987, 'This is Like That: The Use of Earlier Problems and the Separation of Similarity Effects', *Journal of Experimental Psychology: Learning, Memory and Cognition* **13(4)**, 629-639.

Smyth B. & Keane M.T., 1993, 'Retrieving Adaptable Cases: the Role of Adaptation Knowledge in Case Retrieval', Proceedings EWCBR-93, Lecture Notes in Artificial Intelligence 837, Springer-Verlag, 209-220.

Sutcliffe A.G. & Maiden N.A.M., 1992, 'Analysing the Novice Analyst: Cognitive Models in Software Engineering', *International Journal of Man-Machine Studies* **36**, 719-740.

Sutcliffe A.G. & Maiden N.A.M., 1990, 'Software Reusability: Delivering Productivity Gains or Short Cuts', Human-Computer Interaction: Proceedings of INTERACT'90, ed. D. Diaper, G. Cockton, B. Shackel & D. Gilmore, North-Holland, 895-901.

Voss A. & Schmidt-Belz B., 1993, 'Case-Oriented Knowledge Acquisition for Architectural Design', Proceedings of Workshop of 13th IJCAI Conference 'Reuse of Designs: An Interdisciplinary Cognitive Approach', INRIA Technical Report, Domaine de Voluceau, Rocquencourt, BP105, 78153 Le Chesnay, France.

Appendix A

Brockville Precision Tools is a high-tech company manufacturing products (precision tools) using the latest computerised production techniques. The company is moving towards full automation of production facilities, in order to keep human operator intervention to a minimum. Recently a new system was installed, to monitor production. The system identifies delays and potential accidents during production, so that the automated handling system can take appropriate action. The production monitoring system is described in the 2 accompanying data flow diagrams, and in the supporting narrative.

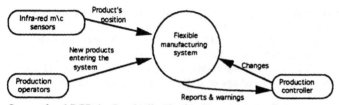

Context-level DFD for Brockville Flexible Manufacturing System

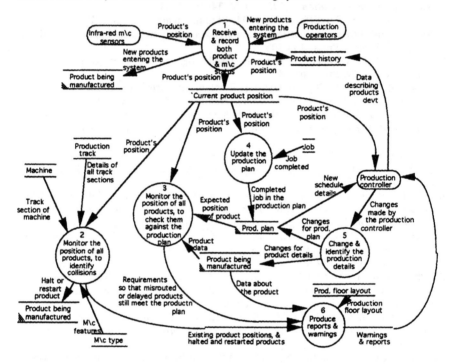

Level-0 DFD for Brockville Flexible Manufacturing System

This narrative explains 3 processes of the level-0 DFD in more detail.

Process 2 - Monitor the position of all products, to avoid collisions
The aim of this process is to ensure no two products being manufactured come together during the manufacturing process. During production products are passed along lines of manufacturing machines by a complicated series of conveyor belts and automatic handlers. Each individual line of machines is called a track, and each track is divided into many sections, which can only legally contain one product at any time. Product positions are determined by infra-red sensors laid along the tracks. This process invesitgates the current position of all products to ensure no track section contains more than one product. If two products are in the

same section one product is halted automatically, and restarted again once the other product has cleared that section. The production controller is warned of any potential accidents, so that he may reroute products.

Process 3 - Monitor the position of all products, to check the production plan is met

A production plan determines the order of machines which a product must follow during manufacture. This process checks to ensure that the tracks followed by a product are those intended, by comparing the current product position with that given in the production plan. Diversions of any sort from the plan are reported to the production controller.

Process 4 - Update the production plan

When sensors detect an individual manufacturing job using one machine has been completed on a product the production plan for that product is updated to indicate a further step in the plan has been fulfilled.

A Case-Based System for Adaptive Hypermedia Navigation

Alessandro Micarelli and Filippo Sciarrone

Dipartimento di Discipline Scientifiche - Sez. Informatica
Università di Roma Tre
Via della Vasca Navale 84, 00146 Roma, Italia
Fax: +39-6-5573030
E-mail: micarel@inf.uniroma3.it

Abstract. One problem posed by the unsupported navigation in a hypermedia system is that users often tend to get lost in the hyperspace. In this paper we describe HYPERCASE, a system for guided knowledge navigation in a hyperspace using a Case-Based Reasoning approach. In the presentation we stress the innovative technique, based on a sub-symbolic approach, we have used to retrieve cases from a case library, and the kind of help given to the user, based on a structural analysis of the hypermedia.

1. Introduction

In this paper we describe a non-intrusive system for guided knowledge navigation in a hypermedia environment using a procedure based on cases. Hypermedia systems are essentially tools that keep a great storage of different kinds of information residing in various media (text, graphics, animations, still images, video, sounds), and permit quick access to such information (Begoray, 1990; Nielsen, 1990a). Typically, in a hypermedia system the user can explore the information in his/her own way, following links between chunks of information. The first example of such systems is the hypertext, which contains only textual information. As the size of the hypermedia data base grows, unsupported navigation often causes the users to get lost in the hyperspace (Nielsen, 1990b). Therefore, adequate aids for navigating through this space are needed (Dillon, McKnight and Richardson, 1990).

In this work we present HYPERCASE, a system for guided knowledge navigation in a hyperspace, under development on a IBM RISC - 6000 platform on the Web environment at the University of Rome 3. In the system the Case-Based Reasoning (CBR) approach (Kolodner, 1993) has been used, in conjunction with a structured analysis of the hypermedia, for guiding the user in finding the desired path according to his/her goals and interests, thus trying to reduce the cognitive load of navigation (Micarelli and Sciarrone, 1996). The CBR approach to knowledge navigation has been explored also in Hammond, Burke and Schmitt (1994) for "data mining" applications.

The paper is structured as follows. In the next Section we present the general architecture of HYPERCASE. In Section 3 we present the method, based on an artificial neural network engine, we have used for the resolution of the indexing problem of the Case-Based reasoner. In Section 4 the kinds of help the recovery module of the system can give the user is described. To this end, the analysis of the structure and metrics of the hypermedia, useful for helping the user during the navigation, is presented. In a concluding Section, we give some final remarks.

2. The Architecture of HYPERCASE

Our main goal is the definition of an approach for knowledge navigation particularly suited for learning purposes. To this end, some specific domains have been chosen and expert tutors have been interviewed. One application domain we have taken into consideration for the definition of our working hypotheses is relative to data on various aspects of the *Neorealism in the Italian Cinema*.

A user can navigate in the hypermedia according to different possible learning goals. Associated with each goal, there is one or more "thematic paths" or "canonical paths", defined by the author of the hypermedia, that must be followed to reach the goal. The user can be allowed to navigate in different ways. The first one is the unsupported navigation or free browsing: it is the usual way, and consists in accessing in a non-linear order by navigating within the hypermedia node network without any help for orientation given by the system (with the limits we previously mentioned).

A way to overcome these limits is to have the possible learning goals and the associated thematic paths prestored in the system. The thematic paths can be viewed as models of "ideal users". At the beginning of a session the user can be presented with a menu of different goals to be chosen, according to his/her interests. For instance, a system on the Italian Neorealist Cinema domain could present a menu containing the various learning goals, fourteen in all, (*Rome in the Neorelism, The War, Rossellini in the Neorealism*, ...) and allow the user to choose one among them. At this point the system could present a suitable prestored path according to the choice of the user, inviting him/her to follow it. With this solution (we can call it constraint navigation) the user-friendliness of the hypermedia system would be strongly reduced, due to the rigid constraints imposed to the user. In Trigg (1988) the use of "guided tours" has been proposed. The user follows a string of linked nodes by pressing a button marked "next". This approach is in fact a means of eliminating navigation in a non-linear document. Our proposed solution tries to go beyond the limits of the previous ones.

The general architecture of HYPERCASE is presented in Fig. 1. The main components of the system (the *Indexing Module*, the *Case Library*, the *Recovery Module* and the *Interface*) are built around the specific hypermedia in which the user navigates. The system is endowed with all the possible thematic paths, defined by an expert on the domain and grouped according to the associated goals. Thematic paths and corresponding goals can be viewed as pre-stored cases of the Case-Based reasoner, and are stored in the *Library of Cases* of Fig. 1. At the beginning of a session the system gives a complete initiative and freedom to the user (*Free Navigation*), hiding the prestored paths from him/her.

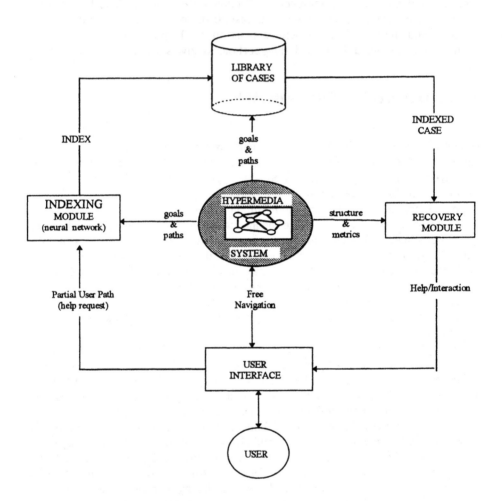

Fig.1. The architecture of the system.

Giving the user the control of the interaction makes him/her an active element during the navigation, improving the effectiveness of the interaction. In fact, as has been pointed out in Stanton and Baber (1992), learning is most effective when it can be directed by the learner. At each moment of the navigation, the user is allowed to ask for help. When help has been requested (*help request*), the system takes into consideration the partial path followed by the user. The *Indexing Module*, in order to determine the presumed user interests, assumes relevant this partial path, and tries to find the thematic path present in the *Library of Cases* that closely matches the user path. The determination of this path allows the system to also determine the (presumed) goal of the user, since this goal is associated with this particular path and pre-stored in the system. This information, associated with a structured representation of the graph that corresponds to the hypermedia (determined in an off-line phase), can then be used by the *Recovery Module* to give the user the right suggestions for the next steps in the navigation as described in Section 4.

The greatest problem in automating this procedure lies in the resolution of the "indexing problem", i.e., in the determination of the prestored case in the case library that corresponds to the user goal. Our working hypothesis is that what is needed from the partial user path is the set of nodes present in the path, regardless of their links (they are in fact predefined in the hypermedia), the time the user spent on each node and the last visited node. According to that hypothesis, the user behaviour can be represented as an "instance of pattern", constituted by a record of attributes relative to the partial user path (see Section 3). The "indexing problem", i.e. the problem of indexing the case library, is therefore reduced to the task of recognizing instances of patterns. For the solution of this problem we have chosen a sub-symbolic approach, consisting in the use of an artificial neural network engine based on a three-layer perceptron (McClelland and Rumelhart, 1986), well suited for pattern recognition, that can be trained by the author of the hypermedia to recognize the right patterns. When a pattern (corresponding to the user behaviour) is presented as input to the network, the network computes an index array that corresponds to a rank ordered list of cases present in the *Library of Cases*, as shown in Fig. 2. The network is described in some detail in the next Section.

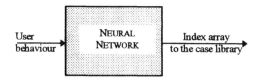

Fig.2. Input and output of the Neural Network.

3. The Indexing Module

In Fig. 3, the input and the output of the neural network used for the *Indexing Module* are shown. The input (Fig. 3a) represents the visited nodes and the time the user spent on each node (time normalized to the range $[0, 1]$, with a zero-value for a node not visited by the user) and the last visited node (normalized over the whole hypermedia).The output (Fig. 3b) represents the structure of an output index array relative to a case library containing m cases. In this case, the *case 2* is the nearest to the user's path while the *case 1* is the farthest.

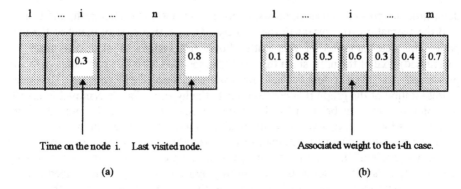

FIG. 3. The structure of the input (a) and of the output (b) of the network.

The network has been realized in the form of a *Multi-Layer-Perceptron* (MLP in the following) (McClelland and Rumelhart, 1986) with three distinct layers (see Fig. 4). The first layer, the *input layer*, is composed of the neurons relative to the nodes of the graph representing the hypermedia, to the last visited node and to the bias value. They are therefore $n + 2$. The *output layer* is composed of as many neurons as the number of the thematic paths, corresponding to the elements of the index array for ordering the prestored cases. In the figure, p_1, p_2, ... p_m are the weights associated with the prestored cases, computed by the network according to a given input.

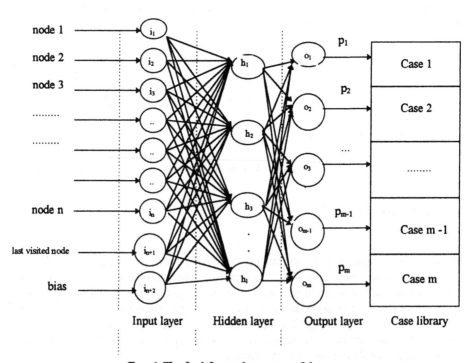

FIG. 4. The feed-forward structure of the perceptron.

Unfortunately there are no theoretical rules for determining the number of *hidden nodes*. We have identified the optimal number of hidden neurons for our application in the context of the training procedure. The chosen learning method belongs to the *Supervised Learning* category (McClelland and Rumelhart, 1986). This procedure consists of the following steps:

a) Collection of a set of *training records*, i.e., a set of input-output pairs, defined by an expert of the domain, where the input is a pattern corresponding to a particuar user path and the output is the index array relative to the thematic paths present in the case library.

b) Test range process. The goal of this phase is to train the network presenting as input some of the already defined training records.

c) Predict range process. In this phase, the network is presented with some inputs for which the output is already known in order to see the forecasting behaviour.

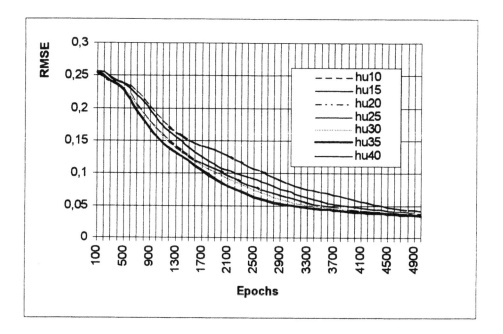

FIG. 5. The error curves in the learning phase.

The *backpropagation* algorithm has been used for training the network. The weight adjustment has followed the rule:

$$\omega_{ij}^{r+1} = \omega_{ij}^{r} + \eta \delta_i x_i + \alpha (\omega_{ij}^{r} - \omega_{ij}^{r-1})$$

where ω_{ij}^{r+1} represents the *synaptic weight* beetwen the i-th and j-th neuron calculated at the (r+1)-th iteration, η the *learning rate* (in the range [0, 1]), δ_i the error relative to the neuron *i* between the calculated output and the true output, x_i the output of the i-th neuron, α the *momentum* factor (in the range [0, 1]). We used $\eta = 0.5$ and $a = 0.9$. The starting values of the weights belonged to the range [-0.3, +0.3]. The following *sigmoid* function has been used as a *transfer function*:

$$o_j = [1 + exp (\Sigma_i \omega_{ij} \ o_i)]^{-1}$$

where o_j represents the output of the j-th neuron, while o_i is the output of the i-th neuron connected to the input of the j-th neuron.

We have tested several configurations of the network for our specific domain (a graph with 70 nodes and fourteen thematic paths) and determined the corresponding error curves. An error curve shows the network throughput during its supervised learning activity. The error is defined by the root mean-square difference between the right output vector (defined in the *training set*) and the output vector generated by the network. Fig. 5 shows the error curve for different numbers of hidden nodes. We have chosen the configuration with 35 hidden units (hu) since it has been the fastest for the error convergence to zero.

Fig. 6 shows the performance of the network as a function of the epochs and of the number of hidden nodes for a given number of training records. The configuration with 35 hidden nodes has reached a satisfactory correctness level (83% performance in the case of 700 training records used in the learning phase).

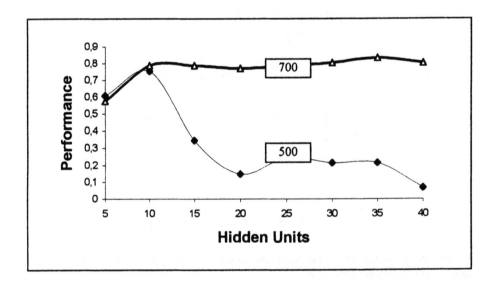

FIG. 6. The performance curves.

4. The Recovery Module

The Recovery Module uses the case retrieved from the *Library of Cases* in conjunction with a structured analysis of the hypermedia (made in an off-line phase) to help the user find the desired path, bringing him/her back if necessary. In the following sub-section we describe the structured analysis of the hypermedia, and in the sub-section 4.2 we present an example of the help given by the system.

4.1. Structure and Metrics of the Hypermedia

Here we describe the structural analysis of the hypermedia we have made, the metrics properties we have defined in order to help the user when he/she gets lost in the hyperspace. According to (Botafogo, Rivlin and Shneiderman, 1992; Charney, 1987), a possible way to help the user in a hyperspace, is to impose a structure on the hyperspace and to identify the user's location within that structure. A natural structure is a hierarchy (Akscyn, McCracken and Yoder, 1988). In order to build a hierarchical structure of the hypermedia, it is necessary first to make the choice of a node as a root and after, by a modified breadth-first search algorithm, to build the associated tree. To this end, we have enhanced the proposal of (Botafogo, Rivlin and Shneiderman, 1992; Rivlin, Botafogo and Shneiderman, 1994) as it is explained in the following.

Given the distance matrix M of the graph representing the hypermedia, a *converted distance matrix C* is defined as follows:

$$C_{ij} = M_{ij} \qquad \text{if } M_{ij} \neq \infty$$
$$C_{ij} = K \qquad \text{if } M_{ij} = \infty$$

where $K = n$ (n = number of the nodes in the graph). Then, the following parameters are defined, in the style of Rivlin, Botafogo and Shneiderman (1994):

The *converted out distance* COD_i for a node i is defined as the sum of all entries in row i in the converted distance matrix C:

$$COD_i = \sum_{j=1}^{n} C_{ij}$$

COD_i is a good indication of the topological centrality of the node i in the hypermedia.

The *converted distance* CD of the whole hypermedia is given by the sum of all entries in the converted distance matrix C:

$$CD = \sum_{i=1}^{n}\sum_{j=1}^{n} C_{ij}$$

This number gives an indication of the general connection of the graph.

The *relative out centrality* ROC_i of a node i is defined as the normalization of COD_i over the whole hypermedia:

$$ROC_i = \frac{CD}{COD_i}$$

A high ROC_i indicates a node i that can easily access other nodes (high out centrality).

The previous metrics are relative to topological properties of the graph. They can be viewed as syntactic properties, since they do not take into consideration the content of the various nodes. We have added to the previous representation another parameter, relative to the thematic relevance of each node in the hypermedia, and have found a metric for determining this relevance.

We define the thematic relevance of a node i as the *canonical multeplicity* CM_i of the node in the thematic paths, that is the number of thematic paths containing the node normalized over all the thematic paths:

$$CM_i = \frac{M_i}{CP}$$

where M_i is the multeplicity of the node i in all the thematic paths and CP is the number of thematic paths. CM_i is a good indication of the importance of the node for reaching the learning goals. We haven't normalized over the number of nodes n since we assume the thematic relevance of a node dimension-independent.

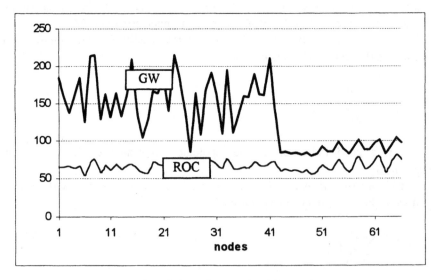

FIG. 7. Complete metric of the graph.

Now, in order to balance both syntactic and thematic relevance all over the graph, we have normalized them imposing the same average on every node:

$$\frac{\sum\limits_{i=1}^{n} ROC_i}{n} = \beta \frac{\sum\limits_{i=1}^{n} CM_i}{n} \Rightarrow \beta = \frac{\sum\limits_{i=1}^{n} ROC_i}{\sum\limits_{i=1}^{n} CM_i}$$

where the number β is a normalization weight.

The *Global weight* GW_i of node i is defined as the sum of the previously defined parameters:

$$GW_i = ROC_i + \beta * CM_i$$

GW_i is an indication of the global relevance of a node within a graph.

In Fig. 7 all the above defined metrics for the graph representing our hypermedia are presented. The calculated β value is: $\beta = 328.66$.

The system is capable to of building a hierarchical structure of the hypermedia whose root is determined according to both topological and semantic relevance of the nodes. We have given the user two possibilities for the choice of the root. The first one is to assume as a root the node with the highest GW. Once the root has been identified, a spanning tree by a modified breadth-first search is built (Botafogo, Rivlin and Shneiderman, 1992; Rivlin, Botafogo and Shneiderman, 1994). The second possibility is to assume as a root the last node of the determined thematic path visited by the user. The former gives the user a wider overview of the hyperspace according to the weights of the various nodes. The latter choice is useful if the retrieved path with the associated didactic goal satisfies the user needs.

4.2. Helping the User

In this sub-section, by means of a simplified example, we describe the kind of help the system can give the user, starting from the partial user path, the nearest thematic path (determined by the artificial neural network in the indexing phase) with the associated learning goal, and the structure of the hypermedia previously defined. The help system tries to answer to the following user's questions: "Where am I?" and "How do I get the right destination?". To answer to these questions, both the hierarchical structure and the retrieved thematic paths have been used.

Suppose that the user is navigating through the graph of Fig. 8, a very semplified subset of the hypermedia, following the goal: *The Wings of Neorealism* that, according to Brunetta, (1993), is composed of twenty-six nodes (65, 28, 47, 22, 25, 26, 48, 33,34, ...). Now suppose that he/she goes to the node 23 from the node 22 (instead of going to the node 25 as from the associated thematic path) and that he/she asks for help just in the node 23 being his/her partial path the following one: 65, 28, 47, 22,23.

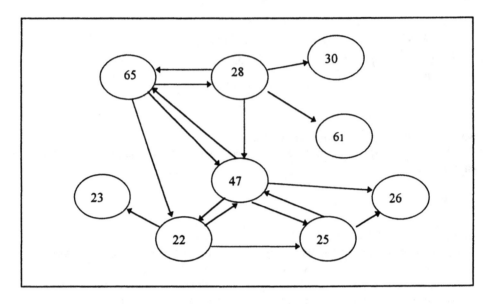

Fig. 8. The example graph.

Given this user behaviour (partial user path, time spent on each visited node and the last visited node) the system retrieves from the case library the thematic path relative to the learning goal: *The Wings of Neorealism* that closely matches the partial user path.

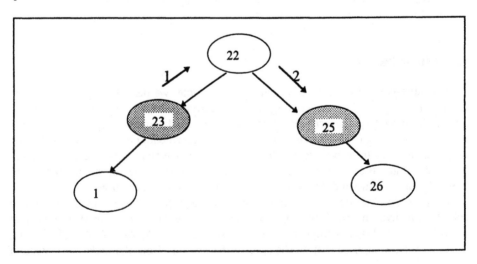

Fig. 9. Help given the user.

At this point the system builds the hierarchical tree whose root is the last node of the retrieved thematic path visited by the user (node 22). In Fig. 9 such a hierarchical tree is shown, where the last visited node in the thematic path is 22 and the user is in the node 23.

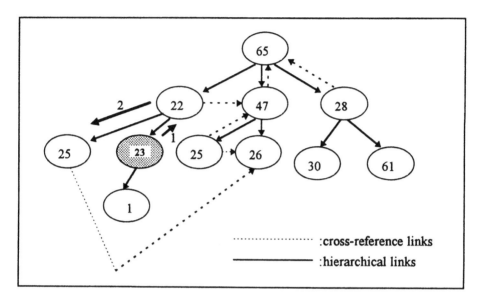

Fig. 10. The hierarchical structure relative to the graph.

Given this tree and the learning goal (associated with the retrieved thematic path) the user can be presented with the suggestions for the next steps to reach the goal: *The Wings of Neorealism*, e.g. "go back to node 22" (line 1) and "jump to node 25 as a next step" (line 2).

If the learning goal doesn't satisfy the user, the system can provide the tree relative to another learning goal (the next case in the rank ordered list of cases computed by the network) or a wider overview of the hyperspace by building a tree whose root is the node with the highest *GW*. In Fig. 10 an example for the graph G is shown, where the root is node 65.

5. Conclusions

Hypermedia systems have become increasingly popular in the last few years, as a basis for electronic encyclopedias, on-line help systems, etc. If the system does not help the user in the navigation, he/she can become easily lost in the hyperspace. In this paper we have proposed a solution for supported navigation, by using a case-based approach. Of particular interest is the solution of the indexing problem (which is critical in any Case-Based Reasoner), obtained by transforming that problem to a pattern recognition problem, and by choosing a neural network, well suited for the task of pattern recognition. One of the advantages of this choice is in that the developer can more easily acquire the knowledge from the expert of the domain. This makes this approach flexible in terms of reusability for other learning goals and for different domains. While our system is deliberately limited to 70 nodes, we feel, on the basis of the success with bigger neural networks (as reported in Hassoun, 1995), that our system can be expanded to handle all hypermedia necessities.

An extensive use of the system for the analysis of the user satisfactions is planned as future work.

References

Akscyn, R.M., McCracken, D.L. and Yoder, E.A. (1988). "KMS: A distributed hypermedia system for managing knowledge in organization". *Commun. ACM*, 31(7), pp. 820-835.

Begoray, J.A. (1990). "An Introduction to Hypermedia Issues, Systems and Application Areas". *Int. J. Human-Computer Studies*, 33, pp. 121-147.

Botafogo, R. A., Rivlin, E., and Shneiderman B. (1992). "Structural Analysis of Hypertexts: Identifying Hierarchies and Useful Metrics". *ACM Trans. Inf. Syst.* 10(2), pp. 142-180.

Brunetta, G. (1993). "Storia Del Cinema Italiano - dal Neorealismo al Miracolo Economico: 1945-1959". *Vol. III*, Editori Riuniti.

Charney, D. (1987). "Comprehending non linear text: The role of discourse cues and reading strategies". In *Proceedings of the Hypertext '87 Conference*, pp. 109-120.

Dillon, A., McKnight, C. and Richardson, J. (1990). "Navigation in Hypertext: A Critical Review of the Concept". In D. Diaper, D. Gilmore, G. Cockton and B. Shackel (Eds.) *Interact '90*, Amsterdam:North Holland.

Hammond, K., Burke, R. and Schmitt, K. (1994). "A Case-Based Approach to Knowledge Navigation". In *Papers of the AAAI Workshop on MultiMedia and Artificial Intelligence*, Seattle, WA.

Hassoun, M.H., (1995). *Fundamentals of Artificial Neural Networks*. The MIT Press.

Kolodner, J. (1993). *Case-Based Reasoning*. San Mateo, Calif., Morgan Kaufmann.

McClelland, J.L., Rumelhart, D.E. (1986). *Parallel Distributed Processing, Explorations in the Microstructure of Cognition, Vol. 1: Foundations*. MIT Press, Cambridge, MA.

Micarelli, A. and Sciarrone, F. (1996). "A Case-Based Toolbox for Guided Hypermedia Navigation". In *Proceedings of The Fifth International Conference on User Modeling UM-96*, Kailua-Kona on the Islands of Hawaii, January 2-5, pp. 129-136.

Nielsen, J. (1990a). *Hypertext and Hypermedia*. San Diego, Calif., Academic Press.

Nielsen, J. (1990b). "The Art of Navigating through Hypertext". *Communications of the ACM,* 33(3), pp. 296-310.

Rivlin, E., Botafogo, R. and Shneiderman B. (1994). "Navigating in Hyperspace: Designing a structure-based toolbox". *Commun. ACM,* 37(2), pp. 87-96.

Stanton, N.A. and Baber, C. (1992). "An Investigation of Styles and Strategies in Self Directed Learning". *Journal of Educational Multimedia and Hypermedia,* 1(2), pp. 147-167.

Trigg, R.H. (1988). "Guided Tours and Tabletops: Tools for Communicating in a Hypertext Environment". *ACM Transactions Office Information Systems,* 6(4), pp. 398-414.

Feature Weighting by Explaining Case-Based Planning Episodes

Héctor Muñoz-Avila & Jochem Hüllen

Centre for Learning Systems and Applications (LSA)
University of Kaiserslautern, Dept. of Computer Science
P.O. Box 3049, D-67653 Kaiserslautern, Germany
E-mail: {munioz|huellen}@informatik.uni-kl.de

Abstract. We present a similarity criterion based on feature weighting. Feature weights are recomputed dynamically according to the performance of cases during planning episodes. We will also present a novel algorithm to analyze and explain the performance of the retrieved cases and to determine the features whose weights need to be recomputed. Experiments show that the integration of our similarity criterion in a feature weighting model and our analysis algorithm improves the adaptability of the retrieved cases over a period of multiple problem solving episodes.

1 Introduction

An essential factor influencing the effectiveness of case-based problem solving is the retrieval phase (Aamodt & Plaza, 1994). In the context of planning and design, retrieval means searching for adaptable cases (Smyth & Keane, 1994; Muñoz-Avila, Paulokat, & Wess, 1995; Smyth & Keane, 1995). Thus, any similarity criterion should measure the adaptation effort of the cases with respect to a new problem. Because the adaptation effort is difficult to determine *a priori*, learning from previous retrieval episodes has been proposed (Veloso, 1992; Fox & Leake, 1995; Ihrig & Kambhampati, 1995).

In *Robbie* (Fox & Leake, 1995), introspective reasoning (Leake, Kinley, & Wilson, 1995) is used to determine the features that should be considered during retrieval. The validity of pre-defined assertions related to indexing criteria is tested after each retrieval episode. If a failure occurs, the criteria is restated resulting in a refinement of the index.

In the context of domain independent planning, EBL (Minton, 1988) has been used in a system called *derSNLP+EBL* (Ihrig & Kambhampati, 1995) to *explain* retrieval failures. An EBL-rule that indicates combinations of features causing a failure is constructed. The rule is used as a filter to avoid selecting the case when a given problem matches the indicated combination of features.

Another approach toward learning from retrieval failures in the context of domain independent planning was proposed in PRODIGY/ANALOGY (Veloso, 1992, 1994a): each feature is assigned a so-called relevance-bias, which is a number indicating the preference of the feature. The relevance-bias of a feature in the case is incremented dynamically when a failure occurs and the feature was not matched in the new problem. PRODIGY/ANALOGY divides features into relevant and non relevant. The *foot-printed similarity metric* counts features of the problem matched by relevant features in the cases. The relevant features are indexed so that features with higher relevance-bias are matched first.

In this paper we will extend PRODIGY/ANALOGY's similarity metric by explicitly incorporating feature weights in a new similarity metric, *the weighted foot-printed similarity metric*. The weighted foot-printed similarity metric counts the weights of relevant features matching features in the new problem and can be integrated with a feature weighting model. We will also present a novel algorithm to analyze and explain the performance of the retrieved cases. This algorithm serves as a bridge between the similarity metric and the weighting model. We will evaluate our approach with experiments and will conclude that the integration in the feature weighting model of the weighted foot-printed similarity metric with the algorithm improves the adaptability of the retrieved cases over a period of multiple problem solving episodes. We will also discuss the convergence to best weights for the relevant features.

This paper is organized as follows: the next section presents the weighted foot-printed similarity metric and a model for feature weighting. Section 3 presents the algorithm for analyzing and explaining the performance of the cases retrieved. Then, the results of the experiments performed are shown. A discussion of our approachis given in section 5. Finally, we make concluding remarks of our work in the last section.

2 Weighting Relevant Features

The foot-printed similarity metric compares relevant features of a case with features of a new problem. Informally, a feature is considered relevant to a goal with respect to a solution, if the feature contributes to achieve the goal in the solution (Veloso, 1994b). This notion can be illustrated with an example in the logistics transportation domain (Veloso, 1994a). A typical problem in this domain is, starting from a certain configuration of objects, locations, and transportation means, to place the objects at different locations. There are different sorts of locations and means of transportation. In addition, the means of transportation have certain operational restrictions. For example, a truck can only be moved between places located within the same city.

Figure 1 (a) shows an example of a possible configuration in this domain describing an initial state. The final state, shown in figure 1 (b), consists of one goal: the object *obj1* must be placed at the post office *post2*. Figure 2 shows a possible solution (i.e., a plan). Continuous boxes represent plan steps and continuous lines represent the order of execution among the plan steps. Dashed boxes represent preconditions of plan steps (in figure 2, only one - *sameCity(post1, post2)*- is shown, which corresponds to a precondition of the plan step *move(truck1, post1, post2)*.). Notice that *truck2* was not used for

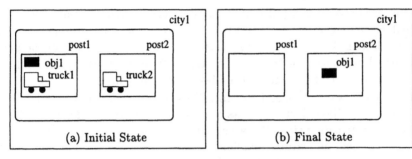

Fig. 1. A problem in the logistics transportation domain

achieving the goal. Thus, *truck2* is not relevant to the goal with respect to this solution.

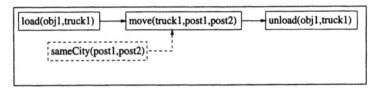

Fig. 2. A plan that, starting with *obj1* and *truck1* in *post1*, places *obj1* in *post2*. This plan supposes that *post1* and *post2* are in the same city

2.1 The Foot-printed Similarity Metric

As defined, the foot-printed similarity metric between a case and a new problem, denoted by $sim_{fp}(case, problem)$, counts the number of relevant features in the case that match features in the new problem. If the percentage of relevant features that are included in the new problem is greater than a certain threshold, the case is retrieved independently of *which features were matched*. However, not all features have the same importance for the solution. To illustrate this affirmation consider the initial state shown in figure 3. Suppose that the final state is to place *obj3* in *post4* and that the problem shown in figure 1 and the solution shown in figure 2 conform a case. The case partially matches the new problem with the substitution: $\{post1 \rightarrow post3, post2 \rightarrow post4, obj1 \rightarrow obj3, truck1 \rightarrow truck3\}$. However, the solution of the case can not be reused in the new problem because *post3* and *post4* are in different cities, so *truck3* can not be moved from *post3* to *post4*. Thus, the retrieval of the case is considered to have failed in this situation.

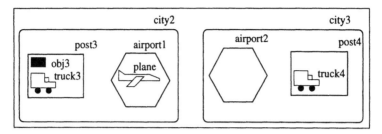

Fig. 3. Initial state of a new problem

2.2 The Weighted Foot-printed Similarity Metric

Incrementing the value of the threshold fixing the percentage of relevant features that must be matched may reduce the number of retrieval failures in a significant way. However, a high value of the threshold over restricts the situations for which the cases can be retrieved, that is, there are situations in which the case is not retrieved although the retrieval would have been adequate.

Ranking the relevant features to establish an order of evaluation improves the adaptability of the cases retrieved (Veloso, 1994a). However, certain features should not only be matched first, but they should be given *more relevance* when deciding if the case is to be retrieved. To illustrate this affirmation, consider the same case as before and a new problem with a similar initial state to the one shown in figure 1. The only difference is that *truck1* is in a third post office, *post3*, placed in the same city as the other two. In this situation 50% of the relevant features in the case match features in the new problem. Thus, unless the threshold has a low value, the case is not retrieved. However, setting the threshold in a lower value increases the number of failed retrievals. Interestingly, retrieving the case may be adequate depending on the adaptation strategy. For example, the new problem can be solved by taking the solution shown in figure 2 and adding *move(truck1, post3, post1)* as first step (i.e., moving *truck1* to *post1* and performing the plan that, starting with *obj1* and *truck1* in *post1*, places *obj1* in *post2*.).

The weighted foot-printed similarity metric overcomes these limitations by counting feature weights. Before continuing, some notation must be introduced: a problem P consists of a pair (I^P, G^P), where I^P is the set of features conforming the initial state and G^P is the set of goals conforming the final state of the problem. Cases consist of pairs $((I^C, G^C), Sol)$, where (I^C, G^C) is a problem and Sol a solution (i.e., a plan). We will suppose for the sake of simplicity that I^C only contains relevant features and that all the goals in G^C interact[1]. We

---

[1] When viewing a partially ordered plan as a graph, the goals achieved in the same connected component of the plan are said to interact (Veloso, 1994a). Each connected component of a plan is considered as a different case that solves the problem consisting of the goals achieved in the connected component and the subset of features

define $sim_{wfp}(C,P)$, the *weighted foot-printed similarity metric* between C and P, as follows

$$sim_{wfp}(C,P) = \begin{cases} |G^C| + \sum_{i \in I^C \bigcap_\theta I^P} \omega_i^C & : \quad G^C\theta \subset G^P \\ 0 & : \quad otherwise \end{cases} \quad (Eq.1),$$

where $G^C\theta \subset G^P$ denotes that G^C matches a subset of G^P with a substitution θ. The factor ω_i^C denotes the weight of the relevant feature i in C, and, $|G^C|$ denotes the number of goals in G^C. Finally, $I^C \bigcap_\theta I^P$ denotes the set of all features in I^C matching a feature in I^P with the substitution θ.

Let P be a new problem, a case, C, is retrieved if: (1) G^C matches a subset of G^P with a substitution θ, and (2) if the weighted proportion of relevant features in I^C matching a feature in I^P is greater than a certain threshold, thr. Condition (2) may be written as follows:

$$(\sum_{i \in I^C \bigcap_\theta I^P} \omega_i^C)/(\sum_{i \in I^C} \omega_i^C) \geq thr \quad (Eq.2)$$

2.3 Weighting Model

For weighting features, a feedback model based on incremental optimizers is used (Salzberg, 1991; Wettschereck & Aha, 1995). Each case, C, contains two counters: k^C and f^C. The first one indicates the number of times a case was adequately retrieved, and the second one the number of times in which not. The weight, ω_i^C, of each relevant feature i is updated according to the following equations, (Eq. 3 and 4 respectively),

$$\omega_i^C = \begin{cases} \omega_i^C + \Delta_{k^C,f^C} & : \quad failed\ retrieval\ and\ i\ was\ not\ matched \\ \omega_i^C - \Delta_{k^C,f^C} & : \quad adequate\ retrieval\ and\ i\ was\ matched \end{cases}$$

where $0 \leq \Delta_{k^C,f^C} \leq \beta \times n^C$. The number of features in the initial state of C is denoted by n^C. Thus, the change in the weight of the features is bound by a factor, $\beta \times n^C$, directly proportional to the number of features in the case.

If the value of ω_i^C is smaller than 1 then ω_i^C is assigned the value 1 and the weights of the other features in the case are incremented proportionally. The incremental factor Δ_{k^C,f^C} depends on the values of k^C and f^C in the following way: the larger the ratio of k^C to f^C, the smaller is the value of Δ_{k^C,f^C}. Thus, as the number of adequate retrieval episodes increases, the effect of a retrieval episode on the feature weights decreases. In contrast, the smaller the ratio of k^C to f^C, the closer is Δ_{k^C,f^C} to $\beta \times n^C$. If the weights of the relevant features were normalized so that $\omega_1^C + \omega_2^C + ... + \omega_{n^C}^C = 1$, then the factor $\sum_{j \neq k} \omega_j^C / \sum_i \omega_i^C$ expresses the *reliability* of making an adequate retrieval, when the feature i_k is the only one not to be matched in the new problem. Thus, the feature weights measure the relative relevance of the features in the case.

---

in the initial state that are relevant to these goals.

3 Analysis of Case-Based Planning Episodes in CAPLAN/CBC

The problem solving cycle in our case-based planner, CAPLAN/CBC (Muñoz-Avila et al., 1995; Muñoz-Avila & Hüllen, 1995), consists of four steps: first, cases meeting the retrieval condition stated in the last section are retrieved. Then, the cases are adapted to the new problem. At the third step, an analysis of the adaptation effort is performed and certain features are identified. Finally, the weights of those features are updated.

3.1 Adaptation Strategy in CAPLAN/CBC

CAPLAN/CBC is built on a first-principles planner called CAPLAN (Weber-skirch, 1995; Paulokat & Wess, 1994) that performs plan-space planning, that is, planning occurs by transforming plans into plans as opposed to state-space planning that transform states into states (McAllester & Rosenblitt, 1991). First-principles planning proceeds in CAPLAN by achieving preconditions of plan steps and solving conflicts. A precondition can be achieved in two ways

1. by *establishing* it with the initial state of the problem, that is, by matching the precondition with a feature in the initial state. For example, in figure 2, the precondition *sameCity(post1, post2)* has been established with the initial state shown in figure 1 (a), or,
2. by *establishing* it with a plan step, that is, by matching the precondition with the effects of the plan step. For example, in figure 2, the plan step *unload(obj1, truck1)* is used to achieve the goal: "the object *obj1* must be placed at the post office *post2*" (The goals of the problem are considered as preconditions of a dummy step called FINISH (Barrett & Weld, 1994).).

The adaptation strategy followed in CAPLAN/CBC is known as eager replay (Ihrig & Kambhampati, 1994). Eager replay is done in two phases: in the first phase, each plan step contained in the retrieved cases is replayed in the new situation if replaying the step does not introduce any inconsistency in the new solution. Once this phase is finished, a partial solution, also known as the "skeletal plan" (Ihrig & Kambhampati, 1994), is obtained. Skeletal plans may contain unsolved preconditions. A precondition remains unsolved because either a corresponding precondition does not exist in the cases or a corresponding precondition exists, but the way it is achieved in the case can not be replayed in the new problem. At the second phase, the skeletal plan is completed by first-principles planning.[2]

---

[2] CAPLAN/CBC implements an extension of eager replay known as complete eager replay in which justifications of failed attempts to obtain the solution are also replayed in the first phase (Muñoz-Avila & Weberskirch, 1996). As a result, in the second phase, the completion effort is reduced. We omit giving further details as this extension goes beyond the purposes of this paper.

3.2 Evaluating the Adaptation Effort

To evaluate the adaptation effort, three numbers are calculated: n_{case}, the number of plan steps in the case, n_{Sk}, the number of plan steps in the skeletal plan, and, n_{SkFin}, the number of plan steps in the skeletal plan that remain after the completion process is finished. The algorithm evaluating the adaptation effort is shown in figure 4. Its input consists of the three numbers, n_{case}, n_{Sk}, and n_{SkFin}, the case, C, and the skeletal plan, Sk. The outcome of this algorithm is the recomputation of the weights of certain relevant features in the case C.

---

evaluateAdaptation$(C, Sk, n_{case}, n_{Sk}, n_{SkFin})$
1. Expl ← FilterFeatures(C,Sk)
2. **If** $(n_{Sk}/n_{case} \leq thr1)$ **or** $(n_{SkFin}/n_{Sk} \leq thr2)$
   For-each $i \in Expl$
     $\omega_i^C = \omega_i^C + \Delta_{kC, fC}$
3. **Else**
   For-each $i \in Expl$
     $\omega_i^C = \omega_i^C - \Delta_{kC, fC}$

Fig. 4. Algorithm evaluating the adaptation effort

If the percentage of plan steps replayed is smaller than a certain threshold, $thr1$, or the percentage of plan steps in the skeletal plan remaining after completion is smaller than another threshold, $thr2$, the retrieval is said to have failed. Otherwise, the retrieval is said to be adequate. In both situations, the weights of the set of features, $Expl$, returned by the function $FilterFeatures(C, Sk)$ are recomputed (this function will be present later).

If the retrieval of the case failed, the weights of features in $Feat$ are increased according to equation 3 (step 2). The argumentation for increasing the weights of those features is that their absence was important in this situation because either only few plan steps were replayed or too many plan steps in the skeletal plan were rejected during the completion process.

If the retrieval of a case is adequate, the weights of the features in $Expl$ are decreased according to equation 4 (step 3). The reason for decreasing the weights of those features is that their absence was not important in the retrieval episode because enough plan steps were replayed and the first-principles planner was able to complete the solution without rejecting too many plan steps of the skeletal plan.

Consider the case formed by the problem and solution shown in figures 1 and 2 respectively and the new problem shown in figure 3. Each of the three plan steps can be replayed in the new situation (i.e., $n_{case} = n_{Sk} = 3$). As a result, the skeletal plan shown in figure 5 is obtained. In this plan, the precondition $sameCity(post3, post4)$ remains unsolved (represented with a question mark, ?).

Because *sameCity*(*post3*, *post4*) cannot be achieved, the first-principles planner rejects the solution step *move*(*truck3*, *post3*, *post4*), and pursues other alternatives (i.e., $n_{SkFin} \leq 2$). Thus, a retrieval failure takes place, if, for example, *thr2* is equal to 2/3.

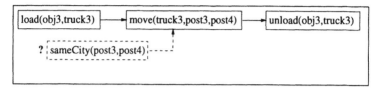

Fig. 5. An skeletal plan

3.3 Filtering Non Matched, Relevant Features

To identify the relevant features whose weights must be recomputed, CA-PLAN/CBC examines the contribution of the feature to the solution of the case by taking as basis the skeletal plan. For example, the precondition *sameCity*(*post3*, *post4*) of the skeletal plan shown in figure 5 was not achieved during replay because it cannot be established with the initial state. Thus, if the retrieval failed, the weight of the corresponding feature in the case, *sameCity*(*post1*, *post2*), must be increased.

In more complex situations non matched, relevant features may not be included in the skeletal plan. Consider, for example, the feature g_3 in the abstract situation described in figure 6.[3] A question arises, namely, whether the weight of g_3 must be recomputed or not. To answer this question, we developed the filtering function, *FilterFeatures*(*C*, *Sk*), that returns a set, *Expl*, of non matched, relevant features whose weight must be recomputed. The set *Expl* meets the following condition:

Expl explains the unsolved preconditions in the skeletal plan.

In the context of this work, explaining an unsolved precondition, *p*, means finding the features in the case such that if they would have been also present in the new problem, the precondition *p* would have been achieved in the skeletal plan. The explanation for an unsolved precondition that is established with the initial state in the case is the feature used to achieve the precondition. Examples

---

[3] As in figure 5, continuous boxes represent plan steps and continuous lines represent the order of execution among the plan steps. Dashed boxes represent preconditions of plan steps. Preconditions remaining unsolved after replay are labelled with a question mark, *?*.

of such preconditions are $sameCity(post3, post4)$ that occurs in the skeletal plan shown in figure 5, and g_1 that occurs in the skeletal plan shown in figure 6. If p is established with a plan step in the case, a careful analysis must be done to explain it. For example, in figure 6, it is assumed that g_2 remains unsolved because a failed establishment with the plan step s_2 occurs.

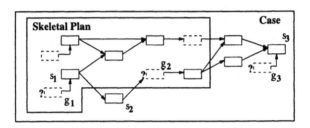

Fig. 6. Abstract configurations of an skeletal plan and a case

The function $FilterFeatures(C, Sk)$ is shown in figure 7. It receives the retrieved case, C, and the skeletal plan, Sk, and returns an explanation, $Expl$. This function uses two global variables: Arg and P. Arg contains all arguments of features in $Expl$ and is computed dynamically. Initially, Arg and $Expl$ are empty (steps 1 and 2). The idea of the function $FilterFeatures(C, Sk)$ is to examine each unsolved precondition in the skeletal plan to obtain an explanation. To accomplish this, P contains the unsolved preconditions in Sk that have not been examined. Initially, P is assigned all unsolved preconditions in Sk.

Recall that a precondition can be achieved by establishing it either with the initial state or with a plan step. Thus, there are only two possible reasons why a precondition, p, was achieved in the case and not in the skeletal plan:

1. The establishment with the initial state can not be performed because there is no feature in the initial state of the new problem that matches the precondition. Examples of failed establishment with the initial state are $sameCity(post3, post4)$ in figure 5 and g_1 in figure 6. This failure is considered in the first control block of the algorithm (step 4): each precondition, p, whose plan step in C is established with the initial state (i.e., $isEstI(p, C)$ is true), is stored in $Expl$ (step e.1) and its arguments are collected in Arg (step e.2). The idea is that if the feature would have been present in the initial state, the precondition p would have been achieved by establishing it with the initial state.

2. The establishment with a plan step can not be performed because an inconsistency in the variable bindings will be introduced. An inconsistency can be expressed as follows (Kambhampati, Katukam, & Qu, 1995): there are two variables x_1 and x_2 bound with the constants a and b respectively, and the constraint $x_1 = x_2$ is stated in the plan step. For example, in figure 6, it is

assumed that s_2 can not be replayed because a failed establishment with a plan step occured. Thus, the precondition g_2 remains unsolved in the skeletal plan. This failure is considered in the second control block of the algorithm (step 5). If the inconsistent arguments of the plan step are included already in Arg, nothing is done (step p2). Otherwise, two steps are performed: first, each argument, c_i, that was not included in Arg already is added to Arg (steps p3.1, e2). Second, for each argument c_i, the feature found by calling the function $searchFeat(p, c_i, C)$ is add to $Expl$ (steps p3.2, e1). This function returns a feature achieving a precondition, p', in the case that has c_i as argument and such that the distance[4] between p' and p is minimal. The point here is that if the feature binding the inconsistent variables would have been present in the initial state, the inconsistency would not have occur and the plan step would have been applicable. Thus, the precondition p would have been established with the plan step.

In resume, one or more features occuring in the case but not in the new problem are identified as the *explanation* for not solving the precondition p in the skeletal plan. In the case C, p is established either with the initial state or with a plan step. In the first situation, the explanation is constitute by the feature in C matching p. In the second situation, the explanation is constitute by the features binding the variables, which caused the inconsistency that made the plan step inapplicable in the new problem.

FilterFeatures(C, Sk)	processEst(p)
1. $Expl \leftarrow \{\}$	e1. Expl $\leftarrow$ Expl $\bigcup \{p\}$
2. $Arg \leftarrow \{\}$	e2. $Arg \leftarrow Arg \bigcup argIn(p)$
3. $P \leftarrow unsolvedPrecond(Sk, C)$.	

FilterFeatures (cont.)	processInconsistency(p,C,Sk)
4. while (exists $p \in P$ with $isEstI(p, C)$)	p1. $I \leftarrow argsInconsistStep(p, C)$
4.1 $processEst(p)$	p2. If $I \subset Arg$ then **skip**
4.2 $P \leftarrow P - \{p\}$	p3. while $(I - Arg)$ isNotEmpty
5. while $(P \neq \{\})$	p3.1 Let $c_i \in I - Arg$
5.1 $processInconsistency(P,C,Sk)$	p3.2 p' $\leftarrow searchFeat(p, c_i, C)$
5.2 $P \leftarrow P - \{p\}$	p3.3 $processEst(p')$
6. **return Expl**	

Fig. 7. Algorithm for filtering features

4 Empirical Results

The experiments were made in two different domains: the logistics transportation domain and the domain of process planning (Muñoz-Avila & Weberskirch,

---

[4] The number of arcs of the shortest path connecting two preconditions in the plan.

1996). During problem solving, the former is characterized by the high number of occurrences of goal blocks caused by goal loops[5] whereas the latter by the high number of interactions between goals. Thus, both domains provide a wide spectrum of problems for our experiments in which we validate the following hypothesis:

Over a period of multiple problem solving episodes, weighting relevant features in a case increases the reliability that the retrieval of the cases is adequate.

4.1 The experiments

This hypothesis was validated with an experiment performed with two collections of problems (one for each domain). The collections were formed in the following way: a problem, that we called the pivot problem, was manually stated. Then, some features in the initial state were randomly fixed. A new goal and new features that do not occur in the pivot problem were also given. Taking as basis the pivot problem, new problems were formed by varying the fixed features, or/and by adding the new goal and the new features. The problem collection met also the following conditions: (1) every problem in the collection can be solved within 300 seconds in the logistics transportation domain and 350 seconds in the domain of process planning. (2) The pivot case meets the foot-printed retrieval condition for every problem with $thr = 75\%$ for the transportation domain and $thr = 80\%$ for the domain of process planning (thr as in equation 2.). The reason for the parameter thr to be higher the domain of process planning is the high level of interactions taking place in this domain, which obligates a more accurate retrieval. (3) The number of times that fixed features where changed in the collection is the same. For example, in the transportation domain, if a truck and a post-office are fixed, then, in the initial state, the number of problems in which the truck is changed of location is the same as the number of times the post office is changed of city. (4) If n denotes the number of fixed features, then problems were ordered in sequences of n problems such that within every sequence, $Problem_{mn+1}, ..., Problem_{mn+n}$, each fixed feature is changed only one time. For this reason, the number of problems in the collection is a multiple of the number of selected features.

The ideal experiment to validate our hypothesis is to form all possible combinations of every collection of problems and show that, in average, our hypothesis holds. Because this implies a combinatorial explosion, we stated conditions (3) and (4), in pursue of equally distributing the effect of every change in the fixed features and of capturing the average situation. Condition (3) ensures that no feature takes advantage of the others by changing them the same number of times. As explained before, the ratio of k_C to f_C determines the incremental rate of the weigths. Thus, if not matching a fixed feature causes an inadequate retrieval, then the change of weights will be greater when problems changing that feature are allocated at the beginning of the collection. In contrast, if those

---

[5] Informally, a goal loop occurs when to achieve a goal, the planner pursues to achieve another goal that unifies the first one.

problems are allocated at the end of the collection, the changes in weights are reduced. For this reason, condition (4) ensures that the final weight of each fixed feature is closer to the average by distributing the problems changing the feature equally throughout the collection.

In each domain a collection of problems was formed. In the transportation domain 6 features were fixed in the collection, and 8 in the domain of process planning. The size of each collection was 5 times the number of fixed features. Before each run, a solution to the pivot problem was found. The pivot problem and its found solution are taken as a pivot case. At each run, each problem in the collection was given and a complete problem-solving episode was performed (see section 3).

4.2 The results

Tables 1 and 2 summarize the results of this experiment for the domain of process planning and for the logistics transportation domain respectively. The first row of these tables present the percentage of times the pivot case was retrieved. The second row of the same tables present the percentage of times that retrieving the pivot case result in a retrieval failure. The first five columns presents the results for each of the 5 sequence of problems $Problem_{mn+1}, ..., Problem_{mn+n}$ ($m = 1, ..., 5$). The last column summarize the results when all the problems in the collections were given without considering the feature weights, that is, by using the foot-printed similarity metric.

Items	1	2	3	4	5	No Weight.
% Cases Retr.	80	70	60	50	50	100
% Retr. Failures	37	29	17	0	0	50

Table 1. Measures of effectiveness of retrieval in the domain of process planning by weighting features and without weighting features.

These experiments show that feature weighting increases the reliability that the retrieval is adequate as the number of problem solving episodes increases. This can be seen by comparing the fifth column with the last column of table 1 (resp. 2). That is, comparing the effectiveness of retrieval by recomputing weights as several problem solving episodes took place and the effectiveness of retrieval without recomputing weights respectively. In the domain of process planning, for example, the pivot case is always retrieved correctly after several problem solving episodes has taken place (see column 5 of table 1). In the logistics transportation domain, the reliability that the retrieval of the pivot case is adequate is increased in a significant way (see column 5 of table 2).

Another interesting result is the convergence to best weights for the features of the pivot cases. In the domain of process planning, the feature weights of

Items	1	2	3	4	5	No Weight.
% Cases Retr.	100	86	71	71	71	100
% Retr. Failures	43	33	17	17	17	43

Table 2. Measures of effectiveness of retrieval in the logistics transportation domain by weighting features and without weighting features.

the pivot case converge after the fourth sequence of problems is given (compare columns 4 and 5 of table 1), and, in the logistics transportation domain, the convergence occur after the third sequence of problems is given (compare columns 3, 4 and 5 of table 2).

5 Discussion

The feature weights may be interpreted as a hypothesis about the relative importance of the features in a case. This hypothesis is validated or rejected in problem solving episodes where one or more relevant features are absent. The effect on the adaptation effort caused by the absence of a relevant feature in a new problem depends on (1) the contribution of the feature to the solution of the case, (2) the characteristics of the domain, (3) the adaptation strategy, and (4) the features that are present in the new problem but not in the case. The first three factors are considered implicitly by the algorithm *evaluateAdaptation*. The last factor could be important in situations in which the retrieval fails, or the retrieval is adequate *exclusively* because of the additional features in the new problem. Thus, in these situations, the feature weights should not be recomputed. Goal regression (Kambhampati et al., 1995) may be used to detect those situations and may speed-up the convergence of the feature weights. However, in the experiments discussed before, goal regression was not necessary because of the uniform distribution of the problems, the domain characteristics, and the adaptation strategy being used.

Another issue to be discussed is the advantage of using the weighted footprinted similarity metric and, particularly, the convergence to best weigths of the relevant features in the case. The experiments show, in average, the advantage of considering feature weights for real-world problems. However, depending on the particular collection of problems given, considering feature weights may be a disadvantage. For example, consider an artificial domain and a case in this domain solving the problem $(\{g_1, g_2, g_4\}, goal)$. Suppose that, when given the problem $(\{g_1, g_4\}, goal)$ or the problem $(\{g_2, g_4\}, goal)$, the retrieval of the case is adequate, and, that the retrieval threshold is set to 60%. Thus, for example, the weight of g_2 in the case is reduced every time the problem $(\{g_1, g_4\}, goal)$ is given. If this problem is given several times, eventually, the weight of g_2 in the case will be so small that, when the problem $(\{g_2, g_4\}, goal)$ is given, the case will not be retrieved. In contrast, the case is always retrieved when using the foot-printed similarity metric (i.e., without considering feature weights). Thus, in this situation, it seems adequate not to consider feature weights. Notice, that the particular sequence of problems given was biased towards a particular subset of features. Equally distributed sequences of problems, however, represent a wider range of sequences for which we have shown a better performance when feature weights are considered.

6 Conclusion

In this paper, we presented the weighting foot-printed similarity metric and an algorithm to analyze and explain the performance of the cases during case-based problem solving episodes. We integrated them in the feature weighting model and performed experiments in two representative domains. Based on these experiments, we conclude that this integration improves the adaptability of the retrieved cases over a period of multiple problem solving episodes.

References

Aamodt, A., & Plaza, E. (1994). Case-based reasoning: Foundation issues, methodological variations and system approaches. *AI-Communications*, 7(1), pp 39–59.

Barrett, A., & Weld, D. (1994). Partial-order planning: Evaluating possible efficiency gains. *Artificial Intelligence*, 67(1), 71–112.

Fox, S., & Leake, D. (1995). Using introspective reasoning to refine indexing. In *(Veloso & Aamodt, 1995)*.

Ihrig, L., & Kambhampati, S. (1994). Derivational replay for partial-order planning. In *Proceedings of AAAI-94*, pp. 116–125.

Ihrig, L., & Kambhampati, S. (1995). Automatic storage and indexing of plan derivations based on replay failures. In *Proceedings of IJCAI-95*.

Kambhampati, S., Katukam, S., & Qu, Y. (1995). Failure driven dynamic search control for partial order planners: An explanation-based approach. *Artificial Intelligence*. (submitted, ASU-CSE-TR-95-010).

Leake, D. B., Kinley, A., & Wilson, D. (1995). Learning to improve case adaptation by introspective reasoning and cbr. In *(Veloso & Aamodt, 1995)*.

McAllester, D., & Rosenblitt, D. (1991). Systematic nonlinear planning. In *Proceedings of AAAI-91*, pp. 634–639.

Minton, S. (1988). *Learning Search Control Knowledge: An Explanation-Based Approach*. Kluwer Academic Publishers, Boston.

Muñoz-Avila, H., & Hüllen, J. (1995). Retrieving relevant cases by using goal dependencies. In *(Veloso & Aamodt, 1995)*.

Muñoz-Avila, H., Paulokat, J., & Wess, S. (1995). Controlling non-linear hierarchical planning by case replay. In Keane, M., Halton, J., & Manago, M. (Eds.), *Advances in Case-Based Reasoning. Selected Papers of the 2nd European Workshop (EWCBR-94)*, No. 984 in Lecture Notes in Artificial Intelligence. Springer.

Muñoz-Avila, H., & Weberskirch, F. (1996). Planning for manufacturing workpieces by storing, indexing and replaying planning decisions. In *Third International Conference on AI Planning Systems (AIPS-96)*. AAAI-Press.

Paulokat, J., & Wess, S. (1994). Planning for machining workpieces with a partial-order nonlinear planner. In Gil, Y., & Veloso, M. (Eds.), *AAAI-Working Notes 'Planning and Learning: On To Real Applications'* New Orleans.

Richter, M., Wess, S., Althoff, K., & Maurer, F. (Eds.). (1994). *First European Workshop on Case-base Reasoning (EWCBR-93)*. No. 837 in Lecture Notes in Artificial Intelligence. Springer Verlag.

Salzberg, S. L. (1991). A nearest hyperrectangle learning method. *Machine Learning, 1*.

Smyth, B., & Keane, M. (1994). Retrieving adaptable cases. In Richter, M., Wess, S., Althoff, K.-D., & Maurer, F. (Eds.), *Proceedings of the 1st European Workshop on Case-Based Reasoning (EWCBR-93)*, No. 837 in LNAI. Springer.

Smyth, B., & Keane, M. (1995). Experiments on adaptation-guided retrieval in case-based design. In *(Veloso & Aamodt, 1995)*.

Veloso, M. (1992). *Learning by Analogical Reasoning in General Problem Solving*. Ph.D. thesis, Carnegie Mellon University.

Veloso, M. (1994a). *Planning and learning by analogical reasoning*. No. 886 in Lecture Notes in Artificial Intelligence. Springer Verlag.

Veloso, M. (1994b). Prodigy/analogy: Analogical reasoning in general problem solving. In *(Richter, Wess, Althoff, & Maurer, 1994)*.

Veloso, M., & Aamodt, A. (Eds.). (1995). *Case-Based Reasoning Research and Development, Proceedings of the 1st International Conference (ICCBR-95)*. No. 1010 in Lecture Notes in Artificial Intelligence. Springer Verlag.

Weberskirch, F. (1995). Combining SNLP-like planning and dependency-maintenance. Tech. rep. LSA-95-10E, Centre for Learning Systems and Applications, University of Kaiserslautern, Germany.

Wettschereck, D., & Aha, D. W. (1995). Weighting features. In *(Veloso & Aamodt, 1995)*.

Classification-Based Problem-Solving in Case-Based Reasoning

Amedeo Napoli, Jean Lieber and Régis Curien

CRIN CNRS – INRIA Lorraine,
BP 239 – 54506 Vandœuvre-lès-Nancy Cedex
Email: {napoli,lieber,curien}@loria.fr

Abstract. In this paper, we present a study on the retrieval and adaptation operations for case-based reasoning, in the context of object-based representations. First, the paper describes the case-based reasoning cycle and the associated problem-solving process. Details are given on problem formalization, the organization and representation of cases and case indexes. Indexes are represented as frames lying in a subsumption hierarchy. Therefore, the links between retrieval, adaptation, and classification, are very close. Retrieval and adaptation are analyzed through three main operations, namely complete, incomplete and approximate classification, corresponding to three different ways for handling indexes and cases in object-based representations. The paper ends with a discussion on the topics presented here, and points out future works completing and extending this study.

1 Introduction

In this paper, we present a study on retrieval and adaptation in an object-based representation environment, relying on a hierarchical representation of knowledge, e.g. object-oriented systems, frame-based systems and description logics. One of the main motivations underlying this study is to investigate the relations between retrieval, adaptation and classification in an object-based representation environment is also called an object-based CBR system.

A CBR system can be considered as a knowledge-based system whose inference procedure relies on retrieval and adaptation (the memorization or learning operation is not directly involved in the inference procedure). The formalism chosen for the representation of cases and case indexes has a direct influence on the characteristics of the inference procedure. In this paper, cases and case indexes are represented as frames lying in a subsumption hierarchy. Therefore, the classification process, that is currently used to manage the hierarchy and more precisely to control the insertion of new frames, is naturally related to the retrieval and adaptation operations.

The paper tries to enlighten the characteristics of retrieval and adaptation in terms of classification and subsumption. It tries also to provide a rigorous description of the behavior of object-based CBR systems. Such a behavior description can be used to evaluate and compare CBR systems, and it can give, as well, guidelines for designing object-based CBR systems.

Some works concerned with a formal study of CBR systems and the relations with classification have already been done. A formalization based on the knowledge acquisition method *Components of expertise* [20] is proposed in terms of strategies, tasks, and procedures, in [1]. In [16], this formalization is extended and considered in terms of concepts and features: cases are represented as structured concepts composed of features lying in a subsumption hierarchy. Then, this study focuses on similarity and case retrieval.

A research on description logics, classification, and case-based planning, is presented in [8] and [9]. In this work, case-based planning is analyzed from two points of view: on the one hand, cases are represented as terms in a temporal logic, on the other hand, indexes associated with cases are represented as concepts in a description logic. Then, the two papers show how these two levels are related and enlighten formal and logical properties of CBR systems.

The study presented in this paper is mainly influenced by [8] and [9]. The retrieval and adaptation operations rely on three distinct classification processes (two classification processes are taken into account in [8] and [9]), depending on the matching between a new problem –the target– and a memorized case –the source– that is reused to solve the target problem. In particular, *approximate* classification –the target problem and the source case have to be transformed to be in correspondence– is introduced and made precise.

The paper is organized as follows. The section 2 introduces the CBR inference procedure, the associated problem-solving process, and details the global characteristics and components of a CBR system, such as the case base, the organization and the indexing of cases. Moreover, relations between problems, the problem solving process and functional types are pointed out. The section 3 makes precise and discusses the three different case retrieval and adaptation operations. Finally, a global discussion, including a note on the learning process, ends the paper.

2   Case-Based Reasoning and Problem-Solving

2.1   The Case-Based Reasoning Cycle

The goal of case-based reasoning is to associate a solution Sol(P) with a given problem P, by reusing the solution Sol(P') of a known problem P'. Case-based reasoning relies on a three-step cycle:

(i) Retrieval: a *source* problem P' *similar* to the *target* problem P is searched in a *case base* containing memorized problems considered as reference cases to solve new problems.

(ii) Adaptation: the solution Sol(P') is transformed –adapted– in order to be reused for solving P.

(iii) Memorization (or learning): the problem P and the building characteristics of the solution Sol(P) can be memorized to be reused in the future.

One can note that these three steps, presented separately here, can be nested. For example, retrieval and adaptation are nested in the case-based systems described in [11], [19] and [18]. Moreover, the learning step can take place within the retrieval and the adaptation steps as well, in order to learn retrieval and adaptation knowledge [10].

The implementation of knowledge-based systems relying on case-based reasoning gives rise to *case-based reasoners* or *case-based reasoning systems*. Given a target problem P, a CBR system takes advantage of a case base and follows the preceding three-step cycle to solve P. The problem P can be of any type, e.g. interpretation, diagnostic, configuration, planning, etc. From a functional point of view, the CBR cycle can be viewed as a function cbr that associates the result Sol(P) with the problem P:

cbr : P $\in$ Problems $\longrightarrow$ Sol(P) $\in$ Solutions $\cup$ $\{\bot\}$

Problems is a space of problem statements and Solutions is a space of solutions of these problems. The special element $\bot$ is interpreted as the lack of solution. The body of the cbr function can be divided into three main operations, namely retrieval, adaptation and memorization:

```
Data: target, Case-Base
1. Retrieval
   source = retrieve(target,Case-Base)
2. Adaptation
   adapted-case = adaptation(source,target)
3. Memorization
   If interesting(adapted-case) then memorize(adapted-case)
```

The cbr function tries to build a solution for the target problem **target**. A similar problem, called **source**, is searched in the case base **Case-Base**, and then is adapted into **adapted-case** to be reused for solving **target**. Finally, when **adapted-case** and the associated building operations appear to be interesting –interesting(adapted-case) is then true– the adapted case and the building operations, are memorized as a new case in the case base.

In the next sections, we make precise the retrieval and adaptation operations of the cbr function.

2.2 A Formal Description of Problems

In the following, the description of problems is based on a classical formalization that does not depend on any representation formalism [15]. A problem P is characterized by a triplet $(I(P), O(P), G(P))$ where:

(i) $I(P)$ is the *initial state* specifying the statement of the problem P,

(ii) $O(P) = \{O_i/i = 1, .., p\}$ is a set of *operators* allowing transitions between states,

(iii) $G(P)$ is the *goal state* that must be met to solve P.

When there is no ambiguity, we will write (I, O, G) for $(I(P), O(P), G(P))$.

A state S_i describes the configuration of the problem at a given step of the resolution process. An operator O_i allows transitions from a state S_i to a state S_{i+1}: it can be seen as a pair $(\text{spec}(O_i), \text{act}(O_i))$, where $\text{spec}(O_i)$ specifies the conditions under which $\text{spec}(O_i)$ is applicable in S_i, and $\text{act}(O_i)$ gives the actions that must be performed to reach −or to produce− the state S_{i+1}.

The *state-space* **State-space(P)** is defined by the set of all states that can be generated from the state I by applying every operators whenever possible. The state-space can be seen as a graph whose vertices denote states and whose edges symbolize transitions −or operator applications− between states.

A *solution* **Sol(P)** is a path in the state-space, consisting of an ordered set of pairs $\text{Sol}(P) = \{(S_i, O_i)/i = 1, .., s\}$, where S_i is a state and O_i is the operator applied in S_i, $S_1 = I$ and $S_s = G$ (note that, for the sake of simplicity, states and operators are supposed to hold same index i).

2.3 The Case Base

A case is a pair problem − solution $(P, \text{Sol}(P))$, where P denotes a triplet (I, O, G) and $\text{Sol}(P)$ an ordered set $\{(S_i, O_i)/i = 1, .., s\}$. The *case base* is a finite set of cases, **Case-Base** $= \{\text{case}_k/k = 1, .., q\}$, where $\text{case}_k = (P_k, \text{Sol}(P_k))$. A target problem P is usually considered as a "new case", denoted in the following by **target**. By contrast, the case belonging to the case base that is reused for solving P is the *source* case, denoted by **source**.

The case base can be flat or partially ordered when there exists an ordering that can be used to compare cases according to their generality. For example, cases can be ordered hierarchically by means of indexes as explained in the section 2.5.

2.4 The Problem Solving Process

Given a problem **target** $= (P, \perp)$, a problem **source** $= (P', \text{Sol}(P'))$ has to be retrieved in **Case-Base** and adapted to build $\text{Sol}(P)$. Thus, the knowledge of $\text{Sol}(P')$ is sufficient to solve P and this statement can be represented by the logical implication $\text{Sol}(P') \longrightarrow \text{Sol}(P)$. As stated in [8], the above implication can be generalized into the *entailment* **source** $\models$ **target**, that can be understood in the following sense: every solution $\text{Sol}(P')$ of P' is a solution of P. In this context, a "solution" can be considered as a "model" and this explains the entailment **source** $\models$ **target**.

Moreover, the entailment **source** $\models$ **target** is equivalent to $\models$ **source** $\longrightarrow$ **target**, and **target** is said to be a *logical consequence* of **source** [9]. The entailment **source** $\models$ **target** can be described in terms of problem states:

$[\models_I]$: $I^{tgt} \models I^{src}$

$[\models_G]$: $G^{src} \models G^{tgt}$

where I^{src}, I^{tgt}, G^{src} and G^{tgt} stand respectively for $I(\text{source})$, $I(\text{target})$, $G(\text{source})$ and $G(\text{target})$.

The equation $[\models_I]$ means that the initial state I^{tgt} of the target problem **target** is a particular case of the initial state I^{src} of the source problem **source**:

the solution associated with the **source** case can be applicable to the new initial state I^{tgt}. For example, the equation $[\models_I]$ holds if $I^{tgt} = Q \wedge R \wedge S$ and $I^{src} = Q \wedge R$, where Q, R and S are propositional variables ($\{Q, R\} \subseteq \{Q, R, S\}$). This example can be generalized as follows:
$$I^{tgt} = I_1^{tgt} \wedge I_2^{tgt} \ldots \wedge I_m^{tgt}, \quad I^{src} = I_1^{src} \wedge I_2^{src} \ldots \wedge I_n^{src}, \text{ with } m \geq n \text{ and}$$
$\{I_1^{src}, I_2^{src}, \ldots, I_n^{src}\} \subseteq \{I_1^{tgt}, I_2^{tgt}, \ldots, I_m^{tgt}\}$, where the terms I_j^{src} and I_k^{tgt} denote *preconditions* in I^{src} and I^{tgt} respectively.

Dually, the equation $[\models_G]$ means that the final state G^{tgt} is a "logical consequence" of the final state G^{src}: whenever the state G^{src} is reached, the state G^{tgt} is reached too. For example, the equation $[\models_G]$ holds if $G^{src} = T \wedge U \wedge V$ and $G^{tgt} = T \wedge U$, where T, U and V are propositional variables ($\{T, U\} \subseteq \{T, U, V\}$). A generalization can be drawn as follows:
$$G^{src} = G_1^{src} \wedge G_2^{src} \ldots \wedge G_{n'}^{src}, \quad G^{tgt} = G_1^{tgt} \wedge G_2^{tgt} \ldots \wedge G_{m'}^{tgt}, \text{ with } m' \leq n' \text{ and}$$
$\{G_1^{tgt}, G_2^{tgt}, \ldots, G_{m'}^{tgt}\} \subseteq \{G_1^{src}, G_2^{src}, \ldots, G_{n'}^{src}\}$, where the terms G_i^{src} and G_j^{tgt} denote *subgoals* of G^{src} and G^{tgt} respectively.

In terms of state-space and paths, the equations $[\models_I]$ and $[\models_G]$ can be read as follows:
$$\text{Sol}(P') = \{(S_1', O_1), \ldots, (S_n', O_n)\}$$
$$\text{Sol}(P) = \{(S_1, O_1), \ldots, (S_m, O_m)\}$$
with $S_1 \longrightarrow S_1'$ and $S_n' \longrightarrow S_m$: the state S_1 is more specific than the first state S_1' of $\text{Sol}(P')$, and thus, the solution $\text{Sol}(P')$ defined in S_1' will be applicable in S_1 to solve the target problem P; the state S_m is a logical consequence of the state S_n', and thus, all subgoals associated with S_m are reached in the last state S_n' of $\text{Sol}(P')$.

We have supposed that the set of operators associated with the source problem P' is reused to build the solution of the target problem P: the preconditions of the first operator associated with the solution $\text{Sol}(P')$, say O_1, must be satisfied in I^{tgt}, so that the application of O_1 can be allowed. Then, a solution of P can be seen as a composition of operators $\{O_i / i = 1, .., s\}$, the final state of an operator application being the initial state of the next operator application. Moreover, the preconditions associated with the initial state S_1 are the preconditions of the global operator composition associated with $\text{Sol}(P)$. These preconditions can be likened to the *footprints* of [21].

2.5   The Organization of Cases

Abstraction and Indexes. The organization of the case base relies on the structure of cases, or on *abstractions* of cases. The first kind of organization is generally used when the problem statements are represented by *structures* that can be –easily– partially ordered. The second kind is used when the problem statements cannot be represented by such structures and must be abstracted to be manipulated, e.g. problem statements given in natural language.

An *abstraction process* is usually based on an *indexing* process, that associates an *index* idx(C) with a case C. The index of C may be seen as a "summary" of C, and must encode the main characteristics of C. For example, cases in the chemical application presented in [14] and [11] are synthesis plans, and they are indexed by molecular structures involved in these synthesis plans. In [8] and [9], the abstraction process is called *encoding scheme*: cases are abstract plans represented by terms in a temporal logic, whereas indexes are concepts in a description logic; plans are not ordered whereas concepts organization relies on a subsumption hierarchy.

The indexing process takes into account the problem formalization as follows: if $P = (I, O, G)$, then $idx(P) = (idx(I), O, idx(G))$ (indexes are not defined for operators). The relations $[\models_I]$ and $[\models_G]$ holding on cases are translated to indexes as follows:

$[\models_I^{idx}]$: $idx(I^{tgt}) \models idx(I^{src})$

$[\models_G^{idx}]$: $idx(G^{src}) \models idx(G^{tgt})$.

The two equations $[\models_I^{idx}]$ and $[\models_G^{idx}]$ leads to two different retrieval processes: *complete retrieval* where cases verifying $[\models_I^{idx}]$ *and* $[\models_G^{idx}]$ are searched, and *incomplete retrieval*, where cases verifying $[\models_I^{idx}]$ *or* $[\models_G^{idx}]$ are searched. The complete and incomplete retrieval processes are called respectively *strong* and *weak* retrievals in [8] and [9].

An important property of the indexing process, namely the *monotonicity property*, is discussed in [8] and [9]: an indexing process satisfies the monotonicity property if the entailments existing between cases are mapped into entailments between indexes, i.e. if `source` $\models$ `target` then $idx(source) \models idx(target)$, meaning that the indexing process preserves an inclusion relation between "set of models". We will not elaborate anymore on this subject, and further details can be found [8] and [9].

An Analogy with Functional Types. It is possible to make a straightforward analogy between the relations $[\models_I^{idx}]$ and $[\models_G^{idx}]$ and the subtyping relation for *functional types* in typed λ-calculus [4].

A functional type $U \longrightarrow V$ describes a family of functions defined on a *domain* U and returning values in the *codomain* V (note that the arrow $\longrightarrow$ denotes the relation between U and V in the present section). A functional type $U_1 \longrightarrow V_1$ is a *subtype* of the functional type $U_2 \longrightarrow V_2$ if and only if $U_2 \leq U_1$ and $V_1 \leq V_2$, where $\leq$ denotes the subtyping relation between domains[1]. In this case, the type $U_1 \longrightarrow V_1$ can be substituted for $U_2 \longrightarrow V_2$ wherever $U_1 \longrightarrow V_1$ is defined.

Following the lines of § 2.2, a problem can be considered as a function the domain of which is an initial state and the codomain of which is a goal state. Then, a functional type $U_1 \longrightarrow V_1$ can be understood as a problem the statement of which is defined in U_1 and the solution of which is defined in V_1. In these terms, the problems `source` and `target` correspond respectively to the functional types $I^{src} \longrightarrow G^{src}$ and $I^{tgt} \longrightarrow G^{tgt}$.

The relations $[\models_I^{idx}]$ and $[\models_G^{idx}]$ can be interpreted in terms of functional types as follows: $idx(I^{tgt}) \longrightarrow idx(I^{src})$ can be read as $idx(I^{tgt}) \leq idx(I^{src})$ and $idx(G^{src}) \longrightarrow idx(G^{tgt})$ can be read as $idx(G^{src}) \leq idx(G^{tgt})$. Then, `source`

---

[1] The subtyping relation is said to be *contravariant* for domains, i.e. U_1 and U_2, and *covariant* for codomains, i.e. V_1 and V_2.

can be substituted for **target** wherever **source** is defined, i.e. **source** can solve the problem **target** wherever **source** is defined.

An Object-Based Representation of Indexes. In this section, we present a practical object-based representation of indexes. This kind of representation is not the unique approach that can be used to represent indexes, but it is the way used currently in our application domain (see for example [13], [14] and [11]). The representation formalism of indexes is important because it has a direct influence on the performances of every steps in the CBR cycle. The abstraction process associating a case with its index will not be detailed here –see [8] or [9] for an extended example– and we focus on the representation of indexes.

An index is represented by a *frame* F composed of a conjunction of attributes $\{a_i/i = 1, .., k\}$ denoted by $F = a_1 \sqcap a_2 ... \sqcap a_k$. Actually, values and constraints such as types, domains, or intervals of values, are attached to attributes. Frames are organized in a hierarchy denoted by $\mathcal{H}_{idx}$ using a *subsumption* relation: a frame F_2 is subsumed by a frame F_1, denoted by $F_2 \sqsubseteq F_1$, if and only if, for every attribute a in F_1, there exists an attribute a in F_2 –the two attributes have the same name– such as the constraints attached to a in F_2 meet the constraints attached to a in F_1. For example, $F_2 = a_1 \sqcap a_2 \sqcap a_3 \sqsubseteq F_1 = a_1 \sqcap a_2$, under the simplifying hypothesis that the constraints attached to the attributes a_1 and a_2 are the same in the frames F_1 and F_2. The hierarchy $\mathcal{H}_{idx}$ has a distinguished frame called **Top**, that subsumes every other frame lying in the hierarchy[2].

The equations $[\models_I^{idx}]$ and $[\models_G^{idx}]$ can be described in terms of subsumption relations as follows:

$[\sqsubseteq_I^{idx}]$: $idx(I^{tgt}) \sqsubseteq idx(I^{src})$
$[\sqsubseteq_I^{idx}]$: $idx(G^{src}) \sqsubseteq idx(G^{tgt})$

For example, let us consider **source** $= (Q \wedge R, T \wedge U \wedge V)$ and **target** $= (Q \wedge R \wedge S, T \wedge U)$. Then $idx(\textbf{source}) = (Q \sqcap R, T \sqcap U \sqcap V)$ and $idx(\textbf{target}) = (Q \sqcap R \sqcap S, T \sqcap U)$, where $X \sqcap Y$ denotes the frame representing the conjunction $X \wedge Y$. Moreover:

$idx(I^{tgt}) = Q \sqcap R \sqcap S \sqsubseteq idx(I^{src}) = Q \sqcap R$
$idx(G^{src}) = T \sqcap U \sqcap V \sqsubseteq idx(G^{tgt}) = T \sqcap U$.

If the equations $[\sqsubseteq_I^{idx}]$ and $[\sqsubseteq_G^{idx}]$ hold, then $idx(\textbf{source})$ is said to be more specific than $idx(\textbf{target})$ in the hierarchy $\mathcal{H}_{idx}$.

3 Retrieval and Adaptation in the Index Hierarchy

In this section, we discuss the behavior of the inference procedure of a CBR system at the index level, in an object-based representation environment. This inference procedure is based on case retrieval and adaptation. Indexes are represented by frames lying in a subsumption hierarchy $\mathcal{H}_{idx}$. Therefore, the retrieval and adaptation operations are deeply related to the classification process controlling the insertion of a new frame in the hierarchy $\mathcal{H}_{idx}$.

---

[2] More details on the subsumption relation are beyond the scope of this paper, see for example [12].

3.1 Retrieval: Complete and Incomplete Classifications

Given a target case **target**, the role of the retrieval process is to find in the case base a source case **source** *similar* to **target**. Most of the time, there exists a similarity measure that computes the similarity between **target** and the source cases in the case base [17] (note that the similarity measure can be defined on cases or on indexes of cases). The most similar source case, i.e. the source case which has the greater similarity with **target**, is selected to be reused.

In an object-based representation environment, retrieval can be considered as a *classification* process, the role of which is to find the most general subsumees of idx(**target**) in the hierarchy $\mathcal{H}_{idx}$: idx(**source**) is more specific than idx(**target**) in $\mathcal{H}_{idx}$. More precisely, case retrieval can be divided into two steps:

(i) Indexing: idx(**target**) = idx(I^{tgt}, G^{tgt}).

(ii) Classification: the index idx(**target**) is classified in the hierarchy $\mathcal{H}_{idx}$, and idx(**source**) $\sqsubseteq$ idx(**target**) if and only if idx(I^{src}) $\sqsubseteq$ idx(I^{tgt}) *and/or* idx(G^{src}) $\sqsubseteq$ idx(G^{tgt}).

The *and* connective corresponds to *complete classification*, and the *or* connective to *incomplete classification*.

For example, if idx(**source**) = ($Q \sqcap R$, $T \sqcap U \sqcap V$) and idx(**target**) = ($Q \sqcap R \sqcap S$, $T \sqcap U$), then idx(**source**) $\sqsubseteq$ idx(**target**), and **source** can be reused for solving **target**. Moreover, every source case the index of which is subsumed by idx(**target**) can be possibly reused for solving **target**. The fact that a retrieved source case provides an actual solution for the target case remains to be checked.

Analogy: Retrieval and Hierarchical Query Answering. Let us draw an analogy giving a different point of view on the retrieval process. Case retrieval in the hierarchy $\mathcal{H}_{idx}$ can be likened to query processing in databases based on a concept hierarchy, say $\mathcal{H}$, of a description logic [2]. This kind of query processing is performed on the hierarchy of concepts $\mathcal{H}$ as follows: the query is represented by a concept Q that is classified in $\mathcal{H}$; the set of potential answers is composed of every individual i being an instance of a concept subsumed by Q. Indeed, it is sure that such an individual i satisfies all the constraints associated with Q. Retrieval of case indexes in the hierarchy $\mathcal{H}_{idx}$ relies on the same idea: if the index of **target** corresponds to a query, say idx(**target**), every index subsumed by idx(**target**) is associated with a source case being a potential solution for the target problem.

3.2 Adaptation

The classification of the index idx(**target**) in $\mathcal{H}_{idx}$ can determine one or more source cases to be reused for solving **target** (note that the situation in which the retrieval process does not return any source case is not taken into account). If only one source case is returned, then the case selection is straightforward and the adaptation process can be performed. If more than one source case is returned, then a criterion selection has to be applied to select the "best" source case, usually the case for which the adaptation cost is the lower. Below, we examine successively what is the meaning of the adaptation process for complete and incomplete classification.

Adaptation and Complete Classification. When the classification process is complete, the equations $[\sqsubseteq_I^{idx}]$ and $[\sqsubseteq_I^{idx}]$ hold. The equation $idx(I^{tgt}) \sqsubseteq idx(I^{src})$ ensures that the solution associated with source can be reused in the context of target. The equation $idx(G^{src}) \sqsubseteq idx(G^{tgt})$ shows that the number of subgoal in G^{src} is greater than in G^{tgt}. Thus, some subgoals in G^{src} are redundant: the adaptation of source consists in ignoring the redundant subgoals[3]. Moreover, the less the source case has redundant subgoals the better the source case is. In terms of the subsumption, this means that the best source candidates are the most general subsumees of $idx(target)$ in the hierarchy $\mathcal{H}_{idx}$. If there is more than one source candidate, an external criterion has to be applied for case selection.

Adaptation and Incomplete Classification. The incomplete classification process divides the case base into three category of cases:

(i) $idx(I^{tgt}) \sqsubseteq idx(I^{src})$ and $idx(G^{src}) \not\sqsubseteq idx(G^{tgt})$.

The solution associated with a source candidate is applicable in the initial state I^{tgt}, e.g. $idx(target) = (Q \sqcap R \sqcap S, T \sqcap U)$ and $idx(source) = (Q \sqcap R, T \sqcap U')$. However, the equation holding on goal states shows that some subgoals of the target goal state G^{tgt} are not reached. Therefore, the source case that reaches the maximum of subgoals is the best case.

(ii) $idx(I^{tgt}) \not\sqsubseteq idx(I^{src})$ and $idx(G^{src}) \sqsubseteq idx(G^{tgt})$.

Contrasting the item (i), all subgoals are reached but all preconditions are not verified, e.g. $idx(target) = (Q \sqcap R \sqcap S, T \sqcap U)$ and $idx(source) = (Q \sqcap R \sqcap S', T \sqcap U)$. Therefore, the source case that meets the maximum of preconditions is the best case.

(iii) $idx(I^{tgt}) \not\sqsubseteq idx(I^{src})$ and $idx(G^{src}) \not\sqsubseteq idx(G^{tgt})$.

For example, $idx(target) = (Q \sqcap R \sqcap S, T \sqcap U)$ and $idx(source) = (Q \sqcap R \sqcap S', T \sqcap U')$. Summarizing the items (i) and (ii), the case that meets the maximum of preconditions and reaches the maximum of subgoals is the best source case.

In [8], it is pointed out that the *adaptation effort* must not be too important: a source case is not a good candidate if it does not share with the target case at least the half of the subgoals or of the preconditions.

A question remains opened: what is the exact meaning of incomplete classification and how incomplete classification and adaptation can be combined? Incomplete classification occurs when matching fails for a precondition or a subgoal, for any of the source cases of the case base. Thus, the best source case cannot be reused directly for solving the target problem. It is then necessary to

---

[3] More precisely, adaptation consists in ignoring in the solution $Sol(P')$ associated with source the steps corresponding to redundant subgoals.

transform –repair– the source case and this is exactly the purpose of *approximate classification*: find the best candidate that can be the most easily transformed to provide the best source case, i.e. the source case for which the adaptation cost is the lower. This approach can be related to adaptation-guided retrieval, as presented and discussed in [18] and [19], a concrete example being given in [11]. In the next section, we make precise approximate classification and adaptation.

3.3   Approximate Classification and Adaptation

Approximate classification operates when the relations $[\sqsubseteq_I^{idx}]$ and $[\sqsubseteq_G^{idx}]$ do not hold, as it is the case for incomplete classification. The idea is to *transform* the source and the target cases so that an approximation of the equations $[\sqsubseteq_I^{idx}]$ and $[\sqsubseteq_G^{idx}]$ can be obtained. The transformations are based on specific operations such as "edit operations" [3]. If approximate classification succeeds, i.e. the approximation of the equations $[\sqsubseteq_I^{idx}]$ and $[\sqsubseteq_G^{idx}]$ hold for the source and the target case, the handling of the transformed cases is done according to the complete classification and adaptation schemes.

We first present an example to show how approximate classification works. Let us suppose that $\mathtt{idx}(\mathtt{I^{tgt}}) = \mathtt{Q} \sqcap \mathtt{R} \sqcap \mathtt{S}$ and $\mathtt{idx}(\mathtt{I^{src}}) = \mathtt{Q} \sqcap \mathtt{R}'$. Thus, $\mathtt{idx}(\mathtt{I^{tgt}}) \not\sqsubseteq \mathtt{idx}(\mathtt{I^{src}})$ and the incomplete classification case occurs. For the sake of simplicity, we suppose that:

(i) only one propositional variable in $\mathtt{idx}(\mathtt{I^{src}})$ does not match any of the propositional variables in $\mathtt{idx}(\mathtt{I^{tgt}})$, e.g. R or S in $\mathtt{idx}(\mathtt{I^{tgt}})$ do not match $\mathtt{R}'$ in $\mathtt{idx}(\mathtt{I^{src}})$,

(ii) the demonstration is restricted to initial states $\mathtt{idx}(\mathtt{I^{tgt}})$ and $\mathtt{idx}(\mathtt{I^{src}})$, but goal states can be handled in the same way.

An index is represented by a frame lying in the hierarchy $\mathcal{H}_{idx}$. Furthermore, the components of frames are also represented as frames lying in this hierarchy. Thus, given two index components $\mathtt{K_1}$ and $\mathtt{K_2}$ that do not match, the *least common subsumer*[4] $\mathtt{lcs}(\mathtt{K_1}, \mathtt{K_2})$ of these two components can be searched in $\mathcal{H}_{idx}$. For example, for $\mathtt{idx}(\mathtt{I^{tgt}}) = \mathtt{Q} \sqcap \mathtt{R} \sqcap \mathtt{S}$ and $\mathtt{idx}(\mathtt{I^{src}}) = \mathtt{Q} \sqcap \mathtt{R}'$, R" $= \mathtt{lcs}(\mathtt{R}, \mathtt{R}')$ or S$' = \mathtt{lcs}(\mathtt{S}, \mathtt{R}')$ are searched in the hierarchy $\mathcal{H}_{idx}$.

Let us suppose that R" $= \mathtt{lcs}(\mathtt{R}, \mathtt{R}')$ exists, then R and $\mathtt{R}'$ are called *unifying components* and R is the *unifying component* of $\mathtt{R}'$. Then, the following equations hold:

$\mathtt{modification}(\mathtt{idx}(\mathtt{I^{tgt}})) = \mathtt{Q} \sqcap \mathtt{R}" \sqcap \mathtt{S}$,

$\mathtt{modification}(\mathtt{idx}(\mathtt{I^{src}})) = \mathtt{Q} \sqcap \mathtt{R}"$,

$\mathtt{modification}(\mathtt{idx}(\mathtt{I^{tgt}})) \sqsubseteq \mathtt{modification}(\mathtt{idx}(\mathtt{I^{src}}))$.

Given two indexes, the function $\mathtt{modification}$ replaces a component in the first index by an unifying component with respect to the second index. After the transformation, $\mathtt{modification}(\mathtt{idx}(\mathtt{I^{tgt}}))$ and $\mathtt{modification}(\mathtt{idx}(\mathtt{I^{src}}))$ can be

---

[4] G is a least common subsumer of $\mathtt{F_1}$ and $\mathtt{F_2}$ if and only if (i) G subsumes both $\mathtt{F_1}$ and $\mathtt{F_2}$, and (ii) no other common subsumer of $\mathtt{F_1}$ and $\mathtt{F_2}$ is strictly subsumed by G. As shown in [5], the least common subsumer can be supposed to be unique.

handled according to the complete classification scheme, and adaptation can be performed.

Three remarks can be done:

(i) The lcs of two components always exist, possibly being equal to Top.

(ii) The search for the lcs must be performed for components of indexes that do not match, e.g. a lcs has to be found for the pairs (R, R') or (S, R'). In this simple situation, the intersection of the sets $Q \sqcap R \sqcap S$ and $Q \sqcap R'$ gives the unifying components.

(iii) Initial states and goal states are handled in the same way.

A generalization of the above example can be drawn as follows (we assume that indexing is "linear" in the sense that $idx(X_1 \sqcap X_2) = idx(X_1) \sqcap idx(X_2)$):

$$idx(I^{tgt}) = idx(I_1^{tgt}) \sqcap idx(I_2^{tgt})...\sqcap idx(I_m^{tgt}),$$

$$idx(I^{src}) = idx(I_1^{src}) \sqcap idx(I_2^{src})...\sqcap idx(I_n^{src}), \text{ with } m \geq n.$$

Unifying components must be searched for any components that do not belong to the set intersection:

$$\{idx(I_1^{src}), idx(I_2^{src}), ..., idx(I_n^{src})\} \cap \{idx(I_1^{tgt}), idx(I_2^{tgt}), ..., idx(I_m^{tgt})\}.$$

The search strategy relies on the following rules:

(i) the components for which exists an unifying component different from Top must be preferred,

(ii) when more than one unifying component exist, the unifying component for which $lcs(idx(I_k^{tgt}), idx(I_j^{src}))$ is the most specific element in the hierarchy is preferred.

The search of unifying components relies on the comparison of sorted lists of subsumers and thus the complexity of the search remains polynomial. If every component in $idx(I^{src})$ has an unifying component in $idx(I^{tgt})$ –and dually every component in $idx(G^{tgt})$ has an unifying component in $idx(G^{src})$– then the approximate classification succeeds, i.e. the equations $[\sqsubseteq_I^{idx}]$ and $[\sqsubseteq_G^{idx}]$ hold for transformed indexes and adaptation can be performed.

We turn now our attention to the adaptation process itself. The search for a least common subsumer lcs is a generalization operation. This generalization must be transferred into the solution $Sol(P')$ associated with the selected source case $(P', Sol(P'))$. Then, the element corresponding to lcs in $Sol(P')$ can be instantiated if necessary to be adapted to the target problem[5].

We now summarize the adaptation in term of situation costs. The best situation is obviously the complete classification situation. The adaptation cost is the same for approximate and incomplete classification: the best source case is the one that shares the maximum of components with the target case, including initial and goal state components. However, the best situation is given by a successful approximate classification and the worst by an incomplete classification that cannot be corrected by an approximate classification.

---

[5] The generalization – instantiation cycle is a classical process associated with adaptation. This cycle can be completed with a transformation step, as shown in [11].

4 Discussion and Future Works

The work presented in this paper is far from being complete and it must be continued and extended in certain directions. This work tries to enlighten some new research topics in the global study of CBR systems: formalization, relations between retrieval, adaptation and classification, relations with knowledge systems such as object-based representation systems. When cases and/or indexes are organized in hierarchies, the links between CBR and classification-based reasoning are very close. Indeed, the representation of cases and indexes are important problems that must be taken into account by CBR system designers: a case should be a structured knowledge unit associated with operating instructions and explanations.

In our context, the learning step of the CBR process is still under study and is not presented explicitly in this paper. The learning step is not only related to the memorization of a new target case $(P, Sol(P))$, but also to the memorization of retrieval and adaptation knowledge, e.g. sequences of operations such as generalization – instantiation associated with the building of $Sol(P)$. Furthermore, the learning step is not considered when complete classification occurs, but a new case has to be built –possibly from scratch– and memorized when (i) the retrieval process fails, i.e. $idx(target)$ has no subsumee in $\mathcal{H}_{idx}$, (ii) the approximate classification fails, (iii) the number of initial and goal states transformations is too high (more than the half of the number of components according to [8]).

Characteristics such as the monotonicity of the indexing process, termination [6] and complexity of the CBR process must also be taken into account in the context of object-based CBR systems. Some opened questions are in relation with termination and complexity of the indexing process (in case of representation changes), matching in the classification processes and search for unifying components. A thorough analysis of these specific points must be carried out. An ultimate remark concerns the evaluation of CBR systems, in accordance with the purpose of [7]. We believe that temporal curves showing the performances of CBR systems must be completed with a study of the formal characteristics of these systems, giving rise to a more rigorous evaluation.

5 Conclusion

In this paper, we have presented a study of retrieval, adaptation and classification for CBR systems in the context of object-based representations. This study relies mainly on the works of J. Koehler presented in [8, 9], and it tries to extend these works in certain directions, concerning especially the object-based representation of indexes, the links between problems, cases and functional types, and the notion of approximate classification.

This study is far from being complete and many points must still be made precise and developed. However, the content of this paper can be viewed as a first synthesis of our studies on a more rigorous understanding and evaluation of CBR systems.

Acknowledgments

The authors would like to thank the "Institut de Recherches Servier" for the financial support provided for the second author, and the referees whose suggestions and comments greatly contributed to improve the first version of this paper.

References

1. E. Armengol and E. Plaza. A Knowledge Level Model of Case-Based Reasoning. In S. Wess, K.-D. Althoff, and M.M. Richter, editors, *Topics in Case-Based Reasoning - First European Workshop (EWCBR'93), Kaiserslautern*, Lecture Notes in Artificial Intelligence 837, pages 53–64. Springer Verlag, Berlin, 1994.
2. A. Borgida. Description Logics in Data Management. *IEEE Transactions on Knowledge and Data Engineering*, 7(5):671–682, 1995.
3. H. Bunke and B.T. Messmer. Similarity Measures for Structured Representations. In M.M. Richter, S. Wess, K.-D. Althoff, and F. Maurer, editors, *Proceedings of the First European Workshop on Case-Based Reasoning (EWCBR'93), Kaiserslautern*, pages 26–31, 1993.
4. L. Cardelli and P. Wegner. On Understanding Types, Data Abstraction and Polymorphism. *ACM Computing Surveys*, 17(4):471–522, 1985.
5. W. Cohen, A. Borgida, and H. Hirsh. Computing Least Common Subsumers in Description Logics. In *Proceedings of AAAI'92, San Jose, California*, pages 754–760, 1992.
6. R. Curien. *Outils pour la preuve par analogie*. Thèse de l'Université Henri Poincaré, Nancy I, 1995.
7. K. Hanney, M. Keane, B. Smyth, and P. Cunningham. Systems, Tasks and Adaptation Knowledge: Revealing Some Revealing Dependencies. In M. Veloso and A. Aamodt, editors, *Case-Based Reasoning. Research and Development, Proceedings of the First International Conference on Case-Based Reasoning (ICCBR'95), Sesimbra, Portugal*, Lecture Notes in Artificial Intelligence 1010, pages 461–470. Springer Verlag, Berlin, 1995.
8. J. Koehler. An Application of Terminological Logics to Case-based Reasoning. In *Proceedings of the Fourth International Conference on Principles of Knowledge Representation and Reasoning (KR'94), Bonn, Germany*, pages 351–362, 1994.
9. J. Koehler. Planning from Second Principles. *Artificial Intelligence*, To Appear in Volume 87, 1996.
10. D.B. Leake, A. Kinley, and D. Wilson. Learning to Improve Case Adaptation by Introspective Reasoning. In M. Veloso and A. Aamodt, editors, *Case-Based Reasoning. Research and Development, Proceedings of the First International Conference on Case-Based Reasoning (ICCBR'95), Sesimbra, Portugal*, Lecture Notes in Artificial Intelligence 1010, pages 229–240. Springer Verlag, Berlin, 1995.
11. J. Lieber and A. Napoli. Using Classification in Case-Based Planning. In W. Wahlster, editor, *European Conference on Artificial Intelligence (ECAI'96), Budapest, Hungary*, pages 132–136. John Wiley & Sons Ltd, 1996.
12. A. Napoli. Objects, Classes, Specialization and Subsumption. In A. Borgida, M. Lenzerini, D. Nardi, and B. Nebel, editors, *Proceedings of the 1995 International Workshop on Description Logics, Universita di Roma (Technical Report 07.95)*, pages 52–55, 1995.

308

13. A. Napoli, C. Laurenço, and R. Ducournau. An object-based representation system for organic synthesis planning. *International Journal of Human-Computer Studies*, 41(1/2):5–32, 1994.
14. A. Napoli and J. Lieber. A First Study on Case-Based Planning in Organic Synthesis. In S. Wess, K.-D. Althoff, and M.M. Richter, editors, *Topics in Case-Based Reasoning – First European Workshop (EWCBR'93), Kaiserslautern*, Lecture Notes in Artificial Intelligence 837, pages 458–469. Springer Verlag, Berlin, 1994.
15. N.J. Nilsson. *Principles of Artificial Intelligence*. Tioga Publishing Co., Palo Alto, California, 1980.
16. E. Plaza. Cases as terms: A feature term approach to the structured representation of cases. In M. Veloso and A. Aamodt, editors, *Case-Based Reasoning. Research and Development, Proceedings of the First International Conference on Case-Based Reasoning (ICCBR'95), Sesimbra, Portugal*, Lecture Notes in Artificial Intelligence 1010, pages 265–275. Springer Verlag, Berlin, 1995.
17. M.M. Richter. Classification and Learning of Similarity Measures. In Opitz, Lausen, and Klar, editors, *Studies in Classification, Data Analysis and Knowledge Organization*. Springer-Verlag, Berlin, 1992.
18. B. Smyth and M.T. Keane. Retrieving Adaptable Cases: The Role of Adaptation Knowledge in Case Retrieval. In S. Wess, K.-D. Althoff, and M.M. Richter, editors, *Topics in Case-Based Reasoning – First European Workshop (EWCBR'93), Kaiserslautern*, Lecture Notes in Artificial Intelligence 837, pages 209–220. Springer Verlag, Berlin, 1994.
19. B. Smyth and M.T. Keane. Experiments on Adaptation-Guided Retrieval in Case-Based Design. In M. Veloso and A. Aamodt, editors, *Case-Based Reasoning. Research and Development, Proceedings of the First International Conference on Case-Based Reasoning (ICCBR'95), Sesimbra, Portugal*, Lecture Notes in Artificial Intelligence 1010, pages 313–324. Springer Verlag, Berlin, 1995.
20. M. Steels. Components of expertise. *The AI Magazine*, 11(2):29–49, 1990.
21. M. M. Veloso. *Planning and Learning by Analogical Reasoning*. Lecture Notes in Artificial Intelligence 886. Springer Verlag, Berlin, 1994.

A Case Base Similarity Framework

Hugh R. Osborne and Derek G. Bridge

University of York

Abstract. Case based systems typically retrieve cases from the case base by applying similarity measures. The measures are usually constructed in an ad hoc manner. This paper presents a theoretical framework for the systematic construction of similarity measures. In addition to paving the way to a design methodology for similarity measures, this systematic approach facilitates the identification of opportunities for parallelisation in case base retrieval.

1 Case Memory Systems

In this paper we present a framework for the construction of similarity measures. Great flexibility is achieved by constructing complex similarity measures from more basic measures using a variety of connectives that we define. The concepts introduced in this paper are illustrated by an extensive example in the appendix.

A case memory system will be considered to consist of a case base and a retrieval mechanism. The case base will be modelled as a finite set, Θ, of cases, equipped with *projection* functions for accessing the component elements of these cases. While the cases in the example in the appendix are all tuples, and the projection functions the standard projection functions for tuples, a case may be a more complex structure, with correspondingly more complex projection functions. The projection functions might even implement considerable inferencing [10, 15], perhaps to obtain "deep" features [3] from "surface" features.

A retrieval request is presented to the system as a pair, consisting of an element, ϑ, of Θ and a similarity measure, σ. The case ϑ, known as the *seed* will, in combination with the similarity measure, represent the "best possible" case. This is in contrast to the earliest approaches, e.g. [12], in which the seed was the ideal case, and the similarity measure measured the closeness of retrieved cases to this ideal. In the approach taken here, the similarity measure can, for example, include negation, so that distance from, rather than closeness to, the seed becomes the measure of suitability.

We take a very general view of what cases are. The problem description, its wider situation or context, its solution, the solution's outcome, etc. may all be features that may be projected from a case. In some case memory implementations, only a subset of these might be stored directly as fields of the cases; others might be part of an indexing structure (as, e.g., with the explanations of case applicability in [6]). However, even in these systems, the information has to be

This research was funded by grant number GR/J99353 in the AIKMS programme of the EPSRC associated with the case in some fashion, and so we can, without loss of generality, assume that the information can be obtained by applying a projection function to a case.

By taking this broad view of what cases are and by allowing similarity measures to apply to any of the features that can be projected from the case, our framework also encompasses proposals that retrieval should be sensitive to aspects of the case other than the problem description (e.g. the adaptability of the solution, as in [13, 25]). If, on the other hand, only problem descriptions are to be compared, σ will be designed to ignore other features.

Finally, we should note that, in systems in which the case memory is indexed, case base interrogation is often a two-stage process [14, 1]: a retrieval step exploits the indexes to restrict computational effort to cases that are similar to the seed on those characteristics encoded as indexes, but the final ranking and case selection requires application of a similarity measure to this retrieved set of cases.

There is a sense in which this two-step process is equivalent to the application of two similarity measures: one that is "hard-coded" as indexes, and one that is then applied to the results of the application of the first. From this point of view, our framework encompasses systems of this kind.

In passing, we note that at stake here is whether to take a *representational* or a *computational* view of similarity [20], or, in Richter's terminology [22], whether the similarity measure is *compiled* knowledge or knowledge that is *interpreted* at run-time. In the representational approach, cases reside in a data structure, such as a DAG, where, e.g., proximity in the data structure denotes similarity. Representational approaches can afford considerable efficiency in retrieval. The data structure is effectively optimised towards retrieval according to the "hard-coded" similarity measure. This can be of especial value when similarity assessment requires the application of large bodies of domain-specific knowledge: that knowledge will be applied once per case at case base update time, rather than being applied afresh on every retrieval [20]. However, this form of optimisation can lead to a loss of flexibility [16] as it may be hard or inefficient to access the case base in different ways as might be needed to give more context-sensitivity or to use the case base for multiple tasks [5]. The computational approach, on the other hand, will, in its most extreme form, compute similarity "from scratch" on each retrieval. This can be a flexible approach as nothing is hard-coded; it may be more amenable to user manipulation of the similarity measure (as allowed in many case-based reasoning shells, e.g., [11]) or even manipulation through some learning process, e.g. [23]; but there may be an efficiency price to be paid. (A "spin-off" of our own work has been the identification of opportunities for parallelisation in pure computational approaches using our similarity framework [19], and this may help to make computational approaches more widely usable. See also [17].) The two-stage process mentioned above is clearly a compromise between pure representational and pure computational approaches. We repeat that (while our implementational work has focused on computational approaches) our framework is general enough to cover the full spectrum of possibilities.

The first half of this paper — Sect. 2 — will discuss "ordinal" similarity measures, both defining simple "atomic" similarity measures and introducing methods of combining these to form more complex measures. A model demonstrating some of the results from Sect. 2 has been implemented [19, 18]. Section 3 will then consider how the results from Sect. 2 can be applied to "cardinal" similarity measures, and how both types of measure may be combined. Finally Sect. 4 draws some conclusions.

2 Ordinal Similarity Measures

This section presents a repertoire of comparison operations, or similarity measures, and operations on these similarity measures used to construct new similarity measures. These similarity measures are *ordinal*, i.e. they are symbolic and do not give a numeric value for cases, but order them in terms of their similarity to a seed, i.e. a similarity measure is a function from (features of) cases to partial orders over (features of) cases: $\sigma :: \Theta \rightarrow \Theta \rightarrow \Theta \rightarrow \textbf{bool}$. Cardinal similarity measures, giving numeric "scores", will be considered in Sect. 3. In this section, Sects. 2.1 and 2.2 will discuss the construction of similarity measures for individual features of cases, while Sects. 2.3, 2.4 and 2.5 will show how to combine these to form more complex similarity measures for complete cases.

2.1 Atomic Similarity Measures

Some standard similarity measures are defined in Fig. 1, and illustrated by an example applied to the set $\{1, 2, 3, 4, 5\}$, with the usual total order $\leq$. The inverse function, $\sigma^{-1}\ \vartheta\ x\ y = \sigma\ \vartheta\ y\ x$, is also defined for similarities, where the inverse of a similarity σ returns the inverse of the order returned by σ.

2.2 Orders from Other Structures

The orders above (with the exception of flat) were all based on an existing ordering. The general approach was to define a function (e.g. is) which given a *seed* (e.g. ϑ) would return an ordering (e.g. is ϑ). This section will discuss the derivation of orderings from other structures. A similar approach will be taken — functions will be defined to generate orders from seeds. These functions will make use of auxiliary functions, again applied to seeds, mapping elements of the domain to some ordered set — e.g. $\mathbf{N}$. These auxiliary functions will reflect some notion of distance from the seed, and will usually be written "⤳".

Trees. A tree in which only leaves contain elements is defined by: Tree *elem* ::= Leaf *elem* | Node [Tree]. The distance of an element from a seed can be defined to be the depth of that element in the smallest subtree containing both the element and the seed. The range of the distance function is the ordered set

flat: No elements are related	flat 3	is: The seed is better than all others	is 3
$$\dfrac{x\ (\text{flat}\ \vartheta)\ y}{x = y}$$	1 2 3 4 5	$$\dfrac{x\ (\text{is}\ \vartheta)\ y}{\dfrac{(y = \vartheta)}{\vee}}$$ $(x = y)$	$\begin{smallmatrix}3\\1\ 2\quad 4\ 5\end{smallmatrix}$
minimal: The seed is a minimum requirement	minimal 3	maximal: The seed is a maximum requirement	maximal 3
$$\dfrac{x\ (\text{minimal}\ \vartheta)\ y}{\begin{array}{c}(x \geq y \wedge x \geq \vartheta)\\ \vee\\ (x = y)\end{array}}$$	$\begin{smallmatrix}5\\\uparrow\\4\\\uparrow\\3\\1\quad 2\end{smallmatrix}$	$$\dfrac{x\ (\text{maximal}\ \vartheta)\ y}{\begin{array}{c}(x \geq y \wedge x \leq \vartheta)\\ \vee\\ (x = y)\end{array}}$$	$\begin{smallmatrix}3\\\uparrow\\2\\\uparrow\\1\\4\quad 5\end{smallmatrix}$
best: The seed is best	best 3	id: Ignore the seed	id 3
$$\dfrac{x\ (\text{best}\ \vartheta)\ y}{\begin{array}{c}(y \leq x \leq \vartheta)\\ \vee\\ (y \geq x \geq \vartheta)\end{array}}$$	$\begin{smallmatrix}3\\2\quad 4\\1\qquad 5\end{smallmatrix}$	$$\dfrac{x\ (\text{id}\ \vartheta)\ y}{x \geq y}$$	$\begin{smallmatrix}5\\\uparrow\\4\\\uparrow\\3\\\uparrow\\2\\\uparrow\\1\\\uparrow\\0\end{smallmatrix}$

Fig. 1. Atomic similarity measures

$N_\infty = N \cup \{\infty\}$. The definition of the distance function $\rightsquigarrow$ makes use of three other functions: depth (giving the depth of an element in a tree), $\in_{\text{Tree}}$ (the subtrees of a tree), and $\in_{\text{Tree}}$ (which tests if an element appears in a tree). These functions are defined in Fig. 2. Since ϑ ($\rightsquigarrow t$) clearly defines a function from elements to the ordered set N_∞, it can be used to define a similarity measure generator for trees, $\sqsubseteq_{\text{Tree}}$, also given in Fig. 2.

Directed Acyclic Graphs. The functions in Fig. 2 have been defined in such a way that they can easily be adapted to apply to DAGs. Details can be found in [18]. The reader should note that graphs are being used in this paper to define distances between elements and seeds. This is quite distinct from assessing the similarity of two graph structures by some sort of subgraph algorithm, as is found in many case based reasoning systems [2, 7]. There is, however, no reason why such an algorithm could not be used to define an ordering on graphs, and

depth :: $elem \to$ Tree $elem \to \mathbf{N}_\infty$

depth e (Leaf l) $= 0$, if $e = l$
$\qquad\qquad\quad = \infty$, otherwise
depth e (Node n) $= 1 + (\min \{\text{depth } e \ t \mid t \in n\})$

$\Subset_{\text{Tree}}$:: Tree $elem \to \{$Tree $elem\}$

$\Subset_{\text{Tree}}$ (Leaf l) $= \{(\text{Leaf } l)\}$
$\Subset_{\text{Tree}}$ (Node n) $= \{(\text{Node } n)\} \cup (\bigcup_{t \in n} \Subset_{\text{Tree}} \ t)$

$\in_{\text{Tree}}$:: $elem \to$ Tree $elem \to \mathbf{bool}$

$e \in_{\text{Tree}}$ (Leaf l) $= e = l$
$e \in_{\text{Tree}}$ (Node n) $= \exists t \in n : e \in_{\text{Tree}} t$

$\rightsquigarrow$:: Tree $elem \to elem \to elem \to \mathbf{N}_\infty$

$\vartheta \ (\rightsquigarrow \ t) \ e = \min \ \{\text{depth } e \ t' \mid t' \in (\Subset_{\text{Tree}} \ t) \wedge \vartheta \in_{\text{Tree}} t'\}$

$\sqsubset_{\text{Tree}}$:: Tree $elem \to elem \to (elem \to elem \to \mathbf{bool})$

$e_1 \ (\sqsubset_{\text{Tree}} \ t \ \vartheta) \ e_2 = \vartheta \ (\rightsquigarrow \ t) \ e_1 < \vartheta \ (\rightsquigarrow \ t) \ e_2$

Fig. 2. Similarity measure generating functions for trees

then apply this ordering in the way presented in this paper.

Graphs. A similar construction can be used for graphs in general, by defining the distance function to return the length of the shortest path between the seed and an element.

User Defined Types. The same method can be applied to user defined types. A metric should be defined giving the "closeness" of an element to a seed, and this can then be used to define an ordering on that type. Indeed this can be used to implement more representational approaches [20], with the user defined type being some representation of the positioning of a case in a structured case base. The similarity measure will then reflect the indexing of cases in the case base structure.

2.3 Boolean Connectives

Sections 2.1 and 2.2 presented a repertoire of similarity measures for individual features of a case. It is now necessary to consider how to combine these similarity measures to form more complex similarity measures for whole cases.

The first obvious candidates for combining orderings are the usual boolean operators. These are covered in this section. The section starts with a present-ation of the application of boolean operators to construct complex similarity measures from simpler ones. This is followed by a discussion of the determination of maxima from these similarity measures. It will then be shown how this can be done in parallel, by transforming similarity measures to a normal form.

Sections 2.4 and 2.5 will then introduce other methods of constructing more complex similarity measures, these being *filters*, *priorities* and *preferences*. These new connectives also allow a normal form to be determined, and the computation of the maxima to be executed in parallel.

Boolean Operators. The usual boolean operators ($\wedge$, $\vee$ and $\neg$) may be applied to similarity measures to form new similarity measures. This is done by "lifting" the point-wise boolean operators to operate on similarities. If $\oplus$ is a binary boolean operator then the lifted operator $\widehat{\oplus}$, acting on similarities σ_1 and σ_2, applied to seed ϑ and cases x and y, is defined by: $(\sigma_1 \widehat{\oplus} \sigma_2) \, \vartheta \, x \, y = (\sigma_1 \, \vartheta \, x \, y) \oplus (\sigma_2 \, \vartheta \, x \, y)$.

Determining Maxima. Note that if $\oplus$ is a boolean operator other than $\wedge$ then, even if $\sigma_1 \, \vartheta$ and $\sigma_2 \, \vartheta$ are partial orders, $(\sigma_1 \widehat{\oplus} \sigma_2) \, \vartheta$ is not necessarily a partial order. Since maxima are not defined for arbitrary relations it is necessary to extend the definition of maxima to do this.

The maxima of a partial order $\sqsubseteq$ are usually defined as

Definition 1. $\sqcap \sqsubseteq S = \{x \in S | \forall y \in S : x \sqsubseteq y \Rightarrow x = y\}$.

The usual method for determining maxima of an arbitrary relation $\oplus$ is to take the reflexive transitive closure, $\oplus^*$, of that relation, thus giving a pre-order, and then taking the maxima of the partial order over the equivalence classes generated by the equivalence relation $\otimes = \{(p, q) | p \oplus^* q \wedge q \oplus^* p\}$. A different approach will be taken here, generalising the concept of maxima to apply to arbitrary relations, avoiding the necessity of generating either the reflexive transitive closure or the equivalence classes.

Since, for a partial order, $(x \sqsubseteq y \Rightarrow x = y) \equiv (x \sqsubseteq y \Rightarrow y \sqsubseteq x)$, Def. 1 is equivalent to

Definition 2. $\sqcap \sqsubseteq S = \{x \in S | \forall y \in S : x \sqsubseteq y \Rightarrow y \sqsubseteq x\}$.

and this will be taken as the definition of the "maxima" of any relation, i.e. '$\sqsubseteq$' in Def. 2 may be any arbitrary relation.

Definition (2) has the following properties:

Property 3. $\sqcap (\widehat{\neg} \oplus) = \sqcap \oplus^{-1}$,

Property 4. $\sqcap (\oplus^1 \widehat{\vee} \oplus^2) \supseteq (\sqcap \oplus^1) \widehat{\cap} (\sqcap \oplus^2)$.

Property (3) states that the maxima of the negation of a relation are equivalent to the maxima of the inverse of the relation. This can be useful, since the inverse of a partial order is a partial order, while the negation is not. Property (4)

ensures that the intersection of the maxima of two relations will be an acceptable approximation of the maxima of the disjunction of those relations.

These, and other properties, given in this paper are stated without proof. Proofs are given in [18].

A sufficient condition for the inclusion in Prop. 4 to be an equality is that the two relations involved have a degree of consistency in their inverses. If x is less than y in the first ordering, and greater than y in the second, then it must also be greater than y in the first, and vice versa. I.e. if, for all x and y in S:

$$(x \oplus^1 y \wedge y \oplus^2 x \Rightarrow y \oplus^1 x) \wedge (x \oplus^2 y \wedge y \oplus^1 x \Rightarrow y \oplus^2 x) \tag{1}$$

then

$$\sqcap (\oplus^1 \hat{\vee} \oplus^2) \, S = ((\sqcap \oplus^1) \hat{\sqcap} (\sqcap \oplus^2)) \, S \ .$$

Since this condition holds if $\oplus^1 \hat{\vee} \oplus^2$ is a partial order, then, in this case, the intersection of the maxima will be the maxima of the disjunction.

These results can be applied to determine the maxima of a relation constructed by application of the boolean operators. This can be done by taking the disjunctive normal form of the boolean expression and determining, in parallel, the maxima of the constituent terms of the normal form, and then taking the intersection.

2.4 Filters

Another possibility is to first "filter" the set through some predicate before applying the maximising function. Normally a filter will take a predicate, and when applied to a set will give a subset of that set. In keeping with the approach taken in the rest of this paper a filter here will take a *relation* over a type, and apply it to a seed to give the predicate that will be applied to a set. The symbol "◁" will be used for filters.

$$◁ :: (\tau \to \tau \to \mathbf{bool}) \to \tau \to \{\tau\} \to \{\tau\}$$
$$◁ \oplus \vartheta \, S = \{x \in S \mid x \oplus \vartheta\}$$

Filters can be used to express concepts such as "only when" and "except when". Filters can also be used to construct more complex preferences. A feature of a case may be a set of constituents. Filters can then be used to select cases containing a minimum (or maximum) set of constituents, to eliminate cases containing (or not containing) some specific constitutent, or even, in combination with the operators given in Sect. 2.1, to order cases according to the closeness of their list of constituents to some ideal.

Filters can be expressed as similarity measures. Given a relation $\ominus$ that is to be applied in a filter, it is possible to define a similarity measure $\sigma_\ominus$ such that, except for one special case, $◁ \oplus = \sqcap \sigma_\oplus$. The exception is when $◁ \ominus S = \emptyset$, in which case $\sqcap \sigma_\oplus S = S$.

Property 5. *Let $\oplus$ be any binary relation. Define $\sigma_\oplus$ by $\sigma_\oplus \vartheta \, x \, y = y \oplus p$. Then* $◁ \oplus = \sqcap \sigma_\oplus$.

Applying $\sigma_\oplus$ makes it possible to combine filters with similarities by applying the two following properties:

Property 6. $(\triangleleft \oplus)\,\widehat{\cdot}\,(\sqcap \sigma) = \sqcap (\sigma_\oplus \,\widehat{\vee}\, \sigma)$,

Property 7. $(\sqcap \sigma)\,\widehat{\cdot}\,(\triangleleft \oplus) = \sqcap (\sigma_\oplus \,\widehat{\vee}\, \sigma \,\widehat{\wedge}\, \sigma_\oplus)$.

2.5   Priorities and Preferences

Another possible type of connective is one which will take one similarity measure as being more significant than another. There are two possible approaches to this. The first applies to the similarity measures themselves, the second to the process of determining maxima. The first of these will be referred to as a *priority* (after [24]), the second as a *preference* (after [9]).

Priorities. The *prioritisation* of relation $\oplus^1$ over relation $\oplus^2$, notation $\oplus^1 \gg \oplus^2$, is a generalisation of lexicographic ordering defined for relations, and is the relation defined by:

Definition 8. $x\,(\oplus^1 \gg \oplus^2)\,y = (x\oplus^1 y \wedge \neg(y\oplus^1 x))\vee(x\oplus^1 y \wedge y\ominus^1 x \wedge x\oplus^2 y)$.

The two terms $(x \oplus^1 y \wedge \neg(y \oplus^1 x)$ and $x \oplus^1 y \wedge y \oplus^1 x \wedge x \oplus^2 y)$ in this disjunction satisfy (1), since both antecedents in this condition will be false. As a consequence, the intersections of the maxima of the two terms will be equal to the maxima of the the prioritisation.

A prioritisation of similarity measures is a prioritisation of relations "lifted" to similarity measures:

$$(\sigma_1 \gg \sigma_2)\,p = (\sigma_1\,p) \gg (\sigma_2\,p)\ .$$

Property 9. *When taking maxima of priorities the first term* $(x\ominus^1 y\wedge\neg(y\oplus^1 x))$ *may be replaced by* $x \oplus^1 y$, *since* $x \oplus^1 y \wedge \neg(y \oplus^1 x) \Rightarrow y \oplus^1 x \wedge \neg(x \oplus^1 y)$ *is equivalent to* $x \oplus^1 y \Rightarrow y \oplus^1 x$.

The prioritisation of similarity σ_1 over similarity σ_2 will therefore be defined as:

Definition 10. $\sigma_1 \gg \sigma_2 = \sigma_1 \,\widehat{\vee}\, (\sigma_1 \,\widehat{\wedge}\, \sigma_1^{-1} \,\widehat{\wedge}\, \sigma_2)$.

thus avoiding the need for negation.

Property 11. *Prioritisation distributes to the right over disjunction and, when taking maxima, if the two similarity measures being disjoined satisfy (1), also to the left.*

Preferences. An alternative approach is to first select maxima for the first similarity measure, and then take the maxima over these according to the second — i.e. the second similarity measure is applied only to discriminate between the maxima of the first. The *preference* of similarity measure σ_1 over similarity measure σ_2 is defined by:

Definition 12. $\sqcap (\sigma_1 \rhd \sigma_2) = (\sqcap \sigma_2) \cdot (\sqcap \sigma_1)$.

Relating Priorities and Preferences. Priorities and preferences satisfy the following, for σ_1, σ_2 pre-order generating similarities:

Property 13. $(\sqcap \sigma_1) \mathbin{\hat{\sqcap}} (\sqcap \sigma_2) \vartheta S \subseteq \sqcap (\sigma_1 \rhd \sigma_2) \vartheta S \subseteq \sqcap (\sigma_1 \gg \sigma_2) \vartheta S \subseteq \sqcap \sigma_1 \vartheta S$.

3 Cardinal Similarity Measures

Another type of similarity measure is one which returns a numeric value for a case, rather than a partial order on cases — i.e. rather than a similarity measure being a function $\sigma :: \Theta \to \Theta \to \Theta \to \mathbf{bool}$ it will be a function that "scores" cases $\sigma_{\mathbf{N}_\infty} :: \Theta \to \Theta \to \mathbf{N}_\infty$, or, alternatively, $\sigma_{[0,1]} :: \Theta \to \Theta \to [0,1]$. This scoring approach is less general that the one developed in Sect. 2 because the orders defined by the scores are always total; it does not, for example, allow the possibility of incomparable cases. But [21] numeric measures may have the advantage of giving cardinal as well as ordinal information to the user.

The definition of cardinal similarity measures again begins by considering comparison of individual elements of a case to seed values, and then considers how to combine the atomic measures, including the use of weightings.

3.1 Atomic Similarity Measures

The particular difficulty in defining numeric measures is how to treat elements of a case that have non-numeric types, e.g. how to score a case whose spiciness is mild, when the seed specifies a desired value of hot. One approach is to order cases as in Sect. 2.1 and then convert from the order to a numeric score. This is discussed in Sect. 3.3, where it is shown that introducing the necessary cardinal information after ordering is problematic.

The alternative is to map non-numeric values to numeric ones. In what follows, functions that carry out this mapping will be denoted as f. Obviously, for numeric valued attributes of cases, f will typically be the identity function, or, if the similarity measures are to return normalised values — i.e. some value in $[0, 1]$, rather than $\mathbf{N}_\infty$ — a normalising function. In most work on numerical measures, equality of a value in a case to the seed is taken as a sign of similarity (corresponding to is below), or the difference between two values is taken as a sign of dissimilarity (corresponding to best below). But numeric correlates of flat, minimal and maximal can also be defined. In the definitions in Fig. 3, the higher the measure, the less similar the cases (some would call this a distance measure or dissimilarity measure). An additional family of similarity measures, $\mathrm{const}_n\ e\ x = n$, can be defined which will be useful in discussing weightings in Sect. 3.2. These measures will return a constant value for any case. Clearly, flat is a special case of const_n, with $n = \infty$, and taking the inverse of a measure (subtracting, rather than adding the score given by that measure) is equivalent to multiplying by const_{-1}.

flat	is
flat $e\ x = \infty$	is $e\ x = 0$, if $f\ x = f\ e$ $= \infty$, otherwise

maximal	minimal
maximal $e\ x = f\ e - f\ x$, if $f\ x \leq f\ e$ $= \infty$, otherwise	minimal $e\ x = f\ e - f\ x$. if $f\ x \geq f\ e$ $= \infty$, otherwise

best	id
best $e\ x = |f\ x - f\ e|$	id $e\ x = f\ x$

Fig. 3. Cardinal similarity measures

Other structures. It is also possible to derive cardinal similarity measures from the structures discussed in Sect. 2.2 — trees, DAGs, graphs, user defined structures. All that is required is that a distance function (such as ⤳ in Sect. 2.2) be defined for these structures which can then be used to give the "score" for each case, rather than using the distance to define an ordering, as was done in Sect. 2.2.

This could even be applied to numeric valued features by defining a distance function on numbers — e.g. a logarithmic distance function — and applying this directly. This provides an alternative to defining some function f and using operations such as best.

3.2   Combining Numeric Measures

Numeric similarity measures can be combined using basic arithmetic operations in a manner analogous to that presented in Sect. 2.3. Using the operators $+$, $-$ (unary and binary), and $\times$, measures can be added, subtracted, multiplied and, using the $const_n$ measures and multiplication, weighted. Again. a normal form can be derived — a sum of products — and the products computed in parallel.

3.3   Switching Types of Similarity Measure

It is fairly easy to switch from cardinal to ordinal similarity measures. To transform a cardinal measure to an ordinal measure the cardinal information can be used to generate an ordinal measure by comparing values. If σ_{N_∞} is a cardinal similarity measure an ordinal measure can be defined:

$$\sigma\ \vartheta\ x\ y = (\sigma_{N_\infty}\ \vartheta\ x) \geq (\sigma_{N_\infty}\ \vartheta\ y),$$

The scores determine the ordering. Obviously the cardinal information — how much more highly one case scores than another — is lost in the transformation.

The transformation from an ordinal measure to a cardinal measure is more complex. The problem is in creating ordinal information where none was previously available, and in transforming a partial order to a total order. One possibility is to take the number of cases that can be found between two cases as an ordinal measure of the similarity of those two cases. Note that, as before, the higher the measure, the less similar the cases. However, if the cases are incomparable, there will be *no* objects between the two cases, and the measure will have to be adapted to deal with this. A possible transformation is, therefore

$$\sigma_{N_\infty} \vartheta \, x = \infty, \text{ if } |\{y|x \, (\sigma \, \vartheta) \, y \, (\sigma \, \vartheta) \, \vartheta \vee \vartheta \, (\sigma \, \vartheta) \, y \, (\sigma \, \vartheta) \, x\}| = 0$$
$$= |\{y|x \, (\sigma \, \vartheta) \, y \, (\sigma \, \vartheta) \, \vartheta \vee \vartheta \, (\sigma \, \vartheta) \, y \, (\sigma \, \vartheta) \, x\}|, \text{ otherwise}$$

Note that if ϑ and x are related, then the cardinality of the set of elements appearing between ϑ and x will never be zero, since both ϑ and x appear "between" ϑ and x.

This measure can, however, give possibly counter-intuitive results. Consider the ordering, for seed A:

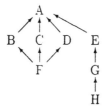

The cardinal measure proposed will return a higher (worse) value for F than for H, because there are five values between A and F (including A and F themselves), and only four between A and H. An alternative would be to take the shortest path between the elements, given by:

$$\text{minpath } x \, \vartheta = \infty, \text{ if } \neg(x \, (\sigma \, \vartheta) \, \vartheta) \wedge \neg(\vartheta \, (\sigma \, \vartheta) \, x)$$
$$= 0, \text{ if } x = \vartheta$$
$$= 1 + \min \, \{\text{minpath } x' \, \vartheta | x' \in \text{neighbours}\}, \text{ otherwise}$$
$$\text{where neighbours} = \{y|x \oplus y \wedge x \neq y \wedge \nexists z \notin \{x, y\} : x \oplus z \oplus y\}$$
$$\oplus = \sigma \, \vartheta, \text{ if } x \, (\sigma \, \vartheta) \, \vartheta$$
$$= (\sigma \, \vartheta)^{-1}, \text{ otherwise }.$$

4 Conclusions

We have presented a repertoire of tools for constructing similarity measures, both numeric and symbolic. These tools make it possible to construct similarity measures systematically and/or incrementally, in which a more refined similarity measure is derived from the result of applying a simpler measure.

The implied loss of efficiency that the use of more flexible similarity measures entails can be compensated for by the opportunities this method offers for parallel evaluation.

A system has been developed that demonstrates the ideas presented [19, 18]. Currently this provides a graphical demonstration of the method. Work is in progress [8] at York to develop this into a realistic, efficient system, and to extend the work to cover other knowledge manipulation systems.

A An Example

A.1 The Case Base

Consider the problem of taking a guest out for a meal. The meals under consideration — the case base — are given in Fig. 4. The fields indicate the name of the dish, the set of ingredients, the type of meat, the degree of spiciness (one of mild, medium mild, medium, medium hot, hot, extra hot, killer and suicide), the number of calories, and the price. These fields will be accessed by the projection functions π_{name}, π_{ingr}, π_{meat}, π_{spic}, π_{cal} and π_{price} respectively. The two letter abbreviations to the left of the cases will be used to identify the cases.

lm	lamb casserole	{meat,tomato}	lamb	medium mild	700	£12
vb	vegetable biryani	{tomato,nuts,chilli}	none	medium	650	£ 8
cv	chicken vindaloo	{meat,nuts,chilli}	chicken	extra hot	700	£15
ps	pasta	{tomato,chilli}	none	extra hot	850	£ 8
tm	truite meuniere	{fish}	fish	mild	650	£16
bb	bœuf bouguignone	{meat,tomato,onion}	beef	medium mild	800	£13
pl	paella	{fish,meat,onion}	chicken	mild	850	£17
cc	couscous	{onion,chilli,tomato}	none	killer	800	£15

| ϑ | seed | {meat,nuts,tomato} | turkey | hot | 0 | £15 |

Fig. 4. A simple case base and a seed

A.2 Atomic Similarity Measures

Assume your guest likes meat, nuts and tomato; their preferred meat is turkey; they like their food hot; and they are watching their weight. In addition, you require the meal to cost less than £15. A seed — also given in Fig. 4 — can be defined reflecting these requirements.

The budgetary restraint can be achieved by applying a filter: $\lhd\,(\pi_{price}\,<)$. The simplest of the guest's requirements to model is their weight watching, as this is simply the inverse of the usual ordering on integers: $\pi_{cal}\,\mathsf{id}^{-1}$. Their desire for hot dishes is also fairly simple, requiring an application of the best similarity measure, which will "break the back" of the spiciness ordering at hot. The required dishes will be selected by π_{spic} best.

The remaining two preferences are slightly more complex. For the desired list of ingredients a directed acyclic graph can be defined — the standard lattice representing the subset ordering on sets of ingredients — and the distance function for DAGs applied to order sets of ingredients according to their proximity to the ideal set of ingredients. The ordering generated — which will be called $\sqsubset_{DAG}$ ingr — reflects the fact that the distance function in this DAG is a measure of the number of elements common to the seed and the set under consideration. The meals best fitting the desired list of ingredients will be selected by $\pi_{ingr}\,(\sqsubset_{DAG}\,\text{ingr})$.

The final preference requires a tree to be defined representing a taxonomy of meat types, to which a distance function can be applied to select those meat types most similar to turkey. This tree is given in Fig. 5. The required meals will be selected by $\pi_{meat}\,(\sqsubset_{Tree}\,\text{meat})$. The four orders discussed here are presented in Fig. 6.

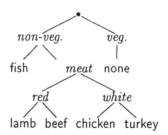

Fig. 5. A taxonomy of meat types

A.3 Retrieval

Assume that we first wish to filter out the more expensive meals, and then select according to our guest's preferences. Assume also that our guest's preferred list of ingredients and desire for meat similar to turkey is to be given priority over their weight watching and preference for hot food. The "best" meals will be selected by: $((\pi_{ingr}\,(\sqsubset_{DAG}\,\text{ingr})\,\hat{\wedge}\,\pi_{meat}\,(\sqsubset_{Tree}\,\text{meat}))\,\gg\,(\pi_{cal}\,\mathsf{id}^{-1}\,\hat{\wedge}\,\pi_{spic}\,\text{best}))\,\hat{\frown}$ $(\pi_{price}\,\lhd\,<)$, applied to ϑ. Application of the transformations presented in this

lm,vb,cv,bb ↑ ps,pl,cc ↑ tm	cv,pl ↑ lm,bb ↑ tm ↑ ps,vb,cc	cv,ps vb ↑ ↑ cc lm,bb ↑ tm,pl	vb,tm ↑ lm,cv ↑ bb,cc ↑ pl,ps
π_{ingr} ($\sqsubseteq_{\text{DAG}}$ ingr)	π_{meat} ($\sqsubseteq_{\text{Tree}}$ meat)	π_{spic} best	π_{cal} id^{-1}

Fig. 6. Some atomic similarity measures

paper shows this to be equivalent to the disjunctive normal form:

$$(\pi_{\text{price}}\ \sigma_<)$$
$$\widehat{\vee}\ (\pi_{\text{ingr}}\ (\sqsubseteq_{\text{DAG}}\ \text{ingr})\ \widehat{\wedge}\ \pi_{\text{meat}}\ (\sqsubseteq_{\text{Tree}}\ \text{meat})\ \widehat{\wedge}\ \pi_{\text{price}}\ \sigma_<)$$
$$\widehat{\vee}\ (\pi_{\text{ingr}}\ (\sqsubseteq_{\text{DAG}}\ \text{ingr})\ \widehat{\wedge}\ \pi_{\text{meat}}\ (\sqsubseteq_{\text{Tree}}\ \text{meat})\ \widehat{\wedge}\ \pi_{\text{ingr}}\ (\sqsubseteq_{\text{DAG}}\ \text{ingr})^{-1}$$
$$\widehat{\wedge}\ \pi_{\text{meat}}\ (\sqsubseteq_{\text{Tree}}\ \text{meat})^{-1}\ \widehat{\wedge}\ \pi_{\text{cal}}\ \text{id}^{-1}\ \widehat{\wedge}\ \pi_{\text{spic}}\ \text{best}\ \widehat{\wedge}\ \pi_{\text{price}}\ \sigma_<)\ .$$

The three terms in this expression will select as maximal cases {lm, vb, ps, bb, pl}, {lm, bb, cv} and {lm, vb, cv, tm, pl, ps, cc} respectively, the intersection of which is {lm}. Consequently, the recommendation will be to serve the lamb casserole.

References

1. A. Aamodt and E. Plaza. Case-based reasoning: Foundational issues, methodological variations, and system approaches. *AI Communications*, 7(1):39–59, 1994.
2. R. Altermann. Adaptive planning. *Cognitive Science*, 12:393–421, 1988.
3. K.D. Ashley and E.L. Rissland. A case-based approach to modeling legal expertise. *IEEE Expert*, 3(3):70–77, 1988.
4. R. Bareiss, J. King, k. Ashley, J.L. Kolodner, B. Porter, and P. Thagard. Panel on "similarity metrics". In *Proceedings of DARPA Case Based Reasoning Workshop*, pages 66–84. Morgan Kaufmann, 1989.
5. R. Bareiss and J.A. King. Similarity assessment in case-based reasoning, 1989. Published as part of [4], pages 67–71.
6. R. Barletta and W. Mark. Explanation-based indexing of cases. In *Proceedings of AAAI-88*, pages 541–546, 1988.
7. M. Brown. *A Memory Model for Case Retrieval by Activation Passing*. PhD thesis, Department of Computer Science, University of Manchester, 1994. Technical report 94-2-1.
8. D.K.G. Campbell, H.R. Osborne, A.M. Wood, and D.G. Bridge. Generic operations for CBR in LINDA. Technical report, Department of Computer Science, University of York, 1996. To appear.

9. A.D. Griffiths and D.G. Bridge. Formalising the knowledge content of case memory systems. In Ian D. Watson, editor, *Progress in Case-Based Reasoning:* First United Kingdom Workshop in Case-Based Reasoning, pages 32–41. Springer Verlag *Lecture Notes in Computer Science; 1020; Lecture Notes in Artificial Intelligence,* 1995.

10. T.R. Hinrichs. *Problem Solving in Open Worlds: A Case Study in Design.* Lawrence Erlbaum, 1992.

11. P. Klahr and G. Vrooman. Commercialising case based reasoning technology. In I.M. Graham and R.W. Milne, editors, *Research and Development in Expert Systems VIII,* pages 18–24. Cambridge University Press, 1991.

12. J.L. Kolodner. Maintaining organization in a dynamic long-term memory. *Cognitive Science,* 7:243–280, 1983.

13. J.L. Kolodner. Judging which is the "best" case for a case-based reasoner, 1989. Published as part of [4], pages 77–81.

14. J.L. Kolodner. *Case-Based Reasoning.* Morgan Kaufmann, 1993.

15. P. Koton. Reasoning about evidence in causal explanations. In *Proceedings of AAAI-88,* pages 256–261, 1988.

16. R. McCartney and K.E. Sanders. The case for cases: A call for purity in case-based reasoning. In *Proceedings of AAAI Symposium on CBR,* pages 12–16, 1990.

17. P. Myllymäki and H. Tirri. Massively parallel case-based reasoning with probabilisitc similarity measures. In S. Wess, K.D. Althoff, and M.M. Richter, editors, *Proceedings of the 1st European Workshop on Case Based Reasoning,* Lecture Notes in Artificial Intelligence No. 837, pages 144–154. Springer Verlag, 1994.

18. H. Osborne and D. Bridge. A formal analysis of case base retrieval. Technical report, Department of Computer Science, University of York, 1996. To appear.

19. H. Osborne and D. Bridge. Parallel retrieval from case bases. In Ian D. Watson, editor, *Progress in Case-Based Reasoning: Proceedings of the 2nd UK CBR Workshop,* pages 43–54, 1996.

20. B.W. Porter. Similarity assessment: Computation vs. representation, 1989. Published as part of [4], pages 82–84.

21. M.M. Richter. Classification and learning of similarity measures. In *Proceedings der Jahrestagung der Gesellschaft für Klassifikation,* Studies in Classification, Data Analyisis and Knowledge Organisation. Springer Verlag, 1992.

22. M.M. Richter. The knowledge content of similarity measures, 1995. Invited talk at ICCBR, Sembria, Portugal.

23. M.M. Richter and S. Wess. Similarity, uncertainty and case-based reasoning in PATDEX. In R.S. Boyer, editor, *Automated Reasoning: Essays in Honour of Noody Bledsoe,* pages 249–265. Kluwer, 1991.

24. M. Ryan. Prioritising preference relations. In S.J.G. Burn and M.D. Ryan, editors, *Theory and Formal Methods 1993: Proc. Imperial College Department of Computer Science Workshop on Theory and Formal Methods.* Springer Verlag, 1993.

25. B. Smyth and M. Keane. Adaptation-guided retrieval: Using adaptation knowledge to guide the retrieval of adaptable cases. In *Proceedings of the 2nd UK Workshop on CBR,* pages 2–15, 1996.

On the Importance of Similitude:
An Entropy-Based Assessment

Enric Plaza, Ramon López de Mántaras, and Eva Armengol

IIIA - Institut d'Investigació en Intel·ligència Artificial

CSIC - Spanish Council for Scientific Research

Campus UAB, 08193 Bellaterra, Catalonia, Spain.

Vox: +34-3-5809570, Fax: +34-3-5809661

{enric,mantaras,eva}@iiia.csic.es

<url:http://www.iiia.csic.es>

Abstract

Assessing the similarity of structured representation of cases in a natural and powerful way is an open issue in case-based reasoning (CBR). In this paper we use the notion of similitude terms, a symbolic representation of structural similarity proposed in an earlier paper. We argue that the issue to be addressed is estimating the relevance of similitude terms with regard to the task at hand, and then we propose a way of using the Case Base to estimate the relevance of similitude terms called the discriminating base. Two specific measures based on Shannon entropy are proposed to assess this relevance: I, the importance of a similitude term, and G, the similitude-based class evidence that estimates class aggregate importance. We show an application of I in the system SPIN for marine sponges identification. A longer version of this paper applies G to two standard Machine Learning datasets for classification tasks [1].

1 Introduction

1.1 Background

Similarity measures are essential in case-based reasoning (CBR) systems. Similarity measures are used in order to select, from a set of potentially relevant precedent cases, a ranked subset of the most useful cases for the particular problem the CBR system is trying to solve. It is commonly argued that 1) similarity-based reasoning is an essential subtask of the whole CBR process, and 2) the key issue in developing a domain-specific CBR system is determining what are the relevant similarities in that domain.

---

[1] Available online as Report de Recerca de l'Institut d'Investigació en Intel·ligència Artificial IIIA-RR-96-14 at <url:http://www.iiia.csic.es/Reports/1996/IIIA-RR-96.html>

The "relevant similarities" in a domain can be determined by knowledge engineering or by a learning method. Some approaches learn weights to be used with a particular similarity [8] measure while other system learn indexes— and inductive as well as EBL methods have been used [5, 4]. However, even approaches that focus on index learning consider indexing as a fast way to assess the similarity between a current case and the precedent cases.

Summarizing, similarity is the intuitive concept that supports case-based reasoning while the problem seems to be engineering a "good" similarity for each application domain.

1.2   Motivation

We argue that similarity is a way to estimate the *relevance* of a precedent case with respect to solving the current case—in a specific domain for a specific goal. The similarity we finally use in a CBR system is one that considers more similar those precedents that can be successfully reused for new problems. In other words, from the different similarity measures we could in principle choose, we are interested in finding one that selects *relevant* precedent cases for our particular task. In this view, learning weights for a similarity measure is a form of specifying a family of similarity measures and defining an optimization method to find a good one.

The approaches using similarity estimates usually deal with attribute-value representations of cases—and there is an extensive literature on this subject matter. Structured representations of cases are more powerful but establishing similarity estimates among them is still an open research issue [6, 7, 9]. Even though the proposed approaches use the notion of *structural similarity* in different ways, they have in common a basic intuition: the similarity between two structured cases to be captured is about the structural relations that are common to both cases.

In [9] we proposed to formalize the notion of structural similarity using the concept of antiunification of cases. First, we required cases to be interpreted as terms in a formal language. The antiunification [11] of two terms is the (set of) most specific term in that language that subsumes both terms. Intuitively, the antiunification of two cases is *all that is common among them*. We showed in [9] how this concept could be used for the feature term formalism for retrieval of cases using domain knowledge or inducing a partial order among retrieved cases using the notion of similitude term. A *similitude term* t_S of a current case t_i with respect to a precedent case t_j is the feature term resulting from the antiunification of both terms $AU(t_i, t_j) = t_{S(t_i, t_j)}$. When no domain knowledge is available for a case base E, a partial ordering among similitude terms $\{t_{S(t_i, t_j)} | t_j \in E\}$ can be computed from more to less specific. Then this partial ordering could be induced over the cases of E as a *preference* on which precedent case were more likely to be useful. Note that the intuition behind the *more to less specific* ordering was the heuristic that, the more a case t_i has in common with a precedent t_j, the more relevant (preferred) is the precedent t_j.

1.3 The proposal

What is needed in addition to this is a measure of whether what is in common among two (structured) cases is *relevant* to the task at hand. However, it is not clear that this could be done just weighting attributes. A problem to be addressed when using weights is how to aggregate the weights of the attributes of a subcomponent to give a weight to the structural attribute that holds this component.

We propose in this article a completely different approach consisting in a measure to estimate the relevance of a similarity term $t_{S(t_i,t_j)}$ based on the discrimination power of that term with respect to the outcomes of a task. The discrimination power of $t_{S(t_i,t_j)}$ will be estimated using an entropy measure of that similitude term over the set of cases in a case base E.

The organization of the paper is as follows. First the entropy-based estimation of similitude relevance is explained. Next an application to case-based identification in the domain of marine sponges identification is presented. Finally we draw some conclusions.

2 Entropy-based Relevance Assessment

The notion of similitude terms [9] allows a symbolic representation of similarities and thus an explicit reasoning about them. Although in [9] similitude terms were defined for the feature term formalism the approach is applicable to any formalism in which subsumption and antiunification can be defined. In this section we first generalize the approach to define symbolic similarities and later we discuss how these similarities can be assessed by their discrimination power using an entropy measure.

2.1 Reasoning About Similitudes

In case-based reasoning the main information source is a case-base E of already solved problems (the precedents). We will assume that, for a particular task, examining E we can determine a finite set of discrete outcomes. We will call C this k possible outcomes classes: $C = C_1, C_2 \ldots, C_k$. All precedents in E are then classified into k classes since their outcome is known, and we will denote by $|C_i|$ the number of cases pertaining to a class C_i.

It may seem this implies a lack of generality of our approach in (1) non-classification tasks like case-based design or planning, and (2) for numerical attributes of cases. However, we claim that the ways in which these two issues are tackled in different CBR systems are applicable in our approach. This claim of course can be endorsed by experimental work, but consider case-based planning. If we take a derivational approach to case-based planning, every case-based decision to select an operator is an instance of a classification framework as presented here–classes are operators and cases situations where operators where applied.

The purpose of this section is to develop a symbolic (i.e. non-numeric) notion of similitude. First, we need to talk about a language for describing instances (cases). In Machine Learning (ML) there is a canonical distinction between the language of instance descriptions and the language of generalization descriptions. However, the so-called *single representation trick*, the amalgamation of both languages, is often performed. In the following, we will develop a framework in which we use the same language for describing instances and generalizations, without loss of generality. If the reader wishes to distinguish between them, what follows is to be understood as the language for generalization descriptions.

We will assume a language L in which cases can be described as terms in L. We will present two examples where L is attribute-value and another one where L is a feature term language. We will only require of language L to have a reflexive and transitive relation (a preorder) $\prec$ among the terms of L, that we will call *subsumption* relation. The intuitive meaning of $\prec$ is that of *informational ordering*.

Definition 2.1 *Let a and b be terms in L. We say that $a \prec b$ (a subsumes b) when all information in a is also contained in b; alternatively we can say that all that is true of a it is also true of b. The subsumption relation can be seen also as the inverse relation to generalization, meaning that $a \prec b$ can be read as a being more general than b.*

Now, having $(L, \prec)$ as a partial order, we can define upon it the notion of antiunification (or least general generalization). The intuition behind antiunification of two terms, $a \sqcap b$, is that of capturing *all* the information common to a and b—and not merely just some information in common. For instance, what is common to a white elephant and a white gorilla—given a taxonomy of abstractions that embodies the $\prec$-ordering—is that both are white mammals. More formally, *antiunification* corresponds to the meet operation on $(L, \prec)$. That is to say, if $s = a \sqcap b$, then $s \prec a$, $s \prec b$, and for any s' that also $s' \prec a$ and $s' \prec b$, it is not the case that $s \prec s'$. Remark that we do not ask s to be such that for all s' then $s' \prec s$. This last condition holds when the result of a meet operation is unique (when there is only one least general generalization), but this need not be the case in all languages L we may be interested in. Without loss of generality, whenever there is more than one term resulting from the antiunification, we can take the set of those terms as the result. This option is the usual in inductive techniques of ML, where that set is considered a disjunctive description that represents the (set of) least general generalizations.

We call the term $s_{ab} = a \sqcap b$ the *similitude term* of a and b [9]. The similitude term $s_{ab} = a \sqcap b$ is a symbolic description of what is common to a and b (since $s_{ab} = a \sqcap b$ generalizes both a and b) and of all that is common to both (since $s_{ab} = a \sqcap b$ is a most specific generalization of a and b). The use of symbolic descriptions was explained in [9], where it is shown that a partial order upon the precedents in E can be computed as follows. For a problem (current case) P we can construct the similitude term set S—that is to say, the set of similitude terms of this case with all the precedents in E:

$$S(P, E) = \{s_{Pe_i} | e_i \in E\}$$

Since similitude terms in set $S(P, E)$ are also terms of L , we can use the partial order to reason about them. In fact, we do not need to define a metric or a distance among them to reason about which precedent is more similar to P. We need only to use the $\prec$-based ordering we have already defined to order the similitude terms in set $S(P, E)$. Then we can map the $\prec$-based ordering over the similitude term set $(S, \prec)$ into a preference ordering upon the case base E forming $(E, \prec_S)$, where $\prec_S$ is defined:

$$e_i, e_j \in E, e_i \prec e_j \text{ iff } s_{Pe_i} \prec_S s_{Pe_j}$$

Now, the most preferred cases in E are the maximals with respect to $\prec_S$. This is what we expected since the maximals in $(E, \prec_S)$ correspond to the maximals in $(S, \prec_S)$, which are those similitude terms s_{Pe_i} that are more specific, i.e. those pairs (P, e_i) that are most similar (i.e. those that have more information in common). In conclusion, we are preferring (considering more relevant) those precedents that have more in common with P to those that have less in common. However, this criterion only takes into account the *amount* of common information. The entropy-based assessment proposed in the next subsection will improve this approach by considering also the discrimination power of these similitude terms with respect to the task at hand.

The bottomline is that the symbolic similitude technique was devised to assess the importance of similitudes. Domain knowledge given by an expert essentially states which predicates are more important when comparing two cases in a for a particular task domain. The question we now pose is *How can we obtain this domain knowledge without an expert?* We propose to extract the knowledge from the case base E itself and the next section presents a particular technique for this purpose.

2.2 Assessing Similitudes

We have now a symbolic definition of similitude between a current problem P and a precedent problem e_i: the similitude term s_{Pe_i}. We can assess how important is this similitude, for a task we have to solve by assessing the similitude term with regard to that task. In other words, we want to assess whether they are similar regarding what is important for solving a task, i.e. whether the similitude s_{Pe_i} is about those aspects of P and e_i that are relevant to solve P. Notice that we are also talking about a sufficient number of similar aspects and of a particular combination of similar aspects that suffice to solve P as it was for solving e_i. And that we want to know it only to the point needed to decide which of the possible outcomes $C = C_1, C_2 \ldots, C_k$ is more likely (or, alternatively to determine the likeliness of every possible outcome $C = C_1, C_2 \ldots, C_k$).

There may be several ways to assess the importance of similitudes, but we will propose in this paper just one criterion based on the discrimination power of the similitude term, which is to be evaluated by an entropy function. The representation of similitude, being symbolic, may support other forms of reasoning for similarity assessment.

We propose to evaluate the importance of the similitude s_{Pe_i} of P and e_i by assessing the discrimination power of s_{Pe_i} with respect to all known solved precedents E in the task at hand.

Definition 2.2 *Since s_{Pe_i} is also a term in the language L, we can define the discriminant base $D(s_{Pe_i})$ of s_{Pe_i} as the set of precedents in E that are subsumed by s_{Pe_i}:*

$$D(s_{Pe_i}) = \{e_j \in E | s_{Pe_i} \prec e_j\}$$

The aim behind D is determining the set of precedents that share the same information as the similitude between P and e_i that we are currently considering (this is the meaning of e_j being subsumed by the similitude term of P and e_i). We can ask now: Does this set of precedents $D(s_{Pe_i})$, that obviously includes e_i, share exactly one and the same outcome, or some few outcomes in common, or any outcome at all? Answering this question is tantamount to giving a measure of how discriminant is the information they all share—namely s_{Pe_i}. If all precedents in $D(s_{Pe_i})$ share a unique outcome C_m, then it is very likely to infer that P will also be in C_m. Conversely, if precedents in $D(s_{Pe_i})$ can have any outcome $C = C_1, C_2 \ldots, C_k$ with the same probability (frequency), it is very likely to infer that P can have any outcome.

A way to estimate the importance of a similitude term s_{Pe_i} is by measuring the entropy of $D(s_{Pe_i})$ with respect to outcomes $C_1, C_2 \ldots, C_k$. Entropy-based measures have been extensively used to measure the randomness of the distribution of a set of elements over the classes of a partition. Shannon entropy-based measures are among the most frequently used measures. The best known example in Machine Learning is the attribute selection measure for topdown induction of decision trees (like the ID3 system [12])

Definition 2.3 *Shannon entropy is given by:*

$$H = -\sum_{i=1}^{n} p_i \log p_i$$

where p_i is the probability of class i in a partition of n classes. In case $p_i = 0$ then $p_i \log p_i = 0$.

We can use Shannon entropy to estimate the randomness of a discriminant base $D(s_{Pe_i})$ as follows.

Definition 2.4 *The entropy of a discriminant base $D(s_{Pe_i})$ of a similitude term s_{Pe_i} is*

$$H(D(s_{Pe_i})) = -\frac{1}{\log k}\sum_{l=1}^{k} p_l^i \log p_l^i \; where \; p_l^i = \frac{|\{e_j \in D(s_{Pe_i})|e_j \in C_l\}|}{D(s_{Pe_i})}$$

Since $\log k$ *is the maximum entropy of a partition of* k *classes,* $\log k$ *normalizes* H *to the* $[0,1]$ *interval.*

We will define an estimate of the relevance of a precedent case with respect to the current problem for a given task called *importance*. We estimate the importance I of a similarity term s_{Pe_i} as the converse of the degree of randomness of a discriminant base $D(s_{Pe_i})$. Using Shannon entropy we can estimate the importance of a similitude as follows.

Definition 2.5 *The importance* I *of a similitude term* s_{Pe_i} *is the converse of the Shannon entropy of the corresponding discriminant base:*

$$I(s_{Pe_i}) = 1 - H(D(s_{Pe_i}))$$

Note that this estimate is individual to pairs (P, e_i). So we have k importance estimates for all precedents in E. An overall decision has to be taken regarding which precedent is best. In order to do so we need an aggregation function—as discussed next.

2.3 Importance Aggregation

Usually in case-based reasoning the retrieval process from the case-base E (the set of precedents) finishes by selecting the *best* precedent, which is estimated as the *most similar* precedent case to the current problem P. This option is independent of the way we estimated similarity, which is any appropriate function of the form $S(P, e_i)$. This *bias* (or option) in CBR retrieval amounts to take as aggregation function the *max* function over $S(P, e_j)$. Given $Sol(e_j) = C_m$, the outcome associated to e_j, such that it is the highest similarity $max\{S(P, e_j)|e_j \in E\}$ then we can infer that also P has as solution C_m, namely that $Sol(P) = C_m$.

Using our estimate of similitude importance, a CBR process is then achieved by taking the maximum importance $I(s_{Pe_i})$ (or the minimum entropy):

$$CBR(P, E, C) = C_m \; such \; that \; Sol(e_j) = C_m \; and \; I(s_{Pe_i}) = \max_{e_j \in E}(I(s_{Pe_j}))$$

However, other aggregation functions can be used to perform case-based reasoning: This different possibilities on case-based reasoning reflect different *biases* on inference we may use while solving a particular task[2].

---

[2]Biases, in the sense of Machine Learning biases, can be used to describe design choices in CBR systems [10].

We now propose a second form of case-based inference that dispenses with the bias of basing inference on a unique precedent (regardless of how it has been selected). In our present framework we can use an aggregation function that is based on all we know about different precedents, the importance of their similitudes with the current problem, and the known outcomes of all the precedents. Specifically, we propose a *class aggregated entropy* estimate K_P that aggregates the entropies for all similitudes with precedents associated with the same outcome class with respect to the current problem P. Intuitively, we weight the entropy of the discriminating base $D(s_{Pe_i})$ with the cardinality of that discriminating base $|D(s_{Pe_i})|$. In this way, the heuristic prefers those similitudes that subsume larger subsets of the Case Base to those that subsume smaller subsets.

Definition 2.6 *The class aggregated entropy K_p for a class C_m is defined as follows:*

$$K_P(C_m) = \frac{\sum_{e_i \in E_{C_m}} |D(s_{Pe_i})| \cdot H(D(s_{Pe_i}))}{\sum_{e_i \in E_{C_m}} |D(s_{Pe_i})|}$$

where $E_{C_m} = \{e_k \mid Sol(e_k) = C_m\}$

Again, for a specific application, now we can take different biases for using K_P as a basis for inference. If we want a unique decision, we can infer that P has outcome $\min_{K_P(C_m)}$. Alternatively, in other domains, we may want display as result a ranking of possible solutions, maybe accompanied by their plausibility degree. In this situation it would be expedient to define a class evidence estimate for each outcome that we will call *similitude-based class evidence*.

Definition 2.7 *The similitude-based class evidence $G(C_m)$ for a class C_m is defined as follows:*

$$G(C_m) = 1 - K_P$$

Then a CBR process can produce a plausible inference where every possible outcome $C_1, C_2, \ldots, C_k$ has a plausibility degree corresponding to $G(C_m)$. We discuss concrete applications of this framework in the next two sections.

3 Similitude Assessment in Marine Sponges

In this section we use the entropy-based assessment of similitude importance I in a particular formalism, namely the feature term formalism used in the Noos representation language [1]. The operations of subsumption and antiunification in feature term formalism are explained in [9] but they can be summarized as follows. A feature term can be considered as a labeled graph with type names in the nodes and feature names in the arcs (see Figure 1). There is a special node, called *root*, that is the outmost node when a feature term is written (in Figure 1 **new-sponge** is the root). The node names are types pertaining to *Type* and there is a type partial order (type subsumption) defined over types: $\langle Type, \prec \rangle$.

Regarding subsumption, the intuitive idea is considering feature terms as descriptions of situations. Then, *subsumption* is the usual one: a description F

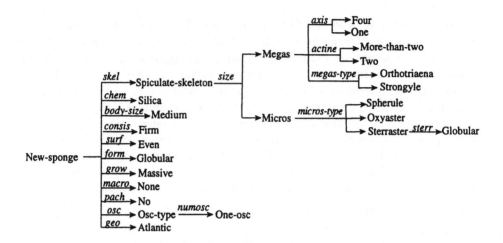

Figure 1: A feature term describing a marine sponge that is to be classified at different levels of the biological taxonomy.

subsumes another description F' if F is more general than F'. Regarding feature terms, the essential idea is that a feature term F subsumes F', written $F \prec F'$, if and only if (1) the type of the root of F' is a subtype in $\langle Type, \prec \rangle$ of the root of F, (2) all features defined in F are also defined in features of F' (3) the feature values of F subsume the corresponding feature values of F', and (4) all path equality constraints in F also hold in F'. Antiunification is an operation $AU(F, F')$ that—as explained in the last section—produces a most specific generalization of F and F'. See [9] for the detailed definitions of subsumption and antiunification.

We will show the entropy-based assessment of similarity importance using the SPIN application, a system for the identification of marine sponges. The SPIN application has been developed using the representation language Noos [1], that integrates CBR with inductive learning methods. This integration is done in a way similar to the CHROMA application [2], but in this paper we will not deal with the integration issues or the inductive methods for structured representation of cases and we will focus exclusively on the assessment of similarity importance using entropy measures.

In the domain of marine sponge identification, a new problem is shown as a sponge description in Figure 1. The task is to classify that sponge description into *taxa* (the outcomes) at several levels of taxonomy—namely class, order, family, genus, and species. Note that the value of a feature can be a set, as in the size feature of Figure 1 that has two values megas and micros.

Now consider a precedent case already solved by the system as that shown in Figure 2. This feature term has a description feature that has a sponge description sponge-1 and a classification feature that holds a solution. The sponge-1 term is similar to that of Figure 1 and the solution object holds the solutions of identifying that sponge at several taxonomic levels.

We can elucidate what is the similitude of both sponges descriptions of Figure

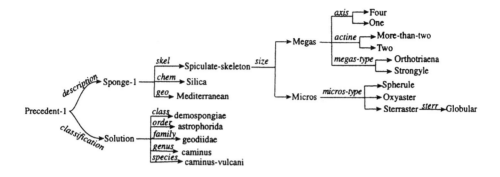

Figure 2: A feature term describing a marine sponge case already classified at different levels of the taxonomy.

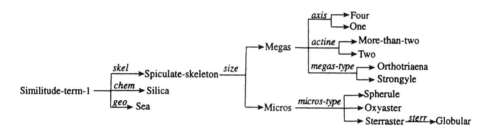

Figure 3: A similitude term describing the shared information of sponges described in Figures 1 and 2.

1 and Figure 2 performing the antiunification of both terms. The result is a similitude term shown in Figure 3 that describes all that is common to both descriptions. Note that, in Figure 3, the **chem** feature is maintained since it is `silica` in both examples, while other features have been eliminated and **geo** is generalized from `atlantic` sea and `mediterranean` sea to `sea`. The most outstanding trait is that the type of skeleton of the sponges, of type `spiculate-skeleton`, forms a complex structure that is shared by both sponges description and is thus included in the similitude term. However, when the new sponge description is matched with another less similar precedent case we obtain a similitude term as that of Figure 4.

Comparing `similitude-term-2` in Figure 4 with the problem described in Figure 1 we can observe that they have less in common—although at first sight this is not obvious. The `similitude-term-2` seem to have more features in common with ourcurrent problem, but in fact the values they share ar much more abstract—i.e. they share less informational content. Indeed, the **megas** object (in the **size** feature of `spiculate-skeleton`) has a feature **megas-type** that has generalized `orthotriaena` to `triaena` and `strongyle` to `a-megas`, both more

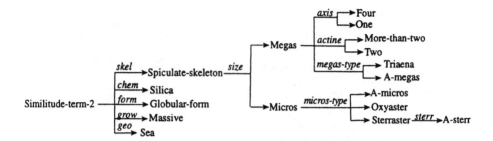

Figure 4: A similitude term describing the shared information of the new sponge described in Figure 1 and another precedent case (not shown).

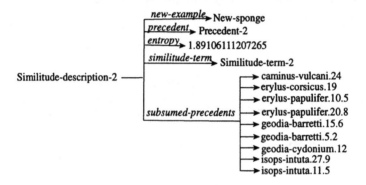

Figure 5: Similitude description showing the entropy of the discrimination base—the precedents subsumed by the similarity term shown in feature **subsumed-precedents**.

abstract types of *megascleras*[3]. Likewise, the **micros-type** feature of **micros** maintains **oxyaster** and **sterraster** but has more abstract values on the rest— namely **globular** has been abstracted to **A-sterr** and **spherule** to **a-micros**.

An entropy measure offers the possibility of evaluating this similitudes against the background knowledge that represents the precedent cases already classified. In the case of **similitude-term-1** of Figure 3, it subsumes only two cases of all the sponges Case Base and both are of species **caminus-vulcani**[4]. Since all elements of discriminating base $D(s_{Np_1})$ for new-sponge N and the first precedent p_1 are in the same outcome class there is no randomness and the entropy for this discriminating base is 0, i.e. $H(D(s_{Np_1})) = 0$, and the importance is 1.

In the case of the similitude term in Figure 4, we show in Figure 5 the (not normalized) entropy and the precedent cases subsumed by the similitude term

---

[3]The name **megas** used is just the short version of *megascleras* as used frequently by bentonic biology experts.

[4]For the sake of simplicity, we will discuss identification of sponges at the *species* level. The rest of taxonomic levels are handled in the same manner

(the 9 cases in the **subsumed-precedents** feature). These 9 cases form the discriminating base $D(s_{Np_2})$ for new-sponge N and precedent p_2 and as can be assumed from their mnemonic names they pertain to different species, genus and family. There is one precedent of species *caminus-vulcani*, *erylus-corsicus*, and *geodia-cydonium*, and there are two precedents of species *erylus-papulifer*, *geodia-barretti*, and *isops-intuta*. The (non normalized) entropy of discriminating base with respect to the species identification task is 1.891. Clearly the entropy with respect to the genus identification task will be different because the discriminating base is assessed against a different partition with less classes—namely taxa *caminus*, *erylus*, *geodia* and *isops*—and that will produce a lesser degree of disorder and thus a lower entropy.

Summarizing, if we use the relevance estimate based on the entropy measure we introduced in section 2.1 that reasons on a case by case basis, we can just take the minimum entropy (conversely, the maximum importance) to select the best precedent. In our example the first precedent p_1 (shown in Fig. 2) is the best and thus the **new-sponge** problem is identified by the SPIN system using entropy assessment as pertaining to the *caminus-vulcani* species—which is correct.

We performed an experiment with 26 marine sponges of the *geodiidae* family. We used this method in order to evaluate the classification of unseen sponges. The experiment is performed on the *genus* taxonomic level consisting in 5 categories, namely *isops* (4 examples), *erylus* (9 examples), *caminus* (3 examples), *pachymatisma* (2 examples), and *geodia* (8 examples), and using the leave-one-out evaluation technique. We have also performed this experiment with INDIE, an inductive learning method[5] also integrated in the SPIN system. Table 1 below shows the result of this experiment for both the SPIN-CBR and SPIN-INDIE methods. The columns in Table 1 report the following: 1) the method used by SPIN applications, 2) the percentage of successful identification. A solution is counted as correct also when more than one solution is given and the correct solution is included, 3) the percentage in which correct solution is not unique, i.e. a multiple solution including the correct one is the outcome of the system, 4) the percentage in which no identification is achieved.

Method	Accuracy	Multiple Solutions	Fails to Answer
SPIN-CBR	73.07	19.23	0.0
SPIN-INDIE	73.07	7.69	19.23

Table 1: Evaluation of the entropy-based assessment of similitude importance I used for case-based reasoning and the inductive method INDIE.

It is worth noting that both provide the same accuracy in the leave-on-out evaluation but with a different bias. SPIN-CBR is always able to yield a plausible identification to a sponge—while SPIN-INDIE fails to give any identification

---

[5]INDIE is a bottom up inductive method based on antiunification of feature terms [3].

19.23% of the times. On the other hand, SPIN-INDIE only gives a multiple identifications 7.69% of the time while SPIN-CBR ratio of multiple identifications is higher, namely 19.23%. Although accuracy is equal for both methods (73.07%) the set of sponges that are correctly classified by each method is not the same. Our future work on this domain intends to use aggregation or consensus measure to provide an identification by considering the outcome of SPIN-INDIE and SPIN-CBR as partial evidence.

4 Conclusion

In order to compare this usage of entropy in case-based reasoning with other uses of entropy in Machine Learning techniques we performed an experimental comparison with program C4.5 in two datasets available at Irvine ML Repository. C4.5 uses Quinlan's Gain [12] (based also on Shannon 's entropy) and is considered a state of the art technique for top down induction of decision trees. In this experiments we used the G estimate since the two datasets we used, the lymphography and the soybean datasets, are tasks of discriminant classification. The G estimate ranked similarly to C4.5 (and with other techniques) regarding precision—but some caveats are in order here. Published results on C4.5 (and other inductive techniques) are based in the assumption that the outcome is discriminant—i. e. C4.5 gives only *one* solution class for any example, and precision is measured against this standard. Since the G measure is numeric, it produces a ranking of solutions with a plausibility degree. In order to compare it with the discrimination-based techniques we just took the maximum solution as the "correct" one. It turned out, however, that in a number of cases of the soybean dataset the G estimate gave two classes with maximum plausibility degree, so comparison with C4.5 is not straightforward. The interested reader is referred to the longer version of this article[6]. Summarizing our conclusions of these experiments, it seems evaluating a case-based reasoning with the G estimate as an absolute discrimination task si quite biased, since G assures only a partial order among possible solutions that can not provide onways a unique solution.

The usability, in general, of entropy-based assessment of similarities requires more empirical work. The kind of evaluation performed on single-solution inductive methods (correct vs. incorrect) appears too simple for a practical evaluation of methods that naturally express the results as a preference ranking or as a set of solutions with a plausibility degree.

Returning to the original rationale for our proposal, estimating structural similarities and its relevance, the proposal we presented allowed us to introduce case-based reasoning to applications like SPIN. The sponge identification task, when using flat representations, proves to be much complex because the number of attributes is very high but the attributes used in describing a particular case is a small subset. This fact causes the well known *missing values* or *inapplicable*

---

[6]Report de Recerca de l'Institut d'Investigació en Intel·ligència Artificial IIIA-RR-96-14, available online at <url:http://www.iiia.csic.es/Reports/1996/IIIA-RR-96.html>

attributes problems that complicate the usage of inductive techniques—or that require, at least, a very large case base. Structured representation avoids this problem because the *inapplicable attributes* problem disappears. The reason is that subcomponents of the cases (like the skeleton of sponges) can have different *types* (like *spiculate* or *fibre* skeletons), and these types have different relevant attributes. The flat representation works always with *all* attributes, in fact introducing the artifactual problems mentioned. Entropy-based estimates of similitude relevance permitted to introduce CBR method in the SPIN application and use a case base of moderate size.

Finally, inductive methods have studied entropy measures and other probability theory measures to estimate the *goodness* of particular inductive descriptions. We think that the notion of symbolic similitudes (of which structural similitudes is one case) can be used to also study these measures for estimating the relevance of precedent cases in case-based reasoning in addition to the specific ones proposed and studied in this article.

Acknowledgments

The authors thank Josep-Lluis Arcos for the discussions and the support he provided in in this and other closely related work. The research reported on this paper has been developed at the IIIA inside the ANA-LOG Project funded by Spanish CICYT grant 122/93, a CICYT fellowship. More information about the ANALOG Project can be found at URL <url:http://www.iiia.csic.es/Projects/analog/analog.html>. A longer version of this article as report IIIA-RR-96-14 is available online at <url:http://www.iiia.csic.es/Reports/1996/IIIA-RR-96.html>

References

[1] Josep Lluís Arcos and Enric Plaza. Inference and reflection in the object-centered representation language Noos. *Journal of Future Generation Computer Systems*, 1996. To appear.

[2] Eva Armengol and Enric Plaza. Integrating induction in a case-based reasoner. In J. P. Haton, M. Keane, and M. Manago, editors, *Advances in Case-Based Reasoning*, number 984 in Lecture Notes in Artificial Intelligence, pages 3–17. Springer-Verlag, 1994.

[3] Eva Armengol and Enric Plaza. Indie: An heuristic induction method based on antiunification. Technical report, IIIA, 1996.

[4] E Auriol, S Wess, M manago, K-D Althoff, and R Traphöner. Inreca: A seamless integrated system based on inductive inference and case-based reasoning. In *Case-Based Reasoning Reseacrh and Development*, number 1010 in Lecture Notes in Artificial Intelligence, pages 371–380. Springer-Verlag, 1995.

[5] C. Bento and E. Costa. A similarity metric for retrieval of cases imperfectly described and explained. In *Proc. 1st European workshop on Case-Based Reasoning*, pages 8–13, 1993.

[6] K Börner. Structural similarity as a guidance in case-based design. In *Topics in Case-Based Reasoning: EWCBR'94*, pages 197–208, 1994.

[7] H Bunke and B T Messmer. Similarity measures for structured representations. In *Topics in Case-Based Reasoning: EWCBR'94*, pages 106–118, 1994.

[8] Beatriz López and Enric Plaza. Case-based planning for medical diagnosis. In Z. Ras, editor, *Methodologies for Intelligent Systems*, volume 689 of *Lecture Notes in Artificial Intelligence*, pages 96–105. Springer Verlag, 1993.

[9] Enric Plaza. Cases as terms: A feature term approach to the structured representation of cases. In Manuela Veloso and Agnar Aamodt, editors, *Case-Based Reasoning, ICCBR-95*, number 1010 in Lecture Notes in Artificial Intelligence, pages 265–276. Springer-Verlag, 1995.

[10] Enric Plaza. Biases in case-based reasoning. Technical report, IIIA, 1996.

[11] Gordon D Plotkin. A note on inductive generalization. In *Machine Intelligence*, number 5. 1970.

[12] J. R. Quinlan. Induction of decision trees. *Machine Learning*, 1:81–106, 1996.

[13] A. Verdaguer, A. Patak, J. J. Sancho, C. Sierra, and F. Sanz. Validation of the medical expert system pneumonia. *Computers and Biomedical Research*, 25(6):511–526, 1992.

Case-Enhanced Configuration by Resource Balancing

Jörg Rahmer[+] and Angi Voß[*]

[+]GMD TKT, Rheinstr.75, D-64295 Darmstadt, Germany, joerg.rahmer@gmd.de
[*]GMD FIT, Schloß Birlinghoven, D-53754 Sankt Augustin, Germany,
angi.voss@gmd.de

Abstract. In this paper we show how an existing problem solver for configuration by resource balancing can be enhanced by cases to become an interactive system for specifying, configuring, and extending complex systems like telecooperation systems. Thereby the integration of case-based reasoning and resource-oriented configuration bases on the observation that both are instances of a more general method. To put this idea into action we are following a pragmatic approach, first supporting manual case retrieval and reuse and then gradually enriching it by automatic methods. Special consideration is given to the reuse of cases. To reuse cases in a new problem context we need adaptation. Adaptation is done by providing cases as a warehouse for our routine design solver. Therefore we do not need special adaptation knowledge, can exploit cases of different quality and size, and can interleave the reuse of multiple cases.

1 Introduction

Configuration is a well-understood routine design task [Brown&Chandrasekaran89] and there is a great number of industrial applications proving the success story of this kind of expert systems. Problem solvers exist, ranging from the pioneering R1/XCON expert system for configuring computer systems [Dermott82] to approaches based on constraints [Mittal&Falkenhainer90], [Faltings&Weigel94], component-composition hierarchies [Günter95] and resource balancing [Kleine-Büning&Stein94]. Our application is the configuration of telecooperation systems[1]. This domain is rapidly growing (new nets, new components, new services and new protocols) and very complex. But the principles are well understood. So a from-scratch configurator can be used to assist the design of a telecooperation system. On the other hand there are millions of existing telecooperation systems and lots of them documented. So that the reuse of old configurations by adaptation to the current situation should be considered, which can be accomplished by CBR. In general the use of cases can improve the efficiency of existing problem solvers, they allow to approximately solve tasks where domain models are missing, and they are more natural for human-machine interactive problem solving than from-scratch solvers. Whether such a routine problem solver can be speeded up by cases, especially for complex systems, depends on the efficiency of the used problem solver and the domain. For our application, this question has not yet been resolved. But there are more compelling arguments for the use of cases: (1) Due to their experience human consultants often know the best solution soon after the beginning of the consultation. This indicates that human experts work in this domain

---

[1]This research is part of the KIKon project [Böhm&Uellner96], [Emde+96] financed by the German Telekom AG.

with cases, so the use of cases is natural. (2) Often, large systems are not configured from scratch, but existing systems are updated or extended. The task of modifying or extending a configuration may be treated as an adaptation task where the old configuration must be adapted to a new problem. But adaptation is one crucial aspect of CBR. (3) Complex systems as in our domain are not specified and configured at one blow. Rather, specification and configuration co-evolve [Emde+96]. But specification is a poorly understood non-routine task and here case-based reasoning could fill a substantial gap. For example, several case-based systems were developed to assist the task of building design (ARCHIE [Domeshek&Kolodner93], PRECEDENTS [Oxman94], FABEL [Voss96c], IDIOM [Smith+95]). They essentially depend on interactive human-machine problem solving, where the cases provide shortcuts for human problem solving.

In this paper we show how an existing problem solver for routine configuration by resource balancing can be enhanced by cases to become an interactive system for specifying, configuring and extending complex systems, like telecooperation systems. Our approach is pragmatic, first supporting manual case retrieval and reuse and then gradually enriching it by automatic methods.

We first motivate why cases are useful in this domain. We justify our choice of methods and then sketch the knowledge sources they need: a resource-oriented model of telecooperation systems and the kinds of cases. We explain how configurations can be specified with a flexible table mechanism by selecting components and cases. Such partial specifications can be configured selectively by an amalgamated resource- and case-based configuration method.

2 Cases are Useful in the Configuration of Telecooperation Systems

World-wide there are millions of telecooperation systems and many are documented, at least on paper [Telekom94]. We do not have to look very far, they are part of our daily life. Every reader will have a telephone at home. This is the simplest example of a telecooperation system. It allows you to communicate with other people using the telephone service. Probably, you also have a PC connected with a modem to the public network. Thus you can use fax-, ftp- or email-services. More sophisticated examples are found in industry, government or academia. There, the members of an institution cooperate using several services supplied by the telecooperation system of their institution, like the telephone service, the file transfer service or the email service.

To answer the question why cases are useful in the configuration of telecooperation systems we first regard a clearly specified configuration problem. A person privately wants to use the telephone service and some information services offered by the WWW. So a compatible combination of telephone, PC, modem, software, and network has to be selected. This is a daily configuration problem in the shops of the German Telecom AG. Instead of respecifying and reconfiguring this routine task from scratch every day, it would be natural for the consultants to have a standard configuration called "private person with PC" which could be selected and adapted.

But in practice, a clear specification in terms of a complete and consistent set of requirements is rare. Often, the customer prefers to select some components rather than specifying his/her needs exactly. And instead of a single concrete component, s/he may select a set of alternatives. For large systems, the selection of elementary components is not feasible, because the systems may consist of hundreds of such components. Here, complex cases of earlier installations are a good starting point. Imagine a company which sells laser technique products and wants to open branches at two new sites. They need services like email, ftp, fax, T-Online, database services, etc. Several of these services shall be realized on a host. The configuration problem becomes more difficult, but again there are some prototypical telecooperation systems which would fit these demands. Nowadays, customer consultants of German Telecom AG configure large telecooperation systems for companies by using available plans of other, similar telecooperation systems and adapting them to the customers demands. A case-based configuration system could assist them with this work by retrieving the available plans as cases and adapting them in the new context.

More and more companies present themselves and their products in the world wide web. They need an internet server and an internet browser, but often the telecooperation systems of the companies do not provide this facility. Extending an existing system is a daily activity. So this is a very important task that has to be supported by our configurator. This task, too, can be simplified by CBR. It is most convenient to fetch the old system configuration and modify its specification according to the new requirements. But that is indeed case adaptation.

3 How to Solve Configuration Problems?

Several knowledge-based methods are available for solving configuration problems. In 3.1 we explain why we have used the resource-oriented method (ROC). For reusing cases, alternatives exist. In 3.2 we motivate our choice of cases for enhancing ROC.

3.1 Choosing a Knowledge-Based Configuration Method

In the literature we find configuration methods using heuristics [Dermott82], constraints [Mittal&Falkenhainer90], [Faltings&Weigel94], component-composition hierarchies [Günter95], and resource balancing [Kleine-Büning&Stein94][2]. Thus, given a particular configuration task, the question is which method and corresponding knowledge models are most appropriate. For the domain of telecooperation systems, we ruled out heuristics because they are poorly structured and hard to maintain. Constraints are insufficient because the structure of the system is not specified in advance, i.e. we first have to figure out the constraint network. Component-composition hierarchies are inadequate because they assume a hierarchical system structure. We chose the resource-oriented approach because it allows to develop arbitrary structures, is easy to maintain and largely self-explanatory [Rahmer&Sprenger96].

ROC relies on a component model. Therefore it needs the domain modeled in terms of components and resources, both of which can be arranged in inheritance hierarchies. Components can be anything material or immaterial you can buy, e.g. service providers. Resources can be any material or immaterial interfaces between components. Wrt. material components and resources, ROC can then be seen as a "plug-and-play"-approach. Two components can be connected by plugging them together via a common resource, one component needing the resource and the other

---

[2]The use of component-composition hierarchies is also called the skeletton-oriented approach whereas the resource-balancing approach is also known as resource-oriented configuration (abbreviated as ROC).

component supplying it. But how can we use this for configuration? The idea is to interpret the user requirements as a list of open resource needs. Now successively all needs are fulfilled by plugging a component to it which supplies the need. Because this component will need further resources, these needs have to be fulfilled as well. This process is iterated until no open resource needs are left and so a correct configuration is obtained.

Resource-oriented domain models are entirely declarative, and they are easy to maintain because resources are assumed to be relatively stable, and introducing a new component with its resource requirements and offers is easy. Resource-oriented configurations are self-explanatory because the components are linked via the resources they offer or provide to each other, and the resources are causal explanations why two components are linked [Heinrich&Jüngst91].

3.2 Choosing a Case-Based Reasoning Method

There are several options in the design of a case reusing method: the approach to adaptation, the kind of cases, and possibly the strategy for handling multiple cases [Voss96a], [Voss96b].

Approach to adaptation: Let us first look at some case-based systems with focus on adaptation. ARCHIE [Domeshek&Kolodner93] and PRECEDENTS [Oxman94], support conceptual building design. They are case browsers and do not support adaptation at all. In Déjà Vu, heuristics are used to configure software from small pieces [Smyth&Keane95]. FABEL´s TOPO heuristically transfers structure from the layout in case [Coulon95] and the adapted layout must be checked and possibly revised by the user. In IDIOM [Smith+95] and COMPOSER [Purvis&Pu95], constraint satisfaction tools are used. This requires that the structure of the constraint network can be copied from the case(s) or is supplied from the user. In FABEL´s AAAO, a knowledge-based from-scratch method is used to adapt the construction from a case [Voss96c]. The same opportunity exists in our application. Our configurator solves configuration problems from scratch and we should exploit it to adapt our cases automatically. So we need not fall back to heuristics for case adaptation. But as in ARCHIE and PRECEDENTS, we should allow the user to browse the case library for specification.

Kind of cases: CBR systems also vary in the kinds of cases. The cases can be abstract or concrete, complete, partial or composite, isolated or related. In our application, complete cases are best suited for initial specification (as in ARCHIE and PRECEDENTS), small cases are needed for extending or completing configurations (as in the other CBR systems mentioned). We already have a good set of complete cases and expect they will contain suitable small cases. Therefore, we will use composite cases. Since our cases shall be processed by our ROC, they must be represented like the input and output of it, that means, as concrete, intermediate configurations. Since we do not have abstract cases at the moment, we do not have any abstraction relations between cases, as for instance in Déjà Vu.

Strategy for multiple cases: To solve a problem, more than one case may be needed. If so, the cases can be retrieved incrementally or simultaneously and, also, they can be adapted incrementally or simultaneously. As our application is highly interactive, the CBR strategy must be comprehensible for the consultant. Since consultants elaborate configurations iteratively, cases should be retrieved iteratively, one by one. As we will explain in 6.4, adaptation need not be done case-wise, but can be interleaved.

4 Knowledge sources

In this section we describe our two knowledge sources: a resource-oriented domain model for ROC and composite cases for CBR.

4.1 The Resource-Oriented Domain Model

ROC needs a description of components and resources. Components are providers like the different kinds of telephones, fax machines, PCs, software, private branch exchanges (PBX) and network terminations. Resources are for example services like the email, ftp, internet or telephone service. Other resources are different kinds of interfaces, like the MAPI or CAPI, telephone slots, PCMCIA-slots, V.24-interfaces, X.21 interfaces.

To systematically describe telecooperation systems, we developed a reference model[3] which can be seen as a unification of the OSI-reference model and the TCP/IP protocol suite[4] for our purposes. This model provides a horizontal structuring: resources (functions, services) required at some layer are either satisfied by components at this level or are passed on to the next lower layer. An orthogonal topological structure is imposed by contexts like the different work places within an office, an infrastructure, a PBX, or computer systems, all of which need to be configured of their own.

Figure 1 shows a simplified configuration of a telecooperation system consisting of three work places and an infrastructure. Rectangles describe components, ellipses resources. Resources link pairs of components. For example the fax machine is connected with the PBX via the access resource. The fax machine and the PBX are at different horizontal layers. These two layers are linked by a resource which can be seen as a service access point. The topological structure of the system is given by the grey boxes which represent the work places and the infrastructure of the system as different contexts.

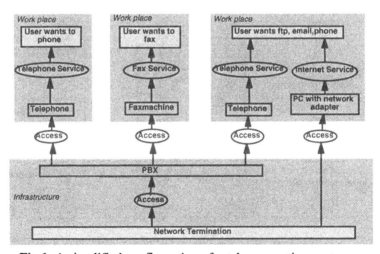

Fig.1. A simplified configuration of a telecooperation system.

---

[3] It also serves as our component model for configuration and specification.
[4] Both are standards for the purpose of systems interconnection.

4.2 Composite Cases for CBR

Cases need to be acquired. This involves two steps. A representative set of meaningful configurations must be elicited, and it must be represented as cases. For retrieval, the cases must be indexed suitably.

Case Elicitation

For developing our configurator, we were given a set of fairly different cases. The set of cases was elicited by a software company and is still being extended[5]. By now we have examples for lawyers, midwives, tax adviser offices, travel agencies, insurance agencies, engineering offices, software companies, medical practices, construction companies, etc. Additional cases can easily be elicited when the configurator is being used: interesting examples configured from scratch can be retained as new cases.

Good candidates for subcases are the different contexts, namely individual branch offices, individual work places, infrastructures, PBX, and computer systems. Theoretically, these cases could be further decomposed along the horizontal layers of our reference model, but this would be counter-intuitive for consultants.

Case Representation

To avoid additional transformation steps and to simplify the integration of CBR and ROC our cases are represented as intermediate configurations of our from-scratch solver. This is a list of balance sheets, which are tables juxtaposing the components offering and needing specific resources. For smaller cases that correspond to a partial configuration balance sheets can be obtained by configuring their components and recording the remaining resource offers and needs. As a result, we get a kind of a complex component. Figure 2 visualizes the process. Rectangles correspond to components, circles to resource offers or needs.

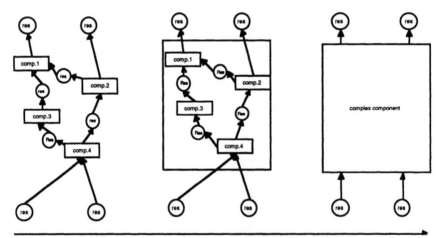

Fig.2. A case turned into a composite component.

Figure 3 gives a concrete example. The case is containing the configuration of a PC that is turned into a composite component "PC for internet services" with the open resource needs "network access" and resource offers "ftp services" and " internet service". Indeed this process of understanding cases as composite components is a kind of abstraction. It is the key to our approach to case-based configuration, as we will see in 6.2.

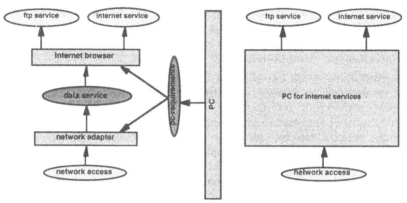

Fig.3. A configuration of a PC (left) as a composite PC component (right).

Case Indexing

Which cases to retrieve depends on context, on the purpose they shall serve. Different purposes may require different indexes for retrieval. For automatic retrieval, cases are sought that best balance the resource needs of the current configuration. This requires a matching of the balance sheets of the case and of the current configuration. So our similarity metric for automatic retrieval should regard how complex a case will be to adapt.

Manual retrieval is useful for specification, because the consultant may look for a good starting point, for a set of alternatives, for a specific alternative, etc. To meet these open-ended demands, we add a set of derived descriptors to the cases. Some of them can be inferred automatically from the case balance sheets: telecommunication networks used, number of offices, number and kind of network accesses, computer networks used, kind of private branch exchanges (PBX), used computer architecture (client-server, ...). Other descriptors must be elicited manually: profession, number of employees, a short verbal characteristic of the system, security, robustness, reliability, extensibility, etc. Providing this information is optional. Remembering that cases are seen as composite components, we can now use the descriptors of cases like the attributes of components. This observation is used for the selection of cases during specification.

5 Interactive Specification

Our configurator is a highly interactive system. It allows the user to incrementally specify the desired system to some degree, and then ask the configurator to extend indicated parts of the configuration. One of the subtasks typically performed by the user is the selection of concrete components. For each components, alternatives may

346

be specified, especially when they are indistinguishable as to their resource needs and offers, e.g. color or costs.

As mentioned in section 2, small telecooperation systems would typically be specified by selecting some concrete components, or sets of alternative components like all fax machines with a particular transmission rate. For complex systems, one would select a complex case or parts from different complex cases as a starting point. For both selection tasks we use a single, flexible table mechanism using the provided understanding of cases as complex components. It is introduced for concrete components in 5.1 and applied to cases in 5.2.

5.1 Selection of Components

Components in our model have a set of features or attributes. In our table, the rows are for features and the columns for components. Features can be composite so that rows can be unfolded (to subfeatures) or folded (to composite features). The columns and rows displayed are automatically changed: components disappear when they do not satisfy the selected features, and they reappear otherwise. Vice versa, selecting components may change the features displayed, dropping all non-discriminating ones. Also, there are elaborate redo mechanisms [Beilken+].

For example, for hardware or software components there are features like color, price, or offered functionality (figure 4). If the customer wants a fax machine with a transmission rate of 14.4 Kbit/s, s/he restricts the feature "offered functionality" to fax service.

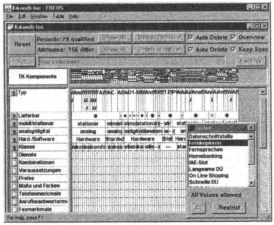

Fig.4. Component table with 79 rows and 156 columns.

Then all components which do not offer a fax service are deleted. The resulting table is displayed in the left hand side of figure 5. Here you see a table with eleven columns. Each column displays three features of a certain fax machine.

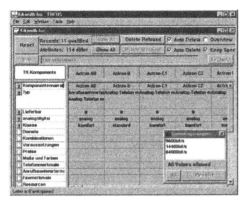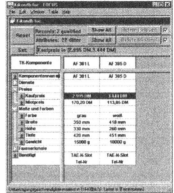

Fig.5. Component table after restricting the feature offered functionality (left) and after restricting the feature transmission rate (right).

After restricting the transmission rate to 14.4 Kbit/s, again several components are deleted and just two fax machines are left. This is displayed in the right of figure 5.

5.2 Selection of Cases

Among the multiple descriptors of a case not all will be relevant for a particular query. Especially for manual retrieval, users must be able to select and change their criteria easily. Therefore, we need a flexible retrieval mechanism. We reuse the described table mechanism to select cases, complete telecooperation systems, and subcases like PBX, computers etc. There is a row for each case characteristic (we have composite characteristics, too) and there is a column for every case. Since only relevant cases and features are displayed, the table mechanism provides a compact, comparative survey at a glance. In Figure 6 thirteen qualified cases are displayed and a possibility for a further restriction is given in the selection menu.

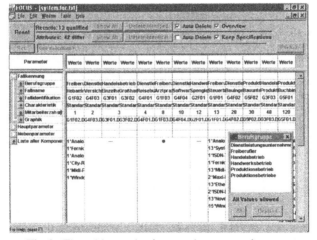

Fig.6. The table mechanism used as a case-browser.

When a new problem has been solved from-scratch, the resulting configuration can be added to the cases and displayed in the table. The user can easily supply any missing characteristics by editing empty fields.

A manually retrieved case can be reused manually be selecting parts, copying and pasting them to the configuration at hand. For automatic reuse we need the knowledge why components were selected and combined in this particular way. This is exactly the knowledge provided by their resource needs and offers. Therefore we apply our ROC for adaptation.

6 Integration of CBR in the Configuration Process

With the addition of cases the question is to combine our resource-oriented configurator with automatic retrieval and adaptation of the cases elicited for manual selection. One possibility is the use of a blackboard architecture. Therefore we would build our two knowledge sources, the resource-oriented configurator and the case-based reasoner. Furthermore we would have to define the blackboard to handle the interaction among the knowledge sources and last but not least a set of control modules to monitor the changes on the blackboard and to decide which actions to take next. Instead of such a loose coupling we propose a new approach which exploits an inherent similarity between the two methods. The result is a simple, amalgamated and new method for case-enhanced configuration.

This method and another idea to adapt cases are described in the rest of this paper. For details on ROC and CBR the reader is referred to the literature [Heinrich&Jüngst91], [Kleine-Büning&Stein94], [Kolodner93].

6.1 Components as Cases?

ROC	CBR

Input:
    a list of balance sheets, open resource offers, and requests
Procedure:
    while there is an open request do:
    1. a) choose a resource requirement to be balanced next;
    b) search all components that could balance the resource requirement;
    c) choose the best among them;
    2. include the component and balance all its resource offers and requirements;
    enddo
Output:
    the solution
	Input:
	    current situation
	Procedure:
	
	    1. Case Retrieval:
	    a) describe (index) situation:
	    b) search for cases with matching index;
	    c) select best case;
	    2. Case adaptation
	
	Output:
	    the solution

Tab.1. ROC and CBR

To motivate our new method, we start with a comparison of ROC and CBR as juxtaposed in table 1 and try to interpret ROC as CBR. That means we assume that components are a very simple kind of cases. Then choosing the next resource requirement can be viewed as a description (index) of the current situation, which is a resource requirement. The next step "search all components that could balance the resource requirement" corresponds to the retrieval of all cases with a matching index. Among them, we have to choose the best case. This is our best component.

So we see that ROC steps 1 a) and b) are a simple form of case retrieval. ROC step 2 is indeed the adaptation step. By including the selected component and balancing its resources we are fitting it into the current situation. This leads to a new situation. The enclosing loop in ROC is just an iteration of CBR.

Interpreting ROC as CBR does not help much, since we already have the configurator but not the case-based reasoner. If, vice versa, we could interpret CBR as ROC we could use our configurator for case-based reasoning. To do this we have to interpret cases as components.

6.2 Cases as Components?

Our cases can contain complete configurations, contexts, or any other partial configurations. Each of them satisfies some external resource requirements and all, except for the complete configurations, have some resource demands to be satisfied externally. Therefore we can describe all cases by their external resource balances. This is a key observation, because all ROC knows about its components is their (external) resource balance. To ROC it makes no difference whether a computer, say, is in reality a complex configuration of hard- and software. Therefore we can interpret our cases as (composite) components. This interpretation was illustrated in figures 2 and 3.

6.3 Amalgamated Case-Based Resource-Oriented Configuration

Table 2 presents CBROC, our amalgamated method for case-enhanced resource-oriented configuration. It iteratively retrieves (elementary or composite) components and adapts them to the current context.

CBROC
Input:
current situation
Procedure:
while(there is an open balance sheet)
do
1. a) describe (index) current situation ;
b) search all components with a matching index
c) select the best among them
2. adapt this component
enddo
Output:
the solution

Tab.2. CBROC

If we replace each occurrence of "component" by "case", we obtain iterated CBR. If we specialize "component" to "elementary component", "describe current situation" to "select an open resource requirement", specialize "matching" to "satisfying the resource requirement", and specialize "adapt" to "adding the component and balancing", we obtain ROC. But we deliberately used the terminology from CBR. It gives us the chance to think about new interpretations which may be less restrictive. Here are three suggestions.

(1) There may be better ways to characterize the current situation than through a single open resource requirement. We could take several or all open resource demands, we could even take the resource offers and thus increase the precision of retrieval. In principle, we could take any of the case characteristics introduced for manual retrieval, provided it can be generated automatically. (2) As explained in 6.2, we can retrieve

elementary components or composite ones (i.e. cases). (3) And for adaptation, we have at least two alternatives.

6.4 Adaptation by Copy and Paste

The straightforward way of reusing cases is to treat cases as (composite) components. We just add their components to the current situation and balance their open resource demands and offers, as is done in ordinary ROC. But this approach may not be optimal. The case may offer more resources than are needed, and then it may well contain unnecessary components. ROC will not recognize them because ROC builds monotonically increasing configurations. A special optimization step would be needed. Better, we could avoid the addition of redundant components.

6.5 Adaptation by Causal Explanation

In order to avoid redundancies ROC must configure a solution from scratch. So we cannot use a case as a prefabricated part. But we can use cases as warehouses or quarries to reduce the search space. More precisely, we can use cases to guide ROC in selecting its candidate components. Therefore, we do not add the components of the case directly to the current situation but into a library of preferred components. This library was originally introduced in order to prefer components preselected by the user to those in the library of all components. Now we interpret the case as a set of recommendations.

Adaptation consists of configuring by preferring the recommended components according to the needs of the current situation. It stops when no more resource requests can be fulfilled by the recommended components or when all of them have been integrated. Since a preferred component is included only if it satisfies an open demand, there are no redundant components and a subsequent optimization step is avoided.

Depending on how well the retrieved case fits the current configuration, all or only some of its components will be included, and they may be included to satisfy different resource needs. When a resource need cannot be satisfied by a preferred component, there are two possibilities. We can first satisfy another need or we can retrieve a non-preferred component. The first alternative means that adaptation will be finished before non-adaptive configuration is continued, the second alternative allows interleaving adaptation with non-adaptive configuration. In particular the adaptation of several cases can be interleaved.

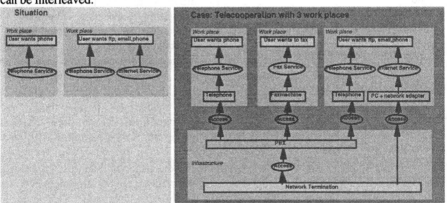

Fig.7. A situation (left) and its matching case (right).

An example is given in figure 7. The user has specified the situation given on the left hand side, the matching case is displayed at the right. The case then is used as a warehouse of components for further configuration. In figure 8 the result of the adaptation step is shown. There is just one component left in the warehouse and a correct configuration is obtained.

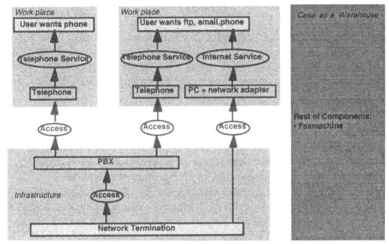

Fig.8. Configuration after adaptation .

Our first alternative for case adaptation in 6.4 is just plain copying and pasting. There is no real adaptation, just integration by balancing. The second alternative could be compared to adaptation by replay where the way a solution was found is replayed [Haig&Veloso95]. But indeed we just give a recommendation for the configuration process. So we construct a new causality for the components from the case. It may or may not turn out to coincide with the causality of the old configuration. Even though the idea is so simple, it has the potential to fit cases nearly perfectly into the actual situation. It can interleave cases, and process cases of any size or quality.

7 Conclusions

This paper presented three simple but appealing ideas for how to enhance configuration by cases. The baseline is an interactive, incrementally operating resource-balancing configurator.

By enhancing it with cases that can be used manually, via an intelligent table, and automatically, by the configurator, the system can be turned into an interactive specification and configuration tool and thus cross the borderline between routine design and non-routine specification.

The second idea concerns the use of cases by the configurator. The key was to recognize resource-balancing configuration and case-based reasoning as instances of a single, more general method. As a consequence, the best of both methods can be used for an amalgamated approach: Cases are treated like (composite) components, component selection is based on more general concepts of suitability, and component integration can be replaced by more flexible adaptation mechanisms.

The third idea concerns the adaptation mechanism. The straightforward solution of adding all components of a case to the evolving configuration may result in redundancies. To avoid them, components must be configured individually, so that they are added only when needed. This is achieved by considering a case as a set of recommendations for components to be configured. Taken as such, cases of different size and quality can be reused and their adaptation be interleaved with each other and with normal configuration.

So far the user interface with the manual retrieval component for our cases is implemented. Also a domain-independent resource-balancing configurator is implemented by a set of logical constraints, which are interpreted by a logical constraint-solver [Emde+96]. Great parts of our domain knowledge have already been modeled. A set of cases is elicited and available for manual retrieval. Future work will concern similarity and retrieval: what makes two balance sheets fit or complement each other and how can this suitability concept be computed fast? At the time of the EWCBR conference we will be able to report on first evaluations.

References

[Aamodt&Veloso95] A.Aamodt, M.Veloso: Case-Based Reasoning Research and Development. In Proceedings of ICCBR-95, Lecture Notes in AI 1010, Springer Verlag 1995

[Amadi95] P.Amadi: Adaptation by Active Autonomous Objects (AAAO). In K.Boerner (ed): Modules for design support, FABEL Report 35, GMD, Sankt Augustin, 1995

[Beilken+] C.Beilken, T.Berlage, M. Spenke: FOCUS: The interactive Table for Product Comparison and Selection, to be published.

[Böhm&Uellner96] A.Böhm, S.Uellner: Application-Specific Configuration of Telecommunciation Systems. In Proceedings of the Ninth International Conference on Industrial & Engineering Applications of Artifical Intelligence & Expert Systems, 1996

[Brown&Chandrasekaran89] D.C. Brown, B. Chandrasekaran: Design Problem Solving: Knowledge Structures and Control Strategies. Morgan Kaufmann Publishers, ISBN 0-273-08766-5, 1989

[Coulon95] C.-H. Coulon. Automatic indexing, retrieval and reuse of topologies in architectural layouts. In CAAD Futures '95, Proceedings of the Fifth International Conference on Computer-Aided Architectural Design Futures, Singapore, 1995. S. 577-586.

[Dermott82] J. Mc Dermott: R1: A Rule-Based Configurer of Computer Systems. In Artificial Intelligence (19) 1982, p.39-88, 1982

[Domeshek&Kolodner93] E.Domeshek, J.Kolodner: Using the points of large cases. AI EDAM 93 7(2), 87-96, 1993.

[Emde+96] W. Emde, C.Beilken, J.Börding, W.Orth, U.Petersen, J.Rahmer, M.Spenke, A.Voss, S.Wrobel: Configuration of Telecommunication Systems in KIKon. To appear in Proceedings AAAI 1996 Fall Symposium Workshop: Configuration. MIT Cambridge, Massachusetts, USA

	(November 1996), R. Weigel, B. Faltings, E. Freuder (eds.), AAAI 1996
[Faltings&Weigel94]	Constraint-based knowledge representation for configuration systems. Technical Report No. TR-94/59, EPFL Lausanne, 1994
[Günter95]	A.Günter: Wissensbasiertes Konfigurieren: Ergebisse aus dem Projekt PROKON. ISBN 3-929037-96-3, Infix Verlag, Sankt Augustin, 1995
[Haig&Veloso95]	K.Z.Haig, M.Veloso: Route Planning by Analogy. In [Aamodt&Veloso95]
[Heinrich&Jüngst91]	M.Heinrich, E. Jüngst: A resource-based paradigm for the configuring of technical systems from modular components. In Proc. CAIA_91, pp257-264.
[Kleine-Büning&Stein94]	H.Kleine Büning, B.Stein: Knowledge-Based Support Within Configuration and Design Tasks. In Proc. ESDA`94, London, pp 435-441, 1994
[Kolodner93]	J. Kolodner: Case-Based Reassoning, Morgan Kaufmann Publishers, ISBN-1-55860-237-2,1993
[Mittal&Falkenhainer90]	Dynamic Constraint Satisfaction Problems. In Proc. of AAAI-90, pages 25-32, Boston, MA, 1990
[Oxman94]	R.E.Oxman: Precedents in Design: a computational model for the organization of precedent knowledge. Design Studies 17 (2),pp.117-134, 1994
[Purvis&Pu95]	L.Purvis, P.Pu: Adaptation using constraint satisfaction techniques. In [Aamodt&Veloso95], pp. 289 - 300.
[Rahmer&Sprenger96]	J.Rahmer, M.Sprenger: Vom strukturorientierten zum ressourcenorientierten Konfigurieren. In Proceedings of 10th Workshop "Planen und Konfigurieren" 1996
[Smith+95]	I. Smith, C.Lottaz, B.Faltings: Spatial composition using cases: IDIOM. In [Aamodt&Veloso95], pp. 88 - 97
[Smyth&Keane95]	B.Smyth and M. Keane: Experiments on Adaptation-Guided Retrieval in Case-Based Design. In [Aamodt&Veloso95], pp. 313 - 324
[Telekom94]	Telekom: Das ISDN-Anwenderbuch. ISBN 3-8203-0308-1, 1994
[Voss96a]	A.Voss: How to solve complex problems with cases. To appear in Engineering Applications of Artificial Intelligence, Special Issue AI in Design, 1996
[Voss96b]	A.Voss: Towards a methodology for case adaptation. To appear in Proc. ECAI'96 W. Wahlster (ed), Chichester, John Wiley and Sons, 1996
[Voss96c]	Voß, A.: Design specialists in FABEL. In: Case-based design (eds. Maher, Pu), Lawrence Erlbaum Associates, Cambridge MA, to appear 1996, 30 pages.

Adaptation Cost as a Criterion for Solution Evaluation

Juho Rousu and Robert J. Aarts

VTT Biotechnology and Food Research
P.O.Box 1500, FIN-02044 VTT, Finland
{Juho.Rousu,Robert.Aarts}@vtt.fi

Abstract. In most case-based systems, the best case is selected by calculating similarities between the surface features of the cases. Sometimes, the most similar case is not the one that is the easiest to adapt. On the other hand, judging the adaptation effort can be tedious. In this paper, we propose case-adaptability to be used as an evaluation criterion as opposed to using it in the case-retrieval phase. Our method can be seen to combine the computational effectiveness of similarity-based retrieval with the better quality solutions of adaptation-guided retrieval.

1. Introduction

The traditional approach to the case-based reasoning has been to retrieve the best case from the casebase by using the surface features associated with the cases. The technique of nearest-neighbor matching is employed in many CBR systems (Kolodner 1993). The case that is deemed to be the nearest to the problem at hand, is selected as the ball-park solution, which is then adapted. An implicit assumption that is present in such methods is that the most similar case in the casebase is also the most adaptable. As noted by Smyth and Keane (1995), this assumption is not always valid; it may even be impossible to adapt the proposed ball-park solution. Similarity metrics often assume that the surface features are independent. This assumption is rarely true, hence interdependencies between surface features are left unnoticed. Unnecessarily large adaptations may result when the goodness of the cases is judged by similarity metrics alone.

In case-based planning systems, adaptation is always a step into an unknown neighborhood. The plan of the ball-park solution can be seen as a 'safe' point in the search space; the outcome of the case is known. Any adaptation to the plan increases the uncertainty about the feasibility of the plan to the new situation. Making large adaptations to the plan reliably requires that our model of the domain is very good. Most often, this kind of models cannot be constructed. Instead, we must resort to incomplete and imprecise models. On the other hand, if a complete and precise model of the domain is available, there is no need for CBR or any other AI methods at all!

Independent of the nature of the model used for adaptation, adapting as little as possible seems to be the natural way to go. The model, even how weak it may be, is likely to incorporate domain knowledge that is useful for adaptation. In contrast, the similarity metrics rarely take any specifities of the application domain into account. Hence, basing the selection of the ball-park case on the required amount of adaptation seems to be a more sound approach than relying on a surface-similarity based method.

An ideal way to take adaptability of the cases into account is to use adaptation-guided retrieval (AGR) as suggested by Smyth and Keane (1995). AGR methods are particularly effective when prediction of the adaptability can be done significantly more quickly than actually performing the adaptations. In such situations it is possible to quickly filter out all the cases that are difficult to adapt or non-adaptable. Obviously, efficient use of AGR requires explicit adaptation knowledge and well-defined criteria for adaptability.

Unfortunately, the above conditions are not fulfilled in the bioprocess planning domain (Aarts 1992, Aarts & Rousu 1996) considered in this paper. In this domain we typically have casebases that are relatively homogeneous on the surface, since the case features consist of standard measurements and specifications, and the plans are constructed from a limited set of actions. Hence, we typically have large numbers of potentially adaptable cases. However, below the surface, the bioprocess planning domain is very complex and the planning problems are hard to decompose: a minor adaptation to the case for fixing one problem may cause several other problems. Consequently, predicting the adaptability is essentially as difficult as actually adapting the cases. In a domain like that, calculating adaptability scores for cases that are totally dissimilar to the new case seems to be an unnecessary large effort; in any case we expect that the distances between surface feature values correlate to some extent with adaptability.

In this paper we propose a case-based planning method that combines similarity-based retrieval with evaluation based on *adaptation cost*. In our method, similarity-based retrieval is used for ordering the cases. An adaptation algorithm then calculates the adaptation cost for each case, in decreasing order of similarity, until a special *stopping criterion* is reached. The plan that was adapted by the least amount is returned as the solution. A necessary component for our approach is defining the adaptation cost of a plan. We base our method on *edit distance* (Wagner & Fischer 1974), a measure that defines the distance between two sequences in terms of *edit operations*, such as *insertions*, *deletions* and *changes*. Since the plans we consider are action sequences, edit distance fits the scheme well.

As application domain we consider bioprocess planning. The applicability of our method, however, is in no way restricted to that domain. The aim in bioprocess planning is to make end-products of constant quality even if the raw materials and production environment varies. Complete recipes, including the ingredients, the production environment, the used process parameter profiles and the product specification, are stored as cases. The cases are automatically adapted using a semi-qualitative model of the bioprocess.

The remainder of this article is organized as follows. In section 2 we describe the domain that we are interested in, namely batch-wise planning of bioprocesses. In section 3 we describe our method for evaluating cases in general level, in section 4 we define the distance measures and in section 5 we present some preliminary experiments.

2. Bioprocess Planning Using Case-Based Methods

A usual goal in bioprocess planning is to obtain products that are of as even quality as possible. Achieving this goal is hindered by several factors. The most common cause of difficulty is that the quality of raw materials varies. Another one is that production schedules may force the plant to use different equipment at different times. These changes in the production environment cause variations in the quality of the product.

To compensate the variations in the production environment, the process should be somehow adapted. On-line control of bioprocesses is difficult for two reasons: Firstly, bioprocesses tend to be sensitive to their past. Failures cannot be fixed after they have happened. Secondly, adequate on-line sensors are not available in many cases. Therefore, the process must be planned in advance, and the potential problems must be taken into account before the batch is started.

From a planning point of view, bioprocess recipes are quite difficult. A minor change to the value of some parameter may result in large, undesired changes in the outcome in the process. For that reason, it is typical of the bioprocess industry that process recipes are not changed very often; recipe modification is perceived as risky. In other words, the plants do not optimize their recipes. Only when severe problems with several batches have occurred, the recipe is changed. Consequently, systematic adaptation knowledge is lacking and recipe adaptation ends up to be an iterative trial and error process.

On the other hand, production data is usually recorded systematically. Hence, ample process experience in the form of successful and unsuccessful recipes is available in corporate databases. As should be clear from this discussion, case-based planning fits this scheme very well: as theoretical knowledge of the process is lacking, building and tuning a model-based planner can be a tedious task. In contrast, a casebase is rather easy to construct, since the production batches are usually well monitored and analyzed, and the measurements are stored in databases anyway.

For recipe adaptation, a large body of biotechnological information is applicable to many processes. An approximate, qualitative model (Cohn 1989) of the bioprocess planning domain[1] can be constructed from this knowledge. Obviously, the model is process specific and has to be constructed anew for each different bioprocess. With the case-based approach we can manage with such a general, qualitative, model of the process. Since the system learns its environment from recipes that were used in production, the model does not need to be as complete as it would otherwise have to be. On the other hand, the suggested adaptations are not so accurate as the ones given by a carefully tuned quantitative model would be. For that reason, avoiding unnecessarily large adaptations is important. The aim of this paper is to develop methods for quantifying the adaptability, or adaptation cost, of the cases and using the methods effectively in terms of computational resources.

---

[1] See Aarts & Rousu (1996) for a description of this model.

3. Evaluation of Cases Using Adaptation Cost

In an industrial setting the casebase consisting of different kinds of recipes may be large. Calculating adaptations for all the cases is clearly not possible. Instead, a filtering scheme is needed. In adaptation-guided retrieval (Smyth & Keane 1995), the filter is based on predicting the adaptability of the cases. This is not feasible in bioprocess planning, since there does not seem to be a quick way of judging the adaptability: Typically, most of the cases in the casebase are adaptable, only the amount of adaptation needed varies. Rapid prediction of the amount of adaptation needed does not seem to be possible. Hence, a different filtering mechanism is needed. We base our filter on the similarity of surface features.

Our planning algorithm is outlined in figure 1. We use the similarity scores to sort the cases. The most similar case is subjected to adaptation first. Remaining cases are treated in the same way in descending order of similarity. A user defined stopping criterion is used; When adaptation cost rises over the best cost found by a fraction δ, the adaptation-performing loop is exited and the cheapest plan in terms of adaptation is returned. Alternatively, the user has always the option to exit the search any time; the best plan that was found so far is returned as the solution.

Although adaptation of the plans using the qualitative model is more difficult than calculating similarities, that is not a problem for our algorithm, since it typically examines only a couple of cases in the adaptation and evaluation phase. Since the casebase is not examined in full, we are not guaranteed to find the case with the absolutely best score. Since the most similar cases are always evaluated, we expect

ConstructPlan(newCase, CaseBase, δ)

1. **For each** *oldCase* ∈ *CaseBase* **do begin**
2.   Compute a similarity score *s(newCase, oldCase)*
3. **end;**
4. Sort the *CaseBase* by the calculated similarity scores.
5. *bestPlan:* = ∅ *, bestCost :=* ∞
6. **For each** *oldCase* ∈ *CaseBase* **do begin**
7.   *newPlan := AdaptPlan(oldCase, newCase).*
8.   Calculate adaptation cost *d(newCase, oldCase).*
9.   **If** *d(newCase, oldCase)* < *bestCost* **then**
10.   *bestPlan := newPlan*
11.   *bestCost := d(newCase, oldCase)*
12.   **Else If** *(d(newCase, oldCase)* > *(bestCost)×(1+δ))*
13.   **or** (user wants to quit) **then break;**
14. **end.**
15. **Return** *bestPlan.*

Figure 1: A planning algorithm with evaluation based on adaptation cost.

to obtain good quality recipes, nonetheless. In comparison to an algorithm that picks only the most similar case for adaptation, we always obtain at least as good solutions and can do significantly better in some situations.

4. Measuring Adaptation Cost

In the bioprocess planning domain, the plan is simply a sequence of actions. Each action is an instance of an *action type*. An action type has an associated set of parameters that define the action. Hence, each action is defined by two aspects: its type and a vector of *action parameter* values. For most action types the parameters are real numbers.

The bioprocess plans that we consider consist of two types of actions: Most actions are targeted to alter reactor conditions such as *temperature*. The second type of actions are additions of some ingredients to the reactor.

As the plans are sequences of actions, it makes sense to define the distance between two plans in terms of *edit distance* (Wagner & Fischer 1974), a measure developed by the string matching community to quantify the distance of two strings. The edit distance is computed as a minimal sum of *edit operations,* namely *insertions, deletions and changes,* that are required to transform a sequence into another. Relatively efficient dynamic programming algorithms for computing the edit distance exist, see e.g. Ukkonen (1985). Note that these algorithms are not needed in our application. The qualitative model is used for generating the adaptation operations and there is no need to search for them using dynamic programming.[2]

In our planning problem, an original plan and the adapted plan are the two 'strings' to be compared. The actions are the 'characters'. Hence, the edit operations in this context are

- *change* of the parameters of an action, or a change of an action to another (denoted by $a{\rightarrow}b$),
- *insertion* of an action into plan ($\varnothing{\rightarrow}b$), and
- *deletion* of an action from the plan ($a{\rightarrow}\varnothing$).

The cost of inserting and deleting and action is the same: $cost(\varnothing{\rightarrow}b)$ $=cost(a{\rightarrow}\varnothing)=1$. The cost of changing an action to another depends on the action types: $cost(a{\rightarrow}b) = 1$, if a and b are of different types, and $cost(a{\rightarrow}b) = m/n$, when the actions are of the same type; m is the number of parameters with different values for a and b, n is the total number of parameters for the action type. The sum of the costs of the individual adaptations is the adaptation cost of the plan.

The above defined measure is unbiased with respect to the number of parameters of the action type. Changing, for example, the values of half of the action parameters costs always 0.5, independent of the total number of parameters.

One could object the simplicity of the measure; it does not take into account the magnitudes of the parameter changes. Indeed, some quantitative properties could be embedded to the measures. We must keep in mind, though, that since our model is qualitative, the adaptation magnitudes suggested by the model cannot possibly be

---

[2] These algorithms could, however, be used as a method for organizing the casebase, by placing similar plans in the proximity of one another.

very accurate. Hence, exact measurement of the adaptation magnitudes seems somewhat inappropriate. Furthermore, a simple quantitative measure would not necessarily make things better; an adaptation that seems large may actually affect the process less than another adaptation that seems small. Another problem in defining distance metrics is that adaptations of the early stages often have greater effect on the outcome of the process than adaptations of the later stages. Thus, it seems to be necessary to utilize the available domain knowledge in the design of more elaborate distance measures.

5. Empirical Evaluation

We have implemented the adaptation-based evaluation method in a bioprocess planning system. In a preliminary experiment we compared the new method to the performance of a similarity-based retrieval method. The casebase consisted of some 15 recipes for mashing, a process that is the first step in the production of beer.

The results of the preliminary experiments were encouraging. The new method was able to find cases that required less adaptations than what the most similar case required. An example of this situation is depicted in figures 2 and 3: In figure 2, the adapted plan for the new recipe ATJT2H is shown against the plan of the most similar case in the casebase, ATJ15. Three parameter changes were suggested by the qualitative model, causing a total adaptation cost of 1.5. Figure 3 depicts the situation in which the plan was adapted from a less similar case ATJ09. Only one parameter-change, of cost 0.5, was required. In all three cases the raw material, malt, was the same. The specifications for the product, the wort, were identical for the cases ATJ15 and ATJT2H, the test case. The case ATJ09 had a different wort specification.

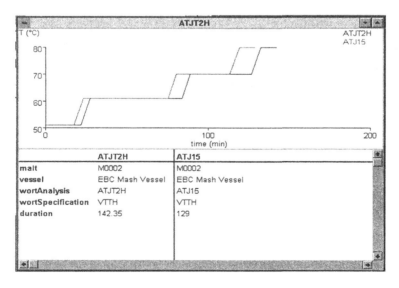

Figure 2. The plan for recipe ATJT2H when adapted from the most similar case ATJ15.

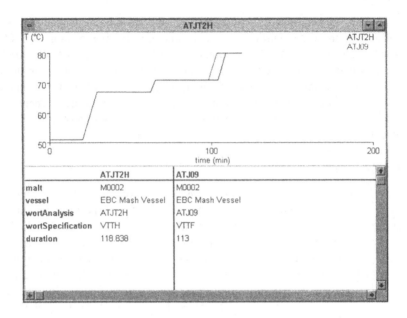

Figure 3. The plan for recipe ATJT2H, adapted from the plan of most adaptable case ATJ09.

In this case, one explanation for this excellent performance is that the case ATJ09 was, in fact, somewhat unsuccessful; the end-product, wort, contained too little sugars compared to the specification VTTF. However, the wort would have met the corresponding requirement in specification VTTH, the specification associated with the case ATJT2H, quite well. Hence only one adaptation is needed.

The fact that the outcome of the case ATJ09 is very good with respect to VTTH is left unnoticed by the retrieval algorithm, as it only compares the similarities of the situations. The retrieval algorithm prefers the case ATJ15 which has the same raw materials and the same wort specification. As the resulting wort of case ATJ15 was not perfectly in line with the specifications, as many as three adaptations were suggested by the domain model in an attempt to get rid of the deviations.

6. Conclusions and Future Work

Similarity metrics have been studied rather extensively in the context of case retrieval. The potential of a similar approach for the solution evaluation phase has, however, been left unrealized. We developed a method that tries to quantify the adaptability by using an edit distance metric as means to measure the adaptation cost. We use the metric in case evaluation: the best recipe is the one requiring the least amount of adaptation.

Our method makes a compromise between the computational efficiency of the similarity-based retrieval methods with the good quality solutions of adaptation-guided retrieval. By setting the stopping criterion for the evaluation algorithm appropriately, the balance between quality and speed can be controlled by the user.

Obviously, as the casebase grows, more and more cases will be examined before the stopping criterion will terminate the adaptation-performing loop, provided that the threshold δ is kept constant. This may potentially have an effect on the efficiency of the algorithm. Case generalization techniques may be used to circumvent this problem. Note that tightening the threshold δ as the casebase grows is not a good idea, since the really alternative ball-park cases will probably drop out.

The preliminary experiments show that the method can actually find better quality solutions in terms of required amount of adaptation. Comprehensive tests in laboratory-scale are still needed, though, in determining the actual benefits to recipe quality. Also, the effect of more elaborate distance measures is still to be investigated. A possible direction is to incorporate some of the process knowledge that is contained in the qualitative model into the distance measures.

Acknowledgments

The authors wish to thank the anonymous reviewers for their suggestions.

References

Aarts, R. J. (1992). *Knowledge-based systems for bioprocesses*. Technical Research Centre of Finland, Publications 120, 116 p.

Aarts, R. J. & Rousu, J. (1996). Towards CBR for Bioprocess Planning. In this volume.

Cohn, A. G. (1989). Approaches to qualitative reasoning. *Artificial Intelligence Rev.* **3**, pp. 177-232.

Kolodner, J. (1993). *Case-Based-Reasoning*. Morgan-Kaufmann Publishers Inc., San Mateo CA, 668 p.

Smyth, B. & Keane, M.T. (1995). Experiments on Adaptation-Guided Retrieval In Case-Based Design. In *Proceedings of First International Conference on Case-Based Reasoning ICCBR-95*, Veloso M., Aamodt, A., (eds.). Springer-Verlag, 1995, pp. 313-324.

Ukkonen, E. (1985). Algorithms for approximate string matching. *Information and Control* **64**, pp. 100-118.

Wagner, R. & Fischer, M. (1974). The string-to-string correction problem. *J. Assoc. Comput. Mach.* **21**, pp. 168-178.

Fish and Shrink. A Next Step Towards Efficient Case Retrieval in Large Scaled Case Bases

Jörg Walter Schaaf

GMD – Artificial Intelligence Research Division
e-mail:Joerg.Schaaf@gmd.de
Sankt Augustin, Germany

Abstract. Keywords: Case-Based Reasoning, case retrieval, case representation
This paper deals with the retrieval of useful cases in case-based reasoning. It focuses on the questions of what "useful" could mean and how the search for useful cases can be organized. We present the new search algorithm *Fish and Shrink* that is able to search quickly through the case base, even if the aspects that define usefulness are spontaneously combined at query time. We compare *Fish and Shrink* to other algorithms and show that most of them make an implicit *closed world assumption*. We finally refer to a realization of the presented idea in the context of the prototype of the FABEL-Project[1].
The scenery is as follows. Previously collected cases are stored in a large scaled case base. An expert describes his problem and gives the aspects in which the requested case should be similar. The similarity measure thus given spontaneously shall now be used to explore the case base within a short time, shall present a required number of cases and make sure that none of the other cases is more similar.
The question is now how to prepare the previously collected cases and how to define a retrieval algorithm which is able to deal with spontaneously user-defined similarity measures.

1 Motivation

Suppose two cases in your domain have just been considered similar with respect to a certain aspect, and just a few minutes later they have to be regarded as to be considerably dissimilar because another aspect is now being regarded.
If that cannot happen in your domain, then a lot of approaches making use of static similarities are available to organize your case base and it would be better to take one of them to realize your retrieval task.
None of them will fit the requirements if similarity between two cases depends on the context in which retrieval is evoked. The reason is that once built up,

---
[1] This research was supported by the German Ministry for Research and Technology (BMFT) within the joint project FABEL under contract no. 01IW104. Project partners in FABEL GMD – German National Research Center for Information Technologie, Sankt Augustin, BSR Consulting GmbH, München, Technical University of Dresden, HTWK Leipzig, University of Freiburg, and University of Karlsruhe.

the relations between cases in the case bases of concurrent approaches remain static over time. These relations always reflect similarity between cases which is calculated once and used to support further retrieval tasks.

The approach presented in this article will help to solve some of your problems if the following statements hold and some basic operations are computable.

- Cases in your domain are complex enough to be worth being regarded from different points of view.
- Frequently changing the point of view is essential to benefit from the knowledge stored in cases.
- Changing the point of view leads to different representations (aspects) of cases, each pointing out what emerges while looking at the cases from that point of view.
- It is possible to evaluate similarity for each pair of cases comparing the corresponding representations.
- Dissimilarity between a query and a case shrinks the possible range of similarity between that case and cases in the neighborhood.

If these preconditions are true, then the presented approach will help to organize, structure and handle your cases.

Each of the cases will be stored in all its possible and meaningful representations, ready to be compared with other cases in the case base. Similarity of all stored cases will be precalculated for each aspect and will be stored. In a retrieval situation you will have the option to select aspects that have to be regarded and to combine them in a weighted manner if more than one aspect should be regarded at a time. The spontaneously defined set of weighted aspects (your actual view on the cases) will be used to calculate similarity between your actual problem (query) and the stored cases. As a result you will get all cases of your case base that deliver useful information to solve your problem, if suitable aspects are represented and regarded in your actual view.

To prevent the user from waiting too long for a retrieval result (until all cases have been checked) a completely new retrieval algorithm is presented in this article. The main idea of this algorithm is to successively shrink the range of possible similarities between the query and an amount of cases by a few explicit tests. Each case can be represented by an interval describing this range. Several different user demands concerning the cases the user wants to get can be answered by interpreting upper and lower bounds of these intervals. The main advantage of this strategy is that the effective use of time depends on the precision the user asked for.

The following article introduces a data structure to hold case representations (aspects) and links to store aspect specific similarities between cases. We explain how changes in point of view on cases can be seen as a spontaneous and weighted combination of aspects. We show that this leads to the possibility of a context dependent redefinition of case similarity by using only low cost calculations.

2 Situation-conform assessment of similarity

What does it mean to assess similarity with respect to a certain situation? First and foremost it means that assessment should change when circumstances change. In this section, I will introduce the elements to construct a situation-specific similarity assessment. They are called "aspects" here. To work with them, cases must be accessible in a format that can be manipulated by computers. In this paper this is called the *source representation* of a case. Many approaches try to interpret or to abstract from the source representation in order to extract the main idea of a case and to make that idea comparable with those of other cases. As a result a case gets a position in a searching structure or an index.

If a position in a searching structure is precalculated, then the query guides through the structure and leads to the most similar case which is part of the structure. This kind of access only works if the meaning of all attributes remains constant throughout all case retrievals. Only then the costs for building the search structure are worthwhile. If, in contrast, spontaneous change of important attributes shall be allowed then a static search structure is not applicable.

If cases are indexed a new possibility of comparison arises. Now it is possible to state at query time which attributes are important and how important they are. There are some approaches in literature, for example [1, 6, 9], that offer spontaneous attribute weighting and try to avoid complete search. These approaches differ from the following one in some important points concerning complexity of attributes and combination.

Complexity of attributes: Attributes of collected cases are often of low complexity. This makes comparison easy. If the cases of a domain can be described sufficiently by using some attributes, then the usage of the concept described here is not indicated. Cases in the domain of building construction need complex attributes to be compared properly. The topology graph of design objects like columns, pipes or furniture is such a complex attribute. Topology of design objects is an essential criterion for reusability of a design. Representation of topology is expensive, and comparison of two topology graphs is NP-complete [14]. Because the term "attribute" hardly fits a topology graph for example, a useful but complex representation like this will be called an "aspect representation" of a case. It is not easy to describe what an aspect itself is. We found that it can be seen as an idea of how to represent a case. To find a good idea to represent cases is a hard problem. Discussion about the quality of suggestions is not the topic of this paper. To define a retrieval algorithm mentioned above, we only need a name for an aspect, a function that represents the case with respect to the aspect and a function that compares the representations of two cases.

Let Ω_0 be the space of potentially all cases in the data exchange format (we sometimes call this format the original representation). That means that each real case is a point in Ω_0.

Definition 1 aspect representation function. Let i be the name of an aspect. An aspect representation function of a case is a function $\alpha_i \colon \Omega_0 \to \Omega_i$. Ω_0 is the set of all cases in their source representation.

Ω_i is the space of all possible representations with respect to aspect i. The aspect representation function α_i assigns a point in Ω_i to each point in Ω_0. In principle the design of the aspect representation function is free but it should be designed to simplify the space and to emphasize certain attributes (the aspects) of cases. The function α_i often has the nature of a transformation or a projection, but sometimes of a knowledge intensive interpretation.

In the project FABEL a case-based reasoner was developed which offers several different tools to retrieve cases [13]. Each tool delivers useful cases under certain conditions. To make them all work together, the main ideas of these methods have been regarded as "aspects" in the sense described above.

Four main parts have been found in each of the developed retrieval methods:

- An idea of what to represent and to compare could be worthwhile.
- A function to represent cases in a specific way.
- A function to compare case representations and to state their distances in terms of a real number.
- A well suited organization of the case base that stores case representations and supports the retrieval of cases that are similar to the query with respect to the representation.

With the help of this analysis, the idea of what a case could b has been elaborated. It should be a set of representations, each regarding one interesting aspect. Figure 1 represents a case as a polyhedron with one face for each aspect.

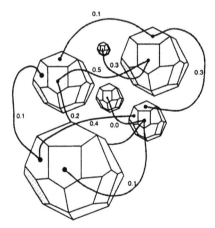

Fig. 1. The case base as a network of cases. A polyhedra corresponds to a case, a face of it to an aspect representation, the label of an edge to a calculated distance between two cases with respect to the connected aspect representations.

A case base can be seen as a network of cases. Weighted edges from face to face connect cases. The weight depends on the distance of the connected cases with respect to a certain aspect. Two cases are called (representation) neighbors with respect to an aspect, if they are connected by an edge concerning this aspect. Edges can be directed if the distance is not symmetric.

Consider the following data structure that defines cases more formal and implies a structure we call case base. It also introduces some terms used in further description.

```
case = record:
  identifier :string;
  representations-list :list of representation-node;
  mindist,maxdist : [0,1].

representation-node = record:
  aspect-name :string;
  aspect-representation :free type;
  neighbor-list :list of representation-neighbor.

representation-neighbor = record:
  reference :pointer to representation-node;
  distance : [0,1].
```

Combination: Comparison between a query and one of the collected cases is the basic operation of the retrieval task. This comparison is done stepwise by comparing aspect by aspect. We call the result of one step the *aspect distance* between two cases.

Definition 2 aspect distance. An aspect distance function δ_i is a distance function in Ω_i. For F_x and $F_y \in \Omega_0$ we abbreviate $\delta_i\big(\alpha_i(F_x), \alpha_i(F_y)\big)$ by $\delta_i(F_x, F_y)$.

The overall similarity between two cases is computed by a combination of the results coming from aspect specific comparisons. To distinguish this combination from an *aspect distance* it is called the *view distance*. The view distance is influenced by the actual importance of each contributing aspect and by the function that calculates the view distance by using the aspect distances as input.

Definition 3 view. A weight vector $\mathbf{W} = (w_1...w_n)$ with $\sum w_i = 1$ defines the "importance" for each aspect i. Each combination of weighted aspects defined by the vector $\mathbf{W}$ is called a view on a case. Aspect i belongs to the actual view if $w_i > 0$.

The importance of each aspect is given by the weight vector *view* $(\mathbf{W})$. The function to calculate the view distance is user defined. We call this function the *view distance function* or SD_{name}.

Definition 4 view distance. The view distance of two cases is defined[2] as a function $SD_{name} : \Omega_0 \times \Omega_0 \times \mathbf{W} \rightarrow [0, 1]$.

The view distance is a combination of aspect distances weighted by the view $\mathbf{W}$. Example:

$$SD_{med}(F_x, F_y, \mathbf{W}) := \sum_{i=1}^{n} w_i \delta_i (F_x, F_y)$$

If, for example, the user wants to consider a set of aspects in a weighted manner, the view distance function SD_{med} in the example above should be used. Further possible and useful view distance functions are discussed in [11]. They lead to more conservative or more creative case proposals.

View distances are calculated between cases. Some of them are of special interest for further explanation so we define them:

Definition 5 Test- and base distance and view neighbor. The view distance between query A and a test case T is called the "test distance". The view distance between test case T and one of its view neighbors V_i is called "base distance [3]". Two cases with a small view distance are called "view neighbors". As a first approach we define two cases as to be view neighbors if their view distance is below 1. As we will see, results of *Fish and Shrink* do not become incorrect by using any other threshold in [0,1].

The input to calculate the *view distance* (actual view and actual view distance function) normally changes when context or user intentions change. *Aspect distances* between two cases normally never change.

Spontaneous changes in case neighborhood (because of changing view distance) will raise difficulties in standard retrieval algorithms. It is principally impossible to precalculate static retrieval structures, like those used in search trees (for example k-d-trees [2, 16, 17]) or networks (for example, shared feature networks or discrimination networks [5]) that are based on a single evaluation of case distance.

3 Retrieval in large scaled case-bases

"Case-based reasoning will be ready for large-scale problems only when its retrieval algorithms are sufficiently robust and efficient to handle thousands and ten thousands of cases." (Kolodner in [8], page 289).

---

[2] Definition of view distances and their influence to case selection is discussed in [11]. $SD(x, x) = 0$ and SD is symmetric if all δ_i are symmetric.

[3] The notion "base distance" shall stress that this particular distance is stored in the case base.

3.1 Approaches with undeclared closed world assumption

We think that retrieval in large scaled case-bases can only be solved if memory is traded against time. The question arises what to store to speed up retrieval without limiting it too much.

In his hillclimbing approach Goos [6] stores distances between entire cases and focuses the search to the neighborhood of a case which are most promising. Other approaches based on case neighborhood are [9] and [18]. They use spreading activation to increase a score for cases with attribute values similar to the query. In the following paragraph I will show that all, [6], [9] and [18], make use of an undeclared, implicit *closed world assumption* and that this assumption is the reason for a lot of problems. The implicit *closed world assumption* is:

If similarity between two cases is not explicitly stated, then these cases are definitively different.

This assumption is not necessary and is not used by the algorithm described in section 3.2.

Goos and Lenz try to benefit from similarities stated and stored between a directly tested case and its neighbors. They use information about the closeness of cases to decide where to go on searching [6] or which cases shall be presented to the user [9]. The authors assume that similarity not stated explicitly is equivalent with stated dissimilarity. They disregard that missing similarity statements can come from at least two reasons. On the one hand missing statements can express dissimilarity, on the other hand they can express that similarity has not yet been checked. That could happen if case representation or comparison is incorrect or if cases have been left unconsidered. The problem has been discussed in both papers without having been solved.

The main idea of the algorithm that I will present here is that only a well known and proven statement of similarity to a definitely dissimilar case leads to the deferment of cases.

Missing representation of important attributes leads to *no delay* and thus to early direct test. If the definitions of dissimilarity in [6], [9] and [18] fail, it is possible that similar cases are not found. According to the definition presented here, similar cases are tested later in the process at the worst.

3.2 Fish and Shrink. Case retrieval without closed world assumption

If one wants to benefit from one direct comparison between a query and a case, a direct test should reduce search space. The *Fish and Shrink* algorithm presented here realizes that without using any *closed world assumption* like this mentioned above. It is based (like the *Fish and Sink* algorithm [12]) on a metaphor of sinking cases and cases being dragged down (Figure 2). *Fish and Shrink* relies on the following assumption:

Presumption 1 *If a case does not fit the actual query, then this may reduce the possible usefulness of its neighbors.*

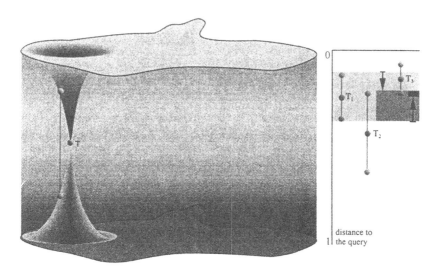

Fig. 2. Metaphor of sinking cases being dragged down by others (left). Intervals, shrinking from both ends, represent the still possible distance to the query (right).

This assumption is supported if the underlying distance function (aspect distance function) fulfills the following condition derived from the triangle inequality.

Presumption 2

$$\delta_i(A, V) \geq \delta_i(A, T) - \delta_i(T, V)$$

If the condition above is true for every triple (A, T, V) the *minimum distance* between the query and some not directly tested neighbors of the directly tested case can be stated. This means that V.mindist can be stated and eventually increased for some cases V, view neighbors of T. If a second condition is valid, an analogue reduction from the other side (V.maxdist) can be achieved. We assume:

Presumption 3

$$\delta_i(A, V) \leq \delta_i(A, T) + \delta_i(T, V)$$

If this condition is true, the interval of possible distances between query and not yet directly tested cases can be shrunk from both sides. That is what we describe with the term "shrink" in the nickname *Fish and Shrink* of the discussed algorithm. "Fishing" refers to the random access to the test case.

If one of the above conditions is violated then an error occurs. A possibility to avoid this is discussed in [11]. Figure 3 shows the algorithm *Fish and Shrink*. The idea of *Fish and Shrink* is that the view distance between the query and a test case restricts both, the minimum distance as well as a maximum distance tested case) and bring it to a single point. Additionally, the intervals of cases in the neighborhood of the tested case will be shortened.

3.3 Results from *Fish and Shrink*

Upon demand, *Fish and Shrink* supplies either all cases that are more similar than a given threshold S or delivers the k best cases optionally including a ranking or giving the exact distance for each of the k best cases.

Suppose the given threshold is S, then it is not necessary to test those cases directly whose maximum distance (maxdist) is lower than S (Figure 4a interval a). Such cases are better than S even if they are finally positioned at maxdist. With an analogue argument those cases whose minimum distance (mindist) is bigger than S (Figure 4a interval b) need not be tested. It cannot overcome the threshold S.

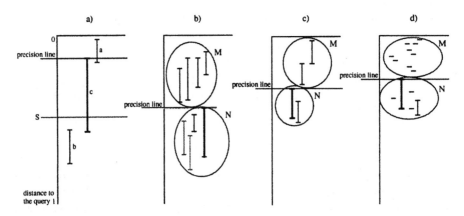

Fig. 4. User demand: all cases better than a threshold (a) and k best cases without giving the partial order of result cases (b). User demand: k best cases of the case base without (c) and with (d) exact distances between query and result cases.

Only those cases have to be tested whose intervals overlap S. The number of overlapping intervals decreases permanently because intervals become shorter. How much the number decreases after one direct test depends on the test distance and on the base distances. The bigger the test distance and the smaller the base distances, the more effective the direct test has been.

Before we give some suggestions for the predicate OK and the movement instructions for the precision line PL to realize various user requirements with *Fish and Shrink* (see Figure 3) we define some help predicates to make further terms more readable.

---

1. Let CB be a list of all cases in the case base.
2. For each case $F \in CB$ let $F.mindist := 0$ and $F.maxdist := 1$;
3. While not OK and not interrupted
   (a) move precision line PL;
   (b) choose (fish) a case T with $T.mindist$ on PL;
   (c) $T.mindist := SD(A, T, \mathbf{W})$;
   (d) $T.maxdist := T.mindist$;
   (e) $\forall$ cases V that are view neighbors of case T
       with $V.mindist \neq V.maxdist$ do
       i. $V.mindist :=$
          $MAX\Big(testdistance - basedistance, \ V.mindist\Big)$;
       ii. $V.maxdist :=$
          $MIN\Big(testdistance + basedistance, \ V.maxdist\Big)$

Fig. 3. *Fish and shrink* algorithm. OK is a predicate which is TRUE if the user demands are fulfilled (see section 3.3). PL marks an increasing distance to the query. All cases with mindist=PL are candidates for the next direct test. All cases whose complete interval is passed by PL are offered to the user.

between query and some of the neighbors of the test case. The algorithm keeps the maximal *minimum distance* and the minimal *maximum distance* for each case. The interval defined by the two values mindist and maxdist describes the range of possible distances to the query for each case. Its upper bound only decreases and the lower bound can only rise. For historical reasons, lowering the upper bounds is also called *sinking*. This term shall stress that cases with bigger mindist are regarded to be not as promising as cases with smaller ones. Both movements of boundaries are results of one direct comparison between query and a test case.

Figure 2 tries to show this on the left. It describes the behavior of a case which is at first the *view neighbor* of test case T_1 and then also *view neighbor* of test cases T_2 and T_3. By knowing the distance between the query and T_1 the interval of possible distances between V and the query can be restricted without having it tested in any way. Direct test of T_2 and T_3 further restricts this interval. The test of T_2 lowers the upper bound (increases mindist), while test of T_3 raises the lower bound (decreases maxdist). To resume, every direct test leads to a further restriction of an interval that describes the possible distances between the not yet directly tested case V and the query.

By this means, derivable guesses become more and more precise until some definitive statements become possible. The ongoing process leads to the exact distance between each case and the query if it runs until its termination. Normally the process is manually or automatically interrupted before termination obtaining the demanded results. A discussion about the best time to interrupt, depending on the demanded results, can be found in the next section. Up to interruption, each direct test will at least shorten one interval (the one of the

$$overlap\_eachother(F_i, F_j) := F_i.mindist \leq F_j.mindist \leq F_i.maxdist$$
$$\vee F_i.mindist \leq F_j.maxdist \leq F_i.maxdist$$
$$\vee F_j.mindist \leq F_i.mindist \leq F_j.maxdist$$
$$overlap(F_i, S) := F.mindist \leq S \leq F.maxdist$$
$$zero\_interval(F) := F.mindist = F.maxdist$$
$$min\_mindist(F_i, M) := F_i \in M \wedge \not\exists F_q \in M : F_q.mindist < F_i.mindist$$

$$PL := F.mindist : overlap(F, S) \wedge min\_mindist(F, CB) \wedge \neg zero\_interval(F).$$
$$OK := \forall F \in CB : \neg overlap(F, S) \vee zero\_interval(F).$$

Fig. 5. Movement of precision line and predicate OK for user demand: cases better than threshold S.

Three more types of user demands shall be discussed here to show how shrinking intervals can be interpreted. Figure 4b shows how to get the k best cases without a ranking (see Figure 4b). The rule is to continue until maxdist of k cases is passed by a line called *precision line*. The precision line is defined by the minimal value of mindist in the case base and marks this value by a line parallel to the X axis (e.g. in Figure 4).
OK and movement of the precision line for the user demand "best k cases without any ranking among them" is described in Figure 6.

$$PL := F.mindist : \neg zero\_interval(F) \wedge \exists M, N \subset CB; M \cap N = \emptyset$$
$$\wedge \forall m \in M, n \in N : m.maxdist \leq n.mindist$$
$$\wedge min\_mindist(F, N).$$
$$OK := |M| \geq k.$$

Fig. 6. Movement of precision line and predicate OK for user demand: k best cases without ranking.

If the user asks for k cases with ranking but without exact distances, *Fish and Shrink* stops if k intervals that do not overlap one another have been passed by the precision line (Figure 4c). OK and movement of the precision line is shown in Figure 7
If the user wants exact distances (and rankings) of the k best cases, *Fish and Shrink* stops if k intervals of length 0 have been passed by the precision line (Figure 4d).

$PL := F.mindist : \neg zero\_interval(F) \wedge \exists M, N \subset CB; M \cap N = \emptyset$
$\quad \wedge \forall m \in M, n \in N : m.maxdist \leq n.mindist$
$\quad \wedge min\_mindist(F, N)$
$\quad \wedge \forall m_1, m_2 \in M : \neg overlap\_eachother(m_1, m_2).$
$OK := |M| \geq k.$

Fig. 7. Movement of precision line and predicate OK for user demand: k best cases with rankings.

$PL := F.mindist : \neg zero\_interval(F) \wedge \exists M, N \subset CB; M \cap N = \emptyset$
$\quad \wedge \forall m \in M, n \in N : m.maxdist \leq n.mindist$
$\quad \wedge min\_mindist(F, N)$
$\quad \wedge \forall m \in M : zero\_interval(m).$
$OK := |M| \geq k.$

Fig. 8. Movement of precision line and predicate OK for user demand: k best cases with exact view distances to the query.

Besides the discussed results one can also activate *Fish and Shrink* to obtain the following:

- a sorted list of cases, recommending the most similar cases first;
- the best cases after a predefined run-time;
- the most promising cases at the time of a spontaneous user interruption;
- a sorted list of best cases up to the point where the quality of the next one is significantly worse than the previously recommended one;
- only one case of each group of very similar cases (a swarm), using a slightly extended algorithm as described below.

Figure 9 shows a diagram to control the ongoing process. It shows all intervals for each direct test, gives an overview to the user and supports the decision whether to interrupt *Fish and Shrink* or not.

4 How Fish and Shrink saves tests

It is an interesting question how *Fish and Shrink* manages to spare expensive direct tests and thereby keeps waiting time short. To explain that we have to look closer into two mechanisms.

First, not promising cases are sunk down so that they are tested – if at all – later in the process. Our last results from tests in the domain of Computer Aided Architectural Design (CAAD) show that *Fish and Shrink* delivers those cases early in the process which fit user specifications without testing too much. Speaking in terms of clusters, one may state that the view distance function

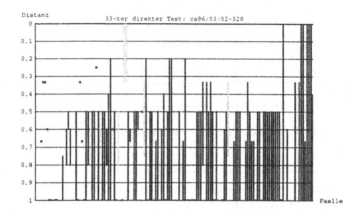

Fig. 9. A visualisation of the intervals in a test with a real database containing 150 cases, each in five different representations.

forms spontaneously a cluster and drags along all neighbors according to their individual (view) distance (see also Figure 2). This leads to a delay of a whole group of cases which can be seen as less promising.

The second mechanism is not yet discussed here and needs a closer look. Keeping with the metaphor of fishing, we call the mechanism the *swarm fishing*. The reason why it has been implemented is easy to explain by telling a joke:

Peter was asked by his teacher to give him ten animals living in Africa. After a short time of thinking he answered: monkey, lion, and ... and eight elephants.

This joke shows what humans expect when they are asked to give examples or even cases. They are expected to give *different* ones. I think it would become boring if the user of an case-based reasoning system would obtain hundreds of nearly equal cases, because he asked for all cases better than some threshold. Even if the user is clever and bounds the number it would be very unsatisfactory if all delivered cases were looking nearly equal. I think users want to get a big variety of cases, that means only one single representative for each cluster.

It is straight forward to satisfy such user demands with *Fish and Shrink*. Knowing the view distance function it is part of the algorithm to calculate the view distance between the test case and its view neighbors in order to sink (and lift) them if necessary. If this distance is recognized as to be below a certain bound, neighbors are seen to belong to the cluster (the swarm) of the test case. Close neighbors are not worthwhile to be tested in the ongoing process. In Figure 9 a case belonging to a swarm is shown in light grey color while intervals of other cases are black.

Further examination of a swarm can be evoked if the user explicitly wants to do that. Experience shows that cases in the swarm of a test case do not differ enough to provide additional information, so tests within a swarm are not recommended.

5 State of the work and outlook

The presented approach is completely worked out, formally described in [11] and implemented as a prototype. The retrieval algorithm *Fish and Shrink* delivers cases from the domain of building design that are similar in five freely combinable aspects. It is now being tested with larger case bases (about 400 cases in five different representations. Empirical results will be available by the end of 1996 ([15]). An evaluation by domain experts with respect to the quality of delivered cases is still to be done.

Up to now, we have integrated the aspects "case silhouette" [4] concerning two subsystems, "Gestalten" [10], "topological structure" [3] and a fuzzy representation of components [7] for cases in the domain of architectural design.

As an interesting additional feature, our concept allows to derive a quality assessment for aspects from working with it. The quality of an aspect could be determined by the support it gives to suggest the case that is finally chosen by the user. Aspects which do not support the delivering of "right" cases can disappear successively. This could happen step by step by disregarding the useless aspects for new cases, deleting aspect representations from older ones and thereby erasing the edges between case representations that are similar. This automatic assessment would make it possible for experts to define their own aspects in their domain, without having to fear that the case-based reasoner will permanently obtain useless cases due to a unfortunate aspect definition. We are still working on that.

References

1. K. D. Ashley and E. L. Rissland, 'Waiting on weighting: A symbolic least commitment approach', in *Proceedings of the Seventh National Conference on Artificial Intelligence*, pp. 239–244. Morgan Kaufmann, St. Paul, MN, (1988).
2. J. L. Bentley, 'Multidimensional binary search trees used for associative searching', *Communications of the ACM*, **18**(9), 509–517, (September 1975).
3. Carl-Helmut Coulon, 'Automatic indexing, retrieval and reuse of topologies in complex designs', in *Proceeding of the sixth International Conference on Computing in Civil and Building Engineering*, eds., Peter Jan Pahl and Heinrich Werner, pp. 749–754, Berlin, (1995). Balkema, Rotterdam.
4. Carl-Helmut Coulon and Ralf Steffens, 'Comparing fragments by their images', in *Similarity concepts and retrieval methods*, ed., Angi Voß, 36–44, GMD, Sankt Augustin, (1994).
5. E. A. Feigenbaum, 'The simulation of natural learning behaviour', in *Computers and Thought*, eds., E. A. Feigenbaum and J. Feldman, 297–309, McGraw-Hill, New-York, (1963).
6. Klaus Goos, *Fallbasiertes Klassifizieren. Methoden, Integration und Evaluation*, Ph.D. dissertation, Bayerische Julius-Maximilians-Universität, Würzburg, 1995.
7. Wolfgang Gräther, 'Computing distances between attribute-value representations in an associative memory', in *Similarity concepts and retrieval methods*, ed., Angi Voß, 12–25, GMD, Sankt Augustin, (1994).
8. Janet L. Kolodner, *Case-Based Reasoning*, Morgan Kaufmann, San Mateo, 1993.

9. M. Lenz and H. D. Burkhard, 'Retrieval ohne Suche', in *Fallbasiertes Schließen – Grundlagen und Anwendungen*, eds., Brigitte Bartsch-Spörl, Dietmar Janetzko, and Stefan Wess, pp. 1–10, Universität Kaiserslautern, Germany, (1995). Zentrum für Lernende Systeme und Anwendungen, Fachbereich Informatik.

10. Jörg W. Schaaf, 'Gestalts in CAD-plans, Analysis of a Similarity Concept', in *AI in Design'94*, eds., J. Gero and F. Sudweeks, pp. 437–446, Lausanne, (1994). Kluwer Academic Publishers, Dordrecht.

11. Jörg W. Schaaf, 'ASPECT: Über die Suche nach situationsgerechten Fällen im Case Based Reasoning', Fabel-Report 31, GMD, Sankt Augustin, (1995).

12. Jörg Walter Schaaf, '"Fish and Sink"; An Anytime-Algorithm to Retrieve Adequate Cases', in *Case-based reasoning research and development: first International Conference, ICCBR-95, proceedings*, eds., Manuela Veloso and Agnar Aamodt, 538–547, Springer, Berlin, (October 1995).

13. Barbara Schmidt-Belz, 'Scenario of FABEL Prototype 3 Supporting Architectural Design', Fabel-Report 40, GMD, Sankt Augustin, (1995).

14. S. Skiena, *Implementing Discrete Mathematics*, Addision-Wesley Publishing Co., 1990.

15. Ralf Steffens, *Kantenreduktion in ASPECT-Fallbasen*, Master's thesis, Universität Bonn, 1995. Diplomarbeit in der Entstehung.

16. Dagmar Steinert, *Effiziente Zugriffsstrukturen für die ähnlichkeitsbasierte Vorauswahl von Fällen*, Master's thesis, Lehrstuhl für Informatik VI (KI) der Universität Würzburg, 1993.

17. S. Wess, K.D. Althoff, and G. Derwand, 'Improving the retrieval step in case-based reasoning', in *Pre-Prints First European Workshop on Case-Based reasoning*, Universität Kaiserslautern, Germany, (1993). Zentrum für Lernende Systeme und Anwendungen, Fachbereich Informatik.

18. M. Wolverton and B. Hayes-Roth, 'Retrieving semantically distant analogies with knowledge-directed spreading activation.', Technical Report KSL 94-19, Knowledge Systems Laboratory, Stanford University, (March 1994).

Abstractions of Data and Time for Multiparametric Time Course Prognoses

Rainer Schmidt [a], Bernhard Heindl [b], Bernhard Pollwein [b], Lothar Gierl [a]

a) Institute for Medical Informatics and Biometry, University of Rostock, Rembrandtstr.
16 / 17, D-18055 Rostock, e-mail: rainer.schmidt@medizin.uni-rostock.de
b) Department of Anaesthesiology of the Ludwig-Maximilians University of Munich

Abstract. In this paper, we describe an approach to utilize Case-Based Reasoning methods for trend prognoses for medical problems. Since using conventional methods for reasoning over time does not fit for course predictions without medical knowledge of typical course pattern, we have developed abstraction methods suitable for integration into our Case-Based Reasoning system ICONS. These methods combine medical experience with prognoses of multiparametric courses. We have chosen the monitoring of the kidney function in an Intensive Care Unit (ICU) setting as an example for diagnostic problems. On the ICU, the monitoring system NIMON provides a daily report based on current measured and calculated kidney function parameters. We subsequently generate course-characteristic trend descriptions of the renal function over the course of time. Using Case-Based Reasoning retrieval methods, we search in the case base for courses similar to the current trend descriptions. Finally, we present the current course together with similar courses as comparisons and as possible prognoses to the user. We applied Case-Based Reasoning methods in a domain which seemed reserved for statistical methods and conventional temporal reasoning.

1. Introduction

Up to 60% of the body mass of an adult person consists of water. The electrolytes dissolved in body water are of great importance for an adequate cell function. The human body tends to balance the fluid and electrolyte situation. But intensive care patients are often no longer able to maintain adequate fluid and electrolyte balances themselves due to impaired organ functions, e.g. renal failure, or medical treatment, e.g. parenteral nutrition of mechanically ventilated patients. The physician therefore needs objective criteria for the monitoring of fluid and electrolyte balances and for choosing therapeutic interventions as necessary.

At our ICU, physicians daily get a printed renal report from the monitoring system NIMON [1] which consists of 13 measured and 33 calculated parameters of those patients where renal function monitoring is applied. For example, the urine osmolality and the plasma osmolality are measured parameters that are used to calculate the osmolar clearance and the osmolar excretion. The interpretation of all reported parameters is quite complex and needs special knowledge of the renal physiology.

The aim of our knowledge based system ICONS is to give an automatic interpretation of the renal state to elicit impairments of the kidney function on time. That means, we need a time course analysis of many parameters without any well-defined standards. At first glance, this seemed to be a field to apply statistical methods. However, our good results of experiments with a Case-Based Reasoning approach and our investigations of the difficulties to handle multiparametric time course problems without a medical domain theory revealed that Case-Based Reasoning methods are more applicable in this field. Although much research has been performed in the field of conventional temporal course analyses in the recent years, none of them is suitable for this problem. Allen's theory of time and action [2] is not appropriate for multiparametric course analysis, because time is represented as just another parameter in the relevant predicates and therefore does not give necessary explicit status [3]. As traditional time series techniques [4] with known periodicities work well unless abrupt changes, they do not fit in a domain characterized by possibilities of abrupt changes and a lack of well-known periodicities at all. One ability of RÉSUMÉ [5] is the abstraction of many parameters into one single parameter and to analyse the course of this abstracted parameter. However, the interpretation of the courses requires complete domain knowledge. Haimowitz and Kohane [6] compare many parameters of current courses with well-known standards. In VIE-VENT [7] both ideas are combined: courses of each quantitativ measured parameter are abstracted into qualitativ course descriptions, that are matched with well-known standards.

However, in the domain of fluid and electrolyte balance, neither a prototypical approach in ICU settings is known nor exists complete knowledge about the kidney function. Especially, knowledge about the behaviour of the various parameters over time is yet incomplete. So we had to design our own method to deal with course analyses of multiple parameters without prototypical courses and without a complete domain theory (see Fig.1.).

2. Methods

2.1. General Model

Our procedure for interpretation of the kidney function corresponds to a general linear model (see Fig. 2). First, the monitoring system NIMON gets 13 measured parameters from the clinical chemistry and calculates 33 meaningful kidney function parameters. To elicit the relationships among these parameters a three dimensional presentation ability was implemented inside the renal monitoring system NIMON. However, complex relations among all parameters are not visible.

We decided to abstract these parameters. For this data abstraction we use states of the renal function which determine states of increasing severity beginning with a normal renal function and ending with a renal failure. Based on these state definitions, we determine the appropriate state of the kidney function per day. Therefore, we present the possible states to the user sorted according to their probability. The physician has to accept one of them. Based on the transitions of the states of one day to the state of the respectively next day, we generate four different trends. These trends, that are abstractions of time, describe the courses of the states. Then we use Case-Based Reasoning retrieval methods [8, 9, 10, 11] to search for similar courses. We present similar courses together with the current one as comparisons to the user, the course continuations of the similar courses serve as prognoses.

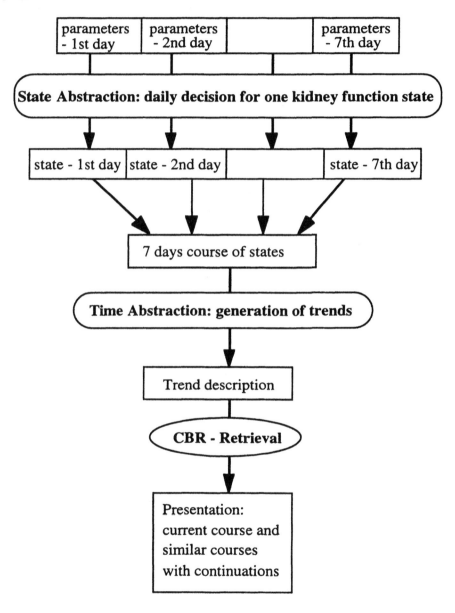

Fig. 1. Abstractions for Multiparametric Prognoses in ICONS

As there may be too many different aspects between both patients, the adaptation of the similar to the current development is not done automatically. ICONS offers only diagnostic and prognostic support, the user has to decide about the relevance of all displayed information. When presenting a comparison of a current course with a similar one, ICONS supplies the user with the ability to access additional renal syndromes and the development of single parameter values during the relevant time period.

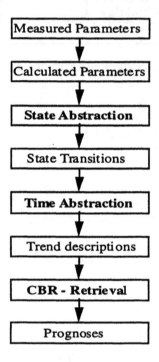

Fig. 2. General model

2.2. Definitions

(kidney function) state := member of
{normal kidney function, selective tubular damage, reduced kidney function, sharply reduced kidney function, filtration rate reduction due to prerenal impairment, kidney failure}

state transition := transition of the function state of one day to the state of the respectively next day

state transition value := difference between the severity value of one day and the severity value of the next day

trend piece := 4-tupel, that describes combined and single state transitions: assessment, first state, number of transitions, last state

381

2.3. Determination of the Kidney Function State

Based on the kidney function states, characterized by obligatory and optional conditions for selected renal parameters, first we check the obligatory conditions. For each state that satisfies the obligatory conditions we calculate a similarity value concerning the optional conditions. We use a variation of Tversky 's [8] measure of dissimilarity between concepts. If two or more states are under consideration, ICONS presents these states sorted to the similarity values together with information about the satisfied and not satisfied optional conditions (see Fig. 3.).

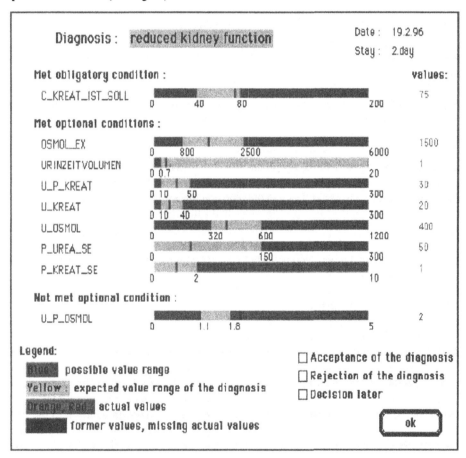

Fig. 3. Presentation of a current kidney function state estimated as reduced kidney function

The user can accept or reject a presented state. When a suggested state has been rejected, ICONS selects another state. The choice depends not only on the computed similarity value, but also on previous decisions of the user and the relation between the states. The states are ordered according to the grade of renal impairment, e.g. it is not necessary to present the state "reduced kidney function", if the user has already accepted the state "sharply reduced kidney function". Finally, we determine the central state of occasionally more than one states the user has accepted. This central state is the closest one towards a kidney failure. Our intention is to find the state indicating the most profound impairment of the kidney function.

When we determine the kidney function states, we abstract all daily measured and calculated quantitative kidney function parameters from the monitoring system NIMON to one single qualitative value. In the next section we describe our course analysis of these qualitative values, which are ordered according to decreasing fluid and electrolyte situations. More than one value can be related to the same severity value.

2.4. Course-characteristic Trend Descriptions

2.4.1. An Intermediate Step: Determination of State Transitions

First, we have fixed five assessment definitions for the transition of the kidney function state of one day to the state of the respectively next day. These assessment definitions are related to the grade of renal impairment:

steady: both states have the same severity value.
increasing: exactly one severity step in the direction towards a normal function.
sharply increasing: at least two severity steps in the direction towards a normal function.
decreasing: exactly one severity step in the direction towards a kidney failure.
sharply decreasing: at least two severity steps in the direction towards a kidney failure.

These assessment definitions are used to determine the state transitions from one qualitative value to another. Neighbouring state transitions with the same assessment are combined into trend pieces.

2.4.2. Trend Descriptions

Based on these trend pieces, we generate three trend descriptions. Two trend descriptions especially consider the current state transitions. The first trend description T1 is equivalent to the current trend piece, the second trend description T2 looks recursively back from the current trend piece to the one before and unites them, if they are both of the same direction or one of them has a "steady" assessment. A third trend description T3 characterizes the whole considered course of at most seven days. In addition to the five former assessment definitions we introduced four new ones. If none of the five former assessments fits the complete considered course, we attempt to fit one of these four definitions in the following order:

alternating: at least two up and two down transitions and all local minima are equal.
oscillating: at least two up and two down transitions.
fluctuating: the distance of the highest to the lowest severity state value is greater than 1.
nearly steady: the distance of the highest to the lowest severity state value equals one.

All three trend descriptions are of the same form as the trend pieces (see 2.2) except that the fourth component of the 4-tupel is unneccessary, because it is the current state, which is considered separately. A fourth trend description T4 assesses the complete considered course with a quantitative value that expresses the average number of state transition values inversely weighted by the distance to the current day. Together with the current kidney function state, these four trend descriptions form a course depiction, that abstracts the sequence of the kidney function states.

Looking back from a time point t, these four trend descriptions form a pattern of the immediate course history of the kidney function considering qualitative and quantitative assessments.

Why these four trend descriptions ?

There are domain specific reasons for defining the three trend descriptions T1, T2 and T3. If physicians evaluate courses of the kidney function, they consider at most one week prior to the current date. Earlier renal function states are irrelevant for the current situation of a patient. Most relevant information is derived from the current function state, the current development and sometimes a current development within a slightly longer time period. That means, very long trends are of no interest in our domain. In fact, sometimes only the current state transition or short continuous or slightly longer developments are crucial.

Our first trend description T1 expresses the current development. For longer time periods, we have defined two trend descriptions T2 and T3, because there are two different phenomena to discover and for each, a special technique is needed. T2 can be used for detecting a continuous trend independant of its length, because equal or steady trend pieces are recursively united beginning with the current one. As the trend description T3 describes a well-defined time period, it is especially useful for detecting fluctuating trends.

As every abstraction loses some specific information, in our second abstraction step, information about the daily kidney function states is lost. The course description contains only information about the current and the start states of the three trend descriptions. The intermediate states are abstracted into trend description assessments.

Only if there are several courses with the same trend description, we use a minor fourth trend description T4 to find the most similar among them. We assess the whole considered course by adding up the state transition values inversely weighted by the distances to the current day. Differences between courses that are observed to be similar can be realized easily.

2.4.3. Example

The following kidney function states (see the current course in Fig. 5.) may be observed in this temporal sequence:

selective tubular damage, reduced kidney function, reduced kidney function, selective tubular damage, reduced kidney function, reduced kidney function, sharply reduced kidney function

So we get these six state transitions:
decreasing, steady, increasing, decreasing, steady, decreasing

with these trend descriptions:
current state: sharply reduced kidney function
T1: decreasing, reduced kidney function, one transition
T2: decreasing, selective tubular damage, three transitions
T3: fluctuating, selective tubular damage, six transitions
T4: 1.23

In this example, trend description T1 assesses the current state transition as "decreasing" from a "reduced kidney function" to a "sharply reduced kidney function". As trend description T2 accumulates steady pieces, this trend assesses a "decrease" in the last four days from a "selective tubular damage" to a "sharply reduced kidney function". Trend description T3 assesses the whole course of seven days as "fluctuating", because there is only one increasing piece and the difference between the severity values of a "selective tubular damage" and a "sharply reduced kidney function" equals two (see the definitions in 2.4.2.).

2.5. Retrieval

We use the parameters of the four trend descriptions and the current kidney function state to search for similar courses. As the aim is to develop an early warning system, we need a prognosis. For this reason and to avoid a sequential runtime search along the whole cases, we store a course of the previous seven days and a maximal projection of three days for each day a patient spent on the intensive care unit.

As there are many different possible continuations for the same previous course, it is necessary to search for two items: similar courses and different projections. Therefore, we divided the search space into nine parts corresponding to the possible continuation directions. Each direction forms an own part of the search space. During the retrieval these parts are searched separately and each part may provide at most one similar case. The similar cases of these parts together are presented in the order of their computed similarity values.

Before the main retrieval, we search for a prototype that matches most of the trend descriptions (the retrieval procedure is shown in Fig.4.). Below this prototype the main retrieval starts. It consists of two steps for each part. First we search with an activation algorithm concerning qualitative features. Our algorithm differs from the common spreading activation algorithm [9] mainly due to the fact that we do not use a net for the similarity relations. Instead, we have defined explicit activation values for each possible feature value. This is possible, because on this abstraction level there are only ten dimensions (see the left column of Table 1) with at most six values. The right column of Table 1 shows the possible activation values for the description parameters. E.g. there are four activation values for the current kidney function state: courses with the same current state as the current course get the value 15, those cases whose distance to the current state of the current course is one step in the severity hierarchy get 7 and so forth.

Subsequently, we check the retrieved cases with an adaptability criterion [10] that looks for sufficient similarity, since even the most similar course may differ from the current one significantly. This may happen at the beginning of the use of ICONS, when there are only a few cases known to ICONS, or when the current course is rather exceptional. Because of the lack of medical knowledge about sufficient similarity, we defined a minimal similarity criterion that may be improved after some experience with ICONS.

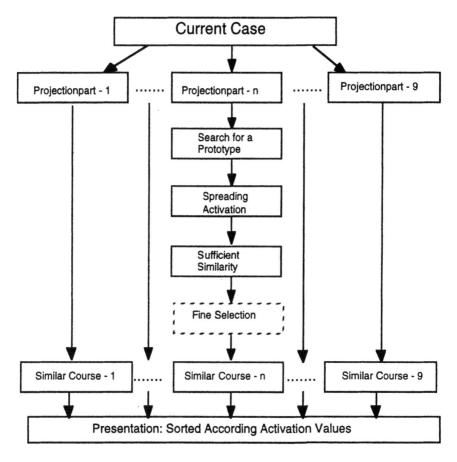

Fig. 4. The retrieval procedure

If several courses are selected in the same projection part, we use a sequential similarity measure concerning the quantitative features in a second step. So far it is only the single parameter of the trend description T4. This measure is a variation of TSCALE [11] and goes back to Tversky [8].

Dimensions	Activation Values
Current State	15, 7, 5, 2
Assessment T1	10, 5, 2
Assessment T2	4, 2, 1
Assessment T3	6, 5, 4, 3, 2, 1
Length T1	10, 5, 3, 1
Length T2	3, 1
Length T3	2, 1
Start State T1	4, 2
Start State T2	4, 2
Start State T3	2, 1

Table 1 : The retrieval dimensions and their activation values

Continuation of the example:
For the example above, we show a retrieval result. A similar course (see Fig. 5.) with the following transitions is found:
decreasing, increasing, decreasing, steady, steady, decreasing

with these trend descriptions:
current state: sharply reduced kidney function
T1: decreasing, reduced kidney function, one transition
T2: decreasing, selective tubular damage, four transitions
T3: oscillating, selective tubular damage, six transitions
T4: 1.17

T1 describes a current "decrease" from a "reduced kidney function" and T2 describes a "decrease" from a "selective tubular damage" to a "sharply reduced kidney function" in the last five days. T3 assesses the whole considered course as "fluctuating" (see again the definitions in 2.4.2.). For T4, a slightly lower value in comparison to the current course has been calculated, because the change from a "selective tubular damage" to a "reduced kidney function" state occurs earlier.

After one more day with a "sharply reduced kidney function" the patient belonging to the similar course had a kidney failure. The physician may notice this as a warning and it is up to him to interpret it.

This course was retrieved, because especially the features with the highest weights (the current state and all assessments) equal the features of the current course. As there is no significant difference between both courses, there is no reason for the sufficient similarity criterion to reject this similar course.

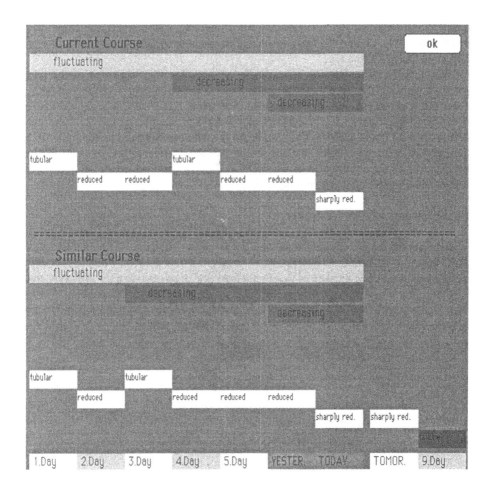

Fig. 5. Screendump of a comparative presentation of a current and a similar course. In the lower part of each course the (abbreviated) kidney function states are depicted. The upper part of each course shows the deduced trend descriptions.

2.6. Learning a Tree of Prototypes

Prognosis of multiparametric courses of the kidney function for ICU patients is a domain without a medical theory. Moreover, we can not expect such a theory to be formulated in the near future. So we attempt to learn prototypical course pattern. Therefore, knowledge on this domain is stored as a tree of prototypes with three levels and a root node (see Fig. 6.). Except for the root, where all not yet united courses are stored, every level corresponds to one of the trend descriptions T1, T2 or T3. As soon as enough courses that share another trend description are stored at a prototype, we create a new prototype with this trend. At a prototype at level 1, we unite courses that share T1, at level 2, courses that share T1 and T2 and at level 3, courses that share all three trend descriptions. We can do this, because regarding their importance, the three trend descriptions T1, T2 and T3 refer to hierarchically related time periods. T1 is more important than T2 and T3.

We start the retrieval with a search for a prototype that has most of the trend descriptions with the current course in common. The search begins at the root with a check for a prototype with the same trend description T1. If such a prototype can be found, the search goes on below this prototype for a prototype that has the same trend descriptions T1 and T2, and so on. If no prototype with another trend in common can be found, we search for a course at the last accepted prototype. If no prototype exists that has the same T1 as the current course, we search at the root node, where all the courses are stored that are not related to a prototype.

Continuation of the example:

In the example above, we can create only one prototype at level one, because at the second level the current course and the similar one, called "similar-1" differ in their length. Although the long-term trend description T3 is equal for both courses, we can not create a prototype at level three because of the strictly hierarical organization of the prototype tree. However, it would be meaningless to learn a prototypical description "fluctuating in seven days from a selective tubular damage to sharply reduced kidney function" which does not consider any more similarities or deviations within this time period.

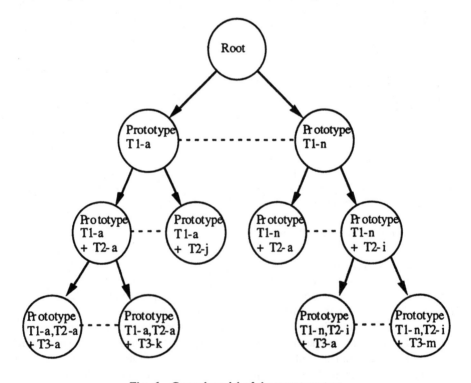

Fig. 6. General model of the prototype tree

Assuming we find another similar course, called "similar-2", for the current case of the example above with the following kidney function states:

reduced kidney function, reduced kidney function, selective tubular damage, selective tubular damage, reduced kidney function, reduced kidney function, sharply reduced kidney function

<u>with these trend descriptions:</u>
current state: sharply reduced kidney function
T1: decreasing, reduced kidney function, one transition
T2: decreasing, selective tubular damage, four transitions
T3: oscillating, reduced kidney function, six transitions
T4: 1.33

The current course, "similar-1" and "similar-2" will be united at level 1 into prototype T1-a, defined by T1 as "decreasing, reduced kidney function, one transition". Afterwards at level 2 the current course and "similar-2" will be united into a prototype T1-a + T2-a, defined by T1 as "decreasing, reduced kidney function, one transition" plus by T2 as "decreasing, selective tubular damage, four transitions". The attempt to create another prototype at level 3 fails, because the trend descriptions T3 have different assessments and start states. The result, a tree of prototypes learned from the three courses is shown in Fig. 7.:

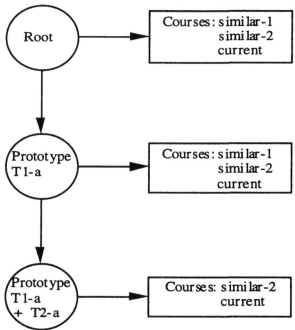

Fig. 7. Prototype tree of the three example courses

3. Related Work

In the field of Case-Based Reasoning, much research is recently going on, but we have not yet heard about a Case-Based comparison of temporal courses. The MetVUW Workbench [12], a system for intelligent retrieval and display of historical meteorological data, analyses a current weather situation and supports an expert user with hints concerning the weather forecast. In AIRQUAP [13], a sytem for prediction of air pollution levels in Athens, the prognostic claim goes further. The aim is a prognosis of the forthcoming air pollution. Both systems use Case-Based Reasoning methods. In contrast to ICONS they do not consider time courses, but they both try to predict from analyses of current situations characterized by well-known models of influence features that can be used for the retrieval. In the domain of kidney function analysis the measured and calculated parameters have not got any influence on the current or future kidney function, but each of them expresses a part of this function.

In the field of time series analyses, efforts are taken in many medical domains. In RÉSUMÉ [5] many temporal abstraction methods are provided. One ability is to abstract the values of different parameters into one value of another parameter and to describe the course of this abstracted parameter. The idea of abstracting many measured parameter values into another parameter and analysing the course of this abstracted parameter is similar to our approach. However, since the result is an abstracted description of the current course without a comparison to a similar course, a prognosis is not possible. The idea to compare a current course with other courses is implemented by Haimowitz and Kohane [6]. However, there is no question of comparing cases with each other, but cases with an expected normal parameter course. Some other systems, e.g. TOPAZ [14] and VIE-VENT [7], also demand the knowledge of expected clinical courses that are unknown in our domain for ICU patients.

4. Conclusion

Our aim is to produce an early warning system that helps to avoid kidney failures. ICONS helps the physicians to abstract from the measured and calculated NIMON parameters to a function state. For time periods up to seven days, we describe courses of function states using four trend descriptions as a second abstraction step. At this double abstraction level, ICONS provides the physicians with courses of other patients with similar developments as potential warnings. As no prototypical courses towards a kidney failure are known, we search for cases with similar courses and present them as possible prognoses. We hope to find some prototypical courses by merging similar courses into prototypes. Up to now, we unify equal courses with each other and join courses with at least one common trend description, create a prototype with the common trend and store the related courses at this prototype. We still need a definition how to join not only equal but similar trend descriptions and a technique to merge courses into prototypes in such a way that we get rid of the courses and keep the prototypes instead. One advantage of combining temporal course analyses with Case-Based Reasoning is the projection. Without medical knowledge about possibilities and probabilities of future developments ICONS shows future developments of patients with similar courses. One part of our future research will be a generalized integration of ICONS and our antibiotic therapy adviser [15] into a Case-Based system for advice in intensive care problems.

Acknowledgement

This research is partly funded by the German Ministry for Research and Technology. It is part of the MEDWIS project of the MEDIS Institute of GSF, Neuherberg, for research on medical knowledge bases.

References

[1]   Wenkebach U., Pollwein B., Finsterer U. (1992): Visualization of large datasets in intensive care, in: Proc Annu Symp Comput Appl Med Care, 18-22

[2]   Allen J.F. (1984): Towards a general theory of action and time, in: Artificial Intelligence, 23 , 123-154

[3]   Keravnou E.T. (1995): Modelling Medical Concepts as Time Objects, in: Barahona P., Stefanelli M., Wyatt J. (Eds.): Artificial Intelligence in Medicine, AIME'95, Berlin, 67-78

[4]   Robeson S.M., Steyn D.G. (1990): Evaluation and comparison of statistical forecast models for daily maximum ozone concentrations, in: Atmospheric Environment 24 B (2), 303-12

[5]   Shahar Y., Musen M.A. (1993): RÉSUMÉ: A Temporal-Abstraction System for Patient Monitoring, in: Computers and Biomedical Research 26 , 255-273

[6]   Haimowitz I.J., Kohane I.S. (1993): Automated Trend Detection with Alternate Temporal Hypotheses, in: Bajcsy R.(ed.), Proceedings of the 13th International Joint Conference on Artificial Intelligence (IJCAI-93), Morgan Kaufmann, San Mateo, CA, 146-151

[7]   Miksch S., Horn W., Popow C., Paky F. (1995): Therapy Planning Using Qualitative Trend Descriptions, in: Barahona P., Stefanelli M., Wyatt J. (Eds.): Artificial Intelligence in Medicine, in: Lecture Notes in Artificial Intelligence 934 , 209-217

[8]   Tversky A. (1977): Features of Similarity, in: Psychological Review 84 , 327-352

[9]   Anderson J.R. (1989): A theory of the origins of human knowledge, in: Artificial Intelligence 40 , 313-351, Special Volume on Machine Learning

[10]   Smyth B, Keane M.T. (1993): Retrieving Adaptable Cases: The Role of Adaptation Knowledge in Case Retrieval. in: First European Workshop on Case-Based Reasoning (EWCBR-93), 76-81

[11]   DeSarbo W.S., Johnson M.D., Manrei A.K., Manrai L.A., Edwards E.A. (1992) : TSCALE: A new multidemensional scaling procedure based on Tversky's contrast model, in: Psychometrika 57 , 43-69

[12   Jones, E.K., Roydhouse A. (1994): Iterative Design of Case Retrieval Systems. Victoria University of Wellington, New Zealand, Technical Report CS_TR-94/6, see: Proc. of the AAAI'94 Workshop on Case-Based Reasoning, Seattle, Washington, 1994

[13]   Lekkas, G.P., Arouris N.M., Viras L.L.: Case-Based Reasoning in Environmental Monitoring Applications. Applied Artificial Intelligence, Vol. 8, 1994, 349-376

[14]   Kahn M.G., Fagan L.M., Sheiner L.B. (1991): Combining Physiologic Models and Symbolic Methods to Interpret Time-Varying Patient Data, in: Methods of Information in Medicine 30 , 167-178

[15]   Schmidt R., Boscher L., Heindl B., Schmid G., Pollwein B., Gierl L.(1995): Adaptation and Abstraction in a Case-Based Antibiotics Therapy Adviser, in: Barahona P., Stefanelli M., Wyatt J. (Eds.): Artificial Intelligence in Medicine, in: Lecture Notes in Artificial Intelligence 934 , 209-217

The Utility Problem Analysed

A Case-Based Reasoning Perspective

Barry Smyth
Department of Computer Science,
University College Dublin,
Belfield, Dublin 2, Ireland.
BSMYTH@cslan.ucd.ie

Pádraig Cunningham
Department of Computer Science,
Trinity College Dublin,
College Green,
Dublin 2, Ireland.
Padraig.Cunningham@cs.tcd.ie

Abstract. In case-based reasoning (CBR) there are compelling arguments in support of large case-bases; greater target problem coverage, better solution quality, improved system efficiency. However a problem known as the *utility problem* dictates that the last of these arguments is not necessarily true. In fact, adding more cases to an already "saturated" case-base will reduce rather than improve system efficiency. Thus, there is a trade-off situation in which adding cases to improve coverage and quality is pitted against efficiency degradation. This paper discusses the utility problem from a case-based reasoning perspective, examining its root causes in an experimental CBR system.

1 Introduction

There are good reasons for supporting large case-bases in CBR systems: improved target problem coverage; better solution quality; more efficient (faster) problem solving. For the relatively small case-bases found in early experimental case-based reasoners, coverage, quality and efficiency were all found to improve with the addition of new cases. However, for the much larger case-bases demanded by many real-world tasks, the efficiency benefit is brought into question. Specifically, a problem known as the "utility problem" means that efficiency will eventually degrade as the case-base becomes "saturated".

The utility problem has been well documented by the machine learning community [1,2,3,4]. Evidently, large amounts if training data will affect the **performance** of the training process. However, in eager learning systems, the **competence** of a system can deteriorate with large amounts of training data - due to over-fitting to the training data for instance. One of the advantages of the lazy learning that is characteristic of CBR is that it should not be possible for system competence to decrease with and increase in case-base size. Instead the Utility Problem manifests itself as a trade-off between the solution quality associated with large case-bases and the efficiency problem of working with a large case-base. This trade-off is not as critical in many machine learning systems, particularly speed-up learners, where limiting the size of their "case-bases" does not affect competence as these systems can always resort to a base-level problem solver. Moreover, similarity-based retrieval and heuristic adaptation mechanisms distinguish CBR from many comparable machine learning methods.

This paper examines the utility problem in CBR. The next section describes the PathFinder system that was used as an experimental test-bed for investigating the CBR utility problem. Section 3 explains the utility problem from a case-based reasoning stand-point and discusses how the relationship between retrieval and adaptation shape its effects in CBR systems. Section 4 presents the results of a series of experiments that show how the PathFinder system in particular is affected by the utility problem and how different algorithmic choices (for example indexing policies) can alter the these outcomes.

2 PathFinder

PathFinder is a case-based reasoning system for optimised route planning [5]. Given a connected graph (e.g. a network of cities) PathFinder will attempt to find the shortest path between any two nodes (cities) on this graph. The traditional brute-force approach epitomised by Dijkstra's greedy algorithm [6] produces optimal paths but is computationally expensive.

The precise details of the PathFinder system are not important here. In brief, the system employs a case-base of previous routes (which are optimal, having been produced by Dijkstra's method) in an attempt to significantly reduce the time needed to construct new routes and without sacrificing the optimality of these new routes. When faced with a new target problem the system will attempt to reuse an existing case or part of an existing case or even chain together a number of cases. Partial routes may then be completed by using Dijkstra's method.

Four basic versions (A,B,C,D) of the PathFinder system will be used in the following experiments. They vary according to the how cases are generated and how cases are indexed (see Figure 1).

	Subsumption Check	Route Indexing
PathFinder A	*Off*	*Off*
PathFinder B	*Off*	*On*
PathFinder C	*On*	*On*
PathFinder D	*On*	*Off*

Figure 1. The PathFinder Test Systems.

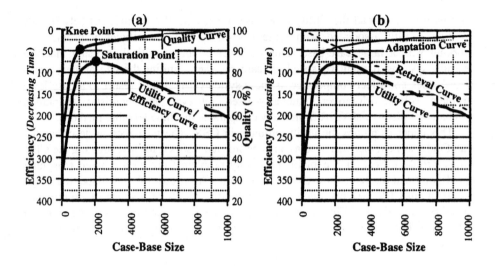

Figure 2. (a) Quality vs. Efficiency   (b) The Utility Factors; Retrieval vs. Adaptation

Cases can be generated with a *subsumption check*, thereby ensuring that potentially redundant routes which are parts of existing routes are not stored in the case-base. During indexing cases can be indexed in terms of their initial and end location cities only or they can be indexed in terms of every city in their route. The former indexing policy (*route indexing* is *off*) means that cases will only be retrieved if their start or end cities match the start or end cities of the target problem. Whereas the latter policy (*route indexing* is *on*) means that cases which intersect the target start or end cities can be reused; of course this means that during retrieval many more cases are considered for reuse and so retrieval is much more expensive.

3 The Utility Problem Explained

In order to properly understand the utility problem in CBR it is critical to appreciate the nature of the relationships between coverage, solution quality, and system efficiency.

3.1 Quality *vs.* Efficiency

Figure 2(a) illustrates how the solution quality and system efficiency of the PathFinder system change as its case-base grows. This is behaviour that is typical of CBR. The x-axis corresponds to the number of cases in the case-base. The left-hand y-axis corresponds to system efficiency which here is measured as the mean time taken to solve a target problem (averaged over 500 random targets); note that decreasing solution times correspond to increasing efficiency. The right-hand y-axis corresponds to increasing solution quality as a percentage of a measurable optimum quality.

Solution quality increases monotonically with case-base size, initially increasing rapidly but eventually tailing off as optimal quality is reached. There is a case-base size (the "knee-point"), less than which the addition of new cases results in significant quality improvements, but greater than which the addition of extra cases results in relatively insignificant quality improvements. For example, the quality curve of Figure 2(a) shows that a case-base of 1000 cases generates solutions within 90% of their optimum while the addition of a further 1000 cases only improves matters by 4%.

System efficiency does *not* increase monotonically with case-base size. Initial efficiency improvements due to the addition of new cases eventually give way to efficiency degradation.

This efficiency degradation is what is meant by the utility problem; for this reason we will often refer to this graph of efficiency versus case-base size as the utility curve. The point at which the positive utility region gives way to the negative region is the saturation point and corresponds to that case-base size that offers optimal efficiency. This case-base size corresponds to the width of the utility curve and the optimal efficiency to the height of the utility curve.

Once the optimal case-base size has been reached there is a trade-off between solution quality and efficiency. As new cases are added to this optimal case-base solution quality will only improve at the expense of efficiency. Furthermore, solution quality may increase much more slowly than system efficiency decreases. In Figure 2(a) it is clear that the optimal case-base (the saturation point) is 2000 cases at which point solution quality is 94% and the average solution time (system efficiency) is 75 msecs. However, by adding a further 2000 cases, solution quality improves by only 2% but system efficiency drops by 50% to 110 msecs.

3.2 The Utility Factors

The utility problem in CBR is caused by two competing factors: (1) the mean retrieval time for a given case-base size and (2) the mean adaptation time for this case-base size. As new cases are added retrieval costs become progressively greater and adaptation savings progressively less. Eventually increases in retrieval time are not compensated for by savings in adaptation time. Figure 2(b) shows the retrieval and adaptation curve that make up the utility curve of Figure 1(a). Retrieval efficiency (mean retrieval time) is seen to degrade and adaptation efficiency (mean adaptation time) is seen to improve (at an ever decreasing rate) as new cases are added.

The adaptation factor is difficult to fully appreciate. The expected adaptation savings due to a new case are related to the coverage offered by that case compared to the coverage of the case-base as a whole; the more target problems that this new case can solve faster than any other case, the greater the adaptation savings afforded by this case. For small case-bases new cases are likely to contribute considerably to coverage and thus significant adaptation savings can be expected. For large case-bases however, case-bases that already cover much of the target problem space, a new case may only improve overall coverage by a small amount resulting in equally small adaptation savings.

The utility curve is simply the addition of these retrieval and adaptation curves. The distance of the intersection point of the retrieval and adaptation curves along the x axis (the case-base size axis) corresponds to the optimal case-base size (the width of the utility curve); 2000 cases in Figure 2(b). The height of this crossing point along the y-axis (the efficiency axis) is related to the optimal efficiency; 37.5 msecs in Figure

1(b) so that the system efficiency at this point is 75 msecs (retrieval time plus adaptation time, 37.5 + 37.5).

4 The Utility Experiments

This section presents experimental results on the effects of the utility problem in the PathFinder systems. Figure 3 shows the results of each system when used to plan routes in a randomly generated network of 200 cities with a mean branching factor of 6. Case-bases of varying sizes were generated using Dijkstra's method and according to the subsumption and indexing constraints imposed by each PathFinder variation.

The graphs of Figure 3 include the four separate curves introduced in the previous section; a utility curve, a quality curve, a retrieval curve, and an adaptation curve. These curves were generated using a set of 500 target problems. A fifth curve shows the mean time for Dijkstra's method to solve the target problems (350 msecs).

We will first look at the relationship between solution efficiency and solution quality by comparing the utility curve to the quality curve. Then we will examine the relationship between retrieval and adaptation efficiency.

4.1 Efficiency vs. Quality

The first curve is the utility curve, a plot of efficiency (the left-hand y-axis, measured as decreasing time) versus case-base size. The first thing to notice is a very distinctive partitioning of the systems, A and D versus B and C. A and D have utility curves which are wider and taller than those of B and C. This increased width allows A and D to support larger case-bases than B and C without suffering from the utility problem. The increased height of the curves mean that the maximum efficiency of A and D is greater than that for B and C.

This division stems from the fact that neither A nor D use route indexing while both B and C do. We shall investigate this further in the next section where we will see how route indexing results in expensive retrieval stages without benefiting from the expected gains in reusability. Remember that using route indexing means that the coverage of individual cases is greatly improved because they can be reused in terms of any city along their routes. In contrast, if route indexing is not employed a case can only be reused if it shares the same start or end city with the target problem.

The fact that route indexing improves case coverage can be seen by looking at the quality curves in Figure 3. The same partitioning exists. This time A and D require many more cases to achieve the same solution quality characteristics as B and C. For example B and C achieve optimal solution quality at around 4500 to 6500 cases, while A and D need about 9000 cases.

However while these quality figures seem good for B and C when we take the utility curves into consideration the result is rather different. When A and D reach optimal solution quality they are still about twice as fast as Dijkstra's method; at 9000 cases A and D have a mean solution time of about 175 msecs. However when B and C reach optimal solution quality they are both *less* efficient that Dijkstra's method; both take about 400msecs to solve target problems.

More importantly perhaps, the knee-point for A and D occurs at 2000 cases and offers 95% quality, while for B and C the knee-point occurs at about 750 cases and offers 90% quality. It is comforting that *all* of the systems have reached their knee-point quality by the time the utility problem takes effect. At this point the efficiency of the systems, A through D, is 73 msecs, 110 msecs, 125 msecs, and 95 msecs, respectively; these correspond to speed-ups over Dijkstra's method of 4.8, 3.1, 2.8, and 3.7, respectively. However, this knee-point quality for A and D is 5% higher than that of B and C. In fact, B and C only achieve the same 95% quality at 2000 cases, well after the utility problem has begun to degrade efficiency, causing an increase in the problem solving time of B and C to 200 msecs (an efficiency decrease of 80% and 60% respectively).

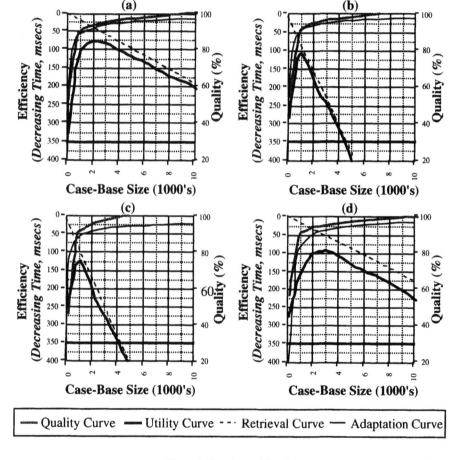

Figure 3. Experimental Results

4.2 Retrieval and Adaptation Efficiency

The third and fourth curves illustrate the retrieval and adaptation efficiency (again displayed as decreasing time on the left-hand y-axis). These two curves show how differences in the case generation and indexing algorithms of the PathFinder systems affect retrieval and adaptation times (again in the 200 city domain).

As expected the retrieval times of A and D are very much less than those of B and C. This delays the crossing point of the retrieval and adaptation curves and results in a widening and heightening of the utility curves. This explains the fact that A and D can accommodate larger case-bases than B and C while at the same time achieving better problem solving efficiency. Case coverage is also sacrificed in A and D and this explains why their adaptation curves are less steep than those of B and C. This again allows for larger case-bases by delaying the crossing point, and also improves optimal efficiency. In general, the cheaper retrieval and more gradual adaptation savings of A and D explain why their utility curves tend to be tall and wide while the curves of B and C are short and narrow.

The effect of subsumption checking is less clear and less prominent, and is only really apparent in this 200 city domain when terminal indexing is used (systems A and D). Although A and D use the same indexing techniques their retrieval times are slightly different; Figure 3(a) and 3(d) show that D's retrieval efficiency is slightly better than A's. This is because subsumption checking tends to produce case-bases that are more regularly distributed, with less clustering and redundancy. This has the net effect of reducing the average number of candidate cases filtered at retrieval time and improves overall retrieval efficiency.

Subsumption checking also flattens the adaptation curve and together the more shallow retrieval and adaptation curves of D mean that their crossover point (the utility saturation point) is delayed. One might expect that this delay would improve the optimal efficiency of D over A? However, when the curves do cross, they cross at a lower point on the efficiency axis and hence optimal efficiency for D is less than that for A; in Figures 3(a) and 3(d) we see that for a 200 city problem A's optimal efficiency is about 73 time units compared to D's 95 time units (in terms of speed-up, this is a factor of 4.8 versus a factor of 3.7 respectively).

5 Conclusions

This paper has investigated the utility problem in CBR using an case-based route planner to demonstrate experimentally how this problem manifests itself in case-based reasoning systems. It was shown that there can be trade-offs in CBR between solution quality and system efficiency, but that a proper understanding of the utility issues can help to minimise these trade-offs. In addition by varying the retrieval, adaptation, and coverage characteristics of the test system we were able to alter significantly the way in which the system responded to differences in problem complexity and case-base size.

In PathFinder increasing case coverage by using sophisticated indexing did not help overall coverage, solution quality or system efficiency in the long run. Instead, simpler indexing and retrieval methods produced the best results overall. Even though they severely limited the coverage of individual cases, in the long run the improved retrieval efficiency meant improved system efficiency. It also meant that larger case-bases could be supported which in turn improved overall coverage and solution quality.

Future work will look at the utility problem in other CBR systems. Finally, by fully analysing the utility problem from a CBR perspective we expect to discover new ways of treating it that are geared towards the specific needs of case-based reasoning. For example, Smyth & Keane [7] describe a newly developed CBR strategy of coping with the CBR utility problem that preserves system efficiency, solution quality, and target coverage, and contrast this with many machine learning methods that concentrate on maintaining efficiency alone [1, 2, 3].

6 Bibliography

[1] Markovitch, S. & Scott, P. D., Information Filtering. Selection mechanisms in Learning Systems. *Machine Learning*, **10**, 113-151, (1993).

[2] Minton, S., Qualitative Results Concerning the Utility of Explanation-Based Learning. *Artificial Intelligence,* **42**, 363-391, (1990).

[3] Tambe, N., Newell, A., and Rosenbloom, P. S., The Problem of Expensive Chunks and is Solution by Restricting Expressiveness. *Machine Learning*, **5**, 299-349, (1990).

[4] Veloso, M., Learning by Analogical Reasoning in General Problem Solving. *Ph.D Thesis* (CMU-CS-92-174). Carnegie Mellon University, Pittsburgh, USA, (1992).

[5] Liu, B., Choo, S. H., Lok, S. L., Leong, S. M., Lee, S. C., Poon, F. P., and Tan, H. H., Finding the Shortest Route Using Cases, Knowledge, and Dijkstra's Algorithm. *IEEE Expert,* **9**(5), 7-11, (1994).

[6] Chen, W. K., *Theory of Nets: Flows in Networks*. John Wiley & Sons, New York. (1990)

[7] Smyth, B. & Keane, M. T., Remembering to Forget: A Competence Preserving deletion Policy for CBR Systems. *Proceedings of the 14th International Joint Conference on Artificial Intelligence*. Montréal Canada., Morgan Kaufmann, (1995).

REPRO: Supporting Flowsheet Design by Case-Base Retrieval

Jerzy Surma, Bertrand Braunschweig
Artificial Intelligence Group
Computer Science and Applied Mathematics Division
Institut Francais du Petrole
1 et 4, av. de Bois-Preau, 92506 Rueil-Malmaison, France
Email: {Jerzy.SURMA │ Bertrand.BRAUNSCHWEIG}@ifp.fr

Case-Based Reasoning (CBR) paradigm is very close to the designer behavior during the conceptual design, and seems to be a fruitable computer aided-design approach if a library of design cases is available. The goal of this paper is to presents the general framework of a case-based retrieval system: REPRO, that supports chemical process design. The crucial problems like the case representation and structural similarity measure are widely described. The presented experimental results and the expert evaluation shows usefulness of the described system in real world problems. The papers ends with discussion concerning research problems and future work.

1 Introduction

This paper presents a prototype of a case-based retrieval system named REPRO (Reutilisation d'Etudes de Procedes) which aims to support a designer through the earliest steps of designing petroleum and chemical processes. REPRO retrieves the best matching flowsheet: Process Flow Diagrams (PFDs) from a library of existing PFDs by computing how they are attributionally and structurally similar to a complete or partial input diagram under preparation. Once the most similar existing flowsheet has been selected, it may be used for:
• completing the partial PFD;
• retrieving other information associated with the reference PFD (such as Piping and Instrumentation Diagrams - P&IDs);
• retrieving other data, e.g. steady-state simulation models, operating conditions etc. which may constitute a good start for the preparation of specific elements for the new process being designed.

PFDs represent complex processes, that can be defined as systems that generate required output products from a given set of input feedstocks under appropriate operating conditions. These processes can be represented at different levels of abstraction corresponding to different phases in the design (Douglas 1988):

• conceptual (synthesis) phase: only the most important functions, connections, and input/output streams are represented in Block Diagrams;

• basic engineering design phase: all equipments, connections, streams, some operating conditions (pressure, temperature, flow rates) are represented in PFDs; additional detailed information such as the control systems, utilities, sensors are represented in the P&IDs; equipment lists are established;

• detailed engineering design: all process-specific information is supplied, including dimensions, materials etc.

In this paper we address both conceptual and the basic engineering design phases where block diagrams and PFDs are used. Drawing a flowsheet is not a simple task. Some PFDs for standard refining processes need several days of designer time and many pages of fine print quality. Designers use highly specific CAD software equipped with time-saving devices such as palettes of equipments. However, when preparing a new process, the designer does not like to start from scratch and always tries to use an existing design as a starting point for the next one (adding and removing process items as needed). The set of existing diagrams in a company, the corporate memory, is a good candidate for case-based retrieval as designers are neither able nor willing to look for the most similar diagram, due to the complexity of the cases and to time constraints.

Computing attributional and structural similarity between complex diagrams such as the PFDs needs to carefully address the complexity aspects, because this similarity implies to compare graphs made of typed nodes and typed links and because most algorithms for graph comparison are NP-complete. In our approach the complexity question is solved by using teleological information, that is defining the function of each equipment in addition to factual data such as the equipment type and connectivity. This functional information saves a lot of computation but implies more input from the user. The paper extends (Surma & Braunschweig 1996) by showing the detailed structural similarity calculation and some results on a relatively complex process example.

At present there is considerable growing interest in the use of CBR in design activities. An overview of the original attempts in case-based design systems has been given by Pu (Pu 1993). A recent general overview the state of art in the field is presented by Maher et al. (Maher et al. 1995). The comprehensive analysis of the computer aided design and presentation of the most important research problems is deeply presented in the FABEL Consortium publications (Voss et. al 1994a, 1994b).

In section 2 we present the object-oriented flowsheet representation. Then in section 3 the two structural similarity measures for flowsheets are introduced. In section 4 the REPRO system is shortly described and in section 5 the evaluation results are presented. The paper concludes with discussions concerning research problems and future work.

2 Flowsheet Representation

The research in knowledge representation for process engineering (Stephanopoulos 1987, Motard 1989, Fraga 1994) suggest object-oriented paradigm as a useful way of representing process information. We adopted this approach (Surma & Braunschweig 1995) and finally the following classes were defined:
• the generalization taxonomy of flowsheet components: the component taxonomy (e.g., Reactor).
• the class defining pipes (stream) connections between components: the class PIPE.
• the generalization taxonomy of available chemical processes: the process taxoxonomy (e.g., Hydrogenation C3).

The instances in the process taxonomy are aggregation taxonomies that represent the flowsheet itself: the flowsheet aggregation (e.g. Flowsheet-1). Aggregation is the relationship (transitive and antisymetric) in which objects representing the components are associated with an object representing the entire assembly (Rumbaugh et al., 1991). Figure 1 illustrates the process taxonomy, and the component taxonomy that is the source of components for a flowsheet aggregation. For example a Flowsheet-1 consists of a Pump-1, Reactor-1, and Pipe-1.

In the component class the following slots concerning case retrieval are defined and are inherited by all the subclasses:

• local-root defines the type for the given object. The objects which belongs to the same local-root are the same kind of objects. For example in fig.1 the local-root for the Pump-1 and Pump-2 is a Pump. In general the local-root defines the sub-tree in generalization taxonomy and is used by similarity measure, for instance by the Most Specific Common Abstraction strategy during local components comparison. The local-root of the component x will be denoted: local-root(x).
• function defines the role (the task) of a given component in a flowsheet aggregation. The function of the component x will be denoted: function(x).
• quantity defines how many identical components perform the function specified in the function slot.
• weight is a real value $\in$ <0;1> that indicates the importance of a given components in the whole assembly. The value of a component x weight will be denoted: weight(x).

Additionally each subclass of the component class has domain-specific slots and methods for computing local similarity between two instance components. Thanks to polymorphism the proper domain specific formula is used.

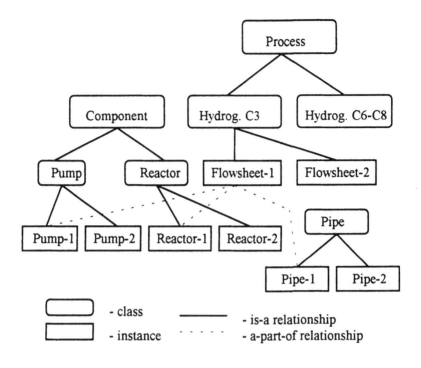

Fig.1. The object-oriented flowsheet representation.

3 Structural Similarity Measure

The similarity measure for flowsheets should interpret them as assemblies of components where the crucial factors are the internal components properties and the pipes connections between components. This mean that in opposite to the most CBR systems the similarity measure for flowsheets should be based not only on the local structure of the objects but on the relational structure existing between them as well. Several approaches were made in this field including: analogical reasoning (Holyoak & Thagard 1989, Falkenhainer et. al. 1989), conceptual graphs (Myaeng & Lopez-Lopez 1992, Maher 1993), and object-oriented representation (Bisson 1995). In CBR the mentioned FABEL project investigates several approaches to structural similarity based on: graph theory, term-based representation, gestalt indices and psychological theories of perception (Voss et al. 1994a).
The flowsheet might be treated as a graph, that implies the use one of the know approaches, which are mostly NP-complete. But the availability of the domain knowledge and the specific nature of the flowsheets allow to create a flowsheet-specific measure that is computationally acceptable. Thanks the local-root slot the set of possible matching components is narrowing to the same type ones. Additionally the function slot selects among the same type components that are

responsible for the same task. In fact in each flowsheet (after careful function labeling) there are no two or more of the same type components performing the same function: the uniqueness property. The practical utilization of this property and the role of the quantity slot is discussed in Surma and Braunschweig paper (Surma & Braunschweig 1996). The uniqueness property fundamentally reduces a complexity of the matching process, but requires deep knowledge acquisition. The similarity measure based only on the same type components is under consideration. One of the most promising approaches for this problem is described in the Bisson paper (Bisson 1995).

Based on the expert suggestions two similarity measures between the input flowsheet aggregation (Ψ_I) and the retrieved flowsheet aggregation (Ψ_R) were created. First, the aggregation similarity treats the flowsheets as a set of components. Second, the connection similarity takes into account connections (pipes) between components. The aggregation and connection similarity measures are normalized, and might be used separately or by a linear combination.

3.1 Aggregation Similarity

The aggregation similarity focuses on the components and on internal (attributional) similarity between common components. Let X be a set of all instances in the component taxonomy, $S_I = \{ x \in X \mid x$ a-part-of $\Psi_I \}$, $S_R = \{ x \in X \mid x$ a-part-of $\Psi_R \}$, and $\Omega = S_I \cap S_R$ this means: $\Omega = \{ (x1 \in S_I, x2 \in S_R) \mid$ local-root(x1)=local-root(x2) $\wedge$ function(x1)=function(x2) $\wedge$ weight(x1) > 0$\}$. The aggregation similarity between the input and the retrieved flowsheets is:

$$\mathrm{SIM}^A(\Psi_I, \Psi_R) = \frac{\mathrm{Card}(\Omega) * \dfrac{\sum\limits_{(x1,x2)\in\Omega} \mathrm{weight}(x1)*\mathrm{sim}(x1,x2)}{\sum\limits_{(x1,x2)\in\Omega} \mathrm{weight}(x1)}}{\mathrm{Card}(S_I) + \mathrm{Card}(S_R) - \mathrm{Card}(\Omega)}$$

where: $\mathrm{sim}(x1,x2) \in <0;1>$ is the similarity between component x1 and x2 computed on the slot (attributes) level.

This measure has the following properties: if for all $(x1,x2)\in\Omega$: $\mathrm{sim}(x1,x2)=1$ then: $\mathrm{SIM}^A(\Psi_I, \Psi_R) = \mathrm{Card}(S_I \cap S_R) / \mathrm{Card}(S_I \cup S_R)$, if $\Omega = \varnothing$ then $\mathrm{SIM}^A(\Psi_I, \Psi_R) = 0$, possibility of using recursively for the nested aggregation taxonomies, and antisimetricy because each argument of the SIM^A function plays a different role (the weights are taking only from an input aggregation).

3.2 Connection Similarity

The connection similarity focuses on the pipe connections between components. Let Y be a set of all instances in the class PIPE, L_I = { $y \in Y$ | y a-part-of Ψ_I }, L_R = { $y \in Y$ | y a-part-of Ψ_R }, in(y) be a component connected at the input of a pipe y, out(y) be a component connected at the output of a pipe y, $\Phi = L_I \cap L_R$ this means: Φ = { (y1 $\in L_I$, y2 $\in L_R$) | (in(y1),in(y2)) $\in \Omega \wedge$ (out(y1),out(y2)) $\in \Omega$ }, sub(Ψ_I ,Ψ_R) = {g | g is the common subgraph between Ψ_I and Ψ_R defined by the elements of a set Φ}, and L_g = { $y \in Y$ | $y \in g$ }. The connection similarity between the input and retrieved flowsheet is:

$$SIM^C(\Psi_I,\Psi_R) = \beta\alpha * \frac{Card(\Phi)}{Card(L_I) + Card(L_R) - Card(\Phi)} + \beta\beta * \frac{\sum_{g \in sub(\Psi_I,\Psi_R)} Card(L_g)^2}{Card(L_I)^2}$$

where: $\beta\alpha$, $\beta\beta \in <0;1> \wedge \beta\alpha+\beta\beta=1$.

This measure has the following properties: if the common subgraph between Ψ_I and Ψ_R is identical to the graph Ψ_I then: $SIM^C(\Psi_I,\Psi_R)$ = $Card(L_I \cap L_R)$ / $Card(L_I \cup L_R)$, if $\Phi = \varnothing$ then $SIM^C(\Psi_I,\Psi_R)$ = 0. The coefficient $\beta\alpha$ concerns the first part of the connection similarity, that interprets connections as a set of pipes. The $\beta\beta$ coefficient concerns the second part of the formula which support the expert heuristic: "it is better to have small number of large common subgraphs than a large number of small ones". Surprisingly this heuristic supports Gentner's systematic principle (Gentner 1993): " A predicate that belongs to a mappable system of mutually interconnecting relationships is more likely to be imported into target than is an isolated predicate".

4 Case Retrieval in REPRO

The knowledge representation and structural similarity for flowsheets introduced in the previous sections have been implemented in the REPRO system (Surma 1996). The main task of REPRO is the case-based retrieval of flowsheets based on the aggregation and/or connection similarity. The system has been implemented on a SUN 10 Sparc workstation with the G2 expert-system development environment. G2 provides an excellent object-oriented representation, a high-level programming language, and a flexible graphical environment. An example of the REPRO user interface is shown in fig.2 and a schematic layout is shown in fig.3.

406

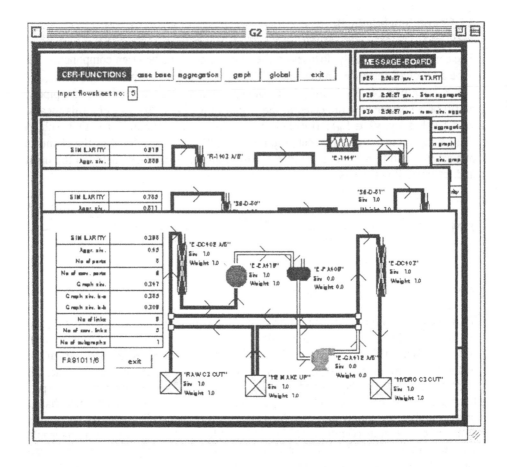

Fig.2. REPRO user interface.

The system consists of four modules: a graphical user interface (GUI), a case manager (CM), a case retrieval module (CR), and a case base / background knowledge repository (CB/BK).

Thanks to the CM module the user can easily define an input flowsheet by selecting the desired components and connecting them graphically with pipes. Additionally CM provide facilities like browsing, deleting, and editing existing flowsheets. A case manager is able to put into the case-retrieval module a draft (incomplete) input flowsheet, so the user (designer) has an opportunity to focus on desired details. After defining an input flowsheet, the CR module is ready for retrieval in the case base in order to find proper existing designs. It starts with automatically selecting the set of flowsheets from the case base. During this preliminary step a set of proper cases (from the same process class) is established.

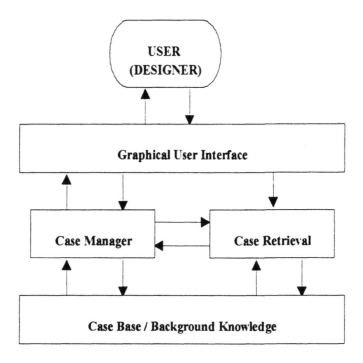

Fig.3. REPRO architecture.

Then the structural similarity between the input flowsheet and the given retrieved one is computed from the formula:

$$SIM(\Psi_I, \Psi_R) = \alpha * SIM^A(\Psi_I, \Psi_R) + \beta * SIM^C(\Psi_I, \Psi_R)$$

where: $\alpha, \beta \in <0;1> \wedge \alpha+\beta=1$

Necessary domain knowledge is taken from the CB/BK repository: for example a components-specific local similarity measure. The value of α and β coefficients are specified by the user, who can focus on the required kind of similarity. After computing the similarities, the CR module ranks the cases and return results to CM. Once relevant cases are retrieved from the case base, the designer can browse those cases in order to select the most applicable ones for the current situation. As it was mentioned in section 4 this approach is computationally tractable because of the flowsheets uniqueness property. In fact this complexity is O(NM) for the aggregation similarity and $O(N^2M^2)$ for the connection similarity in the worst-case performance, where N, M are the number of the components respectively in the input and the retrieved flowsheet.

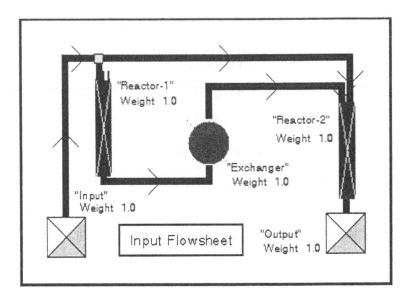

Fig.4. An example of an input flowsheet.

The following example shows the performance of REPRO from the user's point of view. Figure 4 presents a simple input flowsheet that consists of 5 connected components. Each component has a weight that expresses the user preferences. Figure 5 presents an example of a retrieved flowsheet. The results of comparison between an input and a retrieved flowsheets are shown to the user on three levels. First, the local similarity between components is shown next to each component on a retrieved case: sim(x1,x2), see fig.5. Second, the connection similarity is graphically shown by displaying the common pipes with a different color: sub(Ψ_I, Ψ_R), see fig.5. Finally the general quantitative description of the similarity (computed from formulas introduced in sections 3.1 and 3.2) is presented in fig.5 as well. Thanks to this textual and graphical information the designer has a whole overview of the local and global similarity between flowsheets.

5 REPRO evaluation

REPRO was tested on flowsheets for the hydrogenation C3 and hydrogenation C6-C8 processes. The overview of the case base is presented in table 1. The hydrogenation C3 process was selected for introductory tests as a relatively simple and standard type of process. On the contrary the hydrogenation C6-C8 is a complex type of process with a large number of the interconnections. Before being introduced in the case base, all the available flowsheets were especially modified by excluding unimportant control links and by adding function descriptions to all the components. Unfortunately this task required the expert supervision for all the flowsheets.

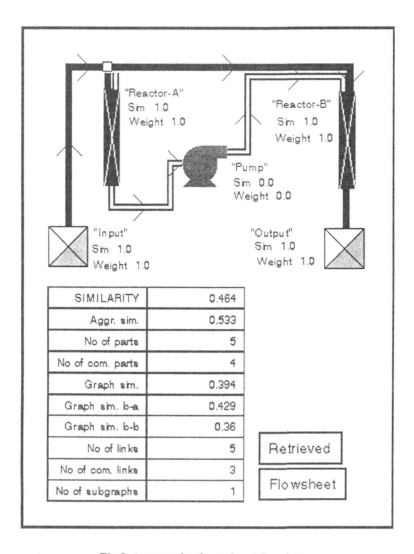

SIMILARITY	0.464
Aggr. sim.	0.533
No of parts	5
No of com. parts	4
Graph sim.	0.394
Graph sim. b-a	0.429
Graph sim. b-b	0.36
No of links	5
No of com. links	3
No of subgraphs	1

Fig.5. An example of a retrieved flowsheet.

Finally the retrieval results and weights for all the available 27 flowsheets were obtained from the expert. Based on this data, REPRO was tested by means of a "leave-one-out" method. For the C3 process the system retrieved the proper cases without error. This result was obtained using only the aggregation similarity ($\alpha=1, \beta=0$). The same results (with longer time of retrieval) were obtained after adding the connection similarity ($\alpha=1/2, \beta=1/2, \beta\alpha=1/2, \beta\beta=1/2$). This means that for simple processes like C3, the whole structure is often determined by the several components and topology of connections is steady, so there is no need for the connection similarity.

Table 1. The case-bases description.

Case-Base Name	Avg. no. of components	Avg. no. of connections	No of cases
Hydrogenation C3	8	8	13
Hydrogenation C6-C8	25	34	14

At it was expected the connection similarity positively influenced the retrieval accuracy for the complex cases. The result of experiments for hydrogenation C6-C8 are summarized in table 2. For the aggregation similarity the accuracy of retrieval was 62 % for the most similar case, and 54 % for the second nearest case. For the connection similarity REPRO achieved 69% accuracy for the most similar case, and increased it up to 77 % for the second nearest case. The superiority of the connection similarity has been confirmed by a qualitative evaluation. The graphical representation of the similarity between flowsheets has been found very useful by the expert.

Table 2. The result of experiments for hydrogenation C6-C8.

Retrieved Flowsheet	Aggregation Similarity $\alpha=1,\beta=0$ $\beta\alpha=0,\beta\beta=0$	Connection Similarity $\alpha=0,\beta=1,$ $\beta\alpha=2/5,\beta\beta=3/5$	Global Similarity $\alpha=1/2,\beta=1/2,$ $\beta\alpha=2/5,\beta\beta=3/5$
first nearest	62 %	69 %	69 %
second nearest	54 %	77 %	69 %

It should be emphasized that table 2 was created based on a binary decision: yes (good retrieval outcome) or no. Several times, when REPRO retrieved an improper flowsheet, very interesting local similarities were discovered that were previously not known by the expert. The performance of the system was very good when an input case was an incomplete flowsheet (part of the whole flowsheet), that is indeed the most common real life situation. Finally, REPRO almost always computed a very low global similarity for the flowsheets that were evaluated by the expert as a definitively not an acceptable solution.

6 Conclusions and Future Directions

The adaptation is well-known as a crucial task for the Case-Based Design Systems. At present this function was not implemented because of two reasons. First, this approach concerns supporting conceptual design and adaptation concerns mostly the final stages of a design. Second, in a flowsheet there are a lot of inter-related components. This means that a change in one of them can not be made without appropriate modifications to the related parts of a flowsheet. We have found very difficult the problem of representing those hidden inter-relations. Unfortunately this kind of knowledge is necessary during the adaptation process for a creation and/or deletion given components and connections.

The importance of the knowledge acquisition in this approach should be clearly underlined. The lack of exponential complexity and the acceptable retrieval outputs have a background in a good domain recognition and careful flowsheets preparation. Disadvantages of this approach are clear, especially during preparation of an input case, where the user must be conscious of a "vocabulary" that was used for describing previous flowsheets. Nevertheless the system at the present level of development was accepted by the experts as a potentially useful tool for supporting the design activity. The integration these CBR functionality with the commercial CAD system is now under consideration.

Acknowledgments

We would like to thank Yves Charlez, Alan Charon, and Jean-Paul Dessapt from the Industrial Division at I.F.P. for providing the domain knowledge and helpful comments.

References

Bisson G. (1995). Why and How to Define a Similarity Measure for Object Based Representation Systems. In *Towards Very Large Knowledge Bases*, pp.236-246, IOS Press, Amsterdam.

Douglas J. (1988). *Conceptual Design of Chemical Processes*. McGraw-Hill.

Gentner (1983). Structure-Mapping: A Theoretical Framework for Analogy. *Cognitive Science*, vol.7, pp. 155-170.

Falkenhainer B., Forbus K., Gentner D. (1989). The Structure-Mapping Engine: Algorithms and Examples. *Artificial Intelligence*, vol.41, no.1, pp.1-64.

Fraga E. (1994) The Implementation of a Portable Object-Oriented Distributed Process Engineering Environment. *Technical Report 1994-17*. Department of Chemical Engineering, Edinburgh University.

Holyoak K., Thagard P. (1989). Analogical Mapping by Constraint Satisfaction. *Cognitive Science*, vol.13, pp.293-355.

Maher M. et al. (1995). *Case-Based Reasoning in Design*. Lawrence Erlbaum.

Maher P. (1993). A Similarity Measure for Conceptual Graphs. *International Journal of Intelligent Systems*, vol.8, pp.819-837.

Motard R. (1989). Integrated Computer-Aided Process Engineering. *Computers & Chemical Engineering* 13(11-12), 1199-1206.

Myaeng S., Lopez-Lopez A. (1992). Conceptual graph matching: a flexible algorithm and experiments. *J.Expt, Theor. Artif. Intell.*, vol.4, pp.107-126.

Pu P. (1993). Introduction: Issues in Case-Based Design Systems. *AI EDAM*, 7(2), 79-85.

Rumbaugh J. et al. (1991). *Object-Oriented Modeling and Design*. Prentice-Hall.

Stephanopoulos G. (1987). Design-Kit: An Object-Oriented Environment For Process Engineering. *Computers & Chemical Engineering* 11(6), 655-674.

Surma J., Braunschweig B (1995). Reutilisation d'Etudes de Procedes. *Proceed. of the XVII Conf. Int. des Industries de Procedes: INTERCHIME '95*, Paris.

Surma J., Braunschweig B. (1996). Case-Based Retrieval in Process Engineering: Supporting Design by Reusing Flowsheets. *Enginnering Applications of Artificial Intelligence, Special Issue: AI in Design Applications* 9(4).

Surma J. (1996). *REPRO ver.1.3. User Manual and Implementation.* IFP Rapport - Juillet 1996.

Voss A. et al. (1994a). *Similarity concepts and retrieval methods.* FABEL Report No.13, Gesellschaft fur Mathematik und Datenverarbeitung mbH, Sankt Augustin.

Voss A. et al. (1994b). Retrieval of Similar Layouts- about a very hybrid approach in FABEL. *Artificial Intelligence in Design '94*, Gero J. and Sudweeks F. (eds.), Kluwer Academic Publ. 625-640.

A Bayesian Framework for Case-Based Reasoning

Henry Tirri, Petri Kontkanen, and Petri Myllymäki

Complex Systems Computation Group (CoSCo)
P.O.Box 26, Department of Computer Science
FIN-00014 University of Helsinki, Finland

Abstract. In this paper we present a probabilistic framework for case-based reasoning in data-intensive domains, where only weak prior knowledge is available. In such a probabilistic viewpoint the attributes are interpreted as random variables, and the case base is used to approximate the underlying joint probability distribution of the attributes. Consequently structural case adaptation (and parameter adjustment in particular) can be viewed as prediction based on the full probability model constructed from the case history. The methodology addresses several problems encountered in building case-based reasoning systems. It provides a computationally efficient structural adaptation algorithm, avoids overfitting by using Bayesian model selection and uses directly probabilities as measures of similarity. The methodology described has been implemented in the D-SIDE software package, and the approach is validated by presenting empirical results of the method's classification prediction performance for a set of public domain data sets.

1 Introduction

In principle any computational system capable of reasoning can be placed somewhere in a spectrum based on the "knowledge-intensiveness" of the underlying approach. At one end of the spectrum are the systems relying on deep causal models [7], closely followed by the classic Knowledge-Based Systems (KBS). At the opposite end of the spectrum are the learning systems with weak prior domain knowledge which base their reasoning on models built from data [8]. Along this spectrum the reasoning process itself gradually changes from the deductive reasoning of knowledge-intensive approaches to inductive reasoning of data-intensive approaches, i.e., from logical inference to statistical inference.

In its most general form, *case-based reasoning* (CBR) can be viewed as an approach to computational reasoning that solves new problems by adapting previously successful solutions to similar problems [20, 39]. This general definition does not by itself place CBR systems in any particular place in the spectrum discussed above—the adaptation step in case-based reasoning can embed a substantial amount of domain knowledge. However, while CBR has its roots in cognitive modeling [34, 20], from an engineering point of view it can be seen as an attempt to address many of the problems recognized in the design of traditional knowledge-intensive systems, in particular the brittleness problem [2]. Consequently, one of the advocated potential advantages of case-based reasoning has been the fact that CBR systems can be built in cases where only weak prior domain knowledge is available [39], and the "top-down" approaches with explicit model representations cannot be applied. In such domains CBR systems construct *implicit domain models*. These models are defined by a case history (a set of past cases) together with the accompanying domain-specific procedures for case matching and adaptation. Such implicit models are then used to solve new problems in the same domain. If we further restrict ourselves to domains where cases can be represented as vectors of attribute values, and allow some of the recorded past cases to be incorrect (both being very realistic assumptions in industrial applications), the CBR approach in such domains can clearly be placed in the data-intensive end of the spectrum. This type of case-based reasoning approaches can be paralleled to the fundamental quest in statistical inference, i.e., finding the most probable model given data and weak prior knowledge. In this view, structural case adaptation [20] (and parameter adjustment in particular) can be seen as probabilistic prediction based on the model constructed from the case history. This observation has been our starting point for developing a probabilistic foundation for data-intensive case-based reasoning.

As discussed in [20], no old situation is ever exactly the same as a new one, hence old solutions must usually be adapted (for more discussion on the importance of adaptation in CBR systems see e.g., [19]). Traditional case-based reasoning systems base their structural adaptation on adjustment heuristics applied to the values of interest in relevant cases. This set of relevant cases is determined during the case retrieval phase typically by using a nearest neighbor matching [32] or indexes created by induction algorithms [33]. For many problem domains the basic approach of storing all the cases suffers from several drawbacks. First, the run-time computational costs for matching algorithms are high when the size of the case base grows large. However, a more fundamental problem in storing all cases in real applications is related to the well-known "overfitting" problem inherent to any inductive model construction method for noisy domains. Finally, the adaptation performance of a case-based system can be very sensitive to the selection of a proper similarity function [39]. In order to address some of these drawbacks of the basic approach, many suggestions for structuring the case storage have been proposed in the literature. From our point of view the most interesting is the "conceptual clustering" approach where *generalized episodes* [26] are used to group similar cases under a more general structure.

The approach presented in this paper adopts a probabilistic viewpoint and argues that the case base stored can be seen to form a probabilistic model of the problem domain, and that (structural) adaptation in such a probabilistic view is equal to prediction based on the model in question. In this approach the attributes are interpreted as random variables, and the case base is used to approximate the underlying joint probability distribution of the attributes. Case adaptation can now be given a rigorous interpretation as follows. Given a new case with some unknown attributes which, if known, could be used to solve the problem at hand, the predictive distributions for these attributes can be constructed by summing the predictions of individual cases weighted by the probability that the new case is a distorted version of the case in question. In this view each case is seen as a component distribution, which contributes to the joint distribution, i.e., the joint distribution is represented as a mixture of "case distributions". This basic case-based approach in numerical domains can in probabilistic terms be understood as a form of using kernel density estimators for inference (see e.g., [35]).

In practice a situation where all the case distributions are required for a good approximation is very rare, as the case base usually exhibits some cluster structure in the attribute domain space. In most cases the joint distribution can be approximated by a simpler mixture of distributions by giving a weighted sum of "cluster distributions", each of which gives the marginal attribute probability distributions conditioned by the cluster index. In fact, construction of prototypical structures such as Generalized Episodes by grouping cases sharing similar properties [26] can be understood as approximations to such simpler mixture structures [11, 38]. Thus the probabilistic approach offers also a natural way of structuring the case storage[1].

There are several advantages of using the above probabilistic view of CBR. If a good approximative representation of the problem domain distribution can be found, we can use a minimum risk Bayes decision rule in the adaptation phase [14]. It should also be observed that although the experimental results presented in Section 5 are only for classification tasks, in our approach *a full probability model is constructed*. Consequently, the predictive distributions can also be used directly for any adaptation task, since when the mixture model is constructed, all attributes are treated equally. In addition, such an adaptation computation can be performed efficiently [31, 30, 29].

As discussed above, to perform successful adaptation in an application with only weak domain knowledge, a model has to be extracted from the (noisy) set of cases. For constructing the component distributions from the case base, we have adopted the Bayesian approach (see e.g., [14]) which allows us to make a tradeoff between the complexity of our distribution structure and fit to the case data, thus resolving the overfitting problem. This combination of probabilistic finite mixture models with Bayesian model selection is akin to the approach adopted in the Autoclass system [5] with the notable difference in our focus to perform adaptation (prediction) rather than exploratory latent class analysis.

In this paper we describe a methodology for probabilistic case-based reasoning with discrete attribute values. The methodology addresses all the drawbacks discussed above: it provides a computationally efficient adaptation algorithm, avoids overfitting by using Bayesian model selection and uses directly probabilities as measures of similarity. The methodology described has been implemented in the D-SIDE software package. In order to validate our approach we present empirical results on a set of classification tasks (for discussion of exemplar-based classification see Chapter 13.1 in [20]). In order to be able to compare the probabilistic exemplar-based method with alternative classification approaches, we have used

---

[1] It should be observed that although not assumed in the discussion below, nothing in our approach prohibits storing also the individual cases in addition to the mixture distribution model. This can sometimes be useful for example for satisfying the needs of the explanation mechanisms.

public domain data sets (including data sets from the StatLog project [28]). Our results clearly demonstrate that the adaptation based on a probabilistic model is highly competitive for a wide spectrum of natural data sets with respect to other model construction approaches including decision trees or neural algorithms.

2 The finite mixture model

We model here the problem domain by m discrete random variables $X_1, \ldots, X_m$ (continuous attributes are at this point discretized by quantization). A *case* $\vec{d}$ is a data instantiation vector where all the variables X_i have been assigned a value, $\vec{d} = (X_1 = x_1, \ldots, X_m = x_m)$, where $x_i \in \{x_{i1}, \ldots, x_{in_i}\}$. A *case base* $D = (\vec{d}_1, \ldots, \vec{d}_N)$ is a set of N i.i.d. (independent and identically distributed) data instantiations, where each $\vec{d}_j$ is sampled from $\mathcal{P}$, the joint distribution of the variables $(X_1, \ldots, X_m)$.

We assume that the case base D is noisy, i.e., the data vectors can be regarded as distorted versions of some unknown "true" case. By noise we do not only mean incorrect or incomplete data caused by measurement errors or other failures in the data sampling process, but also the sampling errors caused by the finite size of the sample D. Consequently, this type of noise is inherently present in all the case bases available. Furthermore, we assume that the noise is not uniformly distributed, but the noisy cases form tightly clustered groups, where all the cases in a group correspond to the same unknown case. We have no means of determining the original unknown cases exactly, but we can form a probability distribution around each cluster of cases, based on the data vectors in the cluster. This probability distribution can be seen as a generalized case representation, a "prototypical case" representing all the data vectors in a cluster[2].

Let us now assume that we are given a clustering of the problem domain, i.e., the data instantiation space is partitioned into K groups of vectors. In finite mixture models [11, 38] the problem domain probability distribution is approximated as a weighted sum of mixture distributions:

$$P(\vec{d}) = \sum_{k=1}^{K} P(Y = y_k) P(\vec{d}|Y = y_k), \tag{1}$$

where the values of the discrete *clustering random variable* Y correspond to the separate clusters of the instantiation space, and each mixture distribution $P(\vec{d}|Y = y_k)$ represents the prototypical case corresponding to cluster k. As the data vectors belonging to the same cluster can be seen as noisy versions of some (unknown) point, we can assume the variables X_i inside each cluster to be independent and thus (1) becomes

$$P(\vec{d}) = P(X_1 = x_1, \ldots, X_m = x_m) = \sum_{k=1}^{K} P(Y = y_k) \prod_{i=1}^{m} P(X_i = x_i|Y = y_k).$$

---

[2] The prototypical cases reduce to normal cases if we allow only one data vector in each cluster.

It should be observed that the use of mixture distributions as prototypical cases implies that a given instance matches to several prototypical cases simultaneously with different probabilities, and thus the predictive distributions of variables can be computed as a weighted estimate from the marginal probability distributions for the variable in question, as shown in Section 3.

In our case both the cluster distribution $P(Y)$ and the intra-class conditional distributions $P(X_i|Y = y_k)$ are assumed to be multinomial. Thus a finite mixture model can be defined by first fixing K, the *model class* (the number of the mixing distributions), and then by determining the values of the model parameters $\Theta = (\alpha, \Phi), \Theta \in \Omega$, where $\alpha = (\alpha_1, \ldots, \alpha_K)$ and $\Phi = (\Phi_{11}, \ldots, \Phi_{1m}, \ldots, \Phi_{K1}, \ldots, \Phi_{Km})$, with the denotations

$$\alpha_k = P(Y = y_k), \Phi_{ki} = (\phi_{ki1}, \ldots, \phi_{kin_i}), \text{ where } \phi_{kil} = P(X_i = x_{il}|Y = y_k).$$

A detailed description of how to determine K and Θ, given a data sample D, can be found in Section 4.

3 Bayesian inference by finite mixture models

Given a finite mixture model, it is possible to solve various probabilistic reasoning tasks in a computationally efficient manner. The Bayesian *predictive inference* (see e.g. [3]) aims at predicting future (yet unobserved) quantities by means of already observed quantities. More precisely, if $\vec{d}$ is an unobserved data vector, its predictive distribution given observed data D is defined as

$$P(\vec{d}|D) = \int_\Omega P(\vec{d}|D, \Theta)P(\Theta|D)d\Theta. \tag{2}$$

So the predictive distribution can be considered as the expected distribution of $\vec{d}$ over all possible parameter settings (models). From (2) we see that the correct Bayesian procedure for making predictions would be to use all possible models by weighting them by their posterior density. However, we currently approximate the predictive distribution by using only a single parameter set $\hat{\Theta}$ which maximizes the density $P(\Theta|D)$, i.e. $\hat{\Theta}$ is a *maximum a posterior* (MAP) estimate of Θ. By setting the probability $P(\hat{\Theta}|D)$ to unity, the approximative predictive distribution becomes simply

$$P(\vec{d}|D) = P(\vec{d}|D, \hat{\Theta}) = P(\vec{d}|\hat{\Theta}), \tag{3}$$

where the last equality follows from the fact that $\vec{d}$ and D are conditionally independent given $\hat{\Theta}$.

With practical applications in mind, we are especially interested in finding the *conditional predictive distribution* of each uninstantiated X_i, given that some of the variables are instantiated, i.e. assigned a fixed value. Let $\mathcal{I} = \{i_1, \ldots, i_t\}$ be the indices of the instantiated variables, and let $\mathcal{X} = \{X_{i_s} = x_{i_s, l_s}, s = 1, \ldots, t\}$ denote the corresponding assignments. Now we want to determine the distribution

$$P(X_i|D, \mathcal{X}) = \int_\Omega P(X_i|\Theta, \mathcal{X})P(\Theta|D)d\Theta \tag{4}$$

for all $i \notin \mathcal{I}$. By using the approximation (3), (4) becomes

$$P(X_i = x_{il}|D, \mathcal{X}) = P(X_i = x_{il}|\hat{\Theta}, \mathcal{X}) = \frac{P(X_i = x_{il}, \mathcal{X}|\hat{\Theta})}{P(\mathcal{X}|\hat{\Theta})}$$

$$= \frac{\sum_{k=1}^{K} \left(P(Y = y_k|\hat{\Theta}) P(X_i = x_{il}|Y = y_k, \hat{\Theta}) \prod_{s=1}^{t} P(X_{i_s} = x_{i_s l_s}|Y = y_k, \hat{\Theta}) \right)}{\sum_{k=1}^{K} \left(P(Y = y_k|\hat{\Theta}) \prod_{s=1}^{t} P(X_{i_s} = x_{i_s l_s}|Y = y_k, \hat{\Theta}) \right)}.$$

The conditional predictive distribution of X_i can clearly be calculated in time $\mathcal{O}(Ktn_i)$, where K is the number of clusters, t the number of instantiated variables and n_i the number of values of X_i. K is usually small compared to the sample size N, and thus the prediction computation can be performed very efficiently[3].

The predictive distributions can be used for classification and regression tasks. In classification problems, we have a special class variable X_c which is used for classifying data. We fix all the other variables and predict the value of X_c by using its conditional predictive distribution. With the simple 0/1-loss function, the predicted value is usually simply taken as the most probable value of the distribution in question, but alternative schemes emerge when using different loss functions. In more general regression tasks, we have more than one variable for which we want to compute the predictive distribution, given that the values of the other variables are instantiated in advance. Alternatively, finite mixture models can also be used for finding the maximal configuration (the most probable value assignment combination) for all the uninstantiated variables, given the values of the instantiated variables.

4   Learning finite mixture models from data

Let $D = (\vec{d}_1, \ldots, \vec{d}_N)$ be a random sample of N data instantiations, sampled from the problem domain distribution $\mathcal{P}$. By learning we mean here the problem of constructing a single finite mixture model $M_K(\Theta)$ which represents $\mathcal{P}$ as accurately as possible. The learning process can be divided into two separate phases: in the first phase we wish to determine the optimal value for K, the number of mixing distributions (the model class), and in the second phase we wish to find MAP parameter values $\hat{\Theta}$ for the chosen model class.

4.1   Determining the model class

In the Bayesian framework, the optimal number of mixing distributions (clusters) can be determined by evaluating the posterior probability for each model class $\mathcal{M}_K$ given the data:

$$P(\mathcal{M}_K|D) \propto P(D|\mathcal{M}_K)P(\mathcal{M}_K), K = 1, \ldots, N,$$

---

[3] If massively parallel hardware is available, the computations can be made even faster since the algorithms can be parallelized easily [30, 29].

where the normalizing constant $P(D)$ can be omitted since we only need to compare different model classes. The number of clusters can safely be assumed to be bounded by N, since otherwise the sample size is clearly too small for the learning problem in question.

Assuming equal priors for the model classes, they can be ranked by evaluating the *evidence* $P(D|\mathcal{M}_K)$ for each model class,

$$P(D|\mathcal{M}_K) = \int_\Omega P(D|\Theta, \mathcal{M}_K) P(\Theta|\mathcal{M}_K) \, d\Theta. \tag{5}$$

This integral can also be given an interpretation in the information-theoretic framework, where the *stochastic complexity* of a model class can be defined as minus the logarithm of the evidence. The evidence integral is very hard to evaluate since the dimension of the parameter space is usually very large ($K(1+\sum_{i=1}^m n_i)$), but the evidence can be approximated by using e.g. Laplace's method [18]. The quality of the approximations has been tested empirically in the finite mixture framework by using both synthetic [23, 6] and natural [24] data.

4.2 Determining the model class parameters

Let us assume that the model class $\mathcal{M}_K$ is fixed. In the Bayesian approach, the goal is to find the MAP (maximum a posteriori) estimate of parameters by maximizing the posterior density $P(\Theta|D)$,

$$P(\Theta|D) = \frac{P(D|\Theta)P(\Theta)}{\int_\Omega P(D|\Theta)P(\Theta) \, d\Theta},$$

where the normalizing factor is the evidence term (5) discussed in the previous section.

We assume that the prior distributions of the parameters are from the family of Dirichlet densities. Assuming that the parameter vectors α and Φ_{ki} are independent, the joint prior distribution of all the parameters is

$$\text{Di}\,(\mu_1, \ldots, \mu_K) \prod_{k=1}^K \prod_{i=1}^m \text{Di}\,(\sigma_{ki1}, \ldots, \sigma_{kin_i}) \tag{6}$$

with density

$$P(\Theta) = \Gamma\left(\sum_{k=1}^K \mu_k\right) \prod_{k=1}^K \left(\frac{\alpha_k^{\mu_k-1}}{\Gamma(\mu_k)}\right) \prod_{k=1}^K \prod_{i=1}^m \left(\Gamma(\sum_{l=1}^{n_i} \sigma_{kil}) \prod_{l=1}^{n_i} \frac{\phi_{kil}^{\sigma_{kil}-1}}{\Gamma(\sigma_{kil})}\right). \tag{7}$$

The family of Dirichlet densities is *conjugate* (see e.g. [9]) to the family of multinomials, i.e. the functional form of parameter distribution remains invariant in the prior-to-posterior transformation, thus the choice of Dirichlet priors is justified.

The likelihood $P(D|\Theta)$ has two different forms depending on whether we know to which cluster each data vector belongs to or not. Let us first consider the positive case, i.e. *supervised learning*. The likelihood term can now be conveniently represented by introducing the *cluster indicator variables* $Z = (z_1, \ldots, z_N)$, $z_j = (z_{j1}, \ldots, z_{jK})$, where

$$z_{jk} = \begin{cases} 1, & \text{if } \vec{d}_j \in y_k, \\ 0, & \text{otherwise.} \end{cases}$$

It follows that

$$P(D|\Theta, \mathcal{M}_K) = \prod_{k=1}^{K} \left(\alpha_k^{h_k} \prod_{i=1}^{m} \prod_{l=1}^{n_i} \phi_{kil}^{f_{kil}} \right),$$

where $h_k = \sum_{j=1}^{N} z_{jk}$ is the number of instantiations in cluster k, and $f_{kil} = \sum_{j=1}^{N} z_{jk} v_{jil}$ is the number of instantiations in cluster k with variable X_i having value x_{il}, where

$$v_{jil} = \begin{cases} 1, & \text{if } d_{ji} = x_{il}, \\ 0, & \text{otherwise.} \end{cases}$$

From the conjugacy property it follows that the posterior distribution is also a product of Dirichlet's and is given by

$$\text{Di}\,(\mu_1 + h_1, \ldots, \mu_K + h_K) \prod_{k=1}^{K} \prod_{i=1}^{m} \text{Di}\,(\sigma_{ki1} + f_{ki1}, \ldots, \sigma_{kin_i} + f_{kin_i})$$

with the corresponding density $P(\Theta|D)$ being analogous to (7). The MAP estimate $\Theta = \hat{\Theta}$ is the mode of this density, and since the parameters α_k and ϕ_{kil} appear disjointly, the mode can be determined by finding the modes of the individual Dirichlet's and is obtained by setting

$$\hat{\alpha}_k = \frac{h_k + \mu_k - 1}{N + \sum_{k=1}^{K} \mu_k - K}, \quad \hat{\phi}_{kil} = \frac{f_{kil} + \sigma_{kil} - 1}{h_k + \sum_{l=1}^{n_i} \sigma_{kil} - n_i}. \tag{8}$$

Assuming that the values of the cluster indicators are part of the training data D results in the simple naive Bayes model (see e.g. [16]). If, however, we do not consider the values of cluster indicators to be known, the learning problem becomes much more complex. In this *unsupervised learning* case we regard z_j's as random variables and assume that Z is a random sample of size N from a multinomial distribution with parameters α. The joint likelihood of D and Z is

$$P(D, Z|\Theta) = \prod_{j=1}^{N} \prod_{k=1}^{K} \left(\alpha_k \prod_{i=1}^{m} \phi_{kid_{ji}} \right)^{z_{jk}}, \tag{9}$$

and the marginal likelihood of D is obtained by summing over Z corresponding to all possible clusterings of data into K clusters. These clusterings are, however, exponential (K^N) in number, so exact MAP estimate cannot be found, and we are forced to use numerical approximation methods. The usual approach is to regard Z as missing data and estimate it iteratively [27]. This estimation can be performed by using the *Expectation-Maximization (EM)* algorithm [10]. The EM algorithm is an iterative algorithm, which monotonically increases the expected value of the posterior corresponding to incomplete data. It consists of two steps: Expectation(E) and Maximization(M). In E step, the expected values of the complete data sufficient statistics given the incomplete data and current parameter estimates are determined. In M step, the parameter values are updated in such a way that the obtained expected value of the posterior is maximized. The detailed derivation of the update formulas in our mixture case is somewhat involved and omitted here, but it is akin to the use of EM in [17]. The detailed derivation of the update formulas in our mixture case can be found in [25].

5   Empirical results

The approach described above has been implemented as part of a more general software package D-SIDE[4] for building systems capable of probabilistic inference. As already discussed in the introduction, we are motivated in finding models with good adaptation performance. In addition we are interested in evaluating the approach against other popular method families such as neural networks or decision tree algorithms.

Below we report results from an ongoing extensive experimentation with the probabilistic case-based reasoning method using publicly available datasets for classification problems. For comparison purposes, we have also collected performance results from the literature for alternative methods using the same datasets. We make no claims that the list of the results of alternative algorithms is exhaustive, however for each dataset we have included the best results we have found in the literature. The selection of datasets was done on the basis of their reported use, i.e., we have preferred datasets that have been used for testing many different methods over datasets with only isolated results. Many of the results are from the StatLog project [28], but we have also included more recent results. The descriptions of the datasets, the testing procedures used, and the best model classes (the number of mixtures) found for each data set are given in Table 1. The last column, the default value, denotes the success rate of a simple classifier, which classifies all the instances to the most common class.

It should be observed that with the exception of the DNA dataset, all our current results are crossvalidated, and when possible (for the StatLog datasets) we have used the same crossvalidation scheme as described in [28]. The same does not hold for many of the results for the other methods. In many cases the testing procedure either was not reported, or the best result with a single test set was given. The current performance results of all the algorithms (measured as classification success percentage) for individual datasets are presented as barcharts in Figures 1 and 2.

Even from these preliminary empirical results it can clearly be seen that our approach performs well not only when compared to memory-based methods

---

[4] A running Java[TM] demo of the D-SIDE software can be accessed through our WWW homepage at URL "http: //www.cs.Helsinki.FI/research/cosco/".

AUSTRALIAN

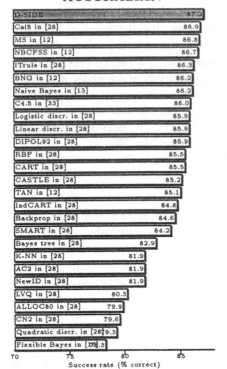

DIABETES

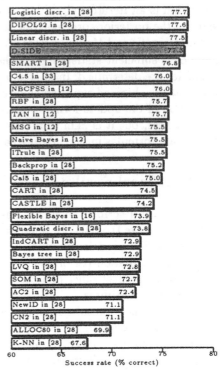

PRIMARY TUMOR

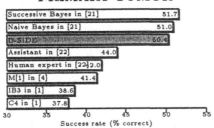

HEPATITIS

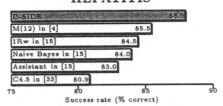

GLASS

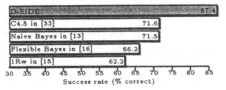

Fig. 1. Experimental results on the Australian, Diabetes, Primary tumor, Hepatitis and Glass datasets.

DNA

RBF in [28]	95.9
DIPOL92 in [28]	95.2
ALLOC80 in [28]	94.3
Linear discr. in [28]	94.1
Quadratic discr. in [28]	94.1
Logistic discr. in [28]	93.9
Naive Bayes in [28]	93.2
CASTLE in [28]	92.8
IndCART in [28]	92.7
C4.5 in [28]	92.4
CART in [28]	91.5
Backprop in [28]	91.2
Bayes tree in [28]	90.5
CN2 in [28]	90.5
AC2 in [28]	90.0
NewID in [28]	90.0
SMART in [28]	88.5
Cal5 in [28]	86.9
ITrule in [28]	86.5
K-NN in [28]	85.4
SOM in [28]	66.1

Success rate (% correct)

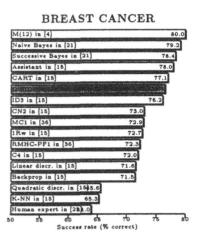

BREAST CANCER

M(12) in [4]	80.0
Naive Bayes in [21]	79.2
Successive Bayes in [21]	78.4
Assistant in [15]	78.0
CART in [15]	77.1
ID3 in [15]	76.2
CN2 in [15]	73.0
MC1 in [36]	72.9
1Rw in [15]	72.7
RMHC-PF1 in [36]	72.3
C4 in [15]	72.0
Linear discr. in [15]	71.6
Backprop in [15]	71.5
Quadratic discr. in [15]	65.6
K-NN in [15]	65.3
Human expert in [21]	2.0

Success rate (% correct)

IRIS

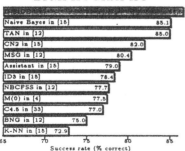

Linear discr. in [15]	98.0
Quadratic discr. in [15]	97.3
Backprop. in [15]	96.7
Naive Bayes in [16]	96.0
K-NN in [15]	96.0
1Rw in [15]	96.0
C4.5 in [16]	95.3
CART in [16]	95.3
Flexible Bayes in [16]	95.3
RMHC-PF1 in [36]	94.7
ID3 in [15]	94.4
MC1 in [36]	93.5

Success rate (% correct)

HEART DISEASE

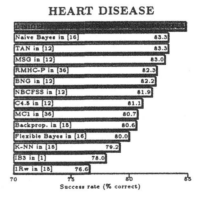

Naive Bayes in [16]	83.3
TAN in [12]	83.3
MSG in [12]	83.0
RMHC-P in [36]	82.3
BNG in [12]	82.2
NBCFSS in [12]	81.9
C4.5 in [12]	81.1
MC1 in [36]	80.7
Backprop. in [15]	80.6
Flexible Bayes in [16]	80.0
K-NN in [15]	79.2
IB3 in [1]	78.0
1Rw in [15]	76.6

Success rate (% correct)

LYMPHOGRAPHY

Naive Bayes in [15]	85.1
TAN in [12]	85.0
CN2 in [15]	82.0
MSG in [12]	80.4
Assistant in [15]	79.0
ID3 in [15]	78.4
NBCFSS in [12]	77.7
M(0) in [4]	77.5
C4.5 in [33]	77.0
BNG in [12]	75.0
K-NN in [15]	72.9

Success rate (% correct)

Fig. 2. Experimental results on the DNA, Breast cancer, Iris, Heart disease and Lymphography databases.

Table 1. The datasets and testing methods used in our experiments.

Data set	Size	#Attrs	#Classes	#Clusters	Test method	Default
Australian	690	15	2	17	10-fold CV	56.0
Breast cancer	286	10	2	21	11-fold CV	70.3
Diabetes	768	9	2	20	12-fold CV	65.0
DNA	3186	181	3	13	train&test	50.8
Glass	214	10	6	30	7-fold CV	40.7
Heart disease	270	14	2	8	9-fold CV	79.4
Hepatitis	150	20	2	9	5-fold CV	55.6
Iris	150	5	3	4	5-fold CV	33.3
Lymphography	148	19	4	19	5-fold CV	54.7
Primary tumor	339	18	21	21	10-fold CV	24.8

such as K-NN, IB3, or ALLOC80, but also with respect to decision tree methods and common neural network approaches such as backpropagation. The goodness of the results with respect to the memory based methods are not especially surprising as they can be seen as approximations to the finite mixture approach presented here [37]. A more interesting observation is that the EM algorithm finds MAP estimates that outperform also all other Bayesian approaches present in the StatLog comparison, including CASTLE, Naive Bayes, and Bayes tree algorithms.

In addition to the adaptation performance, it is also interesting to study if the constructed clusters can indeed be interpreted as "prototypical cases". Hence we investigated the clusters found with the D-SIDE environment, which provides a flexible graphical user interface for displaying predictive distributions and the mixture structure (see Figure 3). Since the meaning of the attributes in the data sets used for the empirical evaluation above were not documented, and thus could not be interpreted by a layman, for this cluster interpretation we used another public domain data set in a credit assessment domain. In this German credit data set we could give clear interpretations for 6 out of the 9 clusters. For example the most influential prototype case could be described consisting of working single women (age < 30, 4 − 7 years in the current job), living in an apartment they owned, and requesting a small loan (less than 1800 DM) for furniture or home appliances with very little savings. It should be emphasized that since, like any case-based system, the mixture model built allows calculation of any predictive distribution, it can also be used explore dependencies between attributes. For example one can investigate what is the effect of being just recently employed to the purpose of the loan.

6 Conclusion

We have discussed the use of a probabilistic framework for building case-based reasoning systems. The presented Bayesian framework is realized by using the

German Problem

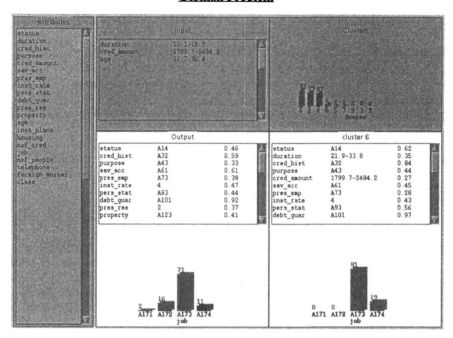

Fig. 3. A snapshot of the interface of the D-SIDE reasoning engine.

Expectation-Maximization (EM) algorithm for finding good models. We also presented empirical results on the method's adaptation performance for a set of public domain classification data sets, and compared the results to the performance of various machine learning and neural network methods. Although the experimentation is still ongoing, the current results clearly demonstrate that our Bayesian approach is highly competitive, and offers a very consistent performance over different types of data.

One should observe that the derivation presented here is given for discrete attributes (but continuous model spaces). The approach extends also to the case where attributes are real-valued. However, some limited experimentation we performed indicated that moving from discrete to continuous values does not necessarily improve the adaptation performance of the model. This is due to the additional assumptions of the distribution form (e.g., modeling continuous attributes with independent Gaussian distributions with appropriate conjugate priors) that are required, as well as to the fact that eventually when computations are performed, only limited numerical accuracy is available. We are currently investigating these issues.

Acknowledgments This research has been supported by the Technology Development Center (TEKES). The Primary Tumor, the Breast Cancer and the Lymphography data were obtained from the University Medical Centre, Institute of Oncology, Ljubljana, Yugoslavia. Thanks go to M. Zwitter and M. Soklič for providing the data.

References

1. D. Aha, D. Kibler, and M. Albert. Instance-based learning algorithms. *Machine Learning*, 6:37–66, 1991.
2. R. Barletta. An introduction to case-based reasoning. *AI Expert*, pages 42–49, 1991.
3. J.M. Bernardo and A.F.M Smith. *Bayesian theory*. John Wiley, 1994.
4. B. Cestnik and I. Bratko. On estimating probabilities in tree pruning. In Y. Kodratoff, editor, *Machine Learning EWSL-91*, pages 138–150. Springer-Verlag, 1991.
5. P. Cheeseman, J. Kelly, M. Self, J. Stutz, W. Taylor, and D. Freeman. Autoclass: A Bayesian classification system. In *Proceedings of the Fifth International Conference on Machine Learning*, pages 54–64, Ann Arbor, June 1988.
6. D.M. Chickering and D. Heckerman. Efficient approximations for the marginal likelihood of incomplete data given a Bayesian network. Technical Report MSR-TR-96-08, Microsoft Research, Advanced Technology Division, 1996.
7. W. Clancey. Heuristic classification. *Artificial Intelligence*, 27:289–350, 1985.
8. T. Cover and P. Hart. Nearest neighbor pattern classification. *IEEE Transactions on Information Theory*, 13:21–27, 1967.
9. M.H. DeGroot. *Optimal statistical decisions*. McGraw-Hill, 1970.
10. A.P. Dempster, N.M. Laird, and D.B. Rubin. Maximum likelihood from incomplete data via the EM algorithm. *Journal of the Royal Statistical Society, Series B*, 39(1):1–38, 1977.
11. B.S. Everitt and D.J. Hand. *Finite Mixture Distributions*. Chapman and Hall, London, 1981.
12. N. Friedman and M. Goldszmidt. Building classifiers using Bayesian networks. In *Proceedings of AAAI-96 (to appear)*, 1996.
13. N. Friedman and M. Goldszmidt. Discretizing continuous attributes while learning Bayesian networks. In L. Saitta, editor, *Machine Learning: Proceedings of the Thirteenth International Conference (to appear)*. Morgan Kaufmann Publishers, 1996.
14. A. Gelman, J. Carlin, H. Stern, and D. Rubin. *Bayesian Data Analysis*. Chapman & Hall, 1995.
15. R.C. Holte. Very simple classification rules perform well on most commonly used datasets. *Machine Learning*, 11:63–91, 1993.
16. G.H. John and P. Langley. Estimating continuous distributions in Bayesian classifiers. In P. Besnard and S. Hanks, editors, *Proceedings of the 11th Conference on Uncertainty in Artificial Intelligence*, pages 338–345. Morgan Kaufmann Publishers, 1995.
17. M.I. Jordan and R.A. Jacobs. Hierarchical mixtures of experts and the EM algorithm. *Neural Computation*, 6:181–214, 1994.
18. R.E. Kass and A.E. Raftery. Bayes factors. Technical Report 254, Department of Statistics, University of Washington, 1994.
19. M. Keane. Analogical asides on case-based reasoning. In S. Wess, K.-D. Althoff, and M Richter, editors, *Topics in Case-Based Reasoning*, volume 837 of *Lecture Notes in Artificial Intelligence*, pages 21–32. Springer-Verlag, 1994.

20. J. Kolodner. *Case-Based Reasoning.* Morgan Kaufmann Publishers, San Mateo, 1993.
21. I. Kononenko. Successive naive Bayesian classifier. *Informatica,* 17:167–174, 1993.
22. I. Kononenko and I. Bratko. Information-based evaluation criterion for classifier's performance. *Machine Learning,* 6:67–80, 1991.
23. P. Kontkanen, P. Myllymäki, and H. Tirri. Unsupervised Bayesian learning of discrete finite mixtures. Manuscript, submitted for publication.
24. P. Kontkanen, P. Myllymäki, and H. Tirri. Comparing Bayesian model class selection criteria by discrete finite mixtures. In *Proceedings of the ISIS (Information, Statistics and Induction in Science) Conference,* Melbourne, Australia, August 1996. (To appear.).
25. P. Kontkanen, P. Myllymäki, and H. Tirri. Constructing Bayesian finite mixture models by the EM algorithm. Technical Report C-1996-9, University of Helsinki, Department of Computer Science, February 1996.
26. P. Koton. *Using experience in learning and problem solving.* PhD thesis, Massachusetts Institute of Technology, 1989.
27. R.J.A. Little and D.B. Rubin. *Statistical analysis with missing data.* Wiley, 1987.
28. D. Michie, D.J. Spiegelhalter, and C.C. Taylor, editors. *Machine Learning, Neural and Statistical Classification.* Ellis Horwood, London, 1994.
29. P. Myllymäki and H. Tirri. Bayesian case-based reasoning with neural networks. In *Proceedings of the IEEE International Conference on Neural Networks,* volume 1, pages 422–427, San Francisco, March 1993. IEEE, Piscataway, NJ.
30. P. Myllymäki and H. Tirri. Massively parallel case-based reasoning with probabilistic similarity metrics. In S. Wess, K.-D. Althoff, and M Richter, editors, *Topics in Case-Based Reasoning,* volume 837 of *Lecture Notes in Artificial Intelligence,* pages 144–154. Springer-Verlag, 1994.
31. P. Myllymäki and H. Tirri. Constructing computationally efficient Bayesian models via unsupervised clustering. In A.Gammerman, editor, *Probabilistic Reasoning and Bayesian Belief Networks,* pages 237–248. Alfred Waller Publishers, Suffolk, 1995.
32. C. Owens. Integrating feature extraction and memory search. *Machine Learning,* 10(3):311–340, 1993.
33. J.R. Quinlan. Improved use of continuous attributes in C4.5. *Journal of Artificial Intelligence Research,* 4:77–90, 1996.
34. R. Schank. *Dynamic Memory: A theory of reminding and learning in computers and people.* Cambridge University Press, 1982.
35. D.W. Scott. *Multivariate Density Estimation. Theory, Practice, and Visualization.* John Wiley & Sons, New York, 1992.
36. D. Skalak. Prototype and feature selection by sampling and random mutation hill climbing algorithms. In *Machine Learning: Proceedings of the Eleventh International Conference,* pages 293–301, 1994.
37. H. Tirri, P. Kontkanen, and P. Myllymäki. Probabilistic instance-based learning. In L. Saitta, editor, *Machine Learning: Proceedings of the Thirteenth International Conference,* pages 507–515. Morgan Kaufmann Publishers, 1996.
38. D.M. Titterington, A.F.M. Smith, and U.E. Makov. *Statistical Analysis of Finite Mixture Distributions.* John Wiley & Sons, New York, 1985.
39. I. Watson and F. Marir. Case-based reasoning: A review. *The Knowledge Engineering Review,* 9(4):327–354, 1994.

Principles of Case Reusing Systems

Angi Voß

GMD – FIT
e-mail:angi.voss@gmd.de
Sankt Augustin, Germany

Abstract. The discipline of case-based reasoning develops techniques
to retrieve and reuse old solutions for new problems. To reuse solutions,
several case adaptation systems have been built and many are under
development. They deal with different tasks in different domains, but
a methodology is still lacking. Based on an analysis of up-to-date case
adaptation systems, this article moves towards a methodology by providing a common framework and some guidelines. As key issues the tailoring
of cases, global strategies, and case adaptation techniques are discussed.

1 Survey

In this paper[1] a framework is proposed that allows to analyze and compare
existing case reusing systems and guides in developing new ones. It identifies
major design decisions, alternative solutions, and from their interdependencies
derives a set of guidelines. Four major aspects in the design of a case reusing
system will be studied:

- The task to be solved by the application, which may be one of three subtasks
  in analysis or synthesis.
- The kinds of cases, which may be complete or partial, abstract or concrete,
  isolated or related.
- The strategy for decomposing the problem, retrieving one or more cases,
  reusing one or more case, and composing the solution.
- The approach to adaptation, which may use a problem solver, a tool, or
  heuristics.

Surveys on case reusing systems can be found in [10] and [8]. Both cover mostly
well published, US-American systems. [10] does not consider reusing multiple
cases. [8] proposes criteria to classify case-based reasoning with multiple cases,
but does not come up with any detailed framework or guidelines.
The present paper has an empirical basis. Several case reusing systems were
analyzed. Figure 1 gives a survey on the systems. They cover multiple kinds

---

[1] This research was supported by the German Ministry for Education and Research
(BMBF) within the joint project FABEL under contract no. 01IW104. Project partners in FABEL are German National Research Center for Computer Science (GMD),
Sankt Augustin, BSR Consulting GmbH, Muenchen, Technical University of Dresden, HTWK Leipzig, University of Freiburg, and University of Karlsruhe.

of tasks with a focus on synthesis tasks where more complex cases are to be expected. All systems are operational, though most are research prototypes, and all are objects of active research.[2]

systems	analytic			synthetic			domain
	classification	diagnosis	decision support	planning	configuration	design	
INRECA	X	X	X				e.g. travels
MoCAS		X					machines
CHESS			X				chess
Déjà Vu				X	X	X	software
EADOCS						X	aircraft panels
AAAO, ToPo						X	buildings
IDIOM					X	X	buildings
Composer				X	X		assembly
RESYN/CBR				X			molecules
PARIS				X			manufacture
PRODIGY/ANALOGY				X			transport, routes
CAPlan/CBC				X			manufacture

Fig. 1. Types of tasks covered by selected, recent adaptation systems.

2 Source cases

2.1 Beyond a single source case: examples

Solving a problem by a single source case is only possible if each source case contains a sufficiently complete solution. There may be several reasons why this condition might be violated: It may be difficult to acquire such source cases, they

---

[2] First contacts were established via questionnaires that were distributed to the participants of the First International Conference on Case-Based Reasoning, ICCBR'95 [15]. Intensive discussions and interviews followed at the conference and at a special session on case adaptation [18]. In [16], [17] first conclusions are published. Further information was obtained in preparation of workshops on case adaptation to be held at the European AI conference, ECAI'96, and at the next European CBR conference, EWCBR'96.

may not be intuitive to the user, they may not be adaptable because adaptation methods are not powerful enough, or problems and solutions are so complex and unique that too many source cases would be needed. Here are some examples.

Abstract cases In model-based diagnosis, a machine is modeled by its components, and their input-output behaviours are modeled by rules. A diagnosis is given together with a causal explanation, which is a trace of rule applications relating the observed symptoms to the diagnosed faults. A forward chaining rule interpreter could perform an exhaustive search to diagnose a faulty machine, but the search space is prohibitively large. To shortcut search, cases could be used as follows: A case with the same symptoms and components is replayed by applying the rules from the case to the new problem. But a large number of cases would be needed. Therefore in the system MoCAS [3], machines are described at different levels of abstraction and cases, too, describe faulty machines at different levels of abstraction. By starting with the most abstract cases, the search space becomes tractable. Usually, the most concrete case that can be replayed is still an abstract case. But it will limit the search space sufficiently so that forward chaining can be used to adapt the case.

Partial cases For assembly sequence planning, a set of components is given that can be assembled in various ways to obtain different products. The problem is that the parts must be assembled in particular order. When there are many parts and many ways to combine them, one would need too many cases to cover all possibilities, even if the cases can be adapted. Therefore, in the system COMPOSER [12] cases contain only assembly plans for very few components. To develop an assembly plan for a larger product, multiple, overlapping cases are retrieved and simultaneously adapted. Assembly plans are represented as constraint networks with a consistent solution and adaptation is performed by a constraint repair algorithm.

Subcases In order to design an apartment, it would be inefficient to adapt the complete plan of another apartment. Human designers select and reuse pieces from different apartments, but they like to have the context provided by the apartment. In the system IDIOM [13], each apartment constitutes a case, which is divided into subcases that can be retrieved and reused individually.

Composite cases A route through a large city could be planned from scratch using a map of the city. But the search space is tremendous, and one should better reuse cases with routes planned previously. The problem is that only parts of these cases will be useful in planning a new route. Storing a route in fragments is no good solution, because practically any fragment may be useful. Statically splitting a case into disjoint subcases is inadequate, because subcases may overlap. Instead, in the system PRODIGY/ANALOGY [7], the route is stored as a whole but indexed by all its intermediate goals (or cross-sections). The indexing scheme superimposes upon a case a flexible, dynamically interpreted subcase structure.

Hierarchical cases Cases contain solutions. If the task is classification, the cases specify classes; for design, they contain designs, for planning they contain plans. Therefore, if a complex problem must be decomposed, cases with decompositions can be used. In the system DéJà Vu[14], two kinds of cases are used, cases that decompose a problem into subproblems, or subproblems into even finer subproblems, and cases that actually solve a small subproblem.

2.2 Principles

Thus, alternative kinds of source cases are encountered in the systems studied. They can be compared with respect to – at least – three features. A source case may contain a *complete* or a *partial* solution. It may be *concrete* or *abstract*, where a concrete source case contains particles that can occur in the final solution, while an abstract source case contains derivational information like a solution path, justifications, or subproblems. A source case can be isolated or related to others, e.g. to subcases or to more abstract cases raising subproblems to be solved. In the systems studied, not all combinations of features occur, and five classes of source cases can be distinguished:

- *Complete source cases* which additionally are concrete and isolated.
- *Partial source cases* which additionally are concrete and isolated.
- *Composite source cases*, which are concrete, complete, and related to concrete but partial *subcases*.
- *Hierachical (sets of) source cases*, which are partial and form a hierarchy with concrete cases at the bottom and abstract cases above.
- *Layered (sets of) source cases*, which are complete and form a hierarchy with concrete cases at the bottom and abstract cases above.

The different kinds of source cases represent compromises between several trade-offs, as shown in figure 2 and explained below.

Complete source cases preserve more context, e.g. the whole building as a context for all its rooms. Users tend to prefer them because of the context. But complete cases may be hard to reuse, especially complex ones as occur in synthesis tasks. Only parts of them may be relevant for the problem at hand. Therefore, parts of a complete case may have to be extracted dynamically, as in TOPO, and possibly, parts from several complete cases are needed.

Partial source cases can be combined flexibly. But one needs more of them and retrieval becomes more difficult because complementary source cases must be found. As COMPOSER demonstrates, partial cases may overlap and one must make sure that the adaptation method can cope with this.

Composite source cases are a good compromise between complete and partial ones. Composite cases preserve the context for their subcases. A composite source case may contain a unique decomposition into subcases, as in IDIOM

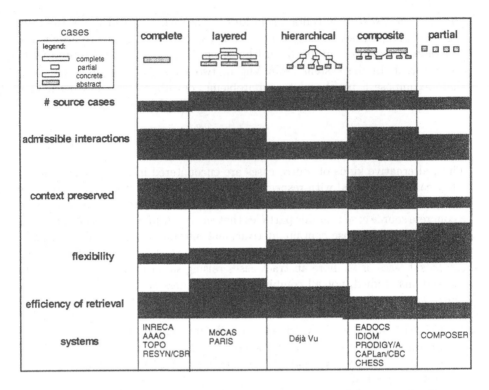

Fig. 2. The kind of source cases is a compromise between different trade-offs.

or CHESS [9], or multiple ones defined by multiple indexes, as in EADOCS [11] or PRODIGY/ANALOGY. Subases may be shared between composite cases, as in EADOCS, or exclusively be part of a single one, as in CHESS. Often both, composite cases and subcases can be accessed directly and indirectly, so that retrieval can be flexible, proceeding from the composite case to its subcases (EADOCS), vice versa from subcases to the composite case (CHESS), or accessing only the subcases (IDIOM, CHESS, PRODIGY/ANALOGY, EADOCS) or only the composites.

Layered source cases Complete or composite source cases are adequate when solutions have strongly interacting parts that should not be broken into independent partial cases. The same is true of layered source cases. As in PARIS [3] and MoCAS, a complete case is represented at different levels of abstraction. At each layer, all relevant interactions are reflected and a complete solution is presented. But abstract cases are more general and can be reused to produce very different solutions. Thus, the number of source cases can be reduced.

Hierachical source cases combine abstract and partial cases. The context of the concrete cases is less preserved than in composite cases, but better than with isolated partial cases. That means interactions within a complete solution should correspondingly be limited in scope. Hierarchical cases are a good means to aquire new decomposition knowledge by explicitly storing it as abstract cases. Retrieval of hierarchical cases is efficient. One has to descend the hierarchy stepwise.

3 Strategies

3.1 The need for strategies

As soon as the problems get more complex, the standard case-based reasoning process becomes more complicated either. The non-shaded parts in figure 3 depict the standard process, and the shaded ones indicate what may have to be added when a single source case is not sufficient. For instance, more than one source case could be retrieved, which can be done iteratively or simultaneously. Next, the cases retrieved have to be adapted, independently, iteratively or simultaneously. The upper, shaded part of the figure suggests an alternative by embedding CBR into an external problem decomposition and solution composition process. If the problem can be decomposed a priori, each subproblem may be solvable with a single source case. And instead of integrating partial solutions during adaptation, this may be done by external composition.

3.2 Principles

In order to characterize the strategy of a particular system, a good notation is needed. It should distinguish expansive steps like multi-case retrieval and problem decomposition, contractive ones like multi-case adaptation and solution composition, and steps that do not essentially affect branching. Also, the notation should allow to distinguish case-based processes from others.

Figure 4 proposes a notation. There are three types of nodes: problem nodes (P) indicating a problem or subproblem to be solved, case nodes (C) indicating a source case that has been retrieved for a problem, and solution nodes (S). Nodes can be linked by 1:1, n:1, 1:n, and n:m edges indicating data flow between the nodes. Edges can be classified by the types of nodes they link. Edges leading to case nodes ($\rightarrow$ C) represent retrieval, edges leaving case nodes (C $\rightarrow$) represent adaptation. Adaptation takes at least two arguments, a query and a source case, but for sake of simplicity, the adaptation edge is not connected to the query case, which can always uniquely be determined from the context. The remaining edges are independent of case-based reasoning.

Interesting is the adaptation edge from a case node to multiple problem nodes. The case must be an abstract case whose adaptation yields a set of subproblems. Two edges stem from iterative strategies that take into account intermediate solutions: An edge from a problem node and a solution node to a case node

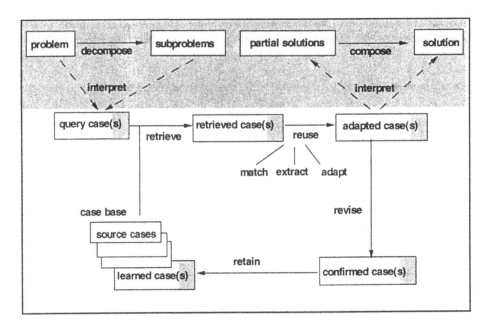

Fig. 3. Reasoning with multiple cases.

	expansion	neutral wrt. branching	iteration	contraction
retrieval	multi-case retrieval	single-case retrieval	iterative retrieval	
adaptation	adaptation of abstract case	single-case adaptation	iterative adaptation	multi-case adaptation
others (knowledge-based)	problem decomposition	single-problem solving		solution composition

Fig. 4. Potential constituents of strategies for case-based reasoning.

indicates iterative retrieval, and an edge from a case node and a solution node to a solution node indicates iterative adaptation and integration.

The major primitives in figure 4 allow to describe the systems studied at a level of abstraction that exhibits both, similarities and differences. The primitives can be combined in multiple ways. Figure 5 shows the combinations realized in the systems studied.

- In the *single concrete case strategy*, a single, complete and concrete source case is retrieved and then reused.
- In the *single abstract case strategy*, a single, complete, abstract case is retrieved and reused. The abstract case contains a problem decomposition, but the subproblems are solved in a simultaneous adaptation step.
- The *iterated abstract case strategy* starts by iteratively retrieving abstract cases, introducing more and finer subproblems. Atomic subproblems are iteratively adapted.
- The *iterated concrete case strategy* retrieves and reuses a single concrete case. But the result may be insufficient so that the procedure must be iterated.
- The *simultaneous strategy* provides a set of source cases in a single retrieval step, and then adapts and integrates them in a single reuse step.
- *Embedded strategies* start with a problem decomposition and end with a solution composition, both of which are in principle independent of case-based reasoning. In between, CBR is applied to all subproblems. The figure shows the strategy of the CHESS system. It embeds an iterated simultaneous strategy with a sophisticated retrieval.

As their names suggest, the strategies are quite closely connected to special kinds of source cases. But the relation is not one-to-one. The iterated concrete case strategy, the simultaneous strategy, and embedded strategies can all operate with composite source cases as well as partial ones.

Apart from the iterated concrete case strategy, all strategies can be split into a half for retrieval and another half for reuse (c.f. the dotted vertical line in figure 5). These halves can be recombined. For instance, simultaneously retrieved source cases could be adapted iteratively, and in the iterated abstract case strategy all concrete source cases could be adapted simultaneously. Indeed, the iterated abstract case strategy can be viewed as an amalgamation of the single abstract case strategy and the iterated conrete case strategy.

In general, the solution need not be composed in the same way as the problem is decomposed, as DéJà Vu demonstrates. But typically, simultaneous retrieval prepares well the ground for simultaneous reuse, because it can select compatible source cases; and incremental retrieval is suited for incremental reuse, because it is more up-to-date: The preceding iteration will have changed the query case and iterative retrieval can take this into account. External solution composition is only required if source cases are adapted independently, as in CHESS.

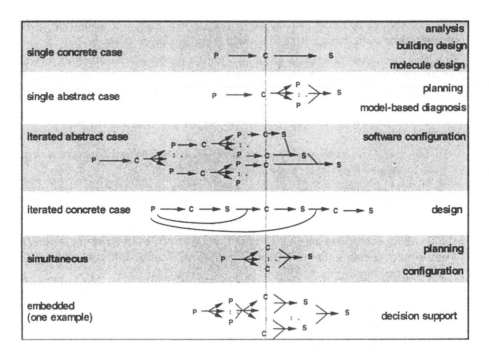

Fig. 5. Some strategies for case-based reasoning.

4 Adaptation

4.1 Examples

Heuristic substitution Historically, if source cases were reused at all, adaptation was done by applying heuristics to parameters transferred from a single source case. A typical example is INRECA [2] where values of attributes are modified. In EADOCS the attributes belong to composite objects and describe their behavior. In CHESS rules generalize or instantiate explanation patterns.

Structure transfer Adaptation by heuristic substitution is often insufficient if the cases are complex structures, like a layout of a large building. To reuse them in another context substructures have to be extracted, copied and fit to the context of a new building, e.g. as in the system TOPO [5].

Tools and problem solvers Heuristic adaptation gives no guarantee that the result will be correct. This is different when CBR is applied in domains where tools or problem solvers exist. Their search space is so huge and sometimes NP-complete that starting from a good guess is necessary. The good guess is the case retrieved, and for adaptation the tool or problem solver is applied. An example is the system AAAO [1]. Given a layout of spaces, it places the columns acoording to statical and aesthetical constraints. Columns are implemented as intelligent agents that negotiate and move around until all are satsified with their positions. This process can be accelerated enormously by starting with a good initial distribution of the columns as obtained from a case with a similar spatial layout.

4.2 Principles

In general, adapting a source case to a query case may be viewed as a kind of problem solving. The query case constitutes the problem, the adapted case contains the solution, and the solution shall be obtained with the help of the source case. Assuming this perspective, it is worth while to look for existing theories that may be used by from-scratch problem solvers or tools. Otherwise, specially tailored adaptation heuristics must be developed. Figure 6 anticipates the options and their trade-offs as described below.

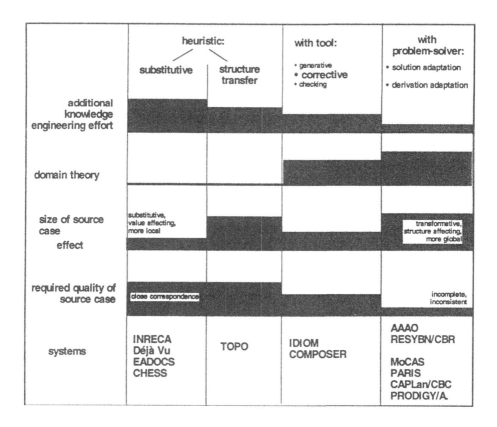

Fig. 6. Adapation techniques are compromises between different trade-offs.

Problem solvers In well-understood domains, there is a *complete theory of problem solving* and there exist from-scratch problem solvers – though they may be prohibitively slow. With them comes a well-defined search space. The source case should help to shortcut exploration of this space and cut down search time. This kind of adaptation shall be called *generative* because a solution can be generated from any starting point.

- There are various ways how information from a source case can influence a problem solver. First, query and source case can be turned into an intermediate point in the search space that acts as a better starting point for the problem solver. This kind of generative adaptation shall be called *solution modification*.
- Alternatively, the problem solver starts from scratch, but information from the source case influences its choices. This variant shall be called *derivation modification* because the path to, or derivation of the solution is reused.
- In its extreme form, called *derivational replay* the problem solver exactly reproduces the problem solving steps from the source case. [3] The border between derivational replay and other derivation modifications is hard to draw, and will not be applied here.

Solution modification and derivation modification lie on a spectrum. Some systems apply a combined approach, and especially for planning systems, the distinction is difficult. On the one hand, a plan is a solution, on the other hand, a plan is a path which planners can replay in order to refine or correct it. To complicate matters, derivation modificiation can be viewed as a solution modification. It transforms a solution that contains a path.

For solution modification, the source case must contain a concrete solution that is (partially) re-used for the query case. For derivational replay, the source case must contain abstract information about the problem solving trace that can be replayed. For derivation modification, both kinds of information can be used. problem solvers can be applied to simultaneously adapt partial cases. But care must be taken that information extracted from the source cases and combined with the query case conform to the problem solver's input conditions so that it can process the case. If the problem solver cannot deal with inconsistencies, it may be possible to remove them before adaptation yielding larger holes for completion; similarly, holes in the intermediate solution may have to be filled tentatively.

If existing problem solvers are applied for adaptation, there is hardly any additional knowledge acquisition effort, and case-based reasoning may achieve sometimes enormous gains in efficiency.Also, requirements on the quality of the case retrieved are not so strong: the lower the quality, the longer adaptation will take,

---

[3] The distinction between solution modification versus derivation modification is old but has been given different names: [4] speaks of transformational versus derivational analogy, while [6] call it substitutive or transformative adaptation versus generative adaptation.

but it will not become infeasible. Last not least, from-scratch problem solvers can achieve powerful transformative effects on both source and query case.

Tools In less-understood domains, there will be no complete theories as a basis for problem solvers but *partial theories* as a basis for *tools* that can support steps in problem solving. Like problem solvers, tools have special input conditions.

- *Corrective tools*, like constraint satisfation algorithms, need a complete network and then compute solutions. Constraint relaxation algorithms even need the network together with tentative values for the variables and then apply corrective substitutions; but they might be able to process inconsistent solutions. The network may be composed of partial source cases, as long as these preconditions are satisfied.
- More rarely, there may be *generative tools* that can complete a partial, but consistent solution.
- More often, there may be *assessment tools* for checking a complete solution. They can be used for adaptation in order to check a tentatively amended query case for correctness. Iterative adaptation may finally lead to a correct solution. This generate-and-test approach is not very efficient.

Tools differ in the kind of effect they can achieve on the source or query case: it can be more global or more local in nature. If a tool does not cover the entire adaptation step it must be supplemented with some heuristic methods or with manual correction. Some knowledge may be needed in order to prepare the source cases for the tool or to postprocess its result. The quality of the source case must be better than for adaptation based on a complete theory, because a tool cannot fall back to from-scratch problem solving.

Heuristics In domains without even partial theories neither problem solvers nor tools can be exploited, but case-based reasoning is particularly attractive because it may help to make formerly unsolvable problems solvable at all. Here, heuristics must be used. They may be elicited from experts, or they may be automatically learnt from source cases.

- *Heuristic adaptation* has long been restricted to rather local effects, usually value substitutions in a complete and concrete source case. More effectful transformative heuristics have been domain-specific. But DéJà Vudemonstrates that heuristic substitution applied to hierarchical source cases allows to tackle synthetic tasks.
- Only in the last few years, inspired from the field of analogical reasoning [4], more general *structural adaptation* methods have been developed which can achieve more global transformations. They require concrete and complete source cases with a rich structure, as can be found in many synthesis applications. Structural adaptation assumes that the structure of a case is meaningful. Though constraints and requirements may be unknown, the source cases comply to them and thus contain implicit, compiled knowledge. Preliminary to structural adaptation, correspondences between query case and

source case must be established to find out which parts or properties of the cases are similar and which are different, and what information to extract. This information can be modified with heuristics while it is transplanted to the query case.

The outcome of heuristic adaptation strongly depends on the quality of the source case to be adapted, because there are no compensatory inference capabilities.

5 More guidelines

Assume a new application is to be built, and the question is whether case reuse would be feasible or even promising. With the application, the task and the domain are predetermined. So one could set out to identify knowledge and methods that are available or easy to obtain. Next, the approach to adaptation could be selected. It constrains the kind of source cases, which in turn is closely related to the strategy.

Figure 7 summarizes the major decisions in the design of the systems studied and relates them to their task. This figure can be interpreted as shown in figure 8.

A single complete source case To keep things simple, one should try to reuse a single, complete and concrete source case. If the problems are sufficiently simple one should try heuristic adaptation. If they contain complex structures, one can try heuristic structure transfer. Otherwise one should try a from-scratch problem solver. Substitutive heuristics are a good candidate for analysis tasks, heuristic structure transfer and solution modification suit design tasks. If a problem cannot be solved by a single case, one may solve it partially, as in TOPO.

A single layered source case As another trick to avoid multiple source cases, it might be possible to formulate and adapt a skeleton case at some higher level of abstraction, as is done in PARIS and MoCAS. Tailored to such layered soure cases are the single abstract case strategy together with a problem solver for adaptation by derivation modification. This is a good choice in hierarchical planning and model-based diagnosis.

Embedded case-based reasoning If a single case is insufficient, one has to reuse multiple source cases. Available static knowledge for problem decomposition knowledge and solution composition should be exploited for an embedded strategy. Depending on the interactions between the subproblems, special adaptation techniques have to be employed. Parallel single-case adaptations, as in CHESS, should only be applied to independent source cases.

One may speculate why, among the systems studied, CHESS is the only one embedding CBR. Maybe, external knowledge often is not available, that it is not so suited, or that the integration of case-based reasoning with other problem

system	task	approach to adaptation	strategy	source cases
INRECA	analysis	heuristic substitution		
AAAO	design	solution modification	single case	complete
ToPo	design	structure transfer		
RESYN/CBR	planning	solution modification		
MoCAS	diagnosis	derivational	abstract case	layered
PARIS	planning			
Déjà Vu	synthesis	heuristic substitution	iterated abstract case	hierarchical
COMPOSER	planning configuration	tool-based	simultaneous	partial
CHESS	decision support	heuristic substitution	embedded	composite
EADOCS	design	heuristic substitution	iterated concretecase	
IDIOM	design configuration	tool-based		composite
PRODIGY/ ANALOGY CAPlan/CbC	planning	derivational	simultaneous	composite

Fig. 7. The major design decisions in the systems studied. The kind of source cases is the primary sorting criterion, the strategy the second one.

solving techniques is yet in its infancy – then CHESS would be a pioneering system. Last not least, multi-case retrieval and reuse may just be flexible enough? Indeed, by retrieving multiple source cases for a single problem, a problem decomposition is achieved a posteriori: every source case defines a subproblem in the query case. And with the addition of new source cases, new problem decompositions may be found. So multi-case retrieval is more flexible than a priori decomposition. To cite Netten, the author of EADOCS: a static decomposition declares how to reformulate a problem, a set of source cases declares what problems can be solved.

Multiple cases and heuristics A compromise between external problem decomposition and a posteriori decomposition by concrete cases is the use of hierarchical cases as in DéJà Vu. They retain previous decompositions explicitly. Tailored to this kind of cases is the iterated abstract case strategy. It allows to tackle syn-

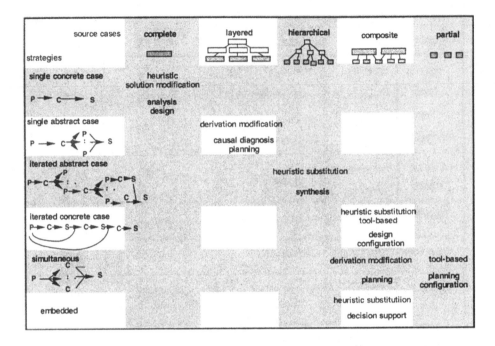

Fig. 8. Combinations of strategy, cases, approach to adaptation, and task in the selected systems.

thetic tasks by a simple adaptation technique like heuristic substitution. This approach must be chosen when the problem is too complex for a single case and only heuristics are available for adaptaiton.

Multiple cases and tools or problem solvers In general, existing problem solvers or tools should be exploited, even if a single source case is not sufficient. Often, the tools or problem solvers can process input that has been assembled from multiple partial or composite source cases, or the input can be preprocessed correspondingly. Composite cases are more versatile than partial ones, because typically both, composite cases and subcases, can be accessed directly and indirectly. In the systems studied, partial source cases are only used simultaneously. Composite source cases are also used for the iterated concrete case strategy, probably because they present the cases in small bits while preserving their context.

Simultaneous adaptation, it seems, can best cope with interactions between partial solutions. Otherwise, one should try to extend a single-case adaptation technique into an iterative one. For that purpose the order in which source cases are adapted may be crucial for the process to converge, a problem recognized in EADOCS. Among the systems studied, the iterated strategy is applied in synthetic tasks for adaptation by heuristic substitution and tools. The simultaneous strategy is used for tool-based adaptation in planning and configuration.

Source case elicitation The problem of eliciting suitably tailored source cases is closely related to the strategy and the adaptation technique. Source cases should be cut so that they fit the query cases and are easy to adapt. Thus, for gaining new source cases, a complex solution should be decomposed using the same heuristics, knowledge or technique that is used to decompose a problem or to retrieve multiple cases. For instance, CHESS decomposes both problems and source cases according to its discrimination tree.

These guidelines conclude the present study. Together with the preceding principles they should help in deciding whether the reuse of cases is a viable approach for a given application. The principles helps to analyze and compare case reusing systems by identifying major characteristics.

References

1. Parivash Adami, 'Adaptation by Active Autonomous Objects (AAAO)', in *Modules for Design Support*, ed., Katy Börner, 46–50, GMD, Sankt Augustin, (June 1995).
2. Eric Auriol, Michel Manago, Klaus-Dieter Althoff, Stefan Wess, and Stefan Dittrich, 'Integrating induction in case-based reasoning: methodological approach and first evaluations', in *Advances in case-based reasoning: second European workshop, EWCBR-94*, eds., J.-P. Haton, M. Keane, and M. Manago, 18–32, Springer, Berlin, (1995).
3. Ralph Bergmann, Gerd Pews, and Wolfgang Wilke, 'Explanation-based similarity: a unifying approach for integrating domain knowledge into case-based reasoning for diagnosis and planning tasks', in *Topics in case-based reasoning: First European Workshop, EWCBR-93, selected papers*, eds., Stefan Wess, Klaus-Dieter Althoff, and Michael M. Richter, number 837 in Lecture Notes in Artificial Intelligence, 182–196, Springer, Berlin, (1994).
4. Jaime G. Carbonell, 'Derivational analogy. A theory of reconstructive problem solving and expertise acquisition', in *Machine learning: an artificial intelligence approach*, eds., R.S. Michalski, J.G. Carbonnel, and T.M. Mitchell, volume 2, 371–392, Morgan Kaufman, Los Altos, CA, (1986).
5. Carl-Helmut Coulon, 'Automatic indexing, retrieval and reuse of topologies in complex designs', in *Proceeding of the sixth International Conference on Computing in Civil and Building Engineering*, eds., Peter Jan Pahl and Heinrich Werner, pp. 749–754, Berlin, (1995). Balkema, Rotterdam.
6. Padraig Cunningham, Donal Finn, and Sean Slattery, 'Knowledge engineering requirements in derivational analogy', in *Topics in case-based reasoning: First European Workshop, EWCBR-93, selected papers*, eds., Stefan Wess, Klaus-Dieter Althoff, and Michael M. Richter, number 837 in Lecture Notes in Artificial Intelligence, 234–245, Springer, Berlin, (1994).
7. Karen Z. Haigh and Manuela M. Veloso, 'Route planning by Analogy', in *Case based reasoning research and development: first international conference, ICCBR-95*, eds., Manuela Veloso and Agnar Aamodt, 169–180, Springer, Berlin, (1995).
8. Kathleen Hanney, Mark T. Keane, Barry Smyth, and Padraig Cunningham, 'Systems, tasks and adaptation knowledge: revealing some revealing dependencies',

in *Case based reasoning research and development: first international conference, ICCBR-95*, eds., Manuela Veloso and Agnar Aamodt, 461–470, Springer, Berlin, (1995).

9. Yaakov Kerner, 'Learning strategies for explanation patterns: basic game patterns with application to chess', in *Case based reasoning research and development: first international conference, ICCBR-95*, eds., Manuela Veloso and Agnar Aamodt, 491–500, Springer, Berlin, (1995).

10. Janet L. Kolodner, *Case-Based Reasoning*, Morgan Kaufmann, San Mateo, 1993.

11. Bart D. Netten, R. A. Vingerhoeds, and H. Koppelaar, 'Expert assisted conceptual design: an application to fibre reinforced composite panels', in *Design research in the Netherlands*, eds., R. Oxman, M. Bax, and H. Achten, 125–139, Faculty of Architecture, Planning, and Building Design Science, Eindhoven University, Eindhoven, (1995).

12. Lisa Purvis and Pearl Pu, 'Adaptation using constraint satisfaction techniques', in *Case based reasoning research and development: first international conference, ICCBR-95*, eds., Manuela Veloso and Agnar Aamodt, 289–300, Springer, Berlin, (1995).

13. Ian Smith, Claudio Lottaz, and Boi Faltings, 'Spatial composition using cases: ID-IOM', in *Case based reasoning research and development: first international conference, ICCBR-95*, eds., Manuela Veloso and Agnar Aamodt, 88–97, Springer, Berlin, (1995).

14. Barry Smyth and Mark T. Keane, 'Retrieval and adaptation in Déjà Vu, a case-based reasoning system for software design', in *Adaptation of knowledge for reuse: a 1995 AAAI Fall Symposium: working notes*, 99–105, MIT, Cambridge, MA, (1995).

15. *Case based reasoning research and development: first international conference, ICCBR-95*, eds., Manuela M. Veloso and Agnar Aamodt, number 1010 in Lecture Notes in Artificial Intelligence, Springer, Berlin, 1995.

16. Angi Voß, 'How to solve complex problems with cases', *Engineering Applications of Artificial Intelligence*, **Special Issue AI in Design**, to appear, (1996).

17. Angi Voß, 'Towards a methodology for case adaptation', in *ECAI'96*, ed., W. Wahlster. John Wiley and Sons, Chichester, (August 1996).

18. Angi Voß, Brigitte Bartsch-Spörl, and Rivka Oxman, 'A study of case adaptation systems', in *AI in Design'96*, eds., J. Gero and F. Sudweeks, p. to appear, Stanford, (1996). Kluwer Academic Publishers, Dordrecht.

Using Typicality Theory to Select the Best Match

Rosina Weber-Lee, Ricardo Miranda Barcia, Alejandro Martins, and
Roberto C. Pacheco

rolee@eps.ufsc.br

Federal University of Santa Catarina, Industrial Engineering,
Florianópolis, SC, BRAZIL.

Abstract. This paper focuses on the problem of choosing the best match among a set of retrieved cases. The *Select* step is the subtask of case retrieval that produces the case that suggests the solution for the input case. There are many different ways to accomplish this task and we propose an automatic means for it. Following the original motivation of paralleling the human similarity heuristic we argue that the selection of the best match is performed by humans choosing the solution that best represents the set of candidate solutions retrieved. The solution that best represents a given data set is the "most typical" solution. Therefore, we describe an application in a Case-Based Reasoning system using the Theory of Typicality to calculate the Most Typical Value of a given set to automatically perform the *Select* task. An example illustrates the application.

1.   Introduction

In a Case-Based Reasoner, the input case is compared with the cases in memory in order to retrieve the set of most similar cases. The case retrieval step is usually referred to as consisting of four subtasks: Identify Features, Initially Match, Search, and *Select* (Aamodt & Plaza, 1994). Here, we address the subtask *Select* that chooses the best match from a set of most similar cases to suggest the solution to the input problem. Several approaches for selecting one best match have been proposed, from developing a separate module to leaving the selection to the user (see section 2). However, one considers that some important piece of information and knowledge may be lost when only one case is used. To overcome such possible loss it might be necessary to select more than one match to produce a good and useful solution, e.g. (Shinn, 1988). This is the situation we have faced when trying to produce a solution in our case-based reasoner developed to predict cash flow accounts (Weber-Lee, Barcia, & Khator, 1995). Hence, we propose to perform the *Select* subtask by means of the Theory of Typicality. It is an attempt to capture all the knowledge embedded in the set of the most similar cases avoiding loosing important information. Building this last subtask of the case retrieval step places us closer to achieving the goal of developing an automatic tool. Whenever knowledge can be manipulated without depending upon humans, we are evolving towards a better Artificial Intelligence tool.

Section 2 discusses the efficient automatization of the *Select* phase in a CBR system. The motivation for this work has its origin in observing that the process starting from identifying a current problem and followed by the search for similar experiences does not stop there. Humans very often retrieve more than one similar case and they go through a selection phase before choosing the solution for the current problem. Section 3 illustrates what we claim to be the human process with examples that show that the human approach actually goes up to the point of selecting the best match. For the purpose of modeling the *Select* phase, we propose the use of the Theory of Typicality (Friedman, M, Ming, M., & Kandel, A., 1995), we comment on the motivation for this choice in section 4. Next, in Section 5 we review this theory that provides a measure of central tendency -- the Most Typical Value of a data set. Then, in Section 6 we demonstrate an example where the Theory of Typicality is applied to select the best match of a set of retrieved cases. We comment on this proposal and indicate future research in Section 7.

2. The Best Match

A CBR system has four major topics to be managed, studied, and developed: retrieve, reuse, revise and retain (Aamodt & Plaza, 1994). All these four topics consist of knowledge engineering tasks that have to be carefully considered within the domain of the application. The system works better with better design of these issues. This is about maximizing the potential of CBR as a tool.

The goal of a CBR system is effectively solving the input problem. The knowledge engineer attempts to optimize the potential of all processes that embody a case-based reasoner. We strive to maximize the efficiency of case-based systems towards continuous improvement. Above all, we seek for ways to improve the CBR as an automatic technique. The automatic selection we are introducing chooses the best match using more cases without increasing computing time. Using more cases increase the chances that no important information is rejected.

Retrieval is the essence of the CBR paradigm. Case retrieval consists of *Identify Features, Initial Match, Search*, and *Select*. All these subtasks are equally important in order to perform an efficient case retrieval. We address the subtask *Select* that chooses the solution for the input case. *Select* step may combine the cases returned by *Initial Match* and produce the solution or simply choose the best match. Besides, when case retrieval is oriented by scores, one needs to set a threshold to limit the amount of cases to be returned. This threshold determines the domain of the *Select* subtask.

According to (Aamodt & Plaza, 1994) the selection of the best match may happen during the *Initial Match* step but usually the *Initial Match* returns a set of cases. However, there are other types of retrieval that searches for matching indexes and the outcome of this retrieval can be of any size. The retrieval may yield either a score meaning the degree of match or assign a yes or no to determine whether the case matches sufficiently or not (Kolodner, 1993).

When retrieving cases one searches for the set of the most similar to the input case. Among this set, the case to be used to solve the input problem must be chosen. There are several ways to determine which one better represents the set of best cases retrieved. In (Kopeikina et al., 1988), it is presented as a separated module, called *Selector*, to perform the choice of the best match. Candidate cases are retrieved and *Selector* determines the most relevant of them identifying more subtle distinctions between them. According to Aamodt and Plaza (1994), *Select* is usually more elaborate than the retrieval itself. They even point out a system where the selection methods generate explanations and the case with the best explanation for the similarity is then selected. The selection may also be performed by a second evaluation of the same retrieval function that then examines closer the first set of retrieved cases. Some systems ask the user either for the choice or for some additional information to perform the choice. The use of heuristics is also employed, (Kolodner, 1989). In Clavier (Hennessy and Hinkle,1992), the system presents candidate layouts and the user chooses the best match. In (Hurley, 1993) the retrieval is divided into two stages. First, *the base filtering* determines a set of broadly similar cases. Second, the *detailed matching* performs the matching trying to verify whether or not the target case satisfies the constraints of the indices of the case base. Another interesting approach is presented in Macchion & Vo, (1993) in which the retrieval phase is split into up to six steps. In searching for the perfect match the system uses *exclusion* and *necessity* indexes to reduce the set.

Most systems tend to perform the *Select* step based on the highest score or on the user. Others choose for *ad hoc* procedures while some do not use any method at all. Next, we present a list of methods for implementing the *Select* subtask followed by the research systems that has adopted it, (Kolodner, 1993). Highest score: ABBY, ACBARR, ARCHIE and ARCHIE-2, CABINS, The Compaq SMART System, SCAVENGER; user: ASK systems, Battle Planner, CLAVIER, CASCADE, REMIND; sort cases in a claim lattice: CABARET, HYPO; no method needed: Parse-O-Matic, PRISM; preference method: CELIA, MEDIC; domain specific metrics: KRITIK, NETTRAC; distance in similarity hierarchy: PERSUADER; plausibility of suggested explanation: SWALE; cases must share surface features and abstract problem types: ORCA; cases that deviates the least along goals and preconditions: Internal Analogy; multiple cases used: IVY; exclusion, then weighted similarity metric: MEDIATOR.

No matter the type of retrieval or case representation used, there is a dilemma regarding efficiency, accuracy, and processing time; that is a cost-effective question. In the system presented in (Kopeikina et al., 1988), they point out that a simple *selector* would choose quickly and imprecisely while a best case would be chosen with the use of more resources. Therefore, a more sophisticated approach should be used to avoid the selection of a sub-optimal result and to avoid wasting processing time with more iterations of a less complex selection.

In our prediction application we have performed tests with different levels of threshold that resulted in different amounts of cases retrieved. Searching for an appropriate threshold turned out to be a difficult task. We have performed tests setting the threshold to higher levels (decreasing the amount of cases retrieved) trying to ensure that very similar cases were not rejected. This is an important cost-effectiveness matter that has to be considered. One may seek for efficiency reducing the cases retrieved and increase the difficulty in choosing the best match or, on the other hand, seek for accuracy and loose efficiency. The solution seems to be keeping a large amount of cases and improve the *Select* task, therefore one may consider all relevant cases without sacrificing efficiency. In order to improve the *Select* task we propose an approach that was motivated by the human behavior as well as the whole philosophy behind CBR: paralleling humans. The choice of the solution to reuse is very often the most frequent and most typical solution in the set, that is the one that better represents the set.

3. CBR Paralleling Humans

Case-Based Reasoning paradigm has been introduced as the Artificial Intelligence technique capable to simulate the similarity heuristic (Whitaker et al., 1990) in a computer program. This behaviour refers to the use of the outcome of a prior similar experience to predict the outcome of a current situation. Such simulation is focused on the use of features to ground the comparison of a current problem in the search for similar ones. The search is for a successful past experience that may provide a proper solution to be reused. In fact, many applications present very good simulations of such human behavior. Most introductory papers, as well as application papers present the CBR philosophy and mechanism with examples that start from the identification of a current problem and the search in memory for a similar situation (DARPA Proceedings, 1988, 1989 & 1991). These examples illustrate how the past experiences can help to provide either a solution, a diagnosis or a prediction for the current problem. Selecting *the* past experience is not highlighted in examples and it may seem as if this final selection is not part of the human approach. However, as the philosophy is originated in simulating the human approach, what actually happens as a result of the search for similar problems? It is not necessarily one similar case that is retrieved. Usually, a number of cases are retrieved and one has to choose one in the set. As we can see through some real life examples, the approach tends to be choosing the most frequent or most typical case. Let us describe some examples to illustrate why we understand that the selection of the best match can also be paralleled like the identification and retrieval of similar cases.

When a crime is committed, police search for all possible characteristics of the crime in order to find enough similarity to other crimes committed in the past. The investigation procedure will point to the criminal whose typical behavior is the most similar to the one under research.

Finding a parking space or the best route to drive to someplace is the type of problem faced by everyone on a daily basis. Humans approach such problem always retrieving past experiences. Sometimes there are more than one choice that has already been successful though the solution chosen is always the route (or the combination of routes) that is typically clearer; or the parking lot which most usually has vacancy.

All these real world situations show that the human approach indeed goes up to the point of selecting the best match and they also provide a strong appeal in considering the choice of the past experience to reuse as one experience that seems to be the most usual, frequent, or typical. Hence, the choice for the best match is, intuitively, a matter of evaluating a set of cases and finding which one(s) better represent this set.

These examples also indicate that the solution to be used in the current problem does not have to be necessarily one solution from one best match. Conversely, they indicate that the best solution may be one obtained by the typical behavior of the set of solutions presented by the most similar cases. In this sense we now search for the best way to automatically calculate this solution.

4. Searching for a Representative Value

A value that is representative of the set of retrieved cases is the solution we want to identify automatically. On this account, we propose an approach that uses the real content of the best matches retrieved to produce a reasonable solution. At this point we have to consider the approaches available to calculate this value and we will have a CBR system that automatically parallels the whole human reasoning when facing a prediction problem. We have to choose an approach that will enable us to implement this automatic selection for the prediction of cash flow accounts. The solution part of the cases in this application is a single numerical attribute. Therefore we have to calculate one value that better represents this set of numbers. The nature of the data is not random, since it is strongly influenced by the economical conditions and top governmental decisions. Under these circumstances, our analysis leads us to prefer a fuzzy approach. There are measures of central tendency that represent attempts to choose one particular event that represents the behavior of a set (numerical averaging). That is not exactly what we are searching for, we want to calculate the most typical behavior of the set of solutions of the retrieved cases, if there is one. This is clearly a problem of representing a data set with a measure of general tendency.

The advantage of obtaining a typical value of a data set grounds on the possibility of having a measure that is representative of this set regardless of central tendency. According to Friedman, Ming, & Kandel, (1995) traditional statistical measures fail on representing data sets containing more than one cluster since these measures are not always able to represent a typical feature of a given set.

The research on measures of general tendency in treating fuzzy sets leads to the development of the Fuzzy Expected Value (FEV), (Kandel, 1982). FEV was meant to present a quantity that would not only replace the arithmetic mean and the median but also be accepted as the typical grade of membership of a given fuzzy set. However, the FEV is not always effective on representing typicality. Two other measures were developed, the Weighted Fuzzy Expected Value (WFEV), (Friedman, Schneider, & Kandel, 1989) and the Clustering Fuzzy Expected Value (CFEV), (Vassilliadis et al., 1994). As a conclusion of these developments, the Most Typical Value (MTV), the Most Typical Deviation (MTD), and the Definite Typical Value (DTV) are presented in the paper *On the Theory of Typicality*, by Friedman, Ming, & Kandel, (1995). At this point, considering the fuzzy nature of the data and the necessity of a measure of central tendency, our analysis shows clear advantages on choosing the Theory of Typicality.

The Theory of Typicality calculates a MTV for the data set after grouping the data into clusters using a geometrical fuzzy clustering algorithm (see section 5.1). The choice for this type of clustering is embedded in the approach, nevertheless it has augmented our decision, as the fuzzy clustering is able to describe ambiguities that often occur in real data, such as bridging objects and outliers (Rousseeuw, 1995). Besides, the fact that fuzzy clusterings are non-exclusive was also relevant (Kim & Novick, 1993).

An alternative to this approach is the probabilistic clustering (Cheeseman & Stutz, 1996). We found that this approach requires several assumptions that are not appropriate in financial environments. Particularly, in CBR applications, the dynamic nature along with small and variable data sets contradict the main assumptions of probabilistic approaches: the requirements for defining the shape of the functions, and the hypothesis of the probabilistic behaviour of the attributes, and the need of the definition of the parameters of the probabilistic functions.

4.1.   Using Typicality to Choose the Best Match

We implement the chosen approach in our prediction systems as follows. A new case is input and the case retrieval returns a set of cases. In the selection of the best match, similarity is no longer considered; conversely we look at the solutions that the retrieved cases offer. These solutions compose a set of data. From this set we employ a fuzzy c-means algorithm (see section 5.1.1) and next calculate the MTV. If a unique solution exists, we then calculate the DTV. If exists one DTV for this set, this value corresponds to the best match, i.e., the value that becomes the solution of the reasoner. If there is not a unique solution to the MTV, we assume the clusters' centers as possible solutions. At this point this second *Select* step is user-driven.

5.   The Theory of Typicality

The expressions MTV, MTD, and DTV are given in Friedman, Ming, & Kandel, (1995). First, one may consider that one typical value of a data set might not exist, what is observed by the failure of the iterative procedure to provide a unique solution. This indicates the existence of multivalue MTV. The MTD measures the grade of typicality of the MTV calculated.

For obtaining the MTV of a given n-dimensional fuzzy set, the set first undergoes a clustering process using a geometrical fuzzy clustering algorithm (Windham, 1983). We present the algorithm briefly.

5.1.   Geometrical Fuzzy Clustering Algorithms

The clustering problem is in essence a task of finding natural groupings in a given data set (Bezdek, 1981). In a fuzzy clustering, the requirements for clusters, classes and blocks are weaker and they generate fuzzy partitions. Hence, in a fuzzy clustering, the clusters are fuzzy subsets of a collection of elements. The clusters are membership functions of the elements in the cluster. Elements in the data set which are similar to each other are identified by the fact that they have high memberships in the same cluster. The memberships are chosen so that the sum for each element is one.

The fuzzy clustering is a non-exclusive method, i.e., each element is assigned to one or more clusters with a degree of inclusion to each cluster in the partition (Kim & Novick, 1993).

The elements to be clustered are represented by vectors in some d-dimensional Euclidean space. We have a set $X=\{x_1,....x_N\} \subset R^p$ where the components of each vector are measurements of one of p features of a particular element. The measure of similarity between the elements can be characterized by a differentiable measure of distance between their corresponding data vectors, i.e. $|x_k - x_l|^2_M = (x_k - x_l)^T M(x_k - v_l)$, for some positive semidefinite matrix, M. Under these assumptions a cluster can be viewed geometrically as a region where the data points are highly concentrated or close together as determined by the metric.

The basis for constructing geometrical fuzzy clustering algorithms that are, in fact, an iterative procedure for choosing membership grades that minimize (Windham, 1983)

$$\sum_i \sum_k \left(u_{ik}\right)^m \left|x_k - v_i\right|_M^2 . \tag{1}$$

5.1.1. Fuzzy c-Means Algorithm

Fuzzy c-means clustering is a geometrical fuzzy clustering algorithm and it differs from the fuzzy equivalence relation-based (the second type of fuzzy clustering) algorithm in the requirement of having the following three values defined beforehand:

1. number of clusters, c
2. a real number $m \in [1, \infty)$
3. a small positive stopping criterion number, ε

See (Windham, 1983), (Bezdek, 1981) and (Klir & Yuan, 1995) for further reading.

5.1.2. Cluster Validity and Unsupervised Tracking

Cluster validity refers to the appropriateness of a partition $U^{(i)}$ resultant from the clustering algorithm. According to Pal & Bezdek, (1995), it depends on what we mean by a good partition. Kim & Novick, (1993), understand that the partition should reflect the inherent organization of the data. They suggest to validate a clustering by verifying that for given c clusters, this organization yields a statistically significant improvement over $c - 1$ and it is only marginally worse than $c+1$. Gath & Geva, (1989), present three requirements to define an *optimal partition*:

" *1) Clear separation between the resulting clusters.*
2) Minimal volume of the clusters.
3) Maximal number of data points concentrated in the vicinity of the cluster centroid."

Unsupervised tracking is required when there is no *a priori* knowledge of the location of the centers for the initial partition. This subject demands proper attention as different initial partitions converge to different local optima. See Gath & Geva, (1989) for a scheme to select the initial clusters' centers.

Under supervised clustering, Rousseeuw (1995) illustrates an example presenting an unidimensional data set graphically showing that this *visual system* can easily reveal the number of clusters.

5.2. MTV

The definition of the MTV is motivated by the following principles:
1. Population effect: Let X consists of two clusters C_1 and C_2 with populations k_1 and k_2 and centers v_1 and v_2 respectively. If $k_1 >> k_2$, then the MTV should be "much closer" to v_1 than to v_2.
2. Distance effect: consider C_i with a center v_i. Then the effect of C_i on the MTV should be a "strong" decreasing monotonic function of $|v_i - \text{MTV}|$.

Definition 1: Let X denote a clustered set $\{ C_i = (k_i, v_i)\}^C_{i=1}$, let $\{\gamma_i \, (u)\}^C_{i=1}$ be nonnegative monotonically decreasing functions defined over the interval $[0, \infty)$ and let λ denote a real number greater than 1. A solution s in R^p to the implicit vector equation

$$s = \frac{v_1\gamma_1\left(\left|v_1 - s\right|\right)k_1^\lambda + v_2\gamma_2\left(\left|v_2 - s\right|\right)k_2^\lambda +......+v_c\gamma_c\left(\left|v_c - s\right|\right)k_c^\lambda}{\gamma_1\left(\left|v_1 - s\right|\right)k_1^\lambda + \gamma_2\left(\left|v_2 - s\right|\right)k_2^\lambda +......+\gamma_c\left(\left|v_c - s\right|\right)k_c^\lambda} \quad (2)$$

is called a most typical value of order λ with the associated weight functions $\{\gamma_i\}^C_{i=1}$, and is denoted by $MTV(\gamma_1,..., \gamma_c, \lambda)$.

The population effect is guaranteed by the request $\lambda > 1$. The functions $\gamma_1(u),..., \gamma_c(u)$ are strong decreasing monotonic functions in order to assure the distance effect. To each cluster we may attach a different weight function.

The next values are as follows:

$$\lambda = 2; \gamma_i\left(u\right) = e^{-\beta u}, 1 \le i \le c \quad (3)$$

where β is a tuning constant that determines the decreasing rate of the weight functions.

A solution s to Equation (2) always exists and can be found by using the standard iteration method. However, this solution is not unique unless one of the clusters is dominant.

5.3. MTD

A solution *s* to Equation (2) is accepted as an MTV if it is not *too far* from *too many* elements of X. To accept and evaluate this measure, another quantity is defined.

The Most Typical Deviation measures the grade of typicality of the MTV: a small MTD indicates that Equation (2) is likely to have a unique solution and that this solution can be accepted as an MTV of the given set. While a large MTD indicates the existence of several typical values.

Definition 2: Let *s* be the solution of Equation (2). The scalar

$$t = \frac{\left|v_1 - s\right|^2\gamma_1\left(\left|v_1 - s\right|\right)k_1^\lambda + \left|v_2 - s\right|^2\gamma_2\left(\left|v_2 - s\right|\right)k_2^\lambda +......+\left|v_c - s\right|^2\gamma_c\left(\left|v_c - s\right|\right)k_c^\lambda}{\gamma_1\left(\left|v_1 - s\right|\right)k_1^\lambda + \gamma_2\left(\left|v_2 - s\right|\right)k_2^\lambda +......+\gamma_c\left(\left|v_c - s\right|\right)k_c^\lambda}$$

$$(4)$$

is called the most typical deviation (MTD) of X, associated with *s*.

If a particular cluster, say C_k, is dominant in the process of determining the MTV, then $s = MTV$ is close to v_k, and due to the choice of λ and $\gamma_1(u),..., \gamma_c(u)$ one gets

$$MTD \sim |v_k - s| \quad (5)$$

In this case, the MTD is small and represents a "typical deviation" from the MTV, considering the population of C_k.

5.4. DTV

The Definite Typical Value (DTV) is the unique solution resulted from Equation (2), after choosing a reasonable β. To verify the existence of a DTV, one has to apply the standard iteration method with the initial conditions:

$$s_0 = v_i, \ 1 \le i \le c \ \text{and see if it converges to the same solution.}$$

6. Example

We illustrate the approach proposed in our case-based reasoner developed to predict cash flow accounts (Weber-Lee, Barcia, & Khator, 1995). This system performs the tasks of identification and prediction. The basic case is represented by a list of attributes that identifies the cases that are cash flow accounts. The cash flow accounts are represented through descriptors related to present and previous amounts, nature and period in time. The system receives as the input problem one cash flow account with the attributes properly assigned. The system searches throughout the memory to identify the most similar cases using a similarity metric that assigns scores representing the degree of matching between the input case and the case being evaluated. There are different levels of importance for the descriptors. The solutions are the amounts that occurred for these accounts in the past -- after an equal period of time as the period described in the input case. The solution is adapted by a *parameter adjustment* (Kolodner,1993) operation to fit to the input case. The solution adapted is the amount forecasted for the account in the cash flow. The system suggests a solution that is an amount that is likely to happen the following period. The solutions of the cases in this set are candidate solutions. In the proposed approach, we evaluate this set of solutions to find out what values represent this set (the typical values) calculating the MTV of the set of cases retrieved.

Suppose we need to estimate an amount that is likely to be spent during next month in administrative expenses. The account named *administrative expenses* is the input case. We want the case-based reasoner to provide this estimate. A sketch of the input case is shown in Table 1.

The reasoner retrieved 26 cases as the set of most similar cases with a threshold defining that only cases yielding a similarity over 33% are retrieved. The search was done in a case base of 624 cases. Table 2 presents the 26 cases, the scores representing the degree of similarity, the period, and the amount estimated for the period. The last column named *estimation* shows the amount provided by each case if it would be chosen. The parameter we are using for measuring the quality of the solutions is the actual amount that was spent, for this input case of *administrative expenses* of June 1987, it was $ 96,745.

Considering the choices for the *Select* step already proposed in the CBR literature, we could, at this point, ask the user for a selection, apply the similarity metric with more detail, exclude some of the cases or even choose the highest score. Also, we could combine these cases in order to produce one single solution. However, we have chosen to group these cases into a set and find out what is the typical value for this set of solutions.

dimensions	values
AccountName	adm. expenses
Amount	119486.99
Month	jun
Year	87
M_1_Density	0.850396
M_2_Density	1.108768
M_3_Density	1.512038
M_4_Density	1.659253
M_5_Density	1.398817
M_6_Density	1.344115
M_7_Density	1.333065
M_8_Density	2.046216
M_9_Density	1.893387
M_10_Density	1.419327
M_11_Density	1.430320
FuzzyLabel	Low

Table 1. Problem description.

Before developing the MTV approach, let us think of applying one of the alternative methods above mentioned. Let us select according to the highest score and asking the user. The selection according to the highest score is *adm.exp. aug82*; the user asked opted for *adm.exp. may87*. Table 4 presents the input case and these two selections for comparison. An explanation for the descriptors that are not self-explanatory follows: Next_Amount, this value refers to the actual amount occurred the following month; M_X_Density, these are seasonality factors, an attempt to represent the behavior of the account for the past months.

It is still important to point out that although the highest score has indeed chosen the best possible forecast for the input problem, one cannot rely on one single example to ground validation. This example has only explanatory purposes.

According to the theory of typicality, in the search for a MTV the data must be first clustered by a geometric fuzzy clustering algorithm and replaced by a finite set of ordered pairs, where each pair consists of a cluster's center and the cluster's size. We want to determine whether there is a DTV to represent the set. The data set is

$X = \{x_1, \ldots, x_{26}\} \subset \Re^1$. We use the fuzzy c-means algorithm to determine the clusters' centers and sizes. The fuzzy c-means algorithm requires that a number of clusters c is given and, also, a particular distance, a real number $m \in (1, \infty)$, and a small positive number ε for a stopping criterion. Let us use $c = 4$, and $m = 1.1$, and $\varepsilon = 0.001$. The choice for ε and m was made after the suggested values in the references Klir & Yuan, (1995), and the value for m worked fine in our tests although Pal & Bezdek (1995) suggest the interval of m to be [1.5,2.5]. The choice for $c = 4$ was based on the visual observation of the data. The resultant partition fit the validity guidelines (see section 5.1.2).

	nature	scores	period	estimate
1	adm exp	55.697	aug82	92444
2	adm exp	55.0982	nov 82	140474
3	adm exp	51.7517	nov81	141733
4	adm exp	50.505	jun83	184256
5	adm exp	50.2867	mar81	172925
6	adm exp	50.0313	jan85	158821
7	adm exp	49.487	mar81	121272
8	adm exp	49.31	dec 84	127859
9	adm exp	48.8606	abr81	334044
10	adm exp	48.0239	feb 81	95496
11	adm exp	47.4461	oct82	200932
12	oth recp	46.6733	aug83	134633
13	adm exp	45.4544	jan81	116865
14	adm exp	45.1228	jan 82	168655
15	adm exp	45.0171	may87	158623
16	oth dis	45.0043	jan 87	142776
17	adm exp	44.7688	feb 82	109315
18	adm exp	44.4445	may87	105113
19	adm exp	44.161	aug83	111196
20	adm exp	44.0656	mar 82	140507
21	adm exp	43.28	sep 82	136687
22	adm exp	41.7466	may81	123876
23	oth recp	39.3639	feb 86	131863
24	adm exp	37.229	feb 85	154815
25	suppl	34.7698	dec 82	143533
26	oth disb	33.9213	nov85	120708

Table 2. Cases retrieved.

The algorithm starts with an initial fuzzy pseudopartition $U^{(0)}$, which is a matrix of u_{ik}, the membership grades of the kth element in the ith cluster. Our initial fuzzy pseudopartition was chosen randomly. The outcome of the algorithm is the optimized fuzzy partition $U^{(t)}$ with the finite set of ordered pairs: the cluster's centers

v={v1,v2,v3,v4}and sizes k={k1,k2,k3,k4}:

v={v1,v2,v3,v4}= {176.950; 139.410 ; 108.820; 333.930}, and

k={k1,k2,k3,k4}= {1, 4, 8, 10}.

Using (3), we calculate MTV by Equation (2) resulting MTV = 132.570, as the unique solution. This means that there is one most typical value of order 2 to represent the given set. To measure the grade of typicality, using the result of (2), we calculate the MTD using (4). The result is MTD = 2.558, which represents a small number confirming that Equation (2) has one unique solution. At this time we verify that a DTV exists for the given data set. The resultant MTV when each center is used as the initial s in Equation (2) is presented in the following table:

Center	MTV
176,950	132,570
139,410	132,570
108,820	132,570
333,930	132,570

Table 3. The centers and the MTV.

Table 3 above demonstrates that there exists one unique MTV to the referred problem and this solution is called the *definite typical value* (DTV), (Friedman, Ming, & Kandel, 1995).

dimensions	input	highest score	user
AccountName	adm. expenses	adm. expenses	adm. expenses
Amount	119486.99	51277.49	101611.26
Month	jun	aug	may
Year	87	82	87
Next_Amount	96745.42	40981.98	119486.99
M_1_Density	0.850396	0.865198	1.303826
M_2_Density	1.108768	1.094545	1.778040
M_3_Density	1.512038	0.971196	1.951153
M_4_Density	1.659253	1.014571	1.644901
M_5_Density	1.398817	0.764248	1.580575
M_6_Density	1.344115	0.939003	1.567582
M_7_Density	1.333065	0.798711	2.406192
M_8_Density	2.046216	0.590103	2.226477
M_9_Density	1.893387	0.670797	1.669020
M_10_Density	1.419327	1.222284	1.681946
M_11_Density	1.430320	1.120506	1.876473
estimate value after adaptation		95496	140507

Table 4. Comparison of two matches.

From our previous assumptions, the MTV represents (is the most typical of) the set of solutions from the retrieved cases. This is the outcome the reasoner produces. The suggested forecast for the account *administrative expenses*, for July 87 is: $ 132,570. This is the result of the run of the automatic *Select* subtask, that combines the solutions of all retrieved cases to solve the input problem. For this example the estimate resulted is worse than the one chosen based on the highest score and a bit better than the one suggested by the user. However this example has only illustrative purposes.

7. Concluding Remarks and Future Work

In this paper, we proposed the use of the Theory of Typicality to perform automatically the *Select* subtask of case retrieval in a CBR system to predict cash flow accounts. The approach demonstrated in section 6 (Example) has produced a solution using all the retrieved cases preventing loss of relevant information.

An important issue to be discussed is about systems that may result in a set of retrieved cases with multivalue MTV. In the example presented, a DTV exists, and consequently it becomes the outcome of the system. On the other hand, if there is not one unique solution to the MTV, the *Select* task is not ready. In some domains, the existence of multivalue MTV may indicate that a CBR system is not able to generate a solution. Striving to achieve the goal of implementing a completely automatic reasoner, the authors are working in an approach to deal with this alternative.

The work presented has been designed to a reasoner in which the solution features of the cases are numeric attributes, enabling us to employ the numerical approach easily. In order to provide a greater contribution to the CBR community, we still have to formulate a similar symbolic method. One alternative is to use an approach similar to the one implemented in PROTOS, making use of the prototypicality (Kolodner, 1993, chapter 2 & 13), where the solutions are previously categorized. The idea of discovering typicality over a set of symbolic cases might be possible with the use of hierarchical clusterings (Fisher, 1996). Again, the directions should be determined by the specific applications, expectations and purposes.

The proposal of selecting the best match through the Theory of Typicality seems to be a very good choice in the development of automated CBR systems. The improvement in accuracy is still to be tested and it may vary depending on the domain. The successful implementation of this approach requires that the solution to the input problem is indeed the most typical of the set in the cases retrieved.

8. References

Aamodt, A. & Plaza, E. (1994). Case-Based Reasoning: Foundational Issues, Methodological Variations, and System Approaches. *Artificial Intelligence Communications, 7* (1), 39-59.

Bezdek, J.C. (1981). *Pattern Recognition with Fuzzy Objective Function Algorithms*. Plenum Press, New York.

Cheeseman, P. and Stutz, J. (1996). Bayesian Classification (AutoClass): Theory and Results, chapter 6, *Advances in Knowledge Discovery and Data Mining*, AAAI Press.

Fisher, D. (1996). Iterative Optimization and Simplification of Hierarchical Clusterings. *Journal of Artificial Intelligence Research*, 4, 147-180.

Friedman, M., Schneider, M., & Kandel, A. (1989). The use of weighted fuzzy expected value (WFEV) in fuzzy expert systems, *Fuzzy Sets and Systems*, 31, 37-45.

Friedman, M, Ming, M., & Kandel, A. (1995). On the Theory of Typicality. *International Journal of Uncertainty, Fuzziness and Knowledge-Based Systems*, 3, 2, 127-142.

Gath, I. & Geva, B. (1989). Unsupervised Optimal Fuzzy Clustering. *IEEE Transactions Pattern Anal. Machine Intelligence*, PAMI-11, 7, 773-781.

Hennessy, D. and Hinkle, D.(1992). Applying Case-Based Reasoning to Autoclave Loading. *IEEE Expert*, 7, 5, 21-26.

Hurley, Neil (1993). A priori Selection of Mesh Densities for Adaptive Finite Element Analysis, using a Case-Based Reasoning Approach. *Topics in Case-Based Reasoning*, (First European Workshop, EWCBR-93). Wess, Stefan, Althoff, Klaus-Dieter & Richter, Michael (editors) Springer-Verlag, 379-391.

Kandel, A. (1982). *Fuzzy Techniques in Pattern Recognition*, John Wiley, New York.

Kaufmann A. (1975). *Introduction to the Theory of Fuzzy Subsets*, vol.1, Academic Press, New York.

Kim, Steven H. & Novick, Mark B.(1993). Using clustering techniques to support case reasoning. *International Journal of Computer Applications in Technology*, 6, 2, 57-73.

Klir, G. & Yuan, B. (1995). *Fuzzy Sets and Fuzzy Logic: theory and applications*. Prentice-Hall Inc., Upper Saddle River, NJ.

Kolodner, J. (1989). Judging Which is the Best Case for a Case-Based Reasoner. *Proceedings of a Workshop on Case-Based Reasoning*, 77-81.

Kolodner, J. (1993). *Case-Based Reasoning*. Morgan Kaufmann, Los Altos, CA,.

Kopeikina, L., Brandau, R. & Lemmon, A. (1988). Case Based Reasoning for Continuous Control. *DARPA Proceedings of a Workshop on Case-Based Reasoning*, Clearwater Beach, Florida, May 10-13, 250-259.

Macchion, D. & Vo, D. P. (1993). Use of case-based reasoning technique in building expert systems. *Future Generation Computer Systems*, 9, 4, 311-319.

Mcintyre, S. H., Achabal, D. D. & Miller, C. M. (1993). Applying Case-Based Reasoning to Forecasting Retail Sales. *Journal of Retailing, 69* (4), 372-398.

Nakatani, Y., Tsukiyama, M. & Fukuda, T. (1991). Case organization in a case-based engineering design support system. *Proceedings of the IEEE International Conference on Systems, Man and Cybernetics, 3*, 1789-1794.

Pal, N. R. & Bezdek, J. C. (1995). On Cluster Validity for the Fuzzy c-Means Model. *IEEE Transactions on Fuzzy Systems*, 3, 3, 370-379.

Riesbeck, C. K. & Schank, R.C. (1989). *Inside Case-Based Reasoning*. Erlbaum, Hillsdale, NJ.

Rousseeuw, P. J. (1995). Discussion: Fuzzy Clustering at the Intersection. *Technometrics*, 37, 3, 283-286.

Shen, Z.L., Lui, H.C. & Ding, L.Y. (1994). Approximate Case-Based Reasoning on Neural Networks. *International Journal of Approximate Reasoning, 10* (1), 75-98.

Shinn, H.S. (1988). Abstractional Analogy: A Model of Analogical Reasoning. DARPA *Proceedings of a Workshop on Case-Based Reasoning*, Florida, May 10-13. Janet Kolodner (ed.) Morgan Kaufmann Publishers, 370-387.

Slade, S. (1991). Case-based reasoning: a research paradigm. *AI Magazine*, 12, 42-55.

Stottler, R. H.(1994). CBR for Cost and Sales Prediction. *AI Expert, (Aug.)*, 25-33.

Sugeno M. (1977). Fuzzy Measures and Fuzzy Integrals - A Survey. In *Fuzzy Automata and Decision Processes*, Gupta Madan M., Saridis, George N. & Gaines, Brian R. (eds.), North-Holland, New York.

Vassilliadis, S., Triantafyllos, G. & Kobrasly, W. (1994). A method for computing the most typical fuzzy expected value, *FUZZ-IEEE'94, Proceedings of the Third IEEE International Conference on Fuzzy Systems* (Orlando, FL), 2040-2045.

Wang, Z. & Klir, G. (1992). *Fuzzy Measure Theory*. Plenum Press, New York.

Weber-Lee, R., Barcia, R. & Khator, S. (1995). Case-based reasoning for cash flow forecasting using fuzzy retrieval. *Case-Based Reasoning Research And Development: First International Conference*; proceedings/ICCBR-95, Sesimbra, Portugal, October 23-26. Manuela Veloso & Agnar Aamodt (ed.) Springer-Verlag, 510-519.

Whalen, T. & Schott, B. (1985). Goal-Directed Approximate Reasoning in a Fuzzy Production System. *Approximate Reasoning in Expert Systems.* M.M.Gupta, A.Kandel, W.Bandler, J.B.Kiszka (editors) Elsevier Science Publishers B.V.(North-Holland).

Whitaker, Leslie A., Stottler, Richard H., Henke, Andrea, e King, James A. (1990). Case-Based Reasoning: Taming the similarity heuristic. *Proceedings of the Human Factors Society*, 312-315.

Windham, Michael P. (1983). Geometrical Fuzzy Clustering Algorithms. *Fuzzy Sets and Systems*, 10, 271-279.

Zadeh, L.A. (1975). The Concept of a Linguistic Variable and it's Application to Approximate Reasoning-I. *Information Sciences, 8*, 199-249.

Considering Decision Cost During Learning of Feature Weights

Wolfgang Wilke and Ralph Bergmann

University of Kaiserslautern
Centre for Learning Systems and Applications (LSA)
Department of Computer Science
P.O. Box 3049, D-67653 Kaiserslautern, Germany
e-Mail: {wilke,bergmann}@informatik.uni-kl.de

Abstract. This paper is to present a new algorithm, called KNN_{cost}, for learning feature weights for CBR systems used for classification. Unlike algorithms known so far, KNN_{cost} considers the profits of a correct and the cost of a wrong decision. The need for this algorithm is motivated from two real-world applications, where cost and profits of decisions play a major role.

We introduce a representation of accuracy, cost and profits of decisions and define the decision cost of a classification system. To compare accuracy optimization with cost optimization, we tested KNN_{acc} against KNN_{cost}. The first one optimizes classification accuracy with a conjugate gradient algorithm. The second one optimizes the decision cost of the CBR system, respecting cost and profits of the classifications. We present experiments with these two algorithms in a real application to demonstrate the usefulness of our approach.

1 Introduction

Developing a case-based reasoning system for a real-world application requires a lot of effort. For example, features must be selected to represent cases, the types of the features must be defined, and the similarity measure for all instances of the attributes must be selected by an expert. One step of the last task of this development process deals with the determination of feature weights. These weights can be acquired from an expert or can be determined by a learning algorithm that tries to extract the importance of the features for a given set of cases. Learning algorithms are required, if no natural weighting can be given for the domain or the weights given by an expert need an improvement. There are several different learning algorithms for feature weights. We focus in this work on algorithms using feedback for learning.

For example, Salzberg's EACH (Salzberg, 1991) proceed as follows: if a correct classification occurs, the weights of the matching features are incremented, while those of mismatching features are decremented of the new query by a fixed amount. If an incorrect classification occurs, matching feature weights are decremented and mismatching feature weights are incremented. Other approaches like VDM (Stanfill and Waltz, 1986), IB4 (Aha, 1991), RELIEF-F

(Kononenko, 1994), PADEX/INRECA (Wess, 1993; Wess, 1995), VSM (Lowe, 1995) or $k - NN_{vsm}$ (Wettschereck, 1994; Wettschereck and Aha, 1995) mostly differ in the way feature weights are modified, but share the main criterion for changing weights, namely: the correctness of the classification. As a consequence, these algorithms optimize classification accuracy only. We argue that this is not an appropriate learning goal for many real-world applications, because *decision cost* play a major role in several domains.

Our view of the problem is motivated by experiences with the following two applications:

Credit Scoring:
The goal of this task is to decide about a business bank customer's credit-worthiness. Available cases consist of the main balance items from the balance sheet, financial index numbers, and other relevant enterprise data, together with the credit-rating. The CBR system classifies new business customers to decide whether the enterprise is creditworthy (class A), or not (class B). In this application, the profits and cost of a right or wrong decision are asymmetric. If the system classifies a creditworthy customer (class A) as not creditworthy (class B) and the bank rejects the credit for the customer, the bank looses only the interest income. On the other hand, if a class B customer is classified as a member of class A, the bank looses the whole credit sum, which is a considerably higher loss. Here, the decision cost of a wrong decision depends strongly on the predicted and the correct class of the customer.

Diagnosing Cases of Poisoning by Psychotropes:
In the INRECA+ project (Althoff et al., 1996), we built a CBR system for diagnosing cases of poisoning by psychotropes. The cases[1] consist of 86 attributes that have been identified as useful for this diagnosis task by experts. The decision classes describe 8 different kinds of possible therapies for treating the poisoning. Of course, the different therapies cause different effects on the patient's constitution. In the worst case a wrong therapy can be mortal for the patient. Thus, it is important to come up with the right diagnosis as quick as possible. However, for a number of diagnoses the respective therapy is identical or, at least, very similar. Therefore making a wrong diagnosis leading to the same (or nearly the same) therapy as the correct diagnosis is no problem. So, in this application decision costs differ significantly.

These two examples show that decision cost may play a major role for the optimization of a CBR system. For that purpose, we developed a feature weight learning algorithm KNN_{cost}, which optimizes the feature weights, with regard to cost and profits of the decisions of a case-based classification system. To compare KNN_{cost} to an algorithm that optimizes classification accuracy only, we first introduce KNN_{acc}, a learning algorithm that uses the same mechanism

---

[1] The application data was provided by the Toxicology Information and Advisory Centre of the Russian Federation Ministry of Health and Medical Industry

as KNN_{cost}, with respect to the accuracy only, yet with another optimization criterion.

The paper is organized as follows: In the next section, we give a short introduction into k−nearest neighbor classification and illustrate our definition of accuracy and cost for a classification system. Section 3 introduces two algorithms KNN_{acc} and KNN_{cost}. After that, we describe an empirical evaluation of the algorithms in the credit scoring application in section 4. We then add a discussion and, finally, give an outlook on future work.

2 Basics

2.1 Case-Based Classification with k−Nearest Neighbors

In a CBR system used for classification tasks, a case $c = (f_1, \ldots, f_n, t_c)$ consists of n describing features f and of the desired class t_c. The set $T = \{t_1, \ldots, t_l\}$ denotes all possible classes in the domain. The case base CB is defined as a set of known cases from the past. Given a new query $q = \{q_1, \ldots, q_n\}$ and a case base CB, the k most similar cases are retrieved to predict the real class t_q of a query q. The similarity $sim(q, c)$ between a query q and a case c from the case base is defined as:

$$sim(q, c) = \sum_{a=1}^{n} w_a * sim_a(q_a, f_a) \tag{1}$$

where w_a is the weight for feature f_a and sim_a is the local similarity measure for attribute a. Further, we assume that $\sum_{a=1}^{n} w_a = 1$ and $sim_a(q_a, f_a) \in [0, 1]$, for all features, yielding the similarity between a query and a case $sim(q, c) \in [0, 1]$. The CBR system predicts the class of the query by retrieving the $q's$ k−nearest neighbors $K = \{r_1, \ldots, r_k\}$ and applying a majority vote method on them, e.g.: Let $p_{q,t}$ denote the probability[2] that a query q is a member of the class $t \in T$ defined as:

$$p_{q,t} = \frac{\sum_{r \in K} \delta_{r,t} * sim(q, r)^2}{\sum_{r \in K} sim(q, r)^2} \tag{2}$$

where $\delta_{r,t}$ is defined as follows:

$$\delta_{r,t} = \begin{cases} 1 & : \quad t_r = t \\ 0 & : \quad t_r \neq t \end{cases} \tag{3}$$

and where $t_r \in T$ denotes the class of case r. Then, the prediction of the CBR system is the class with the highest probability calculated from the set of the k−nearest neighbors.

There are other voting algorithms for the k−nearest neighbor classification, for

---

[2] If the numerator in the definition of $p_{q,t}$ is 0, then $p_{q,t}$ is set to 0. For the later transformation of the error function in an energie function the similarities are squared.

example the single majority vote (Michie et al., 1994)[p. 10 pp], (Weiss and Kulikowski, 1991) [p. 70] that only considers the frequencies of the different classes in the set of nearest neighbors. However, the weighted majority vote has the main advantage that the distance of the neighbors is taken into account for the prediction.

2.2 How to Present Accuracy and Decision Cost

A common representation for the classification accuracy of a system is a confusion matrix (Weiss and Kulikowski, 1991)[p. 18]. For a given set of cases, the entry of such a matrix counts the number of classifications of cases from a class as a member of the predicted class by the system, for a given set of cases. For

$P_{i,j}$	predicted class	
correct class	A	B
A	0.55	0.45
B	0.25	0.75

Table 1. A sample confusion matrix for the credit scoring application

our approach, we modify the entries of the confusion matrix with respect to the probability $p_{q,t}$ from equation (2) to classify that a query q is a member of the class t. So our matrix contains the probabilities for every possible decision of the system for a given set of cases.

For measuring the accuracy of a CBR system during learning, one can use a leave-one-out test (Weiss and Kulikowski, 1991)[p. 31] over a given training set L. Every case from L is used as a query q and classified with the CBR system including all other cases from L except the query q. For every query q, the probabilities $p_{q,t}$ from the retrieved k-nearest neighbors using equation (2) can be calculated for every $t \in T$. This is done for every case from L and the resulting probabilities are combined for every entry of the confusion matrix. After that we normalize every row of the confusion matrix with respect to the occurrences of the correct classes in the given training set. The resulting confusion matrix represents the probabilities for the different outcomes of a classification with the training set L. This matrix is an approximated confusion matrix, because we use probabilities for the decisions, instead of counting the occurrence of the different decisions[3]. Table 1 shows an example of such a matrix for the credit scoring application with the two different classes and predictions. The probability of the correct predictions for each class can be found in the diagonal of the matrix, here 55 and 75 percent. All other entries represent the probabilities of errors for a particular type of misclassification, here 45 and 25 percent.

---

[3] For simplification, we further use the term confusion matrix

To represent cost, (Weiss and Kulikowski, 1991)[p. 21] and (Michie et al., 1994)[p. 224] use a similar matrix called *cost matrix*, in which non-diagonal entries represent cost of a specific misclassification and the fields in the diagonal represent the benefits of a correct classification, explicitly set to 0. We extend this approach by allowing positive and negative entries for representing cost *and* profits in a single matrix. As a result these *decision value matrix* represents the cost and profits for every possible decision of the system. Table 2 shows an example for such a decision value matrix in the credit scoring application. The values

$C_{t_q,t}$	predicted class	
correct class	A	B
A	-1	1
B	10	-10

Table 2. A sample decision value matrix for the credit scoring application

represent the relation between the two possible errors that might occur. Here the cost of misclassifying a bad customer are 10-times higher than misclassifying a good one[4].

In the first case, the bank looses the credit volume, but in the second case only the interest rate is lost. Consequently the profit of detecting a bad one is here 10-times higher than correctly classifying a good one[5].

So, this decision value matrix represents the cost and profits of the different decisions of the classification in the bank application.

With the representation of accuracy from the confusion matrix and the cost from the decision value matrix we can define the *decision cost* of a classification system as:

$$Cost_{decision} = \sum_{i \in T} \sum_{j \in T} P_{i,j} * C_{i,j} \qquad (4)$$

where the $P_{i,j}$ are the probability from the confusion matrix and the $C_{i,j}$ are the corresponding entries from the decision value matrix. This definition is akin to the utility of decisions used in the Bayesian decision theory (Berger, 1985).

3 Incremental Learning of Feature Weights

In this section, we first describe the general algorithm for learning feature weights with a conjugate gradient algorithm. In the next two subsections we specialize this algorithm to the algorithms KNN_{acc} and KNN_{cost}.

---

[4] See the relation between the entries $C_{B,A}$ and $C_{A,B}$ in Table 2.
[5] See the entries $C_{B,B}$ and $C_{A,A}$ in Table 2.

3.1 Learning Weights Guided by the Conjugate Gradient

The conjugate gradient method is a generate-and-test search algorithm with feedback from the test procedure. The algorithm tries to optimize a system with respect to an error function E by adjusting the weights $w = \{w_1, \ldots, w_n\}$. This optimization is realized by an iterative search for a local minimum of the error function E. So E has to be chosen according to the learning goal. A learning rate λ is used to influence the step width for a learning step in the direction of the conjugated gradient. The basic algorithm is follows:

1. initialize the weight-vector w and the learning rate λ
2. compute the error $E(w)$ of the initial system
3. **while** $not(stop - criterion)$ **do**
   learning step: $\forall\ a\ \hat{w}_a := w_a - \frac{\partial E}{\partial w_a} * \lambda$
   compute $E(\hat{w})$
   if $E(\hat{w}) < E(w)$ **then** $w := \hat{w}$ **else** $\lambda := \frac{\lambda}{2}$
4. output w

First, the weights w_i are either initialized to random values, set to the constant $\frac{1}{n}$, or given by an expert. After the calculation of the initial E, the algorithm does a number of learning steps, depending on the stop-criterion. If a learning step is successful ($E(\hat{w}) < E(w)$), the weights are modified to guide E in the direction of a local minimum. Otherwise, the learning rate is decreased. The algorithm terminates and outputs a weight vector as the result of the learning. The use of conjugated gradient methods for feature weight learning is also common in other disciplines like backpropagation (Rummelhart et al., 1986) for Neural Networks.

The choice of the learning rate The choice of a good value for λ is difficult, because it depends on many unknown domain properties. If λ is quite small, many learning steps are needed to find the next local minimum in the neighborhood of the starting point. However, it is guaranteed that the algorithm finds it, respecting the initial starting point. If λ is too large, misleading steps may happen and the algorithm very often decrements the value of λ, before it improves E. It is also possible that a learning step with a large λ leads to an improvement of E, but this improvement is based on a different minimum. So, the algorithm finds a local minimum of E, not respecting to the initial weights. This behavior is illustrated in figure 1. The dotted line shows learning steps which lead to the minimum $w2$, because the value of λ is too large. The solid line shows a learning step with a sufficiently small learning rate. This leads a step forward to a local minimum $w1$ that respects the expert initialization. Thus, if the learning rate is too large, the behavior of the algorithm is not respecting the initialization, because the founded minimum $w2$ is not related to weights given by an expert.

The choice of the stop-criterion The stop-criterion has to ensure the termination of the algorithm. Possible stop criteria for the algorithm are:

- a fixed number of learning steps

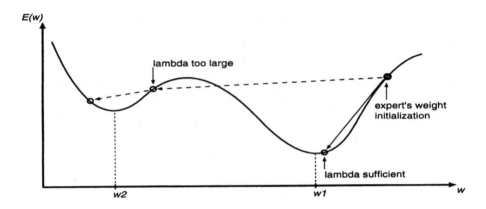

Fig. 1. The effects of different values for the learning rate

- a minimal change of the error function: $\mid E(\hat{w}) - E(w) \mid \, \leq \epsilon$
- a minimal change of the feature weights: $\sum_{a=1}^{n} \mid \frac{\partial E}{\partial w_a} \mid \, \leq \epsilon$
- a minimal learning rate: $\lambda \leq \epsilon$

It is also possible to combine these criteria.

The choice of k A different value of k for the amount of the nearest neighbors taken into account leads to different probabilities for the classifications. The optimal value of k could be computed by a simple generate and test procedure. Here, optimal means a minimal value for the decision cost from equation (4). We used a fixed k from our experience with the domain for the whole learning procedure, like VSM (Lowe, 1995). (Wettschereck and Aha, 1995) calculate an optimal k prior to the first learning step and fix it for the rest of the learning procedure. A computational expensive approach calculates a new optimal k after each learning step. This is necessary, because in general the new weights after a learning step could effect the optimality of the old value of k. The new calculation of an optimal k after every step is costly, but should lead to the best results.

3.2 KNN_{acc} for optimizing classification accuracy

Now we specialize the basic algorithm of the conjugated gradient to KNN_{acc}, which optimizes classification accuracy. This is done by defining a special error functions E for this purpose, together with the required derivation $\frac{\partial E_{acc}}{\partial w_a}$. During the learning we use the leave-one-out test, described in section 2.2 to calculate the value for $E(w)$.

KNN_{acc} is similar to the VSM (Lowe, 1995) and $k-NN_{vsm}$ (Wettschereck and Aha, 1995) algorithms. They also determinate feature weights with a conjugate gradient algorithm. Unlike other approaches, we use a similarity measure to quantify the distance of cases. This measure is not fixed for different types of features.

The error function E_{acc} for optimizing the classification accuracy E_{acc} can be defined as:

$$E_{acc} = \sum_{q \in CB} \sum_{t \in T} (\delta_{q,t} - p_{q,t})^2 \tag{5}$$

For a learning step with the conjugate gradient method, we need the derivation of E_{acc} with respect to the weights w_a from equation (5):

$$\frac{\partial E_{acc}}{\partial w_a} = -2 * \sum_{q \in CB} \sum_{t \in T} (\delta_{q,t} - p_{q,t}) * \frac{\partial p_{q,t}}{\partial w_a} \tag{6}$$

where the derivation of $p_{q,t}$ for the weights w_a is given by[6]:

$$\frac{\partial p_{q,t}}{\partial w_a} = \frac{2 * \sum_{r \in K} [(\delta_{r,t} - p_{q,t}) * sim(q,r) * sim_a(q_a, r_a)]}{\sum_{r \in K} sim(q,r)^2} \tag{7}$$

The KNN_{acc} algorithm is the conjugate gradient algorithm together with the error function from (5) and the derivation given in (6). Minimizing the error function means maximizing the overall probabilities for the prediction of the correct classes and minimizing the overall probabilities of a misclassification for the training set. In the confusion matrix (see Table 1) KNN_{acc} tries to maximize the diagonal and to minimizes the non-diagonal entries.

3.3 KNN_{cost} for Optimizing Decision Cost

The idea of KNN_{cost} is to minimize the decision cost as defined in equation (4). This is done by integrating the decision value matrix (Table 2) into the error function. So every probability in the error function is judged by its respective cost from the decision value matrix. The resulting error function E_{cost}, which defines the error for the respective decision cost, is given by:

$$E_{cost} = \sum_{q \in CB} \sum_{t \in T} sgn(C_{t_q,t}) * C_{t_q,t}^2 * p_{q,t}^2 \tag{8}$$

where $C_{t_q,t}$ is an entry from the decision value matrix and $sgn(C_{t_q,t})$ is the sign of this entry. The derivation $\frac{\partial E_{cost}}{\partial w_a}$ used to calculate the new weights can be computed as follows:

$$\frac{\partial E_{cost}}{\partial w_a} = 2 * \sum_{q \in CB} \sum_{t \in T} sgn(C_{t_q,t}) * C_{t_q,t}^2 * p_{q,t} * \frac{\partial p_{q,t}}{\partial w_a} \tag{9}$$

where $\frac{\partial p_{q,t}}{\partial w_a}$ is the formula from equation (7). Thus, our algorithm KNN_{cost} is the conjugate gradient algorithm from the first part of this section together with the error function E_{cost} and its derivation $\frac{\partial E_{cost}}{\partial w_a}$. With this error function the

---

[6] Please note that these equations are similar to those shown in (Wettschereck, 1994), except for the replacement of distances by similarities

algorithm minimizes the decision cost of the CBR system. In our representation of accuracy and cost this means that KNN_{cost} tries to minimize/maximize the products of every entry of the confusion matrix with a corresponding entry of the decision value matrix, depending on cost and profits[7].

4   Empirical Evaluation of KNN_{acc} and KNN_{cost}

We now present the results of an empirical evaluation of KNN_{acc} and KNN_{cost}. The algorithms were implemented as part of the INRECA[8] CBR - shell. The goal of these tests is to verify or reject our hypothesis:
Classification based on weights learned by KNN_{cost} leads to lower decision cost than classification based on weights learned by KNN_{acc}.

4.1   Experimental Settings

For our experiments we used the the credit scoring domain with 685 cases. A case consists of 136 different features and a class description. There are 20 numeric attributes while the remaining have symbolic values. About 5 percent of the attributes were unknown in each case description.

To test our learning algorithms, we made 5 independent runs. In every run, we divided the case base in a training set with 70 percent randomly selected cases and use the remaining 30 percent as a test set. In each run, we used the training set as case base for the CBR system[9]. The weights were initialized randomly. In each run we learned feature weights using the KNN_{acc} and KNN_{cost} algorithms. The learning process was stopped when a change less than $5 * 10^{-3}$ occured. The initial learning rate λ was set to $5 * 10^{-4}$. In our tests we took $k = 11$ nearest neighbors into account.

4.2   Results

Now we compare the decision cost of the initial CBR systems to those of the resulting systems after learning feature weights with both algorithms. First, we exemplarily show how to calculate the decision cost. We classify the 206 cases from the test set with the initial CBR systems. The left side of the Table 3 shows a confusion matrix with the classification accuracy averaged over the 5 initial systems. Contrary to the matrix introduced in Table 1, the entries denote the average occurrence of classifications for the cases of the test set. We choose this different representation for the classifications to make the entailed cost of

---

[7] This is equal to minimizing the decision cost, because they are computed as the sum of the single products. The squares in equation (8) were only introduced to speed up the learning process.

[8] INRECA (ESPRIT contract P6322, the INRECA project) with the partners: AcknoSoft (prime contractor, France), tecInno (Germany), Irish Medical Systems (Ireland) and the University of Kaiserslautern (Germany)

[9] In the following we name these systems initial CBR systems

correct class	predicted class			
	accuracy		cost	
	A	**B**	**A**	**B**
A	48.6	36.4	-48.6	36.4
B	27.4	93.6	274	-936.0
	decision cost: **-674.2**			

Table 3. The average decision cost of the CBR systems before learning

the systems more explicit. These entries were multiplied with the respective cost from the cost matrix (Table 2). The resulting cost for every possible decision are shown on the right side of the Table 3. The bottom line of the table shows the average decision cost for the 5 initial systems as a result of the sum of all entries of the decision value matrix[10] .

Comparing KNN_{acc} and KNN_{cost} In the following we compare our initial systems with the systems after learning feature weights using KNN_{acc} and KNN_{cost}. After the learning phase, we test the resulting systems with the test set. For both learning algorithms, we calculate the average decision cost of the resulting systems. Table 4 summarizes the entire decision cost of the initial systems and the resulting systems after learning. Both learning algorithms lead to

	Decision cost
Before Learning:	**-674.2**
Learning with KNN_{acc}:	**-756.2**
Learning with KNN_{cost}:	**-1040.6**

Table 4. The decision cost of the CBR systems before and after learning feature weights

an improvement of the decision cost. The average decision cost of the systems with the weights obtained from KNN_{acc} are 82 (= 756.2 − 674.2) lower than the decision cost before learning. We associated profits with right and cost with wrong decisions. So, this improvement represents the benefit of the better classification accuracy after learning. The weights extracted with KNN_{cost} lead to an improvement of 366.4 (= 1040.6 − 674.2) for the decision cost. Especially, the decrease of the decision cost of 284.4 (= 1040.6 − 756.2) obtained by using KNN_{cost} when compared to the results obtained by KNN_{acc} is remarkable.

---

[10] Here, a negative value denotes the profit of the classification systems

The classification accuracy of the systems that use weights learned by KNN_{acc} and of those using weights learned by KNN_{cost} were nearly the same. The reason for the improvement of the decision cost is that KNN_{cost} prefers to classify more costly cases correctly than KNN_{acc}. So, our hypothesis that classification based on weights learned by KNN_{cost} leads to lower decision cost than classification based on weights learned by KNN_{acc}, has been empirically verified in this domain.

5 Summary and Discussion

In this paper, we presented two feature weight learning algorithms, one optimizing classification accuracy only and one optimizing decision cost for a CBR system. Both algorithms use the conjugate gradient to optimize the feature weights for the different criteria. We empirically evaluated these two algorithms in the domain of credit scoring with real bank-customer data. In this evaluation we could verify our hypothesis that cost optimization could be more profitable than classification accuracy optimization.

In (Pazzani et al., 1994) several algorithms are proposed to optimize cost for decision lists, decision trees and rule based expert systems. In this discussion we will focus on algorithms that integrate cost in a CBR system.

It should also be possible to integrate cost into other algorithms for learning feature weights. Especially, the extension of algorithms using feedback seems easy in some cases. Here, the feedback denotes the amount of change for every weight after a learning step to improve the system.

As already stated, EACH (Salzberg, 1991) changes the feature weights by a fixed value depending on whether correct or incorrect classification occured and whether a feature matches or mismatches. To introduce cost, this value could vary according to the decision of the system. EACH has two disadvantages: it is very sensitive to the order of the presentation of the examples and all weights were simultaneously changed by a fixed amount in one learning step.

RELIEF (Kira and Rendell, 1992) selects a random training case c, the most similar case p of the same class, and the most similar case n of a different class. The new feature weights are calculated by:

$$\hat{w}_a = w_a - difference(c_f, p_f) + difference(c_f, n_f) \tag{10}$$

An approach to introduce decision cost in the feedback of RELIEF (in equation 10) could be to judge the differences with the desired cost of the training case c classified as the class of a similar case, here the class of p or n. The original version of RELIEF is limited to two-class problems only, yet this restriction has been removed by (Kononenko, 1994) in RELIEF-F. He takes all different classes in the feedback into account. The extension to decision cost would be quite similar. As in EACH, the problem with these algorithms is the sensitivity to the order of the presentation of the examples.

IB4 (Aha, 1989; Aha, 1991) takes the distribution of the different classes in the case base into account for changing weights. The amount of change is judged

471

with a factor $(1 - \Delta)$ that represents the observed frequency among the different classes. This is a promising approach to optimizing the classification accuracy. To introduce decision cost in this approach could be difficult, because weights are optimized according to two conflicting criteria. If a costly class has a low frequency, the benefits of the two criteria could disappear. The cost criterion argues for a massive change of the feature weights, but the frequency criterion argues for a moderate modification. Otherwise, the factor to change a highly frequent class with low cost is also contrary. So, the feedback of these two criteria would compensate, because the criteria accuracy and cost, as already stated could be contradictory.

Other learning algorithms for improving CBR-Systems could also be modified in order to take decision cost into account. For example, an instance-based learning algorithm (IBL) (Aha, 1989; Aha, 1990) could be extended. Roughly speaking in IBL the cases are rated with their effects on arbitrary classifications and misclassifications. If cases often cause wrong classifications and seldom ensure a right classification, they are removed from the case base. The goal is to keep only those cases in the case base, which ensure a correct classification. To integrate cost, it is possible to rate the cases not only with the classification rating, but with the respective entry from the cost matrix. This will be a topic of our further research in this area.

The price of our approach is that the decision cost must be acquired additionally. However, experts often know the cost and profits for the different outcomes of a classification.

Acknowledgements

The authors would like to thank Prof. Michael M. Richter, Dr. Klaus-Dieter Althoff, Harald Holz and Ivo Vollrath for the useful discussions and for their implementation work. This work was partially funded by the Commision of the European Communities (ESPRIT contract P22196, the INRECA II project: Information and Knowledge Reengineering for Reasoning from Cases) with the partners: AcknoSoft (prime contractor, France), Daimler Benz (Germany), tecInno (Germany), Irish Medical Systems (Ireland) and the University of Kaiserslautern (Germany) and partially funded by the "Stiftung Innovation für Rheinland-Pfalz".

References

Aha, D. W. (1989). Incremental, instance-based learning of independend and graded concepts. In *Proceedings of the 6th international Workshop on Machine Learning*, pages 387–391.

Aha, D. W. (1990). *A Study of Instance-Based Algorithms for supervised Learning*. PhD thesis, University of California at Irvine.

Aha, D. W. (1991). Case-Based Learning Algorithms. In Bareiss, R., editor, *Proceedings CBR Workshop 1991*, pages 147–158. Morgan Kaufmann Publishers.

Althoff, K.-D., Bergmann, R., Wess, S., Manago, M., Auriol, E., Larichev, O. I., Bolotov, A., and Gurov, S. I. (1996). Integration of Induction and case-Based Reasoning for Critical Decision Support Tasks in Medical Domains: The INRECA Approach. *Centre for Learning Systems and Applications Technical Report*, 96-03E.

Berger, J. O. (1985). *Statistical Decision Theory and Bayesian Analysis*. Springer Verlag.

Kira, K. and Rendell, L. A. (1992). A practical approach to feature selection. In *Proccedings of the Ninth International Conference on Machine Learning*, Aberdeen, Scotland. Morgan Kaufmann.

Kononenko, I. (1994). Estimating attributes: Analysis and extensions of relief. In *Proceedings of the 1994 European Conference on Machine Learning*, pages 171–182. Springer Verlag.

Lowe, D. (1995). Similarity metric learning for a variable-kernel classifier. *Neural Computation*, 7:72–85.

Michie, D., Spiegelhalter, D., and Taylor, C. C. (1994). *Machine Learning, Neural and Statistical Classification*. Ellis Horwood.

Pazzani, M. J., Merzi C., Murphy P., Ali K., Hume T. and Brunk C. (1994). Reducing Misclassification Costs. In *Proccedings of the 11th International Conference of Machine Learning*, pages 217–225. Morgan Kaufmann.

Rummelhart, D. E., Hinton, G. E., and Williams, R. J. (1986). *Learning Internal Representations by Error Propagation*, chapter 8, pages 318–364. MIT Press.

Salzberg, S. (1991). A nearest hyperrectangle learning method. *Machine Learning,* 6:277–309.

Stanfill, C. and Waltz, D. (1986). Toward Memory-Based Reasoning. *Communications of the ACM*, 29(12):1213–1229.

Weiss, S. M. and Kulikowski, C. A. (1991). *Computer Systems That Learn – Classification and Prediction Methods from Statistics, Neural Nets, Machine Learning, and Expert Systems*. Morgan Kaufmann.

Wess, S. (1993). PATDEX - Inkrementelle und wissensbasierte Verbesserung von Ähnlichkeitsurteilen in der fallbasierten Diagnostik. In *Tagungsband 2. deutsche Expertensystemtagung XPS-93*, Hamburg. Springer Verlag.

Wess, S. (1995). *Fallbasiertes Problemlösen in wissensbasierten Systemen zur Entscheidungsunterstützung und Diagnostik*. PhD thesis, University of Kaiserslautern.

Wettschereck, D. (1994). *A Study of Distance-Bases Machine Learning Algorithms*. PhD thesis, Oregon State University.

Wettschereck, D. and Aha, D. W. (1995). Weighting features. In Veloso, M. and Aamodt, A., editors, *Case-Based Reasoning Research and Development*, pages 347–358. Springer.

Case-Based Problem Solving Methods for Parametric Design Tasks

Zdenek Zdrahal and Enrico Motta

Knowledge Media Institute, The Open University, UK

Abstract. We discuss a solution to a parametric design problem, which is based on the integration of case-based reasoning and heuristic search techniques. Four algorithms for case-based design are described which exploit both general properties of parametric design tasks and application specific heuristic knowledge.

1 Introduction

Design problems are hard due to the potentially combinatorial explosion of the design space. Designers, both human and artificial, tackle the complexity of the design process by making use of both task-specific heuristics and case-based knowledge. The main focus of this paper is on case-based problem solving methods. In particular, we discuss a case study in the domain of elevator design [10] and we show a solution to this problem which is based on the integration of case-based reasoning (CBR) and heuristic search techniques. This 'hybrid' approach proved particularly important in the elevator design domain, as we found that the original design problem solver, based on a Propose & Revise approach [5], could not solve all the 'obvious' cases. The reason for this limitation was that the available heuristic knowledge provided by domain experts was incomplete. This was probably due to the fact that heuristic problem solving methods, in particular design methods, are difficult to articulate during a knowledge acquisition process – designers' problem solving knowledge is mainly operational. Since we did not have access to an expert designer to ask for assistance with the difficult cases, we followed a different approach. The missing solutions to the 'difficult cases' were calculated by means of best-first search algorithms and stored into a case library and the original design problem solver was replaced by a case-based design module. In this paper we describe four alternative algorithms for performing case-based design and we show how we were able to integrate the pre-existing search control knowledge — originally acquired in the context of a Propose & Revise approach — with a case-based approach to design.

These algorithms exploit both general properties of parametric design and domain specific characteristics of elevator design. The design of even moderately complex artefacts consist of subsystems which are difficult to design and those which are easy to design. In the elevator domain the design of the machinery subsystem is much harder task than the design of the rest. Subsystems which are difficult to design are also difficult to adapt. The case-based algorithms introduced in this paper prefer cases whose difficult subsystems do not need any modifications.

The heuristic knowledge used for adaptation makes it possible to estimate the minimum and the maximum cost of adaptation. Since design task is an optimisation, the upper and lower bounds of the adaptation cost can be used for filtering out cases which cannot minimise the cost criterion. Adaptation consists of elementary corrective steps. Each step represents a modification of the case which increases the cost of the solution. The control of the adaptation algorithm can be broken down into an A* like strategy which evaluates results and costs of the elementary corrections.

Based on these observations which hold in many design domains we have designed and implemented algorithms described in this paper.

2   Parametric Design

The elevator design application is an example of a *parametric design* problem. Parametric design problems are a class of design problems where the solution can be described in terms an assignment of values to a set of *parameters*. This assignment has to satisfy a number of *design constraints* and *requirements*, and should achieve (or at least approximate) some *quality criterion*. A (possibly incomplete) set of parameter assignments is called a *design model*. For example, the elevator domain includes parameters such as the motor model, the motor torque, and the platform weight.

Design requirements are relations which the design model is expected to satisfy. For example, "the number of floors is 6", "the elevator speed is at least 300 ft/min", and "the elevator should be equipped with a telephone" are requirements in the elevator domain. In parametric design problem solving the requirements are often operationalized as an initial assignment of some parameters, e.g. speed = 300. We call these parameters and the resulting design model *initial parameters* and *initial design model*.

Constraints are relations which must not be violated [1]. For instance, the sentences "the minimum safe distance from the counterweight to the rear side of the hoistway is 0.75 inches", and "the weight of the cab is the sum of weights of all its components" express constraints in the elevator domain. In accordance with their role in the design process we can distinguish between *restrictive* and *constructive* constraints. Restrictive constraints eliminate certain combinations of parameter values (the 'safe distance constraint' above). Constructive constraints define legal combinations of parameter values (see the 'total cab weight constraint' above). Constructive constraints can be expressed in a functional notation which indicates the expected way of using the constraint in a design process. Thus, the total cab weight constraint can be operationalised as: "Once the weights of all components are available the weight of the cab can be calculated as their sum".

---

[1] For a given problem some constraints may not be applicable. For example, if a telephone is not required the telephone related constraints are not considered. Therefore a solution is only expected to satisfy the applicable constraints.

It is important to emphasise that while constraints and requirements often appear to be similar (and typically they are both represented as logical sentences over the design domain) they are conceptually distinct. Requirements specify an individual instance of the design problem while constraints describe physical laws and technological principles which must hold — when applicable — for all designs in the domain.

The distinction between constructive and restrictive constraints allows us to distinguish between the parameters which can be calculated by means of operationalised constructive constraints and the other parameters. We call the latter *key design parameters*. Key design parameters and their possible values define the degrees of freedom in the design process and, consequently, the size of the design space. However, the choice of values for key design parameters is not quite free. Instead, the value of a key parameter is restricted to a number of *design choices*. These are normally ordered, according to our preferences for a particular key parameter. For example, in the elevator domain the preferred choice for the motor model selects the cheapest motor which provides the necessary torque. However, if such a motor is too small to be connected with the gearbox already selected on the basis of other requirements, our next choice would be the cheapest motor model providing the necessary torque and compatible with the selected gearbox.

Design is usually a problem of optimisation. We are not satisfied with any design which fulfils requirements and constraints, but we want to achieve (or at least approximate) an optimal one. The optimisation criterion is often complex and may include a number of elements, such as the cost of the artefact, the cost of the design process, expected maintenance costs, customer satisfaction measures, etc. Because the only degrees of freedom we have are the design choices associated with key design parameters, the optimisation criterion must be based on the values of key design parameters. In conclusion, the input to a parametric design task is given by:

1. a set of parameters,
2. a set of key design parameters,
3. a set of design requirements,
4. a set of constraints,
5. a set of design choices associated with each key parameter;
6. preference functions defining an order over the possible design choices for key parameters; and
7. an optimisation criterion.

The goal is to produce a complete design model which satisfies all requirements, does not violate any constraint, and best approximates the optimisation criterion.

Although the elevator design problem has been presented as parametric design it can be also viewed as a configuration task. For example, the design of the machinery consists of selecting motor model, machine model, cables and other components so that the required functionality is achieved and no compatibility constraints are violated. Our domain ontology is based on the part/component hierarchy introduced in [10]. The parameters are associated with the corresponding components and parts. Since the part/component hierarchy of the domain ontology is not essential for the case-based algorithms presented in this paper, we do not discuss this issue in detail.

3 Propose & Revise

Design problem solving often follows a Propose & Revise (P&R) approach [5]. P&R problem solving consists of three main subtasks, which are: (1) proposing a model extension, i.e. selecting an unassigned parameter and calculating its value, (2) evaluating the current design model against the set of applicable constraints, and (3) revising an inconsistent design model. This generic framework can be operationalized into two problem solving methods which we call Extend-Model-then-Revise (EMR) and Complete-Model-then-Revise (CMR). EMR tests and fixes constraint violations after each "propose" step; in other words, violations are resolved as soon as they are generated. In contrast with this approach, CMR first assigns values to all parameters, thus producing a complete design model, and only then attempts to fix constraint violations. A detailed analysis of P&R problem solving methods is presented in [12].

4 Domain Example

The elevator design problem has 220 parameters, 30 of which are key design parameters, and 26 initial parameters. The number of restrictive constraints is 63. The preference functions classify the design choices in 11 classes by providing them with a cost in the integer interval $[0, \ldots, 10]$. A design choice with a low number is meant to be less expensive and therefore preferred to one with a higher rating. Design choices with zero cost are used to provide an initial value to a key design parameter, i.e. they are used during the "propose" phase. Design choices with cost higher than zero are used during the revision phase to fix constraint violations, and are therefore called *fixes*. Figure 1 shows some design elements in the elevator domain. The figure includes five parameters. Hoistway-depth is an initial parameter, i.e. its value is given as part of the design requirements. The other four parameters shown in the figure have instead to be calculated. The Cwt-to-hoistway-rear distance is a key design parameter whose preferred value is calculated so that the counterweight is positioned half way between the rear side of the platform and the rear side of the shaft. If the counterweight plates get too close to the U-bracket, the constraint "Cwt-to-U-bracket < 0.75" is violated. In this case two fixes are applicable: (a) decrease the counterweight plate depth by half-inch step (cost = 1) and (b) increase Cwt-to-platform-rear by the amount by which the constraint is violated (cost = 2).

In general, cheap fixes mean that an alternative design decisions is taken with the same design costs (cost = 1) or, for example, with increased maintenance

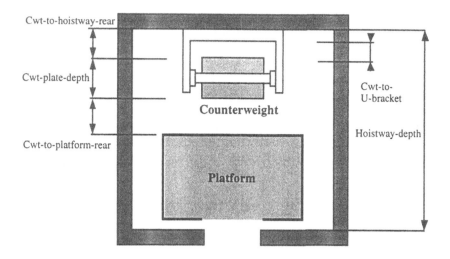

requirements (cost $= 2$). On the other hand, expensive fixes modify the building dimensions (cost $= 9$) or even change major design specifications (cost $= 10$).

5 Heuristic Search in the Elevator Design Problem

The heuristic search control knowledge in the elevator design example has the following characteristics [10]:

1. Fixes are associated with constraints, i.e. a fix can be applied only if the associated constraint is violated. Although the associations of constraints and fixes have been provided by the expert, they can be easily retrieved from the constraint network. We have calculated the associations from the domain dependencies and the result was almost identical with the expert's.
2. As already pointed out, cost is associated with fixes. Fixes associated with the same constraint can be applied in parallel thus forming a *fix combination*. The cost of a fix combination is a composition of the costs of the participating fixes. The composition operation does not necessarily mean an arithmetic addition. For example in the elevator example the designer applies a non-Archimedian composition operation, i.e. the sum of costs is calculated for each cost class separately and the result of a lower class is taken into account only if the costs of higher classes are the same — see [11] for more details. However, for the purpose of this paper we can assume that the cost composition is a simple addition.
3. For a given constraint violation the recommended strategy is to select fixes and their combinations in accordance with the cost minimisation criterion.
4. If a fix removes the associated constraint violation the modified design model becomes permanent. Vice versa, if a new constraint is violated as a result of

a fix application the fix is rejected. The former rule prevents backtracking when the correction happens to result in a dead end, while the latter does not allow us to proceed with inconsistent designs. This *ad hoc* strategy simplifies the search and makes it easy for the designer to supervise the design process. On the other hand it significantly reduces the portion of the design space which is searched and therefore decreases the chances of finding a solution.

Although this framework was proposed originally for the elevator design problem, it can be applied to other design situations. For instance, it has been used for an initial vehicle design application [1] and for sliding bearing design [2].

6   Problems with the Heuristic Search Based Design

An elevator has three main subsystems: i) the driving machinery (e.g. motor, gears, cables, counterweight), ii) the building-related components (e.g. location of the machinery, sheaves, safety, buffers, platform), and iii) the support equipment (e.g. car lantern, phone, door type). Design requirements typically affect more than one subsystem. For instance, the initial parameters related to the machinery design is the speed and capacity [2] of the elevator; while those affecting the building-related design include the shaft dimensions and the number of floors, etc.

The interactions between the subsystems are expressed by constraints and common parameters. The machinery parameters, which are constrained by physical laws, have less degrees of freedom in selecting consistent values than the other subsystems which are typically restricted only by not-so-strict technological rules. Consequently much more effort is needed to find a consistent solution for the machinery subsystem than for the other components of the elevator design. Without a good search strategy many reasonable design requirements cannot be satisfied. We tested the P&R algorithm in accordance with the search strategy described in section 5 on input specifications generated by combining all possible values of speed and capacity. The values of the remaining 24 required parameters were always the same. The competence of the P&R algorithm is shown in table 1. These results are not consistent with our intuition that if a solution (i.e. the machinery subsystem) can be designed for a certain speed and capacity, then some solution will also be found for the same speed and lower capacity, and for the same capacity and lower speed. Based on a simple physical common sense, we expect solutions restricted by the hyperbola $mv = Const$, where m is the elevator mass (i.e. capacity), v is the elevator speed, and $Const$ is a constant proportional to the maximum torque generated by the biggest motor. The hyperbola expresses that the momentum $mv = Const$ of the moving components must not exceed the maximum torque which can be generated by the biggest available motor. Hence the table 1 contradicts our physical common

---

[2] Capacity is the maximum total car weight the system must be able to support, speed is the desired travelling car speed of the elevator.

Speed [ft/min]

Capacity [pound]	200	250	300	350	400
2000	Success	Success	Fail	Success	Success
2500	Fail	Fail	Success	Success	Success
3000	Fail	Success	Success	Success	Success
3500	Success	Fail	Fail	Fail	Fail
4000	Fail	Fail	Fail	Fail	Fail

Table 1. Results of Propose & Revise

sense and this discrepancy can only be attributed to a poor search algorithm and/or to the lack of appropriate search control knowledge.

To improve the competence of our problem solver we tried a more powerful (and computationally expensive) best-first search algorithm, guided by cost-based heuristics. The results are shown in table 2. The results shown in table 2 are intuitively acceptable. The problem is that the search algorithm for those combinations which failed in table 1 and succeeded in table 2 is very slow. For example the combination [speed = 200 ft/min, capacity = 4000 pounds] takes 104 min on our 64 Mb Sparc 5 running Harlequin Common Lisp. For the failed combinations in table 2 the program runs out of memory and it is not clear whether the solution does not exist or whether our computational means are not powerful enough. In any case, the results show that we do not have enough heuristic knowledge to prune sufficiently the design space. The described exper-

Speed [ft/min]

Capacity [pound]	200	250	300	350	400
2000	Success	Success	Success	Success	Success
2500	Success	Success	Success	Success	Success
3000	Success	Success	Success	Success	Success
3500	Success	Success	Success	Fail	Fail
4000	Success	Fail	Fail	Fail	Fail

Table 2. Results of best-first search

iments suggest that the Propose & Revise approach used to design the elevator has limitations and does not adequately capture the design process followed by expert elevator designer. Designers possess a large amount of knowledge which they are unable to communicate. In difficult cases, such as those failed in table 1 the design process probably combines reasoning from first principles, problem decomposition, deep search in a restricted subproblem, and synthesising and merging partial solutions. Such a complex design process would require a large amount of heuristic knowledge because the difficult cases tend to be unique and therefore not easily represented by general design heuristics. Instead of trying to acquire the heuristic knowledge needed for the aforementioned design steps we can employ a case-based approach. We assume that the difficult cases have been resolved and we can access them in a case library. Since we could not get the solution from an expert these cases were resolved by means of an expensive search algorithm.

7 Case-Based Design

The modification required to transform the CMR version of Propose & Revise into a case- based Retrieve & Adapt scheme are relatively straightforward. Propose & Revise consists of three subtasks: Propose, Evaluate and Revise and by different operationalisation we get EMR and CMR. Analogously, we can derive various CBR algorithms by different operationalisation of the Retrieve, Evaluate and Adapt subtasks shown in figure 2.

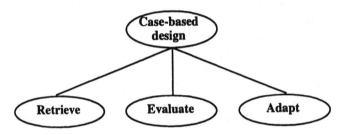

Fig. 2. Subtasks of case-based design

In our experimental case-based design framework each case is represented by a valid design model, i.e. a complete elevator design, with associated cost. The access keys to the case library are lists of 26 initial parameters. The case must be adapted if it does not satisfy the task goal introduced in section 2, i.e. if the design model does not satisfy all design requirements or if it violates some constraints. The goal of the adaptation process is to fix violated constraints and, in addition, to optimise the cost criterion. Since our case library contains only complete and successful solutions, if the retrieved case satisfies all requirements specified by the new problem it also does not violate any constraint. In such a case no adaptation takes place.

Typically the requirements of the new problem are different from those in the case library, and therefore the design model of the retrieved case must be evaluated and modified to satisfy new requirements. The modification results in new constraint violations which are then fixed in the adaptation task.

The cost of the case-based design process includes both the cost of the case and the adaptation cost. Cheap adaptation of an expensive case may produce worse results than expensive adaptation of a cheap case.

We have devised and implemented four case-based design algorithms. They are described in terms of their constituent tasks and the control flow.

7.1 Algorithm 1: A simple match of design requirements

Algorithm 1 operationalizes the task shown in figure 2 as follows:

Retrieve 1: The case which has the maximum number of design requirements identical with the new problem is retrieved. All requirements are taken with the same weight.

Evaluate 1: The design model of the case is modified as follows: The initial parameters of the new problem supersede those of the retrieved case. If some values are different all parameters affected by the changes are recalculated and all relevant constraints are evaluated.

Adapt 1: The adaptation is basically the same as the Revise task of P&R. A violated constraint is selected and the associated fix combinations are applied in accordance with the increasing cost. If a new constraint is violated the fix combination is rejected. This adaptation strategy is based on concepts described in Section 5.

The control flow is defined by the sequence Retrieve, Evaluate, Adapt. Algorithm 1 works well if the case and the new problem differ only in a set of easy-to-fix parameters. If the different initial parameters are the speed or the capacity (see Table 1), the adaptation often fails because of the primitive adaptation algorithm.

7.2 Algorithm 2: A subsystem sensitive match

Algorithm 2 differs from algorithm 1 only in the retrieval phase. We have pointed out that the design of the machinery subsystem is much more complicated than the design of other elevator subsystems. The strategy applied in algorithm 2 selects the cases where the difficult part of design has already been resolved and thus does not need any change. The design requirements are divided into groups corresponding to different subsystems of the designed artefact. The groups are ordered in accordance with the difficulty they represent for the design process.

Retrieve 2: Assign the initial parameters into groups corresponding to different subsystems. Order the groups according to decreasing design difficulty. Select the cases with the best match for the most difficult group. If more than one case is selected, apply the same selection procedure to the selected cases using the next difficulty group, and so on. If more than one case is selected after the last difficulty group was used, select at random.

In the elevator example the best results are achieved if the initial parameters are divided into two groups. The parameters from the first group are called essential. The retrieval algorithm requires that all essential parameters of the selected case match exactly the corresponding parameters of the new problem.

Otherwise the case is not retrieved. The remaining initial parameters are called secondary. The maximum number of identical secondary requirements defines the best match. The essential parameters for the elevator problem are speed and capacity. Algorithm 2 resolved successfully all tested cases providing that a case with corresponding speed and capacity exists. The next two algorithms assume the complete match of the essential parameters. They differ only in the way of exploiting the secondary parameters.

7.3 Algorithm 3: Estimating design costs

Each case in the case library has a cost associated, Q_c. The design cost of the case-based design process, Q, is the sum of the cost of the case before adaptation, Q_c, plus the adaptation cost, Q_a. The adaptation cost Q_a is the sum of the costs of all fixes applied in the process of adaptation. Since the design task has been defined as an optimisation problem the solution must minimise the design cost, i.e. $Q^* = \min\{Q\}$. The case cost Q_c is known in advance for each case. The adaptation cost can be evaluated only during the adaptation process. However, after the evaluation phase and before the start of the adaptation phase, it is possible to estimate the lower and upper bounds of the adaptation cost.

Assume that after completing the Evaluate task we get a set of constraint violations, say CV. In order to remove a constraint violation we apply a fix (or a fix combination). The lower bound Q'_a estimate of the adaptation cost Q_a is based on the best-case scenario for satisfying constraints from CV. Q'_a is the sum of the costs of the fixes selected under the assumption that (1) for each violated constraint, the cheapest fix combination is selected and (2) if a fix can remove multiple constraint violations it will do so. Similarly, the upper bound Q''_a estimate is based on the worst-case scenario. Each constraint violation will have to be removed independently of the others by the most expensive fix combination. In the first step — filtering — the retrieval algorithm eliminates case C_i if a case C_j exists such that the best-case outcome of C_i is worse that the worst-case outcome of C_j, i.e. $Q_c(C_i) + Q'_a(C_i) > Q_c(C_j) + Q''_a(C_j)$. The second step of Algorithm 3 has two alternatives: a retrieval based on $Q_c + Q'_a$ or a retrieval based on $Q_c + Q''_a$. The former one is an optimistic strategy, the latter one is pessimistic. The strategy selection can be grounded on the analysis of the design domain. If the design subtasks have enough degrees of freedom and if they are only loosely coupled, then the optimistic strategy gives good results. Otherwise it is better to be pessimistic. Algorithm 3 consists of the following new subtasks.

Retrieve 3: Retrieve all cases providing a complete match of all essential initial parameters. This subtask is not very difficult because the essential initial parameters can be used as primary indexes to the case library.

Evaluate 3: For each retrieved case calculate Q_c, Q'_a and Q''_a. Calculate $Min = \min\{Q_c + Q''_a\}$ over all retrieved cases. Delete all cases for which $Q_c + Q'_a > Min$. Select retrieve strategy (optimistic or pessimistic) based on the properties of the domain. Order cases in accordance with the selected strategy and take the first case.

7.4 Algorithm 4: Optimising adaptation costs

Algorithm 4 puts even more emphasis on the optimisation character of design. The idea is to control adaptation by continuously updating the estimated cost thus optimising over a number of cases. The result is an A* type of algorithm. The adaptation cost Q_a is divided into two components, Q_g and Q_h, $Q_a = Q_g + Q_h$. Q_g is the cost of the adaptation steps we have carried out so far, Q_h is the cost of the adaptation steps yet to be made. Unless the missing steps are made, Q_h is unknown. However, we can get a lower estimate, Q'_h, and an upper estimate, Q''_h. Q'_h gives an *admissible* search algorithm which always leads to the optimal solution. Q''_h sometimes converges faster but the optimality is not guaranteed. The basic steps are summarised below.

Retrieve 4: The same as Retrieve 3. Denote the set of retrieved cases as $\mathcal{R}$.

Evaluate 4: (Admissible search). Calculate $Q_c + Q'_a$, where $Q'_a = Q_g + Q'_h$ for all cases in $\mathcal{R}$. Initially, $Q_g = 0$ and $Q'_a = Q'_h$. Order cases in terms of the increasing value of $Q_c + Q'_a$ and select the first case. If the case does not violate any constraints report success.

Adapt 4: Select a violated constraint to fix and apply the cheapest associated fix combination. Apply fix combination, calculate Q_g, update $Q_c = Q_g + Q'_h$, and return the result to $\mathcal{R}$.

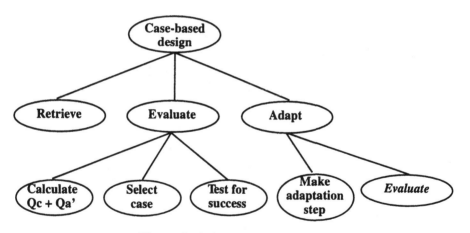

Fig. 3. Optimising case-based design

Algorithm 4 is shown in figure 3, the task Evaluate written by italics is a recursive call. Evaluate 4 can be completed by the filtering technique described in Evaluate 3.

8 Conclusions

Designers use cases. Design is a good application domain for CBR techniques. A number of case-based systems with applications to design are reviewed in [8].

Some of these systems employ similar ideas and techniques with the approach described in this paper. For example, in AAAO, EADOCS, Composer and ID-IOM the design problem is represented as constraint satisfaction, EADOCS and IDIOM take into account the optimisation aspects of the problem. One system (DÉJÀVU, see also [7]) makes use of adaptation knowledge to assist in retrieving the most "adaptable" case. Algorithms 3 and 4 are based on a similar idea but their aim is retrieving not only the most adaptable but also the cheapest solutions.

Detailed discussion of design decomposition into 'nearly independent subproblems' or 'loosely coupled subproblems' is presented in [3]. Several systems in [8] (e.g. Composer, DÉJÀVU, IDIOM) make use of this technique: they divide the problem into subproblems, resolve these subproblems by case-based methods and finally synthesise the solution. The decomposition technique used in this paper is simpler. We identify only one, the most difficult design subproblem. Then the retrieval algorithm searches for a case whose difficult-to-design part can be reused, assuming that the rest will be sorted out in the process of adaptation. Such a technique has its limitations but for simple domains works. In our system, the problem decomposition is derived from the part/component hierarchy and therefore it is a part of domain knowledge. The 'essential' parameters introduced in algorithm 2 are those associated with the difficult-to-design part (the machinery subsystem in the elevator domain). Both the difficult subproblem and the essential parameters are easily identified by the expert.

All four algorithms have been implemented and tested on the elevator design problem. The algorithms derive the adaptation knowledge from the heuristics originally intended for P&R as described in [10]. The performance of algorithm 1 and 2 are discussed in sections 7.1 and 7.2 respectively. These algorithms use the cost of fixes only to control the adaptation (see section 5 paragraph 3). Algorithms 3 and 4 introduce the concept of design cost Q, which is used both for retrieving cases and for optimising solutions. The cost of a solution is the sum of two terms: (i) the cost of the retrieved case, and (ii) the adaptation cost. Cost-based algorithms make it possible to extend the original idea of a cases being only valid design models and exploit also partial and inconsistent cases. The cost of achieving completeness and consistency is incorporated into the second term, i.e. the adaptation cost. Our system can use extended case libraries.

Experiments with the filtering described in section 7.3 indicate that the filtering efficiency depends on the properties of the application domain. In the elevator domain the pruning effect is not significant because when applying the filter almost always an expensive, 'last resort' fix exists (cost = 9 or 10, see section 4) whose cost is significantly higher than the costs of the retrieved case.

Algorithm 4 is a kind of A* and therefore selects always the most promising candidate for the next adaptation step. Its performance depends on the shape of the cost function and on the number of cases applicable to the current design requirements. For the elevator design problem and less than 10 relevant cases the algorithm converges well but for large case libraries with many applicable cases the computation may become expensive.

Two underlying principles employed by the presented algorithms can be summarised as follows:

1. Complex solutions can be better exploited by a case-based approach if they can be broken down into meaningful subsystems.
2. Design is an optimisation problem and the cost function can be used to control all three major subtasks shown in figure 2.

The described algorithms transfer the computational burden from adaptation to early stages, i.e. retrieval and evaluation. For parametric design this approach is justified. The computationally expensive task is adaptation, because it includes various design choices, i.e. search in a potentially large space. Simplifying adaptation at the cost of more complex retrieval may significantly accelerate the whole design process. Parametric design is probably the simplest design task. The structure of the artefact is reduced to a set of parameters, design requirements can be expressed as an initial assignment of values to certain parameters, and constraints are relations over parameter values. Still many complex problems can be expressed as parametric design tasks. The complexity of the designed artefact plays an important role in selecting an appropriate problem solving method. For example, our experiments with the sliding bearing design [2] indicate that for simple domains the case-based approach is not needed. The sliding bearing domain consists of 44 parameters, 5 constraints and 5 fixes. The bearing can be designed only by applying design defaults and heuristic corrections.

References

1. Banecek J., Drvota J.: Problem Analysis and Decomposition of Initial Vehicle Design, TR-Encode-DccS-1-95 (Project Encode report), DccS Engineering, Prague, (1995)
2. Horak J., Valasek M. and Bauma V.: Knowledge Level Analysis of Bearings Design. TR-Encode-CVUT-1-95 (Project Encode report). Czech Technical University, Faculty of Mechanical Engineering. Prague. (1995).
3. Maher M.L.: Process Models for Design Synthesis. AI Magazine, Vol 11, No. 4. pp. 49-58. (1990)
4. Maher M.L., Balachandran M.B. and Zhang D.M.: Case-based reasoning in design. Lawrence Erlbaum Associates, Publishers. Hawah, New Jersey.(1995).
5. Marcus, S., and McDermott, J.: SALT: A Knowledge Acquisition Language for Propose- and-Revise Systems. Journal of Artificial Intelligence, 39(1), 1-37. (1989).
6. Motta E., Stutt A., Zdrahal Z., O'Hara K., Shadbolt N.: Solving VT in VITAL: a study in model construction and knowledge reuse. International Journal of Human- Computer Studies 44. pp. 333-371, (1996).
7. Smyth B., Keane M.T.: Adaptation-Guided Retrieval. 2nd UK CBR workshop (I.D.Watson ed.), Salford. pp. 2-15, (1996).
8. Voss A., Oxman R.: A Study of Case Adaptation Systems. In Artificial Intelligence in Design '96 (J.S.Gero and F. Sudweeks eds.). Kluwer Academic Publishers. pp. 172-189. (1996)

9. Wielinga B.J., Akkermans J.M. and Schreiber A.Th.: A Formal Analysis of Parametric Design Problem Solving. In: Proceedings of the 9th Banff Knowledge Acquisition for KBS Workshop (B.R.Gaines and M.Musen eds.), pp. 37-1–37-15, (1995)
10. Yost G.R., Rothenfluh T.R.: Configuring elevator systems. International Journal of Human-Computer Studies **44**, pp. 521-568, (1996)
11. Zdrahal Z., Motta E.: Optimizing the Revise Task in Propose & Revise Problem Solving. In: Expert Systems 94, British Computer Society Specialist Group on Expert Systems (M.A.Bramer and A.L.Macintosh eds), Cambridge, UK, pp. 245-260, (1994)
12. Zdrahal Z., Motta E.: An In-Depth Analysis of Propose & Revise Problem Solving Methods. In: Proceedings of the 9th Banff Knowledge Acquisition for KBS Workshop (B.R.Gaines and M.Musen eds.), pp. 38-1–38-20, (1995)

Corporate Knowledge Management for the Millennium

James M. Barr[1] and Richard V. Magaldi[2]

This paper discusses how case-based reasoning (CBR) technology could satisfy a new commercial need that has arisen over the past few years: corporate knowledge management. CBR is ideally placed to play a key role in the technological infrastructure required to support this new business paradigm. In what follows we will examine the organisational phenomenon itself, and set out the challenges and opportunities the CBR community faces to create practical systems.

1. The Knowledge-based Enterprise

As we move into the new millennium, traditional approaches to business, in terms of physical assets, and treating workers as standardised units of production, are becoming less appropriate. The static economics of equilibrium has been replaced by a competitive environment characterised by instability, rapid technological advances and uncertainty. With heightened international competition, companies are increasingly having to compete on quality, rapid product life-cycles, customer service, and innovation. Today, a company's value is rooted in its know-how: its technical, professional, operational, marketing or customer service skills.

A measure of the increasing importance of intellectual capital is Tobin's Q, the ratio of a company's stock market value to the replacement value of its physical assets. The more important knowledge is to the company, the greater the ratio. In the United States the ratio is 200-500% and steadily rising.

In response to the new pressures:
a) companies are focusing on core competencies. To be world-class means directing energies at specific areas of skill rather than dissipating them on a range of tasks where performance is mediocre. This requires greater levels of skill and knowledge within the organisation.

---

[1] Samurai Solutions Ltd, 5A Altwood Road, Maidenhead, SL6 4PB, U.K.
   mbarr @ alkhemy.demon.co.uk

[2] British Airways, Information Management, Profit Development,
   AI Consultancy, TBE (E108), PO Box 10, Heathrow Airport,
   Hounslow, Middlesex, TW6 2JA, U.K.
   richard.v.magaldi @ british-airways.com

b) companies are having to use people more effectively. This means de-layering unnecessary levels of management control, more team and project-based work and distributing decision-making power more widely. Consequently the management of knowledge becomes more critical, in terms of acquisition, transfer, and training.

c) organisations are becoming more outward-looking. There are more alliances, joint ventures, and virtual companies. This brings the need to share and co-ordinate knowledge across company boundaries.

A number of authors have sensed this paradigm shift, and coined a variety of terms to describe it:
- the knowledge society (Drucker, 1993)
- the knowledge-creating organisation (Nonaka, 1995)
- the intelligent organisation (Quinn, 1992)
- the learning organisation (Senge, 1990)
- the expert company (Feigenbaum et, al., 1988)
- corporate knowledge (Prahalad & Hamel, 1994)
- organisational memory (Morrison, 1993)
- enterprise knowledge management (Petrie, 1991)
- intellectual capital asset management (e.g. as in a supplement to the financial services company Skandia's annual report).

The new paradigm is creating a demand for a fundamentally new knowledge management technology infrastructure not currently met by conventional data-focused systems. Before discussing the role technology can play to support these new ways of working, we need to clarify some of the concepts around corporate knowledge.

2. What is Corporate Knowledge?

There is no commonly accepted definition of corporate knowledge. A very basic distinction is between data, information and knowledge. Data are basic, raw facts; information places data in a context, while knowledge is a structured network of contexts in which information has meaning. It is a rich concept and can be viewed from many perspectives. One is to break the concept into different categories. Another is to view the various representations of knowledge. A third is to distinguish corporate from individual knowledge.

Categories of Knowledge

At the level of an individual, we suggest there are three layers of knowledge:
- sensori-motor - i.e. finding one's way around the world, lifting, carrying, digging, placing etc. These correspond to manual or so-called unskilled labour.

- common sense - i.e. everyday knowledge of the properties of the world, including people's behaviour and beliefs, plus communication and social skills. This layer of knowledge is particularly important in the service sector.
- specialised domains of expertise, e.g. architectural design, medical diagnosis, providing legal advice etc.

Within each of these layers there are various levels of performance from novice to expert. Both individuals and organisations possess different combinations of such skills.

The artificial intelligence community distinguishes between the different types of specialised expert knowledge required for different activities. Althoff et.al. (1995) suggest a classification scheme beginning with two high-level categories: classification and synthesis tasks. For example diagnosis and process control fall into the former category, and design and configuration into the latter.

The CBR community adds a temporal dimension. Knowledge changes over time, as new experiences are amassed, and less relevant ones forgotten. It distinguishes between abstract, declarative models, and a history of concrete events.

Nonaka & Takeuchi (1995) stress the distinction between the tacit and the explicit. Much of an organisation's knowledge is not represented in a structured form that can be conveyed to others. It is enacted, situated, exists by being put into practice. While Western thought attempts to conceptualise the world from an objective point of view, a Zen approach to knowledge is to relate oneself in a concrete, tactile, interpersonal way. This blurs the distinction between an individual and a community, and encourages multiple perspectives. Nonaka & Takeuchi ascribe recent Japanese success in innovation to a cycle of converting:

- the tacit to the tacit, through socialisation.
- the tacit to the explicit, through deductive, inductive and analogical reasoning.
- the explicit to the tacit, through learning by doing, compiling direct experience.
- the explicit to the explicit, through reconfiguring existing knowledge and formal education.

This approach requires a new paradigm of knowledge creation and sharing. The knowledge used by a living organisation is a far richer entity than that captured by predicate logic or frame systems.

Knowledge Representations

Formal knowledge is represented as written artefacts such as specifications, manuals, blueprints, recipes, etc.

An equally valuable but neglected source are the informal, transitory documents that are part of the creative process, but discarded once a final artefact is produced, e.g. e-mail, minutes, reports, white-papers, notebooks etc.

Knowledge is also 'embodied' in tools, pieces of equipment, plant, incoming materials, layout, and even external, outsourced agencies.

Most knowledge is disembodied 'in people's heads'. Some of it is in a more-or-less structured form that can be explained to other people. Much of it is not.

Corporate Knowledge

In one sense, corporate knowledge is the sum total of knowledge within an organisation. Or it could be that which is not specific to an individual, nor even a department, but shared across an organisation. It is a common set of facts, beliefs and experience. It could also be viewed as meta-knowledge of the organisation itself - its human and physical resources, internal processes, procedures, constraints etc.

Corporate knowledge is greater than the sum of the knowledge of the constituent parts of an organisation in the same way that a football team comprises more than just the skills of the individual players. It is a combination of individual skills with those of others through communication, collaboration and co-ordination.

In a sense, it is a specification of an organisation's competencies. Nelson & Winter (1982) describe the functioning of an organisation as a number of routines, which constitute the day-to-day running of the firm. Corporate knowledge can be viewed as the specification of those routines: how do you make a car? how do you design a bridge? how do you treat an illness? It is a specification in the sense that if the organisation vanished, yet the knowledge remained in some form, if the physical and human resources were replaced, and the knowledge re-introduced, the organisation would function as before. In mass production the routines are highly similar over time. In professional services, the routines are more variable, customised to individual problems. Prahalad & Hamel (1994) describe core competences as those specific routines that confer a unique competitive advantage for the firm.

Knowledge structures are very complex, entailing models of processes within the firm and the outside world. They are also widely dispersed throughout the organisation in a range of representations. The essential point is that a large proportion of what constitutes routines is the interaction between people, and the interpretation of behaviour.

3. The Benefits of Knowledge Management

Knowledge management concerns a range of activities:
- acquisition   - storage   - retrieval mechanisms

- distribution	- embedding in applications	- maintenance
- quality assurance	- training	

It should benefit the enterprise in a number of ways:

- If knowledge adds value to a company, creating and sharing it, adds even more value.

- It can improve the function of the organisation at the level of routines. Applying knowledge where it was not used or misapplied before should improve performance. Quicker, or more informed decisions enable better products to be designed and manufactured, and customers better served.

- It should be applied to improve the quality of training, and to improve the speed with which people reach full productivity when they change roles. This should support more flexible, team-based working.

- Actively managing knowledge should stimulate learning. It should engender a sense of shared understanding and self awareness within the organisation. People can learn from each other's mistakes, avoid re-inventing the wheel, understand why things are done as they are, and stimulate new ideas.

- Knowledge of the external environment can help an organisation track best practice. It can expand on the limited sample of its own experience. It can also be used to spot opportunities and threats, provided it can move quickly to take advantage of them.

- Greater knowledge spawns innovation. More creative solutions can lead to new products and services and improved internal processes.

- Knowledge, when traded can become a revenue stream in its own right. There is already a substantial market for structured data e.g. Reuters, MAID, J.D. Power surveys etc. Structured knowledge should be even more valuable.

4.The Role of Case-based Reasoning

Despite the clear advantages of the new paradigm, existing information systems are not designed to support the knowledge-based company. They are largely concerned with the logistics of data. Coupled with networks it should be possible to leverage knowledge across time and space - enabling companies to learn from the past and distribute expertise across the organisation. On the face of it, case-based reasoning is in an ideal position to become a key part of any new infrastructure.

Opportunities

a) Because CBR is grounded in a model of human cognition based on concrete experience rather than dry abstractions it is natural and easy to grasp. It is therefore more likely to be adopted.
b) Case-retrieval technology is mature and readily integrated with conventional database systems. There are a number of commercially available products.
c) It is at its core, a learning technology.
d) It is applicable to various aspects of knowledge management: representation and storage, retrieval, knowledge-enhanced applications, computer-based training etc.
e) It has wide applicability across all stages of the value chain: design; new product development; various aspects of marketing and sales (e.g. pricing, estimating, bidding); various aspects of operations (e.g. planning, trouble-shooting); customer service; technical support; human resources etc.
f) A further prospect is industry-wide case-bases. Inference Corporation already has a knowledge publishing division specialising in technical domains. The possibilities are endless: para-legal, para-medical, risk assessment, estimating etc.

Two examples of substantial corporate knowledge systems incorporating CBR are already cited in the literature: NEC's SQUAD and Apple's NNable. Both focus on technical, problem-solving knowledge. However, as suggested above, the horizons of corporate knowledge management are far greater.

The Challenges

CBR faces a number of challenges if it is to play a key role in the new knowledge architecture. Some are common to all attempts to use technology to facilitate knowledge management, others are specific to CBR.

General challenges:

a) *Ensure knowledge management is put onto the agenda of senior management.*
Despite the steady flow of books and articles, there is a lack of vision in the potential user community about what the new concepts mean in practice. The importance of knowledge management has not yet gained widespread acceptance. There is a lack of awareness of the benefits that can be achieved. Some form of marketing campaign targeted at senior levels is required to secure investment.

b) *Knowledge management should be a transparent part of working life.*
The cost of managing knowledge may prove prohibitive. Resources devoted to analytical, reflective tasks such as knowledge entry and maintenance will be perceived as an unnecessary overhead in an action-oriented organisation unless very significant benefits are realised. Many engineering companies have in the past appointed project historians or librarians to explicitly retain experience and lessons learned. Typically the person is eventually re-deployed to 'more productive' work

when deadlines tighten, or marginalised as an 'outsider' by project members, or the results of the effort are left to gather dust on a shelf.

Knowledge management has to become a natural part of the normal working process (Conklin, 1996). For example e-mail is a natural process, in which some knowledge is recorded, but it is of little use as a knowledge repository. It is unstructured, stripped of context and therefore difficult to re-use. Knowledge management will require new tools, organisational structures, roles, incentives, ideologies and working methods.

c) *Technology must support the social, collaborative nature of knowledge work.*

Knowledge work is essentially social. Observing customer support teams one is struck by the extent to which informal groups collaborate on an ad hoc basis to solve problems, and share experience. A view of knowledge work as rarefied, abstract and solitary is dangerously restricting. "When you're competing on knowledge, the name of the game is improvisation not standardisation" (Brown & Gray, 1995)

National Semiconductors have set up a Communities of Practice programme as a means of managing corporate knowledge. It is not centred on technology. Each community is an informal grouping of experts. Their corporate knowledge is embedded in a group of people who participate and put their knowledge into practice. The support technology has been designed around their needs.

People generally prefer to consult colleagues rather than a system even when the desired information is available in documents or on-line. It is often quicker, usually more trustworthy, and more interactive. Colleagues can go more deeply into a problem, verify understanding, discuss related issues and brainstorm different solutions. The conversation itself also serves an important social function.

The technology to support knowledge workers should be designed to support collaborative work, rather than attempting to completely automate tasks or provide tools for solitary users.

CBR Challenges

d) *Emphasise that there is more to CBR than helpdesks.*
Commercially, CBR is most commonly viewed as a helpdesk technology. Efforts are needed to raise people's awareness of its much broader applicability.

e) *CBR technology should be integrated with groupware, the intranet, and other approaches to knowledge management such as the knowledge sharing initiative.*

There are already a number of competing technologies, claiming to become the corporate knowledge management infrastructures of the future, that do not take CBR into account.

Groupware. Products such as Collabra's Share, and particularly Lotus Notes (with the full backing of IBM) are laying claim to this territory. Lotus operate a successful Knowledge Management consulting practice and Notes has been used to build systems for several companies including influential management consultancies. Notes is well established in the market-place, robust, well integrated with commercial networks, databases and the internet. As well as knowledge storage and distribution it supports collaborative working. Retrieval can be via structured 'databases' or intelligent text retrieval. Its scripting language also supports the construction of customised applications.

The Intranet. An alternative infrastructure is based on the internet toolbox of web browsers, TCP/IP, HTML, Java etc. National Semiconductor have built a system using Netscape Navigator to support their Communities of Practice approach to acquiring and disseminating corporate knowledge. The intranet can support the storage and distribution of knowledge, offers increasingly intelligent document retrieval engines and the construction of tailored applications.

Other proprietary systems. There are also several in-house corporate knowledge systems based on proprietary technology, e.g. the Eureka project used by Rank Xerox in France. This is a so-called knowledge refinery for technical field staff. It comprises a database of hypertext linked documents, a search engine and expert validation. There is also the NASA Lessons Learned program, and various document-management based approaches.

At the level of knowledge representation there are a number of competitors to CBR.
i) Raw text is by far the most common representation. The biggest advantage is it is natural to enter and store knowledge in this form. It is searchable using intelligent text retrieval. But it is difficult to incorporate into applications that have to interpret data or automate reasoning.
ii) The ARPA knowledge-sharing initiative is a large-scale project to create standards for knowledge sharing and re-use between both applications and organisations. The representations are based on frames, expert-system reasoning mechanisms and ontologies.
iii) CycCorp suggest that their common-sense reasoning system could support corporate knowledge management.
iv) Corporate Memory Systems of Austin Texas, currently sells QuestMap, a display system for corporate knowledge. It focuses on capturing, storing and supporting the use of informal knowledge. It combines hypertext and groupware with a rhetorical problem solving method called IBIS (issue-based information systems).

f) *Emphasise the successes of case retrieval.*
The most accessible and intuitive aspect of CBR is case storage and retrieval. Adaptation is more complex, there is more to go wrong. On the basis of experience with conventional expert systems, adaptation systems are likely to prove more difficult to win users' trust and be deployed.

g) *Establish a standard representation for case-bases.*

h) *Develop richer cases.*
The notion of informal knowledge raises the question of whether cases are a sufficiently rich representation. Cases represent input conditions and an outcome. Their utility could be enhanced by supplementing them with descriptions of the informal rationale by which the final decision was made. Traces may remain in e-mail, memos and minutes but most is dispersed in the memories of the participants. This is often the most important knowledge - how was a solution produced? It comprises items such as: assumptions, questions, decisions, guesses, stories, beliefs, positions.

i) *Use CBR to support double-loop learning.*
Although CBR systems are an improvement over traditional decision support approaches in that they 'learn' with experience, the form of learning is what Argyris & Schon (1978) call single loop learning, or Senge (1990) calls adaptive learning. This concerns correcting errors or refining experience within an existing frame-work. Argyris & Schon, and Senge describe another form of learning which they claim is equally valuable: double loop or generative learning. It involves questioning assumptions, policies etc. - "breaking out of the box" thinking. It would be useful if CBR could support that too.

5. Conclusion

This paper proposes a change in direction for the CBR community. Much of the existing discussion about the way forward concerns integration with specialised AI problem solving methods and models of cognition, rather than groupware and intranet technologies.

There is a window of opportunity for CBR to seize a key role in building an information infrastructure to support the knowledge-based enterprise. The primary challenge for the CBR community is to decide whether this is a goal worth attaining, or whether it should restrict itself to building specialised, domain-specific applications. We believe the benefits of supporting corporate knowledge management would be substantial, and the goal should be pursued.

References

Althoff, K., Auriol, E., Barletta, R. & Manago, M. *A Review of Industrial Case-Based Reasoning Tools.* AI Intelligence, Oxford, 1995.

Argyris, C. & Schon, D.A. *Organizational Learning* Addison-Wesley, Reading, MA, 1978.

Brown, J.S. & Gray, E.S. "The People are the Company" *Fast Magazine,* 1996

Conklin, E.J. "Designing organizational memory: preserving intellectual assets in a knowledge economy." Paper published on the Corporate Memory Systems web-site: http://www.cmsi.com/   ,1996.

Drucker, P.F. *Post Capitalist Society.* Butterworth Heinemann, Oxford, 1993

Feigenbaum, E., McCorduck, P. & Nii, H.P. *The Rise of the Expert Company* MacMillan, London, 1988.

Huber, G.P. "Organizational Learning: The contributing processes and the literatures". *Organization Science* Vol.2 pp.88-115, 1991.

Morrison, J. 1993. "Team Memory: Information management for business teams". *Proceedings of the Twenty-Sixth Hawaii International Conference on System Sciences* CA: IEEE Press, pp.122-131, 1993.

Nelson, R.R. & Winter, S.G. *An Evolutionary Theory of Economic Change* Harvard University Press, Cambridge, Mass, 1982.

Nevis, E. C., DiBella, A. J., and Gould, J. M. "Understanding Organizations as Learning Systems". *Sloan Management Review* Winter: pp.73-85, 1995.

Nonaka, I. & Takeuchi, H. *The Knowledge-creating Company* Oxford University Press, 1995.

Prahalad, C. K. & Hamel, G. *Competing for the Future* Harvard Business School Press, 1994.

Quinn, J.B. *Intelligent Enterprise* The Free Press, New York, 1992.

Senge, P.M. *The Fifth Discipline. The Art and Practice of the Learning Organization.* Doubleday, 1990.

Strassmann, P.A. *The Business Value of Computers - an Executives Guide,* The Information Economics Press, 1990.

Case-Based Reasoning Techniques Applied to Operation Experience Feedback in Nuclear Power Plants

Jean-Louis Bouchet*, Christiane Eichenbaum-Voline**

* Electricité de France, Direction des Etudes et Recherches
Département Surveillance, Diagnostic, Maintenance
6 quai Watier, 78400 Chatou, France
** Commissariat à l'Energie Atomique, Centre d'Etudes de Cadarache
Service des Systèmes d'Aide à l'Exploitation
13108 St Paul-lez-Durance, France

This paper concerns the work being conducted to develop an information retrieval tool for operation feedback in French nuclear power stations, using CBR techniques, to enhance the interactivity and efficiency of information search operations. Experience feedback problem factors are discussed and the specific nature of the data gathered is presented, with particular emphasis being placed on the importance of free-format text.

The principles of the REX plain-language consultation system, based on specialized semantic networks with various points of view, are also briefly described. Reference is made to the conclusions of a study concerning prospects for the application of the main CBR techniques to nearest neighbour event searches, and to the development options adopted for the REX-CASE demonstrator.

This prototype extends the text indexing on specific and structured suject terminology, normally used in REX, to include indexing on the n-uplets of terms significant in the similarity between texts. The various possible interrogation strategies are also presented.

1 Introduction

Since the initial setting up of the French electro-nuclear program (1978), equipment failures and damage during operation in PWR nuclear power plants have been systematically described and referenced. The resulting operation experience feedback is stored in relational databases.

These data constitute a fund of experience, with which any new failure should be compared, enabling full advantage to be taken of the previous analyses, the diagnostics or the actions taken. This reasoning, known as the « case-based » method, requires the exploration of the experience feedback databases, to identify those cases in archives which bear the greatest similarity to the new case.

Unfortunately, the entry quality of the coded data fields, and the considerable volume required for text format information, make any exploration operation extremely delicate. In such a context, the use of SQL queries is complex and is largely dependent upon the individual user's skills and knowledge.

498

These limitations, the strategic importance of operation experience feedback data, and EDF's desire to take full advantage of its expertise, led to the creation of a joint EDF/CEA research project.

Initially, an operation experience feedback consultation tool, REX-EVT, was developed, using an approach similar to that of Electronic Document Management systems. REX-EVT uses a knowledge base, organised in semantic networks. It allows indexing and « full text » search, and queries can also be formulated in plain language. The navigation mechanisms were then completed by nearest neighbour search algorithms, similar to Case Based Reasoning (CBR), and adapted to navigation in terminological knowledge bases.

The implementation of these various mechanisms and their interaction with the search system user are in the process of being evaluated in a prototype : REX-CASE, the general principles and structure of which are defined in this document.

2 Operation Experience Feedback Within Electricité de France

2.1 A Strategic Activity

Operation experience feedback has been systematically gathered since the launching of the French electro-nuclear program, and the resulting advantages have been proved in several strategic programs : evaluation of plant nuclear safety (EPS), and optimisation of preventive maintenance (OMP) or design (CIDEM). This documentary fund now contains more than 120 000 records (or *cards*), each concerning an operating event, and has a growth rate of 10 000 cards per year. Due to the relatively standardised design of the 54 French PWR plants, some of which have been in service for almost 20 years, these files provide the data support for both quantitative and qualitative analyses (/a/).

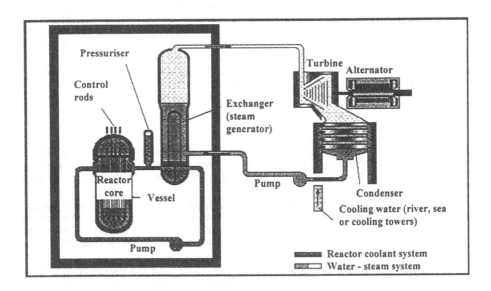

Fig. 1 : French Pressurised Water Reactor (PWR) Operating Principle

Today, the user population has extended beyond its original limits, and now includes many new users. Research staff and management experts have now been joined by operations personnel and outside contractors, with different centres of interest. Thus, the way in which the data are used varies from an in-depth analysis of a few cards, for example to identify a new type of significant operating event, to systematic processing, such as the updating of the reactor operation nuclear safety indicators.

2.2 Structure (Mixed) of Operation Experience Feedback

Operation experience feedback cards are divided into three sections : a set of coded data fields, a set of keywords (up to eight) and a text zone, limited to 400 characters, in which the writer can express himself informally. The appropriate text is mandatory in this zone, which is also known as the *Summary*. The cards describe all types of operating events, ranging from potentially serious equipment or functional failures to simple reactor status information.

Unit code : *****	Equipment ident : 008
Event key : ***********	Defective equipment : PV
Unit name : *********	Equipment affected : PV
Date of event : ******	Cause : ***
Nature of event : ***	Consequence : ***
Date of end of event : *****	Circumstances : ***
Primary system affected : ***	Time to repair : -
Primary system defective : **	AMN code : 050

Keywords : **** ******* **** *****

Summary : LA TRANCHE EST EN ARRET A FROID POUR INTERVENTION. LES VANNES *** 008-009-010 VP SONT OUVERTES ; ELLES SE SONT RENFERMEES INTEMPESTIVEMENT AU BOUT DE UNE A DEUX HEURES D'OUVERTURE. RUPTURE DE LA MEMBRANE DE CHAQUE SERVO-MOTEUR. REOUVERTURE EN MANUEL DE *** 008 VP A 1H06 - *** 009 VP A 2H06 - *** 010 VP A 2H15

Fig. 2 : Example of Operation Experience Feedback card

As shown in the example above, the summary is drafted in a very specific style, known as *telegraphic style*, which has the following three characteristics :

- a restricted and technical vocabulary, mostly concerning nuclear power plant equipments. Words are not always used in their strict meaning, and many terms do not exist in a normal dictionary,

- a syntax adapted to the authoring restrictions, which obliges the author to use short and abbreviated expressions.. Note the use of many codes and abbreviations,

- expression semantics very dependent upon the vocabulary used, due to the nature of the syntax adopted. The semantics field is restricted to nuclear-related principles.

A thorough knowledge of this vocabulary and its syntax rules is indispensable for the analysis of operation experience feedback (/b/).

3 The Importance of Free-Format Text for Operation Experience Feedback

3.1 A Bottleneck - Information Search

Information Search - why ?

The search for information is both an end in itself and a mandatory phase for the processes which use the extracted information. The most common of these processes are :

- the identification of events similar to a given one, to determine its recurrence frequency,

- the identification of events similar to a given one, to facilitate its description, to use the diagnostics and actions of the previous ones or to determine the event recurrence frequency,

- filing, classification and specific distribution of events data.

Remarks : these may be real events, handled in real time or in the operating analysis, or the events may be simulated, for example for nuclear safety studies.

User Requirement - Efficient and Simple Search Procedures

The quality of the operation experience feedback also depends upon the performance of the information search resources.

Among the characteristics of information search, two are frequently put forward by users : *efficiency and simplicity.*

- Efficiency is mainly a question of avoiding silence.

- Simplicity involves speed of operation, the ergonomics of the query entry functions, the reformulation of queries as a function of results obtained, navigation within the information and aid in assessing the relevance of the results.

An Interactive Process, Based on User Knowledge

The consultation of operation experience feedback cards is not simply a question of using menus or entry masks, or even of writing an SQL query.

Data quality (missing data) and the importance of the free-format text involve the user in a process which is frequently exploratory.

Information selection criteria are refined iteratively, as a function of the results obtained and the user's knowledge of power station operation and the operation experience feedback databases (data structure, terminology used in free text, « less than perfect » entries, etc.).

3.2 The Importance of Text

The performance objectives for the various types of utilisation mentioned in paras. 2.1 and 3.1 necessitate the availability of information, the quality of which meets the requirements of the operation experience feedback users.

The text zone was originally conceived to supplement the coded data. However, over the years, it has become an essential resource, while also representing an obstacle to the rapid and rational exploitation of the operation experience feedback databanks.

However, even when this process gives sufficiently accurate results, it is of a transitory nature. The validity and consistency of the results, and the methods used to obtain them, are highly dependent on the expert. The disadvantages are the difficulty of clearly defining silence and noise, poor results tracability and the length of time required for the analyses.

In many information systems like, for example, the one described in (/c/), these problems are solved by imposing strict coding of the data necessary for the various utilisations.

Furthermore, depending upon the nature of the event concerned, not all the coded fields are filled in. This means that the user must differentiate between phenomena identified, and fields left blank by omission or due to lack of knowledge.

However, these solutions are not really suitable for the context considered here. An operation experience feedback database is not simply an archives storage tool, it is also a means of « real time » communication between specialists, notably during the analysis and diagnosis of a new operating event. This further emphasises the value of free-format text, with the emerging of specific advantages, such as :

- it facilitates the authoring of information. This solution is more user friendly than data coding, which may also be impossible, excessively cumbersome, require specific training or knowledge, or expensive resources, etc.,

- it provides a check of the coded data,

- it enables the acquisition of non-quantifiable information (« non-specific » approach), or information supplementing the coded data (new information, not fully identified at the time of the corresponding data coding).

3.3   A Necessity - to Define the Contents of Free-Format Text

The definition of the required processing, and of the data on which the processing will be based, means that the raw facts must be transformed into data enabling the user's real requirements to be met (/d/).

This information and data definition is generally part of an information system design process, and leads to the definition of the various coded data elements which will constitute the system. In our context, free-format text must be analysed to extract its information content, in a « standard » form, usable by computer-based systems, and adapted to the subsequent processing.

Text definition using statistical or linguistic methods will not remove the multitude of authoring ambiguities. The main reason for this is that the texts constitute an information medium which is mainly aimed at the human expert, able to interpret allusions, contradictions or ellipses by using his own personal knowledge, or case-based reasoning processes.

The resolving of these ambiguities by a computer-based tool thus necessitates the construction of a set of references or knowledge, which will extend the tool's means of interpreting a given situation (/e/). Linguists speak of the knowledge of *semantics* (interpretation of meaning, synonyms, etc.) and of *pragmatics* (interpretation based on context).

The definition of texts does not necessitate the compilation of a statement of all the knowledge involved in nuclear powerplant operation. It is basically a question of defining « areas of confidence », a set of facts or concepts which are *indisputable* and *perfectly defined*, based on which technical facts can be integrated, using clearly defined relational procedures. These concepts will be defined with user terminology. The selected degree of detail for this referencing will depend on the methods and resources used and on performance objectives.

4 The REX Method and Tools

4.1 A Knowledge Management Method

REX is a method of knowledge management developed by the CEA (/f/). Its original objective was to save the experience acquired on the start-up of the Super-Phénix reactor. This resulted in the development of a method and tools which, today, enable any enterprise to obtain maximum advantage from, and to distribute, experience acquired during the design, setting up and operation of industrial processes (nuclear power stations, chemical complexes, etc.).

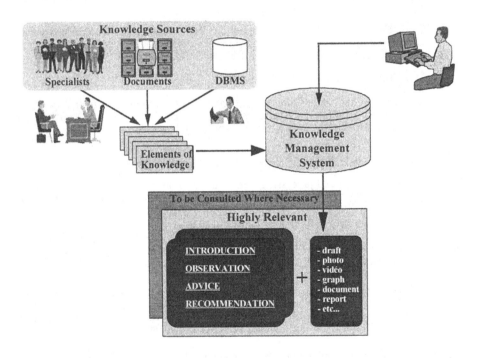

Fig. 3 : Basic Principles of a REX Application

The REX method has been defined (/g/) in the form of eleven procedures concerning the life cycle of a knowledge management application, and in particular concerning the specification, development, operation and maintenance of the application, the composition of *elements of knowledge*, their management using a structured knowledge base for the field concerned, and their access in response to a question formulated in *plain language*.

The method has already been applied in around fifteen industrial applications (CEA, EDF, Aérospatiale, DCN, RATP, Rhône-Poulenc, etc.).

It forms the nucleus of the European EUREKA MNEMOS project, concerning corporate memory. Within this context, development is continuing, notably for the integration of the CBR approach and concepts.

The Specific REX Feature - a Semantic Network for Every « Point of View »

The REX elements of knowledge indexing and search mechanism navigates within a set of *semantic networks*, each corresponding to a « *point of view* » on the information.

These networks can be considered to form a highly detailed thesaurus, which enables links between the terms of the question and the card indexing terms to be dynamically scanned. The links are weighted, and can be activated or de-activated, as a function of the points of view adopted by the user.

This thesaurus is known as the *REX model*, and is built up from the modelling of the knowledge in the technical area concerned, using the existing structured data or documentation, supplemented as appropriate by interviews with experts.

Each node is a keyword or a descriptive object of the knowledge domain. Each branch is a defined link. Each application contains several points of view, and these can be modified and developed as a function of requirements.

This representation creates the « areas of confidence », mentioned in para. 3.3. In the REX-EVT application presented below, the REX networks contain around 20 000 nodes, while the list of the various equipment used in a powerplant (miscellaneous) contains several tens of thousands of elements.

4.2   The REX-EVT Application

This application is dedicated to the consultation of operation experience feedback cards.

The objective was to enable queries to be initiated using both coded fields and free-format text, as simply as possible and with the best possible response quality.

50 000 operation experience feedback cards all constitute elements of knowledge.

Fig. 4, below, shows the basic principles of knowledge representation by networks, in REX, and the method of navigation within the networks.

The terminology used in free-format text is structured in a specific network known as the *lexical network*, which enables queries to be formulated in plain language, as the questions are processed in the same way as a text being indexed.

Each lexical network node is a *lexeme*[1] . From 10 to 20 lexemes are used to index each card.

Lexemes identified in the question are inserted into the lexical network, which enables the description network concepts to be accessed, followed by access to the cards, by navigation within the networks.

The principle adopted is the identification of cards indexed on lexemes which are at least as precise as those of the question. The weighting principle is also incorporated.

Cards identified in response to a question formulated in plain language are classified in order of relevance and are then presented to the user.

---

1 Lexeme - nominal group (or syntagm) belonging to the terminology specific to the subject.

A graphic interface allows the cards to be displayed/viewed, and the links followed to be identified, which enables sorting out of cards or navigation from card to card, through the knowledge base of the subject concerned.

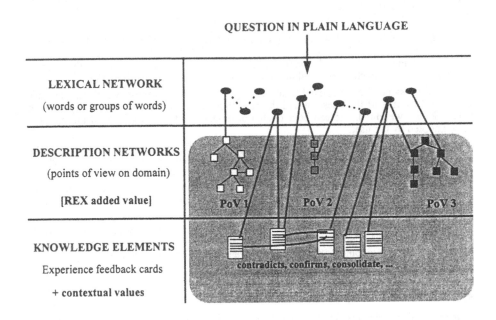

Fig. 4 : Functional Organisation of Knowledge within REX

4.3   Advantages and Limitations of Searching for Data Using REX-EVT

Advantages :

- The knowledge gathered and structured around the subject terminology, in this way, is explicit, adaptable to the user and robust.

- The « terminological meshing » used is fairly general but is also very flexible. It allows an excellent level of performance to be achieved, which is confirmed by the assessments conducted.

- Indexing and search mechanisms can be adapted to the requirements of the various user categories, while conserving overall consistency and avoiding the duplication of information.

- The plain language query interface is highly appreciated.

Limitations :

- At present, the automatic indexing mechanism is only based on lexeme identification. The absence of any syntactic or semantic analysis can generate errors in the positioning of the incident cards

  For example, « VALVE JAMMED » may be either the cause of an incident, or its consequence.

- The work involved in developing the knowledge base is considerable. An efficient search capability depends upon the knowledge base being as complete as possible, together with optimum consideration of possible variations in vocabulary, in both texts and questions.

  The validation and maintenance phases should not be underestimated, and these are also related to performance objectives.

5 CBR Concepts Applied with REX-EVT

5.1 Advantages of Case Based Reasoning

There is no guarantee of success in searching for information using free formulations ! This is because the REX-EVT user expresses his query based upon concepts, the importance of which seems obvious to him. However these concepts are not necessarily sufficiently relevant or numerous to detect similar cases in the base.

The main advantage of CBR in such a context is to *improve the user's interaction with the data source*. The information search based upon « for example » queries is broadened, and their complexity is masked by a *first* plain plain text formulation.

Another advantage of case-based reasoning, as mentioned in the introduction, is improved event analysis, either a posteriori or to determine the appropriate « immediate » action.

Due allowance should also be made for increased operator motivation when completing the cards, which improves both their « completeness » and quality, due to what could be termed « immediate cost-effectiveness ».

5.2 Considerations on Proximity Between Cards

In principle, incident cards are compared based on all available information, whether it be in the coded fields or in the free-format text. However, the informed user only wishes to compare events which are comparable, preselected on the basis of a few significant criteria. If this phase is not performed first, then proximity assessment using NNM (Nearest Neighbour Matching) algorithms has very little physical meaning. This is illustrated in the example given below.

Example:

- *Event considered as the entry case :*

  Free-format text : "AU COURS DE MONTEE DE CHARGE, OBSERVATION PAR L'OPERATEUR D'UNE VARIATION INTEM-PESTIVE DE LA POSITION DEMANDEE DES GRAPPES DE REGULATION DE PUISSANCE

(RGL 80 ID) DE 490A 530 PAS PREMIERES INVESTIGATIONS. LE PROBLEME VIENDRAIT DE LA REGU-LATION TURBINE GRE. CONSEQUENCE : PASSAGE SUR LIMITEUR VOLONTAIRE."

Keywords : DEFAUT, REGULATION, PUISSANCE, TRAVERSEE, LIMITE, GRE

- *Nearest event, found by tested software :*

Free-format text : "REDUCTION DE CHARGE PAR NIVEAU TRES HAUT GSS 202 BA SUITE A UN BLOCAGE DU REGULATEUR VANNE CONDENSATS GSS 206 VL. PERTE DE 300 MW PENDANT 3H."

Keywords : BLOCAGE, BAISSE CHARGE, NIVEAU TRES HAUT, RESERVOIR, GSS

In general terms, these two events are very similar concerning the main coded fields, notably the importance of the incident (which is low here ...), the reactor status and the causes (but the classification of the various causes is too vague). In addition, they have a few similar terms in common. However, the base contains events which are actually nearer, such as :

Free-format text : "LIMITATION PUISSANCE TURBINE PENDANT 4h00 DUE A UN MAUVAIS FONCTIONNEMENT DE RGL de 7h00 A LA SUITE DE LA FERMETURE INTEMPESTIVE DE LA REGULATRICE TURBINE GPV 021 VV"

Keywords : LIMITE, PUISSANCE, TURBINE, ADMISSION, ROBINET

In fact, real proximity would take place in a problem of interaction between NUCLEAR POWER and TURBINE POWER, and this can only be identified by the emphasis placed on proximity in the free text, through a greater number of similar terms in common, after having selected, for example, all the defective equipment, or the consequences of the incident.

Thus, to establish real proximity, i.e. which has a meaning in an analysis context, or point of view, preselection is necessary on a few specific fields or terms. Then, to use an NNM type function, the fields concerned, their relative weighting and the proximity function, should be either completed by an expert, or identified and defined on apprenticeship datasets.

Due to the lack of expert availability, and the workload involved in defining and operating comprehensive apprenticeship datasets which are sufficiently representative of the various types of possible event, it was decided to adopt a generic search mechanism covering the entire base.

As is also shown in the above example, once the values of a limited number of fields have been defined, the proximity between incident cards is mainly dependent on the free-format text. This proximity between free texts can then be considered as an extension of the proximity between question and response, in a REX application.

The possibility of aid in the preselection of discriminatory fields and terms, using induction mechanisms, has also been considered.

5.3 Testing of Main Induction Algorithms

A prospective study has been conducted on the advantages and limitations involved in the use of induction systems for two types of utilisation :

- comparative discrimination of card describers (coded fields and indexing lexemes),

- identification of potentially neighbouring classes of event, which will then be searched for nearest neighbours.

Several commercially available CBR softwares have been tested on a cards sub-set. Card representation has been limited to the most important coded fields and to the free text represented by the list of its indexing terms.

The main observations and the conclusions drawn from these studies are summarised below.

- Firstly, the application of induction algorithms requires a very careful selection of the cases of apprenticeship, which must concern the same problem situation, and with the same fields completed. This constraint is unavoidable, due to the variety of situations described in EVT. These algorithms necessitate the existence of at least one « output field », or a field which can be considered as such in the base. Some of the fields involve an element of interpretation or summary, for example the « TYPE OF EVENT », « DEGREE OF IMPORTANCE » or « CAUSE » fields, which were used in these tests.

- Secondly, induction algorithms such as ID3 and its derivatives, and CART, do not give results which are very easy to use when a high degree of cardinality exists in the list of indexing field values, which is the case in our application. As an example, there are several hundred possible values for the « PRIMARY SYSTEM » field.

  The text field is considered as a list of unordered symbols with a variable cardinality , with a very high number of possible values for the symbols (several thousand). For this field, the generally more discriminatory values of a field have therefore been preselected, using the expedient of induction on the same number of monovalue fields, for the main output fields.

  The induction algorithm considered most suitable to the text data, which is essentially high volume and multi-value, is the Mantaras' distance.

- Finally, the resulting induction trees on several output fields did not show any usable classification criteria.

The principle has therefore been adopted of using induction for data exploration studies, notably for the selection of particularly discriminatory fields or free text terms, both generally for all the fields considered as output fields, and for certain specific fields corresponding to the user's points of view.

6   CBR Functions Demonstrator - REX-CASE Application

6.1   General Specification Principles

As shown in Fig. 5, the demonstrator has been constructed using the REX-EVT application. The demonstrator expands REX-EVT functions to search for events close to a given event.

As mentioned above, generic proximity search mechanisms are used. The user must therefore define his search context, which will activate its related proximity computing parameters : the discriminatory fields for which the value has to be defined, nature and weighting of links to be activated, etc.

REX-EVT knowledge structures are used, with the search algorithms expanded. A REX question becomes longer and more complex when an event is used as an entry case. A search is conducted for close events, in certain contexts which are important for nuclear safety or availability, concerning cause, circumstances, consequences, defective system, etc.

Emphasis is given to proximity between text fields, for which an original algorithm has been developed. This proximity is based on a certain number of significant terms, which are neighbours in the REX networks and in common in the similar texts. « Significant terms » means, in general, terms which are sufficiently discriminatory and present simultaneously in a minimum number of texts.

6.2   Neighbouring Event Search Principles

The search is conducted in two separate phases : event preselection using the coded fields (such as the « DEFECTIVE SYSTEM » field, which is the most discriminatory overall), followed by the neighbour search in the free text, which can also cover the literal value of a few coded fields.

The application knowledge base is enriched with all combinations, known as *n-uplets*, of n lexemes[2] present in at least two free texts of events, and their links with the events concerned.

The various n-uplets which may exist in the entry event are identified. Neighbour n-uplets, and their related events, are found by scanning the networks (RSD).

The n-uplet identification algorithm was developed to identify similar classes of event. The utilisation of this algorithm for text indexing was inspired by the Galois meshes described in /h/.

This approach broadens the principle of indexing and search within REX. Events are not only indexed on lexemes, they are also indexed on n-uplets. The search is based on the following sequences :

- REX question → Lexemes - - RSD - - Indexing lexemes → event

- Event → Lexemes/n-uplets - - RSD - - indexing n-uplets → event

The calculation of proximity between terms in the networks leads to proximity computing between texts, which enables the file of similar events identified to be presented in decreasing proximity sequence.

Remarks : the notion of proximity between texts, and therefore between lexemes, differs from that between the conventional REX question and response file as, in the latter case, the responses must be at least as precise as the questions. For the similar text search, the term « expanded REX search » will be used. As an example, the transition from « ARRET TRANCHE » (« unit shut-down ») to « ARRET » (« shut-down ») will be authorised, but with reduced weighting, and the networks will then be scanned as in the conventional REX search.

6.3   Demonstrator Functions and Design

The demonstrator functional design is shown in Fig. 5.

The following functions are programmed on a UNIX machine and are accessible through a window interface :

a) *Entry* of the event selected as the entry case, and parameters, or selection of an existing event, which may be based on a previous query,

---

[2] At the present time, n is limited to 10

b) *Filtering* where necessary, using the coded fields, to select a consistent search sub-set,

c) *Possible selection of one or more active points of view*, such as, for example : SYSTEM, CAUSE, CONSEQUENCE, CIRCUMSTANCES, PLANT TYPE, FUNCTION-ELEMENT, MISCELLANEOUS, etc.,

d) *Display of discriminatory lexemes* identified in the entry event text, depending on the active points of view,

e) *Search - two methods :*

- « REX broad » search, using discriminatory lexemes in the text, or using a sub-set of these lexemes,

- « REX CBR » search.

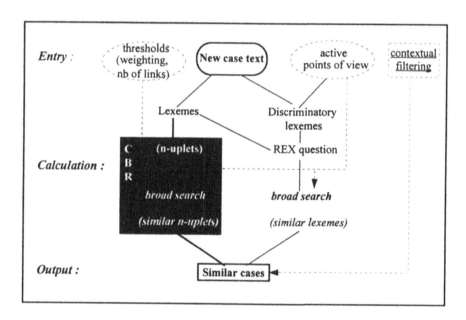

Fig. 5 : REX-CASE Structure

6.4 Example of CBR Search Results

- *Event considered as the entry case :*

Free-format text : « APPLICATION I0 KPS1 : PERTE DE LA FONCTION EBULLIOMETRIE SUITE A LA PERTE CALCULATEUR N1A ET N1B. RELANCE DU CALCULATEUR RAS. ETAT DE REPLI : SANS OBJET.

DELAI DE REPLI : LA REPARATION DEVRA ETRE REALISEE DANS UN DELAI DE UN MOIS. »

Keywords : PANNEAU, SURETE ,CALCULATEUR, KIT

- *This event is indexed with the following lexemes* :

I0 KPS1, PERTE FONCTION, EBULLIOMETRIE, CALCULATEUR, ETAT DE REPLI, OBJET, DELAI DE REPLI, REPARATION, DELAI, PANNEAU DE SURETE, KIT

- Through the use of their indexing n-uplets, these lexemes lead to free-format texts including the following terms :

PERTE FONCTION, CALCULATEUR, KIT, KPS, PANNEAU DE SURETE

- By this way close events are gathered, among which here are two examples :

Free-format text (1) : "KPS : INDISPONIBILITE DE LA FONCTION EBULLIOMETRIE DU KPS SUITE A LA DEFAILLANCE DU CALCULATEUR. APPLICATION DES S.T.E. TABLEAU III/6/7 PKS1 SUITE 25."

Keywords (1) :CALCULATEUR KIT EBULLIOMETRIE MESURE

Free-format text (2) : "INDISPONIBILITE DE LA FONCTION EBULLIOMETRE DU KPS PAR PERTE DES ACQUISITIONS. APRES RELANCE DU CALCULATEUR LA FONCTION EBULLIOMETRE EST A NOUVEAU DISPONIBLE SANS MISE EN EVIDENCE DE DEFAUT PARTICULIER "

Keywords (2) :CALCULATEUR EBULLIOMETRE INDISPONIBLE

Remarks : these events could also be retrieved with REX-EVT, provided that the user is able to write the right query ! When creating a query with REX, a user relies upon his own knowledge of the domain. So he will choose the terms which will be used by REX for the query process, according to the importance he attaches to them, not according to the weight of terms in the indexing scheme - which he is usually not aware of. On the other hand, the CBR approach, with the n-uplets indexing scheme, allows to detect in an entry case the only terms that will lead to close events.

7   Conclusions and Prospects

The application of the CBR process to our own area of activity presented specific difficulties related to the wide diversity of cases, the importance of the free-format text and the variety of the user points of view. An attempt has been made to handle these difficulties separately, using a generic approach, integrating CBR development into REX methods and tools.

The demonstrator developed is of a specific and original nature, due to the following factors :

- the CBR process is applied to text data,

- a generic algorithm is used with specific points of view,

- the interactive selection of semantic links between describers, specific to the points of view selected by the user.

System limitations are due to the scope of the application, which is technical and clearly delimited, for which the terminology is clearly identified and structured, and to the very specific nature of the texts. Like any « intelligent » information search system, these limitations are obviously also related to those of domain knowledge which, ideally, should also be integrated.

The induction mechanisms which, today, are efficient for characterised and structured information, and clearly defined problem situations, are not directly usable for the search for similar events. They may represent a route for future development, which may become feasible when the information system has been developed to provide a more structured form of information recording (/i/).

8 References

/a/ LANNOY A. - the EDF failure reporting system : contribution and prospects - ESREL'96 - PSAM III - Crète (Grèce), juin 1996

/b/ BOUCHET J.-L., HAEUSTLER L. - Construction d'une terminologie sur l'exploitation des centrales nucléaires françaises - Journées sur l'Analyse des Données Textuelles (JADT'95) - Rome (Italie), décembre 1995.

/c/ QUOIDBACH G. - (Tractebel energy engineering, Belgique) - Gestion automatisée des interventions en centrale - Présentation au onzième congrès international des centrales électriques, 1989

/d/ CHASSIGNET C. - Maîtriser et gérer l'information technique - AFNOR, 1991

/e/ LANNOY A. et al. - Analyse automatique de texte libre. Application au codage et à la validation de fiches de retour d'expérience. Communication au λμ10 - Saint-Malo, octobre 1996

/f/ La maîtrise du retour d'expérience avec la méthode REX P. Malvache, Ch. Eichenbaum, P. Prieur - Performances humaines et techniques mars-avril 1994

/g/ Principes et déroulement de la méthode REX Note technique CEA

/h/ Méthodes de classification conceptuelle basées sur les treillis de Galois et applications. Conceptual clustering methods based on Galois lattices and applications Robert Godin, Guy Mineau, Rokia Missaoui, Hafedh Mili - Revue d'Intelligence Artificielle Vol. 9 - n° 2/1995

/i/ BOUCHET J.-L., FERRARO G., LANNOY A., PEREZ F., SABY P. - Cohérence sûreté - maintenance : vers une description générique des défaillances pour le recueil de l'expérience d'exploitation. Communication au λμ10 - Saint-Malo, octobre 1996

Troubleshooting CFM 56-3 Engines for the Boeing 737 Using CBR and Data-Mining

Richard Heider
CFM international
Commercial Product Support
BP 1936 - 77019 Melun Cedex - France

Abstract : This paper describes the industrialisation of a software system to support fault diagnosis of the CFM 56 -3 aircraft engine. The system uses data-mining techniques known as induction and case based reasoning which exploit failure descriptions that are stored in a case base. A first prototype using the induction technique applied on an initial case base has been achieved. The paper presents the main characteristics of the CBR and induction techniques. The modelling of the engine failures and the process of feeding the case base are given next. The system is intended to be used by airline maintenance staff and CFMI specialists. A user friendly environment has been implemented to allow an optimum use of the system as a troubleshooting support.

1   Introduction

CFM-international has developed the CFM 56 engine family that equips Boeing or Airbus planes. Cfm international is a 50% joint venture of the american General Electric and the french SNECMA. One of the goals of Cfm-international is to improve engine maintenance technology in order to reduce the cost of ownership of its engines for its customers.

The *Cassiopee* project was launched in August 1993 with the aim of developing a decision support system for the technical maintenance of the CFM 56-3 engines (which equip the Boeing 737 airplane). The idea was to use inductive and case-based reasoning (CBR) techniques to derive solutions for maintenance problems out of stored experience. The development of the diagnosis software is performed in cooperation with Acknosoft, a specialist of these knowledge discovery techniques [1].

This paper presents the main aspects related to the industrialisation of such a system. A first part deals with the induction and CBR techniques which are incorporated to the system, the second part presents the software itself : purpose of its development, modelling and collection of the data, main results and perspectives of use.

2   Induction and CBR

The term "Data Mining", also called "Knowledge Discovery in Databases", refers to a set of techniques that are used to extract useful decision knowledge from databases. These techniques help turn "Data" into "Knowledge". "Data Mining" is a a general term that covers a wide variety of techniques such as neural nets, statistical analysis as well as sophisticated graphical tools that help discover "Knowledge" hidden in "Data".

Induction and Case-Based Reasoning (CBR) are data mining technologies that solve decision problems by storing, retrieving and adapting past cases. A case is defined as the description of a problem, that has been successfully solved in the past, along with its solution. When a new problem is encountered, CBR recalls similar cases and adapts the solutions that worked in the past for the current problem. Induction extracts a decision tree from the whole case history and then uses this general knowledge for problem solving. Induction and CBR are complementary techniques and their integration improves their capabilities.

Induction automatically builds decision trees from case history. The size of the case database may vary from a dozen to several thousand cases. Induction extracts the knowledge of company specialists from their decision making behaviour as embodied in historical cases. It identifies patterns amongst cases, orders the decision criteria by their discriminatory power, and partitions the cases into families. The user can access cases at any node of the tree, perform data mining using graphical editors and knowledge browsers, and he can also interactively modify the tree manually.

Induction requires that the data is structured, for example by using classes of objets with slots. A standard relational database schema can easily be mapped onto this object model. It allows to define the vocabulary used to describe the cases. For example, the trend of a turbine inlet temperature, the position of a fuel shut-off valve or the value of the rotational fan speed ...

Induction also requires that a target decision slot is defined. For the engine troubleshooting application this slot is defined as the list of spare parts that have been changed in order to solve the problem. Given the data model, the target class and the case data, a fault tree is automatically generated. Induction thus extracts relevant decision knowledge from case history.

Unlike induction, Case-based reasoning does not require that a tree structure be generated before problem solving. A new problem is solved by finding similar, past cases and adapting their solutions. CBR offers flexible indexing and retrieval, and fuzzy matching. For applications where safety is important, the conclusions can be further confirmed, or refuted, by entering additional parameters that may modify the similarity values. CBR particularly appeals to line maintenance specialists who solve an engine failure by recalling what they did in similar situations.

A critical issue, when developing an application using induction or CBR is performance. Tests performed on a standard 486 DX2/66 PC, demonstrate that pure CBR retrieval is fast for databases with fewer than 10,000 cases. Retrieval time using a tree, once the tree has been generated, is instantaneous. When retrieval performances are required on larger case bases, CBR can be combined with a tree generated by induction that is used as an indexing mechanism. Both techniques allow to improve the decision making process by using prior experiences and perform "what-if" analysis [2].

3 Application to Engine Failure Diagnosis

3.1 Business Motivation

Nowadays, it is impossible to sell aircraft engines without reliable customer support. The "cost of ownership" of such a long lasting equipment may exceed its initial value and maintenance costs are increasingly becoming a decision criterion for an airline that wishes to purchase a new engine. By proposing diagnostic software and thus increasing the quality of its customer support, the engine manufacturer will score points against his competitors.

The use of CBR systems and related knowledge discovery techniques to support line maintenance and fault diagnosis activities is becoming a general concern for the civilian aircraft industry. Most engine or airplane manufacturers are known to investigate the subject. Airlines themselves are preparing line maintenance applications based on such systems [3].

The reduction in cost of aircraft ownership is mainly expected from the acceleration of the troubleshooting process. The time required for diagnosis represents about 50% of downtime (the remaining time is used for repair). The use of the system will help to optimise the number of tests required for troubleshooting, to reduce the cost of repair and to minimise airplane downtime. It is expected that the system divides by two the time required for diagnosis. We are thus looking at an overall reduction of 25% in downtime which will result in a proportional reduction of flight delays and cancellations.

Another cost intensive factor to our clients is given by the important number of wrong equipment removals due to troubleshooting errors. It is expected that the system contributes to a more precise diagnosis and a subsequent reduction of wrong removals.

A less measurable but probably as important benefit to CFMI is due to the discipline in formulating and storing the failure cases that is required by a CBR system. The resulting storage of the troubleshooting history will document the expertise of the most skilled maintenance specialists in order to build a corporate memory and help to transfer know-how from the expert to the novice.

3.2 Modelling and Gathering Data

In order to built a decision support system from case history, one must first gather case data. The starting point was a reliability and maintainability database on an IBM mainframe from which 30,000 cases were extracted.

This data base (in the following named *All-Data*) contains failure descriptions which are provided through an electronic network by CFMI's technical on-site representatives at the airlines. Each failure event report contains a structured, formatted part and a free-text narrative which often reproduces the failure event as described by the pilot in his log book. This mainframe database has been created in the past with an aim of statistical exploitation. Therefore only few of the formatted records are of technical interest to the engine trouble-shooter. The technically interesting information is generally given in the free-text narratives which could not directly be fed into the case base of the system.

The acquisition of the first stack of cases could be made in different steps.

A first task was to model the information characteristic to engine failures. It was decided to build a first system using the induction technique. The evaluation of this approach vs. the CBR technique would be made in a second time. Entry points to the system were decided to be the failure symptom (e.g. abnormal noise, thrust deficiency, high oil consumption, ...). The target slot has naturally been defined as the faultive equipment (which is to replace or on which a maintenance action must be undertaken to solve the problem). These slots are present as structured fields in the All-Data mainframe base and could be directly fed into the case base.

A second task consisted in modelling the additional technically relevant information. A team of maintenance specialists have therefore established a list of symptom specific technical parameters that could be found in the All-Data free-text narratives and that were considered important to diagnose the failure. A total of 70 parameters could be defined for approximately 150 failure symptoms, with an average of 15 parameters specific to each symptom.

The following task consisted in a "manual" extraction of the technical information out of the free-text narratives following the above mentioned specifications. Around 14,000 cases out of the 30,000 could be filtered out automatically by elimination of non relevant failure symptoms, cases without given failure cause, etc... It took an average of one specialist during one year to select and feed into the case base the 1500 cases that are representative for the variety of engine failures and provided with a maximum of technical information.

Once the system is put in operation at an airline, electronic case collection questionnaires will allow a direct input of modelled cases into the case base.

3.3 User Interface

The system is designed for airline maintenance crews who perform on-line troubleshooting (i.e., when the airplane is at the departure gate) as well as to assist CFM engineers in offering them a quicker and better advise. A great effort has thus been spent to obtain a user-friendly environment. Fig. 1 illustrates the environment of a *Cassiopee* consultation.

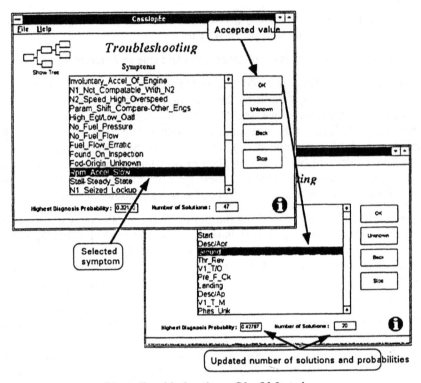

Fig. 1. Troubleshooting a Cfm 56-3 engine

The consultation process runs as follows. New fault trees have been generated by induction. Unlike standard fault trees that are often built during the design stage and that are based on faults that should occur in theory, the fault trees that are built automatically are based on observed faults and can be updated as new faults appear. When browsing such a fault tree, the operator is requested to answer the questions that are in close relationship with the original trouble symptom (figure 1). At the end of the consultation a list of possible solutions is proposed to the operator with their relative frequency. The procedure (test to perform on the engine), to confirm that the selected solution is the accurate one, is obtained by selecting that solution from the list. This is done to improve the accuracy of the system and not to replace the official maintenance documents (it is a add-on to the procedure that is certified by the authorities). Then the cases that support the conclusions are retrieved and the user can browse them in order to confirm or refute the solution.

The system is fully integrated in the end-user environment. Thus, some important achievements are not directly tied to the technology per se: Link of the system with an Illustrated Part Catalogue (IPC) to take into account engine configuration evolution (figure 2), interface the IPC with *Excel* to perform statistics on reliability and maintainability, support electronic mail to collect events world-wide through the X400 network etc.

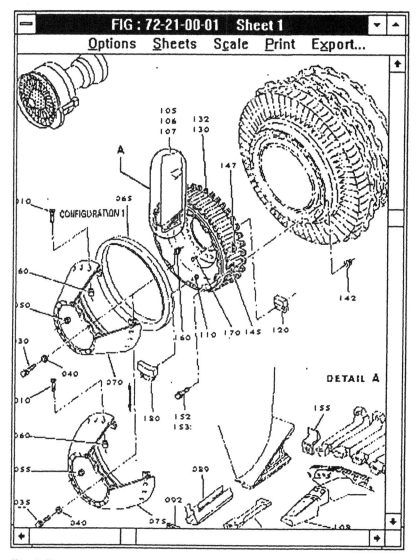

Fig. 2. Part nomenclature is used graphically to design the faulty component

The IPC makes extensive use of hypermedia facilities to navigate between the drawings of the parts and their nomenclature. The system contains over 25,000 images in TIFF format which are highly compressed to fit on a CD-ROM with the diagnostic support system and the case database (it is compressed from 10 Gb down to 230 Mb).

4 Conclusion and Perspectives

A software system to support fault-diagnosis for CFM 56-3 airplane engines has been developed. The core of the system is a data mining algorithm allowing to derive causes for engine failures from past cases. The system relies on a case base which contains modelled engine failures. The modellisation includes the failure symptoms, associated engine operational parameters and the engine part which is or needs to be replaced or readjusted. 1500 failure cases that are considered as representative for a variety of engine problems have been fed into the system's initial version by compiling real fault reports. The system is provided with a user friendly interface that includes a link to an illustrated parts catalogue to support the maintenance action. The system is dedicated to airline engineering or line-maintenance crews and to CFMI's customer support specialists.

The system has achieved a state of maturity that enables tests in an airline environment. The validation of the system by the engineering staff of one or more partner airlines which includes additional feeding of the case base is foreseen. A successful validation should result in a widespread use of the system by CFMI's customers.

References

[1] ALTHOFF, K.-D., AURIOL, E., BARLETTA, R. & MANAGO, M. *A Review of Industrial Case-Based Reasoning Tools.* A. Goodall (Ed.), AI Intelligence, Oxford, 1995.

[2]. AURIOL, E., WESS, S., ALTHOFF, K.-D., MANAGO, M. & TRAPHÖNER, R.. "INRECA: A seamlessly integrated system based on inductive inference and case-based reasoning". ICCBR 95, First International Conference on Case-Based Reasoning, Veloso M. & Aamodt A. (eds), Springer Verlag, Heidelberg, 1995.

[3]. VINGERHOEDS, R.A., JANSSENS, P., NETTEN, B.D. & FERNANDEZ-MONTESINOS "Enhancing off-line and on-line condition monitoring and fault diagnosis". *Control Eng. Practice*, Vol 3, No. 11, pp. 1515-1528, 1995. Elsevier Science Ltd.

Global Case-Base Development and Deployment

Philip Klahr

Inference Corporation
100 Rowland Way
Novato, California 94945 USA
E-mail: klahr@inference.com

Abstract

A major benefit of case-based reasoning (CBR) technology is in the capture and reuse of knowledge to solve problems. Over the past few years, there have been a large number of companies deploying CBR applications in the area of customer support. Since many of these companies are global, there has been increasing interest on building and deploying case bases on a global scale – both to leverage the knowledge and expertise that is distributed around the world, and also to make case bases available to all the regional support organizations to solve customer problems consistently worldwide. These efforts have identified a number of key issues that global companies need to address – issues such as (1) distributed knowledge capture and case authoring, (2) distributing case bases and updates, (3) localization, both for foreign language translation and for incorporating country-specific content, (4) on-going maintenance, and (5) global management and organization. This issues are discussed along with examples of the various approaches companies have taken.

1. Introduction

A major benefit of CBR technology is in the capture and reuse of knowledge to solve problems. Over the past few years, there have been a number of innovative CBR applications in the area of customer support [Acorn & Walden, 1992; Allen, 1994; Nguyen, Czerwinski & Lee, 1993; Hislop & Pracht, 1994]. In this environment, incoming customer telephone calls are handled by support representatives who attempt to answer a customer's question or solve a problem (e.g., about the company's products), or else escalate the call to a technical specialist. As a company grows, both in terms of its customer base, and in the range and complexity of products supported, the customer support organization grows correspondingly. Costs escalate, as does the need for more technically-skilled support staff.

Companies have turned to CBR technology as one method to capture technical expertise and make it available to front-line support staff taking the calls. Previous customer problems and inquiries are incorporated into *cases*, each of which contains descriptive features that define the situation and its uniqueness. Associated with each case is its applicable action or solution, i.e., given the defined situation, it is advisable to suggest the given solution.

Cases are aggregated into a *case base*, or case library, which is then used to search against in response to a new situation or problem. When a similar case is retrieved, it then forms the basis of a solution or response. Case bases evolve as new knowledge is entered, or as modifications and updates occur to existing cases.

The business benefits in using CBR in the area of customer support have been broad and significant, and include:

- ❑ *increasing first-call resolutions* – enabling the front-line staff to answer more of the calls the first time (through use of the case solutions), without the need to escalate.

- ❑ *improving solution quality* – providing technical expertise and best practices (embedded in cases) to the non-technical front-line staff.

- ❑ *establishing consistency* – providing the correct solutions consistently for the same types of problems.

- ❑ *reducing cost per call* – more focused and guided troubleshooting for the support staff, as well as less escalations.

- ❑ *reducing calls to the support desk* – getting it right the first time reduces repeat calls; also some companies have made their case bases available for direct customer access, allowing customers to solve their own problems.

- ❑ *reducing field service costs* – solving problems remotely can eliminate technical field visits for those products that sometime require on-site support.

- ❑ *accelerating training* – support staff's access to the case base becomes part of their job, essentially providing an on-the-job training facility, as well as enabling them to be productive faster.

- ❑ *increasing staff satisfaction* – front-line staff can solve more problems independently and gain confidence in their abilities to do so.

- ❑ *increasing customer satisfaction* – customers get answers faster and with a higher degree of accuracy.

- ❑ *leveraging technical expertise* – embedding expert knowledge in cases frees experts from having to spend large amounts of their time on solving customer problems (repeatedly and redundantly).

❑ *improving management of support knowledge* – standardizing on best practices and making that knowledge available to all support staff.

❑ *increasing sales* – using customer support improvements as an effective marketing weapon; increasing customer loyalty through the quality and responsiveness of customer support service.

Many of the companies that have adopted CBR technology are global companies, i.e., they sell, and support, products worldwide. These companies typically have multiple support organizations distributed around the globe, each supporting a particular country or region where they do business. Since each of these organizations support the company's products, all the support personnel can benefit from the knowledge and experience embedded in cases. As a result, some companies are now beginning to build and distribute case bases with a worldwide perspective.

Building case bases for global use presents some interesting challenges and issues which are the focus of this paper. The issues are generic, i.e., all companies embarking on a global CBR project need to address them. However, the approaches companies take in resolving these issues vary considerably depending on the business strategy, environment and operations of any particular company. The objective of this paper is to outline these issues and present some examples of alternative approaches taken.

2. Global CBR Development

If one examines the above list of benefits companies have achieved with CBR technology, it is clear that these benefits apply to any customer support organization, in any country, in any region. Capturing and reusing knowledge can benefit anyone that needs, and has access to, that knowledge.

When one considers deploying case bases globally, a naïve approach might be to simply take an existing case base (built in one country or region) and distribute it to remote sites. Unfortunately this seldom works – countries typically have varying business requirements, differing operational environments, different customs and cultures (and languages!), and different laws and regulations. While a country may well benefit from a case base built in a different country, that case base most often needs to be customized and localized to meet the country's specific needs – in order for that case base to be most effective.

Another important issue concerns case building. Support organizations build up expertise in solving customer problems. This occurs in all support locations. Why not leverage all the expertise that exists around the world, and embed that knowledge in the case base? Many companies are doing just that, by having cases authored at multiple sites, by multiple authors.

Since case bases contain knowledge (past cases of problems/inquiries and solutions), that knowledge typically grows and changes over time. Problems not experienced before need to be researched and added to the case base. Changes or extensions to the products supported by the case base need to be incorporated. Local cases, appropriate to only one country or region, might need to be included or updated. These types of changes and updates require an on-going maintenance process and a means for distributing updates. How is the new or modified knowledge to be incorporated into the case base, and how are updates to be distributed worldwide?

Finally, or perhaps more correctly "initially," an organizational and management structure needs to be established for managing a global CBR project. Roles and responsibilities need to be defined and managed worldwide.

In summary, the global nature of a CBR project involves the following challenges:

❑ *distributed authoring* – capturing expertise and experience from customer support organizations distributed around the world; embedding that experience in case bases.

❑ *case distribution* – distributing case bases, and updates, and having the local sites incorporate changes and additions.

❑ *localization* – being able to modify global cases and add local cases; customizing to local needs (e.g., language translation, local actions, local questions, local features).

❑ *maintenance* – updating and adding both global and local cases.

❑ *management and organization* – managing a global project and establishing (and enforcing) processes for the above activities; ensuring funding, appropriate staffing, accurate scheduling and other project management activities – on a global scale.

Each global company addresses these issues in different ways depending on their requirements, operations and business objectives. It is important to recognize what the issues are, and the pros and cons of the various alternatives.

3. Case Authoring

3.1 Centralized vs. Distributed Authoring

One approach to building a case base is to do it all in one centralized location – a group of case builders co-located in one area to participate in the case building activities. This facilitates the sharing of ideas, approaches, issues, and techniques. It eases the process of merging cases from the multiple authors, and resolving any problems that might arise. Management of the case building process is also simplified.

For companies that want to leverage the expertise that exists elsewhere around the world, they can attempt to bring in the appropriately knowledgeable people to one location, and provide a centralized case building environment. This entails moving people for (usually) a few months, and requires the selected personnel to have all the expertise themselves, or at least access to it. Typically this expertise is more distributed. Also, costs in bringing everyone together can be extensive, and the impact of losing local expertise for a couple months can be severe. As a result, a more distributed approach to building cases may be preferable.

The approach taken at Reuters [Borron, Morales & Klahr, 1996] distributes the case building process among its support centers around the globe. Each center accepts responsibility for building cases for certain products, those for which the center has the most expertise. These product-oriented case bases are then sent to a global case-base library maintained at one central site. So, in reality, the Reuters approach combines a distributed model (distributed by product) with centralized control.

There are other distributed models as well. An even more distributed approach would allow a product case-base owner to use case authors from multiple worldwide sites. Here the issue is one of intelligently merging cases for the same product from multiple authors and maintaining consistency for each product case base. But clearly the more distributed the authoring process, the more difficult the merging process. The goal is to maximize the capturing of expertise globally, while minimizing the complexity of the processes involved.

3.2 Versions for Different User Types

In developing case bases for global use, one needs to consider the users, most typically the customer support telephone representatives – their skill levels, modes of operation, and business practices. In other situations, users may be on the help desks of customers, or the users may be the customers themselves, having direct access to case bases made available to them either on CD-ROM, or for their direct use on the Internet. Case-base design needs to consider the end users and accommodate their (sometime conflicting) needs.

To service the needs of multiple types of users, one company developed three versions of each solution targeted at the three user groups. All the cases were applicable to all users, but the action differed based on whether the user was on the company's own support staff (supporting customers on the telephone), or whether the user was a distributor of the company's products (i.e., the distributor was providing customer support), or whether the user was the customer directly accessing the case base. A batch process executed over all the cases and extracted the actions applicable to one user type. The resulting system was then given to the appropriate user community.

Other companies provide shortcuts for the more expert users, for example, allowing them to enter free-form descriptions of the problem, which the system can interpret to pre-answer questions (i.e., identify specific features of the problem environment). The non-technical users, alternatively, could be guided step-by-step through the troubleshooting process through a question and answer dialog.

3.3 Managing Local Cases in a Global Context

Typically, global cases contain information that is pertinent worldwide. In some cases, however, it may be important to include local information within global cases. For example, in a 24-hour global support strategy (e.g., a London customer is connected to a London support center during office hours, but is connected to a U.S. support center in the evening, or to an Asia support center in the early morning hours before London is open), it is important to give the correct local information to the customer (who may be on a different continent!). In this situation, local actions for specific regions need to be embedded in the global case base.

3.4 Consistency of Style

Companies typically create a *style guide* to provide guidelines and standards for case authoring (e.g., representational standards, types of questions to ask, formats for case titles and descriptions, types of information to put into actions, annotations and attachments, etc.). The style guide provides the framework for case builders so that the resulting merged case base contains a consistent style and flow for the ultimate user.

Some companies create one global style for all cases created worldwide, while other efforts may require regional styles due to different business practices and requirements. The latter approach creates issues in reusing these case bases in other locations. It does ease the case construction process for the home country (they can do it their way), but burdens other countries as they attempt to reuse a case base – it may require some modifications to meet local needs.

3.5 Authoring by Support Experts vs. Knowledge Engineers

Reuters has used both approaches due to workload constraints in various regions. In North America cases were authored directly by the domain experts. In the United Kingdom, knowledge engineers interviewed domain experts and created all the cases.

As the case base has moved into an operational and maintenance mode, the approach has moved entirely to using knowledge engineers. Content is still obtained from other regions, but formatting, incorporation and testing are done by knowledge engineers.

Both approaches have been successful. The decision on which approach to adopt should be based on skill levels and time commitments of the people involved.

4. Case Distribution

4.1 Central vs. Local Distribution

Reuters chose a central library to be a single repository for case bases. This seemed the best alternative to manage their global approval and distribution processes (through their centralized control model). Another company chose to have two central sites, one in North America and one in Europe principally because their support operations (particularly staff skill level) and types of customers are different. Case bases are still shared and reused, but case bases authored in the two regions have differing styles (aimed at different types of users), and need some restructuring when they cross the Atlantic.

A third company allows each country to build their own case bases – with local autonomy and in the local language. While there is some global coordination and planning, this approach allows each country to proceed with their own business requirements. The resulting case base is made available on a worldwide shared network drive. Other countries can pick up the case bases and then use them for their own needs. This usually involves language translation. The receiving country can then customize, update, and maintain the translated version.

4.2 Content of Distributions

When distributing case-base updates, one can distribute whole case bases or just those cases that have been modified or are new. There are a number of issues to consider here. If whole case bases are distributed each time, then local changes (if there are any) need to be imported for each update. If language translation is involved, whole case bases need to re-translated each time (if the updated cases are not easily identifiable). If only updates are distributed, each local region needs to import the changes (translating first if required) and test the updates to make sure local changes have not been effected by the modifications. If they have been effected, then the local changes need to be re-incorporated. Thus, the business processes and requirements help define what the contents should be for distribution.

The important factors to consider are language requirements, localization needs, and the frequency with which updates are made.

4.3 Frequency and Delivery of Updates

Ideally as soon as there is new case knowledge, it should be distributed immediately. How quickly this can be done is dependent on the delivery mechanism and the processes in place for automating the updating and distribution processes. If the Internet or an intranet is used, distribution can be immediate and updates can occur often. If distribution is through CD-ROM, quarterly (or every other month) updates are common. If distribution to remote sites is through file transfer or a similar electronic transfer mechanism, updates are usually made once or twice a month.

There are also issues in version control and software management that need to be considered in deciding on distribution frequency.

4.4 Foreign Language Translation Requirements

Foreign language translation requirements complicate the distribution process. Issues of sending whole case bases versus updates, and frequency of distribution, are all impacted. Translation could occur before distribution (centrally) or after distribution (locally). This depends on the particular translation process used, and who is designated to manage and control it. Both approaches have been used. Cost and time issues are important as well, limiting the turnaround time for issuing updates in countries requiring language translation.

4.5 Distribution Format

The format in which cases are distributed can vary based on the technical infrastructure available at each site, and the tools and environments that have been established as standards. Simple formatted text files can typically be processed by any site. Those companies that have standardized on a particular database can distribute database records containing the cases. Much of this process can be automated. Reuters, for example, built utilities to identify updated and new cases, to generate a file containing them, and to ship them to remote sites [Borron, Morales & Klahr, 1996].

5. Case Localization

5.1 Incorporating Local Cases

As discussed above, various regions or countries may have differing business practices (e.g., determining when to send out a field engineer), different safety regulations (e.g., in allowing customers to replace parts or components on their own), different legal issues (e.g., liability in performing tests), and different cultures (e.g., customers desire to troubleshoot on the telephone), that make it necessary to modify global cases for local use, or to add local cases.

Local sites need to keep track of their changes and ensure they are accurately reflected (incorporated) in updates. Each local site needs a test environment (for testing updated case bases) and a production environment. A good version control facility is essential.

5.2 Designing Global Cases to Facilitate Local Changes

If there are localization requirements, global cases need to be designed so that local changes can be easily made. An approach one company is taking is to embed local changes in *attachments* to cases. An attachment can be a simple external text file that is attached to a case, and user accessible from the case (e.g., from a case action or from a particular case question/feature). (Some companies use attachments to embed technical notes or documents should the user need more information, or need the original source material for a case.) The advantage of this approach is that the actual contents of global cases need not be changed at all. The attachments contain all the local information. Also these attachments can be maintained at the local level, and in the local language, thereby reducing potential language translation costs, and minimizing local changes to the cases themselves.

Localization needs and requirements need to be identified early on in the design process. This will help case authors build global cases in a way to minimize the work required to customize at the local level.

5.3 Foreign Language Translation

This is a very important issue for every global effort (as discussed above). While some companies (e.g., Reuters) can successful deploy globally in English, other companies cannot. Language translation is costly and time consuming, and adds complexity to the distribution and updating processes. Issues of where translation is done (e.g., centrally, locally), when it is performed (e.g., before distribution, after distribution) and how translation is accomplished (e.g., using automated translation techniques, providing manual translations, or even possibly authoring cases in multiple languages concurrently), all need to be addressed. There is also the issue of who maintains the translated cases, i.e., whether the local country should maintain a case base once translated, or continue to have updates translated when received from other sites.

5.4 Local Infrastructures and Integration Requirements

Again, understanding local requirements (as well as future plans) is critical – client computers, servers, networking, bandwidth, databases, Internet access, etc. all need to be factored in for all the sites to be serviced. This infrastructure impacts system design, automation of processes, and distribution alternatives.

6. Case-Base Maintenance

There are numerous alternatives for case-base maintenance, some of which have been discussed above. Some companies have some subset of the original case authors continue to maintain the case bases. Typically, each case base is assigned to a designated domain owner, who maintains that case base. Some companies transition case-base ownership to a centralized maintenance group, which is assigned responsibility for updating the case bases. Another company, which allows case development locally in the native language, has case bases maintained by the local countries which built the case bases originally. Updates are made available to other countries to be retrieved as needed. Once translated into the local language, the country receiving the case base can then maintain it locally. (Alternatively, rather than maintaining locally, the local country could decide to continue to receive, and translate, updates from the source country.)

7. Management and Organization

7.1 Centralized vs. Distributed Management

There is considerable variation, based on differing models. In the distributed approach, countries are fairly autonomous. with some global coordination. In the centralized approach, there is a centralized *global project leader* to manage the project, and a centralized *global technical manager* to manage the global case-base library. Each region/country then has its own infrastructure for case authoring (and exporting cases to the library) and deployment (receiving global updates and importing cases locally). A *regional coordinator* at each local site is given this responsibility. The central site provides technical assistance to each of the remote centers.

In all situations, however, there needs to be some global coordination and leadership. This is typically accomplished through a *global steering committee*, with representatives from the main global centers, to make sure overall objectives are agreed upon, monitored, and reviewed. These global groups typically meet face-to-face every three to four months, with intermediate conference calls. In addition to providing business focus, the committee resolves funding, staffing and resource issues, as well as ensuring that objectives are met for all the regions and countries involved.

7.2 Case-Base Management

Typically, a *domain supervisor* is responsible for a particular case base. Each case base contains cases concerning a particular domain area – usually a company's product or family of products. This segmentation of knowledge, based on product, seems the most natural for most companies. Customer calls usually focus around a particular product the customer is using, and the problem the customer is having with that product. The domain supervisor is the individual assuming ownership (content, delivery, and potentially maintenance) of a product case base, and has a group of *case authors* to help author the cases for that product.

7.3 Different Cultures

There are often complex cultural issues in working with different countries, with different work ethics, with different approaches to software development, with different business practices, and with different customer expectations. These issues can often dominate global meetings. In this context, it is important to be realistic in deliverable time-scales and the need to remain flexible in achieving results. Aggressive plans can be stalled when authors were not given sufficient time in one region to build global cases; optimistic deadlines to produce working systems can result in brittle and patchy case bases, and inconsistent coverage in the different case bases; giving early incomplete case bases to end users can create negative impressions that are hard to subsequently turnaround. Global managers need to be aware of these issues in managing schedules and deliverables.

7.4 Management Reporting Structure & Communication

Global projects also place unusual demands on reporting structures. For example, domain supervisors typically report to the local customer support center. But they also have responsibilities to the global project, and might also report to the global project leader, or the global steering committee. It is advisable to establish a clearly defined management reporting structure with well-defined roles and responsibilities, and to provide open lines of communication.

8. Summary

Numerous companies have successfully built global CBR systems. They face numerous issues in global organization, management, authoring, distribution, localization, and maintenance. These issues are in no way insurmountable. They just need to be understood, and discussed in relation to the company's business objectives, practices, and operational environments [Klahr, 1996].

Companies implementing global CBR systems have benefited by capturing the expertise of their technical staff from around the world, and making that expertise available to support centers worldwide. Many of these companies are now expanding both case authoring and case access to other parts of the company's operations (e.g., marketing, product development, sales). One company is focusing on building case bases within the product development organization. When a new product is launched, an already built case base is similarly launched to the customer support staff so they can immediately begin to answer customer queries intelligently and consistently. Other companies are making their case bases directly accessible to their customers – a strategy we will see much more of in the future.

References

Acorn, T. L., and Walden, S. 1992. SMART: Support Management Automated Reasoning Technology for Compaq Customer Service. In *Innovative Applications of Artificial Intelligence 4, Proceedings of IAAI-92* (Scott & Klahr, eds.). Menlo Park, California: AAAI Press.

Allen, B. 1994. Case-Based Reasoning: Business Applications. *Communications of the ACM* 37(3): 40-42.

Borron, J., Morales, D., and Klahr, P. 1996. Developing and Deploying Knowledge on a Global Scale. *Proceedings of the Thirteenth National Conference on Artificial Intelligence and the Eighth Conference on Innovative Applications of Artificial Intelligence*. Menlo Park, California: AAAI Press.

Hislop, C., and Pracht, D. 1994. Integrated Problem Resolution for Business Communications. In *Proceedings of the Sixth Innovative Applications of Artificial Intelligence Conference* (Byrnes & Aikins, eds.). Menlo Park, California: AAAI Press.

Klahr, P. 1996. *Seven Principles for Developing an Effective CBR Strategy*. Novato, California: Inference Corporation.

Nguyen, T., Czerwinski, M., and Lee, D. 1993. Compaq QuickSource: Providing the Consumer with the Power of Artificial Intelligence. In *Proceedings of the Fifth Innovative Applications of Artificial Intelligence* (Klahr & Byrnes, eds.). Menlo Park, California: AAAI Press.

Author Index

Lecture Notes in Artificial Intelligence (LNAI)

Lecture Notes in Computer Science